BASIC ISSUES OF AMERICAN DEMOCRACY

THE CENTURY
POLITICAL SCIENCE SERIES

A Book of Readings Selected and Edited by

HILLMAN M. BISHOP and SAMUEL HENDEL
Department of Political Science, The City College of New York

BASIC ISSUES *of* AMERICAN DEMOCRACY

FIFTH  EDITION

New York: APPLETON-CENTURY-CROFTS
Division of Meredith Publishing Company

6124-32

Library of Congress Card Number: 65-11531

PRINTED IN THE UNITED STATES OF AMERICA
E 09573

To Morton Gottschall
Dean Emeritus of

THE CITY COLLEGE OF
THE CITY UNIVERSITY OF NEW YORK

PREFACE

It is appropriate to state, at the outset, what changes are embodied in the fifth edition of *Basic Issues.* Our book has been substantially revised and enlarged to include important controversies that have developed since our fourth edition was published in 1961. New materials include discussions of: the Madisonian system of checks and balances and its contemporary impact on our operative democracy (Topic 6); the Regents' prayer and the "one-man, one-vote" decisions of the Supreme Court (Topics 14 and 16); civil disobedience (Topic 19); judicial activism versus judicial self-restraint (Topic 20); proposals for congressional reform (Topic 23); why democracies fail (Topic 27); the nature of the communist alternative (Topic 29); the meaning and implication of peaceful coexistence (Topic 32); and new directions in American foreign policy (Topic 33). For the rest, a considerable portion of the material found in the previous edition has been retained, supplemented and, we believe, strengthened, by the commentaries of Thomas L. Thorson (Topic 7), J. Roland Pennock (Topic 21); Theodore C. Sorensen (Topic 22), and Walter Lippmann (Topic 24).

The basic premises and objectives reflected in the earlier editions of this book remain unchanged. It is our belief that it is desirable to devote considerable attention to the study of fundamental values and persistent issues of our democracy in the introductory, and frequently terminal, American Government and related courses. This view finds support in the statement by Professor Francis O. Wilcox, Chairman of the American Political Science Association's Committee on Undergraduate Instruction who, in the *American Political Science Review,* wrote:

> [It] must be apparent that we have neglected to give adequate attention to the concept of democracy. We speak at great length about the electoral process, the legislature in action, the Constitution, the courts and the executive, but nowhere do we pause to ponder the real meaning of democracy. Yet here, it seems to me, is the all-important question. What is democracy? What are its weaknesses? Wherein lies its strength? What are its chances to survive? What is the real nature of the alternatives to democracy? It is infinitely more important for a student to think about these questions than it is for him to know the steps a bill must go through before it can become a law.

In the years since 1948, when the first edition of this book appeared, this viewpoint has commanded increasing approval from the political science profession.

A second conviction that guided our selection of materials is that in dealing with controversial issues it is desirable, within limits of space, to present the most persuasively reasoned or authoritative statements obtainable. We agree with John Stuart Mill that full justice can be done to arguments only if they are presented by persons "who actually believe them; who defend them in earnest, and do their utmost for them," and that the "beliefs we have the most warrant for, have no safeguard to rest on, but a standing invitation to the whole world to prove them unfounded." And it is noteworthy that these principles of selection have meant the inclusion of materials representing some of the truly great names in political science.

Inevitably in making selections out of the vast literature of political discourse, some painful choices proved necessary. (To those who may be disappointed because of particular omissions we can only express the hope that compensation will be found in some of the additions and substitutions.) It should be noted, too, that since material on one side of a controversy was not ordinarily written in reply to that on another, direct and sharp conflict will not invariably be found. Notwithstanding these reservations, we believe that there is no other book of readings that gives as much emphasis to, and with as great consistency presents, diverse positions on the fundamental values and problems of American government and democracy.

What purposes are served by the emphasis of *Basic Issues?* We believe that this book contributes to a realization of the following: (*a*) It requires the student to analyze conflicting viewpoints, to weigh evidence and arguments, to make value judgments and reach his own conclusions. This experience may assist him in deciding between alternative policies which confront him as a citizen. (*b*) It increases interest in political discussion and may encourage active participation in public affairs outside the classroom. (*c*) It compels the student to reexamine the foundations of his beliefs and brings "clearer perception and livelier impression" to those to which he adheres; particularly, we think, it heightens his understanding of the meaning and value of democracy.

This volume, we suggest, may be adapted to the primary political science course, or to one semester of an integrated social science course, in a number of ways. At some colleges, for purposes of day-to-day classroom discussion, assignments basically consist of selections from these readings; but in addition, students are required to read particular chapters in a standard textbook (or other materials). While many of the textbook chapters are not discussed in the classroom, knowledge of this largely descriptive, factual material is tested in periodic examinations. At other colleges, instructors prefer to rely upon a standard textbook (or other materials), supplemented at appropriate points with required reading from this volume.*

We are indebted to the authors, editors, and publishers who graciously granted permission to reproduce the material of this volume. Our obligation to members of the department of political science at The City College of New York, past and present, is considerable. We are also grateful to the many members of the profession throughout the country who, from time to time, gave us the benefit of their experience and counsel. To the library staff of The City College for its unfailing cooperation, to Miss Sandra Rosenshein, who supplied extremely competent secretarial and other assistance, and to our wives, Clara Hendel and Georgiana Bishop, for their advice and encouragement, we owe very special thanks.

SAMUEL HENDEL
HILLMAN M. BISHOP

* Teachers and students should note that throughout this book authors' footnotes are numbered, whereas those of the editors are marked by asterisks or other symbols.

CONTENTS

INDEX

(Where an * appears after an author's name the selection is new to this edition of *Basic Issues;* if marked with a † the selection has been substantially revised.)

AUTHORS

CASES

BASIC ISSUES OF AMERICAN DEMOCRACY

HE WHO knows only his own side of the case, knows little of that. His reasons may be good, and no one may have been able to refute them. But if he is equally unable to refute the reasons on the opposite side; if he does not so much as know what they are, he has no ground for preferring either opinion. The rational position for him would be suspension of judgment, and unless he contents himself with that, he is either led by authority, or adopts, like the generality of the world, the side to which he feels most inclination. Nor is it enough that he should hear the arguments of adversaries from his own teachers, presented as they state them, and accompanied by what they offer as refutations. That is not the way to do justice to the arguments, or bring them into real contact with his own mind. He must be able to hear them from persons who actually believe them; who defend them in earnest, and do their very utmost for them. He must know them in their most plausible and persuasive form; he must feel the whole force of the difficulty which the true view of the subject has to encounter and dispose of; else he will never really possess himself of the portion of truth which meets and removes that difficulty.

JOHN STUART MILL—*On Liberty*

Section I

Democracy and Public Opinion

THE NATURE and meaning of democracy have been subjects of considerable controversy. Dispute is in part engendered by confusion between the democratic ideal and the reality. To the early Greeks, democracy simply meant rule by the people; a term derived from *dēmos*-people and *kratein*-to rule. But, as Walter Lippmann makes clear, a false conception of democracy may lead to widespread disillusionment.

Further difficulty arises from the fact that radically different régimes have laid claim to the name and sanction of democracy. One result of this apparent confusion might be to push aside the whole question as a mere matter of semantics. This would be unfortunate; for disagreement over the nature and meaning of democracy may derive from deep-lying differences over values that manifest themselves in the institutions designed to realize these values.

The ensuing section raises several issues. Apart from a general discussion of the nature and meaning of democracy, it considers specifically the relationship of the people and their representatives and the implications to be drawn from the increasing resort to polls to ascertain public opinion. Should the representative simply reflect the public's views of desirable policy or should he, as Burke insisted, refuse to sacrifice "his unbiased opinion, his mature judgment, his enlightened conscience . . . to any man, or any set of men living"?

(For the views of the Founding Fathers on democracy see next section. See also "Democracy Evaluated.")

Topic I

WHAT IS DEMOCRACY?

The Phantom Public

WALTER LIPPMANN *

THE UNATTAINABLE IDEAL

A false ideal of democracy can lead only to disillusionment and to meddlesome tyranny. If democracy cannot direct affairs, then a philosophy which expects it to direct them will encourage the people to attempt the impossible. . . .

The private citizen today has come to feel rather like a deaf spectator in the back row, who ought to keep his mind on the mystery off there, but cannot quite manage to keep awake. He knows he is somehow affected by what is going on. Rules and regulations continually, taxes annually and wars occasionally, remind him that he is being swept along by great drifts of circumstance.

Yet these public affairs are . . . for the most part invisible. They are managed, if they are managed at all, at distant centers, from behind the scenes, by unnamed powers. As a private person he does not know for certain what is going on, or who is doing it, or where he is being carried. No newspaper reports his environment so that he can grasp it; no school has taught him how to imagine it; his ideals, often, do not fit with it; listening to speeches, uttering opinions and voting do not, he finds, enable him to govern it. He lives in a world which he cannot see, does not understand and is unable to direct. . . .

There is then nothing particularly new in the disenchantment which the private citizen expresses by not voting at all, by voting only for the head of the ticket, by staying away from the primaries, by not reading speeches and documents, by the whole list of sins of omission for which he is denounced. I shall not denounce him further. My sympathies are with him, for I believe that he has been saddled with an impossible task and that he is asked to practice an unattainable ideal. I find it so myself for,

* Newspaper columnist. Formerly Editor of *New York World*. Author of *Public Opinion, A Preface to Politics, The Good Society, The Public Philosophy* and numerous other books. The selection is from Walter Lippmann, *The Phantom Public* (New York, The Macmillan Co., 1927), *passim*. By permission.

although public business is my main interest and I give most of my time to watching it, I cannot find time to do what is expected of me in the theory of democracy; that is, to know what is going on and to have an opinion worth expressing on every question which confronts a self-governing community. And I have not happened to meet anybody, from a President of the United States to a professor of political science, who came anywhere near to embodying the accepted ideal of the sovereign and omnipotent citizen. . . .

The actual governing is made up of a multitude of arrangements on specific questions by particular individuals. These rarely become visible to the private citizen. Government, in the long intervals between elections, is carried on by politicians, officeholders and influential men who make settlements with other politicians, officeholders, and influential men. The mass of people see these settlements, judge them, and affect them only now and then. They are altogether too numerous, too complicated, too obscure in their effects to become the subject of any continuing exercise of public opinion.

Nor in any exact and literal sense are those who conduct the daily business of government accountable after the fact to the great mass of the voters. They are accountable only, except in spectacular cases, to the other politicians, officeholders and influential men directly interested in the particular act. Modern society is not visible to anybody, nor intelligible continuously and as a whole. One section is visible to another section, one series of acts is intelligible to this group and another to that.

Even this degree of responsible understanding is attainable only by the development of fact-finding agencies of great scope and complexity. These agencies give only a remote and incidental assistance to the general public. Their findings are too intricate for the casual reader. They are also almost always much too uninteresting. Indeed the popular boredom and contempt for the expert and for statistical measurement are such that the organization of intelligence to administer modern affairs would probably be entirely neglected were it not that departments of government, corporations, trade unions and trade associations are being compelled by their own internal necessities of administration, and by compulsion of other corporate groups, to record their own acts, measure them, publish them and stand accountable for them. . . .

It may be objected at once that an election which turns one set of men out of office and installs another is an expression of public opinion which is neither secondary nor indirect. But what in fact is an election? We call it an expression of the popular will. But is it? We go into a polling booth and mark a cross on a piece of paper for one or two, or perhaps three or four names. Have we expressed our thoughts on the public policy of the United States? Presumably we have a number of thoughts on this and that with many buts and ifs and ors. Surely the cross on a piece of paper does not express them. It would take us hours to express our thoughts, and calling a vote the expression of our mind is an empty fiction.

A vote is a promise of support. It is a way of saying: I am lined up with these men, on this side. I enlist with them. I will follow. . . . The public does not select the candidate, write the platform, outline the policy any more than it builds the automobile or acts the play. It aligns itself for or against somebody who has offered himself, has made a promise, has produced a play, is selling an automobile. The action of a group as a group is the mobilization of the force it possesses. . . .

I do not wish to labor the argument any further than may be necessary to establish the theory that what the public does is not to express its opinions but to align itself for or against a proposal. If that theory is accepted, we must abandon the notion that democratic government can be the direct expression of the will of the people. We must abandon the notion that the people govern. Instead we must adopt the theory that, by their occasional mobilizations as a majority, people support or oppose the individuals who actually govern. We must say that the popular will does not direct continuously but that it intervenes occasionally. . . .

The attempt has been made to ascribe some intrinsic moral and intellectual virtue to majority rule. It was said often in the nineteenth century that there was a deep wisdom in majorities which was the voice of God. Sometimes this flattery was a sincere mysticism, sometimes it was the self-deception which always accompanies the idealization of power. In substance it was nothing but a transfer to the new sovereign of the divine attributes of kings. Yet the inherent absurdity of making virtue and wisdom dependent on 51 per cent of any collection of men has always been apparent. The practical realization that the claim was absurd has resulted in a whole code of civil rights to protect minorities and in all sorts of elaborate methods of subsidizing the arts and sciences and other human interests so they might be independent of the operation of majority rule.

The justification of majority rule in politics is not to be found in its ethical superiority. It is to be found in the sheer necessity of finding a place in civilized society for the force which resides in the weight of numbers. I have called voting an act of enlistment, an alignment for or against, a mobilization. These are military metaphors, and rightly so, I think, for an election based on the principle of majority rule is historically and practically a sublimated and denatured civil war, a paper mobilization without physical violence.

Constitutional democrats, in the intervals when they were not idealizing the majority, have acknowledged that a ballot was a civilized substitute for a bullet. "The French Revolution," says Bernard Shaw, "overthrew one set of rulers and substituted another with different interests and different views. That is what a general election enables the people to do in England every seven years if they choose." . . . Hans Delbrück puts the matter simply when he says that the principle of majority rule is "a purely practical principle. If one wants to avoid a civil war, one lets those rule who in any case would obtain the upper hand if there should be a struggle; and they are the superior numbers." . . .

To support the Ins when things are going well; to support the Outs when they seem to be going badly, this, in spite of all that has been said about tweedledum and tweedledee, is the essence of popular government. Even the most intelligent large public of which we have any experience must determine finally who shall wield the organized power of the state, its army and its police, by a choice between the Ins and Outs. A community where there is no choice does not have popular government. It is subject to some form of dictatorship or it is ruled by the intrigues of the politicians in the lobbies.

Although it is the custom of partisans to speak as if there were radical differences between the Ins and the Outs, it could be demonstrated, I believe, that in stable and mature societies the differences are necessarily not profound. If they were profound, the defeated minority would be constantly on the verge of rebellion. An election would be catastrophic, whereas the assumption in every election is that the victors will do nothing to make life intolerable to the vanquished and that the vanquished will endure with good humor policies which they do not approve.

In the United States, Great Britain, Canada, Australia and in certain of the Continental countries an election rarely means even a fraction of what the campaigners said it would mean. It means some new faces and perhaps a slightly different general tendency in the management of affairs. The Ins may have had a bias toward collectivism; the Outs will lean toward individualism. The Ins may have been suspicious and non-cooperative in foreign affairs; the Outs will perhaps be more trusting or entertain another set of suspicions. The Ins may have favored certain manufacturing interests; the Outs may favor agricultural interests. But even these differing tendencies are very small as compared with the immense area of agreement, established habit and unavoidable necessity. In fact, one might say that a nation is politically stable when nothing of radical consequence is determined by its elections. . . .

The test of whether the Ins are handling affairs effectively is the presence or absence of disturbing problems. . . . It is my opinion that for the most part the general public cannot back each reformer on each issue. It must choose between the Ins and the Outs on the basis of a cumulative judgment as to whether the problems are being solved or aggravated. The particular reformers must look for their support normally to the ruling insiders.

EDUCATION FOR DEMOCRACY

Education has furnished the thesis of the last chapter of every optimistic book on democracy written for one hundred and fifty years. Even Robert Michels, stern and unbending antisentimentalist that he is, says in his "final considerations" that "it is the great task of social education to raise the intellectual level of the masses, so that they may be enabled, within the limits of what is possible, to counteract the oligarchical tendencies" of all collective action. . . .

The usual appeal to education as the remedy for the incompetence of democracy is barren. It is, in effect, a proposal that school teachers shall by some magic of their own fit men to govern after the makers of laws and the preachers of civic ideals have had a free hand in writing the specifications. The reformers do not ask what men can be taught. They say they should be taught whatever may be necessary to fit them to govern the modern world.

The usual appeal to education can bring only disappointment. For the problems of the modern world appear and change faster than any set of teachers can grasp them, much faster than they can convey their substance to a population of children. If the schools attempt to teach children how to solve the problems of the day, they are bound always to be in arrears. The most they can conceivably attempt is the teaching of a pattern of thought and feeling which will enable the citizen to approach a new problem in some useful fashion. But that pattern cannot be invented by the pedagogue. It is the political theorist's business to trace out that pattern. In that task he must not assume that the mass has political genius, but that men, even if they had genius, would give only a little time and attention to public affairs. . . .

At the root of the effort to educate a people for self-government there has, I believe, always been the assumption that the voter should aim to approximate as nearly as he can the knowledge and the point of view of the responsible man. He did not, of course, in the mass, ever approximate it very nearly. But he was supposed to. It was believed that if only he could be taught more facts, if only he would take more interest, if only he would read more and better newspapers, if only he would listen to more lectures and read more reports, he would gradually be trained to direct public affairs. The whole assumption is false. It rests upon a false conception of public opinion and a false conception of the way the public acts. No sound scheme of civic education can come of it. No progress can be made toward this unattainable ideal.

This democratic conception is false because it fails to note the radical difference between the experience of the insider and the outsider; it is fundamentally askew because it asks the outsider to deal as successfully with the substance of a question as the insider. He cannot do it. No scheme of education can equip him in advance for all the problems of mankind; no device of publicity, no machinery of enlightenment, can endow him during a crisis with the antecedent detailed and technical knowledge which is required for executive action. . . .

The fundamental difference which matters is that between insiders and outsiders. Their relations to a problem are radically different. Only the insider can make decisions, not because he is inherently a better man but because he is so placed that he can understand and can act. The outsider is necessarily ignorant, usually irrelevant and often meddlesome, because he is trying to navigate the ship from dry land. That is why excellent automobile manufacturers, literary critics and scientists often talk such nonsense about politics. Their congenital excellence, if it exists, reveals itself only in their own activity. The aristocratic theorists work from the fallacy of supposing that a sufficiently excellent square peg will also fit a round hole. In short, like the democratic theorists, they miss the essence of the matter, which is, that competence exists only in relation to function; that men are not good, but good for something; that men cannot be educated, but only educated for something. . . .

Democracy, therefore, has never developed an education for the public. It has merely given it a smattering of the kind of knowledge which the responsible man requires. It has, in fact, aimed not at making good citizens but at making a mass of amateur executives. It has not taught the child how to act as a member of the public. It has merely given him a hasty, incomplete taste of what he might have to know if he meddled in everything. The result is a bewildered public and a mass of insufficiently trained officials. The responsible men have obtained their training not from the courses in "civics" but in the law schools and law offices and in business. The public at large, which includes everybody outside the field of his own responsible knowledge, has had no coherent political training of any kind. Our civic education does not even begin to tell the voter how he can reduce the maze of public affairs to some intelligible form. . . .

Education for citizenship, for membership in the public, ought, therefore to be distinct from education for public office. Citizenship involves a radically different relation to affairs, requires different intellectual habits and different methods of action. The force of public opinion is partisan, spasmodic, simple-minded and external. It needs for its direction . . . a new intellectual method which shall provide it with its own usable canons of judgment. . . .

THE RÔLE OF THE PUBLIC

If this is the nature of public action, what ideal can be formulated which shall conform to it?

We are bound, I think, to express the ideal in its lowest terms, to state it not as an ideal which might conceivably be realized by exceptional groups now and then or in some distant future but as an ideal which normally might be taught and attained. In estimating the burden which a public can carry, a sound political theory must insist upon the largest factor of safety. It must understate the possibilities of public action. . . .

We cannot, then, think of public opinion as a conserving or creating force directing society to clearly conceived ends, making deliberately toward socialism or away from it, toward nationalism, an empire, a league of nations or any other doctrinal goal. . . .

The work of the world goes on continually without conscious direction from public opinion. At certain junctures problems arise. It is only with the crises of some of these problems that public opinion is concerned. And its object in dealing with a crisis is to help allay that crisis.

I think this conclusion is inescapable. For though we may prefer to believe that the aim of popular action should be to do justice or promote the true, the beautiful and the good, the belief will not maintain itself in the face of plain experience. The public does not know in most crises what specifically is the truth or the justice of the case, and men are not agreed on what is beautiful and good. Nor does the public rouse itself normally at the existence of evil. It is aroused at evil made manifest by the interruption of a habitual process of life. And finally, a problem ceases to occupy attention not when justice, as we happen to define it, has been done but when a workable adjustment that overcomes the crisis has been made. . . .

Thus we strip public opinion of any implied duty to deal with the substance of a problem, to make technical decisions, to attempt justice or impose a moral precept. And instead we say that the ideal of public opinion is to align men during the crisis of a problem in such a way as to favor the action of those individuals who may be able to compose a crisis. The power to discern those individuals is the end of the effort to educate public opinion. The aim of research designed to facilitate public action is the discovery of clear signs by which these individuals may be discerned.

The signs are relevant when they reveal by coarse, simple and objective tests which side in a controversy upholds a workable social rule, or which is attacking an unworkable rule, or which proposes a promising new rule. By following such signs the public might know where to align itself. In such an alignment it does not, let us remember, pass judgment on the intrinsic merits. It merely places its force at the disposal of the side which, according to objective signs, seems to be standing for human adjustments according to a clear rule of behavior and against the side which appears to stand for settlement in accordance with its own unaccountable will.

Public opinion, in this theory, is a reserve of force brought into action during a crisis in public affairs. Though it is itself an irrational force, under favorable institutions, sound leadership and decent training the power of public opinion might be placed at the disposal of those who stood for workable law as against brute assertion. In this theory, public opinion does not make the law. But by canceling lawless power it may establish the condition under which law can be made. It does not reason, investigate, invent, persuade, bargain or settle. But, by holding the aggressive party in check, it may liberate intelligence. Public opinion in its highest ideal will defend those who are prepared to act on their reason against the interrupting force of those who merely assert their will. . . .

These in roughest outline are some of the conclusions, as they appear to me, of the attempt to bring the theory of democracy into somewhat truer alignment with the nature of public opinion. I have conceived public opinion to be, not the voice of God, nor the voice of society, but the voice of the interested spectators of action. I have, therefore, supposed that the opinions of the spectators must be essentially different from those of the actors, and that the kind of action they were capable of taking was essentially different too. It has seemed to me that the public had a function and must have methods of its own in controversies, qualitatively different from those of the executive men; that it was a dangerous confusion to believe that private purposes were a mere emanation of some common purpose. . . .

It is a theory which puts its trust chiefly in the individuals directly concerned. They initiate, they administer, they settle. It would subject them to the least possible interference from ignorant and meddlesome outsiders, for in this theory the public intervenes only when there is a crisis of maladjustment, and then not to deal with the substance of the problem but to neutralize the arbitrary force which prevents adjustment. It is a theory which economizes the attention of men as members of the public, and asks them to do as little as possible in matters where they can do nothing very well. It confines the effort of men, when they are a public, to a part they might fulfill, to a part which corresponds to their own greatest interest in any social disturbance; that is, to an intervention which may help to allay the disturbance, and thus allow them to return to their own affairs.

For it is the pursuit of their special affairs that they are most interested in. It is by the private labors of individuals that life is enhanced. I set no great store on what can be done by public opinion and the action of masses.

I have no legislative program to offer, no new institutions to propose. There are, I believe, immense confusions in the current theory of democracy which frustrate and pervert its action. I have attacked certain of the confusions with no conviction except that a false philosophy tends to stereotype thought against the lessons of experience. I do not know what the lessons will be when we have learned to think of public opinion as it is, and not as the fictitious power we have assumed it to be. It is enough if with Bentham we know that "the perplexity of ambiguous discourse . . . distracts and eludes the apprehension, stimulates and inflames the passions."

Equality and Democracy

HAROLD J. LASKI *

No definition of democracy can adequately comprise the vast history which the concept connotes. To some it is a form of government, to others a way of social life. Men have found its essence in the character of the electorate, the relation between government and the people, the absence of wide economic differences between citizens, the refusal to recognize privileges built on birth or wealth, race or creed. Inevitably it has changed its substance in terms of time and place. What has seemed democracy to a member of some ruling class has seemed to his poorer fellow citizen a narrow and indefensible oligarchy. Democracy has a context in every sphere of life; and in each of those spheres it raises its special problems which do not admit of satisfactory or universal generalization.

The political aspect of democracy has the earliest roots in time. For the most part it remained a negative concept until the seventeenth century. Men protested against systems which upon one ground or another excluded them from a share in power. They were opposed to an oligarchy which exercised privileges confined to a narrow range of persons. They sought the extension of such privileges to more people on the ground that limitation was not justifiable. They felt and argued that exclusion from privilege was exclusion from benefit; and they claimed their equal share in its gains.

That notion of equality points the way to the essence of the democratic idea—the effort of men to affirm their own essence and to remove all barriers to that affirmation. All differentials by which other men exercise authority or influence they do not themselves possess hinder their own self-realization. To give these differentials the protection of the legal order is to prevent the realization of the wishes and interests of the mass of men. The basis of democratic development is therefore the demand for equality, the demand that the system of power be erected upon the similarities and not the differences between men. Of the permanence of this demand there can be no doubt; at the very dawn of political science Aristotle insisted that its denial was the main cause of revolutions. Just as the history of the state can perhaps be most effectively written in terms of the expanding claims of the common man upon the results of its effort, so the development of the realization of equality is the clue to the problem of democracy. . . .

It is because political equality, however profound, does not permit the

* Late Professor of Political Science at London School of Economics and Political Science. The selection is from Harold J. Laski, "Democracy," *Encyclopaedia of Social Sciences* (New York, The Macmillan Co., 1942). By permission.

full affirmation of the common man's essence that the idea of democracy has spread to other spheres. The discovery that men may be politically equal without attaining a genuine realization of their personalities was seen by not a few during the Puritan revolution, and the demand for economic equality was loudly and ably voiced there by Winstanley and his followers. It was only, however, with the French Revolution that economic equality may be said to have become a permanent part of the democratic creed. From that time, particularly in the context of socialist principles, it has been increasingly insisted that in the absence of economic equality no political mechanisms will of themselves enable the common man to realize his wishes and interests. Economic power is regarded as the parent of political power. To make the diffusion of the latter effective, the former also must be widely diffused. To divide a people into rich and poor is to make impossible the attainment of a common interest by state action. Economic equality is then urged as the clue upon which the reality of democracy depends. . . .

The case for democracy is built upon the assumption that in its absence men become the tools of others, without available proof that the common good is inherently involved in this relationship. The case at bottom is an ethical one. It postulates that the right to happiness is inherent in man as a member of society and that any system which denies that right cannot be justified. The main argument in its favor is the important one that in any social order where it has not been accepted a rational analysis finds it difficult to justify the distribution of benefits which occurs. . . .

SOCIALISM AND DEMOCRACY

Democratic government during the nineteenth century may be said to have been successful so long as it confined its activities to the purely political field. While it occupied itself with matters of religious freedom, formal political equality, the abrogation of aristocratic privilege, its conquests were swift and triumphant. But the attainment of these ends did not solve any of the major social and economic issues. The masses still remained poor; a small number of rich men still exercised a predominant influence in the state. With the grant of the franchise to the workers therefore a movement toward collectivism was inevitable. Political parties had to attract their support; the obvious method was to offer the prospect of social and economic legislation which should alleviate the workers' condition. And from the early days of the French Revolution there had appeared the portent of socialism with its insistence that only in the rigorous democratization of economic power could a solution to the social problem be found. Incoherent at first, the development of trade unions and the growth of doctrines like that of Marx made what seemed visionary utopianism into a movement. By the eighties of the nineteenth century socialism could represent itself as the natural and logical outcome of democratic theory. It could outbid the older parties on ground which universal suffrage had made the inevitable territory of conflict. In the opening years of the twentieth century the central theme of debate had become the power of the state to satisfy the economic wants of the working class. . . .

If the hypothesis of self-government is valid in the political sphere it must be valid in the economic sphere also; whence is born the insistence upon constitutional government in industry. Not only must the state interfere to this end in the general details of economic life, but it cannot realize its end if the operation of the profit making motive is admitted in any industry of basic importance to the community. The new ideals of democracy therefore foreshadow a functional society in which the older conception of liberty of contract has no place. Any state in which the economic sphere is left largely uncontrolled is necessarily a class society tilted to the advantage of the rich; it lacks that necessary basis of unity which enables men to compose their differences in peace. The claim for the sovereignty of the state no longer rests upon the strong basis provided by the old liberal hypothesis of a society equal in fact because formally equal in political power. Largely the new democratic theory accepts a quasi-Marxian interpretation of the state while refusing to draw therefrom the inference that revolution is its only satisfactory corrective. . . .

[The new democratic theory] regards the right of men to share in the results of social life as broadly equal; and it regards differences of treatment as justifiable only in so far as they can be shown to be directly relevant to the common good. It takes its stand firmly on the need for a close economic equality on the ground that the benefits a man can obtain from the social process are, at least approximately and in general, a function of his power of effective demand, which in turn depends upon the property he owns. It is thus hostile to all economic privilege as being in its nature fatal to the end at which a democratic society must aim. For the new democratic theory liberty is necessarily a function of equality. . . .

One final remark may be made. It is not the view of modern democratic theory that a political man can be constructed whose interest in the public business of the community is assured. It does believe that increased educational opportunity will increase that interest; a belief which further emphasizes the need for equality. It does argue further that the main result of inequality is so to depress the moral character of those at the base of the social pyramid as to minimize their power to get attention for their experience. Again therefore it sees in equality the path to the end democracy seeks to serve.

The Role of the People

R. M. MACIVER *

Democracy cannot mean the rule of the majority or the rule of the masses. This was the manner in which democracy was interpreted by the Greek philosophers, at a time before there was any representative system or any party system—and this fact may help to explain why they on the whole disapproved of it. The meaning of democracy was then obscure. Even today, with all our experience of democracy, it is often misunderstood. Democracy is not a way of governing, whether by majority or otherwise, but primarily a way of determining who shall govern and, broadly, to what ends. The only way in which the people, *all the people,* can determine who shall govern is by referring the question to public opinion and accepting on each occasion the verdict of the polls. Apart from this activity of the people there is no way of distinguishing democracy from other forms of government.

Any kind of government can claim to rest on "the will of the people," whether it be oligarchy or dictatorship or monarchy. One kind of government alone rests on the constitutional exercise of the will of the people. Every other kind prevents the minority—or the majority—from freely expressing opinion concerning the policies of government, or at the least from making that opinion the free determinant of government. Quite possibly in Russia, at the time of writing, a larger proportion of the people approves and supports its government than may be found in democratic countries to support their governments. But that fact is quite irrelevant to the question of democracy. In the Soviet Union, under these conditions, there is no free exercise of opinion on matters of policy, nor any constitutional means by which the changing currents of opinion can find political expression. It would therefore be the sheerest confusion to classify the Soviet system as democratic.

The growth of democracy has always been associated with the free discussion of political issues, with the right to differ concerning them, and with the settlement of the difference, not *by force majeure* but by resort to the counting of votes. It has always been associated with the growing authority of some assembly of the people or of the people's representatives,

* Professor Emeritus of Political Philosophy and Sociology at Columbia University. Author of *Leviathan and the People, The More Perfect Union* and others. From R. M. MacIver, *The Web of Government* (New York, The Macmillan Co., 1947), pp. 198–199. By permission.

such as the Greek *ecclesia,* the Roman *comitia,* the English parliament. The right to differ did not end with the victory of the majority but was inherent in the system. It was a necessary condition of democracy everywhere that opposing doctrines remained free to express themselves, to seek converts, to form organizations, and so to compete for success before the tribunal of public opinion. Any major trend of opinion could thus register itself in the character and in the policies of government. . . .

THE FUNCTION OF THE PUBLIC *

There are those who condemn democracy because, they say, the people are unfit to rule. And there are those who, in a more friendly spirit, deplore the plight of democracy because the people simply cannot undertake the task it imposes on them, the task of coping with all the complex issues of modern government. In one of his earlier books, *The Phantom Public,* Walter Lippmann put forward the plaint that the democratic man was baffled and disenchanted. He could not make his sovereign voice heard concerning a thousand tangled affairs, and how could he? How could he have an effective opinion about the situation in China today and about the sewers of Brooklyn tomorrow, and the next day about the effects of subsidies to agriculture, and the next day about some deal with Yugoslavia, and so on without end? He gave it up. He was disillusioned about democracy. He could not live up to its demands.

If any "man in the street" holds these views about his democratic obligations it is quite proper he should be disillusionized. But not, we hope, about democracy. Only about his illusions about democracy. Representative democracy, the only kind that has any meaning under modern conditions, does not put any such impossible strain on the citizen. The people, let us repeat, do not and cannot govern; they control the government. In every live democracy they decide the broad march of politics. They decide whether there is to be more social legislation or less, more collectivization or somewhat more play for private enterprise, more dependence on an international system of security or more self-sufficiency and relative isolation, and so forth. They decide these issues, not one at a time but by voting for an administration favorable to one or another "platform." They decide them partly—and in the last resort—at the polls, and partly by the continuously manifested indications of public sentiment. To make decisions easier there is in every community a sense of alternative directions, marked respectively left and right, and a sway of opinion in one or the other direction. . . .

* From R. M. MacIver: *The Ramparts We Guard,* copyright, 1950, by Robert M. MacIver, and used with the permission of The Macmillan Co., pp. 27–30, 49–51.

This incessant activity of popular opinion is the dynamic of democracy. It decides between the larger alternatives of policy-making and in that way has an impact on a thousand issues. Mr. Lippmann, in the book referred to, was clearly off the beam when he suggested that it is not the business of the public to decide the substantive policies of government but merely to see that the government abides by the rules, like a referee who watches the players but takes no part in the game. The great changes in the socio-economic policies of Western European countries in the nineteenth and twentieth centuries—the whole trend toward social legislation and the control of economic power—were due to the swelling currents of public opinion, responsive to changing conditions. Or we may cite the more recent experience of the United States, where a new manifestation of public opinion, opposed by most of the prestige-bearers and of the well-to-do, carried to power and maintained in power the party of the "New Deal."

That is how the citizens of a democracy make their citizenship effective. Not as individuals deciding for themselves the successive problems of politics, each in speculative detachment registering his opinion on every issue. Not merely as units casting their separate votes every few years as election time comes round—the citizens of a democracy are *continuously* engaged in a massive give-and-take of creative opinion-making. Certainly not as experts who must willy-nilly do the job of the administration, that is, by finding the answers to the very specific questions that the administration must face from day to day. No business is run that way, and no government can be. Executive jobs are for executives, whether in business or in government. The public—or the workers or the shareholders—may very well entertain an opinion on whether the management is doing well or badly, but that is a different matter altogether.

We observe in passing that in a democracy there are two stages of decision-making before the *proper* job of the expert begins. First, there is the primary function of policy-making, the choice between directions, the function of the people. Second, there is the delineation of policy by the legislators and the heads of the government—in accordance with the "mandate" thus entrusted to them. Third, there is the implementation of policy. At this third stage the expert finds his place. It is here, and here alone, that he belongs. He is the technician or the craftsman in the art of government.

It is an eminently logical system. The representatives of the people have the authority. They are presumably—they always become at least—more conversant with the ways of governing than are the lay citizens, but they are not experts. They mark out the lines of advance and the experts build the roads. The logic is admirable, but as in all human affairs it is subject to distortion. These three functions are not clear-cut and separable in practice. The limits of each in relation to the others must be discretionary and flexible. Which means also that there may be conflict, confusion, and encroachment between the participants. The legislator may not let the expert do his proper job or, more commonly, he permits the expert to follow his own devices into the area of policy-making. The cabinet officers may ignore the spirit of their mandate, particularly in the screened-off sector of foreign policy. The expert may become a worshipper of routine, a jealous guardian of the secrets of office, a bureaucrat in the less honorable sense of the word.

Such things happen everywhere, and perhaps there is no safeguard except the vigilance of the public, as it becomes better educated in the ways of democracy and armed with fuller knowledge of its practical operation. What indeed appears throughout, as we study democracy at work, is that the defects and shortcomings it exhibits are due not to any inherent weakness in its principle but to the greater responsibilities it imposes on those who carry it out. These responsibilities are in themselves reasonable and never excessive, but interest and pride and office are always at hand, to deflect, to distort, and to betray. The ever-active democratic process checks these tendencies. How effectively it does so is in the keeping of the public, who have the authority and the means to control those whom they entrust with the business of governing. . . .

DEMOCRACY AND FREE EXPRESSION

Democracy constitutionally guarantees certain fundamental rights to all citizens. Apart from these rights—the right to think and believe after one's own mind and heart, the right to express one's opinions and to organize for their furtherance, the right to vote according to one's opinions, and so forth—democracy cannot exist. But the rights in question are not the same thing as a form of government. They may properly be made a *test* of its existence but they do not constitute it. [Former] Secretary of State George C. Marshall applied this test when the Western Powers were in dispute with Soviet Russia regarding the implementation of a pledge made under the Yalta agreement of 1945. The allied plenipotentiaries pledged themselves to use "democratic means" for the solution of the problems of the occupied countries of Europe, and again at the Berlin Conference they gave directions "for the eventual reconstruction of German political life on a democratic basis." But when it came to performance the Soviet Union and the Western Powers were completely opposed, the former claiming that its own restrictive and high-handed methods were in accordance with the democratic pledge.

General Marshall insisted that the essence of democracy was the recognition that "human beings have certain inalienable rights—that is, rights that may not be given or taken away," and that until these rights were granted and guaranteed the pledge was not fulfilled. These rights included "the right of every individual to develop his mind and his soul in the ways of his own choice, free of fear and coercion—provided only that he does not interfere with the rights of others." "To us," he said, "a society is not free if law-abiding citizens live in fear of being denied the right to work or being deprived of life, liberty and the pursuit of happiness."

The argument was just, in the light of the whole history of what the world has known as democracy. For our purpose of definition, however, we must look beyond the possession of such rights to the constitutional order that gives and guards the assurance. This constitutional order, in any of its varieties, *is* democracy. Now then we must ask: what kind of order is it that can *constitutionally* assure these rights? We find that both historically and logically it is an order that, to establish the right of opinion, gives free opinion itself a politically creative role. In other words, the government must be dependent on, and responsive to, the changes of public opinion. More closely, each successive administration is voted into office by an election or series of elections at which the people freely express their effective preference for one group of candidates over another group or other groups. In order that this process may be constitutionally possible the law must bind the relations of men in the areas to which it applies but must not bind their opinions in any areas. (We shall not pause here to examine the apparent but not genuine exceptions to this principle that fall under laws relating to libel, slander, incitement to violence, and so forth.) In a democracy those who oppose the policies of the government lose no civil rights and those who support its policies acquire thereby no civil rights. In a democracy minority opinion remains as untrammeled as majority opinion.

The importance of the creative role assigned to public opinion under democracy lies primarily in the fact that if opinion is free then the whole cultural life of man is free. If opinion is free, then belief is free and science is free and art and philosophy and all the variant styles and modes in which men manifest and develop their values and tastes and ways of living—always up to the limit where they endeavor by oppression or violence to deprive their fellowmen of these same prerogatives. Democracy alone assures the citadel of human personality against the deadly invasions of power. If only we could comprehend what this means we would never let our disappointments with the defects and weaknesses that the workings of democracy may reveal blind us to the intrinsic superiority of democracy over all other systems of government. . . .

"POLITICAL" AND "ECONOMIC" DEMOCRACY *

Some recent writers draw a distinction between "political democracy" and "economic democracy." They regard "economic democracy" as either the complement or the fulfillment of "political democracy." Sometimes they treat "political democracy" as less important than "economic democracy." Not infrequently they refer to the Soviet system as embodying this superior form of democracy. Mr. Harold Laski, who follows this line, writes: "If the hypothesis of self-government is valid in the political sphere it must be valid in the economic sphere also." Now when Mr. Laski speaks of "economic democracy" he is not speaking of *democracy* in any sense. He does not mean that the workers should elect by ballot the managers and the executive boards of industrial corporations or banks and decide what policies they should pursue in the conduct of their business. He certainly can offer no evidence that these democratic procedures are applied in Soviet Russia. Moreover, the economic program he is concerned about is one he wants the state to implement. His program is a *political* one. He wants democratic countries to adopt a collectivist system. But he should not identify a collectivist system with democracy, whether "economic" or "political." A democracy may approve a collectivist program or may reject it. It is still a democracy, and either way it is taking action "in the economic sphere." "The economic sphere" can never be separated from "the political sphere." What policy a democracy follows in this sphere depends on the conditions, and immediately on public opinion.

Mr. Laski, like many others, is apt to identify democracy with the things he would like democracy to do. In some of his writings he suggests that if a democracy should adopt a "revolutionary" socialist program it might meet such resistance from the propertied classes that democracy itself would come to an end and dictatorship take its place. It is indeed possible, but where the democratic spirit prevails, as in England, the United States, the self-governing British Dominions, and the Scandinavian countries, it seeks to avoid such drastic alternatives; it prefers to move to its goals by steps, not by one convulsive act. The point, however, is that should such a convulsion take place Mr. Laski's socialist program would be achieved at the price of democracy. Nor could it reasonably be argued that "economic democracy" had taken the place of "politial democracy." There might be greater economic equality, but we have no ground, either in logic or in history, for assuming that collectivist equality, arrived at on such terms, would become the boon companion of democracy.

* R. M. MacIver, *The Web of Government* (New York, The Macmillan Co., 1947), pp. 206–208. By permission.

Competition for Political Leadership

JOSEPH A. SCHUMPETER *

Our chief troubles about the classical theory [of democracy] † centers in the proposition that "the people" hold a definite and rational opinion about every individual question and that they give effect to this opinion—in a democracy—by choosing "representatives" who will see to it that that opinion is carried out. Thus the selection of the representatives is made secondary to the primary purpose of the democratic arrangement which is to vest the power of deciding political issues in the electorate. Suppose we reverse the roles of these two elements and make the deciding of issues by the electorate secondary to the election of the men who are to do the deciding. To put it differently, we now take the view that the role of the people is to produce a government, or else an intermediate body which in turn will produce a national executive or government. And we define: *the democratic method is that institutional arrangement for arriving at political decisions in which individuals acquire the power to decide by means of a competitive struggle for the people's vote.*

Defense and explanation of this idea will speedily show that, as to both plausibility of assumptions and tenability of propositions, it greatly improves the theory of the democratic process.

First of all, we are provided with a reasonably efficient criterion by which to distinguish democratic governments from others. We have seen that the classical theory meets with difficulties on that score because both the will and the good of the people may be, and in many historical instances have been, served just as well or better by governments that cannot be described as democratic according to any accepted usage of the term. Now we are in a somewhat better position partly because we are resolved to stress a *modus procedendi* the presence or absence of which it is in most cases easy to verify.[1]

For instance, a parliamentary monarchy like the English one fulfills the requirements of the democratic method because the monarch is prac-

* Late Professor of Economics at Harvard University. Former Austrian Minister of Finance. Author of *The Theory of Economic Development, Business Cycles, Imperialism and Social Classes.* The selection is from *Capitalism, Socialism, and Democracy,* 3rd ed. (New York, Harper & Brothers, 1950), pp. 269–273. By permission.

† The author defines the classical theory of democracy as ". . . that institutional arrangement for arriving at political decisions which realizes the common good by making the people itself decide issues through the election of individuals who are to assemble to carry out its will."

[1] See however the fourth point below.

tically constrained to appoint to cabinet office the same people as parliament would elect. A "constitutional" monarchy does not qualify to be called democratic because electorates and parliaments, while having all the other rights that electorates and parliaments have in parliamentary monarchies, lack the power to impose their choice as to the governing committee: the cabinet ministers are in this case servants of the monarch, in substance as well as in name, and can in principle be dismissed as well as appointed by him. Such an arrangement may satisfy the people. The electorate may reaffirm this fact by voting against any proposal for change. The monarch may be so popular as to be able to defeat any competition for the supreme office. But since no machinery is provided for making this competition effective the case does not come within our definition.

Second, the theory embodied in this definition leaves all the room we may wish to have for a proper recognition of the vital fact of leadership. The classical theory did not do this but attributed to the electorate an altogether unrealistic degree of initiative which practically amounted to ignoring leadership. But collectives act almost exclusively by accepting leadership—this is the dominant mechanism of practically any collective action which is more than a reflex. Propositions about the working and the results of the democratic method that take account of this are bound to be infinitely more realistic than propositions which do not. . . .

Third, however, so far as there are genuine group-wise volitions at all —for instance the will of the unemployed to receive unemployment benefit or the will of other groups to help—our theory does not neglect them. On the contrary we are now able to insert them in exactly the role they actually play. Such volitions do not as a rule assert themselves directly. Even if strong and definite they remain latent, often for decades, until they are called to life by some political leader who turns them into political factors. This he does, or else his agents do it for him, by organizing these volitions, by working them up and by including eventually appropriate items in his competitive offering. The interaction between sectional interests and public opinion and the way in which they produce the pattern we call the political situation appear from this angle in a new and much clearer light.

Fourth, our theory is of course no more definite than is the concept of competition for leadership. This concept presents similar difficulties as the concept of competition in the economic sphere, with which it may be usefully compared. In economic life competition is never completely lacking, but hardly ever is it perfect. Similarly, in political life there is always some competition, though perhaps only a potential one, for the allegiance of the people. To simplify matters we have restricted the kind of competition for leadership which is to define democracy to free competition for a free vote. The justification for this is that democracy seems to imply a recognized method by which to conduct the competitive struggle, and that the electoral method is practically the only one available for communities of any size. But though this excludes many ways of securing leadership which should be excluded,[2] such as competition by military insurrection, it does not exclude the cases that are strikingly analogous to the economic phenomena we label "unfair" or "fraudulent" competition or restraint of competition. And we cannot exclude them because if we did we should be left with a completely unrealistic ideal.[3] Between this ideal case which does not exist and the cases in which all competition with the established leader is prevented by force, there is a continuous range of variations within which the democratic method of government shades off into the autocratic one by imperceptible steps. But if we wish to understand and not to philosophize, this is as it should be. The value of our criterion is not seriously impaired thereby.

Fifth, our theory seems to clarify the relation that subsists between democracy and individual freedom. If by the latter we mean the existence of a sphere of individual self-government the boundaries of which are historically variable—*no* society tolerates absolute freedom even of conscience and of speech, *no* society reduces that sphere to zero—the question clearly becomes a matter of degree. We [believe] that the democratic method does not necessarily guarantee a greater amount of individual freedom than another political method would permit in similar circumstances. It may well be the other way round. But there is still a relation between the two. If, on principle at least, everyone is free to compete for political leadership[4] by presenting himself to the electorate, this will in most cases though not in all mean a considerable amount of freedom of discussion *for all*. In particular it will normally mean a considerable amount of freedom of the press. This relation between democracy and freedom is not absolutely stringent and can be tampered with. But, from the standpoint of the intellectual, it is nevertheless very important. At the same time, it is all there is to that relation.

Sixth, it should be observed that in making it the primary function of the electorate to produce a government (directly or through an inter-

[2] It also excludes methods which should not be excluded, for instance, the acquisition of political leadership by the people's tacit acceptance of it or by election *quasi per inspirationem*. The latter differs from election by voting only by a technicality. But the former is not quite without importance even in modern politics; the sway held by a party boss *within his party* is often based on nothing but tacit acceptance of his leadership. Comparatively speaking, however, these are details which may, I think, be neglected in a sketch like this.

[3] As in the economic field, *some* restrictions are implicit in the legal and moral principles of the community.

[4] Free, that is, in the same sense in which everyone is free to start another textile mill.

mediate body) I intended to include in this phrase also the function of evicting it. The one means simply the acceptance of a leader or a group of leaders, the other means simply the withdrawal of this acceptance. This takes care of an element the reader may have missed. He may have thought that the electorate controls as well as installs. But since electorates normally do not control their political leaders in any way except by refusing to reelect them or the parliamentary majorities that support them, it seems well to reduce our ideas about this control in the way indicated by our definition. Occasionally, spontaneous revulsions occur which upset a government or an individual minister directly or else enforce a certain course of action. But they are not only exceptional, they are, as we [believe], contrary to the spirit of the democratic method.

Seventh, our theory sheds much-needed light on an old controversy. Whoever accepts the classical doctrine of democracy and in consequence believes that the democratic method is to guarantee that issues be decided and policies framed according to the will of the people must be struck by the fact that, even if that will were undeniably real and definite, decision by simple majorities would in many cases distort it rather than give effect to it. Evidently the will of the majority is the will of the majority and not the will of "the people." The latter is a mosaic that the former completely fails to "represent." To equate both by definition is not to solve the problem. Attempts at real solutions have however been made by the authors of the various plans for Proportional Representation.

These plans have met with adverse criticism on practical grounds. It is in fact obvious not only that proportional representation will offer opportunities for all sorts of idiosyncrasies to assert themselves but also that it may prevent democracy from producing efficient governments and thus prove a danger in times of stress.[5] But before concluding that democracy becomes unworkable if its principle is carried out consistently, it is just as well to ask ourselves whether this principle really implies proportional representation. As a matter of fact it does not. If acceptance of leadership is the true function of the electorate's vote, the case for proportional representation collapses because its premises are no longer binding. The principle of democracy then merely means that the reins of government should be handed to those who command more support than do any of the competing individuals or teams. And this in turn seems to assure the standing of the majority system within the logic of the democratic method, although we might still condemn it on grounds that lie outside of that logic.

[5] The argument against proportional representation has been ably stated by Professor F. A. Hermens in "The Trojan Horse of Democracy," *Social Research* (November, 1938).

Topic 2

PUBLIC-OPINION POLLS IN A DEMOCRACY

The Pollsters' False Premises

LINDSAY ROGERS *

Public-opinion polling, if not a major, is a large and important American industry whose tycoons and their academic acolytes have been far from reticent in boasting of achievements. "The speed with which sampling referenda can be completed for the entire nation," writes Dr. George Gallup, "is such that public opinion on any given issue can be reported within forty-eight hours if the occasion warrants. Thus the goal has nearly been reached when public opinion can be 'ascertainable at all times.' " . . .

I concede that polls on a wide variety of questions have become a significant feature of journalism in the United States and in other countries, and that they are a new kind of reporting which gives the reading public data that it did not previously possess and that are sometimes worthy of analysis. But the data conceal more than they reveal and will have different meanings for different analysts. And for the pollsters to maintain that percentages of "yeses," "noes," "no opinion," "never heard of it," disclose public opinion on the policy that they have inquired about, and to which many respondents may not have given a moment's thought before they were interrogated, is to advertise a mouthwash as a cure for anemia. If the pollsters sold their product in bottles instead of as news, the Federal Trade Commission would long since have been after them.

Why the misbranding? It results, I think, from two great sins of omission of which the pollsters are guilty. They have never attempted to define what it is they are measuring. . . . And this is the second great omission—that in the now enormous literature on polling methods and the data that have been secured, one never—well almost never—finds any reasoned statement of premises concerning the nature of the political society in

* Formerly Professor of Public Law at Columbia University. Author of *The American Senate, Crisis Government,* and other works. The selection is reprinted from *The Pollsters* by Lindsay Rogers, by permission of Alfred A. Knopf, Inc. Copyright, 1949, by Alfred A. Knopf, Inc.

which public opinion should be the ruler. When, as if by accident, premises are articulated, they prove to be false. They have to be, because, if they were not, the pollsters would not be able to make the exaggerated claims that they do about the meaning of the data they present for consideration. They would see that they are talking nonsense when they speak of "implementing democracy," "making it more articulate," and "speeding up its processes." Moreover, they do not bother to say how they define "democracy," which may be anything from a non-snobbish sentimental interest in the underdog to the system that Stalin and the Politburo impose on Russia. . . .

Most men and women do not study public questions and endeavor to form rational opinions. They have neither time nor interest. What they learn from newspapers or the radio gives them incomplete, ofttimes unintentionally, and sometimes intentionally, distorted information. People follow the "pictures" in their heads, which Lippmann called "stereotypes." There is in fact and need be no public opinion on an issue until it has already been shaped and has its advocates and opponents. Even then people will really concern themselves only if they are directly interested. The Reciprocal Trade Agreements policy, for example, may affect importers and exporters. In the long run it may be of vital importance to the economy of the nation as a whole. Apart from those who feel an immediate self-interest, there are few people—mostly persistent students of public affairs—who know of or care one way or the other about the Reciprocal Trade Agreements.

As Doob wisely remarks, "What is discouraging about democracy in the modern world and what elsewhere has helped give rise to alternate forms of government is the increasing complexity of the affairs with which government must deal. If the forces of democracy have enabled information to be spread at an arithmetically increasing rate, it can be said without much exaggeration that technology and social changes have increased at a geometrical rate the amount of information which needs to be known for the electorate to be intelligent and reasonably expert." The Athenians could choose members of administrative bodies by lot because then any intelligent citizen had sufficient knowledge of the matters that must be dealt with. This is no longer true. . . .

"The task of government, and hence of democracy as a form of government, is not to express an imaginary popular will, but to effect adjustments among the various special wills and purposes which at any given time are pressing for realization." And to do this, I might add, after full discussion in the country and mature deliberation in the representative assembly. . . . The pollsters overlook the really vital role of representative assemblies in focusing attention on political issues. If there were no Congress, with its clash of personalities, parties, and sections, could questions be asked, for example, about the Taft-Hartley Act or the Marshall Plan? If they were, "no opinion" would be by far the most frequent reply. . . .

There are few questions suitable for mass answers by yes or no. This the pollsters must ignore when they talk about sample referenda implementing democracy and making it articulate. A man may say that he is in favor of a protective tariff, but would it be worth while to ask him? No one in his senses would propose that a series of tariff schedules should be submitted for rejection or acceptance at the polls, yet the schedules determine whether there is to be any tariff protection and if so, how much. A man can be for or against the Taft-Hartley Act, but what would this mean? Few who know anything about the statute would say that all its provisions are good or that all are bad.

How, in the postwar period, could any issue of foreign policy have been put to the electorate for decision? The Marshall Plan? Its essence lay in the amounts of money, the strings attached to its use, and the concern of our government in respect of the ancillary measures to be taken by receiving states. Policy toward Russia? What questions could be put to an electorate? In an age when 531 representatives and senators who are paid so well for their time that they do not have to have other means of livelihood, and who are staffed for the investigation of the merits of proposed legislation, have to throw up their hands and say there are many details on which they cannot pass and which they must leave to administrative determination, it is absurd to suggest that counting the public pulse can give any light or leading save on the simplest kind of a proposition. And on such simple propositions the wishes of the public can usually be known without the assistance of a poll.

Harold J. Laski writes:

> If it [a referendum] is confined to obtaining answers to questions of principle, then, in the absence of concrete details, the questions are devoid of real meaning. If it is enlarged to consider the full amplitude of a complicated statute, then it is useless to pretend that a mass judgment upon its clauses is in any way a valid one. . . .

The public's lack of information on certain important issues suggests that in many cases even the pollsters should have viewed their percentages with suspicion and should have boldly declared that there was no opinion for them to try to measure. . . . After the Atlantic Charter had been discussed for some little while, 60 per cent of the population had "never heard of it" and 95 per cent could not name a single one of its provisions. A later poll disclosed eight in ten admitting that they had not read or heard about the Charter. Only one citizen in ten could name the Four Freedoms. Slightly more than one half of the people thought that Lend-Lease operated in reverse, but a majority of these believed that the return was "good will and co-operation" rather than substantial amounts of goods. At the time, polling organizations were telling us what "public opinion" was on the kind of peace settlement that was desirable (1944); and when there was a good deal of discussion of schemes for a new world organization, more than one half of the population thought we had joined the old League of Nations. The same year, seven out of ten did not know that the Senate must approve treaties by a two-thirds vote. . . . In 1946, 31 per cent of a sample had never heard of the Bill of Rights; 36 per cent had heard of it but could not identify it; and 12 per cent gave confused or contradictory answers. . . . And what of opinion on the Taft-Hartley Act? One poll disclosed 61 per cent claiming to have heard of the law, but of this "informed group" 75 per cent could not mention any specific provision that they considered particularly good, and 85 per cent could not pick out a provision that they thought particularly bad. . . .

A premise the pollsters do not make articulate is that if there is a majority public opinion, it should prevail, and presumably at once. They have never bothered to examine what majority rule means in the government the founding fathers proposed, which was accepted, and which, in its main outlines, no section of opinion save the Communists has since challenged. That system is not majority rule pure and simple, which is what the pollsters seem to assume it is. Our arrangements are fashioned as much to protect minorities as they are to enable majority opinion to prevail. Moreover . . . we endeavor to make the arrangements work in a federal system of government. . . . Under the American system of government we take many fateful decisions by less than a majority and sometimes prevent the larger part from having its way against the smaller part. . . .

From the grimness of the contemporary world it is sometimes useful to turn back to a piece of political literature that is still pertinent and suggestive and that deserves rereading. . . . [In 1774, Edmund] Burke made a speech that has been frequently quoted by those who have concerned themselves with the relations between representatives and their constituencies. Burke referred to the fact that his successful colleague at the election (Bristol returned two members to the House of Commons) had declared that "the topic of instructions has occasioned much altercation and uneasiness in this city," and had expressed himself "in favour of the coercive authority of such instructions." That view Burke vehemently repudiated.

> Certainly, gentlemen, [he declared], it ought to be the happiness and glory of a representative to live in the strictest union, the closest correspondence, and the most unreserved communication with his constituents. Their wishes ought to have great weight with him; their opinion high respect; their business unremitted attention. It is his duty to sacrifice his repose, his pleasures, his satisfaction, to theirs; and above all, ever, and in all cases, to prefer their interest to his own. But his unbiased opinion, his mature judgment,

> his enlightened conscience, he ought not to sacrifice to you; to any man, or to any set of men living. These he does not derive from your pleasure; no, nor from the law and the constitution. They are a trust from Providence, for the abuse of which he is deeply answerable. Your representative owes you, not his industry only, but his judgment; and he betrays, instead of serving you, if he sacrifices it to your opinion.

Burke said that his colleague had declared that "his will ought to be subservient to yours." If that were all, there would be no objection.

> If government were a matter of will upon any side, yours, without question, ought to be superior. But government and legislation are matters of reason and judgment, and not of inclination; and what sort of reason is that, in which the determination precedes the discussion; in which one set of men deliberate, and another decide; and where those who form the conclusion are perhaps three hundred miles distant from those who hear the arguments?

Of course it was the right of all men to deliver opinions, and those expressed by constituents would be "weighty and respectable." A representative ought always to be glad to hear them and he ought always most seriously to consider them. "But *authoritative* instructions, *mandates* issued, which the member is bound blindly and implicitly to obey, to vote, and to argue for, although contrary to the clearest conviction of his judgment and conscience—these are things utterly unknown to the laws of this land, and which arise from a fundamental mistake of the whole order and tenor of our constitution."

Then follows the passage that has been quoted most frequently:

> Parliament is not a *congress* of ambassadors from different and hostile interests; which interests each must maintain, as an agent and advocate, against other agents and advocates; but parliament is a *deliberative* assembly of *one* nation, with *one* interest, that of the whole; where, not local purposes, not local prejudices ought to guide, but the general good, resulting from the general reason of the whole. You choose a member indeed; but when you have chosen him, he is not a member of Bristol, but he is a member of *parliament*. If the local constituent should have an interest, or should form an hasty opinion, evidently opposite to the real good of the rest of the community, the member for that place ought to be as far, as any other, from any endeavour to give it effect. . . .

The principles on which Burke insisted are more frequently ignored than honored. He himself stated them in too extreme a form. He was indifferent to the value of discussion, which is indispensable in any community that seeks to govern itself rather than to permit itself to be ruled. As Sir Ernest Barker has suggested, "Burke regarded himself and his fellow members in the light of 'publick-Counsellors,' or as we may say in the language of that book of Ecclesiastes which he knew and quoted, 'leaders of the people by their counsels and by their knowledge of learning meet for the people wise and eloquent instruction.' He remained something of a scholar of

Trinity House, 'damned absolute'; something of a professor who even in the House of Commons was apt to speak *ex cathedra.*"

On the other hand, too many men have thought too exclusively of staying in a legislature or holding onto their seals of office. They have hesitated to express their convictions and have been content to follow rather than to lead public opinion. In Burke, wrote Lord Morley, "there was none of that too familiar casuistry, by which public men argue themselves out of their consciences in a strange syllogism, that they can best serve the country in Parliament; that to keep their seats they must follow their electors; and that, therefore, in the long run they serve the country best by acquiescing in ignorance and prejudice." In other public men who do not thus deceive themselves, hesitation and softness may result from the fact that they are tired; that swimming with the tide requires much less exertion than going against the tide; that plaudits are usually more pleasant than criticism. I could select innumerable illustrations of what I mean, but one will suffice. . . .

In November 1936 Stanley Baldwin told the House of Commons "that not once but on many occasions, in speeches and in various places, when I have been speaking and advocating as far as I am able the democratic principle, I have stated that a democracy is always two years behind the dictator. I believe that to be true." So far as British rearmament was concerned, Mr. Baldwin had made it true as he proceeded to explain to the House with what he himself described as "an appalling frankness." In order to win an election he had deceived Great Britain on Germany's rearmament program.

"Supposing I had gone to the country and said that Germany was rearming and that we must rearm, does anybody think that this pacific democracy would have rallied to that cry at that moment? I cannot think of anything that would have made the loss of the election from my point of view more certain." But the consequences of the policy were far more appalling than the frankness of the statement. To be sure, Mr. Baldwin's successor as Prime Minister had time in which he could have retrieved the error at least partially. But until the war came in September 1939, and Churchill, Eden, and others entered the Cabinet, there had been in the British executive little of that "energy" which in *The Federalist* papers Alexander Hamilton described as "a leading character in the definition of good government."

Energy is not to be found in those who do no more than follow—in those who look upon a legislative assembly as a congress of ambassadors. In Burke's day the sentiment of a constituency had to be ascertained from its leading members. Now legislators quail under a deluge of telegrams or letters, and not only keep their ears to the ground, but wonder whether they would not be wise to use the acousticon of public-opinion polls. . . .

Party first, mandated representatives, sectional and special interests—this is the setting in which free peoples, in Burke's phrase, now expect their governments to be contrivances of human wisdom to provide for human wants. It would be comforting to accept the sales patter of the pollsters and agree that what they call "public-opinion polls" really do "implement democracy." For reasons already given, I think that even to talk in such a fashion discloses reasoning that is fantastically muddled. To do more than talk—to permit the pollsters' pronouncements to influence policy would be disastrous politically. . . .

The great problem, Lord Acton once said, is not to discover "what governments prescribe but what they ought to prescribe." We cannot wait to obtain the prescription from the perfectionists who, as someone remarked, are people who have no solution for any difficulty but are, nevertheless, able to find a difficulty in any proposed solution. The great question so far as public opinion is concerned is not what it wants, but what it ought to want. . . .

During pre-Munich days, for example, the "essential wisdom" of the British people was latent because the nation had no leadership. Every people, it is cynically and untruthfully said, have as good a government as they deserve. But a government may have no better an electorate than it deserves because it fails to give leadership. In the days of Baldwin and Chamberlain, British politicians congratulated themselves on being able to catch buses they were supposed to be driving. Later, as Bertrand Russell said, the British people were magnificent.

"In a multitude of counsellors there is wisdom," wrote Huxley, "but only in a few of them." *Vox populi* cannot help democratic governments to decide what they ought to do. Political and intellectual leaders must propose alternative policies. They must educate the electorate, and if the leadership and education are effective, then the people will demonstrate their "essential wisdom." "It is the few," said Guicciardini, "which commonly give the turn to affairs" and to which "any general temper in a nation" may be traced.

True it is that in a free state public opinion rules, but this is no reason for more than interest in the yeses and noes that may be disclosed by sampling. A baker can ask a sample of consumers whether it wants the loaf of bread sliced or unsliced, and, if the answer is two to one for sliced, can decide to distribute loaves in that proportion. A housing authority *should* ask a sample whether it prefers flats or single dwellings. The British Broadcasting Corporation can ask its listeners whether they prefer jazz or classical music, but the directors of the BBC have a duty that goes beyond satisfying what the public says is its taste. They should endeavor to change that taste for the better.

"Shall income taxes be reduced?" can be asked of a sample, but the

Secretary of the Treasury and congressional committees on appropriations should take note of the answers only for the purpose of endeavoring to change those answers if they do not agree with them.

> It is the business of a statesman to lead [wrote the London *Times*], and with his ear perpetually to the ground he is in no posture of leadership. The honest leader determines his course by the light of his own conscience and the special knowledge available to him, not by ascertaining the views of his necessarily less well-informed followers, in order that he may meekly conform. Having decided for himself what is right, he has then to convince the rank and file, knowing that if he fails to win or hold their support they will dismiss him and transfer their trust to another. That, and that only, is the sanction for the ultimate control of public opinion over policy. By no other means can the general will be formulated and elicited. A leader, in war or peace, who hesitates to take his political life in his hands will not be followed; neither social surveys nor any other mechanical device can be manipulated as an insurance by a politician playing for safety. Democracy implies and demands leadership in the true sense, and flounders without it.

The United States has been fortunate in that it had leadership at critical times. The chief incidents are well known. Jefferson made the Louisiana Purchase without consulting Congress. "A John Randolph," he wrote, "would find means to protract the proceeding on it by Congress until the ensuing spring, by which time new circumstances would change the mind of the other party." Public opinion approved Jefferson's acquisition. President Monroe announced what for a century was the basis of American foreign policy in a message to Congress—the Monroe Doctrine. Abraham Lincoln took courageous action that he admitted was beyond his legal power as President but that he thought was not beyond the constitutional competence of Congress, which would be called upon to approve it. . . .

Franklin Roosevelt made his "New Deal" and took his decisions on the transfer of destroyers in return for the use of British bases and of convoying before he was sure of congressional or public approval. Even if a sample poll had shown majority criticism, and its findings had had support from other quarters, the decisions should have stood and the President could have waited for the "essential wisdom" of the people to manifest itself. The polls did show support for the President, and this was better than if they had shown lack of support, which might have caused a little but only temporary embarrassment.

What of leadership now? What foreign policies should we have? What, domestically, should be our program? Answers to these questions are not my present subject. The pollsters will not be able to discover what our policies should be from samples in which each respondent says "yes" or "no" or "don't know." That method may be suitable for predicting election results, and should work *if the sample is properly chosen.* But the method is not suitable for measuring public opinion on the foreign or domestic proposals that statesmen may make. Each member of the electorate casts a ballot that is the equal of every other ballot. But who are the people who favor certain policies? How influential are they? Whom do they represent? How well are they organized? How much do they care? . . . In politics it is not the accumulation of facts but insight that will find the highroad if and when it is found.

The facts that the pollsters accumulate and endeavor to explain they create themselves. Bernard Shaw once declared that he was unable to see a great deal of difference between the controversies of the schoolmen over how many angels could stand on the point of a needle and the discussions of the physicists over the number of electrons in an atom. There is a difference: the physicist proposes to do something with his answer when he gets it, and he knows that it will be accepted by all other physicists. The pollsters get answers—yeses and noes—that are frequently suspect on their faces, that are not the same answers as other pollsters get, and that sometimes cancel each other out.

Since they must maintain that their work is important, the pollsters use a false premise: that our political system must accept and act on their answers. . . . So far as the pollers of public opinion are concerned, the light they have been following is a will-o'-the-wisp. They have been taking in each other's washing, and have been using statistics in terms of the Frenchman's definition: a means of being precise about matters of which you will remain ignorant.

Do the Polls Serve Democracy?

JOHN C. RANNEY *

Most of the current controversy over public opinion polls has centered about the question of their accuracy: the reliability of the sample taken, the impartiality of the sponsorship, the honesty of the interviewer and the person interviewed, the fairness of the questions, the measurement of intensities or gradations of feeling, and the validity of the analysis or interpretation. These are all, admittedly, important questions; but they tend to ignore or to beg one which is both more important and more theoretical: Assuming that the polls were to attain a miraculously perfect and unchallengeable accuracy, would they, even then, contribute significantly to the working of democracy?

One's first inclination is to take it for granted that the answer is "Yes."

* Late Professor of Government at Smith College. The selection is from John C. Ranney, "Do the Polls Serve Democracy?" *Public Opinion Quarterly*, Vol. 10 (Fall, 1946), pp. 349–360. By permission.

No principle, in democratic theory, has been more fundamental than the belief that political decisions ought to be made by the people as a whole or in accordance with their desires. Yet no principle, in democratic practice, has proved more difficult of precise application. In theory, even when doubts are entertained as to the rationality, the objectivity, and the capacity of the ordinary citizen, modern democratic writers have continued to find the essence of democracy in popular participation in policy-making.[1] But in practice, it has long been apparent that our electoral system, as a reflection of popular wishes and as a channel for popular activity, leaves a good deal to be desired.

Various improvements have been suggested, ranging from the initiative and the referendum to proportional or functional representation. But none of these devices, except by placing an intolerable strain on the voter, has solved the problem of how to reflect simultaneously the great diversity of his interests and attitudes on different issues.[2] The result, under our present system, is that even if one assumes that the voter does anything more than choose between the personalities of rival candidates, an election approximates what has been called "plebiscitary democracy." It is a way of approving or disapproving in the most general terms the policies of the party or individual in office and of renewing or transferring this exceedingly vague mandate for the coming term of office.

Such a check and consultation is much better than none at all. Notwithstanding its resemblance to some of the dictatorial plebiscites, it permits, in a free society, the expression of at least the major discontents. But consultations which are so sweeping and which occur at such rare intervals are only the thinnest caricature of the democratic belief that the health of the community depends upon the personal, active, and continuous political participation of the body of its citizens.

[1] For some recent statements on this subject, see Carl L. Becker, *Modern Democracy* (New Haven, 1941), p. 7; James Bryce, *Modern Democracies* (New York, 1924), Vol. 1, p. 20; Francis Coker, *Recent Political Thought* (New York and London, 1934), p. 293; Carl J. Friedrich, *The New Belief in the Common Man* (Boston, 1942), pp. 31, 221; Harold J. Laski, "Democracy," *Encyclopaedia of the Social Sciences* (New York, 1932), Vol. 3, pp. 80, 84; John D. Lewis, "The Elements of Democracy," *American Political Science Review,* Vol. 34, p. 469 (June, 1940); A. D. Lindsay, *The Modern Democratic State* (London, New York, Toronto, 1943), Vol. 1, pp. 267–268; Charles E. Merriam, *The New Democracy and the New Despotism* (New York, 1939), pp. 11–12; Francis Graham Wilson, *The Elements of Modern Politics* (New York and London, 1936), pp. 189–190, 247.

[2] John Dickinson, "Democratic Realities and the Democratic Dogma," *American Political Science Review,* Vol. 24, p. 300 (May, 1930); Pendleton Herring, *The Politics of Democracy* (New York, 1940), p. 329; E. E. Schattschneider, *Party Government* (New York, 1942), p. 33. For the weaknesses of such devices as the initiative and referendum, see Harold F. Gosnell, "The Polls and Other Mechanisms of Democracy," *Public Opinion Quarterly,* Vol. 4, p. 225 (June, 1940); A. Lawrence Lowell, *Public Opinion and Popular Government* (New York, 1913), pp. 152–235; William B. Munro, "Initiative and Referendum," *Encyclopaedia of the Social Sciences,* Vol. 4, pp. 50–52.

It is here that the polls are supposed to make their great contribution. By separating the issues from one another, by stating them simply and clearly, and by covering the electorate completely and continuously, they avoid the most obvious obscurities, strains, and distortions of the older procedures. If to these virtues one might add unchallengeable accuracy, the well-known dream of Bryce would be realized: the will of the majority of the citizens could be ascertained at all times; representative assemblies and elaborate voting machinery would be unnecessary and obsolete.

ATTACKS ON THE POLLS

Not everyone has rejoiced over this possibility. Anyone who agrees with Hamilton, for example, that the people are turbulent and changing, seldom judging or determining right, is hardly likely to welcome a device to make the voice of the people (which decidedly is not the voice of God) more audible than ever. Nor is this attitude likely to surprise or disturb the genuine democrat.

What should disturb him, however, is the fact that there are many people who consider themselves good democrats and who nevertheless consider the polls a menace to democracy. The objections of this second group deserve more systematic attention than they have yet received.

THE DESTRUCTION OF LEADERSHIP

The first and most frequent of these objections is that the polls destroy political courage and leadership. Every adequate government, it is maintained, requires these qualities in its officials. They can exist, however, only where there is freedom and flexibility and where the statesman is not bound, either in form or in fact, by rigid instructions from the voters. The government official, whether Congressman or administrator, has access to information which is beyond the reach of the ordinary voter, and he has something more than the ordinary voter's leisure in which to consider it. To subject his judgment to the ill-informed and hasty judgment of the electorate is to commit the political crime of rendering a decision before considering the evidence on which it ought to be based. It is true that the polls have no official standing and cannot bind any office-holder. But, the charge runs, the official who wants to keep his job will abandon his duty of analyzing and judging proposed policies in favor of the simpler, and safer, device of deciding as the polls tell him to decide.[3]

[3] For a concise statement of this position, see Eric F. Goldman, "Poll on the Polls," *Public Opinion Quarterly*, Vol. 8, pp. 461–467 (Winter, 1944–45), and the literature there cited.

So far as the legislator is concerned, there are several weaknesses in this argument. Simply as a matter of fact, it would be extremely difficult to show that the polls have had a decisive effect in determining the voting habits of any substantial number of representatives.[4] It is one of the dubious advantages of the American system that it is extremely difficult to allocate responsibility; and even in those cases in which responsibility can be fixed, the ordinary voter is only too likely to be ignorant of the voting record of his representative. The average Congressman on the average issue need not worry too much about the opinion of his constituents in the mass. What he does need to worry about is the opinion of specific organizations and individuals inside his constituency, especially the political machines and the organized pressure groups. Any Congressman who is concerned with political realities knows that it is more important to appease a well-disciplined minority, which can deliver the votes on election day, than to gratify an unorganized and casual majority, the intensity of whose convictions and the efficacy of whose action is far less likely to be decisive. If the polls exert any influence at all, therefore, they tend to moderate or deflate rather than to reinforce the special pressures already influencing legislators.

The absence of scientific methods for measuring opinion, moreover, has never prevented politicians from trying to guess what it is. The representative, if such there be, who follows the polls slavishly would have his ear well to the ground under any circumstances. It is hard to see how democracy is undermined or its moral fibre destroyed simply by providing him with more reliable methods of judgment. It can hardly be urged that so long as a representative is going to vote according to public opinion anyway, the more distorted his picture of it, the better. Nor would it be easy to show that, among those restrained by the polls, the idealists seriously outnumber those who would otherwise follow the dictates of selfish and limited interests.

Finally, it should be remembered that public opinion is not so definite and rigid as the argument implies. In some instances, changes have been both rapid and extreme, and political leaders have often been in a strategic position to influence or shape it. In addition, men of intelligence and foresight who understand the probable effects of an unfortunate policy or the

[4] More Congressmen would be influenced by the polls, and the argument strengthened, if there were more general confidence in their accuracy and if the returns were published by Congressional districts. For evidence of the influence of polls on legislators, see L. E. Gleeck, "96 Congressmen Make Up Their Minds," *Public Opinion Quarterly,* Vol. 4, pp. 3–24 (March, 1940); George W. Hartman, "Judgments of State Legislators Concerning Public Opinion," *Journal of Social Psychology,* Vol. 21, pp. 105–114 (February, 1945); Martin Kriesberg, "What Congressmen and Administrators Think of the Polls," *Public Opinion Quarterly,* Vol. 9, pp. 333–337 (Fall, 1945); George F. Lewis, Jr., "The Congressmen Look at the Polls," *Ibid.,* Vol. 4, pp. 229–231 (June, 1940).

misconceptions on which it is based can anticipate the ultimate revulsion of public feeling and act accordingly. Voters, it should be remembered, do not always show great tolerance for the Congressman who excuses his own past mistakes with the plea that most of the electorate, at the time, shared his way of thinking.

Although the argument concerning the destruction of leadership is usually made with the legislator in mind, it actually has somewhat more factual strength in the case of the policy-making administrator. Surveys indicate that he is more likely to pay attention to the results of the polls, and he is also more likely to have expert or specialized personal knowledge as an alternative basis for decision. There is a possibility, at least, that his interest in the polls may indicate a tendency to subordinate his own well-informed judgment to the opinion of the electorate; and there is a further possibility that he may become so dependent upon it that he will take no action at all when that opinion is confused or divided or simply non-existent.

On the other hand, the administrator is, if anything, subject to even greater and more numerous pressures than is the Congressman. For him, therefore, the polls may be even more important as a basis for resisting minority pressures in the public interest. Moreover, like the legislator, he has considerable power to influence public opinion, although his methods are somewhat different; and a precise knowledge of what that opinion is can be an important help in enlightening or changing it.

The factual basis, or lack of basis, for the argument that the polls destroy leadership is less important, however, than two of the argument's theoretical implications.

The first of these is that government officials, whether legislators or administrators, constitute something of an expert body, possessing unusual intelligence, information, and skill, and that to this body the voter, because of his personal inadequacy, should delegate his power.

This argument, however, proves too much. If expertness is to be the criterion for the right to participate in government, the ordinary Congressman would himself have difficulty in qualifying. Even the policy-making administrator, in an age of increasingly voluminous and technical legislation, is likely to be an expert only in the most attenuated sense of the term. To be sure, both he and the legislator must make use of the knowledge and experience of the expert, especially in determining the technical means to achieve broader and predetermined objectives. But when it comes to determining the objectives themselves—and it is with objectives rather than with means that the polls are primarily concerned—the democratic theorist who would free leaders from the restraint of a less well-informed public opinion is, consciously or unconsciously, on the road to what, since the days of Plato, has been the radically undemocratic position of urging rule by some elite.

The second theoretical implication is the even stranger one that ignorance of what the people want and feel is a positive advantage in a democracy. Yet few defenses of democracy have been more persuasive than the one which insists that democracy alone provides the government with adequate information about the desires and attitudes of the people and that, even if these prove to be ignorant or irrational, it is only on the basis of such information that a government can act intelligently. Legislation cannot be separated from the practical problem of administration and enforcement; and it is of fundamental importance, in framing and administering laws with intelligence, to understand, as one of the vital factors in the situation, the state of public feeling. This is not to say that opinion is the only factor to be considered. It is saying that it is an essential element in the rational analysis of any political situation. People will not refrain from having opinions and acting upon them simply because they are not asked what they are. Yet statesmen, whether legislators or administrators, are unlikely to have direct personal knowledge of these feelings; and the weaknesses of elections, the press, and other methods of identifying them have been obvious for decades. Here, therefore, if anywhere, the polls, far from being a menace to democracy, give substance and meaning to what has always, in theory, been one of its outstanding advantages.[5]

In short, so far as this first set of criticisms is concerned, the polls are neither, in fact, so destructive of leadership and courage as critics suggest nor, in theory, so incompatible with the traditional meaning of democracy. On the contrary, the unstated assumptions of the critics tend logically to a conclusion which is itself basically undemocratic.

THE POLLS AS A BRAKE ON PROGRESS

A second set of charges is remarkable for the way in which it parallels Hamilton's way of thinking for purposes which are quite un-Hamiltonian. Its authors agree that the intelligence and judgment of the people is to be distrusted—not because of their radicalism, however, but because of their conservatism and complacency. Far from being a source of turbulence and unrest and a menace to private property and traditional ways of doing things, the people are so conventional and so contented with things as they are that they constitute a formidable brake upon progress, slow to see the need for drastic social changes and slow to take the necessary steps, always

[5] The use already made of the polls by such governmental agencies as the Department of Agriculture indicates their value in making this theoretical advantage of democracy into a real one. See Friedrich, *op. cit.*, pp. 117, 217–221.

doing too little and always doing it too late. Public opinion polls, by giving publicity to these attitudes, increase their force. In addition, the attention and deference paid them intensify both the complacency of the people and their confidence in their own mystical rightness. What the people need, however, is to develop some realization of their own shortcomings and some willingness to leave to the expert those matters of which he alone can judge.[6]

Here, as in the case of the first set of criticisms, it would be difficult to prove that the people are actually more conservative than their representatives. Some observers, in fact, contend that the polls have repeatedly shown the people to be far readier than Congress to accept progressive ideas.[7] But even if the people proved, as a regular matter, to be a hindrance to progress, certain theoretical difficulties would remain. It is undoubtedly true that the process of modern government is too technical and complex to be directed in detail by the ordinary citizen and that the skill and knowledge of the expert must be tapped in a responsible fashion. Yet this argument is too easily confused with the very different argument that the "responsible" expert must be given the power to introduce, according to his own judgment, drastic social changes. There is, to begin with, a certain lack of logic in an argument which speaks of ultimate responsibility to the public while maintaining that "trained intelligence" must none the less be free to introduce the drastic changes which the uninformed public is not prepared to accept. And the more one tries to avoid this dilemma by limiting responsibility to the voter in favor of government by a disinterested, wise, and public-spirited elite, the more the criticism becomes one, not of the polls as a hindrance to the operation of democracy, but of democracy as a hindrance to progress.

The defense of democracy, which is as old as Aristotle, does not need to be elaborated here. But it is essential to point out, as Plato himself came to recognize, that no government, however well intentioned, can force a community to move in directions in which it does not want to move, or to move much more rapidly than it would otherwise move, without resorting to instruments of force and tyranny which are incompatible with both the spirit and the practice of democracy.

THE POLLS AS A MISCONCEPTION OF DEMOCRACY

The third, and by far the most valid, criticism which can be made of the polls is that they represent a fundamental misconception of the nature of democracy. Bryce's picture of a society in which the will of the majority of

[6] Robert S. Lynd, "Democracy in Reverse," *Public Opinion Quarterly,* Vol. 4, pp. 218–220 (June, 1940). See also Lindsay, *op. cit.*, p. 234.

[7] William A. Lydgate, *What America Thinks* (New York, 1944), pp. 2–8.

the citizens would be ascertainable at all times is neither a very profound nor a very realistic picture of democratic society. Democracy is not simply the ascertaining and the applying of a "will of the people"—a somewhat mystical entity existing in and of itself, independent, unified, and complete. It is the whole long process by which the people and their agents inform themselves, discuss, make compromises, and finally arrive at a decision.

The people are not the only element in this process, and they are not necessarily the agent which is best suited to each part of the task. In general, the executive and the administrative services are best fitted to see policy as a whole and to prepare a coherent program as well as to handle the technical details of legislation. The legislature provides a forum in which the different interests within the country can confront one another in a regularized way, as the people cannot, and acquire something of the mutual understanding and comprehensive outlook which is essential for the satisfactory adjustment of interests. The people themselves, finally, can express better than any other agency what it is they need and want.

None of these functions, it is true, belongs exclusively to any one agency, nor can any be separated rigidly from the others. The process of discussion and adjustment is a continuous one, carried on on all levels. There is a constant interweaving and interpenetration of talk and action subject to no precise demarcation but in which it is none the less essential that each agency refrain from functions which are beyond its competence. In this process the operation of the polls may be positively harmful, not in interfering with "government by experts" as more frequently charged, but in emphasizing the content of the opinion rather than the way in which it is formed and in focussing attention on the divergency of opinion rather than upon the process of adjusting and integrating it.

To say this is not to urge a restriction on popular participation but to emphasize its real nature and function. Popular participation in government is thin and meaningless if it is nothing more than the registering of an opinion. It becomes meaningful to the extent that the opinion is itself the product of information, discussion, and practical political action. There is something not only pathetic but indicative of a basic weakness in the polls' conception of democracy in the stories of those who tell interviewers they could give a "better answer" to the questions if only they had time to read up a bit or think things over. It is precisely this reading up and thinking over which are the essence of political participation and which make politics an educational experience, developing the character and capacity of the citizens.[8]

[8] To some, this is the greatest justification of democracy. C. Delisle Burns, *Democracy* (London, 1929); Coker, *op. cit.;* John Dewey, *The Public and Its Problems* (New York, 1927); John Stuart Mill, *Considerations on Representative Government* (New York, 1862); Alexis de Tocqueville, *Democracy in America* (New York, 1838).

The polls, however, except as their publication tends to stimulate political interest, play almost no part in this process. They make it possible for the people to express their attitude toward specific proposals and even to indicate the intensity of their feeling on the subject; and they can distinguish the attitudes of different social and economic groups from one another. But they provide no mechanism on the popular level for promoting discussion, for reconciling and adjusting conflicting sectional, class, or group interests, or for working out a coherent and comprehensive legislative program.

In fact, far less perfect instruments for discovering the "will" of the voters are often much more effective in arousing popular participation. The initiative and the referendum, for all their weaknesses, stir opponents and advocates of measures to unusual activity and stimulate a large proportion of the voters, rather than a small selected sample, to consider and discuss the issues. Similarly, the privately-conducted British Peace Ballot proved to be an educational experience for the entire British people. Even the much maligned *Literary Digest* Poll performed a greater service in arousing thought and discussion than did its more accurate competitors.

In short, the polls are not concerned with, and provide no remedy for, the gravest weaknesses in the democratic process. If one thinks of democracy in practical terms of discussion and political activity rather than of a disembodied "will," the great need is to get rid of the obstacles to popular education, information, debate, judgment, and enforcement of responsibility. To do this, there must be a multiple effort directed against a multiplicity of evils. To mention only a few of these, the political education in most of our schools, handicapped as they are by conventional schoolboards and the fear of controversy, is wretchedly inadequate. In too many cities the sources of information are insufficient, the news itself distorted, and the free competition of ideas seriously restricted.[9] In general, our facilities for discussion—clubs, unions, pressure organizations, forums, round-tables, and the radio—provide no adequate successor to the town meeting in the sense of active and responsible personal participation.[10] More fundamen-

[9] The development of the one-newspaper pattern is particularly unfortunate. Oswald Garrison Villard, *The Disappearing Daily* (New York, 1944), pp. 3, 5, 10–12. See also Morris L. Ernst, *The First Freedom* (New York, 1946), xii and *passim* for a survey not only of the newspaper but of book publishing, the radio, and the motion picture.

[10] On the need for new devices for discussion, see Harwood L. Childs, *An Introduction to Public Opinion* (New York, 1940), p. 137; Coker, *op. cit.*, p. 373; Harold D. Lasswell, *Democracy through Public Opinion* (Menasha, Wisconsin, 1941), pp. 80–95; Merriam, *On the Agenda of Democracy* (Cambridge, 1941), pp. 21–22; Joseph R. Starr, "Political Parties and Public Opinion," *Public Opinion Quarterly*, Vol. 3, pp. 436–448 (July, 1939). For a more optimistic picture, see Friedrich, *Constitutional Government*, p. 546.

tally, the undemocratic character of much of our economic and social life is a real hindrance to the growth of political democracy.

Moreover, even if our political education were magnificent, the channels of information completely clear, the facilities for discussion abundant, and the spirit of democracy universal, the obscurity and confusion in our political system, resulting from its checks and balances and its lack of party discipline, would make it almost impossible for the ordinary voter to understand what is going on, to pass judgment intelligently, and to place responsibility. Yet any government in which the people are to share must at a minimum be comprehensible. Obscurity and anonymity kill democracy. These defects, however, are present in our government, and about them the polls can do very little.

SUMMARY

The chief advantage of the polls is that, in an age of increasing strain upon traditional democratic procedures, they have made a constructive technical contribution by reflecting sensitively and flexibly the currents of public feeling, by making this information available to political leaders in a way which is neither rigid nor mandatory, and by testing the claims of special interests to represent the desires of the people as a whole. These are services performed by no other agency, and they should not be underestimated.

But if, in a democracy, the health of the community depends upon the personal, active, and continuous political participation of the body of its citizens, this contribution is a limited and even a minor one. Even when used with the greatest accuracy and intelligence, the polls cannot achieve any fundamental improvement until our political system itself is simplified, until the lines of responsibility are clarified, and until devices are discovered for increasing the direct participation of the people, not simply in the registration of their aims, but in the deliberative procedure which is the real heart of democracy.

Section II

Some Fundamental Constitutional Principles

The Constitutional Convention of 1787 met behind closed doors and very early adopted a rule "that nothing spoken in the House be printed, or otherwise published, or communicated without leave." This made it possible for the Framers to speak with greater frankness than one would find in speeches intended for the general public. The debates over suffrage, the term of office, and method of electing congressmen reveal the attitude of the Founding Fathers toward democracy and representative government.

Apart from Benjamin Franklin, few members of the Convention had the great faith in the ultimate wisdom of the people which was characteristic of Jefferson. Many delegates made reference to their assumption that men in politics were usually motivated by self-interest and ambition. Although accepting Hamilton's dictum that "Real liberty is neither found in despotism or the extremes of democracy, but in moderate governments," they rejected, however, Hamilton's conclusion that "the rich and well born" should be given a permanent check on the turbulence and follies of democracy.

While it is something of an exaggeration to call Madison "the Father of the Constitution," it is certainly true that among the delegates he was the most widely read and profound student of political institutions. No other member contributed more to the success of the Convention. "The principal task of modern legislation," said Madison, "is the regulation of the various and conflicting economic interests." Assuming that "justice" should be the aim of government, Madison concluded that since human beings are most likely to be biased by self-interest, no body of men should be allowed to judge in its own cause. In writing to Jefferson about the Constitution, Madison asked: "If two individuals are under the bias of interest or enmity against a third, the rights of the latter could never be safely referred to the majority of the three. Will two thousand individuals be less apt to oppress one thousand, or two hundred thousand one hundred thousand?" Madison's answer to this question was the same as that given later by de Tocqueville and Lippmann—that in a completely democratic form of government the civil rights and the economic interests of the minority would be at the mercy of the majority. Jefferson's greater faith in the majority is supported by Commager's "In Defense of Majority Rule."

Although the American Constitution has been changed by amendments and modified by more than a century and a half of political practice, it still embodies, to a considerable extent, the philosophy of the Founding Fathers. The great object of the Constitution, said Madison in Number 10 of *The Federalist,* is to secure the public good and private rights against the power of popular majorities "and at the same time preserve the spirit and form of popular government." The ideal of Madison was representative government which would, to a much greater extent than under the Articles of Confederation, be independent of the people and yet sufficiently controlled by the people so that it would not serve the interests of the representatives at the expense of general welfare.

Topic 3

DEBATES IN THE CONSTITUTIONAL CONVENTION

Excerpts from the Debates in the Constitutional Convention of 1787

DEBATE ON THE HOUSE OF REPRESENTATIVES *

Resolution: 4. first clause; "that the members of the first branch of the National Legislature ought to be elected by the people of the several states." [under consideration]

Mr. Sherman [Roger Sherman of Connecticut] opposed the election by the people, insisting that it ought to be by the State Legislatures. The people, he said, immediately should have as little to do as may be about the Government. They want information and are constantly liable to be misled.

* This selection is taken from James Madison's Journal of the Debates as reprinted in Max Farrand, ed., *Records of the Federal Convention* (New Haven, Yale University Press, 1927), Vol. I, pp. 48–50. By permission of Yale University Press. The Journal of the Debates was originally published in 1840, after all the members of the Convention had died, as part of *The Papers of James Madison.* Farrand's notations indicating additions and corrections made by Madison in his manuscript in later years have been omitted. The spelling has been modernized and most abbreviations spelled out.

Mr. Gerry [Elbridge Gerry of Massachusetts].* The evils we experience flow from the excess of democracy. The people do not want virtue; but are the dupes of pretended patriots. In Massachusetts it has been fully confirmed by experience that they are daily misled into the most baneful measures and opinions by the false reports circulated by designing men, and which no one on the spot can refute. One principal evil arises from the want of due provision for those employed in the administration of Government. It would seem to be a maxim of democracy to starve the public servants. He mentioned the popular clamor in Massachusetts for the reduction of salaries and the attack made on that of the Governor though secured by the spirit of the Constitution itself. He had he said been too republican heretofore: he was still however republican, but had been taught by experience the danger of the levelling spirit.

Mr. Mason [George Mason of Virginia, author of the Virginia Declaration of Rights] † argued strongly for an election of the larger branch by the people. It was to be the grand depository of the democratic principle of the Government. It was, so to speak, to be our House of Commons— It ought to know and sympathize with every part of the community; and ought therefore to be taken not only from different parts of the whole republic, but also from different districts of the larger members of it, which had in several instances particularly in Virginia, different interests and views arising from difference of produce, of habits &c. &c.

He admitted that we had been too democratic but was afraid we should incautiously run into the opposite extreme. We ought to attend to the rights of every class of the people. He had often wondered at the indifference of the superior classes of society to this dictate of humanity and policy, considering that however affluent their circumstances, or elevated their situations, might be, the course of a few years, not only might but certainly would distribute their posterity throughout the lowest classes of Society. Every selfish motive therefore, every family attachment, ought to recommend such a system of policy as would provide no less carefully for the rights—and happiness of the lowest than of the highest orders of Citizens.

Mr. Wilson [James Wilson of Pennsylvania, member of the first Supreme Court] contended strenuously for drawing the most numerous branch of the Legislature immediately from the people. He was for raising the federal pyramid to a considerable altitude, and for that reason wished to give it as broad a basis as possible. No government could long subsist without the confidence of the people. In a republican Government this confidence was peculiarly essential. He also thought it wrong to increase the weight

* Gerry refused to sign the Constitution and opposed its adoption.
† Mason also refused to sign the Constitution and opposed its adoption.

of the State Legislatures by making them the electors of the national Legislature. All interference between the general and local Governments should be obviated as much as possible. On examination it would be found that the opposition of States to federal measures had proceeded much more from the Officers of the States, than from the people at large.

Mr. Madison [James Madison of Virginia] considered the popular election of one branch of the national Legislature as essential to every plan of free Government. He observed that in some of the States one branch of the Legislature was composed of men already removed from the people by an intervening body of electors. That if the first branch of the general legislature should be elected by the State Legislatures, the second branch elected by the first—the Executive by the second together with the first; and other appointments again made for subordinate purposes by the Executive, the people would be lost sight of altogether; and the necessary sympathy between them and their rulers and officers, too little felt. He was an advocate for the policy of refining the popular appointments by successive filtrations, but thought it might be pushed too far. He wished the expedient to be resorted to only in the appointment of the second branch of the Legislature, and in the Executive and judiciary branches of the Government. He thought too that the great fabric to be raised would be more stable and durable if it should rest on the solid foundation of the people themselves, than if it should stand merely on the pillars of the Legislatures.

Mr. Gerry did not like the election by the people. The maxims taken from the British constitution were often fallacious when applied to our situation which was extremely different. Experience he said had shown that the State Legislatures drawn immediately from the people did not always possess their confidence. He had no objection however to an election by the people if it were so qualified that men of honor and character might not be unwilling to be joined in the appointments. He seemed to think that the people might nominate a certain number out of which the State Legislatures should be bound to choose.

Mr. Butler [Pierce Butler of South Carolina] thought an election by the people an impracticable mode.

On the question for an election of the first branch of the national Legislature, by the people; Massachusetts aye, Connecticut divided, New York aye, New Jersey no, Pennsylvania aye, Delaware divided, Virginia aye, North Carolina aye, South Carolina no, Georgia aye. (Ayes—6; noes—2; divided—2.)

HAMILTON'S PLAN FOR THE CONSTITUTION *

Monday, June 18, In Committee of the Whole

On motion of Mr. Dickinson to postpone the first Resolution in Mr. Patterson's plan, [New Jersey Plan] in order to take up the following, viz: *"that the articles of confederation ought to be revised and amended so as to render the Government of the U.S. adequate to the exigencies, the preservation and the prosperity of the union."* The postponement was agreed to by 10 States, Pennsylvania divided.

Mr. Hamilton. [Alexander Hamilton of New York] Yet, I confess, I see great difficulty of drawing forth a good representation. What, for example, will be the inducements for gentlemen of fortune and abilities to leave their houses and business to attend annually and long? It cannot be the wages; for these, I presume, must be small. Will not the power, therefore, be thrown into the hands of the demagogue or middling politician, who, for the sake of a small stipend and the hopes of advancement, will offer himself as a candidate, and the real men of weight and influence, by remaining at home, add strength to the state governments?

I am at a loss to know what must be done—I despair that a republican form of government can remove the difficulties. Whatever may be my opinion, I would hold it however unwise to change that form of government. I believe the British government forms the best model the world ever produced, and such has been its progress in the minds of the many, that this truth gradually gains ground. This government has for its object *public strength* and *individual security*. It is said with us to be unattainable. If it was once formed it would maintain itself.

All communities divide themselves into the few and the many. The first are the rich and well born, the other the mass of the people. The voice of the people has been said to be the voice of God; and however generally this maxim has been quoted and believed, it is not true in fact. The people are turbulent and changing; they seldom judge or determine right. Give therefore to the first class a distinct, permanent share in the government. They will check the unsteadiness of the second, and as they cannot receive any advantage by a change, they therefore will ever maintain good government. Can a democratic assembly, who annually revolve in the mass

* The selections from Hamilton's speech originally appeared in *Secret Proceedings and Debates of the Convention Assembled at Philadelphia, in the year 1787, for the purpose of forming the Constitution of the United States of America. From Notes taken by the late Robert Yates, Esq. Chief Justice of New York, and copied by John Lansing, Jun, Esq.* Reprinted in Farrand, *Records,* Vol. I, pp. 298–301. Farrand's *Records* contain three other versions of Hamilton's speech. The first paragraph below is from Madison's Journal as reprinted in Farrand, *Records,* Vol. I, p. 282.

of the people, be supposed steadily to pursue the public good? Nothing but a permanent body can check the imprudence of democracy. Their turbulent and uncontrolling disposition requires checks.

The senate of New York, although chosen for four years, we found to be inefficient. Will, on the Virginia plan, a continuance of seven years do it? It is admitted that you cannot have a good executive upon a democratic plan. See the excellency of the British executive— He is placed above temptation— He can have no distinct interests from the public welfare. Nothing short of such an executive can be efficient. The weak side of a republican government is the danger of foreign influence. This is unavoidable, unless it is so constructed as to bring forward its first characters in its support. I am therefore for a general government, yet would wish to go the full length of republican principles.

Let one body of the legislature be constituted during good behavior or life.

Let one executive be appointed who dares execute his powers. It may be asked is this a republican system? It is strictly so, as long as they remain elective.

And let me observe, that an executive is less dangerous to the liberties of the people when in office during life, than for seven years.

It may be said this constitutes an elective monarchy? Pray what is a monarchy? May not the governors of the respective states be considered in that light? But by making the executive subject to impeachment, the term monarchy cannot apply. These elective monarchs have produced tumults in Rome, and are equally dangerous to peace in Poland; but this cannot apply to the mode in which I would propose the election. Let electors be appointed in each of the states to elect the executive.

[Yates' notes indicate that here Hamilton produced his plan for the federal "legislature"] to consist of two branches—and I would give them the unlimited power of passing *all laws* without exception. The assembly to be elected for three years by the people in districts—the senate to be elected by electors to be chosen for that purpose by the people, and to remain in office during life. The executive to have the power of negativing all laws—to make war or peace, with the advice of the senate—to make treaties with their advice, but to have the sole direction of all military operations, and to send ambassadors and appoint all military officers, and to pardon all offenders, treason excepted, unless by advice of the senate. On his death or removal, the president of the senate to officiate, with the same powers, until another is elected. Supreme judicial officers to be appointed by the executive and the senate. The legislature to appoint courts in each state, so as to make the state governments unnecessary to it.

All state laws to be absolutely void which contravene the general laws.

An officer to be appointed in each state to have a negative on all state laws. All the militia and the appointment of officers to be under the national government.

I confess that this plan and that from Virginia are very remote from the idea of the people. Perhaps the Jersey plan is nearest their expectation. But the people are gradually ripening in their opinions of government—they begin to be tired of an excess of democracy—and what even is the Virginia plan, but *pork still, with a little change of the sauce.*

DEBATE ON THE SENATE *

Tuesday, June 26, In Convention

The duration of the second branch under consideration.

Mr. Gorham [Nathaniel Gorham of Massachusetts] moved to fill the blank with "six years," one third of the members to go out every second year.

Mr. Wilson seconded the motion. . . .

Mr. Madison. In order to judge of the form to be given to this institution, it will be proper to take a view of the ends to be served by it. These were first to protect the people against their rulers: secondly to protect [the people] against the transient impressions into which they themselves might be led. A people deliberating in a temperate moment, and with the experience of other nations before them, on the plan of Government most likely to secure their happiness, would first be aware, that those charged with the public happiness, might betray their trust. An obvious precaution against this danger would be to divide the trust between different bodies of men, who might watch and check each other. In this they would be governed by the same prudence which has prevailed in organizing the subordinate departments of Government where all business liable to abuses is made to pass through separate hands, the one being a check on the other.

It would next occur to such a people, that they themselves were liable to temporary errors, through want of information as to their true interest, and that men chosen for a short term, and employed but a small portion of that in public affairs, might err from the same cause. This reflection would naturally suggest that the Government be so constituted, as that one of its branches might have an opportunity of acquiring a competent knowledge of the public interests. Another reflection equally becoming a people on such an occasion, would be that they themselves, as well as a numerous body of Representatives, were liable to err also, from fickleness and passion. A necessary fence against this danger would be to select a portion of

* The following extracts from Madison's Journal of the Debates are reprinted from Farrand, *Records,* Vol. I, pp. 421–426.

enlightened citizens, whose limited number, and firmness might seasonably interpose against impetuous counsels. It ought finally to occur to a people deliberating on a Government for themselves, that as different interests necessarily result from the liberty meant to be secured, the major interest might under sudden impulses be tempted to commit injustice on the minority. In all civilized Countries the people fall into different classes having a real or supposed difference of interests. There will be creditors and debtors, farmers, merchants and manufacturers. There will be particularly the distinction of rich and poor. It was true as had been observed (by Mr. Pinckney) we had not among us those hereditary distinctions of rank which were a great source of contests in the ancient Governments as well as the modern States of Europe, nor those extremes of wealth or poverty which characterize the latter.

We cannot, however, be regarded even at this time, as one homogeneous mass, in which everything that affects a part will affect in the same manner the whole. In framing a system which we wish to last for ages, we should not lose sight of the changes which ages will produce. An increase of population will of necessity increase the proportion of those who will labor under all the hardships of life, and secretly sigh for a more equal distribution of its blessings. These may in time outnumber those who are placed above the feelings of indigence. According to the equal laws of suffrage, the power will slide into the hands of the former. No agrarian attempts have yet been made in this Country, but symptoms of a leveling spirit, as we have understood, have sufficiently appeared in certain quarters to give notice of the future danger.

How is this danger to be guarded against on republican principles? How is the danger in all cases of interested coalitions to oppress the minority to be guarded against? Among other means by the establishment of a body in the Government sufficiently respectable for its wisdom and virtue, to aid, on such emergencies, the preponderance of justice by throwing its weight into the scale. Such being the objects of the second branch in the proposed Government he thought a considerable duration ought be given to it. He did not conceive that the term of nine years could threaten any real danger; but in pursuing his particular ideas on the subject, he should require that the long term allowed to the 2d. branch should not commence till such a period of life as would render a perpetual disqualification to be re-elected little inconvenient either in a public or private view. He observed that as it was more than probable we were now digesting a plan which in its operation would decide forever the fate of Republican Government we ought not only to provide every guard to liberty that its preservation could require, but be equally careful to supply the defects which our own experience had particularly pointed out.

Mr. Sherman. Government is instituted for those who live under it. It ought therefore to be so constituted as not to be dangerous to their liberties. The more permanency it has the worse if it be a bad Government. Frequent elections are necessary to preserve the good behavior of rulers. They also tend to give permanency to the Government, by preserving that good behavior, because it ensures their re-election. In Connecticut elections have been very frequent, yet great stability and uniformity both as to persons and measures have been experienced from its original establishment, to the present time; a period of more than 130 years. He wished to have provisions made for steadiness and wisdom in the system to be adopted; but he thought six or four years would be sufficient. He should be content with either. . . .

Mr. Gerry wished we could be united in our ideas concerning a permanent Government. All aim at the same end, but there are great differences as to the means. One circumstance He thought should be carefully attended to. There were not 1/1000 part of our fellow citizens who were not against every approach toward Monarchy. Will they ever agree to a plan which seems to make such an approach? The Convention ought to be extremely cautious in what they hold out to the people. Whatever plan may be proposed will be espoused with warmth by many out of respect to the quarter it proceeds from as well as from an approbation of the plan itself. And if the plan should be of such a nature as to rouse a violent opposition, it is easy to foresee that discord and confusion will ensue, and it is even possible that we may become a prey to foreign powers.

He did not deny the position of Mr. Madison that the majority will generally violate justice when they have an interest in so doing; but did not think there was any such temptation in this Country. Our situation was different from that of Great Britain: and the great body of lands yet to be parcelled out and settled would very much prolong the difference. Notwithstanding the symptoms of injustice which had marked many of our public Councils, they had not proceeded so far as not to leave hopes, that there would be a sufficient sense of justice and virtue for the purpose of Government. He admitted the evils arising from a frequency of elections: and would agree to give the Senate a duration of four or five years. A longer term would defeat itself. It never would be adopted by the people. . . .

On the question for 9 years; ⅓ to go out triennially: Massachusetts no, Connecticut no, New York no, New Jersey no, Pennsylvania aye, Delaware aye, Maryland no, Virginia aye, North Carolina no, South Carolina no, Georgia no. (Ayes—3; noes—8.)

On the question for 6 years; ⅓ to go out biennially: Massachusetts aye, Connecticut aye, New York no, New Jersey no, Pennsylvania aye, Delaware aye, Maryland aye, Virginia aye, North Carolina aye, South Carolina no, Georgia no. (Ayes—7; noes—4.)

DEBATE ON SUFFRAGE *

Tuesday, August 7th, In Convention

"Article IV. Section 1. (Constitution) taken up."

Article IV, Section 1. "The members of the House of Representatives shall be chosen every second year, by the people of the several States comprehended within this Union. The qualifications of the electors shall be the same, from time to time, as those of the electors in the several States, of the most numerous branch of their own legislatures."

Mr. Gouverneur Morris [of Pennsylvania] moved to strike out the last member of the section beginning with the words "qualifications" of "Electors" in order that some other provision might be substituted which would restrain the right of suffrage to freeholders.

Mr. Fitzsimmons [Thomas Fitzsimmons of Pennsylvania] seconded the motion.

Mr. Williamson [Hugh Williamson of North Carolina] was opposed to it.

Mr. Wilson. This part of the Report was well considered by the Committee, and he did not think it could be changed for the better. It was difficult to form any uniform rule of qualifications for all the States. Unnecessary innovations he thought too should be avoided. It would be very hard and disagreeable for the same persons, at the same time, to vote for representatives in the State Legislature and to be excluded from a vote for those in the National Legislature. . . .

Col. Mason. The force of habit is certainly not attended to by those gentlemen who wish for innovations on this point. Eight or nine States have extended the right of suffrage beyond the freeholders. What will the people there say, if they should be disfranchised? A power to alter the qualifications would be a dangerous power in the hands of the Legislature. . . .

Mr. Dickinson [John Dickinson of Delaware] had a very different idea of the tendency of vesting the right of suffrage in the freeholders of the Country. He considered them as the best guardians of liberty; and the restriction of the right to them as a necessary defense against the dangerous influence of those multitudes without property and without principle, with which our Country like all others, will in time abound. As to the unpopularity of the innovation it was in his opinion chimerical. The great mass of our Citizens is composed at this time of freeholders, and will be pleased with it.

Mr. Ellsworth [Oliver Ellsworth of Connecticut, Chief Justice of the United States 1796–1800]. How shall the freehold be defined? Ought not every man who pays a tax to vote for the representative who is to levy and dispose of his money? Shall the wealthy merchants and manufacturers, who

* The following extracts from Madison's Journal of the Debates are reprinted from Farrand, *Records,* Vol. II, pp. 201–206.

will bear a full share of the public burdens be not allowed a voice in the imposition of them? Taxation and representation ought to go together.

Mr. Gouverneur Morris. He had long learned not to be the dupe of words. The sound of Aristocracy therefore, had no effect on him. It was the thing, not the name, to which he was opposed, and one of his principal objections to the Constitution as it is now before us, is that it threatens this Country with an Aristocracy. The aristocracy will grow out of the House of Representatives. Give the votes to people who have no property, and they will sell them to the rich who will be able to buy them. We should not confine our attention to the present moment. The time is not distant when this Country will abound with mechanics and manufacturers who will receive their bread from their employers. Will such men be the secure and faithful Guardians of liberty? Will they be the impregnable barrier against aristocracy?— He was as little duped by the association of the words, "Taxation and Representation"— The man who does not give his vote freely is not represented. It is the man who dictates the vote. Children do not vote. Why? Because they want prudence, because they have no will of their own. The ignorant and the dependent can be as little trusted with the public interest. He did not conceive the difficulty of defining "freeholders" to be insuperable. Still less that the restriction could be unpopular. $9/10$ of the people are at present freeholders and these will certainly be pleased with it. As to Merchants etc. if they have wealth and value the right they can acquire it. If not they don't deserve it.

Col. Mason. We all feel too strongly the remains of ancient prejudices, and view things too much through a British medium. A Freehold is the qualification in England, and hence it is imagined to be the only proper one. The true idea in his opinion was that every man having evidence of attachment to and permanent common interest with the Society ought to share in all its rights and privileges. Was this qualification restrained to freeholders? Does no other kind of property but land evidence a common interest in the proprietor? Does nothing besides property mark a permanent attachment? Ought the merchant, the monied man, the parent of a number of children whose fortunes are to be pursued in their own Country, to be viewed as suspicious characters, and unworthy to be trusted with the common rights of their fellow Citizens?

Mr. Madison. The right of suffrage is certainly one of the fundamental articles of republican Government, and ought not to be left to be regulated by the Legislature. A gradual abridgment of this right has been the mode in which Aristocracies have been built on the ruins of popular forms. Whether the Constitutional qualification ought to be a freehold would with him depend much on the probable reception such a change would meet with in States where the right was now exercised by every description of people. In several of the States a freehold was now the qualification. Viewing the subject in its merits alone, the freeholders of the Country would be the safest depositories of Republican liberty. In future times a great majority of the people will not only be without landed, but any other sort of property. These will either combine under the influence of their common situation; in which case, the rights of property and the public liberty, will not be secure in their hands; or which is more probable, they will become the tools of opulence and ambition, in which case there will be equal danger on another side. The example of England has been misconceived (by Col. Mason). A very small proportion of the Representatives are there chosen by freeholders. The greatest part are chosen by the Cities and boroughs, in many of which the qualification of suffrage is as low as it is in any one of the U.S. and it was in the boroughs and Cities rather than the Counties, that bribery most prevailed, and the influence of the Crown on elections was most dangerously exerted.

Doctor Franklin. [Benjamin Franklin of Pennsylvania] It is of great consequence that we should not depress the virtue and public spirit of our common people; of which they displayed a great deal during the war, and which contributed principally to the favorable issue of it. He related the honorable refusal of the American seamen who were carried in great numbers into the British Prisons during the war, to redeem themselves from misery or to seek their fortunes, by entering on board the Ships of the Enemies to their Country; contrasting their patriotism with a contemporary instance in which the British seamen made prisoners by the Americans, readily entered on the ships of the latter on being promised a share of the prizes that might be made out of their own Country. This proceeded, he said, from the different manner in which the common people were treated in America and Great Britain. He did not think that the elected had any right in any case to narrow the privileges of the electors. He quoted as arbitrary the British Statute setting forth the danger of tumultuous meetings, and under that pretext, narrowing the right of suffrage to persons having freeholds of a certain value; observing that this Statute was soon followed by another under the succeeding Parliament subjecting the people who had no votes to peculiar labors and hardships. He was persuaded also that such a restriction as was proposed would give great uneasiness in the populous States. The sons of a substantial farmer, not being themselves freeholders, would not be pleased at being disfranchised, and there are a great many persons of that description.

Mr. Mercer. [John Francis Mercer of Maryland] The Constitution is objectionable in many points, but in none more than the present. He objected to the footing on which the qualification was put, but particularly to the *mode of election* by the people. The people can not know and judge of the characters of Candidates. The worse possible choice will be made. He quoted the case of the Senate in Virginia as an example in point— The people in Towns can unite their votes in favor of one favorite; and by that means always prevail over the people of the Country, who being dispersed will scatter their votes among a variety of candidates.

Mr. Rutledge [John Rutledge of South Carolina] thought the idea of restraining the right of suffrage to the freeholders a very ill advised one. It would create division among the people and make enemies of all those who should be excluded.

On the question for striking out as moved by Mr. Gouverneur Morris, from the word "qualifications" to the end of article III: New Hampshire no, Massachusetts no, Connecticut no, Pennsylvania no, Delaware aye, Maryland divided, Virginia no, North Carolina no, South Carolina no, Georgia not present. (Ayes—1; noes—7; divided—1; absent 1.)

Topic 4

THE CONTROL OF MAJORITY "FACTIONS"

The Union as a Safeguard Against Domestic Faction

The Federalist, No. 10

JAMES MADISON

Among the numerous advantages promised by a well-constructed Union, none deserves to be more accurately developed than its tendency to break and control the violence of faction. The friend of popular governments never finds himself so much alarmed for their character and fate, as when he contemplates their propensity to this dangerous vice. He will not fail, therefore, to set a due value on any plan which, without violating the principles to which he is attached, provides a proper cure for it. The instability, injustice, and confusion introduced into the public councils have, in truth, been the mortal diseases under which popular governments have everywhere perished; as they continue to be the favorite and fruitful topics from which the adversaries to liberty derive their most specious declamations.

The valuable improvements made by the American constitutions on the popular models, both ancient and modern, cannot certainly be too much admired; but it would be an unwarrantable partiality, to contend that they have as effectually obviated the danger on this side, as was wished and expected. Complaints are everywhere heard from our most considerate and virtuous citizens, equally the friends of public and private faith, and of public and personal liberty, that our governments are too unstable; that the public good is disregarded in the conflicts of rival parties; and that measures are too often decided, not according to the rules of justice, and the rights of the minor party, but by the superior force of an interested and overbearing majority. However anxiously we may wish that these complaints had no foundation, the evidence of known facts will not permit us to deny that they are in some degree true.

It will be found, indeed, on a candid review of our situation, that some of the distresses under which we labor have been erroneously charged on the operation of our governments; but it will be found, at the same time, that other causes will not alone account for many of our heaviest misfortunes; and, particularly, for that prevailing and increasing distrust of public engagements, and alarm for private rights, which are echoed from one end of the continent to the other. These must be chiefly, if not wholly, effects of the unsteadiness and injustice with which a factious spirit has tainted our public administrations.

By a faction, I understand a number of citizens, whether amounting to a majority or a minority of the whole, who are united and actuated by some common impulse of passion, or of interest, adverse to the rights of other citizens, or to the permanent and aggregate interests of the community.

There are two methods of curing the mischiefs of faction: the one, by removing its causes; the other, by controlling its effects. There are again two methods of removing the causes of faction: the one, by destroying the liberty which is essential to its existence; the other, by giving to every citizen the same opinions, the same passions, and the same interests.

It could never be more truly said than of the first remedy, that it was worse than the disease. Liberty is to faction what air is to fire, an aliment without which it instantly expires. But it could not be less folly to abolish liberty, which is essential to political life, because it nourishes faction, than it would be to wish the annihilation of air, which is essential to animal life, because it imparts to fire its destructive agency.

The second expedient is as impracticable as the first would be unwise. As long as the reason of man continues fallible, and he is at liberty to exercise it, different opinions will be formed. As long as the connection subsists between his reason and his self-love, his opinions and his passions will have a reciprocal influence on each other; and the former will be objects to which the latter will attach themselves. The diversity in the faculties of men, from which the rights of property originate, is not less an insuperable obstacle to a uniformity of interests. The protection of these faculties is the first object of government. From the protection of different and unequal faculties of acquiring property, the possession of different degrees and kinds of property immediately results; and from the influence of these on the sentiments and views of the respective proprietors, ensues a division of the society into different interests and parties.

The latent causes of faction are thus sown in the nature of man; and we see them everywhere brought into different degrees of activity, according to the different circumstances of civil society. A zeal for different opinions concerning religion, concerning government, and many other points, as well of speculation as of practice; an attachment to different leaders ambitiously contending for pre-eminence and power; or to persons of other descriptions whose fortunes have been interesting to the human passions, have, in turn, divided mankind into parties, inflamed them with mutual animosity, and rendered them much more disposed to vex and oppress each other, than to co-operate for their common good. So strong is this propensity of mankind to fall into mutual animosities, that where no substantial occasion presents itself, the most frivolous and fanciful distinctions have been sufficient to kindle their unfriendly passions and excite their most violent conflicts. But the most common and durable source of factions has been the various and unequal distribution of property. Those who hold and those who are without property have ever formed distinct interests in society. Those who are creditors, and those who are debtors, fall under a like discrimination. A landed interest, a manufacturing interest, a mercantile interest, a moneyed interest, with many lesser interests, grow up of necessity in civilized nations, and divide them into different classes, actuated by different sentiments and views. The regulation of these various and interfering interests forms the principal task of modern legislation, and involves the spirit of party and faction in the necessary and ordinary operations of the government.

No man is allowed to be a judge in his own cause, because his interest would certainly bias his judgment and, not improbably, corrupt his integrity. With equal, nay, with greater reason, a body of men are unfit to be both judges and parties at the same time; yet what are many of the most important acts of legislation, but so many judicial determinations, not indeed concerning the rights of single persons, but concerning the rights of large bodies of citizens? And what are the different classes of legislators, but advocates and parties to the causes which they determine? Is a law proposed concerning private debts? It is a question to which the creditors are parties on one side and the debtors on the other. Justice ought to hold the balance between them. Yet the parties are, and must be, themselves the judges; and the most numerous party, or, in other words, the most powerful faction, must be expected to prevail. Shall domestic manufacturers be encouraged, and in what degree, by restrictions on foreign manufactures? are questions which would be differently decided by the landed and the manufacturing classes, and probably by neither with a sole regard to justice and the public good. The apportionment of taxes on the various descriptions of property is an act which seems to require the most exact impartiality; yet there is, perhaps, no legislative act in which greater opportunity and temptation are given to a predominant party, to trample on the rules of justice. Every shilling with which they overburden the inferior number, is a shilling saved to their own pockets.

It is in vain to say that enlightened statesmen will be able to adjust these clashing interests, and render them all subservient to the public good. Enlightened statesmen will not always be at the helm. Nor, in many cases, can such an adjustment be made at all, without taking into view indirect and remote considerations, which will rarely prevail over the immediate interest which one party may find in disregarding the rights of another or the good of the whole. The inference to which we are brought is, that the *causes* of faction cannot be removed, and that relief is only to be sought in the means of controlling its *effects*.

If a faction consists of less than a majority, relief is supplied by the republican principle, which enables the majority to defeat its sinister views by regular vote. It may clog the administration, it may convulse the society; but it will be unable to execute and mask its violence under the forms of the Constitution. When a majority is included in a faction, the form of popular government, on the other hand, enables it to sacrifice to its ruling passion or interest both the public good and the rights of other citizens. To secure the public good and private rights against the danger of such a faction, and at the same time to preserve the spirit and the form of popular government, is then the great object to which our inquiries are directed. Let me add that it is the great desideratum, by which alone this form of government can be rescued from the opprobrium under which it has so long labored, and be recommended to the esteem and adoption of mankind.

By what means is this object attainable? Evidently by one of two only. Either the existence of the same passion or interest in a majority at the same time must be prevented; or the majority, having such coexisting passion or interest, must be rendered, by their number and local situation, unable to concert and carry into effect schemes of oppression. If the impulse and the opportunity be suffered to coincide, we well know that neither moral nor religious motives can be relied on as an adequate control. They are not found to be such on the injustice and violence of individuals, and lose their efficacy in proportion to the number combined together; that is, in proportion as their efficacy becomes needful.

From this view of the subject it may be concluded that a pure democracy, by which I mean a society consisting of a small number of citizens, who assemble and administer the government in person, can admit of no cure for the mischiefs of faction. A common passion or interest will, in almost every case, be felt by a majority of the whole; a communication and concert result from the form of government itself; and there is nothing to check the inducements to sacrifice the weaker party or an obnoxious individual. Hence it is that such democracies have ever been spectacles of turbulence and contention; have ever been found incompatible with personal security, or the rights of property; and have in general been as short in their lives as they have been violent in their deaths. Theoretic politicians, who have patronized this species of government, have erroneously supposed that by reducing mankind to a perfect equality in their political rights, they would at the same time be perfectly equalized and assimilated in their possessions, their opinions, and their passions.

A republic, by which I mean a government in which the scheme of representation takes place, opens a different prospect, and promises the cure for which we are seeking. Let us examine the points in which it varies from pure democracy, and we shall comprehend both the nature of the cure and the efficacy which it must derive from the Union.

The two great points of difference between a democracy and a republic are: first, the delegation of the government, in the latter, to a small number of citizens elected by the rest; secondly, the greater number of citizens, and greater sphere of country, over which the latter may be extended.

The effect of the first difference is, on the one hand, to refine and enlarge the public views, by passing them through the medium of a chosen body of citizens, whose wisdom may best discern the true interests of their country, and whose patriotism and love of justice will be least likely to sacrifice it to temporary or partial considerations. Under such a regulation, it may well happen that the public voice, pronounced by the representatives of the people, will be more consonant to the public good than if pronounced by the people themselves, convened for the purpose. On the other hand, the effect may be inverted. Men of factious tempers, of local prejudices, or of sinister designs, may, by intrigue, by corruption, or by other means, first obtain the suffrages, and then betray the interests of the people. The question resulting is, whether small or extensive republics are more favorable to the election of proper guardians of the public weal; and it is clearly decided in favor of the latter by two obvious considerations.

In the first place, it is to be remarked that, however small the republic may be, the representatives must be raised to a certain number, in order to guard against the cabals of a few; and that, however large it may be, they must be limited to a certain number, in order to guard against the confusion of a multitude. Hence, the number of representatives in the two cases not being in proportion to that of the two constituents, and being proportionally greater in the small republic, it follows that if the proportion of fit characters be not less in the large than in the small republic, the former will present a greater option, and consequently a greater probability of a fit choice.

In the next place, as each representative will be chosen by a greater number of citizens in the large than in the small republic, it will be more difficult for unworthy candidates to practice with success the vicious arts, by which elections are too often carried; and the suffrages of the people, being more free, will be more likely to centre in men who possess the most attractive merit and the most diffusive and established characters.

It must be confessed that in this as in most other cases, there is a mean, on both sides of which inconveniences will be found to lie. By enlarging too much the number of electors, you render the representative too little acquainted with all their local circumstances and lesser interests; as by reducing it too much, you render him unduly attached to these, and too little fit to comprehend and pursue great and national objects. The federal Constitution forms a happy combination in this respect; the great and aggregate interests being referred to the national, the local and particular to the State legislatures.

The other point of difference is, the greater number of citizens and extent of territory which may be brought within the compass of republican than of democratic government; and it is this circumstance principally which renders factious combinations less to be dreaded in the former than in the latter. The smaller the society, the fewer probably will be the distinct parties and interests composing it; the fewer the distinct parties and interests, the more frequently will a majority be found of the same party; and the smaller the number of individuals composing a majority, and the smaller the compass within which they are placed, the more easily will they concert and execute their plans of oppression. Extend the sphere, and you take in a greater variety of parties and interests; you make it less probable that a majority of the whole will have a common motive to invade the rights of other citizens; or if such a common motive exists, it will be more difficult for all who feel it to discover their own strength, and to act in unison with each other. Besides other impediments, it may be remarked that where there is a consciousness of unjust or dishonorable purposes, communication is always checked by distrust in proportion to the number whose concurrence is necessary.

Hence it clearly appears that the same advantage which a republic has over a democracy, in controlling the effects of faction, is enjoyed by a large over a small republic—is enjoyed by the Union over the States composing it. Does the advantage consist in the substitution of representatives, whose enlightened views and virtuous sentiments render them superior to local prejudices, and to schemes of injustice? It will not be denied that the representation of the Union will be most likely to possess these requisite endowments. Does it consist in the greater security afforded by a greater variety of parties, against the event of any one party being able to outnumber and oppress the rest? In an equal degree does the increased variety of parties, comprised within the Union, increase this security? Does it, in fine, consist in the greater obstacles opposed to the concert and accomplishment of the secret wishes of an unjust and interested majority? Here, again, the extent of the Union gives it the most palpable advantage.

The influence of factious leaders may kindle a flame within their particular States, but will be unable to spread a general conflagration through the other States. A religious sect may degenerate into a political faction in a part of the confederacy; but the variety of sects dispersed over the entire face of it must secure the national councils against any danger from that source. A rage for paper money, for an abolition of debts, for an equal division of property, or for any other improper or wicked project will be less apt to pervade the whole body of the Union than a particular member of it; in the same proportion as such a malady is more likely to taint a particular county or district, than an entire State.

In the extent and proper structure of the Union, therefore, we behold a republican remedy for the diseases most incident to republican government. And according to the degree of pleasure and pride we feel in being republicans, ought to be our zeal in cherishing the spirit and supporting the character of federalists.

PUBLIUS

Topic 5

"SINCE ANGELS DO NOT GOVERN MEN"

Separation of Powers

The Federalist, No. 47

JAMES MADISON *

One of the principal objections inculcated by the more respectable adversaries of the Constitution, is its supposed violation of the political maxim that the legislative, executive, and judiciary departments ought to be separate and distinct. In the structure of the federal government, no regard, it is said, seems to have been paid to this essential precaution in favor of liberty. The several departments of power are distributed and blended in such a manner as at once to destroy all symmetry and beauty of form, and to expose some of the essential parts of the edifice to the danger of being crushed by the disproportionate weight of other parts.

No political truth is certainly of greater intrinsic value, or is stamped with the authority of more enlightened patrons of liberty, than that on which the objection is founded. The accumulation of all powers, legislative, executive, and judiciary, in the same hands, whether of one, a few, or many, and whether hereditary, self-appointed, or elective, may justly be pronounced the very definition of tyranny. Were the federal Constitution, therefore, really chargeable with the accumulation of power, or with a mixture of powers, having a dangerous tendency to such an accumulation, no further arguments would be necessary to inspire a universal reprobation of the system. I persuade myself, however, that it will be made apparent to everyone that the charge cannot be supported, and that the maxim on which it relies has been totally misconceived and misapplied. In order to form correct ideas on this important subject, it will be proper to investigate the sense in which the preservation of liberty requires that the three great departments of power should be separate and distinct.

The oracle who is always consulted and cited on this subject is the celebrated Montesquieu. If he be not the author of this invaluable precept in the science of politics, he has the merit at least of displaying and recom-

* Many editions of *The Federalist* credit Hamilton with the authorship of Numbers 47 and 51. Recent research has established that both were written by Madison.

mending it most effectually to the attention of mankind. Let us endeavor, in the first place, to ascertain his meaning on this point.

The British Constitution was to Montesquieu what Homer has been to the didactic writers on epic poetry. As the latter have considered the work of the immortal bard as the perfect model from which the principles and rules of the epic art were to be drawn, and by which all similar works were to be judged, so this great political critic appears to have viewed the Constitution of England as the standard, or to use his own expression, as the mirror of political liberty, and to have delivered, in the form of elementary truths, the several characteristic principles of that particular system. That we may be sure, then, not to mistake his meaning in this case, let us recur to the source from which the maxim was drawn.

On the slightest view of the British Constitution we must perceive that the legislative, executive, and judiciary departments are by no means totally separate and distinct from each other. The executive magistrate forms an integral part of the legislative authority. He alone has the prerogative of making treaties with foreign sovereigns, which, when made, have, under certain limitations, the force of legislative acts. All the members of the judiciary department are appointed by him, can be removed by him on the address of the two Houses of Parliament, and form, when he pleases to consult them, one of his constitutional councils. One branch of the legislative department forms also a great constitutional council to the executive chief; as, on another hand, it is the sole depositary of judicial power in cases of impeachment, and is invested with the supreme appellate jurisdiction in all other cases. The judges, again, are so far connected with the legislative department as often to attend and participate in its deliberations, though not admitted to a legislative vote.

From these facts, by which Montesquieu was guided, it may clearly be inferred that in saying "There can be no liberty where the legislative and executive powers are united in the same person or body of magistrates," or, "if the power of judging be not separated from the legislative and executive powers," he did not mean that these departments ought to have no *partial agency* in, or no *control* over, the acts of each other. His meaning, as his own words import, and still more conclusively as illustrated by the example in his eye, can amount to no more than this, that where the *whole* power of one department is exercised by the same hands which possess the *whole* power of another department, the fundamental principles of a free constitution are subverted. This would have been the case in the Constitution examined by him if the King, who is the sole executive magistrate, had possessed also the complete legislative power, or the supreme administration of justice; or if the entire legislative body had possessed the supreme judiciary or the supreme executive authority.

This, however, is not among the vices of that Constitution. The magistrate in whom the whole executive power resides cannot of himself make a law, though he can put a negative on every law; nor administer justice in person, though he has the appointment of those who do administer it. The judges can exercise no executive prerogative, though they are shoots from the executive stock; nor any legislative function, though they may be advised with by the legislative councils. The entire legislature can perform no judiciary act; though by the joint act of two of its branches the judges may be removed from their offices, and though one of its branches is possessed of the judicial power in the last resort. The entire legislature, again, can exercise no executive prerogative, though one of its branches constitutes the supreme executive magistracy, and another, on the impeachment of a third, can try and condemn all the subordinate officers in the executive department.

The reasons on which Montesquieu grounds his maxim are a further demonstration of his meaning. "When the legislative and executive powers are united in the same person or body," says he, "there can be no liberty, because apprehensions may arise lest *the same* monarch or Senate should *enact* tyrannical laws to *execute* them in a tyrannical manner." Again: "Were the power of judging joined with the legislative, the life and liberty of the subject would be exposed to arbitrary control, for the *judge* would then be the *legislator*. Were it joined to the executive power, the *judge* might behave with all the violence of *an oppressor.*" Some of these reasons are more fully explained in other passages; but briefly stated as they are here, they sufficiently establish the meaning which we have put on this celebrated maxim of this celebrated author.

If we look into the constitutions of the several States, we find that, notwithstanding the emphatical and in some instances the unqualified terms in which this axiom has been laid down, there is not a single instance in which the several departments of power have been kept absolutely separate and distinct. . . .

[Here the author examines the constitutions of the original thirteen states, excepting those of Rhode Island and Connecticut which were formed prior to the American Revolution.]

What I have wished to evince is, that the charge brought against the proposed Constitution, of violating a sacred maxim of free government, is warranted neither by the real meaning annexed to that maxim by its author nor by the sense in which it has hitherto been understood in America.

PUBLIUS

Checks and Balances

The Federalist, No. 51

JAMES MADISON

To what expedient, then, shall we finally resort, for maintaining in practice the necessary partition of power among the several departments, as laid down in the Constitution? The only answer that can be given is, that as all these exterior provisions are found to be inadequate, the defect must be supplied, by so contriving the interior structure of the government as that its several constituent parts may, by their mutual relations, be the means of keeping each other in their proper places. Without presuming to undertake a full development of this important idea, I will hazard a few general observations, which may perhaps place it in a clearer light, and enable us to form a more correct judgment of the principles and structure of the government planned by the Convention.

In order to lay a due foundation for that separate and distinct exercise of the different powers of government, which to a certain extent is admitted on all hands to be essential to the preservation of liberty, it is evident that each department should have a will of its own; and consequently should be so constituted that the members of each should have as little agency as possible in the appointment of the members of the others. Were this principle rigorously adhered to, it would require that all the appointments for the supreme executive, legislative, and judiciary magistracies should be drawn from the same fountain of authority, the people, through channels having no communication whatever with one another.

Perhaps such a plan of constructing the several departments would be less difficult in practice than it may in contemplation appear. Some difficulties, however, and some additional expense would attend the execution of it. Some deviations, therefore, from the principle must be admitted. In the constitution of the judiciary department in particular, it might be inexpedient to insist rigorously on the principle: first, because peculiar qualifications being essential in the members, the primary consideration ought to be to select that mode of choice which best secures these qualifications; secondly, because the permanent tenure by which the appointments are held in that department must soon destroy all sense of dependence on the authority conferring them.

It is equally evident that the members of each department should be as little dependent as possible on those of the others, for the emoluments annexed to their offices. Were the executive magistrate, or the judges, not independent of the Legislature in this particular, their independence in every other would be merely nominal.

But the great security against a gradual concentration of the several powers in the same department consists in giving to those who administer each department the necessary constitutional means and personal motives to resist encroachments of the others. The provision for defence must in this, as in all other cases, be made commensurate to the danger of attack. Ambition must be made to counteract ambition. The interest of the man must be connected with the constitutional rights of the place. It may be a reflection on human nature, that such devices should be necessary to control the abuses of government. But what is government itself, but the greatest of all reflections on human nature? If men were angels, no government would be necessary. If angels were to govern men, neither external nor internal controls on government would be necessary. In framing a government which is to be administered by men over men, the great difficulty lies in this: you must first enable the government to control the governed; and in the next place oblige it to control itself. A dependence on the people is, no doubt, the primary control on the government; but experience has taught mankind the necessity of auxiliary precautions.

This policy of supplying, by opposite and rival interests, the defect of better motives, might be traced through the whole system of human affairs, private as well as public. We see it particularly displayed in all the subordinate distributions of power, where the constant aim is to divide and arrange the several offices in such a manner as that each may be a check on the other—that the private interest of every individual may be a sentinel over the public rights. These inventions of prudence cannot be less requisite in the distribution of the supreme powers of the State.

But it is not possible to give to each department an equal power of self-defence. In republican government, the legislative authority necessarily predominates. The remedy for this inconveniency is to divide the legislature into different branches; and to render them, by different modes of election and different principles of action, as little connected with each other as the nature of their common functions and their common dependence on the society will admit. It may even be necessary to guard against dangerous encroachments by still further precautions. As the weight of the legislative authority requires that it should be thus divided, the weakness of the executive may require, on the other hand, that it should be fortified. An absolute negative on the legislature appears at first view to be the natural defence with which the executive magistrate should be armed. But perhaps it would be neither altogether safe nor alone sufficient. On ordinary occasions it might not be exerted with the requisite firmness, and on extraordinary occasions it might be perfidiously abused. May not this defect of an absolute negative be supplied by some qualified connection between this weaker department and the weaker branch of the stronger department, by which the latter may be led to support the constitutional rights of the former, without being too much detached from the rights of its own department?

If the principles on which these observations are founded be just, as I persuade myself they are, and they be applied as a criterion to the several State constitutions, and to the federal Constitution, it will be found that if the latter does not perfectly correspond with them, the former are infinitely less able to bear such a test.

There are, moreover, two considerations particularly applicable to the federal system of America, which place that system in a very interesting point of view.

First. In a single republic all the power surrendered by the people is submitted to the administration of a single government, and the usurpations are guarded against by a division of the government into distinct and separate departments. In the compound republic of America, the power surrendered by the people is first divided between two distinct governments, and then the portion allotted to each subdivided among distinct and separate departments. Hence a double security arises to the rights of the people. The different governments will control each other, at the same time that each will be controlled by itself.

Second. It is of great importance in a republic not only to guard the society against the oppression of its rulers, but to guard one part of the society against the injustice of the other part. Different interests necessarily exist in different classes of citizens. If a majority be united by a common interest, the rights of the minority will be insecure. There are but two methods of providing against this evil: the one by creating a will in the community independent of the majority, that is, of the society itself; the other by comprehending in the society so many separate descriptions of citizens as will render an unjust combination of a majority of the whole very improbable, if not impracticable.

The first method prevails in all governments possessing an hereditary or self-appointed authority. This, at best, is but a precarious security; because a power independent of the society may as well espouse the unjust views of the major as the rightful interests of the minor party, and may possibly be turned against both parties. The second method will be exemplified in the federal republic of the United States. Whilst all authority in it will be derived from and dependent on the society, the society itself will be broken into so many parts, interests and classes of citizens, that the rights of individuals, or of the minority, will be in little danger from interested combinations of the majority.

In a free government the security for civil rights must be the same as that for religious rights. It consists in the one case in the multiplicity of interests, and in the other in the multiplicity of sects. The degree of security in both cases will depend on the number of interests and sects; and this may be presumed to depend on the extent of country and number of people comprehended under the same government. This view of the subject must particularly recommend a proper federal system to all the sincere and considerate friends of republican government, since it shows that in exact proportion as the territory of the Union may be formed into more circumscribed confederacies, or States, oppressive combinations of a majority will be facilitated; the best security under republican forms, for the rights of every class of citizens, will be diminished; and, consequently, the stability and independence of some member of the government, the only other security, must be proportionally increased.

Justice is the end of government. It is the end of civil society. It ever has been and ever will be pursued until it be obtained, or until liberty be lost in the pursuit. In a society under the forms of which the stronger faction can readily unite and oppress the weaker, anarchy may as truly be said to reign as in a state of nature, where the weaker individual is not secured against the violence of the stronger; and as in the latter state even the stronger individuals are prompted by the uncertainty of their condition to submit to a government which may protect the weak as well as themselves; so, in the former state, will the more powerful factions or parties be gradually induced, by a like motive, to wish for a government which will protect all parties, the weaker as well as the more powerful.

It can be little doubted that if the State of Rhode Island was separated from the confederacy, and left to itself, the insecurity of rights under the popular form of government within such narrow limits would be displayed by such reiterated oppressions of factious majorities that some power altogether independent of the people would soon be called for by the voice of the very factions whose misrule had proved the necessity of it.

In the extended republic of the United States, and among the great variety of interests, parties, and sects which it embraces, a coalition of a majority of the whole society could seldom take place on any other principles than those of justice and the general good; whilst there being thus less danger to a minor from the will of a major party, there must be less pretext, also, to provide for the security of the former, by introducing into the government a will not dependent on the latter; or, in other words, a will independent of the society itself. It is no less certain than it is important, notwithstanding the contrary opinions which have been entertained, that the larger the society, provided it lie within a practical sphere, the more duly capable it will be of self-government. And happily for the *republican cause,* the practicable sphere may be carried to a very great extent, by a judicious modification and mixture of the *federal principle.*

PUBLIUS

Topic 6

"AMBITION MUST BE MADE TO COUNTERACT AMBITION"

[Since Madison contributed to *The Federalist,* his theory that good government required a system of checks and balances so that ambition would counteract ambition has been subjected to continued theoretical analysis and practical test in the actual process of governing over a period of nearly two centuries. In the ensuing discussion, James MacGregor Burns maintains that Madison's theory has "long outlived him" because, even in his own terms, his "first great protection against naked majority rule was the broader diversity of interests in a large republic and hence the greater difficulty in concerting their 'plans of oppression.' " Why, then, Burns asks, "would not any popular majority representing such a variety of interests perforce become so broad and moderate in its goals as never to threaten any major or even minor or individual interest? Why was it necessary to have what Madison called 'auxilliary precautions' of checks and balances built right into the frame of government?" What is more, he argues, the urgency of our modern problems, and the furious pace of social and economic change throughout the world, make protracted delay in governmental action a luxury we can no longer afford. (These views derive support from Professor Commager's explanation of the reasons he prefers "the checks and balances of democratic politics" as against judicial review.)

On the other hand, Reinhold Niebuhr maintains that "it may be taken as axiomatic that great disproportions of power lead to injustice," and he adds that "the larger the group the more certainly will it express itself selfishly in the total community." This is because "it will be more powerful and therefore more able to defy any social restraints which might be devised." He insists that "there has never been a scheme of justice in history which did not have a balance of power at its foundation." But he sees dangers also in the balancing of power which "is always pregnant with the possibility of anarchy." He concludes that "a healthy society must seek to achieve the greatest possible equilibrium of power, the greatest possible number of centers of power, the greatest possible social check upon the administration of power, and the greatest possible inner moral check on human ambition, as well as the most effective use of forms of power in which consent and coercion are compounded."

The viewpoint of Professor Thomas Landon Thorson raises some important questions about majority "rule" and minority "rights." He argues that conceptions or justifications of democracy "that elevate either natural (minority) rights or the principle of majority rule to a position of primacy" are "faulty." He holds, instead, that the principles are "mutually interdependent and essentially equal." Accordingly, the obligation they impose on our political system is that those who operate it "be rational!"]

The Politics of Deadlock

JAMES MACGREGOR BURNS *

THE THEORY OF MINORITY CHECKS

In *The Federalist,* Number 10, Madison came to grips with the crucial problem of breaking and controlling the violence of faction, which he defined as a "number of citizens, whether amounting to a majority or minority of the whole, who are united and actuated by some common impulse of passion, or of interest, adverse to the rights of other citizens, or to the permanent and aggregate interests of the community." The origins of such factions were in the nature of man, in his passions and interests, economic, religious, and otherwise. The cause of faction, Madison wrote, could not and should not be removed, for that cause was liberty, which must never be suppressed. But the effects of faction could be controlled by enlarging the society to be governed, since the larger the society, the greater the "variety of parties and interests" and the less likely that any one faction will have a majority. The greater variety could be found in a broader Republic, with its national Congress representing many sections and groups and hence able to break and control the violence of faction, whether of a popular majority or minority.

Like a careful cook, Madison wanted to dissolve indigestible lumps and fiery spices in the blander waters of a large pot. His crucial assumption here was that the broader republic would overcome faction. Why? If, say, inflationists in one state could get control of the state legislature, why could not inflationists in all states join hands and gain control of the new Congress? Here Madison marshaled his arguments convincingly. For one thing, he said, in a large republic the people would have to delegate decisions to representatives of bigger constituencies, and hence factional feelings would be refined and tempered by carefully chosen leaders whose views were more refined and broad minded than factional leaders. To be sure, factional and even sinister representatives might get elected and betray the people, but this would be less likely where representatives had to appeal to a "greater number of citizens in the large than in the small republic." The new Constitution, providing for two layers of government, would be a fine balance, a "happy combination" of local and general representation. But even more important, under a greater variety of parties and interests, "you make it less probable that a majority of the whole will have a common motive to invade the rights of other

* Professor of Political Science at Williams College. Author of: *Roosevelt: The Lion and the Fox, John Kennedy: A Political Profile, Congress on Trial.* The selection is from *The Deadlock of Democracy,* © 1963 by James MacGregor Burns, pp. 18–23, 1–7, published by Prentice Hall, Inc., Englewood Cliffs, New Jersey. By permission.

citizens; or if such a common motive exists, it will be more difficult for all who feel it to discover their own strength, and to act in unison with one another." Thus inflationists in different states could not easily join together because in the broader sphere other differences would keep them apart—for example, Madison had noted prophetically, the basic conflict between North and South.

But Madison still was not satisfied. There was still the possibility that even in the new Union a majority of the people might gang up on the minority. To be sure, Montesquieu's old safeguard might work: divide up national power among different officials, legislative, executive, and judicial, "for the accumulation of powers . . . in the same hands . . . may justly be pronounced the very definition of tyranny." But even this might not be enough, for what if the different officials—Congressmen, President, and federal judges—got together and pooled their power for the interests of some oppressive majority?

The answer to this question became the archpin of the whole constitutional framework. That answer was the system of checks and balances. "The great security against a gradual concentration of the several powers in the same department, consists in giving to those who administer each department the necessary constitutional means and personal motives to resist encroachments of the others," Madison wrote in the fifty-first paper, which rivals the tenth in intellectual sweep and power. ". . . . Ambition must be made to counteract ambition. The interest of the man must be connected with the constitutional rights of the place." Was it a reflection on human nature that such devices should be necessary to control the abuses of government? Yes, Madison admitted, and reverting to his first premise as to the nature of man, he asked: "But what is government itself, but the greatest of all reflections on human nature? If men were angels, no government would be necessary."

"Ambition must be made to counteract ambition"—in these seven words Madison drove straight to the heart of the whole problem; here he showed his genius as a political scientist. For he was not content with a flimsy separation of power that lunging politicians could smash through like paper. He was calling for barricade after barricade against the thrust of a popular majority—and the ultimate and impassable barricade was a system of checks and balances that would use man's essential human nature—his interests, his passions, his ambitions—to control itself. For Madison's ultimate checks and balances were political; they built into the engine of government automatic stabilizing devices that were sure to counterbalance one another because they were powered by separate sources of political energy. The ambitions of Presidents and Senators and Representatives and judges were bound to collide because each was responsible to separate constituencies in the "greater variety of parties and interests of the new federal republic." And each official, of course, had some kind of constitutional weapon—the President's veto, for example, or the Senators' power over treaties—that could be used against other officials and the sectional or economic or ideological interests they represented.

It was a stunning solution to the Framers' problem of checking the tyranny of the majority. Yet the solution contained a major flaw, or at least inconsistency, in the thinking behind it—a flaw so relevant to our later analysis that we must note it even in the same breath that we pay tribute to this profound scholar and politician.

The trouble was this: if, as Madison said, the first great protection against naked majority rule was the broader diversity of interests in a larger republic and hence the greater difficulty of concerting their "plans of oppression," why was not this enough in itself? Why would not any popular majority representing such a variety of interests perforce become so broad and moderate in its goals as never to threaten any major or even minor or individual interest? Why was it necessary to have what Madison called "auxiliary precautions" of checks and balances built right into the frame of government? Because, he said, experience had taught men the necessity of them. What experience? Madison must have meant the experience of societies so deeply divided between rich and poor, between master and slave, between sections, between religions, that victory for one side meant coercion or annihilation of the other. But the America he knew was not such a society. No ideological conflict racked the nation; as Louis Hartz has shown, Americans were united —to the extent they thought about such things—over the liberal creed of John Locke. No sharp class or religious conflict had torn the country into two warring halves. The same diversity that Madison used as an argument for broader union would have required any majority to appeal to so many interests, to straddle so many issues, that it must act in a moderate, broadly representative fashion.

The key to Madison's thinking is his central aim to stop people from turning easily to government for help. Today, when many people want protection by or through government, and not just protection from government, the power of a minority to stop the majority from acting through government may be as arbitrary as majority rule seemed to Madison. The fact is that Madison believed in a government of sharply limited powers. His efforts at Philadelphia to shift powers from the states to the new national government were intended more to thwart popular majorities in the states from passing laws for their own ends than to empower national majorities to pass laws for *their* ends. For the new national government was supposed to tame and temper popular majorities—which some states had been unable to do. This meant weaker government—but it was Madison, after all, who said that the necessity of any government was a misfortune and a reflection on human nature. Government, in short, was a necessary evil that must be curbed, not an instrument for the realization of men's higher ideals or a nation's broader interests. Hence he could sponsor what Richard Hofstadter has called a harmonious system of mutual frustration.

Still, if Madison was very much a child of his age, his analysis has long outlived him. Because of his brilliant linking of man's basic drives and man's formal institutions, of political forces and governmental mechanisms, Federalist No. 51 is still the best short analysis of the foundations of the American system. How far Madison extended his insights into political dynamics is not wholly clear. His concern—almost obsession—with factions suggests that he well understood the instincts of politicians to collect groups of followers and to build positions of power, for "the interest of the man must be connected with the constitutional rights of the place."

Certainly the implications of Madison's insight are clear today. Around every position established under the new Constitution—around "the interest of the man," whether President, legislator, or even judge or bureaucrat—a circle of sub-leaders and followers would also grow, the size of the circle depending on the importance of the office and the appeal and skills of the leader. Other factions would grow around politicians outside government, trying to get in. And of course the Constitution left intact a proliferation of offices in the states, counties, and localities, which in turn were the centers of thousands of other little circles of political action and influence.

These officeholders, their rivals, and the circles of sub-leaders and personal followers around them comprise a web of influence stretching across the formal governmental system. This is not to deny the importance of political parties and interest groups, of opinion-shaping agencies such as the press, of the thick crust of traditional habits and attitudes, of ideological and social forces, and of other factors. It is to say that, given the stability and durability of our constitutional system, these offices establish the main structure of political combat and governmental power.

Because Madison took the lead in thinking out and articulating this balance of checks, because he helped in masterly fashion to establish it, he stands today as one of the supreme strategists of American politics. . . .

THE POLITICS OF THE CAVE

Behind the fascination with political personalities and election gladiators there is in this country, I think, a vast boredom with politics. Because it has failed to engage itself with the problems that dog us during our working days and haunt our dreams at night, politics has not engaged the best of us, or at least the best in us. If people seem complacent or inert, the cause may lie less in them than in a political system that evades and confuses the real issues rather than sharpening and resolving them. Anyone active in everyday politics knows of concerned, civic-minded people who give hundreds of hours and dollars to fund drives, the Red Cross, and other worthy local causes but will have nothing to do with politics. It frustrates them, alienates them, bores them to tears. They are failing their political obligations—but perhaps politics is failing them.

But never has politics needed them more. We are at the critical stage of a somber and inexorable cycle that seems to have gripped the public affairs of the nation. We have been mired in government deadlock, as Congress blocked or killed most of Mr. Kennedy's bold proposals of 1960, and many planks of the Republican platform as well. Presently we are caught in the politics of drift, as the nation's politicians put off major decisions until after the presidential campaign of 1964. Then we can expect a period of decision, as the voters choose a President, followed by a brief phase of the "politics of the deed," as the President capitalizes on the psychological thrust of his election mandate to put through some bits and pieces of his program. But after the short honeymoon between Congress and President the old cycle of deadlock and drift will reassert itself.

This cycle is one reason for the disenchantment with politics of those most concerned with political issues. It has led to a government by fits and starts, to a statecraft that has not been able to supply the steady leadership and power necessary for the conduct of our affairs. Historically there has been a serious lag—once a near fatal lag—in the speed and effectiveness with which the national government has coped with emerging crises.

The record is a disturbing one. The steady, moderate action on slavery that was so desperately needed in the 1840's and 1850's finally came, immoderately and at frightful cost, in the 1860's and 1870's. American participation in the first real efforts at collective security came after World War II instead of World War I. The anti-depression measures so critically necessary in the 1930's, if not long before, became governmental and political commitments only in the 1940's and 1950's. The most elementary types of federal control over economic power were delayed for years. The social security and other welfare measures needed to protect men against the insecurities of the modern economy should have been adopted at least by the turn of the century; they had to wait for the New Deal of the 1930's. The economic internationalism that characterized the Marshall Plan and its successor programs in the last fifteen years was missing in the 1920's, when our nationalistic economic policies helped bring on the world depression. Our admirable concern today with the developing countries would have paid off many times over if we had come to it sooner; as it is, we are trying to influence revolutions that in many cases have moved out of the narrow orbit of American influence. The cost of delay has also been high in countless other areas of hardly less importance: urban decline, conservation, tax reform, medical care, governmental organization. We have reacted to change rather than dominated it.

We have often been too late, and we have been too late with too little. Whether we can master depression in peacetime is still in doubt, for we pulled ourselves out of the Great Depression only by the bootstrap of war. Currently baffled by a sluggish economy, we seem unable to promote long, sustained economic growth. Negroes still do not share the basic rights of citizenship promised in the 14th and 15th Amendments. We have done almost nothing about the old dream of a coordinated and vitalized transportation policy. Our social welfare measures are inadequate, especially in medical care. We cannot play our full economic role abroad because of inhibiting forces in Congress. Our structure of transportation is inequitable and archaic. We have hardly begun to adapt our federal and state policy-making machinery to the heavy demands on it.

One can view this drift and delay with a certain philosophical calm. In the end American government, like the belated hero in the horse opera, seems to come to the rescue. Delays may be hard, of course, on certain persons. A man whose working life stretched from 1900 to the mid-thirties might be a bit concerned in retrospect over the delay in federal social welfare programs. A twelve-year-old boy working in a textile mill during the 1920's or even in the 1930's, might wonder, if he had a chance to wonder about such things, how a great nation like the United States had been unable to outlaw child labor despite general condemnation of it, while most of the civilized world had accomplished this primitive reform years earlier. A Negro in the 1960's might not be so detached toward states' rights and congressional obstruction as some of his fellow Americans. Still, most of us could reflect that progress has almost always come in the long run, even if the run has been longer for some than for others. And the slowness of change has meant, perhaps, less tension and disruption of the social fabric.

Today, however, the notion of the beneficent inevitability of gradual progress is open to challenge. For one thing, the furious pace of social and economic change at home and abroad makes delay in government action far riskier than before. We do not enjoy a cushion of time in adjusting to such change, just as we no longer enjoy a cushion of time in coping with enemy attack. We may not possess, for example, an extra decade or two to respond to the demands of a revolution in Africa or Asia or Cuba. Then too, crisis does not seem so productive of federal action as in former days. Judging by the Democratic and Republican platforms of 1960, the campaign speeches of the presidential candidates, and the bulk of opinion in the press, at the pulpit, and in academia, most American opinion leaders agree that the international situation calls for mobilization of educational, scientific, industrial, manpower, health, and physical resources, as well as military strength. But despite this weight of opinion, key domestic proposals of both the Eisenhower and Kennedy administrations in such areas have been stalled in Congress. It is notable that Kennedy's major foreign-policy proposal of 1961—long-term financing of foreign aid—failed at the very time that the nation was aroused over crises in Berlin and Southeast Asia. Perhaps the American people have become so benumbed by constant emergency that a crisis no longer serves the old function of providing broad support for government action.

Another reason that the habit of delay and devitalization may have to be abandoned, however, lies in the nature of the competition that the nation faces. Never before have we confronted an enemy that, over so long a period, challenges so formidably as does Soviet Russia, our ideology, our economic system, our democratic ways, and our international role. It is clear in the 1960's that the nation faces a period of years and perhaps decades during which it must strain every nerve and marshal every resource to maintain its own strength and to nourish that of the free world. Soviet Russia has shaped a governmental and political system that, whatever its failings and terrors and deprivations, has shown itself capable of mobilizing Russians for a sustained effort. The Chinese colossus, imposing perhaps even greater sacrifices, is building up its own hard strength. The question is whether Americans, without harming the substance and the processes of democracy, can empower and invigorate their own society for the long pull.

Yet, serious as these failings are, I have still not expressed the main reason that so many concerned people are aliens to the political process. The main reason, I think, is that politics to them seems dominated by old and sterile issues and appears unable to grapple with the two cardinal problems of late 20th Century civilization. These problems are the style of life of urban man, and the need for fresh and creative ventures in foreign policy.

By 1980, it is expected, over four-fifths of all Americans will be living in metropolitan areas. By the year 2000 a nation of 300,000,000 will embrace vast patches of almost solid urban settlement: the Eastern seaboard; the West Coast; and an urban Midwest fusing the urban and suburban areas of a dozen cities from St. Louis to Buffalo. We have become, as Walter Lippmann has said, in large part a mass society living in congested urban agglomerations. This inexorable trend poses the question of whether men will become further dehumanized and corrupted in megalopolis, or whether a national government sensitive to urban needs can take the leadership, through policy on education, cultural subsidies, television and other mass media, city planning and redevelopment, recreation, transportation, expansion of civil rights, in making megalopolis not only habitable but hospitable to man.

The other problem is how to break out of immobilism in foreign and military policy. However much we may be balked by Russian intransigence in such areas as disarmament and East-West trade, there are other creative possibilities that we have hardly begun to exploit. Vastly stepped up educational and cultural exchange, broadening of the powers of the United Nations, more sophisticated and longer range programs of economic aid to the new nations, the establishment of international universities and cultural centers, increased international collaboration in social and natural science and in space technology, follow-up action to President Kennedy's "declaration of interdependence" of the Western nations and to the Test Ban Treaty —the possibilities are almost limitless.

It is in these two areas, with their exciting potential for creative statesmanship, that our politics has, I think, seemed most crabbed and irrelevant. One wonders, indeed, whether we have advanced much beyond the cave man in the stakes and style of our politics. He fashioned shelter, gathered food, and doled out sustenance to the weaker members of the clan; he and his fellows huddled together in defense against the outside foe. And in Plato's famous allegory of another cave, he often took shadow for substance in trying to grasp the great world beyond his narrow vista. So too we produce and distribute goods and grant welfare to the poor; we huddle with our allies behind our nuclear weapons; and we act politically in a shadowland of old governmental fetters and outworn stereotypes. Politics is still mainly a matter of brute economics and sheer survival.

While the main reason for our political futility and frustration is the political system described in this book, the ultimate source is intellectual. The root trouble, I think, is in our own minds. Like the people in the cave, we have been hypnotized by the shadows of our own political images and by the echoes of our old incantations.

We have been too much entranced by the Madisonian model of government. This model was the product of the gifted men who gathered in Philadelphia over 175 years ago, and it deserves much of the admiration and veneration we have accorded it. But this is also the system of checks and balances and interlocked gears of government that requires the consensus of many groups and leaders before the nation can act; and it is the system that exacts the heavy price of delay and devitalization that I have noted.

In glorifying the Madisonian model we . . . have underestimated the powerful balances and safeguards that are built into a system of majority rule and responsible parties. We have thwarted and fragmentized leadership instead of allowing it free play within the boundaries of the democratic process.

Partly because of these miscalculations, we still underestimate the extent to which our system was designed for deadlock and inaction. We look on the current impasse in Washington as something extraordinary rather than as the inevitable consequence of a system we accept. We look on the failure of the national government to act as the result of poor leadership or bad luck or evil men, and we search for scapegoats. Some conceive that Mr. Johnson today can break the impasse by some magic feat of manipulation or some deft bit of persuasion or by some grand appeal to the people, but they are ignoring the weight of American experience. Typically the Madisonian system has made us go slow; only under extraordinary combinations of circumstances have we moved vigorously ahead on many fronts. Even the strongest and ablest Presidents have been, in the end, more the victims of the Madisonian system than the masters of it.

And so today we face the Madisonian idea built into a system of entrenched power. We face a . . . system that compels government by consensus and coalition rather than a two-party system that allows the winning party to govern and the losers to oppose. While the demands on our government pile up at a feverish pace, the system shows no sign of relaxing its grip on the levers of action. This system is rooted in our constitutional arrangements, electoral behavior, party institutions, and machinery of government.

Above all, it is rooted in our minds. "We are at one of those uncommon junctures of human affairs when we can be saved by the solution of intellectual problems and in no other way," John Maynard Keynes said in the 1930's. So we are today. Our need is not to win an election or a leader; we must win a government. To do this we must disenthrall ourselves of the shadows and echoes that draw us away from reality. We cannot unfreeze our politics until we unfreeze our minds.

The Politics of Countervailing Power

REINHOLD NIEBUHR *

All historic forms of justice and injustice are determined to a much larger degree than pure rationalists or idealists realize by the given equilibrium or disproportion within each type of power and by the balance of various types of power in a given community. It may be taken as axiomatic that great disproportions of power lead to injustice, whatever may be the efforts to mitigate it.[1]

All social co-operation on a larger scale than the most intimate social group requires a measure of coercion. While no state can maintain its unity purely by coercion neither can it preserve itself without coercion. Where the factor of mutual consent is strongly developed, and where standardized and approximately fair methods of adjudicating and resolving conflicting interests within an organized group have been established, the coercive factor in social life is frequently covert, and becomes apparent only in moments of crisis and in the group's policy toward recalcitrant individuals. Yet it is never absent. Divergence of interest, based upon geographic and functional differences within a society, is bound to create different social philosophies and

* Professor Emeritus, Union Theological Seminary. Recipient of Presidential Freedom Medal 1964. Author of *The Children of Light and The Children of Darkness, Moral Man and Immoral Society,* fifteen other books, and numerous articles. This compilation is taken from the writings of Reinhold Niebuhr cited at the end of each selection. For a fuller statement of Niebuhr's political philosophy the student is referred to Harry R. Davis and Robert C. Good, eds., *Reinhold Niebuhr on Politics* (New York, Charles Scribner's Sons, 1960). This volume has been of great assistance in the preparation of this compilation.

[1] *Nature and Destiny of Man,* Vol. II. *Human Destiny* (New York, Charles Scribner's Sons, 1943), p. 262. By permission. Cited below as *Human Destiny.*

political attitudes which goodwill and intelligence may partly, but never completely, harmonize. Ultimately, unity, within an organized social group, or a federation of such groups, is created by the ability of the dominant group to impose its will. *Politics will, to the end of history, be an area where conscience and power will meet, where the ethical and coercive forces of human life will interpenetrate and work out their tentative and uneasy compromises.*[2]

AMBIVALENT NATURE OF MAN

Modern developments have proved that there is a more intimate relation between what Madison called man's reason and self-love than the rationalists have assumed.[3] If political issues were really abstract questions of social policy upon which unbiased citizens were asked to commit themselves, the business of voting and the debate which preceded the election might actually be regarded as an educational programme in which a social group discovers its common mind. But the fact is that political questions are inevitably rooted in [self] interest of some kind or other and few citizens can view a social policy without regard to their interest.[4]

The confidence of modern secular idealism in the possibility of an easy resolution of the tension between individual and community, or between classes, races and nations, is derived from a too optimistic view of human nature.[5] All human knowledge is tainted with an "ideological" taint. It pretends to be more true than it is. It is finite knowledge, gained from a particular perspective; but it pretends to be final and ultimate knowledge. Exactly analogous to the cruder pride of power, the pride of intellect is derived on the one hand from ignorance of the finiteness of the human mind and on the other hand from an attempt to obscure the known conditional character of human knowledge and the taint of self-interest in human truth.[6]

Whenever modern idealists are confronted with the divisive and corrosive effects of man's self-love, they look for some immediate cause of this perennial tendency, usually in some specific form of social organization. One school holds that men would be good if only political institutions would not corrupt them; another believes that they would be good if the prior evil of a faulty economic organization could be eliminated. Or another school

[2] *Moral Man and Immoral Society* (New York, Charles Scribner's Sons, 1932), pp. 3, 4. By permission.

[3] "Christianity and Humanism," *Messenger,* Vol. XVII (September 9, 1952), p. 7. By permission.

[4] *Moral Man and Immoral Society,* p. 5.

[5] *The Children of Light and the Children of Darkness* (New York, Charles Scribner's Sons, 1944), p. 18. By permission. Cited below as *The Children of Light.*

[6] *Nature and Destiny of Man,* Vol. I, *Human Nature* (New York, Charles Scribner's Sons, 1941), pp. 194, 195. By permission. Cited below as *Human Nature.*

thinks of this evil as no more than ignorance, and therefore waits for a more perfect educational process to redeem man from his partial and particular loyalties. But no school asks how it is that an essentially good man could have produced corrupting and tyrannical political organizations or exploiting economic organizations, or fanatical and superstitious religious organizations.[7]

"The diversities in the faculties of men," declared James Madison,

> from which the rights of property originate, are . . . an insuperable obstacle to uniformity of interests. The protection of these faculties is the first object of government. From the protection of different and unequal faculties of acquiring property, the possession of different degrees and kinds of property immediately results; and from the influence of these on the sentiments and views of the respective proprietors ensues a division of society into different interests and parties.*

This is a correct analysis of the economic basis of political attitudes, except that too great a significance is attached to faculty as the basis of inequality of privilege. Differences in faculty and function do indeed help to originate inequality of privilege but they never justify the degree of inequality created, and they are frequently not even relevant to the type of inequality perpetuated in a social system.[8]

The selfishness of men and nations is a fixed datum of historical science. Election results can be confidently predicted if the economic interests of the voters can be carefully enough analyzed. Yet this human egotism does not belong to nature. The eighteenth-century rationalists were wrong in asserting that men sought their own, just as every animal seeks to preserve its existence. The human self is different from other creatures in two respects: 1) It is able by its freedom to transmute nature's survival impulse into more potent and more destructive, more subtle and more comprehensive, forms of self-seeking than the one-dimensional survival impulse of nature. 2) It is able to envisage a larger good than its own preservation, to make some fitful responses to this more inclusive obligation and to feel itself guilty for its failure to make a consistent response.[9] Man is the kind of lion who both kills the lamb and also dreams of the day when the lion and the lamb shall lie down together.[10]

The real situation is that the human self is strongly inclined to seek its own but that it has a sufficient dimension of transcendence over self to be unable

[7] *The Children of Light,* p. 17.

* See *The Federalist,* No. 10, in this volume.

[8] *Moral Man and Immoral Society,* pp. 113, 114.

[9] *Faith and History* (New York, Charles Scribner's Sons, 1949), pp. 94, 95. By permission.

[10] Quoted in June Bingham, *Courage to Change* (New York, Charles Scribner's Sons, 1961), p. 67. By permission.

to ascribe this inclination merely to natural necessity. On the other hand, when it strives for a wider good it surreptitiously introduces its own interests into this more inclusive value. This fault may be provisionally regarded as the inevitable consequence of a finite viewpoint. The self sees the larger structure of value from its own standpoint.[11]

The conflicts between men are thus never simple conflicts between competing survival impulses. They are conflicts in which each man or group seeks to guard its power and prestige against the competing expressions of power and pride. Since possession of power and prestige always involves some encroachment upon the prestige and power of others, this conflict is by its very nature a more stubborn and difficult one than the mere competition between various survival impulses in nature. It remains to be added that this conflict expresses itself even more cruelly in collective than in individual terms. Human behavior being less individualistic than secular liberalism assumed, the struggle between classes, races, and other groups in human society is not easily resolved by the expedient of dissolving the groups as liberal democratic idealists assumed.[12]

INDIVIDUAL AND COLLECTIVE MORALITY

Individual men may be moral in the sense that they are able to consider interests other than their own in determining problems of conduct, and are capable, on occasion, of preferring the advantages of others to their own. They are endowed by nature with a measure of sympathy and consideration for their kind, the breath of which may be extended by astute pedagogy. Their rational faculty prompts them to a sense of justice which educational discipline may refine and purge of egoistic elements until they are able to view a social situation, in which their own interests are involved, with a fair measure of objectivity. But all these achievements are more difficult, if not impossible, for human societies and social groups. In every human group there is less reason to guide and check impulse, less capacity for self-transcendence, less ability to comprehend the needs of others and therefore more unrestrained egoism than the individuals, who compose the group, reveal in their personal relations.

The inferiority of the morality of groups to that of individuals is due in part to the difficulty of establishing a rational social force which is powerful enough to cope with the natural impulses by which society achieves its cohesion; but in part it is merely the revelation of a collective egotism, compounded of the egotistic impulses of individuals, which achieve a more vivid expression and a more cumulative effect when they are *united in a common*

[11] *Faith and History,* pp. 95, 96.
[12] *The Children of Light,* pp. 20, 21.

impulse than when they express themselves separately and discretely.* [13]

The group is more arrogant, hypocritical, self-centered and more ruthless in the pursuit of its ends than the individual. An inevitable moral tension between individual and group morality is therefore created. "If," said the great Italian statesman, Cavour, "we did for ourselves what we do for our country, what rascals we would be." This tension is naturally most apparent in the conscience of responsible statesmen, who are bound to feel the disparity between the canons of ordinary morality and the accepted habits of collective and political behavior.[14]

The larger the group the more certainly will it express itself selfishly in the total community. It will be more powerful and therefore more able to defy any social restraints which might be devised. It will also be less subject to internal moral restraints. The larger the group the more difficult it is to achieve a common mind and purpose and the more inevitably will it be united by momentary impulses and immediate and unreflective purposes. The increasing size of the group increases the difficulties of achieving a group self-consciousness, except as it comes in conflict with other groups and is unified by perils and passions. It is a rather pathetic aspect of human social life that conflict is a seemingly unavoidable prerequisite of group solidarity.[15]

The social group asks for the individual's unconditional loyalty, asserting that its necessities are the ultimate law of the individual's existence. But on the other hand it is a pretension which the individual makes for himself, not as an individual but as a member of his group. Collective egotism does indeed offer the individual an opportunity to lose himself in a larger whole; but it also offers him possibilities of self-aggrandizement beside which mere individual pretensions are implausible and incredible. Individuals "join to set up a god whom each then severally and tacitly identifies with himself, to swell the chorus of praise which each then severally and tacitly arrogates to himself." [16] *In its whole range from pride of family to pride of nation, collective egotism and group pride are a more pregnant source of injustice and conflict than purely individual pride.*[17]

Contending factions in a social struggle require morale; and morale is created by the right dogmas, symbols and emotionally potent oversimplifica-

* "By a faction, I understand a number of citizens, whether amounting to a majority or a minority of the whole, *who are united and actuated by some common impulse of passion or of interest,* adverse to the rights of other citizens, or to the permanent and aggregate interests of the community." *The Federalist,* No. 10. (Editor's emphasis.)

[13] *Moral Man and Immoral Society,* pp. xi, xii.

[14] *Human Nature,* pp. 208, 209.

[15] *Moral Man and Immoral Society,* pp. 47, 48.

[16] *Human Nature,* p. 212. The quotation is from Philip Leon, *The Ethics of Power,* p. 140.

[17] *Ibid,* p. 213.

tions.[18] They have to believe more firmly in the justice and probable triumph of their cause, than any impartial science could give them the right to believe, if they are to have enough energy to contest the power of the strong.[19] A too simple social radicalism does not recognize how quickly the poor, the weak, the despised of yesterday, may, on gaining a social victory over their detractors, exhibit the same arrogance and the same will-to-power which they abhored in their opponents and which they were inclined to regard as a congenital sin of their enemies. Every victim of injustice makes the mistake of supposing that the sin from which he suffers is a peculiar vice of his oppressor.[20]

The relations between groups must therefore always be predominantly political rather than ethical, that is they will be determined by the proportion of power which each group possesses at least as much as any rational and moral appraisal of the comparative needs and claims of each group.[21] The peace of the world is always, as St. Augustine observed, something of an armistice between opposing factions.[22]

THE MORAL AMBIGUITY OF GOVERNMENTS

The expectation of changing human nature by the destruction of economic privilege to such a degree that no one will desire to make selfish use of power, must probably be placed in the category of romantic illusions. If power remains in society, mankind will never escape the necessity of endowing those who possess it with the largest measure of ethical self-control. But that does not obviate the necessity of reducing power to a minimum, or bringing the remainder under the strongest measure of social control; and destroying such types of it as are least amenable to social control. For there is no ethical force strong enough to place inner checks upon the use of power if its quantity is inordinate. "The truth is," declared James Madison, "that all men having power ought to be distrusted." [23]

Political power deserves to be placed in a special category, because it results from the ability to use and manipulate other forms of social power for the purpose of organizing and dominating the community.[24] It is obvious that the principle of government, or the organization of the whole realm of social vitalities, stands upon a high plane of moral sanction and social necessity.[25] It is nevertheless important to recognize that government is also morally ambiguous.

[18] *Moral Man and Immoral Society,* p. xv.
[19] *Ibid.* [20] *Human Nature,* p. 226. [21] *Ibid,* p. xxiii.
[22] *Discerning the Signs of the Times* (New York, Charles Scribner's Sons, 1946), p. 187. By permission.
[23] *Moral Man and Immoral Society,* p. 164. The quotation is from *Papers of James Madison,* edited by H. D. Gilpin, Vol. II, p. 1073.
[24] *Human Destiny,* p. 263. [25] *Ibid,* p. 266.

The power of the rulers is subject to two abuses. It may actually be the dominion which one portion of the community exercises over the whole community. But if government does express the imperial impulse of one class or group within the community, it would if its pretensions are not checked, generate imperial impulses of its own towards the community. It would be tempted to destroy the vitality and freedom of component elements in the community in the name of order. It would identify its particular form of order with the principle of order itself. This evil can be fully understood only if it is recognized that all governments and rulers derive a part of their power, not only from the physical instruments of coercion at their disposal, but also from the reality and the pretension of "majesty."

The majesty of the state is legitimate in so far as it embodies and expresses both the authority and power of the total community over all its members and the principles of order and justice as such against the perils of anarchy.[26] But there are no historic expressions of the majesty of state and government without an admixture of illegitimate pretensions of majesty and sanctity. These can be most simply defined as the tendency of states and governments to hide and obscure the contingent and partial character of their rule and to claim unconditional validity for it.[27]

John Adams in his warnings to Thomas Jefferson would seem to have had a premonition of this. At any rate, he understood the human situation well enough to have stated:

> Power always thinks it has a great soul and vast views beyond the comprehension of the weak; and that it is doing God's service when it is violating all His laws. Our passions, ambitions, avarice, love and resentment, etc., possess so much metaphysical subtlety and so much overpowering eloquence that they insinuate themselves into the understanding and the conscience and convert both to their party.

Adams' understanding of the power of self's passions and ambitions to corrupt the self's reason is a simple recognition of the facts of life which refute all theories, whether liberal or Marxist, about the possibility of a completely disinterested self.[28] In political struggles there are no saints but only sinners fighting each other.[29]

Every society uses a degree of coercion in achieving cohesion for the simple reason that the human imagination is too limited and egoistic impulses are too powerful for purely voluntary cooperation on a large scale to be attained. Inevitably the force which society uses for this purpose will seek

[26] *Ibid,* p. 267.
[27] *Human Destiny,* p. 268.
[28] *The Irony of American History* (New York, Charles Scribner's Sons, 1952), pp. 21, 22. By permission.
[29] "Leaves from the Notebook of a War Bound American," *Christian Century,* Vol. LVI (November 15, 1939), p. 1406. Copyright 1939 Christian Century Foundation. Reprinted by permission.

to serve itself more than society. No matter how general the consent which maintains it, the actual social locus from which the initiative of coercion is taken is narrower than the whole of society. Hence in every society there is something like an oligarchy.[30] Modern democracies tend toward a more equal justice partly because they have divorced political power from special social functions. They endowed all men with a measure of it by giving them the right to review the policies of their leaders. This democratic principle does not obviate the formation of oligarchies in society; but it places a check upon their formation, and upon the exercise of their power.[31]

THE BALANCE OF SOCIAL FORCES

The harmony of communities is not simply attained by the authority of law. The social harmony of living communities is achieved by an interaction between the normative conceptions of morality and law and the existing and developing forces and vitalities of the community. Usually the norms of law are compromises between the rational-moral ideals of what ought to be, and the possibilities of the situation as determined by given equilibria of vital forces. The specific legal enactments are, on the one hand, the instruments of the conscience of the community, seeking to subdue the potential anarchy of forces and interests into a tolerable harmony. They are, on the other hand, merely explicit formulations of given tensions and equilibria of life and power, as worked out by the unconscious interactions of social life.

No human community is, in short, a simple construction of conscience or reason. All communities are more or less stable or precarious harmonies of human vital capacities. They are governed by power. The power which determined the quality and harmony is not merely the coercive and organizing power of government. That is only one of the two aspects of social power. The other is the balance of vitalities and forces in any given social situation.[32]

It is our common assumption that political freedom is a simple *summum bonum*. It is not. Freedom must always be related to community and justice. Every community seeks consciously or unconsciously to make social peace and order the first goal of its life. It may pay a very high price in the restriction of freedom so as to establish order; but order is the first desideratum for the simple reason that chaos means non-existence. The situation in the Congo should persuade us of this obvious fact, if we had not been aware of it before.

Order alone can, of course, be bought at a very high price, usually at too high a price from the standpoint of those classes in society who must pay it.

[30] "Russia and Karl Marx," *The Nation,* Vol. CXLVI, (May 7, 1938) pp. 530, 531. By permission.

[31] *Human Destiny,* p. 263. [32] *Ibid,* p. 257.

The second goal of any society therefore is justice. Aristotle defined justice as "giving each man his due." Since in the long history of Western democracy no one has ever offered accurate criteria by which each man's due is measured, we must come to the conclusion that open societies have solved the problem by allowing a free competition of social forces, which enables every force in society to make its claims upon society and to acquire enough social and political power and prestige to enforce its claims.

And liberty and equality are generally recognized as the twin principles of justice. But abstract radical libertarianism and equalitarianism falsely regard them as simple historical possibilities. They cannot be simple possibilities. Liberty must be measured against the community's need for security against internal and external peril. Equality must be measured against the need for the hierarchy of social function by which a community integrates its life and work. That is why history has refuted both Jacobin libertarianism and Marxist equalitarianism.[33]

There are various possibilities of so managing and equilibrating the balance of social forces in a given community that the highest possible justice may be achieved, and since the organizing principle and power in the community is also subject to indeterminate refinement, communal order and justice can approximate a more perfect brotherhood in varying degree. But each principle of communal organization—the organization of power and the balance of power—contains possibilities of contradicting the law of brotherhood. The organizing principle and power may easily degenerate into tyranny. Again the principle of balance of power is always pregnant with the possibility of anarchy. These twin evils, tyranny and anarchy, or authority and liberty, represent the Scylla and Charybdis between which the frail bark of social justice must sail. It is almost certain to founder upon one rock if it makes the mistake of regarding the other as the only peril.[34]

The domination of one life by another is avoided most successfully by an equilibrium of powers and vitalities, so that weakness does not invite enslavement by the strong.[35] Such a balance, once achieved, can be stabilized, embellished, and even, on occasion, perfected by more purely moral considerations. But there has never been a scheme of justice in history which did not have a balance of power at its foundation.[36] It may be wise for the community to sacrifice something in efficiency for the sake of preserving a greater balance of forces and avoiding undue centralization of power.[37]

[33] "Reflections on Democracy as an Alternative to Communism." Reprinted from the *Columbia University Forum* by permission of the publisher Columbia University, Copyright © 1961. Vol. 4 (Summer 1961), pp. 10, 11.

[34] *Human Destiny,* p. 258.

[35] *Ibid.,* p. 265.

[36] *Christianity and Power Politics* (New York, Charles Scribner's Sons, 1940), p. 104. By permission.

[37] *The Children of Light,* p. 115.

But an equilibrium of power is not brotherhood. The restraint of the will-to-power of one member of the community by the counter-pressure of power by another member results in a condition of tension. All tension is covert or potential conflict. The principle of equilibrium of power is thus a principle of justice in so far as it prevents domination and enslavement but it is a principle of anarchy and conflict in so far as its tensions, if unresolved, result in overt conflict. Furthermore social life, when not consciously managed and manipulated, does not develop perfect equilibria of power. Its capricious disproportions of power generate various forms of domination and enslavement. Human society therefore requires a conscious control and manipulation of the various equilibria which exist in it. There must be an organizing center within a given field of social vitalities. This center must arbitrate conflicts from a more impartial perspective than is available to any party of a given conflict; it must manage and manipulate the processes of mutual support so that the tensions inherent in them will not erupt into conflict; it must coerce submission to the social process by superior power whenever the instruments of arbitrating and composing conflict do not suffice; and finally it must seek to redress the disproportion of power by conscious shifts of the balances whenever they make for injustice.[38]

A healthy society must seek to achieve the greatest possible equilibrium of power, the greatest possible number of centers of power, the greatest possible social check upon the administration of power, and the greatest possible inner moral check on human ambition, as well as the most effective use of forms of power in which consent and coercion are compounded.[39]

THE STRATEGY OF DEMOCRACY

A free society requires some confidence in the ability of men to reach tentative and tolerable adjustments between competing interests and to arrive at some common notions of justice which transcend all partial interests. A consistent pessimism in regard to man's rational capacity for justice invariably leads to absolutistic political theories; for they prompt the conviction that only preponderant power can coerce the various vitalities of a community into a working harmony. But a too consistent optimism in regard to man's ability and inclination to grant justice to his fellows obscures the perils of chaos which perennially confront every society, including a free society. In one sense a democratic society is particularly exposed to the dangers of confusion. If these perils are not appreciated they may overtake a free society and invite the alternative of tyranny.[40]

[38] *Ibid,* pp. 265, 266.

[39] Niebuhr, "Coercion, Self-Interest and Love," in K. Boulding, *The Organizational Revolution* (New York, Harper & Brothers, 1953), p. 242. By permission.

[40] *The Children of Light,* pp. xii, xiii.

The preservation of a democratic civilization requires the wisdom of the serpent and the harmlessness of the dove. The children of light must be armed with the wisdom of the children of darkness but remain free from their malice. They must know the power of self-interest in human society without giving it moral justification. They must have this wisdom in order that they may beguile, deflect, harness and restrain self-interest, individual and collective, for the sake of the community.[41]

The whole development of democratic justice in human society has depended upon some comprehension of these moral ambiguities which inhere in both government and the principle of the equilibrium of power. It is the highest achievement of democratic societies that they embody the principle of resistance to government within the principle of government itself. The citizen is thus armed with "constitutional" power to resist the unjust exactions of government. He can do this without creating anarchy within the community if government has been so conceived that criticism of the ruler becomes an instrument of better government and not a threat to government itself.[42]

Thus the democratic strategy is two-fold. First it contributes to the establishment of order and community through the non-violent arbitration and accommodation of social conflict. Second, it seeks to maintain freedom by making power responsible, checking the authority of government and providing a form of social control over the leaders of society.[43]

Contrary to the belief and expectations of eighteenth-century democrats, a national community is both integrated and divided by many ethnic, cultural, religious and economic groups. Of our early constitutionalists, Madison was realistic enough to recognize the inevitability of factions. But even he tried in every way to circumscribe their development.[44] The best political answer to the problem of accommodating and balancing the interests of competing groups is democracy, which is a permanently valid method of holding all cultural viewpoints under criticism and of achieving an uncoerced harmony among the various social and cultural vitalities.[45] An open society manages through this strategy to draw upon the virtues, and to correct the vices, of various components of the community by countervailing influences of other components. The mind of each religious and cultural group is freed by these democratic pressures in exactly the same way as interest groups of various kinds are purged of the virulence of their bias, by the challenge

[41] *Ibid,* pp. 40, 41.

[42] *Human Destiny,* p. 268.

[43] Harry R. Davis and Robert C. Good, editors, *Reinhold Niebuhr On Politics,* p. 183. By permission.

[44] *The Children of Light,* pp. 119, 120.

[45] "The Contribution of Religion to Cultural Unity," Hazen Pamphlet No. 13 (1945), p. 6. By permission.

which they must meet from other groups.[46] In this way a healthy democracy provides for checks and balances upon the pretensions of men and their lust for power.[47]

In this situation the democratic consensus, without which a community cannot survive, must be tentative and precarious; and the required majority, necessary for common action, may be composed from time to time by the various alliances of groups. But history has proved the consequences in justice to be much higher in this freedom than is possible to attain when the "truth" about justice, as defined by any one religious group, [party,] or for that matter, any interest group, remains unchallenged. This is true because the mind by which we define justice is bound, not by ultimate commitments, but by immediate interests. There is no better way of freeing these various minds than the way which has been found in a free society. They would have, if left unchallenged, attempted to dominate the community and provide it with the only ultimate definition of "truth" and "justice." [48]

A free society thus derives general profit from the interested desires of particular groups, each group leaving a deposit of virtue in the community beyond its intentions and interests. The health and justice of the community is preserved, not so much by the discriminate judgment of the whole community, as by the effect of free criticism in moderating the pretensions of every group and by the weight of competing power in balancing power which might become inordinate and oppressive. Democracy in short is not a method which is effective only among virtuous men. It is a method which prevents interested men from following their interests to the detriment of the community—though there must of course be a minimal inclination for justice to furnish a base of community.[49]

The confusions occasioned by the dogmatic assumptions of both Right and Left prove the validity of President Conant's observation that a high degree of empiricism is a basic requirement for democratic health. All sweeping generalizations and assumptions must be eschewed and the questions must be constantly asked, what is the effect of this or that policy in this or that situation; how well does this particular constellation of power satisfy the requirements of justice and freedom? A healthy democracy never gives all power to the proponents of any dogma; it holds all claims to truth under critical review; it balances all social forces, not in an automatic but in a contrived harmony of power. It distills a modicum of truth from a conflict of

[46] "The Commitment of the Self and the Freedom of the Mind," in *Religion and Freedom of Thought,* by Perry Miller, Robert L. Calhoun, Nathan M. Pusey and Reinhold Niebuhr. Copyright 1954 by the Union Theological Seminary. Reprinted by permission of Doubleday & Company, Inc. p. 58.

[47] *Christian Realism and Political Problems,* p. 14.

[48] "The Commitment of the Self and the Freedom of the Mind," p. 59.

[49] *The Self and the Dramas of History* (New York, Charles Scribner's Sons, 1955), p. 198. By permission.

error. In this way pretensions to wisdom are not supported by a monopoly of power and sweeping generalizations may be refuted by daily experience.[50]

Because reason is something more than a weapon of self-interest it can be an instrument of justice; but since reason is never dissociated from the vitalities of life, individual and collective, it cannot be a pure instrument of justice.[51] *Man's capacity for justice makes democracy possible; but man's inclination to injustice makes democracy necessary.*[52]

MADISON THE REALIST

The early American culture was not bereft of a realistic theory. Two strains of thought, Calvinist and Jeffersonian, have entered into our original American heritage. On the problem of the resolution of political conflicts of interest and power in the community, the strain of thought most perfectly expressed by James Madison combined Christian realism in interpretation of human motives and desires with Jefferson's passion for liberty. . . .

Jefferson, and his coterie including Tom Paine, had a vision of an harmonious society in which government would interfere as little as possible with the economic ambitions of the individual. These ambitions were presumed to be moderate; and their satisfaction without friction with the neighbor would be guaranteed by the wide opportunities of the new continent. The subordination of man to man would be prevented by the simple expedient of preferring agriculture to industry. Jefferson's ideal society conformed perfectly to John Locke's conception of men "mixing their labor" with nature and claiming the fruits thereof as their legitimate property.

Madison feared the potential tyranny of government as much as Jefferson; but he understood the necessity of government much more. The Constitution protects the citizen against abuses of government, not so much by keeping government weak as by introducing the principle of balance of power into government. This balance of power between executive, legislative and judicial functions is one method of preventing the abuse of power. European democracies have found other methods of achieving the same end; and their methods may be less likely to issue in a mutual frustration of a community's governing powers. The important fact is that the necessity of a strong government was recognized. Madison was much more conscious than Jefferson of the peril of what he called "faction" in the community. He had no hope of resolving such conflicts by simple prudence. With the realists of every age he knew how intimately man's reason is related to his interests. "As long as any connection exists," he wrote, "between man's reason and his self-love, his opinions and passions will have a reciprocal influence upon each other." He even anticipated Marx in finding disproportions in the possession of

[50] *Christian Realism and Political Problems,* p. 51.
[51] *The Children of Light,* p. 72. [52] *Ibid.,* p. xiii.

property to be the primary cause of political and social friction: "The most common and durable source of faction," he declared, "has been the various and unequal distribution of property." He regarded this inequality as the inevitable consequence of unequal abilities among citizens. One of Madison's most persuasive arguments for a federal union was his belief that a community of wide expanse would so diffuse interests and passions as to prevent the turbulent form of political strife, to which he regarded small communities subject. The development of parties in America has partly refuted the belief that interests could not be nationally organized. Yet the interests which are organized in the two great parties of America are so diverse as to prevent the parties from being unambiguous ideological instruments. Thus, history has partly justified his conviction.

EQUILIBRATED POWER

In any event the political philosophy which underlies our Constitution is characterized by a shrewd awareness of the potential conflicts of power and passion in every community. It knows nothing of a simple harmony in society, analogous to the alleged reciprocity of the free market.

Our political experience has enlarged upon this wisdom without always being in conscious relation to its explicit early formulation. The American labor movement was almost completely bereft of ideological weapons, which the rebellious industrial masses of Europe carried. In its inception it disavowed not only Marxist revolutionary formulas but every kind of political program. It was a pragmatic movement, born of the necessity of setting organized power against organized power in a technical society. Gradually it became conscious of the fact that economic power does try to bend government to its own ends. It has, therefore, decided to challenge a combination of political and economic power with a like combination of its own. These developments have been very recent; but they have also been very rapid.

Naturally, the "semi-official" creed of a bourgeois community, as distinguished from the philosophy which informs our Constitution, was arrayed against this development. The right of collective bargaining was declared to be a violation of the rights of employers to hire or fire whom they would. Supreme Court decisions, directed against the labor movement, were informed by the generally accepted individualistic creed.* But ultimately, in the words of "Mr. Dooley," the court decisions "followed the election returns." Long before the "New Deal" radically changed the climate of American political life the sovereign power of government had been used to enforce taxation laws which embodied social policy as well as revenue

* At the turn of the century a Supreme Court decision declared, "It is the constitutional right of the employer to dispense with the services of an employee because of his membership in a labor union." [Author's footnote.]

necessities; great concentrations of power in industry were broken up by law; necessary monopolies in utilities were brought under political regulation; social welfare, security, and health and other values which proved to be outside the operations of the free market were secured by political policy. More recently, housing and social security have become matters of public and political policy. All this was accomplished on a purely pragmatic basis, without the ideological baggage which European labor carried.

The development of American democracy toward a welfare state has proceeded so rapidly partly because the ideological struggle has not unnecessarily sharpened. It has proceeded so rapidly in fact that the question must be raised in America, as well as in the more collectivist states of Europe, whether the scope of bureaucratic decisions may not become too wide and the room for the automatic balances of unregulated choices too narrow.[53]

The thesis of classical economics was held by the middle classes. The Marxist theory was the weapon of the industrial classes. They both make faulty analysis of the human situation. But the classical theory provides for a multiplicity of powers and the Marxist theory leads to a monopoly of power. All the errors of the first theory are partially relieved by its one virtue; and all the truth in the second theory does not redeem it from this one serious error.[54]

Modern conservativism holds that justice is the inevitable fruit of a free play of economic forces, but fails to recognize that, since these forces are never equally balanced, the disproportions of power actually result in grave injustice. The healthiest Western nations have preserved their economic and political health by following neither the conservative nor the Marxist dogma, but by adopting an empirical wisdom which separates what is true from what is false in each. Thus a political creed which fears the power of the state too much and trusts the automatic balances of the market too uncritically has been balanced by a creed that brings political power to bear upon economic life, though, in its most consistent form, this creed has been too little aware of the peril in a monopoly of political and economic power in the hands of the omnicompetent state.[55]

We have, in short, achieved such justice as we possess in the only way justice can be achieved in a technical society: we have equilibrated power. We have attained a certain equilibrium in economic society itself by setting organized power against organized power. When that did not suffice we used more broadly based political power to redress disproportions and disbalances in the economic society. *A democratic society preserves a modicum of justice by various strategies of distribution and balancing both economic and political power.*[56]

[53] *The Irony of American History,* pp. 96–100.
[54] *Christian Realism and Political Problems,* pp. 99, 100.
[55] *Ibid,* p. 50. [56] *The Irony of American History,* p. 104.

The triumph of the wisdom of common sense over these two types of wisdom is, therefore, primarily the wisdom of democracy itself, which prevents every strategy from being carried through to its logical conclusion. There is an element of truth in each position which becomes falsehood, precisely when it is carried through too consistently. The element of truth in each creed is required to do full justice to man's real situation. For man transcends the social and historical process sufficiently to make it possible and necessary deliberately to contrive common ends of life, particularly the end of justice. He cannot count on inadvertence and the coincidence of private desires alone to achieve common ends. On the other hand, man is too immersed in the welter of interest and passion in history and his survey over the total process is too short-range and limited to justify the endowment of any group or institution of "planners" with complete power. The "purity" of their idealism and the pretensions of their science must always be suspect. Man simply does not have a "pure" reason in human affairs; and if such reason as he has is given complete power to attain its ends, the taint will become the more noxious.

The controversy between those who would "plan" justice and order and those who trust in freedom to establish both is, therefore, an irresolvable one. Every healthy society will live in the tension of that controversy until the end of history; and will prove its health by preventing either side from gaining ultimate victory.[57]

[57] *Ibid,* pp. 107, 108.

Topic 7

MAJORITY RULE AND MINORITY RIGHTS

In Defense of Majority Rule

HENRY STEELE COMMAGER *

It was in America that the doctrine of majority rule was first successfully asserted and effectuated; it was in America that the principle of limited government was first institutionalized and that machinery for maintaining it was first fashioned.

These statements may require some elaboration. What we have here are two fundamental—perhaps the two most fundamental—principles of American politics: the principle that men make government, and the principle that there are limits to the authority of government. The philosophical origins of the first principle may be found in the natural-rights philosophy of the seventeenth century—in the notion that all rights inhered originally in men and that men, living in a state of nature, came together for mutual self-protection and set up government, and that the governments thus instituted derive all their just powers from the consent of the governed. . . .

The second great basic principle—that governments are limited, that there are things no government may do, rights no government may impair, powers no government may exercise—traces its philosophical origins deep into the past but again derives authority from American experience with Parliamentary and royal pretensions. It held, simply enough, that as government was instituted to secure certain rights, its jurisdiction was strictly limited to the fields assigned to it, and that if it over-stepped the bounds of its jurisdiction its acts were not law. In the great words of Samuel Adams, addressed to Shelburne and Rockingham and Camden, "in all free states the constitution is fixed; it is from thence that the legislative derives its authority; therefore it cannot change the constitution without destroying its own foundations." . . .

[The] generation [of the American Revolution], more conscious of the dangers than of the potentialities of government, more concerned with pro-

* Professor of History at Amherst College. Author of *The American Mind*. Co-author of *The Growth of the American Republic, The Heritage of America* and other works. Contributor to many journals and periodicals. The selection is from Henry Steele Commager, *Majority Rule and Minority Rights* (New York, Oxford University Press, 1943), Chs. I and III. By permission of author and publisher.

tection against governmental tyranny than with the promotion of majority welfare, devised cunning mechanisms for putting limitations upon government. When we contemplate the ingenuity of the Fathers in setting up their system of checks and balances we are deeply impressed, almost dismayed. That the limits of governmental authority might not be misunderstood, that authority was described—for the first time—in written constitutions, and to these constitutions were added bills of rights. But this was merely elementary. There were, in addition, the checks and balances of the federal system, of the tripartite division of powers, of the bicameral legislatures, of frequent elections, and of impeachment. And atop all this there developed—I would not say there was established—the practice of judicial review.

But in their laudable zeal to give reality to John Dickinson's description of a free people—"Not those over whom government is reasonably and equitably exercised, but those who live under a government so constitutionally checked and controlled, that proper provision is made against its being otherwise exercised"—the framers of our constitutions confused, it would seem, jurisdiction with power, and the confusion has persisted down to our own day. They failed properly to distinguish between the authority government should have, and the manner in which government might exercise that authority which it did have. They set up limits on the jurisdiction of government, enumerating things no government could do; and this was eminently proper and in harmony with the philosophy of the Revolutionary era. But they went farther. So fearful were they of governmental tyranny that even where they granted to government certain necessary powers they put obstacles in the way of the effective exercise of those powers. They set up not only boundaries to government but impediments in government. Thus they not only made it difficult for government to invade fields denied to it, but they made it difficult for government to operate at all. They created a system where deadlock would be the normal character of the American government—a situation from which political parties rescued us.

So here we have two institutions which are—or would appear to be—fundamentally contradictory. We have first the institutionalization of the principle that men can alter, abolish, and institute governments, can, in short, make government conform to their will. But over against this we have the institutionalization of the principle that governments are limited—that there are things not even a majority may require government to do because they are outside the jurisdiction of any government. If the majority may use government to do its will, is that not an attack upon the inalienable rights of men over against government? if there are limits upon what governments may do, is that not a challenge to or even a denial of the principle of majority rule? Here is a paradox not yet resolved in our political philosophy or our constitutional system.

This paradox is presented in most familiar form in Jefferson's First Inaugural Address: "All, too, will bear in mind this sacred principle, that though the will of the majority is in all cases to prevail, that will to be rightful must be reasonable; that the minority possess their equal rights which equal law must protect, and to violate would be oppression." And throughout our history runs this theme of majority will and minority rights. Jefferson, as we shall see, emphasized majority will, and so did Jefferson's successors, Jackson and Lincoln—Jackson, who brushed aside judicial interposition, Lincoln, who reminded us that

> A majority . . . is the only true sovereign of a free people. Whoever rejects it does, of necessity, fly into anarchy or to despotism. Unanimity is impossible; the rule of a minority, as a permanent arrangement, is wholly inadmissible; so that, rejecting the majority principle, anarchy or despotism in some form is all that is left.

But the emphasis since the Civil War has been increasingly on minority rights—an emphasis so marked, between Reconstruction and the New Deal, that it is no great exaggeration to say that tenderness for the minority became the distinguishing characteristic of the American constitutional system.

Underlying this distinction are, of course, the assumptions that majority will and minority rights are antithetical, that majority rule constantly threatens minority rights, and that the principal function of our constitutional system is to protect minority rights against infringement.

So plausible are these assumptions that there has developed, in course of time, the theory of the "tyranny of the majority"—a theory which derived much support abroad as well as here from the misleading observations of Tocqueville. Tocqueville, who leaned heavily for material and authority on that pillar of conservatism, Joseph Story, confessed that "the very essence of democratic government consists in the absolute sovereignty of the majority," and concluded from this that the prospects for American democracy were bleak indeed. His analysis of the consequences that flow from the tyranny of the majority has given comfort, ever since, to those who fear democracy. So persuasive is this theory of the tyranny of the majority that many Americans have come to believe that our constitutional system is not, in fact, based upon the principle of majority rule. And they have found support and consolation in the curious notion that ours is a "republican" form of government, and that a republic is the very opposite of a democracy.

The fear of the tyranny of the majority has haunted many of the most distinguished and respectable American statesmen and jurists since the days of the founding of the Republic; it persists today, after a century and a half of experience. It was first formulated, in elaborate and coherent fashion, by John Adams in his famous *Defense of the Constitutions of*

Government of the United States of America (1786). The people, Adams urges, are not to be trusted, nor are their representatives, without an adequate system of checks and balances:

> If it is meant by the people . . . a representative assembly, . . . they are not the best keepers of the people's liberties or their own, if you give them all the power, legislative, executive and judicial. They would invade the liberties of the people, at least the majority of them would invade the liberties of the minority, sooner and oftener than any absolute monarch. . . .

[And in No. 51 of *The Federalist,* the warning was given that]

> It is of great importance in a republic not only to guard the society against the oppression of its rulers, but to guard one part of the society against the injustice of the other part. Different interests necessarily exist in different classes of citizens. If a majority be united by a common interest, the rights of the minority will be insecure. . . . Justice is the end of government. It is the end of civil society. . . . In a society under the forms of which the stronger faction can readily unite and oppress the weaker, anarchy may as truly be said to reign as in a state of nature where the weaker individual is not secured against the violence of the stronger. . . .

Confronted by these different interpretations of the American constitutional system, of democracy and of republicanism, we may turn with some confidence to Thomas Jefferson. On these questions he is, indubitably, our leading authority. He helped to create and to establish the new political systems in America, and he furnished them with a good part of their political philosophy. He never wrote a formal treatise on the subject (as did his old friend John Adams), but in his public papers and his private letters we can find the most comprehensive and consistent statement of the nature of American democracy that has come down to us from the generation of the founders.

And it must be observed, first, that Jefferson was by no means unaware of the dangers inherent in majority rule. . . . [To him] majority rule is neither anarchy nor absolutism, but government within self-imposed restraints. And we search in vain through the voluminous writings of Jefferson for any expression of distrust of the virtue or the wisdom of the people. What we do find, on the contrary, from the beginning to the end of Jefferson's career, is an unterrified and unflinching faith in majority rule.

"I am not among those who fear the people," he wrote to Kercheval in 1816; "they and not the rich, are our dependence for continued freedom." . . . Writing to Madison [he said], . . . "After all, it is my principle that the will of the majority should prevail." And to another Virginia friend, Colonel Carrington, went the same reassurance:

> I am persuaded myself that the good sense of the people will always be found to be the best army. They may be led astray for a moment, but will soon correct themselves. The people are the only censors of their governors; and even their errors will tend to keep these to the true principles of their institution.

That the people, if led astray, would "soon correct themselves" was a fixed conviction and one which, *mirabile dictu,* found confirmation in their tenacious support of his own administration. Thus to John Tyler in 1804:

> No experiment can be more interesting than that we are now trying, and which we trust will end in establishing the fact that man may be governed by reason and truth. . . . The firmness with which the people have withstood the late abuses of the press, the discernment that they have manifested between truth and falsehood, show that they may safely be trusted to hear everything true and false, and to form correct judgment between them. . . .

This was the consistent note—that the people may—and must—be trusted. "No government can continue good," he assured John Adams, "but under the control of the people"; and again, to that doughty opponent of judicial pretensions, Spencer Roane, "Independence can be trusted nowhere but with the people in the mass. They are inherently independent of all but the moral law." "I know of no safe depository of the ultimate powers of the society," he told William Jarvis, "but the people themselves; and if we think them not enlightened enough to exercise their control with a wholesome discretion, the remedy is not to take it from them, but to inform their discretion by education." And recalling Hume's argument that "all history and experience" confounded the notion that "the people are the origin of all just power," Jefferson burst out with uncharacteristic violence: "And where else will this degenerate son of science, this traitor to his fellow men, find the origin of just powers, if not in the majority of the society? Will it be in the minority? Or in an individual of that minority?" And we hear an echo of that question which the First Inaugural submits to the contemporary world: "Sometimes it is said that man can not be trusted with the government of himself. Can he, then, be trusted with the government of others? Or have we found angels in the forms of kings to govern him? Let history answer this question." For himself, Jefferson knew the answer. His devotion to the people was not that of the benevolent despot, the party boss, or the dictator, but of the good citizen, and his whole career is a monument to the sincerity of his confession to Du Pont de Nemours. "We both love the people," he said, "but you love them as infants, whom you are afraid to trust without nurses; and I as adults whom I freely leave to self-government."

To all of this many of Jefferson's contemporaries could have subscribed without reservation: he, assuredly, had no monopoly on faith in popular government. "We of the United States," as he explained simply, "are constitutionally and conscientiously democrats." But in one respect Jefferson went farther than most of his contemporaries, went so far, indeed, that his argument sounds bizarre and almost alien to our ears. That was his advocacy of what we may call the doctrine of the continuing majority. It was easy enough for most Americans to subscribe to the compact theory of government—the compact made, of course, by the original majority—

just as it is easy for us to subscribe, now, to the doctrine that we are, all of us, bound by the compact made at Philadelphia in 1787 and ratified by the majority of that time. And just as we have invested that Constitution with sacrosanctity, so—in England, in France, in America of the eighteenth century—there was a tendency to regard the original compact, the product of the Golden Age of the past, with reverence and to invest it with a peculiar sanctity. Such an attitude was foreign to Jefferson. His conviction, however, that each new majority must write its own fundamental law has sometimes been regarded as merely an amusing exaggeration, a whimsey to be indulged along with the whimsey that a little rebellion, now and then, is an excellent thing. But there can be no doubt of Jefferson's sincerity in the matter, nor of his persuasion that the issue was one of fundamental importance.

This problem is more fundamental, and more complex, than might appear at first glance—this problem of the original *versus* the continuing majority. All of us seem to agree that we are bound by the original majority—by the majority of 1787, or that which decreed our state constitutions. But what if the will of the present majority conflicts with that of the original majority? Is majority will valid only for some past generation? The easy answer is that the present majority can, if it chooses, change the original compact by constitutional amendment or by substituting an entirely new constitution. But it takes more than a majority to amend a constitution or to write a new one, and under our present system a determined minority can, if it will, effectively veto any change in the federal document and in most state documents. Not only this, but the courts have pretty consistently held that the current majority may not even interpret the original constitution to accommodate it to felt needs. . . .

Jefferson, as we know, entertained no reverence for the constitutional dogmas of the past. His attitude, set forth in the famous letter to Samuel Kercheval, of July 1816, is too familiar to justify quotation in full:

> Let us [not] weakly believe that one generation is not as capable as another of taking care of itself, and of ordering its own affairs. Let us . . . avail ourselves of our reason and experience, to correct the crude essays of our first and unexperienced, although wise, virtuous and well-meaning counsels. And lastly, let us provide in our Constitution for its revision at stated periods. What these periods should be, nature herself indicates. . . . Each generation is as independent of the one preceding, as that was of all which had gone before. It has, then, like them, a right to choose for itself the form of government it believes most promotive of its own happiness . . . and it is for the peace and good of mankind that a solemn opportunity of doing this every nineteen or twenty years should be provided by the Constitution. . . .

"The People," a distinguished contemporary statesman has said in a phrase already classic, "have no right to do wrong." It is at least suggestive that Eamon de Valera, who has fought pretty consistently for his people and who regards himself as a democrat, should have found it necessary to invoke the techniques of totalitarianism to prevent the people from "doing wrong." And it is a characteristic of almost every anti-democratic philosophy that it purports to serve the welfare of the people but refuses to trust the judgment of the people on questions affecting their welfare. . . .

Our constitutional system, as has already been observed, is one of checks and balances: these have already been noted. It is sometimes forgotten that our political system is one of checks and balances too. Anyone who has followed the slow and tortuous course of a major public issue—the poll tax, for example, or neutrality, through the arena of public opinion, into the party conventions and caucuses, into the halls of Congress and the rooms of appropriate committees, knows how much of delay, of balance, of compromise, is implicit in our political machinery. A good part of our politics, indeed, seems to be concerned with reconciling majority and minority will, class hostilities, sectional differences, the divergent interests of producer and consumer, of agriculture and labor, of creditor and debtor, of city and country, of tax-payer and tax-beneficiary, of the military and the civilian. In small issues as in great, the result is generally a compromise. Democracy, in short, whether from instinct or from necessity, furnishes its own checks and balances—quite aside from such as may be provided in written constitutions.

Indeed it might plausibly be argued that it is one of the major advantages of democracy over other forms of government that it alone can indulge in the luxury of tolerating minority and dissenting groups because it alone has developed the technique for dealing with them. It is sometimes charged as a criticism of democracy that it cannot act speedily and effectively in an emergency—as can totalitarian or despotic governments. The charge is not sound—as witness the efficiency of our own democracy in the spring of 1933 or the winter of 1941–2—but it is true that in a democracy it requires a real emergency to produce prompt and effective action.

But there is this to be said of the checks and balances of democratic politics—that they are natural, not artificial; that they are flexible rather than rigid; that they can yield to public opinion and to necessity. They do, sometimes, enable the majority to ride down the minority; they do, far more frequently, enable the minority to delay and defeat the majority. But the responsibility in all this is with the people themselves—where it belongs. Where they indulge their apathy, their carelessness, their blindness, they pay the price, and it is right that they should pay the price. As the fault is theirs, so, too, the remedy. Where issues appear sufficiently important the majority can have its way even against the recalcitrance of minorities who take refuge in the labyrinths of our party and our legislative systems. But against minorities entrenched in the judiciary there is no effective appeal except through the complicated and slow process of constitutional amendment. Here it is true today as it was in 1801 that the minority can "retire into the judiciary as a stronghold," and "from that battery" beat down the works of republicanism. . . .

This is the crucial objection to judicial nullification of majority will in any field: that "education in the abandonment of foolish legislation is itself a training in liberty." If our democracy is less educated in this respect than we might wish, if our legislatures are less alert to constitutional principles than might seem desirable, a heavy responsibility rests upon the courts. For these, by taking over to themselves the peculiar guardianship of the Constitution and of civil liberties, have discouraged the people's active and intelligent interest in these matters. Judges—and liberals—have ignored what Professor Chafee finely says, that "the victories of liberty of speech must be won in the mind before they are won in the courts." For in the long run only an educated and enlightened democracy can hope to endure. . . .

Our own experience, I believe, justifies Jefferson's faith that men need no masters—not even judges. It justifies us, too, in believing that majority will does not imperil minority rights, either in theory or in operation. It gives us firm basis for a belief that the people themselves can be trusted to realize that the majority has a vital interest in the preservation of an alert and critical minority and that, conversely, the minority can have no rights fundamentally inimical to the commonwealth. It justifies us in the belief that only in a democracy where there is free play of ideas, where issues are freely fought out in the public forum,—where, in short, the safety valves of public discussion and experimentation and reconsideration are always open—can there be assurance that both majority and minority rights will be served. It is the glory of democracy that it—and it alone—can tolerate dissent. It is the strength of democracy that dissent, where tolerated, is helpful rather than harmful.

The Tyranny of the Majority

ALEXIS DE TOCQUEVILLE *

I hold it to be an impious and an execrable maxim that, politically speaking, a people has a right to do whatsoever it pleases, and yet I have asserted that all authority originates in the will of the majority. Am I, then, in contradiction with myself? . . .

* Noted French statesman and critic. Author of *The Old Government and the Revolution* and other works on political and social subjects. The selection is from Alexis de Tocqueville, *Democracy in America* (Henry Reeve translation, 1835), Vol. I, Chs. XIII–XV.

A majority taken collectively may be regarded as a being whose opinions, and most frequently whose interests, are opposed to those of another being, which is styled a minority. If it be admitted that a man, possessing absolute power, may misuse that power by wronging his adversaries, why should a majority not be liable to the same reproach? Men are not apt to change their characters by agglomeration; nor does their patience in the presence of obstacles increase with the consciousness of their strength. And for these reasons I can never willingly invest any number of my fellow creatures with that unlimited authority which I should refuse to any one of them. . . .

I am of opinion that some one social power must always be made to predominate over the others; but I think that liberty is endangered when this power is checked by no obstacles which may retard its course, and force it to moderate its own vehemence.

Unlimited power is in itself a bad and dangerous thing; human beings are not competent to exercise it with discretion, and God alone can be omnipotent, because his wisdom and his justice are always equal to his power. But no power upon earth is so worthy of honor for itself, or of reverential obedience to the rights which it represents, that I would consent to admit its uncontrolled and all-predominant authority. When I see that the right and the means of absolute command are conferred on a people or upon a king, upon an aristocracy or a democracy, a monarchy or a republic, I recognize the germ of tyranny, and I journey onward to a land of more hopeful institutions.

In my opinion the main evil of the present democratic institutions of the United States does not arise, as is often asserted in Europe, from their weakness, but from their overpowering strength; and I am not so much alarmed at the excessive liberty which reigns in that country as at the very inadequate securities which exist against tyranny.

When an individual or a party is wronged in the United States, to whom can he apply for redress? If to public opinion, public opinion constitutes the majority; if to legislature, it represents the majority, and implicitly obeys its injunctions; if to the executive power, it is appointed by the majority, and remains a passive tool in its hands; the public troops consist of the majority under arms; the jury is the majority invested with the right of hearing judicial cases; and in certain States even the judges are elected by the majority. However iniquitous or absurd the evil of which you complain may be, you must submit to it as well as you can. . . .

I do not say that tyrannical abuses frequently occur in America at the present day, but I maintain that no sure barrier is established against them, and that the causes which mitigate the government are to be found in the circumstances and the manners of the country more than in its laws. . . .

In America, the majority raises very formidable barriers to the liberty of opinion: within these barriers an author may write whatever he pleases, but he will repent it if he ever step beyond them. Not that he is exposed to the terrors of an *auto-da-fé,* but he is tormented by the slights and persecutions of daily obloquy. His political career is closed forever, since he has offended the only authority which is able to promote his success. . . .

Monarchical institutions have thrown an odium upon despotism; let us beware lest democratic republics should restore oppression, and should render it less odious and less degrading in the eyes of the many, by making it still more onerous to the few.

The Logic of Democracy

THOMAS LANDON THORSON *

MAJORITY RULE AND MINORITY RIGHTS

The problem that most democratic theorists would regard as the most difficult and most important one arises because of the ever-present possibility under a democratic governmental structure that the right of the majority to rule will come into conflict with the right of individuals and minorities to assert and register in a formal way their political preferences. If, as most democrats in the Western political tradition would admit, democracy necessarily involves the application and utilization of both the principle of majority rule and the principle of minority rights, the potential conflicts can be placed in two broad categories. The first of these is majority action that deprives a minority of its legitimate role in the democratic decision-making process (e.g., by denying free expression or suffrage). The second is action on the part of a minority that deprives a majority of the legitimate right to rule (e.g., the abuse of the power of judicial review by the United States Supreme Court). This problem in its manifold aspects is one which will be quite familiar to anyone who has had contact with democratic government.

The argument I wish to make is that the role of the political philosopher in dealing with this problem has been vastly overestimated. I do not think that it is legitimately a philosophical problem or even, in one sense of the term, legitimately a theoretical problem. By this I mean that the political philosopher *qua* political philosopher cannot solve it. He *can,* however—and this is quite important—show why it cannot be solved by philosophical means and thus clarify the *nature* of the solution.

* Political scientist at the University of Wisconsin. Editor of *Plato: Totalitarian or Democrat.* The selection is from *The Logic of Democracy* (New York, Holt, Rinehart and Winston, Inc., 1962), pp. 151–162. By permission.

There is no single theoretical solution to the problem of majority rule and minority rights; rather, there are solutions of various kinds, the choice of which turns upon the gathering of relevant empirical evidence. The opinion is nonetheless widespread that this is a problem susceptible of theoretical solution. It has in fact been called by reputable authority "the greatest single theoretical controversy about the nature of democracy." [1] That this essentially empirical question should be seen as a theoretical question is, I think, the result of faulty philosophizing.

In one sense, there is an almost infinite variety of writers about democracy, each in one respect or another looking at democracy in a slightly different perspective. However, as was suggested before, so far as the majority rule–minority rights question is concerned, there are two major categories. On the one hand, there are those who see democracy essentially as an instrument for limiting the powers of governmental officials. For them the widest possible freedom for individuals consistent with stable government is the highest value. What they fear most of all is tyranny, and often the sort of tyranny most feared is the tyranny of the majority.[2] To this camp belong the most notable figures in early American democratic thought: surely James Madison, in some measure Thomas Jefferson, and certainly John C. Calhoun. Typically, the philosophical point of departure for democrats of this school is some sort of conception of the natural rights of men. Let us then lump them together under the general rubric "natural rights democrats."

The contrary view, which is generally speaking the more modern one, sees democracy as the method of popular government. The stress here is laid upon popular sovereignty, political equality, and therefore upon majority rule. The test of whether a governmental act is democratic or not is not so much a matter of how it affects individuals as it is of whether the policy has been decided upon by a majority of the citizenry. There is less emphasis upon limiting governmental activity and more emphasis upon allowing the majority to do what it wants. It seems fair to say that this view of democracy is held by jurists such as Felix Frankfurter and Learned Hand and by political scientists such as Austin Ranney and Willmoore Kendall. Such a position can be and has been worked out in a variety of ways. Generally implicit and often explicit in the view, however, is a denial of the possibility of knowing natural law and natural rights and the consequent conclusion that the will of the majority is the only ultimate test in politics. Frankfurter, for example, has had occasion to refer to the Supreme Court as "non-democratic" and "inherently oligarchic," [3] thus implying that for him majority rule is the

[1] Austin Ranney and Willmoore Kendall, *Democracy and the American Party System* (New York, Harcourt, Brace & World, Inc., 1956), p. 29.

[2] Cf. Robert A. Dahl, *A Preface to Democratic Theory*. Copyright 1956 by the University of Chicago. (Chicago, University of Chicago Press), pp. 4–33.

[3] *AFL v. American Sash and Door Co.,* 335 U.S. 538 (1949), 555.

prime element in democracy. . . . These are what we may fairly call "majority rule democrats."

We need to be clear that the difference between "natural rights democrats" and "majority rule democrats," to which I have attempted to call attention, is less a matter of wholly contradictory notions of democracy than a matter of different theoretical casts of mind. All democrats will recognize the need for both majority rule and the protection of minority rights. The difference is a matter of emphasis. As Robert A. Dahl has stated it,[4]

> . . . so far as I am aware, no one has ever advocated, and no one except its enemies has ever defined democracy to mean, that a majority would or should do anything it felt an impulse to do. Every advocate of democracy of whom I am aware, and every friendly definition of it, includes the idea of restraints on majorities. But one central issue is whether these restraints are, or should be, (1) primarily internalized restraints in the individual behavior system, such as the conscience and other products of social indoctrination, (2) primarily social checks and balances of several kinds, or (3) primarily prescribed constitutional checks. Among political systems to which the term "democracy" is commonly applied in the Western world, one important difference is between those which rely primarily on the first two checks, and those like the United States which also employ constitutional checks.

Because of the existence of constitutional checks in the United States, controversy over the proper roles of majority rule and minority rights has flourished among Americans. The questions to confront in this connection are two: (A) Should there be constitutional checks at all? (B) Given that constitutional checks exist, how should they be applied?

The affirmative answer to question A classically takes the following form:

1. All men are endowed with certain natural rights. Among these are life, liberty, property, and the pursuit of happiness.
2. The severe deprivation of these natural rights is tyranny.
3. The true or proper purpose of government is the protection of these rights or, to say the same thing another way, the prevention of tyranny.
4. Minorities can be prevented from depriving other members of the society of their natural rights by the operation of the principle of majority rule.
5. Majorities can be prevented from depriving other members of the society of their natural rights by the operation of constitutional checks on their power.
6. Therefore, constitutional checks on the power of majorities should be employed.

There is no need to elaborate the roles of Locke, Madison, Jefferson, and Calhoun in promoting one or another aspect of this view. Considered historically, this argument represents the mainstream of American democratic thought.

[4] Dahl, *op. cit.*, p. 36.

One can object to the argument in a number of ways. Professor Dahl, for example, is willing in terms of his analysis to grant the natural rights premise but seeks to demonstrate, quite successfully, that the requirement of constitutional checks does not follow on empirical grounds.[5] My quarrel is with the natural rights premise itself. The conception of democracy presented in this argument quite clearly makes natural rights the prime principle and majority rule a secondary one. For this reason its adherents were not content with social and cultural checks upon the power of majorities but demanded constitutional checks as well. Thus, Dahl's argument that constitutional checks do not *necessarily* follow from the premises, while completely accurate as far as it goes, in a certain sense misses a point of great significance. What, most fundamentally, is wrong with this argument is that it identifies the justification of democracy with the justification of natural rights.

The man who sees the protection of natural rights as the very definition of democracy does not need a conclusive demonstration of the necessity of constitutional checks on majorities. For him the likelihood that they will help is enough. But his definition is wrong, because it presumes the existence of a set of qualities or properties that attach to each man. The existence of these qualities or properties is supposedly proved by observation and inductive generalization, or by deductive demonstration from some grand principle—"These truths are self-evident," "All men are endowed with reason," "All men are created in the image of God." We have, I trust, said enough about these lines of argument.

Do not misunderstand my point. My argument is not against constitutional checks on majorities, nor does it suggest that there are no human rights which should be protected. Rather, my contention is that the conception of democracy which holds natural rights to be the prime principle is faulty because it seeks to justify by proof when no proof is possible. When the argument for constitutional checks is contingent upon such proof as it is in the classical argument, it is also faulty.

The contrary theoretical solution to the problem of constitutional checks posed by question A is equally invalid. This position demands, in the words of Professors Ranney and Kendall, that no "*formal* institutional limitations" be placed on the power of popular majorities. This conclusion is said to follow from the definition of democracy in the following way: [6]

[5] *Ibid.*, pp. 11–15.

[6] "*Why 'Absolute' Majority Rule?* For the reasons given in the foregoing pages, any attempt to place *formal* institutional limitations upon the 'absolute' power of popular majorities logically results in the establishment of *minority* rule. And from the standpoint of logic, 'absolute' majority rule must be chosen over minority rule as a principle of ideally democratic government, not because there is any magical or omniscience in popular majorities, but because majority rule is more nearly in accord than minority rule with the other principles of democracy that we have previously discussed." Ranney and Kendall, *op. cit.*, pp. 29–37. (Italics in original.)

1. Political equality and popular sovereignty are principles of democracy.
2. Majority rule alone is compatible with these principles. (Minority rule is incompatible with political equality and popular sovereignty because it violates them by definition, and unanimity is impossible.)
3. Any attempt at formal institutional limitation (e.g., a Supreme Court with the power of judicial review, the requirements for extraordinary majorities) necessarily involves minority rule.
4. Ergo, no formal institutional limitations on the power of majorities are legitimate from a democratic point of view.

This argument seeks by an exercise of "strict logic," as Ranney and Kendall say several times, to solve the problem of constitutional checks by deduction from the basic democratic premises. Again, it may be criticized from several angles. First of all, the conclusion quite simply does not follow from the premises. The conclusion—*no* formal institutional limitations on the power of popular majorities—is too broad. It is quite reasonable to say that, with respect to a wide range of social policy choices, only majority rule is the legitimate democratic principle because of its compatibility with political equality and popular sovereignty. On the other hand, it is hardly reasonable to argue that with respect to majority actions which abrogate political equality and popular sovereignty (e.g., denial of suffrage, free expression, or the opportunity to run for public office) majority rule alone is legitimate because of its compatibility with political equality and popular sovereignty. But this is what the conclusion "*no* constitutional checks" must mean, if it means anything at all. Thus, as an exercise in "strict logic" the argument is a failure.[7]

Because this argument is in large part a modern one, advanced in an era dominated by an empiricist-positivist *Weltanschauung,* questions of philosophical justification are not often explicitly raised in connection with it. Ranney and Kendall, for example, do not explicitly attempt to justify political equality or popular sovereignty; rather, these principles are given. "No one thinks of democracy" without thinking of these two principles.[8] I suspect quite strongly, however, that the implicit justification of the argument is at the core of its inadequacy.

While this argument usually goes by the name "absolute majority rule," it might more precisely be described as absolute "antiminority" rule. The case *for* majority rule is developed wholly from the case *against* minority rule. Here are Ranney and Kendall on this point: [9]

> A policy or procedure, obviously, does not gain in rightness by picking up enough support to justify the claim that it represents the wishes of a majority, or lose in rightness by losing support. But that is not the point at issue, since

[7] See Thomas Landon Thorson, "Epilogue on Absolute Majority Rule," *The Journal of Politics,* vol. XXIII (August, 1961), pp. 557–565.

[8] Ranney and Kendall, *op. cit.,* p. 29. [9] *Ibid.,* p. 32.

> what the majoritarian asserts is not the superior intelligence or wisdom or even morality of popular majorities, but the wrongness, from the democratic point of view, of a state of affairs where the few are in a position to have their way over the wishes of the many.

But what *is* wrong with minority rule? The immediate answer would surely be that "it violates political equality and popular sovereignty." But why these principles? My guess is that the answer we would get to this question, and therefore the real answer to the first question, would be a truncated version of the argument from fallibilism. The reasoning would probably be something like this:

1. No man (or group of men) can demonstrate the rightness of his preferences.
2. Therefore, all men must be treated as equal and allowed to rule.
3. Therefore, no minority should be allowed to rule.
4. If not minority rule, then majority rule.

But this argument *is* truncated; it is oversimplified. Fallibilism prescribes no such simple numerical rule but a general directive on leaving the way open for a change in social goals. The so-called "absolute majority rule" argument eliminates the majority rule–minority rights problem by deductive fiat; and as we have seen, the deduction is faulty.

The conclusion to be drawn from all this is that the controversy over constitutional checks is not to be resolved in either direction by abstract reasoning. The decision to have constitutional checks or not to have them can only turn on an estimate of the empirical situation. The categorical of fallibilism demands that the way be kept open for a change in goals. The categorical, as we have seen, implies the maximization of political equality, popular sovereignty, minority political rights, and majority rule. When faced with the problem of actually designing real-world institutions, this ideal procedure is (or should be) a prime value; but the preservation and stability of the society is also a value. The choice between giving majorities free rein or constitutionally checking them can be sensibly made only by assessing the relative costs of the alternatives. Who in this particular society is more likely to abuse power, a majority or a minority? This is the question, and clearly it is an empirical question, not a theoretical or philosophical one.

Treating the majority rule–minority rights problem as essentially resolved by either a natural rights argument or an "absolute majority rule" argument can lead to very important practical consequences. A good deal of American constitutional history can be understood in these terms. It would be beyond the scope of this essay to discuss this history in any detail. Let me instead discuss a hypothetical society, which I suspect will nonetheless sound a bit familiar. This discussion will deal with question B: given that constitutional checks exist, how should they be applied?

Imagine a society with a democratic governmental structure. This democratic structure is provided for in a written constitution that is to be the supreme law of society. To the legislature and the executive is given a general grant of power to promote the general welfare. The legislature and the executive are specifically prohibited from abridging free expression, suffrage, the right to run for public office, and the right peacably to assemble. The legislature and the executive are also prohibited from expropriating private property without due process of law. A supreme judicial body with the power of judicial review is also provided for. The constitution is very difficult to amend, so that the exercise of the power of judicial review is quite effective.

This is clearly a constitutional-check situation. The supreme judicial body, a minority, is given the power to check the action of majorities. The delegation of this power is anything but clear. When does a legislative act promote the general welfare, and when is it deleterious to the general welfare? What are the limits on free expression? What is a peaceful assembly? What is due process of law? All these questions will require answers from the members of the supreme judicial body, and it is clear that a mere reading of the constitution, no matter how assiduous, cannot provide them. The judges will therefore have to define their role in this democratic process which the constitution attempts to create. How the judges do this will surely in part turn on their conceptions of democracy. Undoubtedly the formation of attitudes on these questions will be the result of a wide variety of environmental factors, including presumably socio-economic class origins, experience prior to appointment, and education. A particular judge's conception of democracy will be here created and there reinforced by these factors, but he is likely to have a conception of democracy at the level of articulation.

Suppose a majority of judges share a natural rights conception of democracy and see democratic government basically as limited government. How are these judges likely to react to cases that involve a conflict between the wishes of the majority as reflected by the legislature and the freedom to act of individuals affected by the statute in question? Surely it would not be surprising to find them using their power of judicial review aggressively—striking down what they consider to be majority infringement on the freedom of individuals. For these judges "the general welfare" would likely be defined in terms of the freedom to act of individuals. For them "due process of law" might come to mean not only a set of regular procedures but also a substantive directive with regard to the wisdom of certain policies. That this conception of democracy might lead to a frustration of majority desires, to a blocking of the possibility of change with respect to social goals, appears rather clear. That statutes limiting child labor, fixing maximum hours and minimum wages, or coercing payment for old-age pensions might be struck down as infringing freedom of contract or as deleterious to the general welfare would not be surprising.

Suppose, on the other hand, that the court majority held a majority rule conception of democracy. Would not this majority be likely to regard its whole position as somewhat tenuous? Might not judges holding this view see the judicial body of which they were a part as "non-democratic" and "inherently oligarchic," to use words written by Mr. Justice Frankfurter in a not dissimilar context. Majority rule democrats on the court might adopt, as the rule of behavior with respect to the use of the power of judicial review, not the aggressiveness of the natural rights democrats but a doctrine of self-restraint toward the preferences of majorities.

If the legislature were to adopt a statute limiting the right to speak and write of a group of social, political, or economic heretics, a judge who held majority rule to be the very definition of democracy might be quite reluctant to employ judicial review against it. If free expression is limited by a frightened and myopic majority, the possibility of changing social goals is blocked to that extent.

My line of argument, I hope, is now clear. Conceptions of democracy, justifications of democracy that elevate either natural rights or the principle of majority rule to a position of primacy, can lead to practical consequences of great importance. We have tried to show that such justifications are faulty, and we call instead for a conception of democracy which makes no institutional principle supreme but which holds that the principles are mutually interdependent and essentially equal. They are the spelling out of the general categorical recommendation "Be rational" when setting up a political system. According to this view, it is quite consistent for judges empowered with judicial review to be self-restrained in the face of majority preferences on general social policy *and* to be aggressive in the use of their power when free expression, suffrage, or the right to run for public office is in question. Thus, thinking through the logic of democracy can be of great importance to actors in the democratic process.

There is no suggestion here that all the problems involved in implementing democracy will be magically solved if "the proper" justification of democracy is adopted. The categorical of rationality is no Euclidean theorem from which the answers to all problems follow by demonstration. Empirical concerns, or matters of fact, are crucial to every political problem; but matters of choice are equally crucial. One of the functions of the political scientist, the economist, the sociologist, the psychologist, and the anthropologist is to find and present the facts relevant to these problems.

The political philosopher, on the contrary, is not a superscientist. The definition of his task does not include the possession of a superior insight into the way the world *is*. He tries instead to think through matters of choice, often of ultimate choice, for citizens who have not the time or resources to do it for themselves. Unless one is willing to adopt the metaphysic that human beings are Pavlovian dogs whose behavior is *entirely* to be understood as a set of responses to irrational stimuli, this is a task of greatest importance, and it should not be rejected because political philosophers have at times been far too pretentious or because they have made mistakes. Political philosophy can be good or bad, helpful or useless. If it is wrong, it should be criticized, but it should be criticized in its own terms. It is recommendation, not fact. To criticize political philosophy because it is not fact is no criticism at all. Like all political philosophers, Plato made many mistakes, but he made no mistake when he cast the first political philosophy in the form of a dialogue. Mistakes call for criticism, and if he understands his role, the political philosopher welcomes them.

Section III

The Constitution: "Road or Gate"?

MARBURY *v.* MADISON established the power of the Supreme Court to declare Acts of Congress unconstitutional and unenforceable. The Constitution explicitly provided for the exercise of similar power by the Court with respect to state legislation. Thus the limits of both federal and state power have been determined, in the final analysis, by the Supreme Court except in those rare instances where the Constitution has been changed by amendment. That the Court has enjoyed considerable discretion in defining those limits is illustrated by the cases in this section.

McCulloch *v.* Maryland, in which Chief Justice Marshall gave elastic scope to Congressional power generally under the Constitution, is not merely of historic interest but proved of great importance in helping to sustain much of the New Deal legislation and continues as the foundation of broad federal authority.

On the other hand, the Schechter case, in which the Supreme Court unanimously invalidated the National Industrial Recovery Act, reflects a restricted view of delegated congressional power. This was one of several blows to New Deal legislation which led President Roosevelt in 1937 to seek to reorganize the Supreme Court. Wickard *v.* Filburn, decided in the decade of the 40's, is representative of sweeping extensions of federal power over the economy upheld by the Court in its greatly expanded view of Congressional prerogative under the Constitution.

Similarly, with respect to the power of the state to legislate in the interests of the health, safety, and welfare of its inhabitants (the so-called police power), the Court for many decades, beginning in the late 1800's, while reflecting a dominant *laissez faire* philosophy, often invoked general clauses of the Constitution, such as the due process and contract clauses, to curb social legislation. However, during President Roosevelt's second term, in the midst of depression, the Court began to give expanded scope to the police power of the states; and this liberal attitude toward social legislation has characterized the decisions of the Supreme Court ever since. The due process (like the equal protection) clause has now served chiefly as a restraint upon state action in denigration of civil liberties and civil rights.

[Further discussion of the role of the Court will be found in the section titled "Judicial Review."]

Topic 8

FOUNDATION OF JUDICIAL REVIEW

The Judicial Power

MARBURY *V.* MADISON

1 Cranch 137 (1803)

[On March 2, 1801, two days before the close of his term, President John Adams appointed William Marbury, among others, as a justice of the peace in the District of Columbia. Through some inadvertence the commission was left on the desk of the Secretary of State when President Adams' term expired at midnight, March 3rd. Upon Thomas Jefferson's accession to the presidency, he directed his Secretary of State, James Madison, to refuse delivery of the commission. Marbury applied to the Supreme Court, sitting as a court of original jurisdiction, for a writ of mandamus to compel delivery of the commission. This specific writ was sought under section 13 of the Judiciary Act of 1789.]

The following opinion of the court was delivered by the CHIEF JUSTICE [Marshall]. . . .

The first object of inquiry is, 1st. Has the applicant a right to the commission he demands? . . . Mr. Marbury, then, since his commission was signed by the President and sealed by the Secretary of State, was appointed; and as the law creating the office gave the officer a right to hold for five years, independent of the executive, the appointment was not revocable, but vested in the officer legal rights, which are protected by the laws of his country. To withhold his commission, therefore, is an act deemed by the court not warranted by law, but violative of a vested legal right.

This brings us to the second inquiry, which is, 2d. If he has a right, and that right has been violated, do the laws of his country afford him a remedy? . . .

It is then the opinion of the court,

1st. That by signing the commission of Mr. Marbury, the President of the United States appointed him a justice of peace for the county of Washington, in the District of Columbia; and that the seal of the United States, affixed thereto by the Secretary of State, is conclusive testimony of the verity of the signature, and of the completion of the appointment; and that the appointment conferred on him a legal right to the office for the space of five years.

2dly. That, having this legal title to the office, he has a consequent right to the commission; a refusal to deliver which is a plain violation of that right, for which the laws of his country afford him a remedy.

It remains to be inquired whether, 3dly. He is entitled to the remedy for which he applies. This depends on,

1st. The nature of the writ applied for; and, 2dly. The power of this court.

[As to the 1st, in light of the facts, this was held to be] a plain case for a mandamus, either to deliver the commission, or a copy of it from the record; and it only remains to be inquired, whether it can issue from this court.

[The Court then decided that the portion of Section 13 of the Judiciary Act of 1789 which provided that "The Supreme Court . . . shall have power to issue . . . writs of mandamus in cases warranted by the principles and usages of law, to any persons holding office, under the authority of the United States," was in conflict with the constitution as an attempt to enlarge the original jurisdiction of the Supreme Court beyond that provided by Article III, Section 2 of the Constitution of the United States which reads in part as follows: "In all cases affecting ambassadors, other public ministers and consuls, and those in which a State shall be Party, the Supreme Court shall have *original jurisdiction*."]

[Chief Justice Marshall continued:] The question, whether an act, repugnant to the constitution, can become the law of the land, is a question deeply interesting to the United States; but, happily, not of an intricacy proportioned to its interest. It seems only necessary to recognize certain principles, supposed to have been long and well established, to decide it. That the people have an original right to establish, for their future government, such principles as, in their opinion shall most conduce to their own happiness, is the basis on which the whole American fabric has been erected. The exercise of this original right is a very great exertion; nor can it, nor ought it, to be frequently repeated. The principles, therefore, so established, are deemed fundamental; and as the authority from which they proceed is supreme, and can seldom act, they are designed to be permanent.

This original and supreme will organizes the government, and assigns to different departments their respective powers. It may either stop here, or establish certain limits not to be transcended by those departments. The government of the United States is of the latter description. The powers of the legislature are defined and limited; and that those limits may not be mistaken, or forgotten, the constitution is written. To what purpose are powers limited, and to what purpose is that limitation committed to writing, if these limits may, at any time, be passed by those intended to be restrained? The distinction between a government with limited and unlimited powers is abolished, if those limits do not confine the persons on whom they are imposed, and if acts prohibited and acts allowed, are of equal obligation. It is a proposition too plain to be contested, that the constitution controls any legislative act repugnant to it; or that the legislature may alter the constitution by an ordinary act.

Between these alternatives, there is no middle ground. The constitution is either a superior paramount law, unchangeable by ordinary means, or it is on a level with ordinary legislative acts, and, like other acts, is alterable when the legislature shall please to alter it. If the former part of the alternative be true, then a legislative act, contrary to the constitution, is not law; if the latter part be true, then written constitutions are absurd attempts, on the part of the people, to limit a power, in its own nature, illimitable.

Certainly, all those who have framed written constitutions contemplate them as forming the fundamental and paramount law of the nation, and consequently, the theory of every such government must be, that an act of the legislature, repugnant to the constitution, is void. This theory is essentially attached to a written constitution, and is, consequently, to be considered, by this court, as one of the fundamental principles of our society. It is not, therefore, to be lost sight of, in the further consideration of this subject.

If an act of the legislature, repugnant to the constitution, is void, does it, notwithstanding its invalidity, bind the courts, and oblige them to give it effect? Or, in other words, though it be not law, does it constitute a rule as operative as if it was a law? This would be to overthrow, in fact, what was established in theory; and would seem, at first view, an absurdity too gross to be insisted on. It shall, however, receive a more attentive consideration.

It is, emphatically, the province and duty of the judicial department, to say what the law is. Those who apply the rule to particular cases, must of necessity expound and interpret that rule. If two laws conflict with each other, the courts must decide on the operation of each. So, if a law be in opposition to the constitution; if both the law and the constitution apply to a particular case, so that the court must either decide that case, conformably to the law, disregarding the constitution; or conformably to the constitution, disregarding the law; the court must determine which of these conflicting rules governs the case; this is of the very essence of judicial duty. If then, the courts are to regard the constitution, and the constitution is superior to any ordinary act of the legislature, the constitution, and not such ordinary act, must govern the case to which they both apply.

Those, then, who controvert the principle, that the constitution is to be considered, in court, as a paramount law, are reduced to the necessity of maintaining that courts must close their eyes on the constitution, and see only the law. This doctrine would subvert the very foundation of all written constitutions. It would declare that an act which, according to the principles and theory of our government, is entirely void, is yet, in practice, completely obligatory. It would declare, that if the legislature shall do what is expressly forbidden, such act, notwithstanding the express prohibition, is in reality effectual. It would be giving to the legislature a practical and real omnipotence, with the same breath which professes to restrict their powers within narrow limits. It is prescribing limits, and declaring that those limits may be passed at pleasure. That it thus reduces to nothing, what we have deemed the greatest improvement on political institutions, a written constitution, would of itself, be sufficient, in America, where written constitutions have been viewed with so much reverence, for rejecting the construction.

But the peculiar expressions of the constitution of the United States furnish additional arguments in favor of its rejection. The judicial power of the United States is extended to all cases arising under the constitution. Could it be the intention of those who gave this power, to say, that in using it, the constitution should not be looked into? That a case arising under the constitution should be decided, without examining the instrument under which it arises? This is too extravagant to be maintained. In some cases, then, the constitution must be looked into by the judges. And if they can open it at all, what part of it are they forbidden to read or to obey?

There are many other parts of the constitution which serve to illustrate this subject. It is declared, that "no tax or duty shall be laid on articles exported from any state." Suppose, a duty on the export of cotton, of tobacco, or of flour; and a suit instituted to recover it. Ought judgment to be rendered in such a case? ought the judges to close their eyes on the constitution, and only see the law?

The constitution declares "that no bill of attainder or *ex post facto* law shall be passed." If, however, such a bill should be passed, and a person should be prosecuted under it; must the court condemn to death those victims whom the constitution endeavors to preserve?

"No person," says the constitution, "shall be convicted of treason, unless on the testimony of two witnesses to the same overt act, or on confession in open court." Here, the language of the constitution is addressed especially to the courts. It prescribes, directly for them, a rule of evidence not to be departed from. If the legislature should change that rule, and declare one witness, or a confession out of court, sufficient for conviction, must the constitutional principle yield to the legislative act?

From these, and many other selections which might be made, it is apparent, that the framers of the constitution contemplated that instrument as a rule for the government of courts, as well as of the legislature. Why otherwise does it direct the judges to take an oath to support it? This oath certainly applies in an especial manner, to their conduct in their official character. How immoral to impose it on them, if they were to be used as the instruments, and the knowing instruments, for violating what they swear to support!

The oath of office, too, imposed by the legislature, is completely demonstrative of the legislative opinion on this subject. It is in these words: "I do solemnly swear, that I will administer justice, without respect to persons, and do equal right to the poor and to the rich; and that I will faithfully and impartially discharge all the duties incumbent on me as ——, according to the best of my abilities and understanding, agreeably to the constitution and laws of the United States." Why does a judge swear to discharge his duties agreeably to the constitution of the United States, if that constitution forms no rule for his government? if it is closed upon him, and cannot be inspected by him? If such be the real state of things, this is worse than solemn mockery. To prescribe, or to take this oath, becomes equally a crime.

It is also not entirely unworthy of observation, that in declaring what shall be the supreme law of the land, the constitution itself is first mentioned; and not the laws of the United States, generally, but those only which shall be made in pursuance of the constitution, have that rank.

Thus, the particular phraseology of the constitution of the United States confirms and strengthens the principle, supposed to be essential to all written constitutions, that a law repugnant to the constitution is void; and that courts, as well as other departments, are bound by that instrument.

The rule must be discharged.

Critique of Marbury v. *Madison*

EAKIN *v.* RAUB

12 Sergeant and Rawle (Pennsylvania Supreme Court) 330 (1825).

GIBSON, J. (dissenting) . . .

I am aware, that a [judicial] right to declare all unconstitutional acts void . . . is generally held as a professional dogma; but, I apprehend, rather as a matter of faith than of reason. I admit that I once embraced the same doctrine, but without examination, and I shall therefore state the arguments that impelled me to abandon it, with great respect for those by whom it is still maintained. But I may premise, that it is not a little remarkable, that although the right in question has all along been claimed by the judiciary, no judge has ventured to discuss it, except Chief Justice Marshall (in Marbury *v.* Madison, 1 Cranch, 176), and if the argument of a jurist so distinguished for the strength of his ratiocinative powers be found inconclusive, it may fairly be set down to the weakness of the position which he attempts to defend. . . .

The Constitution and the right of the legislature to pass the act, may be in collision. But is that a legitimate subject for judicial determination? If it be, the judiciary must be a peculiar organ, to revise the proceedings of the legislature, and to correct its mistakes; and in what part of the Constitution are we to look for this proud pre-eminence? Viewing the matter in the opposite direction, what would be thought of an act of assembly in which it should be declared that the Supreme Court had, in a particular case, put a wrong construction on the Constitution of the United States, and that the judgment should therefore be reversed? It would doubtless be thought a usurpation of judicial power. But it is by no means clear, that to declare a law void which has been enacted according to the forms prescribed in the Constitution, is not a usurpation of legislative power. It is an act of sovereignty; and sovereignty and legislative power are said by Sir William Blackstone to be convertible terms. It is the business of the judiciary to interpret the laws, not scan the authority of the lawgiver; and without the latter, it cannot take cognizance of a collision between a law and the Constitution. So that to affirm that the judiciary has a right to judge of the existence of such collision, is to take for granted the very thing to be proved. And, that a very cogent argument may be made in this way, I am not disposed to deny; for no conclusions are so strong as those that are drawn from the *petitio principii.*

But it has been said to be emphatically the business of the judiciary, to ascertain and pronounce what the law is; and that this necessarily involves a consideration of the Constitution. It does so: but how far? If the judiciary will inquire into anything besides the form of enactment, where shall it stop? There must be some point of limitation to such an inquiry; for no one will pretend that a judge would be justifiable in calling for the election returns, or scrutinizing the qualifications of those who composed the legislature. . . .

In theory, all the organs of the government are of equal capacity; or, if not equal, each must be supposed to have superior capacity only for those things which peculiarly belong to it; and, as legislation peculiarly involves the consideration of those limitations which are put on the law-making power, and the interpretation of the laws when made, involves only the construction of the laws themselves, it follows that the construction of the constitution in this particular belongs to the legislature, which ought therefore to be taken to have superior capacity to judge of the constitutionality of its own acts. But suppose all to be of equal capacity in every respect, why should one exercise a controlling power over the rest? That the judiciary is of superior rank, has never been pretended, although it has been said to be co-ordinate. It is not easy, however, to comprehend how the power which gives law to all the rest, can be of no more than equal rank with one which receives it, and is answerable to the former for the observance of its statutes. . . .

Everyone knows how seldom men think exactly alike on ordinary subjects; and a government constructed on the principle of assent by all its parts, would be inadequate to the most simple operations. The notion of a complication of counter checks has been carried to an extent in theory, of which the framers of the Constitution never dreamt. When the entire sovereignty was separated into its elementary parts, and distributed to the appropriate branches, all things incident to the exercise of its powers were committed to each branch exclusively. The negative which each part of the legislature may exercise, in regard to the acts of the other, was thought sufficient to prevent material infractions of the restraints which were put on the power of the whole; for, had it been intended to interpose the judiciary as an additional barrier, the matter would surely not have been left in doubt. The judges would not have been left to stand on the insecure and ever shifting ground of public opinion as to constructive powers; they would have been placed on the impregnable ground of an express grant. . . .

But the judges are sworn to support the Constitution, and are they not bound by it as the law of the land? In some respects they are. In the very few cases in which the judiciary, and not the legislature, is the immediate organ to execute its provisions, they are bound by it in preference to any act of assembly to the contrary. In such cases, the Constitution is a rule to the courts. But what I have in view in this inquiry, is the supposed right of the judiciary to interfere, in cases where the Constitution is to be carried into effect through the instrumentality of the legislature, and where that organ must necessarily first decide on the constitutionality of its own act.

The oath to support the Constitution is not peculiar to the judges, but is taken indiscriminately by every officer of the government, and is designed rather as a test of the political principles of the man, than to bind the officer in the discharge of his duty: otherwise it were difficult to determine what operation it is to have in the case of a recorder of deeds, for instance, who, in the execution of his office, has nothing to do with the Constitution. But granting it to relate to the official conduct of the judge, as well as every other officer, and not to his political principles, still it must be understood in reference to supporting the Constitution, only as far as that may be involved in his official duty; and, consequently, if his official duty does not comprehend an inquiry into the authority of the legislature, neither does his oath.

It is worthy of remark here, that the foundation of every argument in favor of the right of the judiciary, is found at last to be an assumption of the whole ground in dispute. Granting that the object of the oath is to secure a support of the Constitution in the discharge of official duty, its terms may be satisfied by restraining it to official duty in the exercise of the ordinary judicial powers. Thus, the Constitution may furnish a rule of construction, where a particular interpretation of a law would conflict with some constitutional principle; and such interpretation, where it may, is always to be avoided. But the oath was more probably designed to secure the powers of each of the different branches from being usurped by any of the rest: for instance, to prevent the House of Representatives from erecting itself into a court of judicature, or the Supreme Court from attempting to control the legislature; and, in this view, the oath furnishes an argument equally plausible against the right of the judiciary. But if it require a support of the Constitution in anything beside official duty, it is in fact an oath of allegiance to a particular form of government; and, considered as such, it is not easy to see why it should not be taken by the citizens at large, as well as by the officers of the government. It has never been thought that an officer is under greater restraint as to measures which have for their avowed end a total change of the Constitution, than a citizen who has taken no oath at all. The official oath, then, relates only to the official conduct of the officer, and does not prove that he ought to stray from the path of his ordinary business to search for violations of duty in the business of others; nor does it, as supposed, define the powers of the officer.

But do not the judges do a positive act in violation of the Constitution, when they give effect to an unconstitutional law? Not if the law has been passed according to the forms established in the Constitution. The fallacy of the question is, in supposing that the judiciary adopts the acts of the legislature as its own; whereas the enactment of a law and the interpretation of it are not concurrent acts, and as the judiciary is not required to concur in the enactment, neither is it in the breach of the Constitution which may be the consequence of the enactment. The fault is imputable to the legislature, and on it the responsibility exclusively rests. . . .

For these reasons, I am of opinion that it rests [ultimately] with the people, in whom full and absolute sovereign power resides, to correct abuses in legislation, by instructing their representatives to repeal the obnoxious act. What is wanting to plenary power in the government, is reserved by the people for their own immediate use; and to redress an infringement of their rights in this respect, would seem to be an accessory of the power thus reserved. It might, perhaps, have been better to vest the power in the judiciary; as it might be expected that its habits of deliberation, and the aid derived from the arguments of counsel, would more frequently lead to accurate conclusions. On the other hand, the judiciary is not infallible; and an error by it would admit of no remedy but a more distinct expression of the public will, through the extraordinary medium of a convention; whereas, an error by the legislature admits of a remedy by an exertion of the same will, in the ordinary exercise of the right of suffrage,—a mode better calculated to attain the end, without popular excitement.

Topic 9

THE BASES OF NATIONAL POWER

"It Is a Constitution We Are Expounding"

McCULLOCH *v.* MARYLAND

4 Wheaton 316 (1819)

Error to the Court of Appeals of the State of Maryland.

[Congress in 1816 passed an act to incorporate the Bank of the United States, and in the following year the bank established a branch in Baltimore. In 1818 the state of Maryland required all banks not chartered by the state to pay an annual tax of $15,000 or to pay a stamp tax on each bank note issued. McCulloch, the cashier of the Baltimore branch of the Bank of the United States, issued bank notes in violation of the state law whereupon the state of Maryland brought suit against him. The state courts decided in favour of Maryland. McCulloch appealed the case to the United States Supreme Court on a writ of error.]

MARSHALL, Chief Justice, delivered the opinion of the court. . . .

The first question made in the cause is, has congress power to incorporate a bank? . . . The power now contested was exercised by the first congress elected under the present constitution. The bill for incorporating the Bank of the United States did not steal upon an unsuspecting legislature, and pass unobserved. Its principle was completely understood, and was opposed with equal zeal and ability. After being resisted, first in the fair and open field of debate, and afterwards in the executive cabinet, with as much persevering talent as any measure has ever experienced, and being supported by arguments which convinced minds as pure and as intelligent as this country can boast, it became a law.

The original act was permitted to expire; but a short experience of the embarrassments to which the refusal to revive it exposed the government, convinced those who were most prejudiced against the measure of its necessity, and induced the passage of the present law. It would require no ordinary share of intrepidity to assert, that a measure adopted under these circumstances, was a bold and plain usurpation, to which the constitution gave no countenance. These observations belong to the cause: but they are not made under the impression that, were the question entirely new, the law would be found irreconcilable with the constitution.

In discussing this question, the counsel for the state of Maryland have deemed it of some importance, in the construction of the constitution, to consider that instrument not as emanating from the people, but as the act of sovereign and independent states. The powers of the general government, it has been said, are delegated by the states, who alone are truly sovereign; and must be exercised in subordination to the states, who alone possess supreme dominion. It would be difficult to sustain this proposition.

The convention which framed the constitution was, indeed, elected by the state legislatures. But the instrument, when it came from their hands, was a mere proposal, without obligation, or pretensions to it. It was reported to the then existing congress of the United States, with a request that it might "be submitted to a convention of delegates, chosen in each state by the people thereof, under the recommendation of its legislature, for their assent and ratification." This mode of proceeding was adopted; and by the convention, by congress, and by the state legislatures, the instrument was submitted to the *people*. They acted upon it, in the only manner in which they can act safely, effectively, and wisely, on such a subject, by assembling in convention. . . . From these conventions, the constitution derives its whole authority. The government proceeds directly from the people; is "ordained and established" in the name of the people; and is declared to be ordained, "in order to form a more perfect union, establish justice, insure domestic tranquility, and secure the blessings of liberty to themselves and to their posterity." . . . The government of the Union, then, is emphatically and truly, a government of the people. In form, and in substance, it emanates from them. Its powers are granted by them, and are to be exercised directly on them, and for their benefit.

This government is acknowledged by all, to be one of enumerated powers. The principle, that it can exercise only the powers granted to it, would seem too apparent, to have required to be enforced by all those arguments, which its enlightened friends, while it was depending before the people, found it necessary to urge; that principle is now universally admitted. But the question respecting the extent of the powers actually granted, is perpetually arising, and will probably continue to arise, as long as our system shall exist. In discussing these questions, the conflicting powers of the general and state governments must be brought into view, and the supremacy of their respective laws, when they are in opposition, must be settled.

If any one proposition could command the universal assent of mankind, we might expect that it would be this—that the government of the Union, though limited in its powers, is supreme within its sphere of action. This would seem to result, necessarily, from its nature. It is the government of all; its powers are delegated by all; it represents all, and acts for all. Though any one state may be willing to control its operations, no state is willing to allow others to control them. The nation, on those subjects on which it can act, must necessarily bind its component parts. But this question is not left to mere reason: the people have, in express terms, decided it, by saying, "this constitution, and the laws of the United States, which shall be made in pursuance thereof," "shall be the supreme law of the land," and by requiring that the members of the state legislatures, and the officers of the executive and judicial departments of the state, shall take the oath of fidelity to it. The government of the United States, then, though limited in its powers, is supreme; and its laws, when made in pursuance of the constitution, form the supreme law of the land, "anything in the constitution or laws of any state, to the contrary notwithstanding."

Among the enumerated powers, we do not find that of establishing a bank or creating a corporation. But there is no phrase in the instrument which, like the articles of confederation, excludes incidental or implied powers; and which requires that everything granted shall be expressly and minutely described. Even the 10th amendment, which was framed for the purpose of quieting the excessive jealousies which had been excited, omits the word "expressly," and declares only that the powers "not delegated to the United States, nor prohibited to the states, are reserved to the states or to the people"; thus leaving the question, whether the particular power which may become the subject of contest, has been delegated to the one government, or prohibited to the other, to depend on a fair construction of the whole instrument.

The men who drew and adopted this amendment had experienced the embarrassments resulting from the insertion of this word in the articles of confederation, and probably omitted it, to avoid those embarrassments. A constitution, to contain an accurate detail of all the subdivisions of which its great powers will admit, and of all the means by which they may be carried into execution, would partake of the prolixity of a legal code, and could scarcely be embraced by the human mind. It would, probably, never be understood by the public. Its nature, therefore, requires, that only its great outlines should be marked, its important objects designated, and the minor ingredients which compose those objects, be deduced from the nature of the objects themselves. That this idea was entertained by the framers of the American constitution, is not only to be inferred from the nature of the instrument, but from the language. Why else were some of the limitations, found in the 9th section of the 1st article, introduced? It is also, in some degree, warranted, by their having omitted to use any restrictive term which might prevent its receiving a fair and just interpretation. In considering this question, then, we must never forget, that it is a *constitution* we are expounding.

Although, among the enumerated powers of government, we do not find the word "bank," or "incorporation," we find the great powers, to lay and collect taxes; to borrow money; to regulate commerce; to declare and conduct war; and to raise and support armies and navies. . . . A government, intrusted with such ample powers, on the due execution of which the happiness and prosperity of the nation so vitally depends, must also be intrusted with ample means for their execution. The power being given, it is the interest of the nation to facilitate its execution. It can never be their interest, and cannot be presumed to have been their intention, to clog and embarrass its execution, by withholding the most appropriate means.

Throughout this vast republic, from the St. Croix to the Gulf of Mexico, from the Atlantic to the Pacific, revenue is to be collected and expended, armies are to be marched and supported. The exigencies of the nation may require, that the treasure raised in the north should be transported to the south, that raised in the east, conveyed to the west, or that this order should be reversed. Is that construction of the constitution to be preferred, which would render these operations difficult, hazardous, and expensive? Can we adopt that construction (unless the words imperiously require it), which would impute to the framers of that instrument, when granting these powers for the public good, the intention of impeding their exercise by withholding a choice of means? If, indeed, such be the mandate of the constitution, we have only to obey; but that instrument does not profess to enumerate the means by which the powers it confers may be executed; nor does it prohibit the creation of a corporation, if the existence of such a being be essential, to the beneficial exercise of those powers. It is, then, the subject of fair inquiry, how far such means may be employed.

It is not denied, that the powers given to the government imply the ordinary means of execution. That, for example, of raising revenue, and applying it to national purposes, is admitted to imply the power of conveying money from place to place, as the exigencies of the nation may require, and of employing the usual means of conveyance. But it is denied, that the government has its choice of means, or, that it may employ the most convenient means, if, to employ them, it be necessary to erect a corporation. . . . The government which has a right to do an act, and has imposed on it the duty of performing that act, must, according to the dictates of reason, be allowed to select the means; and those who contend that it may not select any appropriate means, that one particular mode of effecting the object is excepted, take upon themselves the burden of establishing that exception. . . .

But the constitution of the United States has not left the right of congress to employ the necessary means, for the execution of the powers conferred on the government, to general reasoning. To its enumeration of powers is added, that of making "all laws which shall be necessary and proper, for carrying into execution the foregoing powers, and all other powers vested by this constitution, in the government of the United States, or in any department thereof." . . .

The argument on which most reliance is placed, is drawn from the peculiar language of this clause. Congress is not empowered by it to make all laws, which may have relation to the powers conferred on the government, but only such as may be "necessary and proper" for carrying them into execution. The word "necessary" is considered as controlling the whole sentence, and as limiting the right to pass laws for the execution of the granted powers, to such as are indispensable, and without which the power would be nugatory. That it excludes the choice of means, and leaves to congress, in each case, that only which is most direct and simple.

Is it true, that this is the sense in which the word "necessary" is always used? Does it always import an absolute physical necessity, so strong, that one thing, to which another may be termed necessary, cannot exist without that other? We think it does not. If reference be had to its use, in the common affairs of the world, or in approved authors, we find that it frequently imports no more than that one thing is convenient, or useful, or essential to another. . . . A thing may be necessary, very necessary, absolutely or indispensably necessary. To no mind would the same idea be conveyed by these several phrases. This comment on the word is well illustrated by the passage cited at the bar, from the 10th section of the 1st article of the constitution. It is, we think, impossible to compare the sentence which prohibits a State from laying "imposts, or duties on imports or exports, except what may be absolutely necessary for executing its inspection laws," with that which authorizes congress "to make all laws which shall be necessary and proper for carrying into execution" the powers of the general government, without feeling a conviction, that the convention understood itself to change materially the meaning of the word "necessary" by prefixing the word "absolutely." This word, then, like others, is used in various senses; and, in its construction, the subject, the context, the intention of the person using them, are all to be taken into view.

Let this be done in the case under consideration. The subject is the execution of those great powers on which the welfare of a nation essentially depends. It must have been the intention of those who gave these powers, to insure, as far as human prudence could insure, their beneficial execution. This could not be done, by confining the choice of means to such narrow limits as not to leave it in the power of congress to adopt any which might be appropriate, and which were conducive to the end. This provision is made in a constitution, intended to endure for ages to come, and consequently, to be adapted to the various crises of human affairs. To have prescribed the means by which government should, in all future time, execute its powers, would have been to change, entirely, the character of the instrument, and give it the properties of a legal code. It would have been an unwise attempt to provide, by immutable rules, for exigencies which, if foreseen at all, must have been seen dimly, and which can be best provided for as they occur. To have declared, that the best means shall not be used, but those alone, without which the power given would be nugatory, would have been to deprive the legislature of the capacity to avail itself of experience, to exercise its reason, and to accommodate its legislation to circumstances. If we apply this principle of construction to any of the powers of the government, we shall find it so pernicious in its operation that we shall be compelled to discard it. [The Court here cites the law requiring an oath of office in addition to the oath prescribed by the Constitution.]

So, with respect to the whole penal code of the United States whence arises the power to punish, in cases not prescribed by the constitution? All admit, that the government may, legitimately, punish any violation of its laws; and yet, this is not among the enumerated powers of congress. . . .

If this limited construction of the word "necessary" must be abandoned, in order to punish, whence is derived the rule which would reinstate it, when the government would carry its powers into execution, by means not vindictive in their nature? If the word "necessary" means "needful," "requisite," "essential," "conducive to," in order to let in the power of punishment for the infraction of law; why is it not equally comprehensive, when required to authorize the use of means which facilitate the execution of the powers of government, without the infliction of punishment? . . .

We admit, as all must admit, that the powers of the government are limited, and that its limits are not to be transcended. But we think the sound construction of the constitution must allow to the national legislature that discretion, with respect to the means by which the powers it confers are to be carried into execution, which will enable that body to perform the high duties assigned to it, in the manner most beneficial to the people. Let the end be legitimate, let it be within the scope of the constitution, and all means which are appropriate, which are plainly adapted to that end, which are not prohibited, but consist[ent] with the letter and spirit of the constitution, are constitutional.

That a corporation must be considered as a means not less usual, not of higher dignity, not more requiring a particular specification than other means, has been sufficiently proved. . . . If a corporation may be employed, indiscriminately with other means, to carry into execution the powers of the government, no particular reason can be assigned for excluding the use of a bank, if required for its fiscal operations. To use one, must be within the discretion of congress, if it be an appropriate mode of executing the powers of government. That it is a convenient, a useful, and essential instrument in the prosecution of its fiscal operations, is not now a subject of controversy. . . .

After the most deliberate consideration, it is the unanimous and decided opinion of this court, that the act to incorporate the Bank of the United States is a law made in pursuance of the constitution, and is a part of the supreme law of the land.

The branches, proceeding from the same stock, and being conducive to the complete accomplishment of the object, are equally constitutional. . . .

It being the opinion of the court that the act incorporating the bank is constitutional, and that the power of establishing a branch in the state of Maryland might be properly exercised by the bank itself, we proceed to inquire:

2. Whether the State of Maryland may, without violating the constitution, tax that branch?

That the power of taxation is one of vital importance; that it is retained by the States; that it is not abridged by the grant of a similar power to the government of the Union; that it is to be concurrently exercised by the two governments: are truths which have never been denied. But, such is the paramount character of the constitution that its capacity to withdraw any subject from the action of even this power, is admitted. The States are expressly forbidden to lay any duties on imports or exports, except what may be absolutely necessary for executing their inspection laws. If the obligation of this prohibition must be conceded—if it may restrain a State from the exercise of its taxing power on imports and exports; the same paramount character would seem to restrain, as it certainly may restrain, a State from such other exercise of this power, as is in its nature incompatible with, and repugnant to, the constitutional laws of the Union. A law, absolutely repugnant to another, as entirely repeals that other as if express terms of repeal were used. . . .

This great principle is, that the constitution and the laws made in pursuance thereof are supreme; that they control the constitution and laws of the respective States, and cannot be controlled by them. From this, which may be almost termed an axiom, other propositions are deduced as corollaries, on the truth or error of which, and on their application to this case, the cause has been supposed to depend. These are, 1st. That a power to create implies a power to preserve. 2d. That a power to destroy, if wielded by a different hand, is hostile to, and incompatible with these powers to create and to preserve. 3d. That where this repugnancy exists, that authority which is supreme must control, not yield to that over which it is supreme. . . .

The sovereignty of a State extends to everything which exists by its own authority, or is introduced by its permission; but does it extend to those means which are employed by Congress to carry into execution powers conferred on that body by the people of the United States? We think it demonstrable that it does not. Those powers are not given by the people of a single State. They are given by the people of the United States, to a government whose laws, made in pursuance of the constitution, are declared to be supreme. Consequently, the people of a single State cannot confer a sovereignty which will extend over them.

If we measure the power of taxation residing in a State, by the extent of sovereignty which the people of a single State possess, and can confer on its government, we have an intelligible standard, applicable to every case to which the power may be applied. We have a principle which leaves the power of taxing the people and property of a state unimpaired; which leaves to a State the command of all its resources, and which places beyond its reach, all those powers which are conferred by the people of the United States on the government of the Union, and all those means which are given for the purpose of carrying those powers into execution. We have a principle which is safe for the States, and safe for the Union. We are relieved, as we ought to be, from clashing sovereignty; from interfering powers; from a repugnancy between a right in one government to pull down what there is an acknowledged right in another to build up; from the incompatibility of a right in one government to destroy what there is a right in another to preserve. We are not driven to the perplexing inquiry, so unfit for the judicial department, what degree of taxation is the legitimate use, and what degree may amount to the abuse of the power. The attempt to use it on the means employed by the government of the Union, in pursuance of the constitution, is itself an abuse, because it is the usurpation of a power which the people of a single State cannot give. . . .

That the power to tax involves the power to destroy; that the power to destroy may defeat and render useless the power to create; that there is a plain repugnance, in conferring on one government a power to control the constitutional measures of another, which other, with respect to those very measures, is declared to be supreme over that which exerts the control, are propositions not to be denied. . . .

If the States may tax one instrument, employed by the government in the execution of its powers, they may tax any and every other instrument. They may tax the mail; they may tax the mint; they may tax patent rights; they may tax the papers of the customhouse; they may tax judicial process; they may tax all the means employed by the government, to an excess which would defeat all the ends of government. . . .

The Court has bestowed on this subject its most deliberate consideration. The result is a conviction that the States have no power, by taxation or otherwise, to retard, impede, burden, or in any manner control, the operations of the constitutional laws enacted by Congress to carry into execution the powers vested in the general government. This is, we think, the unavoidable consequence of that supremacy which the constitution has declared.

We are unanimously of opinion, that the law passed by the legislature of Maryland, imposing a tax on the Bank of the United States, is unconstitutional and void. . . .

Topic 10

NATIONAL POWER OVER THE ECONOMY

The Commerce Power: A Restricted View

SCHECHTER POULTRY CORP. *V.* UNITED STATES

295 U.S. 495 (1935)

[In 1933 Congress passed the National Industrial Recovery Act. In signing the bill President Roosevelt said, "History probably will record the National Industrial Recovery Act as the most important and far-reaching legislation ever enacted by the American Congress." The purpose of the law, according to the President, was to promote re-employment, to shorten hours and increase wages, and to prevent unfair competition.

The first section of the act attempted to provide a constitutional basis for the legislation, stating:

"Section 1. A national emergency productive of widespread unemployment and disorganization of industry, which burdens interstate and foreign commerce, affects the public welfare, and undermines the standards of living of the American people, is hereby declared to exist. It is hereby declared to be the policy of Congress to remove obstructions to the free flow of interstate and foreign commerce which tend to diminish the amount thereof; and to provide for the general welfare by promoting the organization of industry for the purpose of cooperative action among trade groups, to induce and maintain united action of labor and management under adequate competitive practices, to promote the fullest possible utilization of the present productive capacity of industries, to avoid restriction of production (except as may be temporarily required), to increase the consumption of industrial and agricultural products by increasing purchasing power, to reduce and relieve unemployment, to improve standards of labor, and otherwise to rehabilitate industry and to conserve natural resources."

On May 27, 1935 the Supreme Court in a unanimous opinion declared the National Industrial Recovery Act unconstitutional on the grounds that (1), it "attempted delegation of legislative power" and (2), it "attempted regulation of intrastate transactions which affect interstate commerce only indirectly."

In the case at issue, The Schechter Poultry Corporation conducted a wholesale poultry slaughterhouse market in Brooklyn. It ordinarily purchased live poultry from commission men in New York City or at the railroad terminals and after slaughtering the poultry sold it to retail dealers and butchers. The Court stated that "New York City is the largest live-poultry market in the United States. Ninety-six per cent of the live poultry there marketed comes from other States."]

MR. CHIEF JUSTICE HUGHES delivered the opinion of the court.

Penalties are confined to violations of a code provision "in any transaction in or affecting interstate or foreign commerce." This aspect of the case presents the question whether the particular provisions of the Live Poultry Code, which the defendants were convicted for violating and for having conspired to violate, were within the regulating powers of Congress.

These provisions relate to the hours and wages of those employed by defendants in their slaughterhouses in Brooklyn and to the sales there made to retail dealers and butchers.

(1) Were these transactions "in" interstate commerce? Much is made of the fact that almost all the poultry coming to New York is sent there from other states. But the code provisions as here applied do not concern the transportation of the poultry from other states to New York, or the transactions of the commission men or others to whom it is consigned, or the sales made by such consignees to defendants.

When defendants had made their purchases, whether at the West Washington Market in New York City or at the railroad terminals serving the city, or elsewhere, the poultry was trucked to their slaughterhouses in Brooklyn for local disposition. The interstate transactions in relation to that poultry then ended. Defendants held the poultry at their slaughterhouse markets for slaughter and local sale to retail dealers and butchers, who in turn sold directly to consumers.

Neither the slaughtering nor the sales by defendants were transactions in interstate commerce. . . . The undisputed facts thus afford no warrant for the argument that the poultry handled by defendants at their slaughterhouse markets was in "current" or "flow" of interstate commerce and was thus subject to congressional regulation.

The mere fact that there may be a constant flow of commodities into a state does not mean that the flow continues after the property has arrived and has become commingled with the mass of property within the state and is there held solely for local disposition and use. So far as the poultry here in question is concerned, the flow in interstate commerce had ceased. The poultry had come to a permanent rest within the state. It was not held, used or sold by defendants in relation to any further transaction in interstate commerce and was not destined for transportation to other states. Hence, decisions which deal with a stream of interstate commerce—where goods come to rest within a state temporarily and are later to go forward in interstate commerce—and with the regulations of transactions involved in that practical continuity of movement, are not applicable here. . . .

(2) Did the defendant's transactions directly "affect" interstate commerce so as to be subject to federal regulation? The power of Congress extends not only to the regulation of transactions which are part of inter-

state commerce, but to the protection of that commerce from injury. It matters not that the injury may be due to the conduct of those engaged in intrastate operations. Thus, Congress may protect the safety of those employed in interstate transportation "no matter what may be the source of the dangers which threaten it." . . .

Defendants have been convicted, not upon direct charges of injury to interstate commerce or of interference with persons engaged in that commerce, but of violations of certain provisions of the Live Poultry Code and of conspiracy to commit these violations. Interstate commerce is brought in only upon the charge that violations of these provisions—as to hours and wages of employes and local sales—"affected" interstate commerce.

In determining how far the federal government may go in controlling intrastate transactions upon the ground that they "affect" interstate commerce, there is a necessary and well-established distinction between direct and indirect effects. The precise line can be drawn only as individual cases arise, but the distinction is clear in principle. . . . [And] where the effect of intrastate transactions upon interstate commerce is merely indirect, such transactions remain within the domain of state power. . . .

The question of chief importance relates to the provision of the Code as to the hours and wages of those employed in defendants' slaughterhouse markets. It is plain that these requirements are imposed in order to govern the details of defendants' management of their local business. The persons employed in slaughtering and selling in local trade are not employed in interstate commerce. Their hours and wages have no direct relation to interstate commerce. . . . If the federal government may determine the wages and hours of employees in the internal commerce of a State, because of their relation to cost and prices and their indirect effect upon interstate commerce, it would seem that a similar control might be exerted over other elements of cost, also affecting prices, such as the number of employees, rents, advertising, methods of doing business, etc. All the processes of production and distribution that enter into cost could likewise be controlled. If the cost of doing an intrastate business is in itself the permitted object of federal control, the extent of the regulation of cost would be a question of discretion and not of power.

The government also makes the point that efforts to enact state legislation establishing high labor standards have been impeded by the belief that, unless similar action is taken generally, commerce will be diverted from the states adopting such standards, and that this fear of diversion has led to demands for federal legislation on the subject of wages and hours. The apparent implication is that the federal authority under the commerce clause should be deemed to extend to the establishment of rules to govern wages and hours in intrastate trade and industry generally throughout the country, thus overriding the authority of the states to deal with domestic problems arising from labor conditions in their internal commerce.

It is not the province of the Court to consider the economic advantages or disadvantages of such a centralized system. It is sufficient to say that the Federal Constitution does not provide for it. Our growth and development have called for wide use of the commerce power of the federal government in its control over the expanded activities of interstate commerce and in protecting that commerce from burdens, interferences, and conspiracies to restrain and monopolize it. But the authority of the federal government may not be pushed to such an extreme as to destroy the distinction, which the commerce clause itself establishes, between commerce "among the several States" and the internal concerns of a State. The same answer must be made to the contention that is based upon the serious economic situation which led to the passage of the Recovery Act,—the fall in prices, the decline in wages and employment, and the curtailment of the market for commodities. Stress is laid upon the great importance of maintaining wage distributions which would provide the necessary stimulus in starting "the cumulative forces making for expanding commercial activity." Without in any way disparaging this motive, it is enough to say that the recuperative efforts of the federal government must be made in a manner consistent with the authority granted by the Constitution.

[The portion of the opinion dealing with the "attempted delegation of legislative power" is omitted.]

MR. JUSTICE CARDOZO, concurring . . .

There is another objection, far-reaching and incurable, aside from any defect of unlawful delegation.

If this code had been adopted by Congress itself, and not by the President on the advice of an industrial association, it would even then be void unless authority to adopt it is included in the grant of power "to regulate commerce with foreign nations and among the several states." United States Constitution, Art. I, Sec. 8, Clause 3.

I find no authority in that grant for the regulation of wages and hours of labor in the intrastate transactions that make up the defendants' business. As to this feature of the case little can be added to the opinion of the court. There is a view of causation that would obliterate the distinction between what is national and what is local in the activities of commerce. Motion at the outer rim is communicated perceptibly, though minutely, to recording instruments at the center. A society such as ours "is an elastic medium which transmits all tremors through its territory; the only question is of their size." Per Learned Hand, J., in the court below. The law is not indifferent to considerations of degree. Activities local in their immediacy do not become interstate and national because of distant repercussions. What is near and what is distant may at times be uncertain. Cf. Board of Trade v. Olsen, 262

U.S. 1. There is no penumbra of uncertainty obscuring judgment here. To find immediacy or directness here is to find it almost everywhere. If centripetal forces are to be isolated to the exclusion of the forces that oppose and counteract them, there will be an end to our federal system.

To take from this code the provisions as to wages and the hours of labor is to destroy it altogether. If a trade or an industry is so predominantly local as to be exempt from regulation by the Congress in respect of matters such as these, there can be no "code" for it at all. This is clear from the provisions of § 7a of the Act with its explicit disclosure of the statutory scheme. Wages and the hours of labor are essential features of the plan, its very bone and sinew. There is no opportunity in such circumstances for the severance of the infected parts in the hope of saving the remainder. A code collapses utterly with bone and sinew gone.

I am authorized to state that MR. JUSTICE STONE joins in this opinion.

[The following year, in Carter *v.* Carter Coal Co., 298 U.S. 238, the Supreme Court took the occasion to say: "Whether the effect of a given activity or condition is direct or indirect is not always easy to determine. The word 'direct' implies that the activity or condition invoked or blamed shall operate proximately—not mediately, remotely, or collaterally—to produce the effect. It connotes the absence of an efficient intervening agency or condition. And the extent of the effect bears no logical relation to its character."]

The Commerce Power: An Expanded View

WICKARD *V.* FILBURN

317 U.S. 111 (1942)

[The Agricultural Adjustment Act of 1938, as related to wheat, sought to control the volume moving in interstate and foreign commerce in order to avoid surpluses and shortages and consequent abnormalities of price and obstructions to commerce. The Act, as amended, provided procedures which resulted in the fixing of a market quota applicable to each farm and laid a penalty upon any excess brought to market by the farmer. The basic provision of this law was sustained in Mulford *v.* Smith, 307 U.S. 38 (1939).

The question in the instant case is whether Congress may constitutionally regulate *production* of wheat, not intended in any part for commerce, but wholly for *consumption* on the farm.]

MR. JUSTICE JACKSON delivered the opinion of the Court. . . .

[Filburn] says that this is a regulation of production and consumption of wheat. Such activities are, he urges, beyond the reach of congressional power under the commerce clause, since they are local in character, and their effects upon interstate commerce are at most "indirect." In answer the government argues that the statute regulates neither production nor consumption, but only marketing; and, in the alternative, that if the Act does go beyond the regulation of marketing it is sustainable as a "necessary and proper" implementation of the power of Congress over interstate commerce.

The government's concern lest the Act be held to be a regulation of production or consumption rather than of marketing is attributable to a few dicta and decisions of this Court which might be understood to lay it down that activities such as "production," "manufacturing," and "mining" are strictly "local" and, except in special circumstances which are not present here, cannot be regulated under the commerce power because their effects upon interstate commerce are, as matter of law, only "indirect." Even today, when this power has been held to have great latitude, there is no decision of this Court that such activities may be regulated where no part of the product is intended for interstate commerce or intermingled with the subjects thereof. We believe that a review of the course of decision under the commerce clause will make plain, however, that questions of the power of Congress are not to be decided by reference to any formula which would give controlling force to nomenclature such as "production" and "indirect" and foreclose consideration of the actual effects of the activity in question upon interstate commerce.

At the beginning Chief Justice Marshall described the federal commerce power with a breadth never yet exceeded. Gibbons *v.* Ogden, 9 Wheat. 1, 194, 195. He made emphatic the embracing and penetrating nature of this power by warning that effective restraints on its exercise must proceed from political rather than from judicial processes. 9 Wheat. at page 197.

For nearly a century, however, decisions of this Court under the commerce clause dealt rarely with questions of what Congress might do in the exercise of its granted power under the clause and almost entirely with the permissibility of state activity which it was claimed discriminated against or burdened interstate commerce. During this period there was perhaps little occasion for the affirmative exercise of the commerce power, and the influence of the clause on American life and law was a negative one, resulting almost wholly from its operation as a restraint upon the powers of the states. In discussion and decision the point of reference instead of being what was "necessary and proper" to the exercise by Congress of its granted power, was often some concept of sovereignty thought to be implicit in the status of statehood. Certain activities such as "production," "manufacturing," and "mining" were occasionally said to be within the province of state governments and beyond the power of Congress under the commerce clause.

It was not until 1887 with the enactment of the Interstate Commerce Act that the interstate commerce power began to exert positive influence in American law and life. This first important federal resort to the commerce power was followed in 1890 by the Sherman Anti-Trust Act and, thereafter, mainly after 1903, by many others. These statutes ushered in new phases of adjudication, which required the Court to approach the interpretation of the commerce clause in the light of an actual exercise by Congress of its power thereunder.

When it first dealt with this new legislation, the Court adhered to its earlier pronouncements, and allowed but little scope to the power of Congress. United States *v.* E. C. Knight Co., 156 U.S. 1. These earlier pronouncements also played an important part in several of the five cases in which this Court later held that acts of Congress under the commerce clause were in excess of its power.

Even while important opinions in this line of restrictive authority were being written, however, other cases called forth broader interpretations of the commerce clause destined to supersede the earlier ones, and to bring about a return to the principles first enunciated by Chief Justice Marshall in Gibbons *v.* Ogden, *supra.*

Not long after the decision of United States *v.* E. C. Knight Co., *supra,* Mr. Justice Holmes, in sustaining the exercise of national power over intrastate activity, stated for the Court that "commerce among the states is not a technical legal conception, but a practical one, drawn from the course of business." Swift & Co. *v.* United States, 196 U.S. 375, 398. It was soon demonstrated that the effects of many kinds of intrastate activity upon interstate commerce were such as to make them a proper subject of federal regulation. In some cases sustaining the exercise of federal power over intrastate matters the term "direct" was used for the purpose of stating, rather than of reaching, a result; in others it was treated as synonymous with "substantial" or "material"; and in others it was not used at all. Of late its use has been abandoned in cases dealing with questions of federal power under the commerce clause.

In the Shreveport Rate Cases (Houston, E. & W. T. R. Co. *v.* United States), 234 U.S. 342, the Court held that railroad rates of an admittedly intrastate character and fixed by authority of the state might, nevertheless, be revised by the federal government because of the economic effects which they had upon interstate commerce. The opinion of Mr. Justice Hughes found federal intervention constitutionally authorized because of "matters having such a close and substantial relation to interstate traffic that the control is essential or appropriate to the security of that traffic, to the efficiency of the interstate service, and to the maintenance of the conditions under which interstate commerce may be conducted upon fair terms and without molestation or hindrance." 234 U.S. at page 351.

The Court's recognition of the relevance of the economic effects in the application of the commerce clause exemplified by this statement has made the mechanical application of legal formulas no longer feasible. Once an economic measure of the reach of the power granted to Congress in the commerce clause is accepted, questions of federal power cannot be decided simply by finding the activity in question to be "production" nor can consideration of its economic effects be foreclosed by calling them "indirect." The present Chief Justice has said in summary of the present state of the law: "The commerce power is not confined in its exercise to the regulation of commerce among the states. It extends to those activities intrastate which so affect interstate commerce or the exertion of the power of Congress over it, as to make regulation of them appropriate means to the attainment of a legitimate end, the effective execution of the granted power to regulate interstate commerce. . . . The power of Congress over interstate commerce is plenary and complete in itself, may be exercised to its utmost extent, and acknowledges no limitations other than are prescribed in the Constitution. . . . It follows that no form of state activity can constitutionally thwart the regulatory power granted by the commerce clause to Congress. Hence the reach of that power extends to those intrastate activities which in a substantial way interfere with or obstruct the exercise of the granted power." United States *v.* Wrightwood Dairy Co., 315 U.S. 110, 119.

Whether the subject of the regulation in question was "production," "consumption," or "marketing" is, therefore, not material for purposes of deciding the question of federal power before us. That an activity is of local character may help in a doubtful case to determine whether Congress intended to reach it. The same consideration might help in determining whether in the absence of congressional action it would be permissible for the state to exert its power on the subject matter, even though in so doing it to some degree affected interstate commerce. But even if appellant's activity be local and though it may not be regarded as commerce, it may still, whatever its nature, be reached by Congress if it exerts a substantial economic effect on interstate commerce and this irrespective of whether such effect is what might at some earlier time have been defined as "direct" or "indirect."

The parties have stipulated a summary of the economics of the wheat industry. Commerce among the states in wheat is large and important. Although wheat is raised in every state but one, production in most states is not equal to consumption. Sixteen states on average have had a surplus of wheat above their own requirements for feed, seed, and food. Thirty-two states and the District of Columbia, where production has been below consumption, have looked to these surplus-producing states for their supply as well as for wheat for export and carryover.

The wheat industry has been a problem industry for some years. Largely as a result of increased foreign production and import restrictions, annual exports of wheat and flour from the United States during the ten-year period ending in 1940 averaged less than 10 per cent of total production, while during the 1920's they averaged more than 25 per cent. The decline in the export trade has left a large surplus in production which in connection with an abnormally large supply of wheat and other grains in recent years caused congestion in a number of markets; tied up railroad cars; and caused elevators in some instances to turn away grains, and railroads to institute embargoes to prevent further congestion. . . .

In the absence of regulation the price of wheat in the United States would be much affected by world conditions. During 1941 producers who co-operated with the Agricultural Adjustment program received an average price on the farm of about $1.16 a bushel as compared with the world market price of 40 cents a bushel. . . .

The effect of consumption of home-grown wheat on interstate commerce is due to the fact that it constitutes the most variable factor in the disappearance of the wheat crop. Consumption on the farm where grown appears to vary in an amount greater than 20 per cent of average production. The total amount of wheat consumed as food varies but relatively little, and use as seed is relatively constant.

The maintenance by government regulation of a price for wheat undoubtedly can be accomplished as effectively by sustaining or increasing the demand as by limiting the supply. The effect of the statute before us is to restrict the amount which may be produced for market and the extent as well to which one may forestall resort to the market by producing to meet his own needs. That [Filburn's] own contribution to the demand for wheat may be trivial by itself is not enough to remove him from the scope of federal regulation where, as here, his contribution, taken together with that of many others similarly situated, is far from trivial. National Labor Relations Board *v.* Fainblatt, 306 U.S. 601, 606, *et seq.,* 307 U.S. 609; United States *v.* Darby, *supra,* 312 U.S. at page 123.

It is well established by decisions of this Court that the power to regulate commerce includes the power to regulate the prices at which commodities in that commerce are dealt in and practices affecting such prices. One of the primary purposes of the Act in question was to increase the market price of wheat and to that end to limit the volume thereof that could affect the market. It can hardly be denied that a factor of such volume and variability as home consumed wheat would have a substantial influence on price and market conditions. This may arise because being in marketable condition such wheat overhangs the market and, if induced by rising prices, tends to flow in to the market and check price increases. But if we assume that it is never marketed, it supplies a need of the man who grew it which would otherwise be reflected by purchases in the open market. Home-grown wheat in this sense competes with wheat in commerce. The stimulation of commerce is a use of the regulatory function quite as definitely as prohibitions or restrictions thereon. This record leaves us in no doubt that Congress may properly have considered that wheat consumed on the farm where grown if wholly outside the scheme of regulation would have a substantial effect in defeating and obstructing its purpose to stimulate trade therein at increased prices. . . .

[The decision of the lower court is reversed.]

Section IV

What Limits on Free Speech?

THE AGE WHICH acclaimed the Declaration of Independence and added a Bill of Rights to the Federal Constitution considered freedom of expression one of the great natural rights which governments were instituted to protect. It believed that this sacred and inalienable right could not be justly impaired by any government, even with the consent of the majority. Today, many "truths" which appeared to Jefferson "self-evident" seem to have less influence on "the opinions of mankind," and the case for freedom of opinion must find a more pragmatic basis.

Most Americans would agree that freedom of speech and of the press is essential to self-government. Many, however, may not adequately comprehend *why* freedom of discussion is fundamental to our democratic way of life, or why we should allow the propagation of doctrines which we regard as false, or even loathsome.

The words of the First Amendment are absolute and unqualified: "Congress shall make *no* law . . . abridging the freedom of speech, or of the press. . . ." If taken literally this would seem to prohibit *all* legislation by Congress which in any degree interferes with freedom of opinion. However, very few serious thinkers have maintained that freedom of speech should be entirely unlimited, and even many libertarian members of the Supreme Court have recognized that freedom of speech cannot be an unqualified right.

The cornerstone of most contemporary judicial discussion of freedom of speech is the so-called "clear and present" danger test first enunciated in the case of Schenck *v.* United States. "The question in every case," wrote Mr. Justice Holmes, "is whether the words used are used in such circumstances and are of such a nature as to create a clear and present danger that they will bring about the substantative evils that Congress has a right to prevent." Since, as Mr. Justice Holmes added, "It is a question of proximity and degree," it is not surprising that the Supreme Court justices should frequently disagree in their interpretation and application of this test.

Should freedom of speech include the right to advocate revolution and dictatorship? Should those who seek to destroy constitutional liberties be allowed to take advantage of the very liberties which they aim to destroy? To answer these questions requires an examination of the limits of freedom of discussion, an evaluation of our present loyalty-security program in public service, and related problems of individual liberties.

In the case of Gitlow *v.* New York, 268 U.S. 652, the majority of the Supreme Court took the position that freedom of the press did not include the right to publish a manifesto which contained an "incitement" to violent revolution. In sustaining the Criminal Anarchy law of New York, Mr. Justice Sanford, writing for the majority of the Supreme Court, said in 1925:

"A single revolutionary spark may kindle a fire that, smouldering for a time, may burst into a sweeping and destructive conflagration. It cannot be said that the State is acting arbitrarily or unreasonably when in the exercise of its judgment as to the measures necessary to protect the public peace and safety, it seeks to extinguish the spark without waiting until it has enkindled the flame or blazed into the conflagration."

The dissent of Justice Holmes regarded this decision as a departure from the clear and present danger test enunciated in the Schenck case. He said:

"If what I think the correct test is applied it is manifest that there was no present danger of an attempt to overthrow the government by force on the part of the admittedly small minority who shared the defendant's view. . . . Whatever may be thought of the redundant discourse before us, it had no chance of starting a present conflagration. If in the long run the beliefs expressed in proletarian dictatorship are destined to be accepted by the dominant forces of the community, the only meaning of free speech is that they should be given their chance and have their way."

Without overruling the Gitlow case, the Supreme Court in the thirties tended to return to the "clear and present danger test" as interpreted by Holmes and Brandeis. The extreme libertarian position was reached by the "Roosevelt Court" in 1941 in the case of Bridges *v.* California, 314 U.S. 252. In a 5-to-4 opinion Mr. Justice Black, writing for the majority, said: "What finally emerges from the 'clear and present danger' cases is a working principle that the substantive evil must be *extremely serious* and the degree of *imminence extremely high* before utterances can be punished." This victory for the extreme libertarian position in the Supreme Court, however, was only temporary.

The case of Dennis *v.* United States, decided in 1951, by a 6-to-2 vote, upheld the constitutionality of the Smith Act which punishes those who "knowingly or willfully advocate" the destruction of "any government in the United States by force or violence." The justices follow at least four different lines of reasoning in reaching their conclusions and none of these opinions was subscribed to by a majority of the Court.

It should be observed that in Yates *v.* United States, decided in 1957 after some changes in the composition of the Court, it took pains to emphasize that its decision was consistent with that in the Dennis case. However, it is pertinent to inquire whether the Court's narrow construction of the meaning of the word "organize" in the

Smith Act and its insistence that advocacy, to serve as a basis for conviction, must be directed toward *action,* do not, in fact suggest, a return to a somewhat more libertarian position.

We suggest, finally, that the ultimate issue is not one of constitutionality but of wisdom.

Topic 11

THE DILEMMAS OF FREEDOM

"Clear and Present Danger"

SCHENCK *V.* UNITED STATES

249 U.S. 47 (1919).

Error to the District Court of the United States for the Eastern District of Pennsylvania.

MR. JUSTICE HOLMES delivered the opinion of the court.

This is an indictment in three counts. The first charges a conspiracy to violate the Espionage Act of June 15, 1917, c. 30, § 3, 40 Stat. 217, 219, by causing and attempting to cause insubordination, &c., in the military and naval forces of the United States, and to obstruct the recruiting and enlistment service of the United States, when the United States was at war with the German Empire, to-wit, that the defendants wilfully conspired to have printed and circulated to men who had been called and accepted for military service under the Act of May 18, 1917, a document set forth and alleged to be calculated to cause such insubordination and obstruction. The count alleges overt acts in pursuance of the conspiracy, ending in the distribution of the document set forth. The second count alleges a conspiracy to commit an offense against the United States, to-wit, to use the mails for the transmission of matter declared to be non-mailable by Title XII, § 2 of the Act of June 15, 1917, to-wit, the above mentioned document, with an averment of the same overt acts. The third count charges an unlawful use of the mails for the transmission of the same matter and otherwise as above. The defendants were found guilty on all the counts. They set up the First Amendment to the Constitution forbidding Congress to make any law abridging the freedom of speech, or of the press, and bringing the case here on that ground have argued some other points also of which we must dispose. . . .

The document in question upon its first printed side recited the first section of the Thirteenth Amendment, said that the idea embodied in it was violated by the Conscription Act and that a conscript is little better than a convict. In impassioned language it intimated that conscription was despotism in its worst form and a monstrous wrong against humanity in the interest of Wall Street's chosen few. It said, "Do not submit to intimidation," but in form at least confined itself to peaceful measures such as a petition for the repeal of the act.

The other and later printed side of the sheet was headed "Assert Your Rights." It stated reasons for alleging that any one violated the Constitution when he refused to recognize "your right to assert your opposition to the draft," and went on, "If you do not assert and support your rights, you are helping to deny or disparage rights which it is the solemn duty of all citizens and residents of the United States to retain." It described the arguments on the other side as coming from cunning politicians and a mercenary capitalist press, and even silent consent to the conscription law as helping to support an infamous conspiracy. It denied the power to send our citizens away to foreign shores to shoot up the people of other lands, and added that words could not express the condemnation such coldblooded ruthlessness deserves, &c., winding up, "You must do your share to maintain, support and uphold the rights of the people of this country." Of course the document would not have been sent unless it had been intended to have some effect, and we do not see what effect it could be expected to have upon persons subject to the draft except to influence them to obstruct the carrying of it out. The defendants do not deny that the jury might find against them on this point.

But it is said, suppose that that was the tendency of this circular, it is protected by the First Amendment to the Constitution. Two of the strongest expressions are said to be quoted respectively from well-known public men. It well may be that the prohibition of laws abridging the freedom of speech is not confined to previous restraints, although to prevent them may have been the main purpose, as intimated in Patterson *v*. Colorado, 205 U.S. 454, 462. We admit that in many places and in ordinary times the defendants in saying all that was said in the circular would have been within their constitutional rights. But the character of every act depends upon the circumstances in which it is done. Aikens *v*. Wisconsin, 195 U.S. 194, 205, 206. The most stringent protection of free speech would not protect a man in falsely shouting fire in a theatre and causing a panic. It does not even protect a man from an injunction against uttering words that may have all the effect of force. Gompers *v.* Buck Stove & Range Co., 221 U.S. 418, 439.

The question in every case is whether the words used are used in such circumstances and are of such a nature as to create a clear and present danger that they will bring about the substantive evils that Congress has a right to prevent. It is a question of proximity and degree. When a nation is at war many things that might be said in time of peace are such a hindrance to its effort that their utterance will not be endured so long as men fight and that no Court could regard them as protected by any constitutional right. It seems to be admitted that if an actual obstruction of the recruiting service were proved, liability for words that produced that effect might be enforced. The statute of 1917 in § 4 punishes conspiracies to obstruct as well as actual obstruction. If the act (speaking, or circulating a paper), its tendency and the intent with which it is done are the same, we perceive no ground for saying that success alone warrants making the act a crime. Goldman *v.* United States, 245 U.S. 474, 477. Indeed that case might be said to dispose of the present contention if the precedent covers all *media concludendi.* But as the right to free speech was not referred to specially, we have thought fit to add a few words. . . .

Judgments affirmed.

"Free Trade in Ideas"

JUSTICE OLIVER WENDELL HOLMES, JR.*

Persecution for the expression of opinions seems to me perfectly logical. If you have no doubt of your premises or your power and want a certain result with all your heart you naturally express your wishes in law and sweep away all opposition. To allow opposition by speech seems to indicate that you think the speech impotent, as when a man says that he has squared the circle, or that you do not care wholeheartedly for the result, or that you doubt either your power or your premises. But when men have realized that time has upset many fighting faiths, they may come to believe even more than they believe the very foundations of their own conduct that the ultimate good desired is better reached by free trade in ideas—that the best test of truth is the power of the thought to get itself accepted in the competition of the market, and that truth is the only ground upon which their wishes safely can be carried out. That, at any rate, is the theory of our Constitution. It is an experiment, as all life is an experiment. Every

* The selection is from his dissenting opinion in Abrams *v.* United States, 250 U.S. 616, 624 (1919).

year if not every day we have to wager our salvation upon some prophecy based upon imperfect knowledge. While that experiment is part of our system I think that we should be eternally vigilant against attempts to check the expression of opinions that we loathe and believe to be fraught with death, unless they so imminently threaten immediate interference with the lawful and pressing purposes of the law that an immediate check is required to save the country.

I wholly disagree with the argument of the Government that the First Amendment left the common law as to seditious libel in force. History seems to me against the notion. I had conceived that the United States through many years had shown its repentance for the Sedition Act of 1798 by repaying fines that it imposed. Only the emergency that makes it immediately dangerous to leave the correction of evil counsels to time warrants making any exception to the sweeping command, "Congress shall make no law . . . abridging the freedom of speech." Of course I am speaking only of expressions of opinion and exhortations, which were all that were uttered here, but I regret that I cannot put into more impressive words my belief that in their conviction upon this indictment the defendants were deprived of their rights under the Constitution of the United States.

Free Speech and Self-Government

ALEXANDER MEIKLEJOHN *

The First Amendment to the Constitution, as we all know, forbids the federal Congress to make any law which shall abridge the freedom of speech. In recent years, however, the government of the United States has in many ways limited the freedom of public discussion. For example, the Federal Bureau of Investigation has built up, throughout the country, a system of espionage, of secret police, by which hundreds of thousands of our people have been listed as holding this or that set of opinions. The only conceivable justification of that listing by a government agency is to provide a basis for action by the government in dealing with those persons. And that procedure reveals an attitude toward freedom of speech which is widely held in the United States. Many of us are now convinced that, under the Constitution, the government is justified in bringing pressure to bear against the holding or expressing of beliefs which are labeled "dangerous." Congress, we think, may rightly abridge the freedom of such beliefs.

* Former President, Amherst College. Author of *The Liberal College, Freedom and the College* and other works. The selection is from Alexander Meiklejohn, *Free Speech and Its Relation to Self-Government* (New York, Harper & Brothers, 1948), *passim.* Reprinted by permission of author and publisher.

Again, the legislative committees, federal and state, which have been appointed to investigate un-American activities, express the same interpretation of the Constitution. All the inquirings and questionings of those committees are based upon the assumption that certain forms of political opinion and advocacy should be, and legitimately may be, suppressed. And, further, the Department of Justice, acting on the same assumption, has recently listed some sixty or more organizations, association with which may be taken by the government to raise the question of "disloyalty" to the United States. And finally, the President's Loyalty Order, moving with somewhat uncertain steps, follows the same road. We are officially engaged in the suppression of "dangerous" speech.

Now, these practices would seem to be flatly contradictory of the First Amendment. Are they? What do we mean when we say that "Congress shall make no law . . . abridging the freedom of speech . . . ?" What is this "freedom of speech" which we guard against invasion by our chosen and authorized representatives? Why may not a man be prevented from speaking if, in the judgment of Congress, his ideas are hostile and harmful to the general welfare of the nation? Are we, for example, required by the First Amendment to give men freedom to advocate the abolition of the First Amendment? Are we bound to grant freedom of speech to those who, if they had the power, would refuse it to us? The First Amendment, taken literally, seems to answer "Yes" to those questions. It seems to say that no speech, however dangerous, may, for that reason, be suppressed. But the Federal Bureau of Investigation, the un-American Activities Committees, the Department of Justice, the President, are, at the same time, answering "No" to the same question. Which answer is right? What is the valid American doctrine concerning the freedom of speech? . . .

When men govern themselves, it is they—and no one else—who must pass judgment upon unwisdom and unfairness and danger. And that means that unwise ideas must have a hearing as well as wise ones, unfair as well as fair, dangerous as well as safe, un-American as well as American. Just so far as, at any point, the citizens who are to decide an issue are denied acquaintance with information or opinion or doubt or disbelief or criticism which is relevant to that issue, just so far the result must be ill-considered, ill-balanced planning for the general good. *It is that mutilation of the thinking process of the community against which the First Amendment to the Constitution is directed.* The principle of the freedom of speech springs from the necessities of the program of self-government. It is not a Law of Nature or of Reason in the abstract. It is a deduction from the basic American agreement that public issues shall be decided by universal suffrage.

If, then, on any occasion in the United States it is allowable to say that the Constitution is a good document it is equally allowable, in that situation, to say that the Constitution is a bad document. If a public building may be used in which to say, in time of war, that the war is justified, then the same building may be used in which to say that it is not justified. If it be publicly argued that conscription for armed service is moral and necessary, it may likewise be publicly argued that it is immoral and unnecessary. If it may be said that American political institutions are superior to those of England or Russia or Germany, it may, with equal freedom, be said that those of England or Russia or Germany are superior to ours. These conflicting views may be expressed, must be expressed, not because they are valid, but because they are relevant. If they are responsibly entertained by anyone, we, the voters, need to hear them. When a question of policy is "before the house," free men choose to meet it not with their eyes shut, but with their eyes open. To be afraid of ideas, any idea, is to be unfit for self-government. Any such suppression of ideas about the common good, the First Amendment condemns with its absolute disapproval. The freedom of ideas shall not be abridged. . . .

In the course of his argument [in Schenck *v.* United States] Mr. Holmes says, "The question in every case is whether the words used are used in such circumstances and are of such a nature as to create a clear and present danger that they will bring about the substantive evils that Congress has a right to prevent." And to this he adds, a few sentences later, "It seems to be admitted that, if an actual obstruction of the recruiting service were proved, liability for words that produced that effect might be enforced."

As one reads these words of Mr. Holmes, one is uneasily aware of the dangers of his rhetorical skill. At two points the argument seems at first much more convincing than it turns out to be. First, the phrase, "substantive evils that Congress has a right to prevent," seems to settle the issue by presumption, seems to establish the right of legislative control. If the legislature has both the right and the duty to prevent certain evils, then apparently it follows that the legislature must be authorized to take whatever action is needed for the preventing of those evils. But our plan of government by limited powers forbids that that inference be drawn. The Bill of Rights, for example, is a series of denials that the inference is valid. It lists, one after the other, forms of action which, however useful they might be in the service of the general welfare, the legislature is forbidden to take. And, that being true, the "right to prevent evils" does not give unqualifiedly the right to prevent evils. In the judgment of the Constitution, some preventions are more evil than are the evils from which they would save us. And the First Amendment is a case in point. If that amendment means anything, it means that certain substantive evils which, in principle, Congress has a right to prevent, must be endured if the only way of avoiding them is by the abridging of that freedom of speech upon which the entire structure of our free institutions rests. . . .

But, second, the "clear and present danger" argument which Mr. Holmes here offers, moves quickly from deliberate obstruction of a law to reasonable protest against it. Taken as it stands, his formula tells us that whenever the expression of a minority opinion involves clear and present danger to the public safety it may be denied the protection of the First Amendment. And that means that whenever crucial and dangerous issues have come upon the nation, free and unhindered discussion of them must stop. If, for example, a majority in Congress is taking action against "substantive evils which Congress has a right to prevent," a minority which opposes such action is not entitled to the freedom of speech of Article I, section 6.* Under that ruling, dissenting judges might, in "dangerous" situations, be forbidden to record their dissents. Minority citizens might, in like situations, be required to hold their peace. No one, of course, believes that this is what Mr. Holmes or the court intended to say. But it is what, in plain words, they did say. The "clear and present danger" opinion stands on the record of the court as a peculiarly inept and unsuccessful attempt to formulate an exception to the principle of the freedom of speech. . . .

Human discourse, as the First Amendment sees it, is not "a mere academic and harmless discussion." If it were, the advocates of self-government would be as little concerned about it as they would be concerned about the freedom of men playing solitaire or chess. The First Amendment was not written primarily for the protection of those intellectual aristocrats who pursue knowledge solely for the fun of the game, whose search for truth expresses nothing more than a private intellectual curiosity or an equally private delight and pride in mental achievement. It was written to clear the way for thinking which serves the general welfare. It offers defense to men who plan and advocate and incite toward corporate action for the common good. On behalf of such men it tells us that every plan of action must have a hearing, every relevant idea of fact or value must have full consideration, whatever may be the dangers which that activity involves. It makes no difference whether a man is advocating conscription or opposing it, speaking in favor of a war or against it, defending democracy or attacking it, planning a communist reconstruction of our economy or criticising it. So long as his active words are those of participation in public discussion and public decision of matters of public policy, the freedom of those words may not be abridged. That freedom is the basic postulate of a society which is governed by the votes of its citizens.

"If, in the long run, the beliefs expressed in proletarian dictatorship are destined to be accepted by the dominant forces of the community, the only meaning of free speech is that they should be given their chance and

* Article I, section 6, of the Constitution defining the duties and privileges of the members of Congress, says, ". . . and for any speech or debate in either House, they shall not be questioned in any other place."

have their way." [The quote is from Justice Holmes' dissent in Gitlow *v.* New York, 268 U.S. 652 (1925).] That is Americanism. In these wretched days of postwar and, it may be, of prewar, hysterical brutality, when we Americans, from the president down, are seeking to thrust back Communist belief by jailing its advocates, by debarring them from office, by expelling them from the country, by hating them, the gallant, uncompromising words of Mr. Holmes, if we would listen to them, might help to restore our sanity, our understanding of the principles of the Constitution. They might arouse in us something of the sense of shame which the nation so sorely needs. . . .

We Americans, in choosing our form of government, have made, at this point, a momentous decision. We have decided to be self-governed. We have measured the dangers and the values of the suppression of the freedom of public inquiry and debate. And, on the basis of that measurement, having regard for the public safety, we have decided that the destruction of freedom is always unwise, that freedom is always expedient. The conviction recorded by that decision is not a sentimental vagary about the "natural rights" of individuals. It is a reasoned and sober judgment as to the best available method of guarding the public safety. We, the People, as we plan for the general welfare, do not choose to be "protected" from the "search for truth." On the contrary, we have adopted it as our "way of life," our method of doing the work of governing for which, as citizens, we are responsible. Shall we, then, as practitioners of freedom, listen to ideas which, being opposed to our own, might destroy confidence in our form of government? Shall we give a hearing to those who hate and despise freedom, to those who, if they had the power, would destroy our institutions? Certainly, yes! Our action must be guided, not by their principles, but by ours. We listen, not because they desire to speak, but because we need to hear. If there are arguments against our theory of government, our policies in war or in peace, we the citizens, the rulers, must hear and consider them for ourselves. That is the way of public safety. It is the program of self-government.

In his study, *Free Speech in the United States,* Mr. Chafee gives abundant evidence in support of this criticism. . . . The suppression of freedom of speech, he finds, has been throughout our history a disastrous threat to the public safety. As he sums up his results, he takes as a kind of motto the words of John Stuart Mill: "A State which dwarfs its men in order that they may be more docile instruments in its hands even for beneficial purposes, will find that with small men no great thing can really be accomplished." Mr. Chafee tells the story, as he sees it, of the futility and disaster which came upon the efforts of President Wilson in World War I as he was driven, by the threat of clear and present dangers, into the suppressions of the Espionage Act.

President Wilson's tragic failure, according to Mr. Chafee, was his blindness to the imperative need of public information and public discussion bearing on the issues of war and peace. He felt bound to prevent imminent substantive evils which might arise from that discussion. In the attempt to do so, nearly two thousand persons, Mr. Chafee tells us, were prosecuted. The fruits of those prosecutions he sums up as follows: ". . . tens of thousands among those 'forward-looking men and women' to whom President Wilson had appealed in earlier years were bewildered and depressed and silenced by the negation of freedom in the twenty-year sentences requested by his legal subordinates from complacent judges. So we had plenty of patriotism and very little criticism, except of the slowness of ammunition production. Wrong courses were followed like the dispatch of troops to Archangel in 1918, which fatally alienated Russia from Wilson's aims for a peaceful Europe. Harmful facts like the secret treaties were concealed while they could have been cured, only to bob up later and wreck everything." . . .

And the final argument upon which the absoluteness of the First Amendment rests [is that] it does not balance intellectual freedom against public safety. On the contrary, its great declaration is that intellectual freedom is the necessary bulwark of the public safety. That declaration admits of no exceptions. If, by suppression, we attempt to avoid lesser evils, we create greater evils. We buy temporary and partial advantage at the cost of permanent and dreadful disaster. That disaster is the breakdown of self-government. Free men need the truth as they need nothing else. In the last resort, it is only the search for and the dissemination of truth that can keep our country safe.*

* It should be noted that, according to Meiklejohn, the word *liberty* in the due process clause of the Fifth Amendment has been "construed by the Supreme Court to include 'the liberty of speech.' The Fifth Amendment is, then, saying that the people of the United States have a *civil* liberty of speech which, *by due legal process,* the government may limit or suppress." It is Meiklejohn's view, therefore, that the Constitution recognizes "two radically different kinds of utterances." The first—relating to "discussion of public policy"—is in the realm of "absolute freedom of speech." But "the constitutional status of a merchant advertising his wares" and of similar activities "is utterly different" and subject to regulation and limitation.

Freedom to Destroy Freedom?

FREDERICK BERNAYS WIENER *

As our legislatures and courts come to closer grips with the nature—and the menace—of world communism, Americans are necessarily forced to inquire whether there is anything in the Constitution of the United States that guarantees immunity, or even possible success, for those who seek to replace the model of government fashioned at Philadelphia in 1787 with the pattern forged at Petrograd in 1917–1918 and since further developed in the Kremlin at Moscow.

To what extent, if at all, is "freedom for the thought that we hate" a principle of our Constitution? Is it the theory of our fundamental law "that the best test of the truth is the power of the thought to get itself accepted in the competition of the market"? Is there anything in the Constitution that requires the Government to stay its hand against those who would overthrow it, and to "let them stand undisturbed as monuments of the safety with which error of opinion may be tolerated when reason is left free to combat it"? . . .

FRAMERS INTENDED TO LEAVE NO SCOPE FOR ANTI-REPUBLICAN GOVERNMENT

Having fought monarchy for long and hard years in the face of terrible odds, the Framers were not quixotic enough to cast away the prize of independence by providing new sanctuaries where that hated institution might conveniently reappear. They had not turned the other cheek when George III struck at their liberties; now, having secured those liberties, they were not with the other hand preparing to endanger the hard-won prize by providing freedom for the hated thought of monarchy. Indeed, they intended to leave no scope for any antirepublican form of government. For those men of 1787, though they knew nothing of swastikas, or dictatorship of the proletariat, or fascism, or communism, were yet fully aware, good classicists that they were, of the excesses of tyranny in the days of ancient Greece and Rome. And for anti-republican ideas, whether of kings by divine right or of tyrants by irresistible force, of totalitarianism whether in the name of blood unity or in the name of economic interest, they never intended to provide a foothold. They not

* Member of the District of Columbia Bar. Professorial Lecturer in Law, George Washington University. Formerly with the Department of Justice. Author of *Effective Appellate Advocacy*. This selection is from Frederick Bernays Wiener, " 'Freedom for the Thought That We Hate': Is It a Principle of the Constitution?" *American Bar Association Journal,* Vol. 37 (March 1951). By permission.

only presupposed the orthodoxy of republicanism, they guaranteed its continuance.

At this point it will doubtless be urged, however, that the writings of Thomas Jefferson reflect the very ideas that Mr. Justice Holmes expressed, and Mr. Justice Brandeis elaborated, over a century later. Reliance is generally had on the one sentence from Jefferson's First Inaugural:

> If there be any among us who would wish to dissolve this Union or to change its republican form, let them stand undisturbed as monuments of the safety with which error of opinion may be tolerated where reason is left free to combat it.

The hard fact of the matter is, however, that Jefferson is far from being a safe guide on the issues now under consideration. He was not a member of the Constitutional Convention, being at the time Minister to France, and had no access to its records during his lifetime. His letter to Kercheval, written in 1816, in which he deprecates looking at constitutions with sanctimonious reverence, is merely an individual attitude, which is far from representative of the views of those who framed the Constitution in 1787, or of those who in 1795 decided to admit to citizenship only those aliens who were "attached to the principles of the Constitution of the United States."[1] In that connection, it is significant that Madison, then in Congress, opposed the latter requirement. "It was hard to make a man swear that he preferred the Constitution of the United States, or to give any general opinion, because he may, in his own private judgment, think Monarchy or Aristocracy better, and yet be honestly determined to support this Government as he finds it."[2] But Congress adopted the provision over Madison's objections.[3] . . .

Moreover, since Inaugural Addresses traditionally and normally have partisan connotations, Jefferson's First Inaugural must be read in the light of the political controversies of the day. It must be read with an eye to the Sedition Act, and to that measure's partisan, even virulent, enforcement by the Federalists; and pre-eminently, it must be read in the light of the vital circumstance, always overlooked by those who uncritically accept that document as constitutional gospel, that Jefferson was the real author of the Kentucky and Virginia Resolutions and hence the spiritual ancestor of nullification and of its progeny, secession.

The Southern leaders of 1860–1861 relied upon the Jeffersonian doctrine of noninterference when they left the Union. But the course of American history did not follow the Jeffersonian view. For if Jefferson was right, if those "who would wish to dissolve this Union" should "stand undisturbed as monuments of the safety with which error of opinion may be tolerated where reason is left free to combat it," then Lincoln was

[1] Secs. 1 (*Thirdly*) and 2, Act Jan. 29, 1795, c. 20, 1 Stat. 414, 414–415.
[2] 4 *Annals of Congress* 1023. [3] *Ibid.*

wrong, and the men who fought to preserve the Union were wrong, and we should now be two nations instead of one. Holmes himself asserted the error of the Jeffersonian view at the Marshall centennial in 1901, when, as Chief Justice of Massachusetts, he noted "The fact that time has been on Marshall's side, and that the theory for which Hamilton argued, and he decided, and Webster spoke, and Grant fought, and Lincoln died, is now our cornerstone." [4] Moreover, Holmes, on the United States Supreme Court, wrote the opinions upholding the convictions of Schenck [5] and Frohwerk [6] and Debs,[7] in which the "clear and present danger" test was first enunciated; if Jefferson was right, these persons should never have been convicted, they should have been permitted to stand undisturbed. Indeed, it is not amiss to point out that, much earlier, Jefferson had backtracked also; the treason prosecutions of his Administration indicated a strong disinclination to let Aaron Burr *et al.* pursue their machinations without interference.[8] . . .

WE NEED NOT FOLLOW WEIMAR EXAMPLE

These are not mere theoretical abstractions; the views herein discussed can be illustrated and illustrated by the sorry spectacle of the demise of republican governments elsewhere.

The record in the Knauer denaturalization case [9] showed that Hitler prior to 1923 "never had any intention of trying to obtain political power in Germany except by means of force, except by violence, by a *coup d'état,* or a similar direct action method." It was only after the failure of the 1923 *Putsch* "that he with his advisers decided that the way to do away with democracy in Germany was to use democracy—was to use democratic rights and privileges with the explicit aim of paralyzing democracy and the democratic procedures. . . ." [10] By allowing full "freedom for the thought that we hate," by opening its marketplaces in ideas to "the monstrous and debauching power of the organized lie," [11] the

[4] Holmes, "John Marshall," in *Collected Legal Papers* 87, 90–91.

[5] Schenck *v.* United States, 249 U.S. 47.

[6] Frohwerk *v.* United States, 249 U.S. 204.

[7] Debs *v.* United States, 249 U.S. 211.

[8] United States *v.* Burr, Fed. Case No. 14693 (C.C.D. Va.); *Ex parte Bollman,* 4 Cranch 75. See also 4 Channing, *History of the United States,* 335–343; 3 Beveridge, *The Life of John Marshall,* 274–545; Channing, *The Jeffersonian System,* 155–168.

[9] Knauer *v.* United States, 328 U.S. 654.

[10] Consolidated transcript in Knauer *v.* United States, *supra,* pages 611 *et seq.* (not printed).

[11] Gilbert Murray, quoted in Kimball, "The Espionage Acts and the Limits of Legal Toleration," 33 *Harv. L. Rev.,* 442, 447, note 36, which is an exceptionally well-reasoned defense of Abrams *v.* United States, 250 U.S. 616.

Germany of the Weimar Republic effectively signed its own death warrant. Nothing in the Constitution of the United States requires us to follow the German example.

The sad history of the second overthrow of Czechoslovakia in 1948 by the Communists illuminates the practical difficulties in the way of applying the "clear and present danger" test to the purposeful underground plottings of organized communism. Those who parrot the Holmes' formula in a vacuum of their own devising—ignoring, by the way, Holmes' warning about the consequences which follow when thoughts become encysted in fine phrases [12]—have yet to indicate the point at which, in their view, the Czechoslovak Government would have been free to move against those who eventually overthrew it. What was said in reply to a similar argument in a treason case affords an ample answer to most of the contentions drawn from a too literal application of "clear and present danger" to the machinations of the Communist Party: "And after this kind of reasoning they will not be guilty till they have success; and if they have success enough, it will be too late to question them." [13] Judge Learned Hand's Dennis opinion [14] blows a welcome breath of fresh realistic air through a good deal of abstract libertarianism. That opinion holds, in substance and effect, that nothing in the Constitution of the United States requires this country to suffer the Czechoslovak experience in the name of freedom of thought. . . .

The truth of the matter is that "freedom for the thought that we hate" is not, certainly in any absolute sense, a principle of our Constitution. And the present paper suggests that it would be well to remember that fact whenever we have occasion to deal with those who seek to use the protections of the Constitution in order to undermine the Constitution, who take advantage of American freedom only that they may be the better able to destroy it.*

[12] "It is one of the misfortunes of the law that ideas become encysted in phrases and thereafter for a long time cease to provoke further analysis." Holmes, J., dissenting in Hyde *v.* United States, 225 U.S. 347, 384, 391.

"To rest upon a formula is a slumber that, prolonged, means death." Holmes, "Ideals and Doubts," in *Collected Legal Papers,* 303, 306.

[13] Lord Chief Justice Treby in *Trial of Captain Vaughan,* 13 How. St. Tr. 485, 533.

[14] 183 F. (2d) 201 (C.A. 2d), decided August 1, 1950. [See next Topic.] Holmes' dissent in the Abrams case was cited by Dennis *et al.* in their brief some eleven times, Brandeis' concurring opinion in the Whitney case no less than nineteen times. Counsel for Dennis *et al.* had not progressed beyond page 14 of the transcript of his oral argument in the Second Circuit before he quoted the sentence beginning, "If there be any among us who would wish to dissolve this Union or to change its republican form," etc.

* For a reply to the above article see Arthur S. Katz, "Freedom for the Thought We Hate," *American Bar Association Journal* (December, 1951), Vol. 37, pp. 901–904.

Topic 12

FREEDOM TO ADVOCATE REVOLUTION?

Democracy May Defend Itself

DENNIS ET AL. *V.* UNITED STATES

341 U.S. 494 (1951)

MR. CHIEF JUSTICE VINSON announced the judgment of the Court and an opinion in which MR. JUSTICE REED, MR. JUSTICE BURTON and MR. JUSTICE MINTON join.

Petitioners were indicted in July, 1948, for violation of the conspiracy provisions of the Smith Act, . . . § 11, during the period of April, 1945, to July, 1948. . . . We granted certiorari, 340 U.S. 863, limited to the following two questions: (1) Whether either § 2 or § 3 of the Smith Act, inherently or as construed and applied in the instant case, violates the First Amendment and other provisions of the Bill of Rights; (2) whether either § 2 or § 3 of the Act, inherently or as construed and applied in the instant case, violates the First and Fifth Amendments because of indefiniteness.

Sections 2 and 3 of the Smith Act, . . . provide as follows:

> SEC. 2.
> (a) It shall be unlawful for any person—
> (1) to knowingly or willfully advocate, abet, advise, or teach the duty, necessity, desirability, or propriety of overthrowing or destroying any government in the United States by force or violence, or by the assassination of any officer of such government;
> (3) to organize or help to organize any society, group, or assembly of persons who teach, advocate, or encourage the overthrow or destruction of any government in the United States by force or violence; or to be or become a member of, or affiliate with, any such society, group, or assembly of persons, knowing the purpose thereof. . . .
> SEC. 3. It shall be unlawful for any person to attempt to commit, or to conspire to commit, any of the acts prohibited by the provisions of . . . this title.

The indictment charged the petitioners with wilfully and knowingly conspiring (1) to organize as the Communist Party of the United States of America a society, group and assembly of persons who teach and advocate the overthrow and destruction of the Government of the United States by force and violence, and (2) knowingly and wilfully to advocate and teach the duty and necessity of overthrowing and destroying the Government of the United States by force and violence. The indictment further alleged that § 2 of the Smith Act proscribes these acts and that any conspiracy to take such action is a violation of § 3 of the Act.

The trial of the case extended over nine months, six of which were devoted to the taking of evidence, resulting in a record of 16,000 pages. . . . Petitioners dispute the meaning to be drawn from the evidence, contending that the Marxist-Leninist doctrine they advocated taught that force and violence to achieve a Communist form of government in an existing democratic state would be necessary only because the ruling classes of that state would never permit the transformation to be accomplished peacefully, but would use force and violence to defeat any peaceful political and economic gain the Communists could achieve.

But the Court of Appeals held that the record supports the following broad conclusions: By virtue of their control over the political apparatus of the Communist Political Association,[1] petitioners were able to transform that organization into the Communist Party; that the policies of the Association were changed from peaceful cooperation with the United States and its economic and political structure to a policy which had existed before the United States and the Soviet Union were fighting a common enemy, namely, a policy which worked for the overthrow of the Government by force and violence; that the Communist Party is a highly disciplined organization, adept at infiltration into strategic positions, use of aliases, and double-meaning language; that the Party is rigidly controlled; that Communists, unlike other political parties, tolerate no dissension from the policy laid down by the guiding forces, but that the approved program is slavishly followed by the members of the Party; that the literature of the Party and the statements and activities of its leaders, petitioners here, advocate, and the general goal of the Party was, during the period in question, to achieve a successful overthrow of the existing order by force and violence.

It will be helpful in clarifying the issues to treat next the contention that the trial judge improperly interpreted the statute by charging that the statute required an unlawful intent before the jury could convict. More specifically, he charged that the jury could not find the petitioners guilty under the indictment unless they found that petitioners had the intent "to overthrow the government by force and violence as speedily as circumstances permit. . . ."

The structure and purpose of the statute demand the inclusion of intent as an element of the crime. Congress was concerned with those who ad-

[1] Following the dissolution of the Communist International in 1943, the Communist Party of the United States dissolved and was reconstituted as the Communist Political Association. The program of this Association was one of cooperation between labor and management, and, in general, one designed to achieve national unity and peace and prosperity in the post-war period.

vocate and organize for the overthrow of the Government. Certainly those who recruit and combine for the purpose of advocating overthrow intend to bring about that overthrow. We hold that the statute requires as an essential element of the crime proof of the intent of those who are charged with its violation to overthrow the Government by force and violence. . . .

Nor does the fact that there must be an investigation of a state of mind under this interpretation afford any basis for rejection of that meaning. A survey of Title 18 of the U.S. Code indicates that the vast majority of the crimes designated by that Title require, by express language, proof of the existence of a certain mental state, in words such as "knowingly," "maliciously," "wilfully," "with the purpose of," "with intent to," or combinations or permutations of these and synonymous terms. The existence of a *mens rea* is the rule of, rather than the exception to, the principles of Anglo-American criminal jurisprudence. See American Communications Assn. *v.* Douds, 339 U.S. 382, 411 (1950). . . .

The obvious purpose of the statute is to protect existing Government, not from change by peaceable, lawful and constitutional means, but from change by violence, revolution and terrorism. That it is within the *power* of the Congress to protect the Government of the United States from armed rebellion is a proposition which requires little discussion. Whatever theoretical merit there may be to the argument that there is a "right" to rebellion against dictatorial governments is without force where the existing structure of the government provides for peaceful and orderly change. We reject any principle of governmental helplessness in the face of preparation for revolution, which principle, carried to its logical conclusion, must lead to anarchy. No one could conceive that it is not within the power of Congress to prohibit acts intended to overthrow the Government by force and violence. The question with which we are concerned here is not whether Congress has such *power,* but whether the *means* which it has employed conflict with the First and Fifth Amendments to the Constitution.

One of the bases for the contention that the means which Congress has employed are invalid takes the form of an attack on the face of the statute on the grounds that by its terms it prohibits academic discussion of the merits of Marxism-Leninism, that it stifles ideas and is contrary to all concepts of a free speech and a free press. . . .

The very language of the Smith Act negates the interpretation which petitioners would have us impose on that Act. It is directed at advocacy, not discussion. Thus, the trial judge properly charged the jury that they could not convict if they found that petitioners did "no more than pursue peaceful studies and discussions or teaching and advocacy in the realm of ideas." He further charged that it was not unlawful "to conduct in an American college and university a course explaining the philosophical theories set forth in the books which have been placed in evidence." Such a charge is in strict accord with the statutory language, and illustrates the meaning to be placed on those words. Congress did not intend to eradicate the free discussion of political theories, to destroy the traditional rights of Americans to discuss and evaluate ideas without fear of governmental sanction. Rather Congress was concerned with the very kind of activity in which the evidence showed these petitioners engaged. . . .

We pointed out in Douds, *supra,* that the basis of the First Amendment is the hypothesis that speech can rebut speech, propaganda will answer propaganda, free debate of ideas will result in the wisest governmental policies. It is for this reason that this Court has recognized the inherent value of free discourse. An analysis of the leading cases in this Court which have involved direct limitations on speech, however, will demonstrate that both the majority of the Court and the dissenters in particular cases have recognized that this is not an unlimited, unqualified right, but that the societal value of speech must, on occasion, be subordinated to other values and considerations.

No important case involving free speech was decided by this Court prior to Schenck *v.* United States, 249 U.S. 47 (1919). . . . Writing for a unanimous Court, Justice Holmes stated that the "question in every case is whether the words used are used in such circumstances and are of such a nature as to create a clear and present danger that they will bring about the substantive evils that Congress has a right to prevent." 249 U.S. at 52. But the force of even this expression is considerably weakened by the reference at the end of the opinion to Goldman *v.* United States, 245 U.S. 474 (1918), a prosecution under the same statute. Said Justice Holmes, "Indeed [Goldman] might be said to dispose of the present contention if the precedent covers all *media concludendi,* but as the right to free speech was not referred to specially, we have thought fit to add a few words." 249 U.S. at 52.

The fact is inescapable, too, that the phrase bore no connotation that the danger was to be any threat to the safety of the Republic. The charge was causing and attempting to cause insubordination in the military forces and obstruct recruiting. The objectionable document denounced conscription and its most inciting sentence was, "You must do your share to maintain, support and uphold the rights of the people of this country." 249 U.S. at 51. Fifteen thousand copies were printed and some circulated. This insubstantial gesture toward insubordination in 1917 during war was held to be a clear and present danger of bringing about the evil of military insubordination. . . .

The rule we deduce . . . is that where an offense is specified by a statute in nonspeech or nonpress terms, a conviction relying upon speech or press as evidence of violation may be sustained only when the speech or publication created a "clear and present danger" of attempting or accomplishing the prohibited crime, *e. g.,* interference with enlistment. . . .

Neither Justice Holmes (nor Justice Brandeis) ever envisioned that a shorthand phrase should be crystallized into a rigid rule to be applied inflexibly without regard to the circumstances of each case. Speech is not an absolute, above and beyond control by the legislature when its judgment, subject to review here, is that certain kinds of speech are so undesirable as to warrant criminal sanction. Nothing is more certain in modern society than the principle that there are no absolutes, that a name, a phrase, a standard has meaning only when associated with the considerations which gave birth to the nomenclature. See Douds, 339 U.S. at 397. To those who would paralyze our Government in the face of impending threat by encasing it in a semantic straitjacket we must reply that all concepts are relative.

In this case we are squarely presented with the application of the "clear and present danger" test, and must decide what that phrase imports. We first note that many of the cases in which this Court has reversed convictions by use of this or similar tests have been based on the fact that the interest which the State was attempting to protect was itself too insubstantial to warrant restriction of speech. . . .

Overthrow of the Government by force and violence is certainly a substantial enough interest for the Government to limit speech. Indeed, this is the ultimate value of any society, for if a society cannot protect its very structure from armed internal attack, it must follow that no subordinate value can be protected. If, then, this interest may be protected, the literal problem which is presented is what has been meant by the use of the phrase "clear and present danger" of the utterances bringing about the evil within the power of Congress to punish.

Obviously, the words cannot mean that before the Government may act, it must wait until the *putsch* is about to be executed, the plans have been laid and the signal is awaited. If Government is aware that a group aiming at its overthrow is attempting to indoctrinate its members and to commit them to a course whereby they will strike when the leaders feel the circumstances permit, action by the Government is required. The argument that there is no need for Government to concern itself, for Government is strong, it possesses ample powers to put down a rebellion, it may defeat the revolution with ease needs no answer. For that is not the question. Certainly an attempt to overthrow the Government by force, even though doomed from the outset because of inadequate numbers or power of the revolutionists, is a sufficient evil for Congress to prevent. The damage which such attempts create both physically and politically to a nation makes it impossible to measure the validity in terms of the probability of success, or the immediacy of a successful attempt.

In the instant case the trial judge charged the jury that they could not convict unless they found that petitioners intended to overthrow the Government "as speedily as circumstances would permit." This does not mean, and could not properly mean, that they would not strike until there was certainty of success. What was meant was that the revolutionists would strike when they thought the time was ripe. We must therefore reject the contention that success or probability of success is the criterion.

The situation with which Justices Holmes and Brandeis were concerned in Gitlow was a comparatively isolated event, bearing little relation in their minds to any substantial threat to the safety of the community. Such also is true of cases like Fiske *v.* Kansas, 274 U.S. 380 (1927), and DeJonge *v.* Oregon, 299 U.S. 353 (1937); but cf. Lazar *v.* Pennsylvania, 286 U.S. 532 (1932). They were not confronted with any situation comparable to the instant one—the development of an apparatus designed and dedicated to the overthrow of the Government, in the context of world crisis after crisis.

Chief Judge Learned Hand, writing for the majority below, interpreted the phrase as follows: "In each case [courts] must ask whether the gravity of the 'evil,' discounted by its improbability, justifies such invasion of free speech as is necessary to avoid the danger." 183 F. 2d at 212. We adopt this statement of the rule. As articulated by Chief Judge Hand, it is as succinct and inclusive as any other we might devise at this time. It takes into consideration those factors which we deem relevant, and relates their significances. More we cannot expect from words.

Likewise, we are in accord with the court below, which affirmed the trial court's finding that the requisite danger existed. The mere fact that from the period 1945 to 1948 petitioners' activities did not result in an attempt to overthrow the Government by force and violence is of course no answer to the fact that there was a group that was ready to make the attempt. The formation by petitioners of such a highly organized conspiracy, with rigidly disciplined members subject to call when the leaders, these petitioners, felt that the time had come for action, coupled with the inflammable nature of world conditions, similar uprisings in other countries, and the touch-and-go nature of our relations with countries with whom petitioners were in the very least ideologically attuned, convince us that their convictions were justified on this score. And this analysis disposes of the contention that a conspiracy to advocate, as distinguished from the advocacy itself, cannot be constitutionally restrained, because it comprises only the preparation. It is the existence of the conspiracy which creates the danger. [Citations omitted.] If the ingredients of the reaction are present, we cannot bind the Government to wait until the catalyst is added. . . .

The argument that the action of the trial court is erroneous, in declaring as a matter of law that such violation shows sufficient danger to justify the punishment despite the First Amendment, rests on the theory that a jury must decide a question of the application of the First Amendment. We do not agree.

When facts are found that establish the violation of a statute the protection against conviction afforded by the First Amendment is a matter of law. The doctrine that there must be a clear and present danger of a substantive evil that Congress has a right to prevent is a judicial rule to be applied as a matter of law by the courts. The guilt is established by proof of facts. Whether the First Amendment protects the activity which constitutes the violation of the statute must depend upon a judicial determination of the scope of the First Amendment applied to the circumstances of the case. . . .

The question in this case is whether the statute which the legislature has enacted may be constitutionally applied. In other words, the Court must examine judicially the application of the statute to the particular situation, to ascertain if the Constitution prohibits the conviction. We hold that the statute may be applied where there is a "clear and present danger" of the substantive evil which the legislature had the right to prevent. Bearing as it does, the marks of a "question of law," the issue is properly one for the judge to decide. . . .

Petitioners intended to overthrow the Government of the United States as speedily as the circumstances would permit. Their conspiracy to organize the Communist Party and to teach and advocate the overthrow of the Government of the United States by force and violence created a "clear and present danger" of an attempt to overthrow the Government by force and violence. They were properly and constitutionally convicted for violation of the Smith Act. The judgments of conviction are

Affirmed.

MR. JUSTICE CLARK took no part in the consideration or decision of this case.

MR. JUSTICE FRANKFURTER, concurring in affirmance of the judgment.

The First Amendment categorically demands that "Congress shall make no law respecting an establishment of religion, or prohibiting the free exercise thereof; or abridging the freedom of speech, or of the press; or the right of the people peaceably to assemble, and to petition the Government for a redress of grievances." The right of a man to think what he pleases, to write what he thinks, and to have his thoughts made available for others to hear or read has an engaging ring of universality. The Smith Act and this conviction under it no doubt restrict the exercise of free speech and assembly. Does that, without more, dispose of the matter?

Just as there are those who regard as invulnerable every measure for which the claim of national survival is invoked, there are those who find in the Constitution a wholly unfettered right of expression. Such literalness treats the words of the Constitution as though they were found on a piece of outworn parchment instead of being words that have called into being a nation with a past to be preserved for the future. The soil in which the Bill of Rights grew was not a soil of arid pedantry. The historic antecedents of the First Amendment preclude the notion that its purpose was to give unqualified immunity to every expression that touched on matters within the range of political interest.

The Massachusetts Constitution of 1780 guaranteed free speech; yet there are records of at least three convictions for political libels obtained between 1799 and 1803. The Pennsylvania Constitution of 1790 and the Delaware Constitution of 1792 expressly imposed liability for abuse of the right of free speech. Madison's own State put on its books in 1792 a statute confining the abusive exercise of the right of utterance. And it deserves to be noted that in writing to John Adams' wife, Jefferson did not rest his condemnation of the Sedition Act of 1798 on his belief in unrestrained utterance as to political matter. The First Amendment, he argued, reflected a limitation upon Federal power, leaving the right to enforce restrictions on speech to the States.

The language of the First Amendment is to be read not as barren words found in a dictionary but as symbols of historic experience illumined by the presuppositions of those who employed them. Not what words did Madison and Hamilton use, but what was it in their minds which they conveyed? Free speech is subject to prohibition of those abuses of expression which a civilized society may forbid. As in the case of every other provision of the Constitution that is not crystallized by the nature of its technical concepts, the fact that the First Amendment is not self-defining and self-enforcing neither impairs its usefulness nor compels its paralysis as a living instrument. . . .

Absolute rules would inevitably lead to absolute exceptions, and such exceptions would eventually corrode the rules. The demands of free speech in a democratic society as well as the interest in national security are better served by candid and informed weighing of the competing interests, within the confines of the judicial process, than by announcing dogmas too inflexible for the non-Euclidian problems to be solved.

But how are competing interests to be assessed? Since they are not subject to quantitative ascertainment, the issue necessarily resolves itself into asking, who is to make the adjustment?—who is to balance the relevant factors and ascertain which interest is in the circumstances to prevail? Full responsibility for the choice cannot be given to the courts. Courts are not representative bodies. They are not designed to be a good reflex of a democratic society. Their judgment is best informed, and therefore most dependable, within narrow limits. Their essential quality is detachment, founded on independence. History teaches that the independence of the judiciary is jeopardized when courts become embroiled in the passions of the day and assume primary responsibility in choosing between competing political, economic and social pressures.

Primary responsibility for adjusting the interests which compete in the situation before us of necessity belongs to the Congress. The nature of the power to be exercised by this Court has been delineated in decisions not charged with the emotional appeal of situations such as that now before us. We are to set aside the judgment of those whose duty it is to legislate only if there is no reasonable basis for it. [Citations omitted.] . . .

In all fairness, the argument cannot be met by reinterpreting the Court's frequent use of "clear" and "present" to mean an entertainable "probability." In giving this meaning to the phrase "clear and present danger," the Court of Appeals was fastidiously confining the rhetoric of opinions to the exact scope of what was decided by them. We have greater responsibility for having given constitutional support, over repeated protests, to uncritical libertarian generalities.

Nor is the argument of the defendants adequately met by citing isolated cases. Adjustment of clash of interests which are at once subtle and fundamental is not likely to reveal entire consistency in a series of instances presenting the clash. It is not too difficult to find what one seeks in the language of decisions reporting the effort to reconcile free speech with the interests with which it conflicts. The case for the defendants requires that their conviction be tested against the entire body of our relevant decisions. Since the significance of every expression of thought derives from the circumstances evoking it, results reached rather than language employed give the vital meaning. . . .

[After reviewing a number of decisions of the Court, MR. JUSTICE FRANKFURTER continued:] I must leave to others the ungrateful task of trying to reconcile all these decisions. In some instances we have too readily permitted juries to infer deception from error, or intention from argumentative or critical statements. Abrams *v.* United States; Schaefer *v.* United States; Pierce *v.* United States; Gilbert *v.* Minnesota, 254 U.S. 325. In other instances we weighted the interest in free speech so heavily that we permitted essential conflicting values to be destroyed. Bridges *v.* California; Craig *v.* Harney. Viewed as a whole, however, the decisions express an attitude toward the judicial function and a standard of values which for me are decisive of the case before us.

First.—Free-speech cases are not an exception to the principle that we are not legislators, that direct policy-making is not our province. How best to reconcile competing interests is the business of legislatures, and the balance they strike is a judgment not to be displaced by ours, but to be respected unless outside the pale of fair judgment. . .

Second.—A survey of the relevant decisions indicates that the results which we have reached are on the whole those that would ensue from careful weighing of conflicting interests. The complex issues presented by regulation of speech in public places, by picketing, and by legislation prohibiting advocacy of crime have been resolved by scrutiny of many factors besides the imminence and gravity of the evil threatened.

The matter has been well summarized by a reflective student of the Court's work. "The truth is that the clear-and-present-danger test is an oversimplified judgment unless it takes account also of a number of other factors: the relative seriousness of the danger in comparison with the value of the occasion for speech or political activity; the availability of more moderate controls than those which the state has imposed; and perhaps the specific intent with which the speech or activity is launched. No matter how rapidly we utter the phrase 'clear and present danger,' or how closely we hyphenate the words, they are not a substitute for the weighing of values. They tend to convey a delusion of certitude when what is most certain is the complexity of the strands in the web of freedoms which the judge must disentangle." Freund, *On Understanding the Supreme Court,* 27–28. . . .

Bearing in mind that Mr. Justice Holmes regarded questions under the First Amendment as questions of "proximity and degree," Schenck *v.* United States, 249 U.S. at 52, it would be a distortion, indeed a mockery, of his reasoning to compare the "puny anonymities," 250 U.S. at 629, to which he was addressing himself in the Abrams case in 1919 or the publication that was "futile and too remote from possible consequences," 268 U.S. at 673, in the Gitlow case in 1925 with the setting of events in this case in 1950.

"It does an ill-service to the author of the most quoted judicial phrases regarding freedom of speech, to make him the victim of a tendency which he fought all his life, whereby phrases are made to do service for critical analysis by being turned into dogma. 'It is one of the misfortunes of the law that ideas become encysted in phrases and thereafter for a long time cease to provoke further analysis.' Holmes, J., dissenting, in Hyde *v.* United States, 225 U.S. 347, 384, at 391." . . . It were far better that the phrase be abandoned than that it be sounded once more to hide from the believers in an absolute right of free speech the plain fact that the interest in speech, profoundly important as it is, is no more conclusive in judicial review than other attributes of democracy or than a determination of the people's representatives that a measure is necessary to assure the safety of government itself.

Third.—Not every type of speech occupies the same position on the scale of values. There is no substantial public interest in permitting certain kinds of utterances: "the lewd and obscene, the profane, the libelous, and the insulting or 'fighting' words—those which by their very utterance inflict injury or tend to incite an immediate breach of the peace." Chaplinsky *v.* New Hampshire, 315 U.S. 568, 572. We have frequently indicated that the interest in protecting speech depends on the circumstances of the occasion. See Niemotko *v.* Maryland, 340 U.S. at 275–283. It is pertinent to the decision before us to consider where on the scale of values we have in the past placed the type of speech now claiming constitutional immunity.

The defendants have been convicted of conspiring to organize a party of persons who advocate the overthrow of the Government by force and violence. The jury has found that the object of the conspiracy is advocacy as "a rule or principle of action," "by language reasonably and ordinarily calculated to incite persons to such action," and with the intent to cause the overthrow "as speedily as circumstances would permit."

On any scale of values which we have hitherto recognized, speech of this sort ranks low.

Throughout our decisions there has recurred a distinction between the statement of an idea which may prompt its hearers to take unlawful action, and advocacy that such action be taken. The distinction has its root in the conception of the common law that a person who procures another to do an act is responsible for that act as though he had done it himself. . . . We frequently have distinguished protected forms of expression from statements which "incite to violence and crime and threaten the overthrow of organized government by unlawful means." Stromberg *v.* California, 283 U.S. at 369. . . .

The object of the conspiracy before us is clear enough that the chance of error in saying that the defendants conspired to advocate rather than to express ideas is slight. MR. JUSTICE DOUGLAS quite properly points out that the conspiracy before us is not a conspiracy to overthrow the Government. But it would be equally wrong to treat it as a seminar in political theory.

These general considerations underlie decision of the case before us.

On the one hand is the interest in security. The Communist Party was not designed by these defendants as an ordinary political party. For the circumstances of its organization, its aims and methods, and the relation of the defendants to its organization and aims we are concluded by the jury's verdict. The jury found that the Party rejects the basic premise of our political system—that change is to be brought about by nonviolent constitutional process. The jury found that the Party advocates the theory that there is a duty and necessity to overthrow the Government by force and violence. It found that the Party entertains and promotes this view, not as a prophetic insight or as a bit of unworldly speculation, but as a program for winning adherents and as a policy to be translated into action.

In finding that the defendants violated the statute, we may not treat as established fact that the Communist Party in this country is of significant size, well-organized, well-disciplined, conditioned to embark on unlawful activity when given the command. But in determining whether application of the statute to the defendants is within the constitutional powers of Congress, we are not limited to the facts found by the jury. We must view such a question in the light of whatever is relevant to a legislative judgment. We may take judicial notice that the Communist doctrines which these defendants have conspired to advocate are in the ascendency in powerful nations who cannot be acquitted of unfriendliness to the institutions of this country. We may take account of evidence brought forward at this trial and elsewhere, much of which has long been common knowledge. In sum, it would amply justify a legislature in concluding that recruitment of additional members for the Party would create a substantial danger to national security.

In 1947, it has been reliably reported, at least 60,000 members were enrolled in the Party. Evidence was introduced in this case that the membership was organized in small units, linked by an intricate chain of command, and protected by elaborate precautions designed to prevent disclosure of individual identity. There are no reliable data tracing acts of sabotage or espionage directly to these defendants. But a Canadian Royal Commission appointed in 1946 to investigate espionage reported that it was "overwhelmingly established" that "the Communist movement was the principal base within which the espionage network was recruited." The most notorious spy in recent history was led into the service of the Soviet Union through Communist indoctrination. Evidence supports the conclusion that members of the Party seek and occupy positions of importance in political and labor organizations. Congress was not barred by the Constitution from believing that indifference to such experience would be an exercise not of freedom but of irresponsibility.

On the other hand is the interest in free speech. The right to exert all governmental powers in aid of maintaining our institutions and resisting their physical overthrow does not include intolerance of opinions and speech that cannot do harm although opposed and perhaps alien to dominant, traditional opinion. The treatment of its minorities, especially their legal position, is among the most searching tests of the level of civilization attained by a society. It is better for those who have almost unlimited power of government in their hands to err on the side of freedom. We have enjoyed so much freedom for so long that we are perhaps in danger of forgetting how much blood it cost to establish the Bill of Rights. . . .

We must not overlook the value of that interchange. Freedom of expression is the well-spring of our civilization—the civilization we seek to maintain and further by recognizing the right of Congress to put some limitation upon expression. Such are the paradoxes of life. For social development of trial and error, the fullest possible opportunity for the free play of the human mind is an indispensable prerequisite. The history of civilization is in considerable measure the displacement of error which once held sway as official truth by beliefs which in turn have yielded to other truths. Therefore the liberty of man to search for truth ought not to be fettered, no matter what orthodoxies he may challenge. Liberty of thought soon shrivels without freedom of expression. Nor can truth be pursued in an atmosphere hostile to the endeavor or under dangers which are hazarded only by heroes. . . .

It is not for us to decide how we would adjust the clash of interests which this case presents were the primary responsibility for reconciling it ours. Congress has determined that the danger created by advocacy of overthrow justifies the ensuing restriction on freedom of speech. The determination was made after due deliberation, and the seriousness of the congressional purpose is attested by the volume of legislation passed to effectuate the same ends.

Can we then say that the judgment Congress exercised was denied it by the Constitution? Can we establish a constitutional doctrine which forbids the elected representatives of the people to make this choice? Can we hold that the First Amendment deprives Congress of what it deemed necessary for the Government's protection?

To make validity of legislation depend on judicial reading of events still in the womb of time—a forecast, that is, of the outcome of forces at best appreciated only with knowledge of the topmost secrets of nations—is to charge the judiciary with duties beyond its equipment. We do not expect courts to pronounce historic verdicts on bygone events. Even historians have conflicting views to this day on the origin and conduct of the French Revolution. It is as absurd to be confident that we can measure the present clash of forces and their outcome as to ask us to read history still enveloped in clouds of controversy. . . .

Even when moving strictly within the limits of constitutional adjudication, judges are concerned with issues that may be said to involve vital finalities. The too easy transition from disapproval of what is undesirable to condemnation as unconstitutional, has led some of the wisest judges to question the wisdom of our scheme in lodging such authority in courts. But it is relevant to remind that in sustaining the power of Congress in a case like this nothing irrevocable is done. The democratic process at all events is not impaired or restricted. Power and responsibility remain with the people and immediately with their representation. All the Court says is that Congress was not forbidden by the Constitution to pass this enactment and a prosecution under it may be brought against a conspiracy such as the one before us.

The wisdom of the assumptions underlying the legislation and prosecution is another matter. In finding that Congress has acted within its power, a judge does not remotely imply that he favors the implications that lie beneath the legal issues. Considerations there enter which go beyond the criteria that are binding upon judges within the narrow confines of their legitimate authority. . . .

Civil liberties draw at best only limited strength from legal guaranties. Preoccupation by our people with the constitutionality, instead of with the wisdom of legislation or of executive action, is preoccupation with a false value. Even those who would most freely use the judicial brake on the democratic process by invalidating legislation that goes deeply against their grain, acknowledge, at least by paying lip service, that constitutionality does not exact a sense of proportion or the sanity of humor or an absence of fear. Focusing attention on constitutionality tends to make constitutionality synonymous with wisdom. When legislation touches freedom of thought and freedom of speech, such a tendency is a formidable enemy of the free spirit.

Much that should be rejected as illiberal, because repressive and envenoming, may well be not unconstitutional. The ultimate reliance for the deepest needs of civilization must be found outside their vindication in courts of law; apart from all else, judges, howsoever they may conscientiously seek to discipline themselves against it, unconsciously are too apt to be moved by the deep undercurrents of public feeling. A persistent, positive translation of the liberating faith into the feelings and thoughts and actions of men and women is the real protection against attempts to strait-jacket the human mind. Such temptations will have their way, if fear and hatred are not exorcized. The mark of a truly civilized man is confidence in the strength and security derived from the inquiring mind. We may be grateful for such honest comforts as it supports, but we must be unafraid of its uncertitudes. Without open minds there can be no open society. And if society be not open the spirit of man is mutilated and becomes enslaved.

MR. JUSTICE JACKSON, concurring.

This prosecution is the latest of never-ending, because never successful, quests for some legal formula that will secure an existing order against revolutionary radicalism. It requires us to reappraise, in the light of our own times and conditions, constitutional doctrines devised under other circumstances to strike a balance between authority and liberty.

Activity here charged to be criminal is conspiracy—that defendants conspired to teach and advocate, and to organize the Communist Party to teach and advocate, overthrow and destruction of the Government by force and violence. There is no charge of actual violence or attempt at overthrow.

The principal reliance of the defense in this Court is that the conviction cannot stand under the Constitution because the conspiracy of these defendants presents no "clear and present danger" of imminent or foreseeable overthrow.

Communism . . . appears today as a closed system of thought representing Stalin's version of Lenin's version of Marxism. As an ideology, it is not one of spontaneous protest arising from American working-class experience. It is a complicated system of assumptions, based on European history and conditions, shrouded in an obscure and ambiguous vocabulary, which allures our ultrasophisticated intelligentsia more than our hard-headed working people. From time to time it champions all manner of causes and grievances and makes alliances that may add to its foothold in government or embarrass the authorities.

The Communist Party, nevertheless, does not seek its strength primarily in numbers. Its aim is a relatively small party whose strength is in selected, dedicated, indoctrinated, and rigidly disciplined members. From established policy it tolerates no deviation and no debate. It seeks members that are, or may be, secreted in strategic posts in transportation, communications, industry, government, and especially in labor unions where it can compel employers to accept and retain its members. It also seeks to infiltrate and control organizations of professional and other groups. Through these placements in positions of power it seeks a leverage over society that will make up in power of coercion what it lacks in power of persuasion.

The Communists have no scruples against sabotage, terrorism, assassination, or mob disorder; but violence is not with them, as with the anarchists, an end in itself. The Communist Party advocates force only when prudent and profitable. Their strategy of stealth precludes premature or uncoordinated outbursts of violence, except, of course, when the blame will be placed on shoulders other than their own. They resort to violence as to truth, not as a principle but as an expedient. Force or violence, as they would resort to it, may never be necessary, because infiltration and deception may be enough.

Force would be utilized by the Communist Party not to destroy government but for its capture. The Communist recognizes that an established government in control of modern technology cannot be overthrown by force until it is about ready to fall of its own weight. Concerted uprising, therefore, is to await that contingency and revolution is seen, not as a sudden episode, but as the consummation of a long process.

The United States, fortunately, has experienced Communism only in its preparatory stages and for its pattern of final action must look abroad. Russia, of course, was the pilot Communist revolution, which to the Marxist confirms the Party's assumptions and oints its destiny. But Communist technique in the overturn of a free government was disclosed by the *coup d'état* in which they seized power in Czechoslovakia. There the Communist Party during its preparatory stage claimed and received protection for its freedoms of speech, press, and assembly. Pretending to be but another political party, it eventually was conceded participation in government, where it entrenched reliable members chiefly in control of police and information services. When the government faced a foreign and domestic crisis, the Communist Party had established a leverage strong enough to threaten civil war.

In a period of confusion the Communist plan unfolded and the underground organization came to the surface throughout the country in the form chiefly of labor "action committees." Communist officers of the unions took over transportation and allowed only persons with party permits to travel. Communist printers took over the newspapers and radio and put out only party-approved versions of events. Possession was taken of telegraph and telephone systems and communications were cut off whereever directed by party heads. Communist unions took over the factories, and in the cities a partisan distribution of food was managed by the Communist organization. A virtually bloodless abdication by the elected government admitted the Communists to power, whereupon they instituted a reign of oppression and terror, and ruthlessly denied to all others the freedoms which had sheltered their conspiracy.

The foregoing is enough to indicate that, either by accident or design, the Communist stratagem outwits the anti-anarchist pattern of statute aimed against "overthrow by force and violence" if qualified by the doctrine that only "clear and present danger" of accomplishing that result will sustain the prosecution.

The "clear and present danger" test was an innovation by Mr. Justice Holmes in the Schenck case, reiterated and refined by him and Mr. Justice Brandeis in later cases, all arising before the era of World War II revealed the subtlety and efficacy of modernized revolutionary techniques used by totalitarian parties. In those cases, they were faced with convictions under so-called criminal syndicalism statutes aimed at anarchists but which, loosely construed, had been applied to punish socialism, pacifism, and left-wing ideologies, the charges often resting on far-fetched inferences which, if true, would establish only technical or trivial violations. They proposed "clear and present danger" as a test for the sufficiency of evidence in particular cases.

I would save it, unmodified, for application as a "rule of reason" in the kind of case for which it was devised. When the issue is criminality of a hot-headed speech on a street corner, or circulation of a few incendiary pamphlets, or parading by some zealots behind a red flag, or refusal of a handful of school children to salute our flag, it is not beyond the capacity of the judicial process to gather, comprehend, and weigh the necessary materials for decision whether it is a clear and present danger of substantive evil or a harmless letting off of steam. It is not a prophecy, for the danger in such cases has matured by the time of trial or it was never present.

The test applies and has meaning where a conviction is sought to be based on a speech or writing which does not directly or explicitly advocate a crime but to which such tendency is sought to be attributed by construction or by implication from external circumstances. The formula in such cases favors freedoms that are vital to our society, and, even if sometimes applied too generously, the consequences cannot be grave. But its recent expansion has extended, in particular to Communists, unprecedented immunities. Unless we are to hold our Government captive in a judge-made verbal trap, we must approach the problem of a well-organized, nation-wide conspiracy, such as I have described, as realistically as our predecessors faced the trivialities that were being prosecuted until they were checked with a rule of reason.

I think reason is lacking for applying that test to this case.

If we must decide that this Act and its application are constitutional only if we are convinced that petitioner's conduct creates a "clear and present danger" of violent overthrow, we must appraise imponderables, including international and national phenomena which baffle the best informed foreign offices and our most experienced politicians. We would have to foresee and predict the effectiveness of Communist propaganda, opportunities for infiltration, whether, and when, a time will come that they consider propitious for action, and whether and how fast our existing government will deteriorate. And we would have to speculate as to whether an approaching Communist *coup* would not be anticipated by a nationalistic fascist movement. No doctrine can be sound whose application requires us to make a prophecy of that sort in the guise of a legal decision. The judicial process simply is not adequate to a trial of such far-flung issues. The answers given would reflect our own political predilections and nothing more.

The authors of the clear and present danger test never applied it to a case like this, nor would I. If applied as it is proposed here, it means that the Communist plotting is protected during its period of incubation; its preliminary stages of organization and preparation are immune from the law; the Government can move only after imminent action is manifest, when it would, of course, be too late.

The highest degree of constitutional protection is due to the individual acting without conspiracy. But even an individual cannot claim that the Constitution protects him in advocating or teaching overthrow of government by force or violence. I should suppose no one would doubt that Congress has power to make such attempted overthrow a crime. But the contention is that one has the constitutional right to work up a public desire and will to do what is a crime to attempt. I think direct incitement by speech or writing can be made a crime, and I think there can be a conviction without also proving that the odds favored its success by 99 to 1, or some other extremely high ratio. . . .

As aptly stated by Judge Learned Hand in Masses Publishing Co. *v.*

Patten, 244 F. 535, 540: "One may not counsel or advise others to violate the law as it stands. Words are not only the keys of persuasion, but the triggers of action, and those which have no purport but to counsel the violation of law cannot by any latitude of interpretation be a part of that public opinion which is the final source of government in a democratic state."

Of course, it is not always easy to distinguish teaching or advocacy in the sense of incitement from teaching or advocacy in the sense of exposition or explanation. It is a question of fact in each case.

What really is under review here is a conviction of conspiracy, after a trial for conspiracy, on an indictment charging conspiracy, brought under a statute outlawing conspiracy. With due respect to my colleagues, they seem to me to discuss anything under the sun except the law of conspiracy. One of the dissenting opinions even appears to chide me for "invoking the law of conspiracy." As that is the case before us, it may be more amazing that its reversal can be proposed without even considering the law of conspiracy.

The Constitution does not make conspiracy a civil right. The Court has never before done so and I think it should not do so now. Conspiracies of labor unions, trade associations, and news agencies have been condemned, although accomplished, evidenced and carried out, like the conspiracy here, chiefly by letter-writing, meetings, speeches and organization. Indeed, this Court seems, particularly in cases where the conspiracy has economic ends, to be applying its doctrines with increasing severity. While I consider criminal conspiracy a dragnet device capable of perversion into an instrument of injustice in the hands of a partisan or complacent judiciary, it has an established place in our system of law, and no reason appears for applying it only to concerted action claimed to disturb interstate commerce and withholding it from those claimed to undermine our whole Government.

The basic rationale of the law of conspiracy is that a conspiracy may be an evil in itself, independently of any other evil it seeks to accomplish. Thus, we recently held in Pinkerton *v.* United States, 328 U.S. 640, 643–644, "It has been long and consistently recognized by the Court that the commission of the substantive offense and a conspiracy to commit it are separate and distinct offenses. The power of Congress to separate the two and to affix to each a different penalty is well established. . . . And the plea of double jeopardy is no defense to a conviction for both offenses. . . ."

So far does this doctrine reach that it is well settled that Congress may make it a crime to conspire with others to do what an individual may lawfully do on his own. This principle is illustrated in conspiracies that violate the antitrust laws as sustained and applied by this Court. Although one may raise the prices of his own products, and many, acting without concert, may do so, the moment they conspire to that end they are punishable. The same principle is applied to organized labor. Any workman may quit his work for any reason, but concerted actions to the same end are in some circumstances forbidden. Labor Management Relations Act, 61 Stat. 136, § 8 (b), 29 U.S.C. § 158 (b).

The reasons underlying the doctrine that conspiracy may be a substantive evil in itself, apart from any evil it may threaten, attempt, or accomplish are peculiarly appropriate to conspiratorial Communism.

> The reason for finding criminal liability in case of a combination to effect an unlawful end or to use unlawful means, where none would exist, even though the act contemplated were actually committed by an individual, is that a combination of persons to commit a wrong, either as an end or as a means to an end, is so much more dangerous, because of its increased power to do wrong, because it is more difficult to guard against and prevent the evil designs of a group of persons than of a single person, and because of the terror which fear of such a combination tends to create in the minds of people.[2]

There is lamentation in the dissents about the injustice of conviction in the absence of some overt act. Of course, there has been no general uprising against the Government, but the record is replete with acts to carry out the conspiracy alleged, acts such as always are held sufficient to consummate the crime where the statute requires an overt act.

But the shorter answer is that no overt act is or need be required. The Court, in antitrust cases, early upheld the power of Congress to adopt the ancient common law that makes conspiracy itself a crime. Through Mr. Justice Holmes, it said: "Coming next to the objection that no overt act is laid, the answer is that the Sherman Act punished the conspiracies at which it is aimed on the common law footing—that is to say, it does not make the doing of any act other than the act of conspiring a condition of liability." Nash *v.* United States, 229 U.S. 373, 378. Reiterated, United States *v.* Socony-Vacuum Oil Co., 310 U.S. 150, 252. It is not to be supposed that the power of Congress to protect the Nation's existence is more limited than its power to protect interstate commerce.

Also, it is urged that since the conviction is for conspiracy to teach and advocate, and to organize the Communist Party to teach and advocate, the First Amendment is violated, because freedoms of speech and press protect teaching and advocacy regardless of what is taught or advocated. I have never thought that to be the law.

I do not suggest that Congress could punish conspiracy to advocate something, the doing of which it may not punish. Advocacy or exposition of the doctrine of communal property ownership, or any political philosophy unassociated with advocacy of its imposition by force or seizure of govern-

[2] Miller on Criminal Law, 110.

ment by unlawful means could not be reached through conspiracy prosecution. But it is not forbidden to put down force or violence, it is not forbidden to punish its teaching or advocacy, and the end being punishable, there is no doubt of the power to punish conspiracy for the purpose.

The defense of freedom of speech or press has often been raised in conspiracy cases, because, whether committed by Communists, by businessmen, or by common criminals, it usually consists of words written or spoken, evidenced by letters, conversations, speeches or documents. Communication is the essence of every conspiracy, for only by it can common purpose and concert of action be brought about or be proved. However, when labor unions raised the defense of free speech against a conspiracy charge, we unanimously said:

> It rarely has been suggested that the constitutional freedom for speech and press extends its immunity to speech or writing used as an integral part of conduct in violation of a valid criminal statute. We reject the contention now. . . .
>
> Such an expansive interpretation of the constitutional guaranties of speech and press would make it practically impossible ever to enforce laws against agreements in restraint of trade as well as many other agreements and conspiracies deemed injurious to society. Giboney *v.* Empire Storage & Ice Co., 336 U.S. 490, 498, 502. . . .

In conspiracy cases the Court not only has dispensed with proof of clear and present danger but even of power to create a danger: "It long has been settled, however, that a 'conspiracy to commit a crime is a different offense from the crime that is the object of the conspiracy.' Petitioners, for example, might have been convicted here of a conspiracy to monopolize without ever having acquired the power to carry out the object of the conspiracy. . . ." American Tobacco Co. *v.* United States, 328 U.S. 781, 789.

Having held that a conspiracy alone is a crime and its consummation is another, it would be weird legal reasoning to hold that Congress could punish the one only if there was "clear and present danger" of the second. This would compel the Government to prove two crimes in order to convict for one.

When our constitutional provisions were written, the chief forces recognized as antagonists in the struggle between authority and liberty were the Government on the one hand and the individual citizen on the other. It was thought that if the state could be kept in its place the individual could take care of himself.

In more recent times these problems have been complicated by the intervention between the state and the citizen of permanently organized, well-financed, semi-secret and highly disciplined political organizations.

Totalitarian groups here and abroad perfected the technique of creating private paramilitary organizations to coerce both the public government and its citizens. These organizations assert as against our Government all of the constitutional rights and immunities of individuals and at the same time exercise over their followers much of the authority which they deny to the Government. The Communist Party realistically is a state within a state, an authoritarian dictatorship within a republic. It demands these freedoms, not for its members, but for the organized party. It denies to its own members at the same time the freedom to dissent, to debate, to deviate from the party line, and enforces its authoritarian rule by crude purges, if nothing more violent.

The law of conspiracy has been the chief means at the Government's disposal to deal with the growing problems created by such organizations. I happen to think it is an awkward and inept remedy, but I find no constitutional authority for taking this weapon from the Government. There is no constitutional right to "gang up" on the Government.

While I think there was power in Congress to enact this statute and that, as applied in this case, it cannot be held unconstitutional, I add that I have little faith in the long-range effectiveness of this conviction to stop the rise of the Communist movement. Communism will not go to jail with these Communists. No decision by this Court can forestall revolution whenever the existing government fails to command the respect and loyalty of the people and sufficient distress and discontent are allowed to grow up among the masses. Many failures by fallen governments attest that no government can long prevent revolution by outlawry. Corruption, ineptitude, inflation, oppressive taxation, militarization, injustice, and loss of leadership capable of intellectual initiative in domestic or foreign affairs are allies on which the Communists count to bring opportunity knocking to their door. Sometimes I think they may be mistaken. But the Communists are not building just for today—the rest of us might profit by their example.

MR. JUSTICE BLACK, dissenting.

At the outset I want to emphasize what the crime involved in this case is, and what it is not. These petitioners were not charged with an attempt to overthrow the Government. They were not charged with overt acts of any kind designed to overthrow the Government. They were not even charged with saying anything or writing anything designed to overthrow the Government. The charge was that they agreed to assemble and to talk and publish certain ideas at a later date: The indictment is that they conspired to organize the Communist Party and to use speech or newspapers and other publications in the future to teach and advocate the forcible overthrow of the Government. No matter how it is worded, this is a virulent form of prior censorship of speech and press, which I believe the First Amendment forbids. I would hold § 3 of the Smith Act authorizing this prior restraint unconstitutional on its face and as applied.

But let us assume, contrary to all constitutional ideas of fair criminal procedure, that petitioners although not indicted for the crime of actual advocacy, may be punished for it. Even on this radical assumption, the other opinions in this case show that the only way to affirm these convictions is to repudiate directly or indirectly the established "clear and present danger" rule. This the Court does in a way which greatly restricts the protections afforded by the First Amendment. The opinions for affirmance indicate that the chief reason for jettisoning the rule is the expressed fear that advocacy of Communist doctrine endangers the safety of the Republic.

Undoubtedly, a governmental policy of unfettered communication of ideas does entail dangers. To the Founders of this Nation, however, the benefits derived from free expression were worth the risk. They embodied this philosophy in the First Amendment's command that Congress "shall make no law abridging . . . the freedom of speech, or of the press. . . ." I have always believed that the First Amendment is the keystone of our Government, that the freedoms it guarantees provide the best insurance against destruction of all freedom. At least as to speech in the realm of public matters, I believe that the "clear and present danger" test does not "mark the furthermost constitutional boundaries of protected expression" but does "no more than recognize a minimum compulsion of the Bill of Rights." Bridges *v.* California, 314 U.S. 252, 263.

So long as this Court exercises the power of judicial review of legislation, I cannot agree that the First Amendment permits us to sustain laws suppressing freedom of speech and press on the basis of Congress' or our own notions of mere "reasonableness." Such a doctrine waters down the First Amendment so that it amounts to little more than an admonition to Congress. The Amendment as so construed is not likely to protect any but those "safe" or orthodox views which rarely need its protection. I must also express my objection to the holding because, as MR. JUSTICE DOUGLAS' dissent shows, it sanctions the determination of a crucial issue of fact by the judge rather than by the jury. . . .

Public opinion being what it now is, few will protest the conviction of these Communist petitioners. There is hope, however, that in calmer times, when present pressures, passions and fears subside, this or some later Court will restore the First Amendment liberties to the high preferred place where they belong in a free society.

MR. JUSTICE DOUGLAS, dissenting.

If this were a case where those who claimed protection under the First Amendment were teaching the techniques of sabotage, the assassination of the President, the filching of documents from public files, the planting of bombs, the art of street warfare, and the like, I would have no doubts. The freedom to speak is not absolute; the teaching of methods of terror and other seditious conduct should be beyond the pale along with obscenity and immorality. This case was argued as if those were the facts. The argument imported much seditious conduct into the record. That is easy and it has popular appeal, for the activities of Communists in plotting and scheming against the free world are common knowledge.

But the fact is that no such evidence was introduced at the trial. There is a statute which makes a seditious conspiracy unlawful.[3] Petitioners, however, were not charged with a "conspiracy to overthrow" the Government. They were charged with a conspiracy to form a party and groups and assemblies of people who teach and advocate the overthrow of our Government by force or violence and with a conspiracy to advocate and teach its overthrow by force and violence. It may well be that indoctrination in the techniques of terror to destroy the Government would be indictable under either statute. But the teaching which is condemned here is of a different character.

So far as the present record is concerned, what petitioners did was to organize people to teach and themselves teach the Marxist-Leninist doctrine contained chiefly in four books: *Foundations of Leninism* by Stalin (1924), *The Communist Manifesto* by Marx and Engels (1848), *State and Revolution* by Lenin (1917), *History of the Communist Party of the Soviet Union (B)* (1939).[4]

Those books are to Soviet Communism what *Mein Kampf* was to Nazism. If they are understood, the ugliness of Communism is revealed, its deceit and cunning are exposed, the nature of its activities becomes apparent, and the chances of its success less likely. That is not, of course, the reason why petitioners chose these books for their classrooms. They are fervent Communists to whom these volumes are gospel. They preached the creed with the hope that some day it would be acted upon.

The opinion of the Court does not outlaw these texts nor condemn them to the fire, as the Communists do literature offensive to their creed. But if the books themselves are not outlawed, if they can lawfully remain on library shelves, by what reasoning does their use in a classroom become a

[3] 18 U.S.C. § 2384 provides: "If two or more persons in any State or Territory, or in any place subject to the jurisdiction of the United States, conspire to overthrow, put down, or to destroy by force the Government of the United States, or to levy war against them, or to oppose by force the authority thereof, or by force to prevent, hinder, or delay the execution of any law of the United States, or by force to seize, take, or possess any property of the United States contrary to the authority thereof, they shall each be fined not more than $5,000 or imprisoned not more than six years, or both."

[4] Other books taught were *Problems of Leninism* by Stalin, *Strategy and Tactics of World Communism* (H. Doc. No. 619, 80th Cong., 2d Sess.), and *Program of the Communist International.*

crime? It would not be a crime under the Act to introduce these books to a class, though that would be teaching what the creed of violent overthrow of the government is. The Act, as construed, requires the element of intent —that those who teach the creed believe in it. The crime then depends not on what is taught but on who the teacher is. That is to make freedom of speech turn not on *what is said,* but on the *intent* with which it is said. Once we start down that road we enter territory dangerous to the liberties of every citizen.

There was a time in England when the concept of constructive treason flourished. Men were punished not for raising a hand against the king but for thinking murderous thoughts about him. The Framers of the Constitution were alive to that abuse and took steps to see that the practice would not flourish here. Treason was defined to require overt acts—the evolution of a plot against the country into an actual project. The present case is not one of treason. But the analogy is close when the illegality is made to turn on intent, not on the nature of the act. We then start probing men's minds for motive and purpose; they become entangled in the law not for what they did but *for what they thought;* they get convicted not for what they said but for the purpose with which they said it. . . .

The vice of treating speech as the equivalent of overt acts of a treasonable or seditious character is emphasized by a concurring opinion, which by invoking the law of conspiracy makes speech do service for deeds which are dangerous to society. The doctrine of conspiracy has served divers and oppressive purposes and in its broad reach can be made to do great evil. But never until today has anyone seriously thought that the ancient law of conspiracy could constitutionally be used to turn speech into seditious conduct. Yet that is precisely what is suggested.

I repeat that we deal here with speech alone, not with speech *plus* acts of sabotage or unlawful conduct. Not a single seditious act is charged in the indictment. To make a lawful speech unlawful because two men conceive it is to raise the law of conspiracy to appalling proportions. That course is to make a radical break with the past and to violate one of the cardinal principles of our constitutional scheme.

Free speech has occupied an exalted position because of the high service it has given our society. Its protection is essential to the very existence of a democracy. The airing of ideas releases pressures which otherwise might become destructive. When ideas compete in the market for acceptance, full and free discussion exposes the false and they gain few adherents. Full and free discussion even of ideas we hate encourages the testing of our own prejudices and preconceptions. Full and free discussion keeps a society from becoming stagnant and unprepared for the stresses and strains that work to tear all civilizations apart.

Full and free discussion has indeed been the first article of our faith. We have founded our political system on it. It has been the safeguard of every religious, political, philosophical, economic, and racial group amongst us. We have counted on it to keep us from embracing what is cheap and false; we have trusted the common sense of our people to choose the doctrine true to our genius and to reject the rest. This has been the one single outstanding tenet that has made our institutions the symbol of freedom and equality. We have deemed it more costly to liberty to suppress a despised minority than to let them vent their spleen. We have above all else feared the political censor. We have wanted a land where our people can be exposed to all the diverse creeds and cultures of the world.

There comes a time when even speech loses its constitutional immunity. Speech innocuous one year may at another time fan such destructive flames that it must be halted in the interests of the safety of the Republic. That is the meaning of the clear and present danger test. When conditions are so critical that there will be no time to avoid the evil that the speech threatens, it is time to call a halt. Otherwise, free speech which is the strength of the Nation will be the cause of its destruction.

Yet free speech is the rule, not the exception. The restraint to be constitutional must be based on more than fear, on more than passionate opposition against the speech, on more than a revolted dislike for its contents. There must be some immediate injury to society that is likely if speech is allowed. The classic statement of these conditions was made by Mr. Justice Brandeis in his concurring opinion in Whitney *v*. California, 274 U.S. 357, 376–377,

> Fear of serious injury cannot alone justify suppression of free speech and assembly. Men feared witches and burnt women. It is the function of speech to free men from the bondage of irrational fears. To justify suppression of free speech there must be reasonable ground to fear that serious evil will result if free speech is practiced. There must be reasonable ground to believe that the danger apprehended is imminent. There must be reasonable ground to believe that the evil to be prevented is a serious one. Every denunciation of existing law tends in some measure to increase the probability that there will be violation of it. Condonation of a breach enhances the probability. Expressions of approval add to the probability. Propagation of the criminal state of mind by teaching syndicalism increases it. Advocacy of law-breaking heightens it still further. But even advocacy of violation, however reprehensible morally, is not a justification for denying free speech where the advocacy falls short of incitement and there is nothing to indicate that the advocacy would be immediately acted on. The wide difference between advocacy and incitement, between preparation and attempt, between assembling and conspiracy, must be borne in mind. In order to support a finding of a clear and present danger it must be shown either that immediate serious violence was to be expected or was advocated, or that the past conduct furnished reason to believe that such advocacy was then contemplated.
>
> Those who won our independence by revolution were not cowards. They did not fear political change. They did not exalt order at the cost of liberty.

> To courageous, self-reliant men, with confidence in the power of free and fearless reasoning applied through the processes of popular government, no danger flowing from speech can be deemed clear and present, unless the incidence of the evil apprehended is so imminent that it may befall before there is opportunity for full discussion. *If there be time to expose through discussion the falsehood and fallacies to avert the evil by the processes of education, the remedy to be applied is more speech, not enforced silence.* [Italics added by Mr. Justice Douglas.]

I had assumed that the question of the clear and present danger, being so critical an issue in the case, would be a matter for submission to the jury. . . . Yet, whether the question is one for the Court or the jury, there should be evidence of record on the issue.

This record, however, contains no evidence whatsoever showing that the acts charged, *viz.*, the teaching of the Soviet theory of revolution with the hope that it will be realized, have created any clear and present danger to the Nation. The Court, however, rules to the contrary. It says, "The formation by petitioners of such a highly organized conspiracy, with rigidly disciplined members subject to call when the leaders, these petitioners, felt that the time had come for action, coupled with the inflammable nature of world conditions, similar uprisings in other countries, and the touch-and-go nature of our relations with countries with whom petitioners were in the very least ideologically attuned, convince us that their convictions were justified on this score."

That ruling is in my view not responsive to the issue in the case. We might as well say that the speech of petitioners is outlawed because Soviet Russia and her Red Army are a threat to world peace.

The nature of Communism as a force on the world scene would, of course, be relevant to the issue of clear and present danger of petitioners' advocacy within the United States. But the primary consideration is the strength and tactical position of petitioners and their converts in this country. On that there is no evidence in the record. If we are to take judicial notice of the threat of Communists within the nation, it should not be difficult to conclude that *as a political party* they are of little consequence. Communists in this country have never made a respectable or serious showing in any election. I would doubt that there is a village, let alone a city or county or state which the Communists could carry.

Communism in the world scene is no bogey-man; but Communists as a political faction or party in this country plainly is. Communism has been so thoroughly exposed in this country that it has been crippled as a political force. Free speech has destroyed it as an effective political party. It is inconceivable that those who went up and down this country preaching the doctrine of revolution which petitioners espouse would have any success. In days of trouble and confusion when bread lines were long, when the unemployed walked the streets, when people were starving, the advocates of a short-cut by revolution might have a chance to gain adherents. But today there are no such conditions. The country is not in despair; the people know Soviet Communism; the doctrine of Soviet revolution is exposed in all of its ugliness and the American people want none of it.

How it can be said that there is a clear and present danger that this advocacy will succeed is, therefore, a mystery. Some nations less resilient than the United States, where illiteracy is high and where democratic traditions are only budding, might have to take drastic steps and jail these men for merely speaking their creed. But in America they are miserable merchants of unwanted ideas; their wares remain unsold. The fact that their ideas are abhorrent does not make them powerful. . . .

The First Amendment provides that "Congress shall make no law . . . abridging the freedom of speech." The Constitution provides no exception. This does not mean, however, that the Nation need hold its hand until it is in such weakened condition that there is no time to protect itself from incitement to revolution. Seditious conduct can always be punished. But the command of the First Amendment is so clear that we should not allow Congress to call a halt to free speech except in the extreme case of peril from the speech itself.

The First Amendment makes confidence in the common sense of our people and in their maturity of judgment the great postulate of our democracy. Its philosophy is that violence is rarely, if ever, stopped by denying civil liberties to those advocating resort to force. The First Amendment reflects the philosophy of Jefferson "that it is time enough for the rightful purposes of civil government for its officers to interfere when principles break out into overt acts against peace and good order." The political censor has no place in our public debates. Unless and until extreme and necessitous circumstances are shown our aim should be to keep speech unfettered and to allow the processes of law to be invoked only when the provocateurs among us move from speech to action.

Vishinsky wrote in 1948 in *The Law of the Soviet State,* "In our state, naturally there can be no place for freedom of speech, press, and so on for the foes of socialism."

Our concern should be that we accept no such standard for the United States. Our faith should be that our people will never give support to these advocates of revolution, so long as we remain loyal to the purposes for which our Nation was founded.

[Most of the footnotes and many citations to cases have been omitted.]

Distinguishing Forms of Advocacy

YATES ET AL. *V.* UNITED STATES

354 U.S. 298 (1957)

MR. JUSTICE HARLAN delivered the opinion of the Court.

These 14 petitioners stand convicted, after a jury trial in the United States District Court for the Southern District of California, upon a single count indictment charging them with conspiring (1) to advocate and teach the duty and necessity of overthrowing the Government of the United States by force and violence, and (2) to organize, as the Communist Party of the United States, a society of persons who so advocate and teach, all with the intent of causing the overthrow of the Government by force and violence as speedily as circumstances would permit. . . . The conspiracy is alleged to have originated in 1940 and continued down to the date of the indictment in 1951. . . . Upon conviction each of the petitioners was sentenced to five years' imprisonment and a fine of $10,000. . . .

INSTRUCTIONS TO THE JURY

Petitioners contend that the instructions to the jury were fatally defective in that the trial court refused to charge that, in order to convict, the jury must find that the advocacy which the defendants conspired to promote was of a kind calculated to "incite" persons to action for the forcible overthrow of the Government. It is argued that advocacy of forcible overthrow as mere *abstract doctrine* is within the free speech protection of the First Amendment; that the Smith Act, consistently with that constitutional provision, must be taken as proscribing only the sort of advocacy which incites to illegal *action;* and that the trial court's charge, by permitting conviction for mere advocacy, unrelated to its tendency to produce forcible action, resulted in an unconstitutional application of the Smith Act. The Government, which at the trial also requested the court to charge in terms of "incitement," now takes the position, however, that the true constitutional dividing line is not between inciting and abstract advocacy of forcible overthrow, but rather between advocacy as such, irrespective of its inciting qualities, and the mere discussion or exposition of violent overthrow as an abstract theory. . . .

After telling the jury that it could not convict the defendants for holding or expressing mere opinions, beliefs, or predictions relating to violent overthrow, the trial court defined the content of the proscribed advocacy or teaching in the following terms, which are crucial here:

> Any advocacy or teaching which does not include the urging of force and violence as the means of overthrowing and destroying the Government of the United States is not within the issue of the indictment here and can constitute no basis for any finding against the defendants.
>
> The kind of advocacy and teaching which is charged and upon which your verdict must be reached is not merely a desirability but a necessity that the Government of the United States be overthrown and destroyed by force and violence and not merely a propriety but a duty to overthrow and destroy the Government of the United States by force and violence.

There can be no doubt from the record that in so instructing the jury the court regarded as immaterial, and intended to withdraw from the jury's consideration, any issue as to the character of the advocacy in terms of its capacity to stir listeners to forcible action. Both the petitioners and the Government submitted proposed instructions which would have required the jury to find that the proscribed advocacy was not of a mere abstract doctrine of forcible overthrow, but of action to that end, by the use of language reasonably and ordinarily calculated to incite persons to such action. The trial court rejected these proposed instructions on the ground that any necessity for giving them which may have existed at the time the Dennis case was tried was removed by this Court's subsequent decision in that case. The court made it clear in colloquy with counsel that in its view the illegal advocacy was made out simply by showing that what was said dealt with forcible overthrow and that it was uttered with a specific intent to accomplish that purpose, insisting that all such advocacy was punishable "whether in language of incitement or not." . . .

We are thus faced with the question whether the Smith Act prohibits advocacy and teaching of forcible overthrow as an abstract principle, divorced from any effort to instigate action to that end, so long as such advocacy or teaching is engaged in with evil intent. We hold that it does not.

The distinction between advocacy of abstract doctrine and advocacy directed at promoting unlawful action is one that has been consistently recognized in the opinions of this Court, beginning with Fox *v.* Washington, 236 U.S. 273, and Schenck *v.* United States, 249 U.S. 47. This distinction was heavily underscored in Gitlow *v.* New York, 268 U.S. 652, in which the statute involved was nearly identical with the one now before us. . . . The legislative history of the Smith Act and related bills shows beyond all question that Congress was aware of the distinction between the advocacy or teaching of abstract doctrine and the advocacy or teaching of action, and that it did not intend to disregard it. . . .

In failing to distinguish between advocacy of forcible overthrow as an abstract doctrine and advocacy of action to that end, the District Court appears to have been led astray by the holding in Dennis that advocacy of violent action to be taken at some future time was enough. It seems to have considered that, since "inciting" speech is usually thought of as calculated to induce immediate action, and since Dennis held advocacy of action for future overthrow sufficient, this meant that advocacy, irrespective of its tendency to generate action, is punishable, provided only that it is uttered with a specific intent to accomplish overthrow. In other words, the District Court apparently thought that Dennis obliterated the traditional dividing line between advocacy of abstract doctrine and advocacy of action. . . .

In light of the foregoing we are unable to regard the District Court's charge upon this aspect of the case as adequate. The jury was never told that the Smith Act does not denounce advocacy in the sense of preaching abstractly the forcible overthrow of the Government. We think that the trial court's statement that the proscribed advocacy must include the "urging," "necessity," and "duty" of forcible overthrow, and not merely its "desirability" and "propriety," may not be regarded as a sufficient substitute for charging that the Smith Act reaches only advocacy of action for the overthrow of government by force and violence. The essential distinction is that those to whom the advocacy is addressed must be urged to *do* something, now or in the future, rather than merely to *believe* in something. . . .

Granting . . . that it was not necessary even that the trial court should have employed the particular term "incite," it was nevertheless incumbent on the court to make clear in some fashion that the advocacy must be of action and not merely abstract doctrine. The instructions given not only do not employ the word "incite," but also avoid the use of such terms and phrases as "action," "call for action," "as a rule or principle of action," and so on, all of which were offered in one form or another by both the petitioners and the Government.

What we find lacking in the instructions here is illustrated by contrasting them with the instructions given to the Dennis jury, upon which this Court's sustaining of the convictions in that case was bottomed. There the trial court charged:

> In further construction and interpretation of the statute [the Smith Act] I charge you that it is *not the abstract doctrine* of overthrowing or destroying organized government by unlawful means which is denounced by this law, but the teaching and advocacy *of action* for the accomplishment of that purpose, *by language reasonably and ordinarily calculated to incite persons to such action.* Accordingly, you cannot find the defendants or any of them guilty of the crime charged unless you are satisfied beyond a reasonable doubt that they conspired . . . to advocate and teach the duty

and necessity of overthrowing or destroying the Government of the United States by force and violence, with the intent that such teaching and advocacy *be of a rule or principle of action* and *by language reasonably and ordinarily calculated to incite persons to such action,* all with the intent to cause the overthrow . . . as speedily as circumstances would permit. (Emphasis added.) 341 U.S., at 511–512.

We recognize that distinctions between advocacy or teaching of abstract doctrines, with evil intent, and that which is directed to stirring people to action, are often subtle and difficult to grasp, for in a broad sense, as Mr. Justice Holmes said in his dissenting opinion in Gitlow, *supra,* at 673: "Every idea is an incitement." But the very subtlety of these distinctions required the most clear and explicit instructions with reference to them, for they concerned an issue which went to the very heart of the charges against these petitioners. . . .

The judgment of the Court of Appeals is reversed, and the case remanded to the District Court for further proceedings consistent with this opinion.

It is so ordered.

[Mr. Justice Burton concurred in the result and agreed with the above portion of the Court's opinion. Justices Brennan and Whittaker took no part in the consideration of this case.]

MR. JUSTICE BLACK, with whom MR. JUSTICE DOUGLAS joins, concurring in part and dissenting in part.

I agree with the Court insofar as it holds that the trial judge erred in instructing that persons could be punished under the Smith Act for teaching and advocating forceful overthrow as an abstract principle. But on the other hand, I cannot agree that the instruction which the Court indicates it might approve is constitutionally permissible. The Court says that persons can be punished for advocating action to overthrow the Government by force and violence, where those to whom the advocacy is addressed are urged "to *do* something, now or in the future, rather than merely to *believe* in something." Under the Court's approach, defendants could still be convicted simply for agreeing to talk as distinguished from agreeing to act. I believe that the First Amendment forbids Congress to punish people for talking about public affairs, whether or not such discussion incites to action, legal or illegal. See Meiklejohn, *Free Speech and Its Relation to Self-Government.* Cf. Chafee, "Book Review," 62 *Harv. L. Rev.* 891. As the Virginia Assembly said in 1785, in its "Statute for Religious Liberty," written by Thomas Jefferson, "it is time enough for the rightful purposes of civil government, for its officers to interfere when principles break out into overt acts against peace and good order. . . ."

MR. JUSTICE CLARK, dissenting. . . .

The conspiracy includes the same group of defendants as in the Dennis case though petitioners here occupied a lower echelon in the party hierarchy. They, nevertheless, served in the same army and were engaged in the same mission. The convictions here were based upon evidence closely paralleling that adduced in Dennis and in United States *v.* Flynn, 216 F. (2d) 354 (C.A. 2d Cir. 1954), both of which resulted in convictions. This Court laid down in Dennis the principles governing such prosecutions and they were closely adhered to here, although the nature of the two cases did not permit identical handling. . . .

I have studied the section of the opinion concerning the instructions and frankly its "artillery of words" leaves me confused as to why the majority concludes that the charge as given was insufficient. I thought that Dennis merely held that a charge was sufficient where it requires a finding that "the Party advocates the theory that there is a duty and necessity to overthrow the Government by force and violence. . . . not as a prophetic insight or as a bit of . . . speculation, but as a program for winning adherents and as a policy to be translated into action" as soon as the circumstances permit. 341 U.S., at 546–547 (concurring opinion). I notice however that to the majority

> The essence of the Dennis holding was that indoctrination of a group in preparation for future violent action, as well as exhortation to immediate action, by advocacy found to be directed to "action for the accomplishment" of forcible overthrow, to violence "as a rule or principle of action," and employing "language of incitement," *id.*, at 511–512, is not constitutionally protected when the group is of sufficient size and cohesiveness, is sufficiently oriented towards action, and other circumstances are such as reasonably to justify apprehension that action will occur.

I have read this statement over and over but do not seem to grasp its meaning for I see no resemblance between it and what the respected Chief Justice wrote in Dennis, nor do I find any such theory in the concurring opinions. As I see it, the trial judge charged in essence all that was required under the Dennis opinions, whether one takes the view of the Chief Justice or of those concurring in the judgment. Apparently what disturbs the Court now is that the trial judge here did not give the Dennis charge although both the prosecution and the defense asked that it be given. Since he refused to grant these requests I suppose the majority feels that there must be some difference between the two charges, else the one that was given in Dennis would have been followed here. While there may be some distinctions between the charges, as I view them they are without material difference. I find, as the majority intimates, that the distinctions are too "subtle and difficult to grasp."

Topic 13

LOYALTY AND SECURITY

Security and Freedom

SIDNEY HOOK *

The quest for security in human life, like the quest for certainty in human knowledge, has many sources. All are rooted in man's finitude in a complex world of danger and mystery. Of the varied methods man has pursued to reduce the dangers and cope with the mysteries, the way of piecemeal knowledge and continuous experiment has been most fruitful. For it is in the fields in which human knowledge has foresworn the quest for absolute certainty, as in the scientific disciplines, that it has proved both reliable and capable of winning universal agreement. On the other hand, in the fields in which the strongest claims to certainty have been made—politics and philosophy—there is the least agreement.

Because absolute certainty in human affairs is impossible, absolute security is impossible. Unless we are aware of this, the price we pay for straining to achieve an impossible ideal may result in netting us less security than would otherwise be attainable. This is not an unusual phenomenon: it is observable in large things and small. The man who strives for absolute health may end up a valetudinarian. The man who won't venture on the highways until they are accident-proof may as well not own an automobile; and if he crawls along playing it supersafe, traffic-enforcement authorities tell us he adds to the dangers of the road.

The real problem, then, is not one of absolute security, or security in general. It is always one of achieving more and better security in meeting specific hazards in a particular area of risk and uncertainty—and meeting them in such a way that we do not lose more by the methods we use than by the disasters we would prevent. . . .

The McCarthy episode in American history was a test of political judgment and political morality. Those who dismissed him as an unimportant phenomenon or extenuated his methods in the light of his goals

* Chairman of the Department of Philosophy, New York University. Author of *Heresy, Yes—Conspiracy, No!; Common Sense and the Fifth Amendment;* and other books. The selection is from *Political Power and Personal Freedom* (New York, Criterion Books, Inc., 1959), pp. 235–249. By permission.

failed the tests of both judgment and morality. So did those who exaggerated his power, who proclaimed that he had transformed America into a police state, and who fought McCarthy with the weapons of McCarthy instead of the weapons of truth. Even at the height of McCarthy's power a more rational view was not impossible. . . .

"Security is like liberty," writes Mr. Justice Jackson in one of his dissenting opinions, "in that many are the crimes that have been committed in its name." Yet he would be the first to admit that this is no more warrant for abandoning the quest for reasonable rules of security than for relinquishing the struggle for a more humane conception of liberty. . . .

After the Seventh Congress of the Communist International, the Communists kidnaped the vocabulary of American liberalism. This "corruption of the word," as I called it then, made it easier for some sentimental liberals to interpret sharp criticisms of Communism as oblique attacks on liberalism, if not a first step towards Fascism. In liberal circles to be an anti-Fascist was always honorable. But to be anti-Communist, especially during the war years, invited distrust. That liberals had a stake in the survival of the democratic system whose defects they could freely criticize under the ground rules of the Bill of Rights was granted, of course. That they therefore also had a stake in preventing the ground rules from being abused, that they had a responsibility to think about the problem, was resolutely ignored. . . .

Instead of offering a viable alternative to eliminate or reduce these injustices, they wrote as if the only problem was to develop more efficient methods of detecting acts of espionage *after* they had been committed. They thereby revealed the extent of their misunderstanding. Not the acts prevented but those which are discovered create public disquietude, because they give the impression that many more remain undiscovered and beyond the reach of prosecution in virtue of the statute of limitations. . . .

Recent experience, or a study of recent history, should make it possible for the liberal to acquire a reliable knowledge of the whole costumer's shop of organizational masks cleverly designed by Communist technicians to take in the unwary until the time comes for the sacrificial slaughter. If he believes that there is a foreign threat to the survival of the liberal community, he cannot withhold assent from the dictum of Roger Baldwin, former head of the American Civil Liberties Union, that "a superior loyalty to a foreign government disqualifies a citizen from service to our own." It does not disqualify the citizen from protection of the Bill of Rights, but the right to government service is not an integral part of the Bill of Rights.

It is the liberal *attitude,* however, which is most crucial in the reasonable administration of a security program. Just as only those who love children can be trusted to discipline them without doing psychological harm, so only those who love freedom can be trusted to devise appropriate safeguards without throttling intellectual independence or smothering all but the mediocre in blankets of regulations. No safeguards are appropriate or even efficient which impose conformity of belief or inhibit intellectual spontaneity. The fresh and unfamiliar solution to difficulties depends on a certain imaginative daring and a receptivity to such solutions by those in a position of authority. A liberal with a sense of history is aware of the possibility that in a specific situation there may be a sharp conflict between the legitimate demands of national security and the freedom of the individual. But on balance, and in perspective, he is convinced that the two are not in opposition. In the very interest of a freely expressed dissent, some security measures are required to protect the institutional processes which, however imperfectly, reflect a freely given consent. At the same time, the faith and practices of freedom, indeed, an almost religious veneration for the *élan* of the free spirit, may generate a sense of security even in the shadows of war. . . .

The argument and evidence can be put briefly. The one unshakeable dogma in the Bolshevik faith is that the Soviet Union is not safe from attack so long as the "capitalistic democracies" of the West—and not only the United States but also countries like Great Britain and France—exist. Let not those who in the past assured us that Hitler's racial myth and ideology of world conquest were "just words" tell us again that ideologies do not count in politics and history. If anything, the Kremlin has gone further than Hitler because it has publicly proclaimed that "encirclement" is a *political,* not a geographical, concept. The Communist parties of the West . . . have as their *first* function the defense of the Soviet Union. Instructions are explicit to all of them to organize secretly (as well as publicly) even in "the freest" and "most democratic" countries and to infiltrate into strategic centers. This type of activity has been extensively carried on for years especially during the days of the popular front struggle against the Nazis. Even during the war which Hitler forced on the Soviets, the Kremlin engaged in the most comprehensive types of espionage against its Allies as part of the underlying struggle which, according to their fanatical conviction, must end either with the victory of the West or the Soviet power.

Because it can count on the devotion *à outrance* of Communist nationals of other countries, many of them highly trained, intelligent and inspired by a misguided idealism which does not see under the flowers of official rhetoric the chains of Soviet control on its own people, the Kremlin possesses an incomparable advantage over the West. For one thing, it is the best informed regime in the world. . . .

Although one would hardly suspect it from present attitudes to security in many circles in those countries, it is from Canadian and British sources that we have the most incontrovertible, if not the weightiest evidence, of how Communist parties are involved in the espionage nets the Soviet Union has spun around the free world.[1]

Since the Kremlin combines this belief in the inevitablity of war with a dialectical conception according to which a sudden attack or offense, as in Korea, is the best method of defense and because of the centralized organization of western industrial life, the location of America's undispersed plants, and the evolution of thermonuclear weapons, an attempt at a sudden knockout blow cannot be ruled out as a possibility. Since Bolshevik morality is confessedly subordinate to what will further the victory of the "proletarian dictatorship"—indeed, this is *the whole* of their morality—the possession of information about strategic weakness on the part of the West, or the hope that a sudden blow may prevent instant retaliatory action, may make a decisive difference to the Kremlin in resolving to launch the Blitzkreig which will end "the final struggle." It does not require many persons to betray the key secrets of the radar defense of a nation.

The consequences of less extreme suppositions may be equally disastrous. The free world cannot deploy its defense forces everywhere. Its decisions where to stand, where to fight, once known to the Kremlin, give the latter a flexibility that it can exploit most skillfully to draw the world bit by bit into its orbit. On the other hand, there is no possibility for the free world to build up a counterweight within the Soviet sphere to redress the balance. No democratic Jeffersonian or Millsian International exists with affiliated parties in the Soviet world.

Does it follow that *every* member of the Communist party is an espionage agent ready to do the bidding of his superiors and betray his country? Is it not possible that some members of the Communist party may be loyal to their own government rather than to the Soviet Union? The best answer to these questions was made by Mr. Clement Attlee, Prime Minister at the time when Pontecorvo, scientifically a much more gifted man than Fuchs, fled from England. "There is no way," said Mr. Attlee who never chased a witch in his life, "of distinguishing such people [hypothetically loyal Communists] from those who, if opportunity offered, would be prepared to endanger the security of the state in the interests of another power. The Government has, therefore, reached the conclusion that the only prudent course to adopt is to ensure that no one who is known to be

[1] Cf. *The Report of the Royal Commission to Investigate the Facts Relating to and Circumstances Surrounding the Communication by Public Officials and Other Persons in Positions of Trust of Secret and Confidential Information to Agents of a Foreign Power* (Ottawa, 1946); also Alexander Foote's *Handbook for Spies* (London, 1949).

a member of the Communist party, *or to be associated with it in such a way as to raise legitimate doubts about his or her reliability* (my italics), is employed in connection with work, the nature of which is vital to the security of the State." It is well to remember that a clerk in a code office or even those who empty trash baskets may have access to material bearing on national security. Mr. Attlee apparently believes that if we distinguish between legal guilt and *moral* or professional guilt or unfitness, and between association by happenstance and association by cooperation, then there certainly can be and is "guilt by association." . . .

It is the gravest error to imagine that anyone in America, even Senator McCarthy who helped the Communist cause throughout the world, believed for a moment that the Communists constituted a domestic danger. But American public opinion was aroused by a series of incidents over a span of three years which seemed to show that in the international field the position of the American government was being weakened by Soviet agents.

The first was the Hiss case and the revelations that several interlocking rings of Communist conspirators had been active in high places for years. It remains mystifying that many of these individuals continued working in strategic places, one even at the Aberdeen Weapons Proving Grounds, many years after the chief operatives had been identified by former members of the Communist party. The worst of these revelations came after Mr. Truman had dismissed the Hiss case as a "red herring." Following Hiss's conviction, Wadleigh's confession, and a long line of refusals to answer questions about espionage on the ground that a truthful answer would tend to be self-incriminating, the implication was natural, and in part justified, that the government had been lax or indifferent in taking intelligent safeguards. As the Dexter White case shows, the Truman administration feared that its opponents would make political capital out of the presence of Communist espionage agents in the government and tried to hush up matters. This narrow political partisanship by no means warranted the charge of "treason" or of coddling treason hurled by some Republicans against the Democrats. There is no reason to believe that had the former been in power, they would have acted more wisely. But the country never really recovered from the shock of learning that publicly sworn testimony, some of it legally substantiated where the charges were contested, showed that persons holding the following positions were members of the secret Communist underground apparatus:

an Executive Assistant to the President of the United States
an Assistant Secretary of the Treasury
the Director of the Office of Special Political Affairs for the State Department
the Secretary of the International Monetary Fund

Head of Latin-American Division of the Office of Strategic Services
a member of the National Labor Relations Board
Secretary of the National Labor Relations Board
Chief Counsel, Senate Subcommittee on Civil Liberties
Chief, Statistical Analysis Branch, War Production Board
Treasury Department Representative and Adviser in Financial Control Division of the North African Board of UNRRA, and at the meeting of the Council of Foreign Ministers in Moscow
Director, National Research Project of the Works Progress Administration

These were not the only, but only the most conspicuous, positions Communists filled. The *actual* amount of damage done, however, is difficult to assess and probably will never be known. But no reasonable person can doubt the existence of a planned pattern of infiltration whose significance can be better gauged by the European reader if he draws up a comparable list of posts in his own government and fills them, in his mind's eye, with Communist espionage agents.

The second series of incidents began with the Fuchs case which broke after several outstanding scientists had dismissed the idea that atomic espionage was possible. "There are no secrets" declared the very scientists who in 1939 and 1940 had imposed upon themselves a voluntary secrecy in publications to prevent Hitler from developing nuclear power. Subsequent trials in the United States of the Communist spies associated with Fuchs produced evidence that there were others deep underground.

All this was still very much in the public mind when Truman announced that the Soviet Union had exploded its first atomic bomb, thus eliminating the monopoly of atomic power which, according to Churchill and other Europeans, had prevented the Red Army from marching west after American and British demobilization. The head of the United States Atomic Energy Commission observed that Soviet espionage had made it possible for the Soviet Union to save years of costly experiment (an observation officially repeated by President Eisenhower on October 8, 1953, after the U.S.S.R. had exploded a thermonuclear bomb).[2]

[2] As early as 1950 some scientists holding high official positions had charged that the Soviet Union had acquired through espionage the "know-how" to make hydrogen bombs. *The New York Times* of July 20, 1950, quoted François Perrin, Joint Commissioner for Atomic Energy in France, as saying that Russia, through its espionage network, had certainly obtained the know-how to make the hydrogen bomb. The same report appeared in *The San Francisco Chronicle* of July 23, 1950. At the time Professor Perrin's co-commissioner was Irene Joliot-Curie, wife of Frederic Joliot-Curie, later dismissed from the post as High Commissioner for Atomic Energy because of his pro-Soviet activities. Frederic Joliot-Curie subsequently charged that the U.S. was waging bacterial germ warfare in Korea and spurned the proposal of a Committee of Nobel Prize Winners to conduct an objective international inquiry into the truth of his charges.

Finally came the loss of China and the charge that some of the advisors and consultants to the State Department on Far Eastern affairs not only had long records of Communist association but had followed the twists and turns of the Party line. Some like L. Rossinger who fell back on the Fifth Amendment were identified as members of the Communist party. Although there was no legal proof of the identification by Budenz of Lattimore as a top Soviet agent, there could be no reasonable doubt that he was a fellow-traveler whose justification of the Moscow frame-up trials was very brazen. Whatever the degree of their Communism, it seemed indisputable that a group in the State Department had been urging the abandonment of all support to Chiang Kai-shek despite the absence of any alternative to Communist triumph. The defeat of Chiang may have been unavoidable, but the evidence that American Communists and their sympathizers had actively worked for his downfall by attempting to influence official channels was unmistakable.

These events, together with other trials involving Communist espionage and perjury, and the multiplication of cases of refusal to answer questions on the ground that a truthful answer would tend to be self-incriminatory, contributed to the prevalent feeling that the United States was being weakened in the cold war on whose outcome so many things, both domestic and international, depend. The Korean war exacerbated the mood. Had these events, especially the pattern of their succession, occurred in other countries, it is not likely that they would have been met with complacency.

The concern of the American people with the question of Communist penetration, in the light of the evidence, was legitimate enough. Questionable only was the character of the reaction to it on the part of the government. Buffeted by cultural vigilantes on the one side and ritualistic liberals on the other, it swung from one position to another, pleasing no one with its eclecticism. Almost all of the excesses of loyalty and security programs are attributable to the incredible political ignorance and naiveté of the personnel of the Review Boards. It was not the procedures themselves which were at fault, because oddly enough American procedures in crucial respects are fairer than the English. For example, in hearings before English boards, civil servants under investigation are rarely, if ever, told of the evidence against them. They are also denied rights of legal counsel, and even of representation. Nonetheless, American procedures worked hardship and injustices because instead of being administered by knowledgeable men and women with a little common sense who had some political experience, they were entrusted to investment bankers, corporation lawyers, army and navy officers, small town officials, or Republican or Democratic party regulars to whom Communist language was gobbledygook, Communist ideas suspiciously like the ideas of socialists, do-gooders and even New Dealers, and Communist organizations with the distinctions between member, sympathizer, front, dupe, innocent, and honest mistaken liberal, as mysterious as the order of beings in the science of angelology.

In the light of the above, the answer to our final question regarding the relative unconcern of other nations to the problem of Communist penetration is not hard to give. The greatest Soviet effort was directed against the United States as the Kremlin's chief and strongest enemy. Since 1939 the United States has been the center of atomic weapons research and development. Its policies are more fateful for the U.S.S.R. than those of any other single nation. To make these policies miscarry, to delay, distort and abort government directives pays rich political dividends. The Kremlin is quite aware of the fact that a defeat or paralysis of the United States would mean the end of the independence of Austria, France and Italy. Further, the Communist movement in the United States is not a mass party and, in all likelihood, will never become one. But it has a solid core of some thousands of hardened "professional revolutionists." From the Soviet viewpoint they are expendable. What is more natural, therefore, than to employ them for all sorts of conspiratorial purposes from direct espionage to the capture of small but key unions, to the seeding of government services with "sleepers"? A few thousand totally dedicated persons, working underground with the help of a sympathetic periphery of several times that size, can cause a great many headaches. Countries like Austria need not worry about the problem, one is tempted to observe, because it wouldn't make a difference if they did. There isn't much the Kremlin can learn from them and an attempt at a Communist putsch on Czechoslovakian lines, so long as the United States is still strong, risks a war for which at the moment the U.S.S.R. is unready. Countries like France and Italy, on the other hand, which have mass Communist parties and where infiltration and underground organization are not inconsiderable can hardly solve the problem without facing crippling strikes and extensive public disorders. Too weak to act they sometimes pretend that there is no need for action. *They can live with the Communist menace only because the United States is free of it and only so long as the United States is strong enough to restrain the Soviet Union from overrunning the free world.*

Only those who are ignorant of the stupendous extent of Soviet infiltration and espionage over the years, the complexity of its patterns and its potential for harm, can sneer at the problems of security in the free world. It is not enough to shout slogans—whether of security or freedom. What is required is creative intelligence to devise just and effective procedures which will protect the free cultures of the world from their hidden enemies without making less free those who are not its hidden enemies.

These procedures must be flexible. They cannot be formalized into a code without inviting abuses. They must be devised and administered by civil libertarians who are familiar with Communist theory and who have studied Communist conspiratorial practice. They must be applied discreetly, without fanfare, without developing a climate of public concern. And their primary function must be effective prevention rather than exemplary punishment.

Critique of the Loyalty Program

L. A. NIKOLORIĆ *

Established by the President's Executive Order 9835 in March, 1947, the government's loyalty program . . . presents a complex problem: whether, in the name of "loyalty" and "national security," our society is justified in abusing most of the basic tenets of Anglo-American jurisprudence and legal philosophy traditional since the seventeenth century.

The purpose of the program is not to discharge employees expressly because of what they have done in the past. President Truman has stated that it is aimed at "potentially disloyal" persons who, because of attitudes and ideas they entertain today or subscribed to yesterday, might in the future undertake action contrary to the best interests of the United States. The basic concept of the program—to ferret out the "potentially disloyal" —violates a most important principle of Anglo-American law: that one cannot be punished for merely considering the commission of a crime, or for thinking in such a way that a body determines that one might undertake action contrary to the law. . . .

The loyalty program also distorts the concept of equal justice under the law. It assumes that a democratic government may exact from its employees special standards of conduct wholly offensive to constitutional guarantees of freedom and justice as applied to ordinary citizens. We deny two and a half million government employees political and intellectual freedoms in order to protect ourselves from the potentially subversive.

These innovations are spreading not only to some three and a half million state and local employees (the County of Los Angeles, among other local governments, has instituted a loyalty check), but elsewhere. The AFL and the CIO have undertaken to purge the Communists. The Army, the Navy and the Air Force pass on the loyalty of the employees of private

* Washington attorney associated with the firm of Arnold, Fortas and Porter. The selection is from L. A. Nikolorić, "The Government Loyalty Program," *The American Scholar,* Vol. XIX (Summer, 1950). Copyright of United Chapters of Phi Beta Kappa. By permission.

contractors who bid successfully on government jobs having to do with classified material. Congressmen have urged that all employees working for industries connected with the national security be subjected to a similar screening. Presumably this concerns the various utilities—in steel, automobile, transportation and others. Teachers and scientists have been discharged for entertaining unpopular ideas. Even veterans' organizations have pledged themselves to loyalty programs. The most liberal of these, the American Veterans Committee, has adopted resolutions directing its officers to purge the Communists.

Since we are rapidly accepting the proposition that American institutions have a right to examine their membership on the basis of their "loyalty," it is appropriate to determine what the government's loyalty program is and how it operates, its ideology, and the concrete effects of its operation. . . .

It is the duty of the [Loyalty] Boards to determine the existence of a nebulous state of mind which might lead an employee to commit in the future a disloyal act, either willfully or through an indiscretion. The most important elements of consideration are of necessity the employee's political beliefs, the organizations to which he has belonged, and the associations he has had.

Experience proves that it is not necessary for the employee to have been a member of either a Communist or Fascist organization. He will be found wanting if he has been "sympathetic" to communism or fascism, friendly to persons or organizations that are sympathetic, associated with such persons or organizations, or even "unduly talkative" in the presence of persons who are associated with sympathetic persons. The Boards do not find it necessary to prove any of these matters. They are required only to find "a reasonable doubt."

In order to assist the Boards, the Attorney General, in December, 1947, and by various supplements, designated some 150 organizations—membership in or sympathy for which is held to be indicative of disloyalty. These lists were promulgated without hearings. No explanation for the inclusion of any organization was given. . . .

Although the order provides that the employee is entitled to a charge stating the offense with some particularity, this is limited by the discretion of the agency in the interest of security considerations. Practice has shown that it has been almost impossible for an employee or his lawyer to secure a full or complete statement of the offenses.

Defending against such charges is difficult. The burden is placed on the employee to recall all the persons with whom, and organizations with which, he has ever been in contact, and to explain them. He must also prove affirmatively that he adheres to certain nebulous standards that might be construed by the Board as indicative of so loyal a state of mind that the employee will never commit a disloyal act.

The following quotation demonstrates the position in which an employee finds himself. In this case, Mr. A was faced with an unexplained action of the State Department in dismissing him "for security reasons." A asked the Board to tell him what he had done to justify the action, so that he might defend himself. The Board representative said:

> Well, we realize the difficulty you are in, in this position; on the other hand, I'd suggest that you might think back over your own career and perhaps in your own mind delve into some of the factors that have gone into your career which you think might have been subject to question and see what they are and see whether you'd like to explain or make any statement with regard to any of them. . . .

None of these things could happen in any other court or board proceeding directed against an individual in the United States. Axis Sally and Judith Coplon, who were charged with overt acts of treason and espionage, have received more procedural protection than is accorded the potentially disloyal. A common pickpocket may insist on every traditional and fundamental safeguard. A government employee may not. No one would dream of indicting Axis Sally for merely contemplating broadcasting Nazi propaganda; we would not consider putting a petty thief in jail for thinking about picking his neighbor's pocket. Yet we discharge and publicly smear government employees who have done nothing wrongful, who may not consider committing an act of disloyalty. We fire them because, on the basis of standards of the status quo, the Board suspects that they might do so in the future.

Those who would defend the program argue that the government is not required to secure to its employees procedural safeguards when it fires them. It is said that no citizen has an inherent right to government employment. Thus the government may fire arbitrarily—because it does not like the color of the employee's hair, because he is inefficient, or because the government fears that the employee may become a security risk. The procedural safeguards that are provided—charges and a hearing—are a matter of the sovereign's largess. They do not accrue to the employee as a matter of constitutional right. Therefore, the employee may not ask for other safeguards as a matter of constitutional right.

The opponents have a convincing case. Many judges, notably Mr. Justice Black, have argued that once having been hired, a government employee does secure a vested interest in his job which shall not be taken from him without cause. Cause may not be a matter of speculation; it must be a reality—such as inefficiency or overt acts of disloyalty.

Furthermore, a dismissal for disloyalty entails a permanent brand amounting to treason. Experience has shown that an employee who has been discharged under the loyalty program is unable to get another job; his career is ruined; he loses the respect of the community. Dismissal on loyalty or security grounds transcends the arbitrary right to fire. It amounts to punishment by government, which is protected by the Constitution. If this be the case, an employee who is fired on these grounds does have the constitutional right to traditional due process and safeguards.

Regardless of the coldly legal interpretation of the situation, it is obvious that a loyalty proceeding is a serious matter. On moral grounds, the government should not ruin an employee's career on a conjectural determination that he may in the future become disloyal. It must be remembered that the loyalty program was not designed or intended to punish people who have committed overt acts of disloyalty or treason. Not an employee fired has been charged with the commission of a wrongful act. During a recent public discussion with me, Mr. Seth Richardson, Chairman of the Loyalty Review Board, stated that the loyalty program has not discovered a single instance of espionage or any other overt action contrary to the best interests of the United States.

There are innumerable statutes calculated to deal with persons who are or have been acting contrary to our best interests. They include sanctions against espionage, sabotage, treason or advocacy of the overthrow of the government by force. More important to the inquiry here, any government agency may fire an employee for cause. "Cause" includes everything from simple inefficiency to disagreement with the agency's policy. Every applicant for government employment must sign, under oath, a statement that he does not subscribe to subversive doctrines and does not belong to any organization that does. Failure to make full disclosure is punishable as a criminal offense. . . .

A troublesome question is whether the loyalty program should be retained in the so-called "sensitive" agencies—the Atomic Energy Commission, the Department of Defense, and the State Department. Dr. Klaus Fuchs has done much for the proponents of the argument that in these areas, at least, we must examine employees for potential disloyalty because of the greater dangers involved.

My own view is a minority one. The proponents of the "sensitive agency" argument assume that this program is capable of catching the potentially disloyal. Even if we had the necessary instruments to accomplish this, I believe that if free institutions are to survive, they cannot be compromised in this way. A citizen in the Atomic Energy Commission should not be subjected to arbitrary treatment merely because his contribution is the more sensitive. Once the scientist or State Department official becomes a second class citizen, he will not be alone in this classification for long; he will be joined by the employee who deals in foreign trade and commerce, the expert whose concern is labor in the defense industries, and government men who deal with education and health—all fields fertile for sabotage or infiltration.

But the record speaks for itself. The loyalty program has proved to be a miserable failure as far as security is concerned. It has found no spies or security violations in sensitive areas or otherwise. Nor is it geared to; it is geared to accomplish the impossible—determine who tomorrow's spies will be. Let the FBI attend to the business of sabotage and espionage on the basis of the actual, not the potential—on the basis of acts, not possibilities. Let every agency continue to screen applicants for employment carefully; but let us not, in our fear of the police state, compromise free institutions.

The atmosphere in government is one of fear—fear of ideas and of irresponsible and unknown informers. Government employees are afraid to attend meetings of politically minded groups; they are afraid to read "liberal" publications; they screen their friends carefully for "left-wing" ideas. Government employees are in very real danger of dying intellectually and politically. Everyone knows of someone who has been accused of disloyalty—and it amounts to an accusation of treason—on ridiculous charges. Nobody wants to go through a lengthy "loyalty" investigation. The inclination and inevitable result are simply to restrict one's own freedoms.

All Americans suffer thereby. Political growth and progressive evolution depend on a vital and enthusiastic corps of government workers. Democracy can survive only upon the condition of a constant flexibility in its institutions to meet growing social and economic needs. Good government incorporates varying shades of opinion into a synthesis of action in behalf of the greatest good. Synthesis and flexibility are impossible when dissenters or the unorthodox are ruthlessly stamped out. The suppression of opposition can only mean the retention of outmoded and useless institutions, the impossibility of compromise and adjustment.

History has demonstrated again and again that freedom and the maturity of democratic processes cannot survive when the politically and economically dominant suspend traditional safeguards to the unorthodox. This is true, regardless of whether the suspension is undertaken because of fear of outside forces, or whether it is because a society has frozen in its evolutionary progress toward the fuller dignity of man. Surely it cannot be said that the United States, entering into a period of world leadership and enjoying the greatest prosperity in our history, has ceased growing. Let us not through hysteria and the uncertainty engendered by new responsibilities abdicate the basic standards of freedom which made us great. This is what we have done in the government's loyalty program; and this is what we threaten to do in the extension of that program to other segments of our society.

What Limits on the Security Program?

WALTER GELLHORN *

Wholly unrelated to the "sensitive areas," some thirty thousand civilians have professional civil-service ratings in federal agencies as chemists, physicists, meteorologists, entomologists, geologists, bacteriologists, pathologists, astronomers, and so on. To that number must be added the many thousands of supporting technical personnel and the yet further thousands of doctors, dentists, psychologists, and the like who are employed by the Veterans Administration, the Public Health Service, and other departments. Even those scientists who do have access to restricted data possess, for the most part, few real secrets—certainly far fewer than many normally self-assertive men ever permit their acquaintances to suppose. As for the scientists who will be discussed in the present piece, there is no room whatsoever for speculation on this score. They are factually, officially, and unqualifiedly barren of state secrets. They have not the slightest opportunity to deal in restricted data or to magnify their own importance by multiplying the number of hushes in hush-hush.

The inconspicuous ichthyologist of the Fish and Wildlife Service knows many secrets, to be sure, but they are the secrets of the speckled trout rather than the secrets of national defense. The mine safety engineer in the Department of the Interior peers into dark and hidden places, but the information he acquires has no element of confidentiality. The researcher at the National Cancer Institute explores the unknown, but there is certainly no disposition to conceal whatever he may discover. The Liberian scientific mission of the Public Health Service and the Agriculture Department is engaged in work of national importance, but whatever it learns about *Strophanthus sarmentosus* as a ready source of adrenocorticotrophic hormone will not be withheld from the rheumatoid arthritis sufferers of the world. . . . Yet the political views and the associations of all these men, and of others like them, have been a matter of governmental scrutiny almost as though they were entrusted with the latest developments in chemical warfare or rocket design. . . .

In the field of science, the crudities of the loyalty program discourage efforts to draw into public service the live-minded and experienced men

* Betts Professor of Law at Columbia University. Former Law secretary to Justice Harlan Fiske Stone. Author of *Individual Freedom and Governmental Restraints, American Rights,* and many other books. The selection is from *Security, Loyalty, and Science* (Ithaca, Cornell University Press, 1950), pp. 127–129, 158, 173–174. By permission.

whose talents are needed in many agencies. The distress occasioned by an unwarranted inquisition by a loyalty board is felt by a wide circle of friends and fellow-workers. Especially in the case of scientists there is a realization that even after a man has been exonerated following a hearing, he may still be subjected to a renewal of the charges and a dusting off of the same evidence if the winds of politics continue to blow strongly. On September 6, 1948, eight of America's great scientists, joining in a message to President Truman and Governor Dewey, deplored the disastrous effects upon scientific recruitment that followed the denunciatory sensationalism of the House Committee on Un-American Activities. . . . [They] concluded that the atmosphere of suspicion surrounding scientists in government was an effective deterrent to procurement and use of their services. What these men said publicly has been echoed privately by scientific men of every level of eminence.

The negative consequences of the Loyalty Order are dramatically realized when able men refuse to engage in public service or choose to leave it for less harassing occupations. All in all, however, the more serious though perhaps more subtle impact is on those who remain in federal service. . . .

Those difficulties would be diminished if we ceased searching for "disloyalty" as a general abstraction and became concerned exclusively with "security." Concededly there are positions outside the "sensitive agencies" that directly involve national safety. Occasionally an entire section or division of an organization may have occasion to deal with classified matters or may be so immediately involved in the formulation of international policy as to render it "sensitive" even though the agency as a whole may not be so. . . .

The solution here is to authorize the head of each department and agency to designate the units or particular positions in his department which he believes to be "sensitive." Persons who may be employed in these sensitive posts may properly be investigated in order that there may be full confidence in them. But as for the rest—the typists in the Veterans Administration or the Federal Housing Administration, the scientists in the Allergen Research Division or the Mycology and Disease Survey of the Bureau of Plant Industry—experience under the Loyalty Order demonstrates that constant peering over their shoulders endangers liberty without enhancing loyalty.

This is the administrative device that has been tried with reasonable success in Great Britain. There the power is lodged in each Minister to decide what parts of his ministry require the equivalent of our security clearance. In all, about 100,000 jobs were identified as having security significance. The Admiralty, as has our Department of the Army, concluded that everyone, from the highest to the lowest, must be cleared. Other ministries found no "sensitive" jobs at all. And this is as it should be, for in the variety of modern governmental activities there is room for both extremes.

If this approach be adopted, it will not mean an abandonment of interest in the probity of "nonsensitive" personnel. It will mean merely that observations will be related to behavior rather than belief. Government employees who improperly discharge their duties, whether motivated by disloyalty or mere slovenliness of habit, should of course be identified and appropriately disciplined. This, however, is a matter of administration rather than of detection. The supervisory officials of a functioning unit can more readily determine a staff member's misconduct or carelessness than can even the most vigilant agent of the FBI. The responsibility for efficiency should rest squarely on them. They cannot fulfill their responsibility if they tolerate on their staffs employees who are not actively loyal to their jobs. As for misdeeds unrelated to the direct performance of an employee's work, reliance must be placed upon the excellent counterespionage staffs of federal investigating agencies. The thorough work of the Federal Bureau of Investigation has given that bureau the place of public esteem that it occupies. The inherent absurdities of the loyalty program threaten the FBI's deservedly high reputation, for its "loyalty probers" must expend their energies in recording the often ambiguous pettinesses of political expression rather than in uncovering criminality. Releasing the FBI from the thankless and fruitless work to which it is now assigned will enhance the nation's safety. The more broadly we define the limits of our concern with personnel security, the more thinly we must spread attention to it. As has been true so often in matters of public administration, the scattershot of the blunderbuss is less effective than the aimed bullet of the rifle.

More than one hundred and fifty years ago a great friend of American democracy, Edmund Burke, argued that while restraint upon liberty may sometimes be required if liberty itself is to survive, "it ought to be the constant aim of every wise public council to find out by cautious experiments, and cool rational endeavors, with how little, not how much, of this restraint the community can subsist; for liberty is a good to be improved, and not an evil to be lessened." Burke's words are as true today as when he uttered them in 1777. The country will be the stronger for discovering that the restraints of the present loyalty program exceed the needs of national preservation.

Section V

Separation of Church and State

THE FIRST AMENDMENT of the Constitution debars Congress not only from abridging freedom of expression but specifically mandates that "it make no law respecting an establishment of religion, or prohibiting the free exercise thereof." This prohibition has been extended and applied to the states by the Supreme Court through its reading of the same limitations into the due process clause of the Fourteenth Amendment.

Although the First Amendment has been construed by a majority of the Supreme Court, in Jefferson's words, to require "a wall of separation between Church and State," in practice, as Mr. Justice Robert Jackson has pointed out, "the wall of separation has become like Jefferson's famous wall at the University of Virginia a serpentine wall." In point of fact, real and passionate differences have arisen, and continue to arise, as to both the legal and socially desirable scope and reach of the First Amendment inhibitions of governmental action affecting religion. Among the more important of these issues has been whether a state may, consistently with the Constitution, direct that a prayer be said aloud by each class during each school day. That is the subject matter of the decision in Engel *v.* Vitale, contained herein. Opponents of that decision are urging a constitutional amendment to reverse its effect. The Republican party platform in 1964 contained a plank pledging support for such an amendment.

Since that decision, in School District *v.* Schempp, 203 U.S. 374, decided in 1963, the Supreme Court, in an opinion by Mr. Justice Clark, held that state action, requiring that schools begin each day with readings from the Bible, was unconstitutional since it constituted "religious exercises" in violation of the command "that the Government maintain strict neutrality, neither aiding nor opposing religion." Only Mr. Justice Stewart dissented.

Topic 14

"ESTABLISHMENT" OF RELIGION

Regents' Prayer Case

ENGLE *V.* VITALE
370 U.S. 421 (1962)

MR. JUSTICE BLACK delivered the opinion of the Court.

The respondent Board of Education of Union Free School District No. 9, New Hyde Park, New York, acting in its official capacity under state law, directed the School District's principal to cause the following prayer to be said aloud by each class in the presence of a teacher at the beginning of each school day:

> Almighty God, we acknowledge our dependence upon Thee, and we beg Thy blessings upon us, our parents, our teachers and our country.

This daily procedure was adopted on the recommendation of the State Board of Regents, a governmental agency created by the State Constitution to which the New York Legislature has granted broad supervisory, executive, and legislative powers over the State's public school system. These state officials composed the prayer which they recommended and published as a part of their "Statement on Moral and Spiritual Training in the Schools," saying: "We believe that this Statement will be subscribed to by all men and women of good will, and we call upon all of them to aid in giving life to our program."

Shortly after the practice of reciting the Regents' prayer was adopted by the School District, the parents of ten pupils brought this action in a New York State Court insisting that use of this official prayer in the public schools was contrary to the beliefs, religions, or religious practices of both themselves and their children. Among other things, these parents challenged the constitutionality of both the state law authorizing the School District to direct the use of prayer in public schools and the School District's regulation ordering the recitation of this particular prayer on the ground that these actions of official governmental agencies violate that part of the First Amendment of the Federal Constitution which commands that "Congress shall make no law respecting an establishment of religion"—a command which was "made applicable to the State of New York by the Fourteenth Amendment of the said Constitution." . . .

We think that by using its public school system to encourage recitation of the Regent's prayer, the State of New York has adopted a practice wholly inconsistent with the Establishment Clause. There can, of course, be no doubt that New York's program of daily classroom invocation of God's blessings as prescribed in the Regents' prayer is a religious activity. It is a solemn avowal of divine faith and supplication for the blessings of the Almighty. The nature of such a prayer has always been religious, none of the respondents has denied this and the trial court expressly so found:

> The religious nature of prayer was recognized by Jefferson and has been concurred in by theological writers, the United States Supreme Court and State courts and administrative officials, including New York's Commissioner of Education. A committee of the New York Legislature has agreed.
>
> The Board of Regents as *amicus curiae,* the respondents and intervenors all concede the religious nature of prayer, but seek to distinguish this prayer because it is based on our spiritual heritage. . . .

The petitioners contend among other things that the state laws requiring or permitting use of the Regents' prayer must be struck down as a violation of the Establishment Clause because that prayer was composed by governmental officials as a part of a governmental program to further religious beliefs. For this reason, petitioners argue, the State's use of the Regent's prayer in its public school system breaches the constitutional wall of separation between Church and State. We agree with that contention since we think that the constitutional prohibition against laws respecting an establishment of religion must at least mean that in this country it is no part of the business of government to compose official prayers for any group of the American people to recite as a part of a religious program carried on by government.

It is a matter of history that this very practice of establishing governmentally composed prayers for religious services was one of the reasons which caused many of our early colonists to leave England and seek religious freedom in America. The Book of Common Prayer, which was created under governmental direction and which was approved by Acts of Parliament in 1548 and 1549, set out in minute detail the accepted form and content of prayer and other religious ceremonies to be used in the established, tax-supported Church of England. The controversies over the Book and what should be its content repeatedly threatened to disrupt the peace of that country as the accepted forms of prayer in the established church changed with the views of the particular ruler that happened to be in control at the time. Powerful groups representing some of the varying religious views of the people struggled among themselves to impress their particular views upon the Government and obtain amendments of the Book more suitable to their respective notions of how religious services should be conducted in order that the official religious establishment would advance their particular religious beliefs. Other groups, lacking the necessary political power to influence the Government on the matter, decided to leave England and its established church and seek freedom in America from England's governmentally ordained and supported religion.

It is an unfortunate fact of history that when some of the very groups which had most strenuously opposed the established Church of England found themselves sufficiently in control of colonial governments in this country to write their own prayers into law, they passed laws making their own religion the official religion of their respective colonies. Indeed, as late as the time of the Revolutionary War, there were established churches in at least eight of the thirteen former colonies and established religions in at least four of the other five. But the successful Revolution against English political domination was shortly followed by intense opposition to the practice of establishing religion by law. This opposition crystallized rapidly into an effective political force in Virginia where the minority religious groups such as Presbyterians, Lutherans, Quakers and Baptists had gained such strength that the adherents to the established Episcopal Church were actually a minority themselves. In 1785–1786, those opposed to the established Church, led by James Madison and Thomas Jefferson, who though themselves not members of any of these dissenting religious groups, opposed all religious establishments by law on grounds of principle, obtained the enactment of the famous "Virginia Bill for Religious Liberty" by which all religious groups were placed on an equal footing so far as the State was concerned. Similar though less far-reaching legislation was being considered and passed in other States.

By the time of the adoption of the Constitution, our history shows that there was a widespread awareness among many Americans of the dangers of a union of Church and State. These people knew, some of them from bitter personal experience, that one of the greatest dangers to the freedom of the individual to worship in his own way lay in the Government's placing its official stamp of approval upon one particular kind of prayer or one particular form of religious services. They knew the anguish, hardship and bitter strife that could come when zealous groups struggled with one another to obtain the Government's stamp of approval from each King, Queen, or Protector that came to temporary power.

The Constitution was intended to avert a part of this danger by leaving the government of this country in the hands of the people rather than in the hands of any monarch. But this safeguard was not enough. Our Founders were no more willing to let the content of their prayers and their privilege of praying whenever they pleased be influenced by the ballot box than they were to let these vital matters of personal conscience depend upon the succession of monarchs. The First Amendment was added to the Constitution to stand as a guarantee that neither the power nor the prestige of the Federal Government would be used to control, support or influence the kinds of prayer the American people can say—that the people's religions must not be subjected to the pressures of government for change each time a new political administration is elected to office. Under that Amendment's prohibition against governmental establishment of religion, as reinforced by the provisions of the Fourteenth Amendment, government in this country, be it state or federal, is without power to prescribe by law any particular form of prayer which is to be used as an official prayer in carrying on any program of governmentally sponsored religious activity.

There can be no doubt that New York's state prayer program officially establishes the religious beliefs embodied in the Regents' prayer. The respondents' argument to the contrary, which is largely based upon the contention that the Regents' prayer is "non-denominational" and the fact that the program, as modified and approved by state courts, does not require all pupils to recite the prayer but permits those who wish to do so to remain silent or be excused from the room, ignores the essential nature of the program's constitutional defects. Neither the fact that the prayer may be denominationally neutral, nor the fact that its observance on the part of the students is voluntary can serve to free it from the limitations of the Establishment Clause, as it might from the Free Exercise Clause, of the First Amendment, both of which are operative against the States by virtue of the Fourteenth Amendment. Although these two clauses may in certain instances overlap, they forbid two quite different kinds of governmental encroachment upon religious freedom.

The Establishment Clause, unlike the Free Exercise Clause, does not depend upon any showing of direct governmental compulsion and is violated by the enactment of laws which establish an official religion whether those laws operate directly to coerce nonobserving individuals or not. This is not to say, of course, that laws officially prescribing a particular form of religious worship do not involve coercion of such individuals. When the power, prestige and financial support of government is placed behind a particular religious belief, the indirect coercive pressure upon religious minorities to conform to the prevailing officially approved religion is plain. But the purposes underlying the Establishment Clause go much further than that. Its first and most immediate purpose rested on the belief that a union of government and religion tends to destroy government and to degrade religion. The history of governmentally established religion, both in England and in this country, showed that whenever government had allied itself with one particular form of religion, the inevitable result had been that it had incurred the hatred, disrespect and even contempt of those who held contrary beliefs.[1]

[1] "[A]ttempts to enforce by legal sanctions, acts obnoxious to so great a proportion of Citizens, tend to enervate the laws in general, and to slacken the bonds of Society.

That same history showed that many people had lost their respect for any religion that had relied upon the support of government to spread its faith. The Establishment Clause thus stands as an expression of principle on the part of the Founders of our Constitution that religion is too personal, too sacred, too holy, to permit its "unhallowed perversion" by a civil magistrate. Another purpose of the Establishment Clause rested upon an awareness of the historical fact that governmentally established religions and religious persecutions go hand in hand.[2] The Founders knew that only a few years after the Book of Common Prayer became the only accepted form of religious services in the established Church of England, an Act of Uniformity was passed to compel all Englishmen to attend those services and to make it a criminal offense to conduct or attend religious gatherings of any other kind—a law which was consistently flouted by dissenting religious groups in England and which contributed to widespread persecutions of people like John Bunyan who persisted in holding "unlawful [religious] meetings . . . to the great disturbance and distraction of the good subjects of this kingdom. . . ."[3] And they knew that similar persecutions had received the sanction of law in several of the colonies in this country soon after the establishment of official religions in those colonies.[4] It was in large part to get completely away from this sort of systematic religious persecution that the Founders brought into being our Nation, our Constitution, and our Bill of Rights with its prohibition against any governmental establishment of religion. The New York laws officially prescribing the Regents' prayer are inconsistent with both the purposes of the Establishment Clause and with the Establishment Clause itself.

It has been argued that to apply the Constitution in such a way as to prohibit state laws respecting an establishment of religious services in public

---

If it be difficult to execute any law which is not generally deemed necessary or salutary, what must be the case where it is deemed invalid and dangerous? and what may be the effect of so striking an example of impotency in the Government, on its general authority." Memorial and Remonstrance against Religious Assessments, II Writings of Madison 183, 190.

[2] "[T]he proposed establishment is a departure from that generous policy, which, offering an asylum to the persecuted and oppressed of every Nation and Religion, promised a lustre to our country, and an accession to the number of its citizens. What a melancholy mark is the Bill of sudden degeneracy? Instead of holding forth an asylum to the persecuted, it is itself a signal of persecution. . . . Distant as it may be, in its present form, from the Inquisition it differs from it only in degree. The one is the first step, the other the last in the career of intolerance. The magnanimous sufferer under this cruel scourge in foreign Regions, must view the Bill as a Beacon on our Coast, warning him to seek some other haven, where liberty and philanthropy in their due extent may offer a more certain repose from his troubles." *Id.*, at 188.

[3] Bunyan's own account of his trial is set forth in A Relation of the Imprisonment of Mr. John Bunyan, reprinted in Grace Abounding and The Pilgrim's Progress (Brown ed. 1907), at 103–132.

[4] For a vivid account of some of these persecutions, see Wertenbaker, The Puritan Oligarchy (1947).

schools is to indicate a hostility toward religion or toward prayer. Nothing, of course, could be more wrong. The history of man is inseparable from the history of religion. And perhaps it is not too much to say that since the beginning of that history many people have devoutly believed that "More things are wrought by prayer than this world dreams of." It was doubtless largely due to men who believed this that there grew up a sentiment that caused men to leave the cross-currents of officially established state religions and religious persecution in Europe and come to this country filled with the hope that they could find a place in which they could pray when they pleased to the God of their faith in the language they chose.[5] And there were men of this same faith in the power of prayer who led the fight for adoption of our Constitution and also for our Bill of Rights with the very guarantees of religious freedom that forbid the sort of governmental activity which New York has attempted here. These men knew that the First Amendment, which tried to put an end to governmental control of religion and of prayer, was not written to destroy either. They knew rather that it was written to quiet well-justified fears which nearly all of them felt arising out of an awareness that governments of the past had shackled men's tongues to make them speak only the religious thoughts that government wanted them to speak and to pray only to the God that government wanted them to pray to. It is neither sacrilegious nor antireligious to say that each separate government in this country should stay out of the business of writing or sanctioning official prayers and leave that purely religious function to the people themselves and to those the people choose to look to for religious guidance.[6]

It is true that New York's establishment of its Regents' prayer as an officially approved religious doctrine of that State does not amount to a total establishment of one particular religious sect to the exclusion of all others—that, indeed, the governmental endorsement of that prayer seems relatively insignificant when compared to the governmental encroachments upon religion which were commonplace 200 years ago. To those who may sub-

[5] Perhaps the best example of the sort of men who came to this country for precisely that reason is Roger Williams, the founder of Rhode Island, who has been described as "the truest Christian amongst many who sincerely desired to be Christian." Parrington, Main Currents of American Thought (1930), Vol. 1, at p. 74. Williams, who was one of the earliest exponents of the doctrine of separation of church and state, believed that separation was necessary in order to protect the church from the danger of destruction which he thought inevitably flowed from control by even the best-intentioned civil authorities. . . .

[6] There is of course nothing in the decision reached here that is inconsistent with the fact that school children and others are officially encouraged to express love for our country by reciting historical documents such as the Declaration of Independence which contain references to the Deity or by singing officially espoused anthems which include the composer's professions of faith in a Supreme Being, or with the fact that there are many manifestations in our public life of belief in God. Such patriotic or ceremonial occasions bear no true resemblance to the unquestioned religious exercise that the State of New York has sponsored in this instance.

scribe to the view that because the Regents' official prayer is so brief and general there can be no danger to religious freedom in its governmental establishment, however, it may be appropriate to say in the words of James Madison, the author of the First Amendment:

> [I]t is proper to take alarm at the first experiment on our liberties. . . . Who does not see that the same authority which can establish Christianity, in exclusion of all other Religions, may establish with the same ease any particular sect of Christians, in exclusion of all other Sects? That the same authority which can force a citizen to contribute three pence only of his property for the support of any one establishment, may force him to conform to any other establishment in all cases whatsoever? [7]

The judgment of the Court of Appeals of New York is reversed and the cause remanded for further proceedings not inconsistent with this opinion.

Reversed and remanded.

[MR. JUSTICE FRANKFURTER took no part in the decision of this case.]

[MR. JUSTICE WHITE took no part in the consideration or decision of this case.]

MR. JUSTICE DOUGLAS, concurring.

It is customary in deciding a constitutional question to treat it in its narrowest form. Yet at times the setting of the question gives it a form and content which no abstract treatment could do. The point for decision is whether the Government can constitutionally finance a religious exercise. Our system at the federal and state levels is presently honeycombed with such financing.[8] Nevertheless, I think it is an unconstitutional undertaking whatever form it takes.

[7] Memorial and Remonstrance against Religious Assessments, II Writings of Madison 183, at 185–186.

[8] "There are many 'aids' to religion in this country at all levels of government. To mention but a few at the federal level, one might begin by observing that the very First Congress which wrote the First Amendment provided for chaplains in both Houses and in the armed services. There is compulsory chapel at the service academies, and religious services are held in federal hospitals and prisons. The President issues religious proclamations. The Bible is used for the administration of oaths. N. Y. A. and W. P. A. funds were available to parochial schools during the depression. Veterans receiving money under the 'G. I.' Bill of 1944 could attend denominational schools, to which payments were made directly by the government. During World War II, federal money was contributed to denominational schools for the training of nurses. The benefits of the National School Lunch Act are available to students in private as well as public schools. The Hospital Survey and Construction Act of 1946 specifically made money available to non-public hospitals. The slogan 'In God We Trust' is used by the Treasury Department, and Congress recently added God to the pledge of allegiance. There is Bible-reading in the schools of the District of Columbia, and Religious instruction is given in the District's National Training School for Boys. Religious organizations are exempt from the federal income tax and are granted postal privileges. Up to defined limits—15 per cent of the adjusted gross income of individ-

First, a word as to what this case does not involve.

Plainly, our Bill of Rights would not permit a State or the Federal Government to adopt an official prayer and penalize anyone who would not utter it. This, however, is not that case, for there is no element of compulsion or coercion in New York's regulation requiring that public schools be opened each day with the following prayer:

> Almighty God, we acknowledge our dependence upon Thee, and we beg Thy blessings upon us, our parents, our teachers and our Country.

The prayer is said upon the commencement of the school day, immediately following the pledge of allegiance to the flag. The prayer is said aloud in the presence of a teacher, who either leads the recitation or selects a student to do so. No student, however, is compelled to take part. The respondents have adopted a regulation which provides that "neither teachers nor any school authority shall comment on participation or nonparticipation . . . nor suggest or request that any posture or language be used or dress be worn or be not used or not worn." Provision is also made for excusing children, upon written request of a parent or guardian, from the saying of the prayer or from the room in which the prayer is said. A letter implementing and explaining this regulation has been sent to each taxpayer and parent in the school district. As I read this regulation, a child is free to stand or not stand, to recite or not recite, without fear of reprisal or even comment by the teacher or any other school official.

In short, the only one who need utter the prayer is the teacher; and no teacher is complaining of it. Students can stand mute or even leave the classroom, if they desire. . . . The question presented by this case is therefore an extremely narrow one. It is whether New York oversteps the bounds when it finances a religious exercise.

What New York does on the opening of its public schools is what we do when we open court. Our Marshal has from the beginning announced the convening of the Court and then added "God save the United States and this honorable court." That utterance is a supplication, a prayer in which we, the judges, are free to join, but which we need not recite any more than the students need recite the New York prayer.

What New York does on the opening of its public schools is what each House of Congress does at the opening of each day's business. Reverend Frederick B. Harris is Chaplain of the Senate; Reverend Bernard Braskamp

---

uals and 5 per cent of the net income of corporations—contributions to religious organizations are deductible for federal income tax purposes. There are limits to the deductibility of gifts and bequests to religious institutions made under the federal gift and estate tax laws. This list of federal 'aids' could easily be expanded, and of course there is a long list in each state." Fellman, The Limits of Freedom (1959), pp. 40–41.

is Chaplain of the House. Guest chaplains of various denominations also officiate.[9]

In New York the teacher who leads in prayer is on the public payroll; and the time she takes seems minuscule as compared with the salaries appropriated by state legislatures and Congress for chaplains to conduct prayers in the legislative halls. Only a bare fraction of the teacher's time is given to reciting this short 22-word prayer, about the same amount of time that our Marshal spends announcing the opening of our sessions and offering a prayer for this Court. Yet for me the principle is the same, no matter how briefly the prayer is said, for in each of the instances given the person praying is a public official on the public payroll, performing a religious exercise in a governmental institution. It is said that the element of coercion is inherent in the giving of this prayer. If that is true here, it is also true of the prayer with which this Court is convened, and with those that open the Congress. Few adults, let alone children, would leave our courtroom or the Senate or the House while those prayers are being given. Every such audience is in a sense a "captive" audience.

At the same time I cannot say that to authorize this prayer is to establish a religion in the strictly historic meaning of those words. A religion is not established in the usual sense merely by letting those who choose to do so say the prayer that the public school teacher leads. Yet once government finances a religious exercise it inserts a divisive influence into our communities. The New York court said that the prayer given does not conform to all of the tenets of the Jewish, Unitarian, and Ethical Culture groups. One of petitioners is an agnostic.

"We are a religious people whose institutions presuppose a Supreme Being." *Zorach* v. *Clauson,* 343 U.S. 306, 313. Under our Bill of Rights free play is given for making religion an active force in our lives. But "if a religious leaven is to be worked into the affairs of our people, it is to be done by individuals and groups, not by the Government." *McGowan* v. *Maryland,* 366 U.S. 420, 563 (dissenting opinion). By reason of the First Amendment government is commanded "to have no interest in theology or ritual" (*id.,* at 564), for on those matters "government must be neutral."

[9] It would, I assume, make no difference in the present case if a different prayer were said every day or if the ministers of the community rotated, each giving his own prayer. For some of the petitioners in the present case profess no religion.

The Pledge of Allegiance, like the prayer, recognizes the existence of a Supreme Being. Since 1954 it has contained the words "one nation *under God,* indivisible, with liberty and justice for all." 36 U. S. C. 172. The House Report, recommending the addition of the words "under God" stated that those words in no way run contrary to the First Amendment but recognize "only the guidance of God in our national affairs." H. R. Rep. No. 1693, 83d Cong., 2d Sess., p. 3. And see S. Rep. No. 1287, 83d Cong., 2d Sess. Senator Ferguson, who sponsored the measure in the Senate, pointed out that the words "In God We Trust" are over the entrance to the Senate Chamber. . . .

Ibid. The First Amendment leaves the Government in a position not of hostility to religion but of neutrality. The philosophy is that the atheist or agnostic—the nonbeliever—is entitled to go his own way. The philosophy is that if government interferes in matters spiritual, it will be a divisive force. The First Amendment teaches that a government neutral in the field of religion better serves all religious interests.

MR. JUSTICE STEWART, dissenting.

A local school board in New York has provided that those pupils who wish to do so may join in a brief prayer at the beginning of each school day, acknowledging their dependence upon God and asking His blessing upon them and upon their parents, their teachers, and their country. The Court today decides that in permitting this brief non-denominational prayer the school board has violated the Constitution of the United States. I think this decision is wrong.

The Court does not hold, nor could it, that New York has interfered with the free exercise of anybody's religion. For the state courts have made clear that those who object to reciting the prayer must be entirely free of any compulsion to do so, including any "embarrassments and pressures." Cf. *West Virginia State Board of Education* v. *Barnette,* 319 U.S. 624. But the Court says that in permitting school children to say this simple prayer, the New York authorities have established "an official religion."

With all respect, I think the Court has misapplied a great constitutional principle. I cannot see how an "official religion" is established by letting those who want to say a prayer say it. On the contrary, I think that to deny the wish of these school children to join in reciting this prayer is to deny them the opportunity of sharing in the spiritual heritage of our Nation.

The Court's historical review of the quarrels over the Book of Common Prayer in England throws no light for me on the issue before us in this case. England had then and has now an established church. Equally unenlightening, I think, is the history of the early establishment and later rejection of an official church in our own States. For we deal here not with the establishment of a state church, which would, of course, be constitutionally impermissible, but with whether school children who want to begin their day by joining in prayer must be prohibited from doing so. Moreover, I think that the Court's task, in this as in all areas of constitutional adjudication, is not responsibly aided by the uncritical invocation of metaphors like the "wall of separation," a phrase nowhere to be found in the Constitution. What is relevant to the issue here is not the history of an established church in sixteenth century England or in eighteenth century America, but the history of the religious traditions of our people, reflected in countless practices of the institutions and officials of our government.

At the opening of each day's Session of this Court we stand, while one of our officials invokes the protection of God. Since the days of John Marshall our Crier has said, "God save the United States and this Honorable Court." Both the Senate and the House of Representatives open their daily Sessions with prayer. Each of our Presidents, from George Washington to John F. Kennedy, has upon assuming his Office asked the protection and help of God.[10]

The Court today says that the state and federal governments are without constitutional power to prescribe any particular form of words to be recited by any group of the American people on any subject touching religion.[11] The third stanza of "The Star-Spangled Banner," made our National Anthem by Act of Congress in 1931, contains these verses:

Blest with victory and peace, may the heav'n rescued land
    Praise the Pow'r that hath made and preserved us a nation!
Then conquer we must, when our cause it is just,
    And this be our motto "In God is our Trust."

In 1954 Congress added a phrase to the Pledge of Allegiance to the Flag so that it now contains the words "one Nation *under God,* indivisible, with liberty and justice for all." In 1952 Congress enacted legislation calling upon the President each year to proclaim a National Day of Prayer. Since 1865 the words "IN GOD WE TRUST" have been impressed on our coins.

[10] For example:

On April 30, 1789, President George Washington said:

". . . it would be peculiarly improper to omit in this first official act my fervent supplications to that Almighty Being who rules over the universe, who presides in the councils of nations, and whose providential aids can supply every human defect, that His benediction may consecrate to the liberties and happiness of the people of the United States a Government instituted by themselves for these essential purposes, and may enable every instrument employed in its administration to execute with success the functions allotted to His charge.

On March 4, 1933, President Franklin D. Roosevelt said:

"In this dedication of a Nation we humbly ask the blessing of God. May He protect each and every one of us. May He guide me in the days to come."

On January 21, 1957, President Dwight D. Eisenhower said:

"Before all else, we seek, upon our common labor as a nation, the blessings of Almighty God. And the hopes in our hearts fashion the deepest prayers of our whole people."

On January 20, 1961, President John F. Kennedy said:

"The world is very different now. . . . And yet the same revolutionary beliefs for which our forebears fought are still at issue around the globe—the belief that the rights of man come not from the generosity of the state, but from the hand of God. . . .

"With a good conscience our only sure reward, with history the final judge of our deeds, let us go forth to lead the land we love, asking His blessing and His help, but knowing that here on earth God's work must truly be our own."

[11] My brother DOUGLAS says that the only question before us is whether government "can constitutionally finance a religious exercise." The official chaplains of Congress are paid with public money. So are military chaplains. So are state and federal prison chaplains.

Countless similar examples could be listed, but there is no need to belabor the obvious.[12] It was all summed up by this Court just ten years ago in a single sentence: "We are a religious people whose institutions presuppose a Supreme Being." *Zorach* v. *Clauson,* 343 U.S. 306, 313.

I do not believe that this Court, or the Congress, or the President has by the actions and practices I have mentioned established an "official religion" in violation of the Constitution. And I do not believe the State of New York has done so in this case. What each has done has been to recognize and to follow the deeply entrenched and highly cherished spiritual traditions of our Nation—traditions which come down to us from those who almost two hundred years ago avowed their "firm reliance on the Protection of Divine Providence" when they proclaimed the freedom and independence of this brave new world.[13]

I dissent.

[12] I am at a loss to understand the Court's unsupported *ipse dixit* that these official expressions of religious faith in and reliance upon a Supreme Being "bear no true resemblance to the unquestioned religious exercise that the State of New York has sponsored in this instance." I can hardly think that the Court means to say that the First Amendment imposes a lesser restriction upon the Federal Government than does the Fourteenth Amendment upon the States. Or is the Court suggesting that the Constitution permits judges and Congressmen and Presidents to join in prayer, but prohibits school children from doing so?

[13] The Declaration of Independence ends with this sentence: "And for the support of this Declaration, with a firm reliance on the Protection of Divine Providence, we mutually pledge to each other our Lives, our Fortunes and our Sacred Honor."

Section VI

Federalism

THE UNITED STATES is the first great experiment in federalism. Prior to the framing of the Constitution in 1787, history had witnessed the rise and fall of a number of confederacies, and the world had experienced numberless centralized or unitary states.

Our Constitution establishes a system under which, generally speaking, the federal government, subject to specific prohibitions, enjoys supremacy in the exercise of delegated sovereign powers, while the states, also subject to specific prohibitions and those inferred from grants to the federal government, exercise reserved sovereign powers. Theoretically this distribution of powers can be changed only by constitutional amendment. In actual practice, however, the elastic scope accorded by the Supreme Court to federal power, in spheres previously regarded as reserved to state action, demonstrates that the balance is a changing one.

Although some criticism of our federal structure has been far-reaching, no serious student of politics would suggest the substitution—in our vast and complex land with its long tradition of state sovereignty—of a unitary system of government. The real issues are concerned, rather, with establishing the appropriate spheres of national and state activities. To do this requires regard not only for tradition but for many other considerations including basic democratic values, experience, resources, and changing social needs.

One position that is often urged is that the emphases should be on decentralization and that ground should seldom, if ever, be yielded to the national power. Another persistently seeks to expand national control as necessary to efficiency and uniformity of social benefit. A third view would increase political centralization only when problems have clearly assumed national proportions with which the states cannot successfully cope and, at the same time, would maintain, whenever possible, administrative decentralization.

The relationship between federalism and freedom is the subject of special consideration. So, also, is the controversy over the extent to which the fashioning of legislative districts is the special prerogative of state legislatures, or the appropriate subject of control by the Supreme Court—at least in terms of defining basic, guiding principles—under that provision of the Fourteenth Amendment which bars the state from denying "to any person within its jurisdiction the equal protection of the laws."

Topic 15

CENTRALIZATION AND DECENTRALIZATION

Centralization and Democracy

PAUL STUDENSKI AND PAUL R. MORT *

Theoretically central versus local control is an issue between extreme centralization of government on the one hand, and extreme decentralization of it on the other. In actual practice, however, the issue is generally far from being so broad in character. It is limited in most cases to a consideration of whether certain functions of government should be centralized or decentralized, and of the extent to which such centralization or decentralization of them should be carried. The discussions of these narrower issues are generally carried on in much more realistic terms than the discussions of the broader theoretical issues, for they take into account particular situations and problems. . . .

The necessity of complete and direct central control over certain spheres of public affairs, such as national defense, foreign affairs, and foreign trade, is admitted by all writers. No one would seriously propose today that these functions be administered locally.

In most spheres of public affairs, however, the sharing of control by the central and local authorities is generally deemed most advisable. Central and local control are considered to possess different advantages deemed equally essential to the national welfare in the administration of public services. This sharing of control, it is noted, may take the form of (*a*) the exercise by the central and local governments, respectively, of independent authority over different spheres of the same functions as exemplified by the present control of most of the federal and state functions, (*b*) the supervision by the central government of the operations of

* Paul Studenski, former Professor of Economics, New York University. Author of *The Income of Nations, Financial History of the United States,* and other books and articles. Paul R. Mort, former Professor of Education, Teachers College, Columbia University. Author of *Principles of School Administration* and other books. The selection is from Paul Studenski and Paul R. Mort, *Centralized vs. Decentralized Government in Relation to Democracy* (New York, Bureau of Publications, Teachers College, Columbia University, 1941), *passim* as specially rearranged. By permission.

the local governments, as exemplified by state supervision over local educational administration and, more recently, by federal supervision over state administration of highways, social security, relief, etc., or (*c*) joint or cooperative management by the central government and the local authorities of certain of their affairs as exemplified by the proposals for a joint federal-state management of specific public works. . . .

MERITS OF LOCAL CONTROL

Local control (and by this is meant well-conceived local control) possesses the following principal merits, according to its advocates: (1) it promotes local unity, sense of neighborhood responsibility, spirit of self-reliance and capacity for group action; (2) it secures a close adaptation of public services to local needs; (3) it promotes and safeguards freedom, democracy, and responsible governments; (4) it promotes socially beneficial inter-community competition; (5) it permits safe experimentation with new forms and methods of government, thus fostering a gradual improvement in government throughout the country; . . . (6) it relieves the national government of congestion of business. Each one of these contentions will be reviewed below.

PROMOTION OF SELF-RELIANCE

Much emphasis is placed on the fact that overcentralization destroys civic interest, individual initiative, and the moral fiber of the nation. Citizens are discouraged from participating actively in civic affairs either as candidates for public office, or as voters, or as members of civic organizations, inasmuch as they are unable to influence materially the public policy under a system of this sort. Their freedom is restricted by the rules promulgated by the national administrative officers. Not being allowed to exercise their initiative, they become subservient subjects of a national bureaucracy. . . .

ADAPTATION TO LOCAL NEEDS

Extreme centralization, according to many writers in political science, results in a neglect of local needs. The national legislature is too absorbed with national affairs to give adequate attention to local matters. It tends to pass general laws relating to localities, which cannot possibly take care of special local situations, or else to make provision for the special conditions only of such communities as have substantial representation. . . .

The national administrative officers who dispose of the local affairs are even more inclined than the national legislature to apply uniform rules to varying situations. Uniformity of treatment simplifies their tasks. That such uniformity does violence to local development often concerns them little. They generally lack intimate acquaintance with the situations of the particular localities and therefore are unable to consider these situations even if they wished to do so. . . .

Most of the advocates of local self-government stress the fact that it secures a close adaptation of the public services to local needs. They contend that each locality has peculiar needs, predicated by its peculiar location, physical, social, and economic advantages, stage of development, historical tradition, and similar factors. In speaking of the needs of the locality, they have in mind, of course, the needs of the people inhabiting the locality. They maintain that the nation as a whole is advantaged by the intensive care which local governments are able to give to these peculiar local needs and by the close adaptation of the public services, under home rule, to peculiar local situations. They insist that the local people know best how to utilize the special advantages of their locality for their own collective benefit, and that their own self-interest prompts them to exercise their intelligence to the utmost to that end. Adequate consideration of local needs, they say, is assured under local government by the fact that the officials who formulate and execute local policy thereunder are residents of the locality and hence are interested in its welfare; that these officials are close to the citizens and susceptible to pressure on their part; and that the structure and the procedure of the local government generally become, in the course of the evolution, well adjusted to the peculiar local situation. . . .

PROMOTION OF FREEDOM AND RESPONSIBLE GOVERNMENT

The trump card of the advocates of local government, at least in England and the United States, seems to be the argument that it promotes freedom, democracy, and responsible government. This argument is developed by writers in these countries with great eloquence and conviction. The ideals of freedom, democracy, and responsible government are held by these writers to be among the highest ever conceived by man. It is contended by them that an institution that promotes these ideals deserves to be cherished and revered.

It is stated that under local self-government, local groups are free to manage their own affairs as they deem best, to venture on new undertakings, to make mistakes and to correct them in the light of experience, and that every active and interested member of the group is free to partake in this collective privilege. It is [evident] that under local self-government the individual has a wide opportunity for self-expression; that he can influence the course of public affairs in the local group much more effectively than in the national group; and that his importance in the local group is considerable, whereas in the national group it is exceedingly small. Thus, local self-government enlarges the freedom of the individual. . . .

It is pointed out by the advocates of local home rule that local public policy thereunder is determined by the people concerned, through their own democratically elected government and not by some central officials over whom they have no control. It is shown that, under local self-government, civic interest is stimulated and responsibility of the officials to the people is readily enforced. Local officials act as the servants of the people and not as their rulers. Inasmuch as each locality has its own policy-making body and its own elected officials, the opportunity for the ordinary citizen to hold public office is multiplied. Since the local government is so close at hand it tends to be responsive to the public will. The officials are accessible to the people. Although it is impossible in most of the local governments to have town meetings attended by all the citizens, an effective substitute therefor is frequently provided in the form of local referenda. All these factors help to make local government a popular government.

It is also contended that local self-government is the training school of national democracy. Local democratic processes, it is held, are simpler than the national democratic procedures. By learning how to manage democratically local affairs, it is said, a people becomes better fitted to manage democratically its national concerns. In the local democracies leaders are developed who eventually qualify for leadership in the national democracy. . . .

PROMOTION OF SOCIALLY BENEFICIAL INTER-COMMUNITY COMPETITION

Very few writers call attention to the fact that local self-government permits a healthy competition between local communities in the matter of civic improvements, and in this way promotes good government and social and economic progress. Students of government can furnish many illustrations of the fact that states and cities are trying to outdo each other in the construction of highways, development of port facilities and parks, building of schools, and similar improvements. This civic competition is due to some extent to the influence of the realtors, shopkeepers, and other commercial interests in the communities that seek to attract business and population to their localities for their own private benefit. But to some extent this competition is also due to the unselfish devotion of local civic leaders to the welfare of their respective local people. Laski says: "The only way to make municipal life an adequate thing is to set city striving against city in a consistent conflict of progressive improvement."

POSSIBILITY FOR SAFE EXPERIMENTATION WITH NEW FORMS AND METHODS OF GOVERNMENT

Many advocates of local self-government list among its merits the fact that it permits safe experimentation with new methods and forms of government, and fosters thereby a gradual improvement in government throughout the country. Groups of citizens in a locality, dissatisfied with the existing structure or procedure of their local government, may formulate programs for its reorganization along new lines and secure the consent of the local electorate to a trial of their proposals. If the experiment proves successful, it becomes established permanently in the political or administrative system of their community and is soon copied by other localities, or possibly even by the national government itself. If the experiment with a new form or method of government proves a partial or total failure, it may be reconsidered by the local people and either modified in some respects or abandoned in favor of some other, more promising arrangement. By securing a local trial for their advanced ideas, progressive citizens who enjoy a substantial local influence but have no national following may indirectly affect the course of political development in the country as a whole.

Since each experiment involves only a local area, it is held that mistakes cannot be very costly from a national point of view. Experimentation can be carried on, therefore, relatively freely. Thus, in the United States, local political experimentation has resulted in the development of the city manager form of government and the introduction in this country of the executive budget, proportional representation, the unicameral legislature, city planning, central purchasing, and a number of similar reforms.

Some writers also stress the fact that experimentation under local self-government is safe in the sense that it is carried on under conditions of a full democratic discussion and a vigilant critical observation by dissenting groups. . . .

LIGHTENING THE TASK OF THE NATIONAL AUTHORITY

It is [quite evident] that local self-government relieves the national government of the details of local administration and permits it to concentrate on the affairs which are truly national in character. National needs are better cared for as a result. Prior to the extension of the powers of local government in England during the eighties, a substantial portion of the time of Parliament was consumed annually by the consideration of local bills. There was general complaint of the congestion of the Parliamentary business which interfered with the proper consideration of national measures. The widening of the powers of self-government was urged on the ground that it would reduce this congestion. The term "specialization or division of labor" was commonly used in the English political literature of the time in the sense of a distribution of powers between the central and local governments. . . .

Excessive centralization of government, according to many scholars, promotes the rule of an irresponsible national bureaucracy and destroys democracy. The reason given is that the national legislature generally has so many measures of national importance to consider that it has no time to consider measures of only local importance. It must, therefore, delegate the local matters to the heads of the administrative departments even though those matters involve questions of public policy. Thus, in contravention of democratic principles, policy making is delegated to administrative officers. Moreover, the local questions involved are left to be decided finally, not by the heads of the departments who are responsible to the national legislature or to the elected national executive, but by the subordinate employees of the department, the permanent civil servants who are practically irremovable, and responsible to no one. Since the heads of the departments generally hold office only temporarily, they have no opportunity to acquire the expert knowledge necessary for a decision on the matters presented to them. Nor is it humanly possible for them to be acquainted with the multiple angles of the problems that are brought before them. Therefore, they must depend for advice on their subordinates—the civil servants, and sign documents which the latter present to them, even though they may not know their true implications.

The civil servants gain dominance not only over the ministers but also over the legislators, who depend on them for information, advice, and special favors. They form a closely-knit self-perpetuating group. They are bound together by common tradition and self-interest, a common distrust of the intelligence of the common citizens, and common contempt for popular government; and they shield one another. They become, in time, an entrenched and independent power in the country, in fact, its real government. Where a bureaucracy develops, democracy comes to an end. Thus runs the argument against excessive centralization.

There is wide agreement in the literature that bureaucracy lacks imagination, discourages initiative, and exercises a deadening influence on national life. It is not only oppressive, it is also slow and inefficient.

The evils of bureaucracy are so dreaded in a democratic country that the very mention of the word condemns the system of which it is a part. The argument of bureaucracy is, therefore, the most potent of all arguments advanced in American political discussion against excessive centralization. Brun, a French writer, says: [1]

> Centralization promotes bureaucracy, the dangers of which have sufficiently been demonstrated. The civil servants, greater in number from day to day, are powerful, and in practice almost irresponsible. They weigh heavily on the budget, and as if in spite of themselves, upon individual enterprises, which often appear to them suspicious . . . thus France is not a democracy; it is a bureaucracy.
>
> Bureaucracy engenders red tape, multiplies and complicates administration. The most elementary matters drag indefinitely, demanding an excessive amount of work, time, and the expenditure of money which is an actual waste.

SHORTCOMINGS OF DECENTRALIZATION

The principal shortcomings of extreme decentralization may be summarized as follows: (1) it results in an inefficient and an uneconomic management of local affairs; (2) it fosters local autocratic rule by petty officials and powerful minority groups; (3) it breeds narrow parochialism, and produces national and regional disunity and disorganization; (4) it results in extreme inequality in the standards of public service and protection of civil rights throughout the country or the region; (5) central government unifies the nation.

INEFFICIENT AND UNECONOMIC MANAGEMENT OF LOCAL AFFAIRS

Central government is in many respects more efficient and economical than are local governments, all other conditions being the same. First of all, central government generally attracts a more competent personnel for its policy-making body and its administrative departments than do local governments. The prestige attached to the holding of a national political office is far greater than that attached to the holding of a local one. The number of leading national offices in the country is smaller than the number of local ones, and the competition for them is therefore much keener. Each national legislator represents a larger area and a larger population, is concerned with more important affairs, and receives wider publicity than does a local councilman. The possibility for elevation to a higher office is greater in the case of a member of the national legislature than

[1] Charles T. Brun, *Le Regionalisme* (Paris, Bloud & Cie, 1911), pp. 15–16.

in that of a member of a municipal council. The compensation of a national representative is generally greater too. All these circumstances are responsible for the fact that capable men who are willing to devote their time to political affairs, as a rule, more readily aspire to a national political office than to a local one.

The central government has a wider choice of candidates for administrative positions than have local governments. It recruits its personnel wherever it can find suitable material. It is not obligated to employ local men for local offices. It can hire men in one locality and employ them in another. By advertising nationally the vacancies which it wishes to fill, it invites active competition for the positions from applicants all over the country. Inasmuch as the higher positions in the national administration involve greater responsibilities, enjoy greater prestige, and generally offer better pay than do the higher positions in the sphere of local government, they naturally attract more able and ambitious men. The greater opportunities which the national service offers for promotion to higher positions and also the more secure tenure of office it provides tend to secure for the national government a better personnel. In view of all these facts, the national government can afford to be more selective in its choice of employees than can the local governments.

Second, the national government has much wider sources of information than have local governments. It is in a position to collect through its local agents data on existing conditions in the various sections of the country and to base its policies on information of a comparative sort. The national service provides better opportunities to the men engaged therein to acquire wide experience than does the municipal service. The national administrators in the course of their careers are often shifted from one locality to another or travel extensively over the country and in this manner become familiar with the situations in various localities or regions.

Third, the central government can introduce much greater functional specialization in its administrative services than can local governments. It can subdivide the work into minute specialities to a much greater degree and thus can secure greater efficiency and economy of operation.

In the fourth place, the national government affords greater opportunities for centralization of administrative responsibility in a few key offices than does local government. This centralization of responsibility enables the government better to coordinate the activities of its officials. It makes possible quick and decisive action.

In the fifth place, the national government possesses the advantages of large-scale enterprise. One of these advantages, that of division or specialization of labor, has already been noted. The central government is in a better position to employ experts to use elaborate and highly efficient equipment. Moreover, it can execute large projects affecting substantial areas, which the localities in these areas cannot possibly accomplish, separately or jointly, themselves. Large projects of this sort can be executed more economically and are much more efficient than are the smaller projects which local governments can undertake. The central government is able to perform, in cases of this sort, the same amount of work as the local governments with a smaller number of employees. It can eliminate duplicate functions and positions and use its personnel more effectively and economically. . . .

FOSTERING LOCAL AUTOCRATIC RULE BY PETTY OFFICIALS AND POWERFUL MINORITY GROUPS

Extreme decentralization fosters local autocratic rule by petty officials and powerful minority groups. The smaller the local area, the more static are likely to be the social, economic, and political conditions therein. Old-time residents cling together in an effort to preserve the traditional policies of the community and lend loyal support to a common leader, an old resident like themselves, who becomes the local dictator in all the spheres of the local public life—political, economic, and the like. Newcomers who have different ideas of the development of the community are not permitted by the dominant local clique to take active part in the management of local affairs. The jobs in the local government are distributed by the local "boss" among his faithful followers, and a job once granted to a follower readily becomes a sinecure. . . .

NARROW PAROCHIALISM AND NATIONAL AND REGIONAL DISUNITY AND DISORGANIZATION

Extreme decentralization results in the disorganization of government in the country or the region. Confusing and conflicting regulations are enacted by the various local governments. Projects conceived in the interest of the entire territory are often blocked by the refusal of a small local area to join in the undertaking or to permit its facilities to be extended through its territory. The officials of the local government are unwilling to cooperate. They fear that intergovernmental cooperation of this sort may bring in its wake the unification of government, the abolition of their local independence, and a loss of their jobs; or that in some other way it may result in the lowering of their prestige and influence in the eyes of their own citizens. . . .

The vesting of excessively wide powers in state governments and of totally inadequate powers in the central government in this country, after the War of Independence, produced disunity and a breakdown of government. As soon as a strong central government was provided under the new constitution, the disintegrating tendencies came to an end. In like manner, in later times the exercise by the states of complete authority over the institution of slavery, over banks, railroads, monopolies and trusts, liquor traffic, and other economic and social matters produced chaos in these spheres of the national economy. With the partial or complete centralization of authority over these spheres in the national government, however, their administration became more orderly in character. The multiplication of local governments in densely populated metropolitan regions has produced serious evils. The small rural governments which, years ago, performed a useful function have become in recent times a bar to governmental and social progress.

Professor Munro refers to the shortcomings of extreme decentralization of government in this country as represented by excessive grants of power to state governments and inadequate grants of them to the Federal authority, as follows: [2]

> In their relation to the problems of American economic and social life, the states have been gradually receding as entities of political action, whether regulative or constructive, until today they are all but powerless in some of the fields ostensibly reserved to them by our scheme of government. . . . When a problem of industry or social welfare becomes too big to be handled by the authorities of the individual states, there are only two alternatives under present conditions. One is to confess our helplessness and bear the evils as best we can; the other is to demand that Washington take the problem in hand, whether it belongs there or not. It is natural that a practical people should prefer the latter alternative. They will continue to prefer it, and no theory of division of powers will stand in their way. Jurists may sob over the "vanishing rights of the states," but it is a fair guess that these rights will continue to dwindle as our problems keep growing in size. The steady erosion of state powers is bound to go hand in hand with the increasing complexity of our economic and social life. Nothing in the realm of political prophecy can be more certain than that the intrepid rear guards of the states' rights army are fighting for a lost cause. . . .

EXTREME INEQUALITY IN STANDARDS OF PUBLIC SERVICE AND PROTECTION OF CIVIL RIGHTS

Under an extremely decentralized government, the standards of public service and of the protection of civil rights, it is said, vary greatly from area to area. The maintenance by some areas of high standards benefits

[2] W. B. Munro, "Do We Need Regional Government?" *Forum* (January, 1928), p. 109.

the nation or the region. But the maintenance by others of low standards injures the neighboring communities and the country or region as a whole. For the evil conditions resulting from such low standards spread far beyond the boundaries of the areas responsible for them. The low standards maintained by these areas nullify the efforts of the other areas to maintain a high record of performance and eventually cause the latter to relax in their zeal. As a result, the quality of public services throughout the entire country or region is lowered. To prevent this eventuality, the neighboring communities and the state must take some action that would raise the standards of service in the backward areas. . . .

Swift, an American authority on education, points out that: [8]

> . . . a condition essential to democracy is equality of opportunity. . . . Inequalities of educational opportunity in the United States today are directly proportional to the degree of autonomy in matters of school support and control granted to the local communities. Any system which creates, perpetuates, and increases educational inequalities is undemocratic; and these are beyond all doubt the characteristics and results of our decentralized systems.

NATIONAL UNIFICATION AND THE SERVICE OF THE NATIONAL INTEREST

A properly conceived central government promotes national unity. It provides for the common needs of the population and for the coordinated development of all the social and economic factors upon which the welfare of the nation depends. And it obviously provides for the security of the nation. The centralized government organizes the creative forces of the nation and its resources for the achievement of these important ends. Advocates of centralization strongly emphasize the importance of these unifying functions of the central government. The need for the unification which centralization provides is admitted in many fields of public administration, even by the strongest advocates of local self-government. Thus, it is generally admitted that uniformity of regulation of interstate commerce, throughout the country, is essential for national prosperity, and that the central government, which alone can provide uniform regulation over the country as a whole, should exercise jurisdiction over this sphere of the economic life of the people. It is admitted by the advocates of modern centralization that in certain spheres of public affairs there is no need for unified administration and uniformity of regulation.

Central government equalizes the social, economic, and educational op-

[8] Fletcher H. Swift, *Federal and State Policies in Public School Finance in the United States* (New York, Ginn and Company), p. 85.

portunities available to the people in various sections of the country. It develops backward territories in accordance with national requirements. It promotes the national economy and the national culture. Well-conceived centralization enables the government to respond quickly to rapid nation-wide social and economic changes. The information which indicates occurrence of such changes and the type of adjustment required to meet them is readily available to the central government. The whole huge machinery of the government may be mobilized at a moment's notice to meet the national emergency or changed situation. Thousands of employees may be shifted from one type of activity to another or from one section of the country to another, as conditions require that this be done.

Proper centralization of government stimulates the civic interest of the people and broadens their civic outlook. It fosters broad national ideals, it gives rise to momentous political issues which profoundly stir the people, and it provides, if the people so desire, its own democratic processes for the consideration of public issues, which are just as effective as the democratic processes provided by the local government for the disposition of local affairs.

A properly conceived central government does not restrict the freedom of the individual. On the contrary, it often proves to be the most effective instrument for safeguarding the civil liberties of the people and their democratic institutions. It endeavors, in a democratic country, to guarantee fundamental civil rights to all the citizens in any portion of the country. Wherever undemocratic local pressure groups gain dominance and deny to some citizens their fundamental civil rights, the national government may intervene and may force upon these pressure groups the observance of these civil rights.

A well-conceived central government enlarges individual freedoms also by guaranteeing to the individuals freedom of enterprise over the entire national territory and by affording them an opportunity for a wider sphere of creative activity. The individual shares, in a democracy, in the determination of the large affairs with which the central government is concerned. The greater the scope of the public affairs, the greater the importance and responsibility of the individuals who share in their disposition. . . .

Some students of political science also emphasize the fact that the country which is exposed to attack requires a more centralized government than one whose natural location affords it relative security. It is significant that the tendencies toward the centralization of government become most pronounced in a country in times of war or when war is imminent.

CONCLUSION

The national interest can best be served by striking a fair balance between centralization and decentralization so that the advantages of both of those types of control may be maintained and the disadvantages of their extreme manifestations avoided. The exact degree of centralization and decentralization which may be advisable in the case of different countries must necessarily depend on the size of the country, the stage of its economic development, and the particular political, social, and economic situation with which it may be confronted at the moment. A small country would necessarily require a more centralized government than a large one. So, too, a country exposed to the dangers of attack requires a more centralized organization than one that is relatively secure from external aggression. Each country should seek to blend central control with local control in its major public services so as best to promote its social ideals under the particular circumstances of its life.

Federalism and Freedom: A Critique

FRANZ L. NEUMANN *

The theoretical argument for federalism revolves around the potential of political power for evil. Federalism is seen as one of the devices to curb the evil use of power by dividing power among a number of competing power-units.

The underlying sentiment—the corruptive influence of power—is often not clearly formulated and the consequences thus not clearly seen. . . .

1. It is Lord Acton's statement on the corruptive effect of political power which appears to have today the greatest influence. Three statements of his on political power are:

a. ". . . power tends to expand indefinitely, and will transcend all barriers, abroad and at home, until met by superior forces."
b. "History is not a web woven with innocent hands. Among all the causes which degrade and demoralize men, power is the most constant and the most active."
c. To Creighton: "I cannot accept your canon that we are to judge Pope

* Late Professor of Public Law and Government, Columbia University. Author of *Behemoth* and other publications. The selection is from Franz L. Neumann, "Federalism and Freedom: A Critique," in A. W. Macmahon, ed., *Federalism: Mature and Emergent* (New York, Doubleday & Co. Inc., 1955), pp. 45–49. By permission of the Trustees of Columbia University.

> and King unlike other men, with a favorable presumption that they did no wrong. If there is any presumption it is the other way against holders of power, increasing as the power increases. Historic responsibility has to make up for the want of legal responsibility. Power tends to corrupt and absolute power corrupts absolutely. Great men are almost always bad men, even when they exercise influence and not authority: still more when you superadd the tendency or the certainty of corruption by authority. There is no worse heresy than that the office sanctifies the holder of it."

These statements have two aspects. The first one is, indeed, unobjectionable and, of course, not very original. Thucydides said much the same:

> *Melians*—You may be sure that we are as well aware as you of the difficulty of contending against your power and fortune, unless the terms be equal. But we trust that the gods may grant us fortune as good as yours, since we are just men fighting against unjust, and that what we want in power will be made up by the alliance of the Lacedaemonians, who are bound, if only for very shame, to come to the aid of their kindred. Our confidence, therefore, after all is not so utterly irrational.
>
> *Athenians*—When you speak of the favour of the gods, we may as fairly hope for that as yourselves; neither our pretensions nor our conduct being in any way contrary to what men believe of the gods, or practise among themselves. *Of the gods we believe, and of men we know, that by a necessary law of their nature they rule wherever they can.* And it is not as if we were the first to make this law, or to act upon it when made: we found it existing before us, and shall leave it to exist for ever after us; all we do is to make use of it, knowing that you and everybody else, having the same power as we have, would do the same as we do. (Emphasis supplied.)

And Montesquieu said this even more clearly. According to him power could be checked only by power—a statement that few would be willing to quarrel with. Not ideologies and beliefs but only a counter-power can check power. In this he applies Cartesian principles and stands in the tradition of Spinoza who saw no way of limiting the state's absoluteness (which was logical consequence of his assumptions and of his geometric method) except by a counter-power.

The Montesquieu generalization is, of course, designed to give his doctrine of the separation of powers an adequate theoretical base. But as little as the theory of separate powers follows from his sociological observation, as little does that of the preferability of the federal state. Bentham rejected the separation of powers not only as incompatible with democracy but also because it could not really maximize freedom if the three organs of government were controlled by the same social group. A quite similar argument can be raised against federalism as a guarantee for liberty. Those who assert that the federal state through the diffusion of *constitutional* powers actually diffuses *political* power often overlook the fact that the real cause for the existence of liberty is the pluralist structure of society and the multi-party (or two-party) system. Federalism is not identical with social pluralism; and neither the two-party nor the multi-party system is the product of the federal state or the condition for its functioning.

2. Whether the federal state does indeed increase freedom cannot be abstractly determined. We have some evidence that the federal state as such (that is, regardless of the form of government) has not fulfilled this role. The German Imperial Constitution certainly created a federal state but there is little doubt that politically it had a dual purpose: to be a dynastic alliance against the forces of liberalism and democracy, and to secure the hegemony of Prussia. One may argue that a unitary state may even have been worse than the federal solution: that is quite possible. Nevertheless one may say, with reason, that the archaic Prussian three-class franchise could not possibly have been introduced as the system for a unitary German state. Thus a unitary German state in all likelihood would have been more progressive than the Bismarckian system. The Austro-Hungarian Dual Monarchy, after the *Ausgleich* of 1867, was an attempt to ensure the rule of the Germans and Magyars over all other nationalities. The Dual Monarchy most certainly did not maximize freedom except for the oligarchies in its two constituent states.

Perhaps more striking are the respective roles of federalism and centralism in the coming to power of National Socialism. Some believe, indeed, that the centralization under the Weimar Republic is wholly or at least partly responsible for the rise of National Socialism. But there is no evidence for this statement—nor indeed for the opposite one. It is certain that Bavaria, with the strongest states' rights tradition, gave shelter to the National Socialist movement and it is equally certain that the federal character of the Weimar Republic did not, after Hitler's appointment, delay the process of synchronization (*Gleichschaltung*) of the various state governments. Nor is there any definable relation between democratic conviction and federalist (or unitary) sympathies. The National Socialists were both centralists and reactionary, as were the Nationalists. Democrats and Social Democrats were antifederalists and committed to the preservation of political freedom. The Catholic center was not wholeheartedly committed to any position, and the Communists were, in theory, for the unitary state but did not hesitate, during the revolution of 1918, to advocate the secession of Brunswick which they believed they had in their pocket.

3. But perhaps what is meant by saying that federalism maximizes freedom is that only in a democracy does the division of constitutional power among various autonomous territorial units effect a maximum of political liberty; in other words, that democracy and the federal state go

together, even that federalism is necessary for democracy. Literally taken, this statement is most certainly untrue. The United Kingdom is a proof against it. Weimar Germany cannot be cited either for or against it. Bavaria—the most states' rights-conscious *land*—was certainly the most reactionary; Prussia, the most democratic. Insofar as the United States is concerned, it seems almost impossible to make any statement because of the extreme difficulty of attributing to the federal system—in isolation from other elements—any specific function. There are, perhaps, some tests like the protection of civil liberties. For a criminal, the federal system has obvious advantages in that it increases his margin of safety from prosecution. The need for extradition may, in isolated cases, permit a criminal to escape punishment. It is doubtful, however, that this can be taken as a compliment to federalism. Of real importance would be a study designed to prove or disprove that the federal nature of American government has strengthened civil liberties. The criminal syndicalism legislation of the post World War I period does not permit us to pass a final judgment. The "red hysteria" of that period "practically assured . . . passage (of this type of legislation) with only slight examination." The bills were passed with "breath-taking swiftness and little debate, or with a great outburst of oratory characterized more by passion, prejudice, and misinformation than by a reasoned effort to get at the facts." There seemed to be a race among the various states for the most drastic legislation, and vested interests, their influence enhanced by the makeup of the state legislatures, pushed through the bills. Simultaneously, efforts to enact a federal bill failed from 1917 to 1920. On the other hand, however, it is possible that without state laws a federal bill may have been enacted, and it is also true that in a few states no legislation was enacted. On the whole, one may perhaps say that the federal system may have speeded up inroads into the civil liberties rather than have protected them.

The same, perhaps, may be said of the present situation. The evidence is certainly too slight to be of great value in determining whether the federal system is preferable to the unitary state as an instrument to preserve or enhance civil liberties. Nor is it likely that convincing evidence can be obtained, since other factors—the plurality of the social structure, the functioning of a truly competitive party system, the strength of a favorable tradition, the intellectual level of the population, the attitude of the courts—do far more easily permit the formation of a counter-power against forces hostile to civil liberties than does the federal structure of the government.

4. Lord Acton's statements, however, are also concerned with a second aspect: namely, the corruptive influence of power. This brilliant formula

that power tends to corrupt and absolute power corrupts absolutely has attained the position of a classical remark; but, inevitably, it has also become a cliché of which neither the meaning nor the validity is ever questioned. The content of the statement is certainly not very original. While Plato's discussion of the same problem shows a much deeper insight, Lord Acton's has the undoubted merits of brevity and of quotability.

Lord Acton asserts that the character of the man who has power is corrupted by the exercise of power, or as the German adage has it: Politics corrupts the character. This is probably a valid generalization—but what is its significance for politics, in general, and for our problem, in particular? A morally evil ruler does not necessarily make a bad ruler—he may accumulate riches, indulge in all kinds of vices—and yet his rule may be beneficial; while the paragon of virtue may lead his country to destruction. But if we turn from monarchy or tyranny to representative government, the applicability of the formula to politics is quite certainly small.

However, we may well redefine the formula to mean that too much power concentrated in any organ of government has evil consequences for the people and that federalism, by dividing power among independent territorial units, checks these evil potentialities.

Thus redefined, the statement is no longer defensible because the opposite may equally be true. It is, indeed, also true: Too little power tends to corrupt and absolute lack of power corrupts absolutely; or, as Edmund Burke put it: "Nothing turns out to be so oppressive and unjust as a feeble government." One can accept Burke's assertion as absolute truth as little as one can Lord Acton's. Both are partially true generalizations, Burke's being, perhaps, a more realistic description of marginal situations than Lord Acton's. If one shares Burke's hatred of revolution, one may keep in mind that modern revolutions such as the French of 1789, the two Russian ones of 1917, and the German of 1918, had their immediate cause in the lack of power of the central governments and not in the excessive use or abuse of power.

It thus seems impossible to attribute to federalism, as such, a value; or to assert that the federal state—as contrasted to the unitary state—enhances political and civil freedom by dividing power among autonomous territorial subdivisions.

Topic 16

"ONE MAN, ONE VOTE"

Legislative Apportionment

REYNOLDS *V.* SIMS
377 U.S. 533 (1964)

[In eight cases, decided on June 15, 1964, the apportionment of state legislatures in six states (Alabama, New York, Maryland, Virginia, Delaware and Colorado) was attacked as violative of the provision of the Fourteenth Amendment of the Constitution which provides that "no state shall deny to any person within its jurisdiction the equal protection of the laws." In each case, but one, a gross inequality of population in state legislative districts existed with the result that a vote in one district was, for all practical purposes, worth much more than a vote in other districts.]

MR. CHIEF JUSTICE WARREN delivered the opinion of the Court.

Undeniably the Constitution of the United States protects the right of all qualified citizens to vote, in state as well as in federal elections. A consistent line of decisions by this Court in cases involving attempts to deny or restrict the right of suffrage has made this indelibly clear. . . . The right to vote freely for the candidate of one's choice is of the essence of a democratic society, and any restrictions on that right strike at the heart of representative government. And the right of suffrage can be denied by a debasement or dilution of the weight of a citizen's vote just as effectively as by wholly prohibiting the free exercise of the franchise. . . .

In *Baker* v. *Carr,* 369 U.S. 186, we held that a claim asserted under the Equal Protection Clause challenging the constitutionality of a State's apportionment of seats in its legislature, on the ground that the right to vote of certain citizens was effectively impaired since debased and diluted in effect, presented a justiciable controversy subject to adjudication by federal courts. The spate of similar cases filed and decided by lower courts since our decision in *Baker* amply shows that the problem of state legislative malapportionment is one that is perceived to exist in a large number of the States.[1]

[1] Litigation challenging the constitutionality of state legislative apportionment schemes had been instituted in at least 34 States prior to end of 1962—within nine months of our decision in *Baker* v. *Carr.*

In *Baker,* a suit involving an attack on the apportionment of seats in the Tennessee Legislature, we remanded to the District Court, which had dismissed the action, for consideration on the merits. We intimated no view as to the proper constitutional standards for evaluating the validity of a state legislative apportionment scheme. Nor did we give any consideration to the question of appropriate remedies. Rather, we simply stated:

> Beyond noting that we have no cause at this stage to doubt the District Court will be able to fashion relief if violations of constitutional rights are found, it is improper now to consider what remedy would be most appropriate if appellants prevail at trial. . . .

In *Gray* v. *Sanders,* 372 U.S. 368, we held that the Georgia county unit system, applicable in statewide primary elections, was unconstitutional since it resulted in a dilution of the weight of the votes of certain Georgia voters merely because of where they resided. . . .

In *Wesberry* v. *Sanders,* 376 U.S. 1, decided earlier this Term, we held that attacks on the constitutionality of congressional districting plans enacted by state legislatures do not present nonjusticiable questions and should not be dismissed generally for "want of equity." We determined that the constitutional test for the validity of congressional districting schemes was one of substantial equality of population among the various districts established by a state legislature for the election of members of the Federal House of Representatives.

In that case we decided that an apportionment of congressional seats which "contracts the value of some votes and expands that of others" is unconstitutional, since "the Federal Constitution intends that when qualified voters elect members of Congress each vote be given as much weight as any other vote. . . ." We concluded that the constitutional prescription for election of members of the House of Representatives "by the People," construed in its historical context, "means that as nearly as is practicable one man's vote in a congressional election is to be worth as much as another's." We further stated:

> It would defeat the principle solemnly embodied in the Great Compromise—equal representation in the House for equal numbers of people—for us to hold that, within the States, legislatures may draw the lines of congressional districts in such a way as to give some voters a greater voice in choosing a Congressman than others.

We found further, in *Wesberry,* that "our Constitution's plain objective" was that "of making equal representation for equal numbers of people the fundamental goal . . . ." We conclude by stating:

> No right is more precious in a free country than that of having a voice in the election of those who make the laws under which, as good citizens, we must live. Other rights, even the most basic, are illusory if the right to vote is under-

mined. Our Constitution leaves no room for classification of people in a way that unnecessarily abridges this right.

Gray and *Wesberry* are of course not dispositive of or directly controlling on our decision in these cases involving state legislative apportionment controversies. Admittedly, those decisions, in which we held that, in statewide and in congressional elections, one person's vote must be counted equally with those of all other voters in a State, were based on different constitutional considerations and were addressed to rather distinct problems. But neither are they wholly inapposite. . . . Our decision in *Wesberry* was of course grounded on that language of the Constitution which prescribes that members of the Federal House of Representatives are to be chosen "by the People," while attacks on state legislative apportionment schemes, such as that involved in the instant cases, are principally based on the Equal Protection Clause of the Fourteenth Amendment. Nevertheless, *Wesberry* clearly established that the fundamental principle of representative government in this country is one of equal representation for equal numbers of people, without regard to race, sex, economic status, or place of residence within a State. Our problem, then, is to ascertain, in the instant cases, whether there are any constitutionally cognizable principles which would justify departures from the basic standard of equality among voters in the apportionment of seats in state legislatures.

A predominant consideration in determining whether a State's legislative apportionment scheme constitutes an invidious discrimination violative of rights asserted under the Equal Protection Clause is that the rights allegedly impaired are individual and personal in nature. . . . Undoubtedly, the right of suffrage is a fundamental matter in a free and democratic society. Especially since the right to exercise the franchise in a free and unimpaired manner is preservative of other basic civil and political rights, any alleged infringement of the right of citizens to vote must be carefully and meticulously scrutinized. Almost a century ago, in *Yick Wo* v. *Hopkins,* 118 U.S. 356, the Court referred to "the political franchise of voting" as "a fundamental political right, because preservative of all rights."

Legislators represent people, not trees or acres. Legislators are elected by voters, not farms or cities or economic interests. As long as ours is a representative form of government, and our legislatures are those instruments of government elected directly by and directly representative of the people, the right to elect legislators in a free and unimpaired fashion is a bedrock of our political system. It could hardly be gainsaid that a constitutional claim had been asserted by an allegation that certain otherwise qualified voters had been entirely prohibited from voting for members of their state legislature. And, if a State should provide that the votes of citizens in one part of the State should be given two times, or five times, or 10 times the weight of votes of citizens in another part of the State, it could hardly be contended that the right to vote of those residing in the disfavored areas had not been effectively diluted. It would appear extraordinary to suggest that a state could be constitutionally permitted to enact a law providing that certain of the state's voters could vote two, five, or 10 times for their legislative representatives, while voters living elsewhere could vote only once. And it is inconceivable that a state law to the effect that, in counting votes for legislators, the votes of citizens in one part of the State would be multiplied by two, five, or 10, while the votes of persons in another area would be counted only at face value, could be constitutionally sustainable. Of course, the effect of state legislative districting schemes which give the same number of representatives to unequal numbers of constituents is identical. Overweighting and overvaluation of the votes of those living here has the certain effect of dilution and undervaluation of the votes of those living there. The resulting discrimination against those individual voters living in disfavored areas is easily demonstrable mathematically. Their right to vote is simply not the same right to vote as that of those living in a favored part of the State. Two, five, or 10 of them must vote before the effect of their voting is equivalent to that of their favored neighbor. Weighting the votes of citizens differently, by any method or means, merely because of where they happen to reside, hardly seems justifiable. One must be ever aware that the Constitution forbids "sophisticated as well as simple-minded modes of discrimination." *Lane* v. *Wilson,* 307 U.S. 268, 275, *Gomillion* v. *Lightfoot,* 364 U.S. 339, 342. . . .

Representative government is in essence self-government through the medium of elected representatives of the people, and each and every citizen has an inalienable right to full and effective participation in the political processes of his State's legislative bodies. Most citizens can achieve this participation only as qualified voters through the election of legislators to represent them. Full and effective participation by all citizens in state government requires, therefore, that each citizen has an equally effective voice in the election of members of his state legislature. Modern and viable state government needs, and the Constitution demands, no less.

Logically, in a society ostensibly grounded on representative government, it would seem reasonable that a majority of the people of a State could elect a majority of that State's legislators. To conclude differently, and to sanction minority control of state legislative bodies, would appear to deny majority rights in a way that far surpasses any possible denial of minority rights that might otherwise be thought to result. Since legislatures are responsible for enacting laws by which all citizens are to be governed, they should be bodies which are collectively responsive to the popular will. And the concept of equal protection has been traditionally viewed as requiring the uniform treatment of persons standing in the same relation to the governmental action questioned or challenged. With respect to the allocation of legislative representation, all voters, as citizens of a State, stand in the same relation regardless of where they live. Any suggested criteria for the differentiation of citizens are insufficient to justify any discrimination, as to the weight of their votes, unless relevant to the permissible purposes of legislative apportionment. Since the achieving of fair and effective representation for all citizens is concededly the basic aim of legislative apportionment, we conclude that the Equal Protection Clause guarantees the opportunity for equal participation by all voters in the election of state legislators. Diluting the weight of votes because of place of residence impairs basic constitutional rights under the Fourteenth Amendment just as much as invidious discriminations based upon factors such as race, *Brown* v. *Board of Education,* 347 U.S. 483, or economic status, *Griffin* v. *Illinois,* 351 U.S. 12, *Douglas* v. *California,* 372 U.S. 353. Our constitutional system amply provides for the protection of minorities by means other than giving them majority control of state legislatures. And the democratic ideals of equality and majority rule, which have served this Nation so well in the past, are hardly of any less significance for the present and the future.

We are told that the matter of apportioning representation in a state legislature is a complex and many-faceted one. We are advised that States can rationally consider factors other than population in apportioning legislative representation. We are admonished not to restrict the power of the States to impose differing views as to political philosophy on their citizens. We are cautioned about the dangers of entering into political thickets and mathematical quagmires. Our answer is this: a denial of constitutionally protected rights demands judicial protection; our oath and our office require no less of us. . . . To the extent that a citizen's right to vote is debased, he is that much less a citizen. The fact that an individual lives here or there is not a legitimate reason for overweighting or diluting the efficacy of his vote. The complexions of societies and civilizations change, often with amazing rapidity. A nation once primarily rural in character becomes predominantly urban.[2] Representation schemes once fair and equitable become archaic and outdated. But the basic principle of representative government remains, and must remain, unchanged—the weight of a citizen's vote cannot be made to depend on where he lives. Population is, of necessity, the starting point for consideration and the controlling criterion for judgment in legislative apportionment controversies. A citizen, a qualified voter, is no more nor no less so because he lives in the city or on the farm. This is the clear and strong command of our Constitution's Equal Protection Clause. This is an essential part of the concept of a government of laws and not men. This is at the heart

[2] Although legislative apportionment controversies are generally viewed as involving urban-rural conflicts, much evidence indicates that presently it is the fast-growing suburban areas which are probably the most seriously underrepresented in many of our state legislatures.

of Lincoln's vision of "government of the people, by the people, [and] for the people." The Equal Protection Clause demands no less than substantially equal state legislative representation for all citizens, of all places as well as of all races.

We hold that, as a basic constitutional standard, the Equal Protection Clause requires that the seats in both houses of a bicameral state legislature must be apportioned on a population basis. Simply stated, an individual's right to vote for state legislators is unconstitutionally impaired when its weight is in a substantial fashion diluted when compared with votes of citizens living in other parts of the State. . . .

Much has been written since our decision in *Baker* v. *Carr* about the applicability of the so-called federal analogy * to state legislative apportionment arrangements. . . .

Attempted reliance on the federal analogy appears often to be little more than an after-the-fact rationalization offered in defense of maladjusted state apportionment arrangements. The original constitutions of 36 of our States provided that representation in both houses of the state legislatures would be based completely, or predominantly, on population. And the Founding Fathers clearly had no intention of establishing a pattern or model for the apportionment of seats in state legislatures when the system of representation in the Federal Congress was adopted. Demonstrative of this is the fact that the Northwest Ordinance, adopted in the same year, 1787, as the Federal Constitution, provided for the apportionment of seats in territorial legislatures solely on the basis of population.

The system of representation in the two Houses of the Federal Congress is one ingrained in our Constitution, as part of the law of the land. It is one conceived out of compromise and concession indispensable to the establishment of our federal republic. Arising from unique historical circumstances, it is based on the consideration that in establishing our type of federalism a group of formerly independent States bound themselves together under one national government. . . . The developing history and growth of our republic cannot cloud the fact that, at the time of the inception of the system of representation in the Federal Congress, a compromise between the larger and smaller States on this matter averted a deadlock in the constitutional convention which had threatened to abort the birth of our Nation. . . .

Political subdivisions of States—counties, cities, or whatever—never were and never have been considered as sovereign entities. Rather, they have been traditionally regarded as subordinate governmental instrumentalities created by the State to assist in the carrying out of state governmental functions. . . .

* [Representation according to population in the House and equal representation for each state in the Senate.]

Since we find the so-called federal analogy inapposite to a consideration of the constitutional validity of state legislative apportionment schemes, we necessarily hold that the Equal Protection Clause requires both houses of a state legislature to be apportioned on a population basis. The right of a citizen to equal representation and to have his vote weighted equally with those of all other citizens in the election of members of one house of a bicameral state legislature would amount to little if States could effectively submerge the equal-population principle in the apportionment of seats in the other house.

If such a scheme were permissible, an individual citizen's ability to exercise an effective voice in the only instrument of state government directly representative of the people might be almost as effectively thwarted as if neither house were apportioned on a population basis. Deadlock between the two bodies might result in compromise and concession on some issues. But in all too many cases the more probable result would be frustration of the majority will through minority veto in the house not apportioned on a population basis, stemming directly from the failure to accord adequate overall legislative representation to all of the State's citizens on a nondiscriminatory basis. In summary, we can perceive no constitutional difference, with respect to the geographical distribution of state legislative representation, between the two houses of a bicameral state legislature.

We do not believe that the concept of bicameralism is rendered anachronistic and meaningless when the predominant basis of representation in the two state legislative bodies is required to be the same—population. A prime reason for bicameralism, modernly considered, is to insure mature and deliberate consideration of, and to prevent precipitate action on, proposed legislative measures. Simply because the controlling criterion for apportioning representation is required to be the same in both houses does not mean that there will be no differences in the composition and complexion of the two bodies. Different constituencies can be represented in the two houses. One body could be composed of single-member districts while the other could have at least some multimember districts. The length of terms of the legislators in the separate bodies could differ. The numerical size of the two bodies could be made to differ, even significantly, and the geographical size of districts from which legislators are elected could also be made to differ. And apportionment in one house could be arranged so as to balance off minor inequities in the representation of certain areas in the other house. In summary, these and other factors could be, and are presently in many States, utilized to engender differing complexions and collective attitudes in the two bodies of a state legislature, although both are apportioned substantially on a population basis.

By holding that as a federal constitutional requisite both houses of a state legislature must be apportioned on a population basis, we mean that the

Equal Protection Clause requires that a State make an honest and good faith effort to construct districts, in both houses of its legislature, as nearly of equal population as is practicable. We realize that it is a practical impossibility to arrange legislative districts so that each one has an identical number of residents, or citizens, or voters. Mathematical exactness or precision is hardly a workable constitutional requirement. . . .

A State may legitimately desire to maintain the integrity of various political subdivisions, insofar as possible, and provide for compact districts of contiguous territory in designing a legislative apportionment scheme. Valid considerations may underlie such aims. Indiscriminate districting, without any regard for political subdivision or natural or historical boundary lines, may be little more than an open invitation to partisan gerrymandering. Single-member districts may be the rule in one State, while another State might desire to achieve some flexibility by creating multimember or floterial districts. Whatever the means of accomplishment, the overriding objective must be substantial equality of population among the various districts, so that the vote of any citizen is approximately equal in weight to that of any other citizen in the State.

[Mr. Justice Clark and Mr. Justice Stewart substantially disagreed with the reasoning of the majority in *Reynolds* v. *Sims* but concurred in the judgment of the Court. However, these Justices dissented in *Lucas* v. *Colorado* which follows hereafter.]

MR. JUSTICE HARLAN, dissenting.

In these cases the Court holds that seats in the legislatures of six States are apportioned in ways that violate the Federal Constitution. Under the Court's ruling it is bound to follow that the legislatures in all but a few of the other 44 States will meet the same fate. These decisions, with *Wesberry* v. *Sanders,* 376 U.S. 1, involving congressional districting by the States, and *Gray* v. *Sanders,* 372 U.S. 368, relating to elections for statewide office, have the effect of placing basic aspects of state political systems under the pervasive overlordship of the federal judiciary. Once again,[3] I must register my protest.

Today's holding is that the Equal Protection Clause of the Fourteenth Amendment requires every State to structure its legislature so that all the members of each house represent substantially the same number of people; other factors may be given play only to the extent that they do not significantly encroach on this basic "population" principle. Whatever may be

[3] See *Baker* v. *Carr,* 369 U.S. 186, 330, and the dissenting opinion of Frankfurter, J., in which I joined, *id.,* at 266; *Gray* v. *Sanders,* 372 U.S. 368, 382; *Wesberry* v. *Sanders,* 376 U.S. 1, 20.

thought of this holding as a piece of political ideology—and even on that score the political history and practices of this country from its earliest beginnings leave wide room for debate (see the dissenting opinion of Frankfurter, J., in *Baker* v. *Carr,* 369 U.S. 186, 266, 301–323)—I think it demonstrable that the Fourteenth Amendment does not impose this political tenet on the States or authorize this Court to do so.

The Court's constitutional discussion, found in its opinion in the Alabama cases is remarkable (as, indeed, is that found in the separate opinions of my Brothers STEWART and CLARK) for its failure to address itself at all to the Fourteenth Amendment as a whole or to the legislative history of the Amendment pertinent to the matter at hand. Stripped of aphorisms, the Court's argument boils down to the assertion that petitioners' right to vote has been invidiously "debased" or "diluted" by systems of apportionment which entitle them to vote for fewer legislators than other voters, an assertion which is tied to the Equal Protection Clause only by the constitutionally frail tautology that "equal" means "equal."

Had the Court paused to probe more deeply into the matter, it would have found that the Equal Protection Clause was never intended to inhibit the States in choosing any democratic method they pleased for the apportionment of their legislatures. This is shown by the language of the Fourteenth Amendment taken as a whole, by the understanding of those who proposed and ratified it, and by the political practices of the States at the time the Amendment was adopted. It is confirmed by numerous state and congressional actions since the adoption of the Fourteenth Amendment, and by the common understanding of the Amendment as evidenced by subsequent constitutional amendments and decisions of this Court before *Baker* v. *Carr, supra,* made an abrupt break with the past in 1962.

The failure of the Court to consider any of these matters cannot be excused or explained by any concept of "developing" constitutionalism. It is meaningless to speak of constitutional "development" when both the language and history of the controlling provisions of the Constitution are wholly ignored. Since it can, I think, be shown beyond doubt that state legislative apportionments, as such, are wholly free of constitutional limitations, save such as may be imposed by the Republican Form of Government Clause (Const., Art. IV, § 4), the Court's action now bringing them within the purview of the Fourteenth Amendment amounts to nothing less than an exercise of the amending power by this Court.

So far as the Federal Constitution is concerned, the complaints in these cases should all have been dismissed below for failure to state a cause of action, because what has been alleged or proved shows no violation of any constitutional right. . . .

[In the appendix to his opinion Mr. Justice Harlan quotes from the speeches of eleven members of the House of Representatives and five members of the Senate to support the view that the purpose of the Fourteenth Amendment was to reduce the number of Representatives in the House and the Electoral College vote of states that denied Negro suffrage. Several of these speakers stated that while they would have preferred an unequivocal guarantee of universal suffrage in the Constitution, they were supporting the Fourteenth Amendment as a step in this direction.]

LUCAS *V.* COLORADO

377 U.S. 713 (1964)

[The important distinguishing elements in the Colorado case were that: (1) The parties conceded that one house of the Colorado state legislature was apportioned "as nearly equal in population" as may be practical (while a majority of the other house was elected by 33.2 per cent of the population*), and (2) the whole scheme of districting for both houses was approved by a referendum vote of nearly 2 to 1, with a majority obtained in each county, including those urban counties allegedly discriminated against.]

MR. CHIEF JUSTICE WARREN delivered the opinion of the Court. . . .

At the November 1962 general election, the Colorado electorate adopted proposed Amendment No. 7 by a vote of 305,700 to 172,725, and defeated proposed Amendment No. 8 by a vote of 311,749 to 149,822. Amendment No. 8, rejected by a majority of the voters, prescribed an apportionment plan pursuant to which seats in both houses of the Colorado Legislature would purportedly be apportioned on a population basis. Amendment No. 7, on the other hand, provided for the apportionment of the House of Representatives on the basis of population, but essentially maintained the existing apportionment in the Senate, which was based on a combination of population and various other factors. . . .

[Additionally,] this case differs from the others decided this date in that the initiative device provides a practicable political remedy to obtain relief against alleged legislative malapportionment in Colorado. An initiated measure proposing a constitutional amendment or a statutory enactment is entitled to be placed on the ballot if the signatures of 8% of those voting for the Secretary of State in the last election are obtained. No geographical distribution of petition signers is required. Initiative and referendum has been frequently utilized throughout Colorado's history.

We find no significance in the fact that a nonjudicial, political remedy may be available for the effectuation of asserted rights to equal representation in a state legislature. Courts sit to adjudicate controversies involving

* The dissenting opinion states the percentage as 36.

alleged denials of constitutional rights. While a court sitting as a court of equity might be justified in temporarily refraining from the issuance of injunctive relief in an apportionment case in order to allow for resort to an available political remedy, such as initiative and referendum, individual constitutional rights cannot be deprived, or denied judicial effectuation, because of the existence of a nonjudicial remedy through which relief against the alleged malapportionment, which the individual voters seek, might be achieved. An individual's constitutionally protected right to cast an equally weighted vote cannot be denied even by a vote of a majority of a State's electorate, if the apportionment scheme adopted by the voters fails to measure up to the requirements of the Equal Protection Clause.

Manifestly, the fact that an apportionment plan is adopted in a popular referendum is insufficient to sustain its constitutionality or to induce a court of equity to refuse to act. As stated by this Court in *West Virginia State Bd. of Educ.* v. *Barnette,* 319 U.S. 624, 638, "One's right to life, liberty, and property . . . and other fundamental rights may not be submitted to vote; they depend on the outcome of no elections." [1] A citizen's constitutional rights can hardly be infringed simply because a majority of the people choose to do so. We hold that the fact that a challenged legislative apportionment plan was approved by the electorate is without federal constitutional significance, if the scheme adopted fails to satisfy the basic requirements of the Equal Protection Clause, as delineated in our opinion in *Reynolds* v. *Sims.* And we conclude that the fact that a practicably available political remedy, such as initiative and referendum, exists under state law provides justification only for a court of equity to stay its hand temporarily while recourse to such a remedial device is attempted or while proposed initiated measures relating to legislative apportionment are pending and will be submitted to the State's voters at the next election. . . .

Since the apportionment of seats in the Colorado Legislature, under the provisions of Amendment No. 7, fails to comport with the requirements of the Equal Protection Clause, the decision below must be reversed. Beyond what we said in our opinion in *Reynolds,* we express no view on questions relating to remedies at the present time. On remand, the District Court must now determine whether the imminence of the 1964 primary and general elections requires that utilization of the apportionment scheme contained in the constitutional amendment be permitted, for purposes of those elections, or whether the circumstances in Colorado are such that appellants' right to cast adequately weighted votes for members of the State Legislature can practicably be effectuated in 1964. Accordingly, we reverse the decision

[1] And, as stated by the court in *Hall* v. *St. Helena Parish School Bd.,* 197 F. Supp. 649, 659 (D. C. E. D. La. 1961), aff'd, 368 U.S. 515, "No plebiscite can legalize an unjust discrimination."

of the court below and remand the case for further proceedings consistent with the views stated here and in our opinion in *Reynolds* v. *Sims*.

It is so ordered.

MR. JUSTICE STEWART, whom MR. JUSTICE CLARK joins, dissenting.*

It is important to make clear at the outset what these cases are not about. They have nothing to do with the denial or impairment of any person's right to vote. Nobody's right to vote has been denied. Nobody's right to vote has been restricted. Nobody has been deprived of the right to have his vote counted. The voting right cases which the Court cites are, therefore, completely wide of the mark. Secondly, these cases have nothing to do with the "weighting" or "diluting" of votes cast within any electoral unit. The rule of *Gray* v. *Sanders,* 372 U.S. 368, is, therefore, completely without relevance here. Thirdly, these cases are not concerned with the election of members of the Congress of the United States, governed by Article I of the Constitution. Consequently, the Court's decision in *Wesberry* v. *Sanders,* 376 U.S. 1, throws no light at all on the basic issue now before us.

The question involved in these cases is quite a different one. Simply stated, the question is to what degree, if at all, the Equal Protection Clause of the Fourteenth Amendment limits each sovereign State's freedom to establish appropriate electoral constituencies from which representatives to the State's bicameral legislative assembly are to be chosen. The Court's answer is a blunt one, and, I think, woefully wrong. The Equal Protection Clause, says the Court, "requires that the seats in both houses of a bicameral state legislature must be apportioned on a population basis."

After searching carefully through the Court's opinions in these and their companion cases, I have been able to find but two reasons offered in support of this rule. First, says the Court, it is "established that the fundamental principle of representative government in this country is one of equal representation for equal numbers of people. . . ." With all respect, I think that this is not correct, simply as a matter of fact. It has been unanswerably demonstrated before now that this "was not the colonial system, it was not the system chosen for the national government by the Constitution, it was not the system exclusively or even predominantly practiced by the States at the time of adoption of the Fourteenth Amendment, it is not predominantly practiced by the States today." [2] Secondly, says the Court, unless legislative

* This dissent applied to both the Colorado and New York cases.

[2] *Baker* v. *Carr,* 369 U.S. 186, 266, 301 (Frankfurter, J., dissenting).

See also the excellent analysis of the relevant historical materials contained in MR. JUSTICE HARLAN's dissenting opinion filed this day in these and their companion cases.

districts are equal in population, voters in the more populous districts will suffer a "debasement" amounting to a constitutional injury. As the Court explains it, "To the extent that a citizen's right to vote is debased, he is that much less a citizen." We are not told how or why the vote of a person in a more populated legislative district is "debased," or how or why he is less a citizen, nor is the proposition self-evident. I find it impossible to understand how or why a voter in California, for instance, either feels or is less a citizen than a voter in Nevada, simply because, despite their population disparities, each of those States is represented by two United States Senators.

To put the matter plainly, there is nothing in all the history of this Court's decisions which supports this constitutional rule. The Court's draconian pronouncement, which makes unconstitutional the legislatures of most of the 50 States, finds no support in the words of the Constitution, in any prior decision of this Court, or in the 175-year political history of our Federal Union. With all respect, I am convinced these decisions mark a long step backward into that unhappy era when a majority of the members of this Court were thought by many to have convinced themselves and each other that the demands of the Constitution were to be measured not by what it says, but by their own notions of wise political theory. The rule announced today is at odds with long-established principles of constitutional adjudication under the Equal Protection Clause, and it stifles values of local individuality and initiative vital to the character of the Federal Union which it was the genius of our Constitution to create.

I.

What the Court has done is to convert a particular political philosophy into a constitutional rule, binding upon each of the 50 States, from Maine to Hawaii, from Alaska to Texas, without regard and without respect for the many individualized and differentiated characteristics of each State, characteristics stemming from each State's distinct history, distinct geography, distinct distribution of population, and distinct political heritage. My own understanding of the various theories of representative government is that no one theory has ever commanded unanimous assent among political scientists, historians, or others who have considered the problem. But even if it were thought that the rule announced today by the Court is, as a matter of political theory, the most desirable general rule which can be devised as a basis for the make-up of the representative assembly of a typical State, I could not join in the fabrication of a constitutional mandate which imports and forever freezes one theory of political thought into our Constitution, and forever denies to every State any opportunity for enlightened and progressive innovation in the design of its democratic institutions, so as to accommodate within a system of representative government the interests and aspirations of diverse groups of people, without subjecting any group or class to absolute domination by a geographically concentrated or highly organized majority.

Representative government is a process of accommodating group interests through democratic institutional arrangements. Its function is to channel the numerous opinions, interests, and abilities of the people of a State into the making of the State's public policy. Appropriate legislative apportionment, therefore, should ideally be designed to insure effective representation in the State's legislature, in cooperation with the other organs of political power, of the various groups and interests making up the electorate. In practice, of course, this ideal is approximated in the particular apportionment system of any State by a realistic accommodation of the diverse and often conflicting political forces operating within the State. . . .

I do know enough to be aware of the great variations among the several States in their historic manner of distributing legislative power—of the Governors' Councils in New England, of the broad powers of initiative and referendum retained in some States by the people, of the legislative power which some States give to their Governors, by the right of veto or otherwise, of the widely autonomous home rule which many States give to their cities. The Court today declines to give any recognition to these considerations and countless others, tangible and intangible, in holding unconstitutional the particular systems of legislative apportionment which these States have chosen. Instead, the Court says that the requirements of the Equal Protection Clause can be met in any State only by the uncritical, simplistic, and heavy-handed application of sixth-grade arithmetic.

But legislators do not represent faceless numbers. They represent people, or, more accurately, a majority of the voters in their districts—people with identifiable needs and interests which require legislative representation, and which can often be related to the geographical areas in which these people live. The very fact of geographic districting, the constitutional validity of which the Court does not question, carries with it an acceptance of the idea of legislative representation of regional needs and interests. Yet if geographical residence is irrelevant, as the Court suggests, and the goal is solely that of equally "weighted" votes, I do not understand why the Court's constitutional rule does not require the abolition of districts and the holding of all elections at large.[3]

[3] Even with legislative districts of exactly equal voter population, 26% of the electorate (a bare majority of the voters in a bare majority of the districts) can, as a matter of the kind of theoretical mathematics embraced by the Court, elect a majority of the legislature under our simple majority electoral system. Thus, the Court's constitutional rule permits minority rule.

Students of the mechanics of voting systems tell us that if all that matters is that votes count equally, the best vote-counting electoral system is proportional representation in state-wide elections. . . . It is just because electoral systems are intended to serve functions other than satisfying mathematical theories, however, that the system of proportional representation has not been widely adopted.

The fact is, of course, that population factors must often to some degree be subordinated in devising a legislative apportionment plan which is to achieve the important goal of ensuring a fair, effective, and balanced representation of the regional, social, and economic interests within a State. And the further fact is that throughout our history the apportionments of State Legislatures have reflected the strongly felt American tradition that the public interest is composed of many diverse interests, and that in the long run it can better be expressed by a medley of component voices than by the majority's monolithic command. What constitutes a rational plan reasonably designed to achieve this objective will vary from State to State, since each State is unique, in terms of topography, geography, demography, history, heterogeneity and concentration of population, variety of social and economic interests, and in the operation and interrelation of its political institutions. But so long as a State's apportionment plan reasonably achieves, in the light of the State's own characteristics, effective and balanced representation of all substantial interests, without sacrificing the principle of effective majority rule, that plan cannot be considered irrational.

II.

This brings me to what I consider to be the proper constitutional standards to be applied in these cases. Quite simply, I think the cases should be decided by application of accepted principles of constitutional adjudication under the Equal Protection Clause. A recent expression by the Court of these principles will serve as a generalized compendium:

> [T]he Fourteenth Amendment permits the States a wide scope of discretion in enacting laws which affect some groups of citizens differently than others. The constitutional safeguard is offended only if the classification rests on grounds wholly irrelevant to the achievement of the State's objective. State legislatures are presumed to have acted within their constitutional power despite the fact that, in practice, their laws result in some inequality. A statutory discrimination will not be set aside if any state of facts reasonably may be conceived to justify it. *McGowan* v. *Maryland,* 366 U.S. 420, 425-426.

These principles reflect an understanding respect for the unique values inherent in the Federal Union of States established by our Constitution. They reflect, too, a wise perception of this Court's role in that constitutional system. The point was never better made than by Mr. Justice Brandeis, dissenting in *New State Ice Co.* v. *Leibmann,* 285 U.S. 262, 280. The final paragraph of that classic dissent is worth repeating here:

> To stay experimentation in things social and economic is a grave responsibility. Denial of the right to experiment may be fraught with serious consequences to the Nation. It is one of the happy incidents of the federal system that a single courageous State may, if its citizens choose, serve as a laboratory; and try novel social and economic experiments without risk to the rest of the

> country. This Court has the power to prevent an experiment. We may strike down the statute which embodies it on the ground that, in our opinion, the measure is arbitrary, capricious or unreasonable. . . . But in the exercise of this high power, we must be ever on our guard, lest we erect our prejudices into legal principles. If we would guide by the light of reason, we must let our minds be bold. 285 U.S., at 311. . . .

Moving from the general to the specific, I think that the Equal Protection Clause demands but two basic attributes of any plan of state legislative apportionment. First, it demands that, in the light of the State's own characteristics and needs, the plan must be a rational one. Secondly, it demands that the plan must be such as not to permit the systematic frustration of the will of a majority of the electorate of the State. I think it is apparent that any plan of legislative apportionment which could be shown to reflect no policy, but simply arbitrary and capricious action or inaction, and that any plan which could be shown systematically to prevent ultimate effective majority rule, would be invalid under accepted Equal Protection Clause standards. But, beyond this, I think there is nothing in the Federal Constitution to prevent a State from choosing any electoral legislative structure it thinks best suited to the interests, temper, and customs of its people. In the light of these standards, I turn to the Colorado . . . plan of legislative apportionment.

III.

COLORADO.

The Colorado plan creates a General Assembly composed of a Senate of 39 members and a House of 65 members. The State is divided into 65 equal population representative districts, with one representative to be elected from each district, and 39 senatorial districts, 14 of which include more than one county. In the Colorado House, the majority unquestionably rules supreme, with the population factor untempered by other considerations. In the Senate rural minorities do not have effective control, and therefore do not have even a veto power over the will of the urban majorities. It is true that, as a matter of theoretical arithmetic, a minority of 36% of the voters could elect a majority of the Senate, but this percentage has no real meaning in terms of the legislative process. Under the Colorado plan, no possible combination of Colorado senators from rural districts, even assuming *arguendo* that they would vote as a bloc, could control the Senate. To arrive at the 36% figure, one must include with the rural districts a substantial number of urban districts, districts with substantially dissimilar interests. There is absolutely no reason to assume that this theoretical majority would ever vote together on any issue so as to thwart the wishes of the majority of the voters of Colorado. Indeed, when we eschew the world of numbers, and look to the real world of effective representation, the simple fact of the matter is that Colorado's three metropolitan areas, Denver, Pueblo, and Colorado Springs, elect a majority of the Senate. . . .

The present apportionment was proposed and supported by many of Colorado's leading citizens. The factual data underlying the apportionment were prepared by the wholly independent Denver Research Institute of the University of Denver. Finally, the apportionment was adopted by a popular referendum in which not only a 2–1 majority of all the voters in Colorado, but a majority in each county, including those urban counties allegedly discriminated against, voted for the present plan in preference to an alternative proposal providing for equal representation per capita in both legislative houses. As the District Court said:

> The contention that the voters have discriminated against themselves appalls rather than convinces. Difficult as it may be at times to understand mass behaviour of human beings, a proper recognition of the judicial function precludes a court from holding that the free choice of the voters between two conflicting theories of apportionment is irrational or the result arbitrary.

The present apportionment, adopted overwhelmingly by the people in a 1962 popular referendum as a state constitutional amendment, is entirely rational, and the amendment by its terms provides for keeping the apportionment current. Thus the majority has consciously chosen to protect the minority's interests, and under the liberal initiative provisions of the Colorado Constitution, it retains the power to reverse its decision to do so. Therefore, there can be no question of frustration of the basic principle of majority rule.

Section VII

The Problem of Desegregation

OF THE MANY problems with which our country has been troubled in recent decades, few if any have assumed the great importance and engendered the deep bitterness that has been true of the controversy over racial desegregation.

Despite the unanimity of the Supreme Court in the school desegregation cases, powerful and often dominant forces in a number of states have resorted to various tactics of obstructionism and delay. A case in point is Prince Edward County in Virginia, which was one of the defendants in the 1954 cases, but by the summer of 1964 had not provided even token desegregation. This resistance is based essentially upon certain social and cultural arguments which are openly and seriously discussed in this section.

In the attempt to break down racial discrimination, and promote greater equality, Negro leaders (with white supporters) have increasingly resorted to "civil disobedience." The meaning, limits, and the arguments for and against this "weapon," are also the subject of special and full consideration.

Topic 17

IS THE CONSTITUTION "COLOR BLIND"?

"Separate But Equal"

PLESSY *V.* FERGUSON

163 U.S. 537 (1896)

[A Louisiana statute of 1890 imposed a twenty-five dollar fine on persons of Negro blood who attempted to enter railway train coaches set aside for whites. The statute also required railroads to furnish "separate but equal" railway accommodations for white and colored people. Plessy was one-eighth Negro but appeared white. He occupied a vacant seat in a railway coach reserved for white passengers, to which his ticket otherwise entitled him. He was fined as provided in the statute. On appeal, the higher state courts held the statute constitutional.]

MR. JUSTICE BROWN . . . delivered the opinion of the Court:

This case turns upon the constitutionality of an act of the General Assembly of the state of Louisiana, passed in 1890, providing for separate railway carriages for the white and colored races. . . .

The constitutionality of this act is attacked upon the ground that it conflicts both with the Thirteenth Amendment of the Constitution, abolishing slavery, and the Fourteenth Amendment, which prohibits certain restrictive legislation on the part of the states.

1. That it does not conflict with the Thirteenth Amendment, which abolished slavery and involuntary servitude, except as a punishment for crime, is too clear for argument. . . .

2. By the Fourteenth Amendment, all persons born or naturalized in the United States, and subject to the jurisdiction thereof, are made citizens of the United States and of the state wherein they reside; and the states are forbidden from making or enforcing any law which shall abridge the privileges or immunities of citizens of the United States, or shall deprive any person of life, liberty or property without due process of law, or deny to any person within their jurisdiction the equal protection of the laws. . . .

The object of the amendment was undoubtedly to enforce the absolute equality of the two races before the law, but in the nature of things it could not have been intended to abolish distinctions based upon color, or to enforce social, as distinguished from political, equality, or a commingling of the two races upon terms unsatisfactory to either. Laws permitting, and even requiring, their separation in places where they are liable to be brought into contact do not necessarily imply the inferiority of either race to the other, and have been generally, if not universally, recognized as within the competency of the state legislatures in the exercise of their police power. The most common instance of this is connected with the establishment of separate schools for white and colored children, which has been held to be a valid exercise of the legislative power even by courts of states where the political rights of the colored race have been longest and most earnestly enforced.

One of the earliest of these cases is that of Roberts *v.* City of Boston, 5 Cush. 198 (1849), in which the Supreme Judicial Court of Massachusetts held that the general school committee of Boston had power to make provision for the instruction of colored children in separate schools established exclusively for them, and to prohibit their attendance upon the other schools. "The great principle," said Chief Justice Shaw, p. 206, "advanced by the learned and eloquent advocate for the plaintiff" (Mr. Charles Sumner), "is, that by the constitution and laws of Massachusetts, all persons without distinction of age or sex, birth or color, origin or condition, are equal before the law. . . . But, when this great principle comes to be applied to the actual and various conditions of persons in society, it will not warrant the assertion, that men and women are legally clothed with the same civil and political powers, and that children and adults are legally to have the same functions and be subject to the same treatment; but only that the rights of all, as they are settled and regulated by law, are equally entitled to the paternal consideration and protection of the law for their maintenance and security." It was held that the powers of the committee extended to the establishment of separate schools for children of different ages, sexes and colors, and that they might also establish special schools for poor and neglected children, who have become too old to attend the primary school, and yet have not acquired the rudiments of learning, to enable them to enter the ordinary schools. Similar laws have been enacted by Congress under its general power of legislation over the District of Columbia . . . as well as by the legislatures of many of the states, and have been generally, if not uniformly, sustained by the courts. . . .

The distinction between laws interfering with the political equality of the Negro and those requiring the separation of the two races in schools, theatres, and railway carriages has been frequently drawn by this court. Thus in Strauder *v.* West Virginia, 100 U.S. 303, it was held that a law of West Virginia limiting to white male persons, 21 years of age and citizens of the state, the right to sit upon juries, was a discrimination which implied a legal inferiority in civil society, which lessened the security of the right of the colored race. and was a step toward reducing them to a condition of servility. Indeed, the right of a colored man that, in the selection of jurors to pass upon his life, liberty and property, there shall be no exclusion of his race, and no discrimination against them because of color, has been asserted in a number of cases. . . .

So far, then, as a conflict with the Fourteenth Amendment is concerned, the case reduces itself to the question whether the statute of Louisiana is a reasonable regulation, and with respect to this there must necessarily be a large discretion on the part of the legislature. In determining the question of reasonableness it is at liberty to act with reference to the established usages, customs and traditions of the people, and with a view to the promotion of their comfort, and the preservation of the public peace and good order. Gauged by this standard, we cannot say that a law which authorizes or even requires the separation of the two races in public conveyances is unreasonable or more obnoxious to the Fourteenth Amendment than the acts of Congress requiring separate schools for colored children in the District of Columbia, the constitutionality of which does not seem to have been questioned, or the corresponding acts of state legislatures.

We consider the underlying fallacy of the plaintiff's argument to consist in the assumption that the enforced separation of the two races stamps the colored race with a badge of inferiority. If this be so, it is not by reason of anything found in the act, but solely because the colored race chooses to put that construction upon it. The argument necessarily assumes that if, as has been more than once the case, and is not unlikely to be so again, the colored race should become the dominant power in the state legislature, and should enact a law in precisely similar terms, it would thereby relegate the white race to an inferior position. We imagine that the white race, at least, would not acquiesce in this assumption. The argument also assumes that social prejudices may be overcome by legislation and that equal rights cannot be secured to the Negro except by an enforced commingling of the two races. We cannot accept this proposition. If the two races are to meet upon terms of social equality, it must be the result of natural affinities, a mutual appreciation of each other's merits, and a voluntary consent of individuals. As was said by the Court of Appeals of New York in People *v.* Gallagher, 93 N.Y. 438, 448,

> this end can neither be accomplished nor prompted by laws which conflict with the general sentiment of the community upon whom they are designed to operate.
>
> When the government, therefore, has secured to each of its citizens equal rights before the law and equal opportunities for improvement and progress, it has accomplished the end for which it was organized and performed all of the functions respecting social advantages with which it is endowed.

Legislation is powerless to eradicate racial instincts or to abolish distinctions based upon physical differences, and the attempt to do so can only result in accentuating the difficulties of the present situation. If the civil and political rights of both races be equal, one cannot be inferior to the other civilly or politically. If one race be inferior to the other socially, the Constitution of the United States cannot put them upon the same plane. . . .

The judgment of the court below is, therefore, affirmed.

MR. JUSTICE HARLAN, dissenting:

In respect of civil rights, common to all citizens, the Constitution of the United States does not, I think, permit any public authority to know the race of those entitled to be protected in the enjoyment of such rights. Every true man has pride of race, and under appropriate circumstances when the rights of others, his equals before the law, are not to be affected, it is his privilege to express such pride and to take such action based upon it as to him seems proper. But I deny that any legislative body or judicial tribunal may have regard to the race of citizens when the civil rights of those citizens are involved. Indeed, such legislation as that here in question is inconsistent not only with that equality of rights which pertains to citizenship, national and state, but with the personal liberty enjoyed by everyone within the United States. . . .

It was said in argument that the statute of Louisiana does not discriminate against either race but prescribes a rule applicable alike to white and colored citizens. But this argument does not meet the difficulty. Everyone knows that the statute in question had its origin in the purpose, not so much to exclude white persons from railroad cars occupied by blacks, as to exclude colored people from coaches occupied by or assigned to white persons. Railroad corporations of Louisiana did not make discrimination among whites in the matter of accommodation for travellers. The thing to accomplish was, under the guise of giving equal accommodations for whites and blacks, to compel the latter to keep to themselves while travelling in railroad passenger coaches. No one would be so wanting in candor as to assert the contrary. The fundamental objection, therefore, to the statute is that it interferes with the personal freedom of citizens. . . . If a white man and a black man choose to occupy the same public conveyance on a public highway, it is their right to do so, and no government, proceeding alone on grounds of race, can prevent it without infringing the personal liberty of each. . . .

The white race deems itself to be the dominant race in this country. And so it is, in prestige, in achievements, in education, in wealth, and in power. So, I doubt not, it will continue to be for all time, if it remains true to its great heritage and holds fast to the principles of constitutional liberty. But in the view of the Constitution, in the eye of the law, there is in this country no superior, dominant, ruling class of citizens. There is no caste here. Our Constitution is color-blind and neither knows nor tolerates classes among citizens. In respect of civil rights, all citizens are equal before the law. The humblest is the peer of the most powerful. The law regards man as man and takes no account of his surroundings or of his color when his civil rights as guaranteed by the supreme law of the land are involved. . . .

The arbitrary separation of citizens, on the basis of race, while they are on a public highway, is a badge of servitude wholly inconsistent with the civil freedom and the equality before the law established by the Constitution. It cannot be justified upon any legal grounds.

If evils will result from the commingling of the two races upon public highways established for the benefit of all, they will be infinitely less than those that will surely come from state legislation regulating the enjoyment of civil rights upon the basis of race. We boast of the freedom enjoyed by our people above all other peoples. But it is difficult to reconcile that boast with a state of the law which, practically, puts the brand of servitude and degradation upon a large class of our fellow citizens, our equals before the law. The thin disguise of "equal" accommodations for passengers in railroad coaches will not mislead anyone, nor atone for the wrong this day done. . . .

I do not deem it necessary to review the decisions of state courts to which reference was made in argument. Some, and the most important, of them are wholly inapplicable, because rendered prior to the adoption of the last amendments of the Constitution, when colored people had very few rights which the dominant race felt obliged to respect. Others were made at a time when public opinion, in many localities, was dominated by the institution of slavery; when it would not have been safe to do justice to the black man; and when, so far as the rights of blacks were concerned, race prejudice was, practically, the supreme law of the land. Those decisions cannot be guides in the era introduced by the recent amendments of the supreme law, which established universal civil freedom, gave citizenship to all born or naturalized in the United States and residing here, obliterated the race line from our systems of governments, national and state, and placed our free institutions upon the broad and sure foundation of the equality of all men before the law. . . .

For the reasons stated, I am constrained to withhold my assent from the opinion and judgment of the majority.

"Separate Educational Facilities Are Inherently Unequal"

BROWN *V.* BOARD OF EDUCATION OF TOPEKA

347 U.S. 483 (1954)

MR. CHIEF JUSTICE WARREN delivered the opinion of the Court.

These cases come to us from the States of Kansas, South Carolina, Virginia, and Delaware. They are premised on different facts and different local conditions, but a common legal question justifies their consideration together in this consolidated opinion.

In each of the cases, minors of the Negro race, through their legal representatives, seek the aid of the courts in obtaining admission to the public schools of their community on a nonsegregated basis. In each instance, they had been denied admission to schools attended by white children under laws requiring or permitting segregation according to race. This segregation was alleged to deprive the plaintiffs of the equal protection of the laws under the Fourteenth Amendment. In each of the cases other than the Delaware case, a three-judge federal district court denied relief to the plaintiffs on the so-called "separate but equal" doctrine announced by this Court in Plessy *v.* Ferguson, 163 U.S. 537. Under that doctrine, equality of treatment is accorded when the races are provided substantially equal facilities, even though these facilities be separate. In the Delaware case, the Supreme Court of Delaware adhered to that doctrine, but ordered that the plaintiffs be admitted to the white schools because of their superiority to the Negro schools.

The plaintiffs contend that segregated public schools are not "equal" and cannot be made "equal," and that hence they are deprived of the equal protection of the laws. Because of the obvious importance of the question presented, the Court took jurisdiction. Argument was heard in the 1952 Term, and reargument was heard this Term on certain questions propounded by the Court.

Reargument was largely devoted to the circumstances surrounding the adoption of the Fourteenth Amendment in 1868. It covered exhaustively consideration of the Amendment in Congress, ratification by the states, then existing practices in racial segregation, and the views of proponents and opponents of the Amendment. This discussion and our own investigation convince us that, although these sources cast some light, it is not enough to resolve the problem with which we are faced. At best, they are inconclusive. The most avid proponents of the post-War Amendments undoubtedly intended them to remove all legal distinctions among "all persons born or naturalized in the United States." Their opponents, just as certainly, were antagonistic to both the letter and the spirit of the Amendments and wished them to have the most limited effect. What others in Congress and the state legislatures had in mind cannot be determined with any degree of certainty.

An additional reason for the inconclusive nature of the Amendment's history, with respect to segregated schools, is the status of public education at that time. In the South, the movement toward free common schools, supported by general taxation, had not yet taken hold. Education of white children was largely in the hands of private groups. Education of Negroes was almost nonexistent, and practically all of the race were illiterate. In fact, any education of Negroes was forbidden by law in some states. Today, in contrast, many Negroes have achieved outstanding success in the arts and sciences as well as in the business and professional world. It is true that public school education had advanced further in the North, but the effect of the Amendment on Northern States was generally ignored in the congressional debates. Even in the North, the conditions of public education did not approximate those existing today. The curriculum was usually rudimentary; ungraded schools were common in rural areas; the school term was but three months a year in many states; and compulsory school attendance was virtually unknown. As a consequence, it is not surprising that there should be so little in the history of the Fourteenth Amendment relating to its intended effect on public education.

In the first cases in this Court construing the Fourteenth Amendment, decided shortly after its adoption, the Court interpreted it as proscribing all state-imposed discriminations against the Negro race. The doctrine of "separate but equal" did not make its appearance in this Court until 1896 in the case of Plessy *v.* Ferguson, *supra,* involving not education but transportation. American courts have since labored with the doctrine for over half a century. In this Court, there have been six cases involving the "separate but equal" doctrine in the field of public education. In Cumming *v.* County Board of Education, 175 U.S. 528, and Gong Lum *v.* Rice, 275 U.S. 78, the validity of the doctrine itself was not challenged. In more recent cases, all on the graduate school level, inequality was found in that specific benefits enjoyed by white students were denied to Negro students of the same educational qualifications. Missouri ex rel. Gaines *v.* Canada, 305 U.S. 337; Sipuel *v.* Oklahoma, 332 U.S. 631; Sweatt *v.* Painter, 339 U.S. 629; McLaurin *v.* Oklahoma State Regents, 339 U.S. 637. In none of these cases was it necessary to reexamine the doctrine to grant relief to the Negro plaintiff. And in Sweatt *v.* Painter, *supra,* the Court expressly reserved decision on the question whether Plessy *v.* Ferguson should be held inapplicable to public education.

In the instant cases, that question is directly presented. Here, unlike Sweatt *v.* Painter, there are findings below that the Negro and white schools involved have been equalized, or are being equalized, with respect to buildings, curricula, qualifications and salaries of teachers, and other "tangible" factors. Our decision, therefore, cannot turn on merely a comparison of these tangible factors in the Negro and white schools involved in each of the cases. We must look instead to the effect of segregation itself on public education.

In approaching this problem, we cannot turn the clock back to 1868 when the Amendment was adopted, or even to 1896 when Plessy *v.* Ferguson was written. We must consider public education in the light of its full development and its present place in American life throughout the Nation. Only in this way can it be determined if segregation in public schools deprives these plaintiffs of the equal protection of the laws.

Today, education is perhaps the most important function of state and local governments. Compulsory school attendance laws and the great expenditures for education both demonstrate our recognition of the importance of education to our democratic society. It is required in the performance of our most basic public responsibilities, even service in the armed forces. It is the very foundation of good citizenship. Today it is a principal instrument in awakening the child to cultural values, in preparing him for later professional training, and in helping him to adjust normally to his environment. In these days, it is doubtful that any child may reasonably be expected to succeed in life if he is denied the opportunity of an education. Such an opportunity, where the state has undertaken to provide it, is a right which must be made available to all on equal terms.

We come then to the question presented: Does segregation of children in public schools solely on the basis of race, even though the physical facilities and other "tangible" factors may be equal, deprive the children of the minority group of equal educational opportunities? We believe that it does.

In Sweatt *v.* Painter, *supra,* in finding that a segregated law school for Negroes could not provide them equal educational opportunities, this Court relied in large part on "those qualities which are incapable of objective measurement but which make for greatness in a law school." In McLaurin *v.* Oklahoma State Regents, *supra,* the Court, in requiring that a Negro admitted to a white graduate school be treated like all other students, again resorted to intangible considerations: ". . . his ability to study, to engage in discussions and exchange views with other students, and, in general, to learn his profession." Such considerations apply with added force to children in grade and high schools. To separate them from others of similar age and qualifications solely because of their race generates a feeling of inferiority as to their status in the community that may affect their hearts and minds in a way unlikely ever to be undone. The effect of this separation on their educational opportunities was well stated by a finding in the Kansas case by a court which nevertheless felt compelled to rule against the Negro plaintiffs:

> Segregation of white and colored children in public schools has a detrimental effect upon the colored children. The impact is greater when it has the sanction of the law; for the policy of separating the races is usually interpreted as denoting the inferiority of the Negro group. A sense of inferiority affects the motivation of a child to learn. Segregation with the sanction of law, therefore, has a tendency to retard the educational and mental development of Negro children and to deprive them of some of the benefits they would receive in a racially integrated school system.

Whatever may have been the extent of psychological knowledge at the time of Plessy *v.* Ferguson, this finding is amply supported by modern authority. Any language in Plessy *v.* Ferguson contrary to this finding is rejected.

We conclude that in the field of public education the doctrine of "separate but equal" has no place. Separate educational facilities are inherently unequal. Therefore, we hold that the plaintiffs and others similarly situated for whom the actions have been brought are, by reason of the segregation complained of, deprived of the equal protection of the laws guaranteed by the Fourteenth Amendment. This disposition makes unnecessary any discussion whether such segregation also violates the Due Process Clause of the Fourteenth Amendment.

Because these are class actions, because of the wide applicability of this decision, and because of the great variety of local conditions, the formulation of decrees in these cases presents problems of considerable complexity. On reargument, the consideration of appropriate relief was necessarily subordinated to the primary question—the constitutionality of segregation in public education. We have now announced that such segregation is a denial of the equal protection of the laws. In order that we may have the full assistance of the parties in formulating decrees, the cases will be restored to the docket, and the parties are requested to present further argument on Questions 4 and 5 previously propounded by the Court for the reargument this Term.*

The Attorney General of the United States is again invited to participate. The Attorneys General of the states requiring or permitting segregation in public education will also be permitted to appear as *amici curiae* upon request to do so by September 15, 1954, and submission of briefs by October 1, 1954.

It is so ordered.

* These questions were designed to aid the Court to formulate specific decrees to effectuate its decision declaring segregation in public education a denial of equal protection of the laws.

BOLLING *V*. SHARPE

347 U.S. 497 (1954)

[In this case involving racial segregation in the public schools of the *District of Columbia,* the Court said, in part:]

We have this day held that the equal protection clause of the Fourteenth Amendment prohibits the states from maintaining racially segregated public schools. The legal problem in the District of Columbia is somewhat different, however. The Fifth Amendment, which is applicable in the District of Columbia, does not contain an equal protection clause as does the Fourteenth Amendment which applies only to the states. But the concepts of equal protection and due process, both stemming from our American ideal of fairness, are not mutually exclusive. The "equal protection of the laws" is a more explicit safeguard of prohibited unfairness than "due process of law," and therefore, we do not imply that the two are always interchangeable phrases. . . .

Segregation in public education is not reasonably related to any proper governmental objective, and thus it imposes on Negro children of the District of Columbia a burden that constitutes an arbitrary deprivation of their liberty in violation of the due process clause. In view of our decision that the Constitution prohibits the states from maintaining racially segregated public schools, it would be unthinkable that the same Constitution would impose a lesser duty on the Federal Government. We hold that racial segregation in the public schools of the District of Columbia is a denial of the due process of law guaranteed by the Fifth Amendment to the Constitution.

BROWN *V*. BOARD OF EDUCATION OF TOPEKA

349 U.S. 294 (1955)

[In its earlier decision in the Brown case, the Court requested further argument on the form of relief to be granted. See footnote, above. After weighing the presentations, the Court, on May 31, 1955, rendered its opinion in part, as follows.]

MR. CHIEF JUSTICE WARREN delivered the opinion of the Court.

Full implementation of these constitutional principles may require solution of varied local school problems. School authorities have the primary responsibility for elucidating, assessing, and solving these problems; courts will have to consider whether the action of school authorities constitutes good faith implementation of the governing constitutional principles. Because of their proximity to local conditions and the possible need for further hearings, the courts which originally heard these cases can best perform this judicial appraisal. Accordingly, we believe it appropriate to remand the cases to those courts.

In fashioning and effectuating the decrees, the courts will be guided by equitable principles. Traditionally, equity has been characterized by a practical flexibility in shaping its remedies and by a facility for adjusting and reconciling public and private needs. . . .

While giving weight to these public and private considerations, the courts will require that the defendants make a prompt and reasonable start toward full compliance with our May 17, 1954, ruling. Once such a start has been made, the courts may find that additional time is necessary to carry out the ruling in an effective manner. The burden rests upon the defendants to establish that such time is necessary in the public interest and is consistent with good faith compliance at the earliest practicable date. To that end, the courts may consider problems related to administration, arising from the physical condition of the school plant, the school transportation system, personnel, revision of school districts and attendance areas into compact units to achieve a system of determining admission to the public schools on a nonracial basis, and revision of local laws and regulations which may be necessary in solving the foregoing problems. They will also consider the adequacy of any plans the defendants may propose to meet these problems and to effectuate a transition to a racially nondiscriminatory school system. During this period of transition, the courts will retain jurisdiction of these cases.

The judgments below, except that in the Delaware case, are accordingly reversed and remanded to the District Courts to take such proceedings and enter such orders and decrees consistent with this opinion as are necessary and proper to admit to public schools on a racially nondiscriminatory basis with all deliberate speed the parties to these cases. The judgment in the Delaware case—ordering the immediate admission of the plaintiffs to schools previously attended only by white children—is affirmed on the basis of the principles stated in our May 17, 1954, opinion. . . .

It is so ordered.

[In 1964, in Griffin v. Prince Edward School Board, 377 U.S. 218, the Court held unanimously that the closing of public schools in Prince Edward County, Virginia, while public schools in all the other counties of Virginia were being maintained, constituted a denial of equal protection of the laws. The Court commented that "there has been entirely too much deliberation and not enough speed in enforcing the constitutional rights which we held in Brown v. Board of Education had been denied," and added, "relief needs to be quick and effective. . . . The time for mere 'deliberate speed' has run out. . . ."]

Topic 18

THE SOCIAL ISSUES

The Southern Case Against Desegregation

THOMAS R. WARING *

Although the Supreme Court has declared that separation of the races in public schools is unconstitutional, few white Southerners are able to accept the prospect of mingling white and Negro pupils. Resistance to the court decree is stiffening throughout the region.

Many white Northerners are unable to understand the depth of feeling in the Southern states, whose area is about a sixth of the nation and whose population is roughly a fourth of the total. The purpose of this article is to try to put before open-minded readers the point of view of the Southerner—whom the rest of the United States apparently cannot believe to be open-minded at all on the subject of race.

At the outset it is only fair to warn the Northern reader that he may be infuriated long before he reaches the end. This, I suspect, is just as inevitable as the outraged feelings of the Southerner when he reads the Northern press with its own interpretation of the American dilemma. Both sides have been shouting at each other so loudly that it is difficult any longer to hear facts through the din of name-calling. If, in the course of speaking for the South, I should raise blood pressure among some Northerners, I apologize for causing pain—with the hope that I may be able to reach Northern minds that are truly open so that some good may come along with the discomfort.

The reader outside the South may, unfortunately, react in still another way. He may find it difficult, if not impossible, to believe much of what I say. To this I can only reply that as editor of a South Carolina newspaper with a circulation of 56,000, with twenty-eight years of journalistic experience in both the North and the South, I have had to be in possession of accurate information on this as on any other subject covered in my work. Across an editor's desk pass, day by day and year after year, reports, letters, statistics—in other words, facts. By means of these facts,

* Managing Editor of the *News and Courier,* Charleston, South Carolina. The selection is from "The Southern Case Against Desegregation," *Harper's Magazine,* Vol. 212 (January, 1956), pp. 39–45. By permission.

plus personal conversations with people from all over the world, an editor manages to keep in touch with public opinion.

It is the public opinion of the South that I am about to report. That opinion is a fact. It exists, and can be demonstrated. What I am saying is documented by facts and statistics. If these should seem to the reader to add up merely to bias, bigotry, and even untruth, I shall regret it. Facts, however, remain facts.

One of the reasons these facts may be unfamiliar—and therefore incredible—is the almost unanimous attitude of the national press—daily and weekly—toward the subject of race. I read many newspapers and news magazines, and people send me clippings from others that I do not see regularly. From my observation, the testimony these publications print is almost entirely one-sided. While less violent than the Negro press—which understandably presents only the militant anti-segregation case—the metropolitan press almost without exception has abandoned fair and objective reporting of the race story. For facts it frequently substitutes propaganda.

Furthermore, with the exception of a small coterie of Southern writers whom Northern editors regard as "enlightened," spokesmen for the Southern view cannot gain access to Northern ears. . . . The South, alas, lacks a magazine or other organ with nationwide distribution.

Perhaps my first assertion of a seldom realized truth will be the most difficult to believe. This statement is that white Southerners of good will—and the percentage of decency runs about the same in the South as anywhere else—favor uplift of the Negro, and that these white Southerners are in the vast majority. If it is impossible to prove the percentage of decency among Southerners, it is equally impossible to show that people in the North—or any other region—have a monopoly of it. But the South fears, and with reason, that the uplift is being forced at too fast a pace. The vagaries of custom and race taboos have many inconsistencies. The rules of segregation, both written and unwritten, change with conditions. And the sudden rewriting by the Supreme Court of regional laws and state constitutions has stirred as much resentment in Southern breasts as would be aroused among Northerners if suddenly their own freedom from race restrictions were denied by federal fiat. (Do I hear a muffled cheer from one or two Northerners who may take a dim view of mingling the races?)

Interference with sovereignty usually produces rage. In matters of education, the states long have been sovereign—until suddenly nine men have held otherwise. Is it any wonder that the Southerner is bitter over what he believes to be a flouting of the Constitution for political reasons?

Aside from legal questions—and they are deep and broad—the Southerner believes that as a practical matter, he is better equipped by experience to cope with race problems than people from other regions, no matter what their intellectual or political attainments. One of the proofs that this belief is founded not merely on pride or emotional prejudice lies in the fact that Northerners who spend some time in the South—not tourists or weekend visitors, but people who make their homes here—come rather sooner than later to agree that this is so. These transplanted Northerners come to see that there are far more bonds of friendship and active, productive good will between the white Southerner and his Negro neighbor than they had believed—or could believe until they became eye-witnesses and partakers of this relationship.

Although the South is both willing and eager to have the Negro earn greater acceptance on many levels—especially economic—it does not consider, for reasons that I shall submit, that mixed education is the way to achieve this acceptance—certainly not at this stage of affairs.

What may lie in the distant future is more than any of us can predict with accuracy. Southerners know that race problems are as old as history. While views and philosophies may change through the ages, some basic truths stand out like the Ten Commandments. Southerners are not yet ready to accept an eleventh, "Thou shalt not protect the purity of thy race."

THE CLASH OF CULTURES

Before going into the actual reasons for the Southerner's objections to mixed education—before asking the burning question, how can the races best live together—let us examine for a moment the pattern of separation. It is a pattern that Thomas Jefferson, Abraham Lincoln, and at one time Dwight D. Eisenhower have favored as best for both races. In 1888, Henry W. Grady, Atlanta editor—described by Don Shoemaker of the Southern Education Reporting Service as a Southern "liberal" of his time—summed up the situation as follows:

> Neither "provincialism" nor "sectionalism" holds the South together but something deeper than these and essential to our system. The problem is how to carry within her body politic two separate races, and nearly equal in numbers. [Since Grady spoke, the whites in the South have come to outnumber the Negroes four to one, but the proportions vary greatly by neighborhoods.] She must carry these races in peace—for discord means ruin. She must carry them separately—for assimilation means debasement. She must carry them in equal justice—for to this she is pledged in honor and gratitude. She must carry them to the end, for in human probability she will never be quit of either.

While Grady's statements were made nearly seventy years ago and therefore are subject to the criticism that they do not reflect "modern conditions," to many Southerners they are true both now and for the future.

The presence of large numbers of Negroes—especially in the tidewater regions of Virginia, the Carolinas, and Georgia, and the plantation country of Alabama and Louisiana, Mississippi and East Texas—means that the races necessarily live in intimate daily association. Why, then, should not the children of people who live in the same community—sometimes as close neighbors—attend the same schools?

Southerners believe they have valid reasons, aside from "prejudice" about the color of skin, for their insistence on sending white children to exclusively white schools. Without debating superiority of either race, they are keenly aware of cultural differences. In some ways the standards of white people are none too high. The same economic conditions that have held back Negroes have worked against the whites. The increasing prosperity of the South is removing some of these disadvantages for both races, though not necessarily in precisely the same way.

Whether all the differences will eventually be removed, or enough of them to make mixed education acceptable to a substantial number of white people, the differences are too great *at present* to encourage white parents to permit their children to mingle freely in school. This has nothing to do with the frequent practice of children of both races of playing together when young, or with cordial relationships in many other contacts of ordinary life.

Volumes could be written on racial differences from many angles, including anthropology and sociology. I shall merely try to summarize five of the differences that most immediately come to the minds of white parents in the South. These are health; home environment; marital standards; crime; and a wide disparity in average intellectual development.

(1) *Health.* Negro parents as a whole—for reasons that white people may sympathetically deplore but which nevertheless exist—are not so careful on the average as their white neighbors in looking after the health and cleanliness of their children. The incidence of venereal disease for instance is much greater among Negroes than among whites.

Statistics to document this statement are difficult to come by, though the statement itself would be generally accepted in the South. The U.S. Public Health Service some years ago quietly stopped identifying statistics by races. South Carolina figures, available for 1952–53, give a clue to the situation in that state; it probably is much the same elsewhere in the South. Out of a population 60 per cent white and 40 per cent Negro, 6,315 cases of syphilis were reported, of which 89 per cent were among Negroes. Infection with gonorrhea was found in six Negroes to one white person, but some physicians report that many cases of gonorrhea among Negroes go unrecorded.

During the same period—1952–53—a campaign against venereal disease was carried on, county by county. A spot check of four representative counties in different parts of South Carolina showed that cases of syphilis were found among 1.3 per cent of the white persons examined. This was a fairly constant percentage. The percentage of infection among Negroes ranged in the same counties from 8.5 to 10.8 per cent, averaging more than 9 per cent.

Fastidious parents do not favor joint use of school washrooms when they would not permit it at home—and there's no use to tell them that it is unlikely that anyone will catch venereal disease from a toilet seat. They just don't want to take risks of any kind with their children.

(2) *Home environment.* For most colored children in the South the cultural background is different in many ways from that of their white neighbors—and while these differences may have various explanations, they add up in the public's mind as racial. Slavery is so long in the past that nobody thinks about it any more, but the master and servant, or boss and laborer, relationship between whites and Negroes is still the rule rather than the exception. The emergence of a middle class among the Negroes has been extremely slow—again, the reasons count for less in the minds of white parents than the fact itself. Indeed, the professional and commercial class among Negroes is so small that its members are in perhaps the most unenviable position of all. They have progressed beyond the cultural level of the vast bulk of their own people, but are not accepted among the whites, who fear to let down any dikes lest they be engulfed in a black flood.

Someone may suggest that here is an opening wedge for integration in the schools, by admitting a few well scrubbed and polished colored children of cultivated parents. In reply, let me say that this would be no more acceptable to the colored people than to the whites. The solution, perhaps—as it is among upper-bracket white people who do not send their children to public schools—might be private schools for prosperous Negroes as for prosperous whites. In any case, white people feel that cultural gaps on other levels should be filled in before discussing integrated schools.

(3) *Marital habits.* Among many Southern Negroes they are, to state it mildly, casual—even more so, in fact, than among the often-divorced personalities of Northern café society. Many Negro couples—the statistics are not readily available, for obvious reasons—do not bother with divorce because there was no actual marriage in the first place. Statistics on the results of such casual unions, however, are available. On the average one Southern Negro child in five is illegitimate. It is possible the figure may be even higher, since illegitimate births are more likely to go unrecorded. Even among Negroes who observe marriage conventions, illegitimacy has little if any stigma.

Many white persons believe that morals among their own race are lax enough as it is, without exposing their children to an even more primitive view of sex habits. Moreover, while these parents do not believe there is any surge of desire among their offspring to mate with colored people, they abhor any steps that might encourage intermarriage. They believe that lifting the racial school barriers would be such a step. Miscegenation has been on the wane of recent years. Whatever mixing of blood may have occurred—and admittedly that was due largely to lustful white men seeking out acquiescent Negro women—has been without benefit of either law or custom. On some levels of society, breaking the racial barriers might lead to mixed marriages. The mixture of races which white Southerners have observed in Latin American countries gives them a dim view of legalizing cohabitation with Negroes.

(4) *Crime.* For many years, crime in the South has been more prevalent among Negroes than among white people. Though the Northern press no longer identifies criminals by race, white Southerners have reason to believe that much of the outbreak of crime and juvenile delinquency in Northern cities is due to the influx of Negro population. They believe the North now is getting a taste of the same race troubles that the South fears would grow out of mixed schooling, on a much bigger scale. They want no "Blackboard Jungles" in the South.

Maintaining order is a first concern of Southerners. What they have heard about the fruits of integration in the North does not encourage them to adopt the Northern race pattern. In Chicago, three hundred policemen have been assigned for a year or more to guard a nonsegregated housing project, with no bigger population than a Southern village where a single constable keeps the peace. In the County of Charleston, South Carolina—with 190,000 population, nearly half Negro—the total law enforcement manpower of combined city and county forces is 175.

While the homicide rate in the South is high, it is due in large measure to knifings and shootings among the colored people. Interracial homicide is relatively rare. (One of the reasons why the ghastly killing of Emmett Till in Mississippi made hot news—and some of that news was superheated and garnished with prejudice for the Northern press—was the very fact that it *was* unusual. No lynching, as even most Northerners now realize, has occurred in years.)

With racial bars down and rowdies of both races daring one another to make something of the vast increase in daily contacts, opportunities for interracial strife are frightening. Conservative, law-abiding people—and believe it or not, they constitute the bulk of Southern whites—are deeply fearful that hatred and bloodshed would increase without separation of the races.

And they know that, in the long run, if there is riotous bloodshed it will be for the most part Negroes' blood. The thin tolerance of the ruffian and lower elements of the white people could erupt into animosity and brutality if race pressure became unbearable. Schools would be a focal point for such disturbance, first among pupils themselves and later by enraged parents. Instead of learning out of books, the younger generation would be schooled in survival—as several Northern sources have told me already is happening in some areas of New York, Philadelphia, and Washington, D. C.

(5) *Intellectual development.* Again for whatever the reasons may be, Southern Negroes usually are below the intellectual level of their white counterparts. *U.S. News and World Report*—the fairest nationally circulated publication I am acquainted with in its treatment of the race issue—has reported that in Washington, colored children are about two grades behind the whites in attainment. This discrepancy, I believe, is about par for other communities. In Washington it was found that there were even language difficulties to surmount. The children used different terms for some things.

Some advocates of integration say the way to cure these differences is to let the children mingle so that the Negroes will learn from the whites. The trouble with this theory is that even if it works, a single generation of white children will bear the brunt of the load. While they are rubbing off white civilization onto the colored children, Negro culture will also rub off onto the whites.

Few Southern parents are willing to sacrifice their own offspring in order to level off intellectual differences in this fashion. They reason that their children will get along better in later life if they have, as youngsters, the best available cultural contacts. Such an attitude is not, I understand, altogether unknown in the North. Many parents in New York City, for example, make considerable financial sacrifices to send their children to private schools, to spare them the undesirable associations and the low-geared teaching standards of most public schools.

If this sounds snobbish to a Northern reader, let me ask you to examine your own conscience. Can you honestly say that you are eager to send your own child to a classroom where the majority of other pupils will be considerably more backward in their studies, and extremely different in social background and cultural attainment? Which would you *really* put first: your theory of racial justice, or justice to your own child?

THE NEGROES' CRUSADE

In reply to objections to integration by white Southerners, someone may ask: What about the Negroes? What do they think?

At the outset, let me say that as a person who has spent most of his life in the South, has known Negroes from earliest childhood, and as a newspaperman has been dealing with race matters every day for many years, I cannot say just what goes on in the minds of the Negroes. Nor do I believe that a white man can put himself in the place of a colored man any more than he can, by taking thought, add a cubit to his stature. Until the school question became agitated in recent years, however, race relations on the whole were good. Since the agitation, relations are not yet bad in a broad sense—but they are not improving by reason of the crusade for integration.

The leadership in that crusade comes from outside the South. It is sparked by the National Association for the Advancement of Colored People. Southerners have reason to believe that this organization has a very large measure of white influence among its leaders. They recognize that both major political parties are courting the Negro vote, which holds the balance of power in key cities of populous Northern states. They are bewildered by the array of power aligned on the side of the NAACP in press, pulpit, and politics. The NAACP and its allies seem well supplied with money. They have won legal victories and they are not disposed to compromise on any front. In fact, the NAACP seems—to white Southerners—more interested in forcing the Negro into the white man's company than in equipping the Negro to qualify fully for such association.

A small but pointed illustration occurred in Charleston when a white community theater group tried to produce "Porgy" (the original play, not the opera) with a Negro cast in the city where the story is laid. There was a grave question about how the community, in a time when racial agitation was so bitter, would accept a play performed almost exclusively by Negroes. Many difficulties had to be surmounted in casting and production. But the sponsoring group, in consultation with NAACP and other Negro spokesmen, decided to proceed, and spent a sizable amount of money getting the production under way.

One of the key questions was the seating of the audience. Under South Carolina law separate seating for the races is required. The chairman of the local NAACP chapter agreed in writing, I have been informed, to an arrangement for separate seating by means of a vertical line down the center aisle, whites on one side and Negroes on the other. At the last moment, with the play already in rehearsal, the NAACP repudiated the agreement.

The Negro cast pleaded with the white sponsors to go through with the production in spite of the NAACP. By this time, however, it became obvious that the delicate circumstances had become too explosive and the production was canceled. A possible good-will gesture, opening a new line of communication, thus was halted because the NAACP would accept nothing less than complete integration—regardless of both state law and local custom.

Whether the NAACP really speaks for the rank and file of Negroes is debatable. Public expressions of opinion from Negroes in the South, other than the NAACP, are relatively few. Some white people feel that a Negro is so accustomed to telling a white man what he thinks the white man wants to hear, that they put little stock in whatever the Negro says on race. It would not be hard to believe that, given a choice, a Negro naturally would prefer all restrictions to be removed. That does not mean, however, that all Negroes want to associate with white people. Far from it; many Negroes prefer their own churches and, it stands to reason, should be equally satisfied with their own schools, so long as an equal allotment of public money is given them.

While the allotment has not always been equal—Negroes pay only a small fraction of taxes—the sums of money spent on Negro schooling have increased by leaps and bounds. On the average the South spends a greater percentage of its per capita income on schools than other regions, and nowadays the Negroes are getting their share in most areas. One thing is certain: if the schools were integrated, many a Negro school teacher would lose his or her job. Even if the white people would accept mixed pupils—and few apparently would do so—they would insist on white teachers.

Whenever a Southern Negro does object to the drive for integration, he is subject to pressure from his own people. Two Negro clergymen—what are known as "local preachers"—recently wrote letters to newspapers in lower South Carolina opposing the mixing of schools. Both were disciplined by their church superiors. Many white people on friendly terms with Negroes are convinced that as a rule, the Negroes are not eager for mixed schools so long as the schools for Negroes are adequate.

BOOTLEG SEGREGATION?

This conviction leads them to hope that a voluntary approach eventually may help to solve the problem within the Supreme Court ruling. Judge John J. Parker of Charlotte, North Carolina, senior judge of the Fourth Circuit Court of Appeals, has said:

> It is important that we point out exactly what the Supreme Court has decided and what it has not decided in this [the Clarendon County] case. . . . It has not decided that the states must mix persons of different races in the schools. . . . Nothing in the Constitution or in the decision of the Supreme Court takes away from the people freedom to choose the schools they attend. The Constitution, in other words, does not require integration. It does not forbid such segregation as occurs as the result of voluntary action. It merely forbids the use of governmental power to enforce segregation. The Fourteenth Amendment is a limitation upon the exercise of power by the state or state agencies, not a limitation upon the freedom of individuals.

The Alabama state legislature has set up a new basis for assignment of pupils which does not mention race, though its provisions might tend to keep white and Negro pupils apart. In South Carolina, a committee of fifty-two representative citizens is circulating a resolution—already signed by many thousands—asking the State Legislature to interpose its authority between the federal government and local school boards to maintain segregation. Such a move would be based on the Tenth Amendment to the U.S. Constitution, reserving to the states and the people all powers not specifically granted to the federal government.

These are only two of many tentative plans to get around the Supreme Court's decision by methods of law. Another proposal is revival of the principle of nullification, which states both in the North and South have used in years gone by. A recent example was the public disregard of Prohibition. Segregation, perhaps, may be bootlegged in some regions. How that can be done is not immediately apparent—but the resourcefulness of the rum-runners and speakeasies was not foreseen by sponsors of the Volstead Act.

As in Prohibition, there is danger that white hoodlums may enter the picture. Sporadic outbreaks of the Ku Klux Klan have been reported. To combat the lawless element, law-abiding white men—who are determined not to yield to pressures they still regard as contrary to the guarantees of the Constitution—have been forming protective organizations. These go under many names. In Mississippi, South Carolina, and some of the other states they are called Citizens Councils.

Much has been said about the adoption of "economic pressure" as a weapon by these white groups. In some instances Negroes have reported that their sharecropper contracts have not been renewed because they signed petitions to integrate schools. Other forms of pressure have been reported, and in some localities Negroes have retaliated with boycotts against white merchants who were active in the Councils. White leaders of the resistance movements repeatedly have said they were not organizing boycotts and pressures against the Negroes and that they are determined there shall be no reign of terror as predicted by some of the Negro spokesmen.

Hodding Carter—one of a handful of Southern writers granted access to the national magazines—has predicted that attempts to enforce integration in the public schools of Mississippi would be likely to create violence. White leaders are exploring many other avenues in hopes of preventing strong-arm methods from being tried. They fear also that the very existence of the public schools is in peril. Rather than accept mixed public schools, some white Southerners may seek other means of educating their children.

Even if the schools are not abandoned, it seems unlikely that the white people will submit to heavy taxation to operate schools that many of them refuse to patronize. If they are not throttled outright, the public school systems in some areas may be starved to death. The spread of resistance organizations, far from being the product of demagogues, is at the local level among ordinary people, without "big-name" leadership. School trustees and other officials are getting the message from the grass roots.

Acceptance of the Supreme Court's order in border states and lip service in some other quarters have encouraged some advocates to believe that many Southern communities soon will yield to integration. While the borders of the old Confederacy may narrow, the determination of white people in areas with heavy Negro population is not relaxing. Not only regions where Negroes predominate by ten to one are rejecting the prospect of mixed schools. Pickens County in Piedmont South Carolina has the smallest number of Negroes (about one in ten) of any county in the state; its grand jury—most fundamental of all bodies safeguarding the people's liberty—has gone on record against mixed schools. On Edisto Island, at the opposite side of the state, where a white face looks out of place, insistence on mingling would be almost academic. If any attempt were made to force white children into Negro schools, the white people would move off the island, or find other means of educating their children.

Talk about segregation may promote migration of Negroes from the South. Already thousands have left the cotton fields and villages to seek jobs in Northern cities. On the farms, machines have replaced them. With the minimum wage advancing to $1 an hour, Southern employers will demand production from their laborers that not all Negroes will be able or willing to supply. These employers also may seek ways to mechanize or to employ white labor. As industries move South, more attractive opportunities for white people are opening.

If the North continues to appeal to Negroes as a land of integration and the South continues to attract white settlers, the racial proportions may grow more nearly equal. Then the North may become more tolerant of the Southerners' view of race problems, and the South better able to handle its dwindling Negro problem. Southerners will gladly share the load.

Meanwhile, stripped of emotions, the race problem for both Southern whites and Negroes is a practical matter of daily living. The problem has been recognized by thoughtful Americans from the early days of the Republic. It would be foolish to deny that any Negro pupils ever will enter Southern white schools. (Some already have.) But it would be equally foolhardy to predict that their numbers will be significant at an early date.

Psychological Aspects of Desegregation

A REPORT BY PSYCHIATRISTS *

INTRODUCTION

School segregation has been declared illegal throughout the country. We share the widespread belief that desegregation will inevitably occur. It is already occurring, and people everywhere are aroused to the strongest emotions by the legal, economic, and social problems it entails. Some have taken firm stands for desegregation, even when this has resulted in economic sanctions and ensuing hardships. Others have openly defied the law, thereby risking arrest and punishment. In actual fact, although desegregation presents various legal, social, and economic problems, it is above all a psychological problem. Were it not for the violent feelings which are involved, it would be possible to solve the legal, economic, and social difficulties.

This report represents the pooled experience of an interracial group of psychiatrists from different parts of the country, aided by consultant social scientists. In it we shall attempt to explore some of the psychological bases for the strong personal involvement on the part of those who oppose desegregation in the hope that a better understanding of individual and group behavior will facilitate the process. We will then discuss the difficulties which retard the solution of problems connected with desegregation and the possible contribution of psychological principles for dealing with them.

Let us begin by examining the adverse psychological effects which our previous segregational policies have had on the country as a whole, on the community, and, finally, on the individual.

1. The country. For the country as a whole, the tension, ill-feeling, and disunity engendered by the segregation issue interfere with and hamper constructive activities both at home and abroad. Furthermore, segregation and racial prejudice are extremely damaging to our prestige and friendships overseas, particularly among the non-white people of the world. Finally, we have been deprived of a substantial part of our human resources because a large proportion of our population is underprivileged, economically, educationally, and socially, and is therefore unable to make its potentially valuable contribution to our nation.

* The selection is from *Emotional Aspects of School Desegregation, passim,* published by The Group for the Advancement of Psychiatry, New York, 1960. By permission.

2. *The community.* Segregation must inevitably lower the well-being of the community. A lack of educational and economic opportunities, high disease and death rates, crime and delinquency, sub-standard living conditions are all directly related to segregation. For example, if the local government must provide health, welfare, and educational services in duplicate, the budget for each must be lowered by the expense of the other. If sub-standard housing leads to a high rate of contagious disease among Negroes, the health of the white group is jeopardized as well. Contagiousness does not discriminate. Economic and social deprivation contribute to crime and delinquency. By limiting communication between groups, segregation promotes a social climate which is conducive to violent outbreaks of racial tension.

3. *The individual.* Under segregation, the Negro occupies an inferior social status. He cannot live in the neighborhood of his choice; he is not permitted to occupy certain positions; he is denied certain educational opportunities, etc. As a result of being treated as though he were unworthy, he can come to feel unworthy. These feelings of inferiority and humiliation often lead to a strong resentment of all white people, or of all Negroes, or, indeed, of all mankind. Energies which might otherwise be directed toward self-development are instead consumed by his bitterness at his lot in life.

The white person, on the other hand, may gain a false sense of superiority from the mere existence in his community of an "inferior" group. This will lead him to a self-evaluation based merely on the fact that his social, economic, and political situations compare favorably with those of the Negro. Moreover, segregation, by its very nature, is conducive to and encourages the expression of hostility and aggression, thus providing the white person with a tempting means of escape from recognizing and coping with his own problems realistically. For when feelings of self-hatred or of anger toward significant people in one's environment become too painful to face, and yet demand some outlet, they may find their target in the Negro.

We do not wish to imply that all those who believe in and advocate segregation are psychologically abnormal. There is some element of the irrational in all of us. Many people in the United States who are essentially sound psychiatrically, strongly favor segregation for many reasons, aside from obvious personal gain, including, for example, social conformity and consciously high-minded considerations. On the other hand, prejudices may be a symptom of deep emotional disorder.

By the same token, it would be an error to regard desegregation as a purely Southern issue. Anti-Negro discrimination exists in the North, and there are many segregated schools in the North. In fact, the basic issue of equal rights for Negroes and whites, and the psychological attitudes which give rise to such inequalities, exist everywhere in the United States.

OPPOSITION TO DESEGREGATION

What are some of the psychological reasons for the strong adverse response to desegregation? To begin with, it may be helpful to point out that the majority of the current generation have lived all of their lives in a segregated society. The beliefs and feelings of that society have been absorbed in their adult personalities and must, therefore, affect their attitudes toward desegregation. Some of these beliefs are related to real social and economic differences which existed in the previously segregated community. Others are associated with the racial myths that have sprung up under such conditions.

Functions of Racial Myths and Prejudices

In the myths which have grown up about the Negro he is depicted as little better than a savage animal, intellectually and normally inferior, childish and irresponsible. (Nor are such myths limited to beliefs about Negroes. For example, many people believe that all Scots are misers, all Englishmen stuffed shirts, all Frenchmen lascivious, etc.) In the case of the Negro, however, these myths serve to rationalize and justify the white person's disparaging attitudes, because he cannot clearly recognize or understand the real source of his prejudice. If we realize that myth-formation, psychologically, seeks to protect individual and group security against a sense of threat and to diminish anxiety, we can better understand why the myths of prejudice are so resistive to logic: The powerful need for safety, which the myth is created to insure, explains why it is clung to despite facts and logic to the contrary.

Myths as a Defense

During any individual's life-time, he is frequently faced with highly complicated problems which appear to him to be insoluble. At such times he may feel helpless, torn by indecision; he may not know how to solve or even approach his problem. These dilemmas provoke feelings of uneasiness that may reach proportions of extreme anxiety. In order to cope with this anxiety, he may resort to the prevailing myths to provide a seemingly rational solution to his problem. Although such myths are without objective validity, they are maintained and transmitted in the culture as a powerful influence by virtue of the fact that they have their deep roots in individual childhood experience. To illustrate: in the United States white people have had to reconcile their belief in equality and

Christian principles with their actual inhuman treatment of Negroes. In trying to solve this dilemma they have created and defended the various myths about the stereotyped Negro described above. Having created such myths, it becomes easier to justify their conduct, for principles of equality need not apply to so unworthy and inferior a group. Furthermore, through a vicious circle these myths are nourished, sustained, and perpetuated by actual present-day social and economic deprivations of Negroes.

The damaging consequences of racial myths are misconstrued as evidence to support them. American Negroes as a group are in fact multiply handicapped: socially, politically, educationally, and economically. But these handicaps are a consequence of racial discrimination rather than of racial inferiority.

The myth may serve another purpose. Individuals of any race will, from time to time, experience acute doubts about their own worth, their sexual adequacy, their acceptability. These fears and misgivings do not seem quite so intense if one focuses one's attention upon the deficiencies of others. The individual who is filled with self-contempt because of his lack of efficiency and progress on his job may turn this contempt onto the members of a racial minority, represented in myths as being stupid, lazy, irresponsible, etc. He then obtains some consolation from the thought that at least he is better than they are. But such methods of dealing with one's problems fail to reach a realistic solution of the original difficulty. Furthermore, they result in increased guilt and anxiety.

Effect on Negro-white Relationships

In addition to their effect on the psyche of the individual, these concepts of the Negro's inferiority have, of course, severely affected Negro-white relationships. Merely because of his membership in the white group, one individual is accorded certain social privileges and is regarded as "better" or higher class. Merely because of his membership in the Negro group, another is deprived of certain social privileges and is regarded as a "second-class citizen." Thus the Negro is usually expected to show deference to all white people, regardless of whether or not the white individual has reached his own stage of intellectual and social development. By contrast, the white person, with no claim to his fellow citizen's respect other than his skin color, may derive a sense of heightened worth because of this deference. This feeling of security is a fleeting one, however. The white person is well aware that the Negro has been forced to assume his attitude of deference. He cannot entirely believe his own feelings of superiority, since they are not based on actual evidence of personal growth and achievement.

This difference in social status is accompanied by differences in political and economic status. The Negro is typically a source of low-paid unskilled labor on farms, in domestic service, in industry. Because his employer or supervisor is usually white, this economic relationship has reinforced the inequities of his social situation.

The racial myth helps to maintain the Negro's political subordination. His right to vote has been curtailed, and as a result, a large part of our population has been deprived of its share in the government process.[1] He has also been excluded from governmental positions of authority and consequently almost all the positions of leadership in our society have been filled by its white members. In his deprived state, this very real lack of power and representation in community and national affairs feeds back into the Negro's feelings of inferiority to lower his self-esteem still further.

In accordance with the myth, both Negro and white are expected to assume certain roles in their relationship with each other. The Negro should be fun-loving, irresponsible, deferential, deeply loyal, dependent, afraid of whites, and capable of hard physical labor and little need for rest or relaxation. Conversely, the white person should enjoy pleasure but not live for it, plan for the future, be independent and unafraid, and utilize Negroes for the hard labor and menial tasks he considers beneath him.

The fact is, of course, that the Negro possesses the same capacities and potentialities as does the white and experiences the same basic emotions. Therefore, a relationship based on the characterizations described above must of necessity be subject to a great deal of strain and resentment. The Negro is expected to repress his ambitions, his desires for self-realization and development. In return for the Negro's acceptance of low status and dependent servility, the white offers him such advantages as freedom from responsibility and paternalistic protectiveness.

No matter how well such a Negro-white relationship may appear to function on the surface, underlying the apparent conformity and compliance are deep anger, fear, and resentment. If the myth is firmly believed, Negro-white relationships tend to become mere rituals, without genuine human significance. Even when people consciously reject the myth, there still remain deep-rooted prejudices and anxieties in Negro-white interaction.

Still another aspect of the myth derives its strength from the emotional attitudes which have come to be associated with different forms, colors, and textures of the skin. The feelings and meanings attached to different skin colors vary between cultures and subcultures in relation to patterns of emotional conditioning. For example, several studies carried

[1] Among the paradoxes of social change in the South is that Negroes are being courted for their much needed votes and purchasing power, while at the same time they are subjected to discrimination.

out in this country have indicated that most small children—both white and Negro—prefer light dolls to dark ones, even though they are not antagonistic to the dark dolls. Psychological studies of adults show that many people equate a rough, dark skin with "wrong" or with "dirtiness"; smoothness or whiteness, on the other hand, symbolize "right" or purity. Since the skin cloaks the entire body, it becomes the part of the person most accessible to superficial perception and evaluation.

In our culture yellow, brown, and black tend to be associated with ideas of evil or destructiveness; white and pink represent cleanliness, virtue, chastity. Consequently, the negative associations to his skin color may contribute and lend support to myths which have evolved about the Negro.

The Negro, in turn, long victimized as a result of the myth, may himself come to believe it. He is often as frightened as the white person by the mythical image of the dirty, aggressive Negro. Indeed, caste systems have grown up among some Negroes on the basis of how close skin color approaches white, and how close social and sexual customs approach supposed white middle-class standards. It is well known how much money and time many Negroes feel driven to spend on cosmetics, clothes, showy automobiles, etc. in an effort to break away from the devaluing self-concept fostered by the myth.

Fears Related to Sex

As a result of the myth of the Negro's sexual aggressiveness and virility, desegregation has been severely handicapped by widespread fears that the traditional barriers against sexual relationships between whites and Negroes will break down. Let us examine some of the psychological bases for such fears.

Quite apart from questions of race, unrealistic emotions and attitudes toward sex abound in our culture. In general, our attitudes toward sex are split: Sex represents the culmination of tenderness and love, but it is also regarded in our society as dirty and degrading, and as an outlet for aggressive impulses. To those who look upon another group as inferior or exploitative, sex relations with members of that group express aggression rather than love.

As part of the process of growing up we have all had to learn to give up some childish wishes, to control our impulses, to modify our sexual drives and aggressions in accordance with social prohibitions. However, these deep sexual urges do not disappear. We carry them with us into adulthood to varying degrees as conscious or unconscious fantasies. One of the prejudices learned in childhood is the belief that people of lower status groups are more primitive, aggressive, and potent sexually. According to the distortions of myths, the Negro male has great sexual prowess, the Negro female is invariably responsive. This concept of the aggressive, primitive, potent Negro represents all that is bad and forbidden, all that the white adult, when reared to conform to middle-class social mores, has been denied. Because these adults fear to allow themselves to play the leading roles in fantasies of violent primitive sexual behavior, they more readily assign such roles to the Negro.

Unacknowledged white male jealousy of the Negro male's fantasied advantage as a sexual rival for the white female is an emotional source of power behind the extreme taboo, maintained by the white-supremacy code, ostensibly to protect white womanhood. This code sanctions the most savage reprisals for Negro male violation, or even the most realistically flimsy suspicion of it, as in the Emmett Till "wolf whistle" case. The irrational emotionality of a lynch mob reveals the terrible antisocial power of racial myth. The white-supremacy code also provides immunity to the white male from Negro resistance or retaliation for the white's sexual freedom with Negro females. And so, fear and hate, founded and maintained by racial sex mythology, breeds ever more fear and hate within members of both races.

The stereotype of the sexual Negro has entered deeply into the emotions of many white people. To such people this image is very real, although objectively it is groundless. Unfortunately, certain surface facts do seem to lend it credence. Let us discuss these:

Psychiatric experience and delinquency studies have indicated that antisocial and impulsive sexual behavior is more prevalent among those persons, whether Negro or white, who have been raised under conditions of social and economic deprivation and disorganized family and community living. When statistical evidence is cited of the comparatively poor sexual restraint among Negroes, the figures may be right. However, they require interpretation. Granted that the Negro is economically underprivileged, poverty in itself does not lead to promiscuity. Such figures are actually a clue to social differences between certain Negro and white groups. There is a correlation between social disorganization and similar sexual patterns for any racial group, but in this country discrimination has caused a greater proportion of Negroes to live under such conditions. The seriousness of antisocial sex behavior cannot be minimized, but its sources should not be falsely attributed to mythological folk tales rather than to social and psychological forces which can be constructively dealt with.

Interracial Unions: Marital and Extramarital

White arguments in defense of segregation which are based primarily on the myth of Negro sexuality invariably focus on the fear of intermarriage and the desire to preserve racial purity. Do these fears stem from facts, or are they rationalizations designed to mask deep emotional confusion?

There are many people, throughout the North, as well as the South, who oppose the idea of Negro-white union. Such opposition may, of course, be attributed to biological concepts of heredity, although there is no available scientific evidence that Negro stock is genetically inferior. However, if this were really the only reason, two of its rather curious aspects would require further explanation. First, while intermarriage is prohibited by law in some states and by severe social penalties in the rest, out-of-wedlock and casual relations between the races are condoned and even expected to occur in some sections of the country. Yet genetic transmission is, of course, the same for progeny born in or out of wedlock.

Secondly, as mentioned previously, these relations are condoned only in combinations of white male and Negro female. Since the mingling of white and Negro genes occurs whether the man is white and the woman Negro or vice versa, the fear of interracial union on the basis of loss of racial purity would appear to be based on illogical rather than rational thought.

Those who oppose school desegregation on the grounds that it will encourage racial amalgamation further fail to recognize that such a process was already underway as an accomplished fact prior to the desegregation decision. Racial admixture began more than two hundred and fifty years ago with the first importation of Negro slaves, and according to several studies it has continued to increase steadily—to the same degree in segregated sections of the country as elsewhere.

As further proof of the increased white admixture to the Negro population, despite segregation one might point out the increase over the years in the practice of "passing" by light-skinned individuals of Caucasian appearance who have some fraction of Negro ancestry, but who do not identify themselves socially as Negroes. The intensity of the Negro's desire to "pass" is, of course, due to the inferior position assigned to him in American life. An individual's skin color and facial appearance, which permit his "passing," are by no means reliable indicators of his genetic endowment. Therefore, "passing" facilitates interracial union. Since discrimination provides the incentive for "passing," and "passing" increases the opportunities for admixture of white and Negro genes, this is an instance of how segregationists actually defeat their ostensible goal of preserving racial purity.

The fear that school desegregation will result in increased intermarriage, which is related to but far from identical with interracial union, expresses an emotional attitude or ignorance rather than a valid prediction.

Available data about intermarriage rates from Northern cities legally desegregated for years, is too limited and confusing for social scientists to interpret. They cannot satisfactorily account for the ups and downs of intermarriage rates in desegregated communities at different periods. Reliable predictions, therefore, as to whether, how, and when extending school desegregation to the South will influence the rate of intermarriage cannot yet be made. The readiness to predict, and with such certainty, by opponents of school desegregation would thus seem to bespeak their own bias, or be designed to arouse the emotions of others, whatever the objective facts in the matter may prove to be. Many complicated factors determine marital choice, and some of these are as yet unknown.

Perhaps, rather than focusing our attention on the effects of desegregation on intermarriage or interracial union, we might think of the over-all changes in Negro-white relationships it will bring about. As a result of school desegregation, Negroes and whites will share many experiences on an equal level. In the course of time this may lead to a great degree of interaction and mutuality in many aspects of living. Rather than leading to increased illicit, antisocial behavior, one might predict that it will lead to greater respect and responsibility in relationships between the races. . . .

ATTITUDE CHANGES

Intensification of Hostility

Among the reasons for the intense opposition of many white persons to desegregation is the fear that Negroes will gain power and use it for retaliation, physical aggression, and even role reversal—that is, the fear that the Negroes will become the dominant race and the whites the subjugated group. On the contrary, the facts show that the influential Negro leadership and organizations have conducted the struggle against discrimination through legal and other democratic means of social action. During the effective boycott of segregated buses in Montgomery, Alabama, 50,000 Negroes practiced nonviolence;[2] they refrained from retaliating to provocations ranging from insults to dynamite by white segregationists. From

[2] At present (March 1960) recent Negro student "sit-in" strikes and demonstrations against eating facilities have spread to six southern states. With few exceptions these Negroes have not retaliated with violence to verbal and physical harassment by whites. Indeed, this is their stated policy. What rioting has occurred, so far, in relation to these disciplined protests, appears to involve some members of both races whose general proneness for aggressive outbreak is triggered by the racial issue pretext. The increase of nonviolent protest techniques may reflect Negro dissatisfaction with delays in the litigation process and such anti-integration devices as pupil-placement laws which have slowed down even token desegregation.

the evidence, ideas of Negro-white role reversal seem limited to fantasies of individual Negroes and whites under conditions of segregation. . . .

Leadership

Unsettled by these inner and outer contradictions many people become very susceptible to the authority of firm and decisive leadership which can tip the scales of their opposing feelings, in either direction. We have seen this demonstrated by the power of some segregationist leaders to sway public support to "a crusade" against integrated schooling or directly or indirectly to sanction mob violence against desegregation. On the other hand, prompt, clear-cut and resolute action to uphold the Federal law by those in authority has proved effective in preventing and reducing the uncertainties stirred up by the social change-over to desegregation.

The direction in which a white person is apt to be swayed by such external authority on the issue of desegregation depends, in large part, on the development of his general attitudes by specific authority influences in his childhood. Thus, many white people conform to the practice of segregation less because of prejudice against Negroes than because of their need to conform to group patterns. These are the people who also usually require a great deal of support and approval by authority figures, however, so that typically they can readjust more readily to desegregation when it is firmly prescribed by those in authority. . . .

RESPONSES OF VARIOUS GROUPS TO DESEGREGATION

The Children

. . . The wide differences in achievement level between white and Negro children of the same age level accounts for another possible source of difficulty. Segregationists consider this further evidence of the inequality of Negroes. Actually, Negro children are at a disadvantage in this regard because the quality of schooling to which they have been exposed has been inferior, coupled with their parents' poorer educational level. Experts maintain that there is no scientific evidence of inborn differences in intelligence between Negroes and whites. Rather, the relative academic retardation of Negroes as compared to whites is due to the Negro's inferior opportunities. "I.Q." tests do not allow for the different cultural experiences of Negro children and are, therefore, inaccurate measures of Negro intelligence potential. The fact that such academic differences do exist, statistically at least, between the Negro and white groups does mean, however, that for a time the slower child will be under pressure, and that the faster child may be held back to some degree. This must be taken into account in scholastic planning. . . .

The Parents

Although children are the direct participants in school desegregation, their attitudes and behavior reflect to a great extent the attitudes and behavior of their parents. Parents in our society are immensely concerned about the welfare and future of their children. There is almost no sacrifice too great to be made for their benefit. It is because of this dedication that the threat of possible damage to the children has proved so effective a force against desegregation. Parents are concerned about the alleged dangers in intermarriage, about the psychological problems with which their children will have to cope, about the educational problems which will arise.

White parents may fear that the school their child attends will have to lower its academic standards because of the admission of Negroes. They may fear that the child, as well as the family, will lose status in the community if he attends a desegregated school, that their child will be exposed to the Negro's lower moral standards, to communicable diseases. They may also have fears with regard to future contact with Negro parents at PTA meetings, etc.

Negro parents worry about whether their children will be able to compete satisfactorily in schools with higher scholastic standards. Will they be treated fairly by their teachers? Will they be hurt physically or emotionally by the white children? Will they, as parents, be humiliated at PTA meetings, or subject to reprisals in other direct contact with whites?

CONCLUSION

In preparing this report on desegregation we have tried to bring together some facts and principles drawn from general knowledge of human behavior, as well as from our special experience in the particular aspects of prejudice and discrimination. There are inevitable strains inherent in any social change of this magnitude. We cannot hope that school desegregation will banish prejudices, but it is a step toward reversing the damage of discrimination. We believe that insight and understanding, that is, a rational approach to the profoundly irrational forces which move man, are essential and appropriate ways of dealing with desegregation issues.

Topic 19

CIVIL DISOBEDIENCE

Meaning of Civil Disobedience

HUGO A. BEDAU *

Since I have been unable to find a suitably detailed analysis of what civil disobedience is and of its role in turning dissent into resistance, I have decided to try to provide such an analysis myself. . . .

A dissenter performs an act of civil disobedience only if he acts *illegally;* i.e., if he violates some positive law, because of (one of) the laws, policies, or decisions of his government which he finds objectionable. Acts of protest directed at government, no matter how conscientious or effective, in which no law is violated (as is usually the case with a poster parade, voluntary boycott, or refusal to accept government employment), are not acts of civil disobedience. Civil disobedience, after all, is not just done; it is committed. It is always the sort of thing that can send one to jail. . . .

It is also possible to distinguish between those acts of dissent which, though illegal according to the authorities at hand, are believed by the dissenter to be within his legal rights as defined by the "fundamental law" or constitution as interpreted by the highest courts of the land and those acts which are committed without any belief in their judicial vindication (e.g., helping an escaped slave to keep his freedom in a slave state in the period immediately following the Supreme Court's decision in the Dred Scott case). . . .

Usually, though not always, it is essential to the purpose of the dissenter that both the public and the government should know what he intends to do. At least, it is essential that the government know of his act if it is intended that the government shall change its policy because of the act. This is one reason why the authorities are customarily notified in advance by those intending to commit civil disobedience. More fundamental still is the fact that the dissenter views what he does as a civic act, an act that properly belongs to the public life of the community. This derives from the fact that he thinks of himself as acting to thwart some law, policy, etc., that deviates

* Department of Philosophy at Reed College. Editor of *The Death Penalty in America*. The selection is from "On Civil Disobedience," *Journal of Philosophy,* Vol. 58 (1961), pp. 653–661. By permission.

from the true purpose of government as he sees it. Thus, his act draws attention to something he thinks the whole community should be brought to consider, since the community has as much interest in the act as he does. For these reasons, civil disobedience is necessarily *public*.

Not every illegal act of public resistance to government, however, is an act of civil disobedience. Anytime the dissenter resists government by deliberately destroying property, endangering life and limb, inciting to riot (e.g., sabotage, assassination, street fighting), he has not committed *civil* disobedience. The pun on 'civil' is essential; only *nonviolent* acts thus can qualify. . . .

Here we meet an important distinction. Some acts of civil disobedience intend to achieve this aim by *directly* violating the objectionable law (e.g., refusing to register for the military draft), whereas other acts, like Thoreau's, intend to achieve this aim by violating some other law and are thus aimed at the objectionable law only *indirectly* (e.g., withholding from payment that portion of one's income taxes used to support the "defense" establishment). . . .

Civil disobedience is, finally, a *conscientious* act. That is, the dissenter proposes to justify his disobedience by an appeal to the incompatibility between his political circumstances and his moral convictions. Usually, this requires that he be convinced that it would be worse for everyone to suffer the consequences of the objectionable law than it would be for everyone to suffer the consequences of his (and, conceivably, of everyone else's) civil disobedience. . . .

In the light of the foregoing examination, I suggest the following definition: Anyone commits an act of civil disobedience if and only if he acts illegally, publicly, nonviolently, and conscientiously with the intent to frustrate (one of) the laws, policies, or decisions of his government.

What's Become of "Law and Order"?

DAVID LAWRENCE *

This period may go down in history as the "era of confusion." For many people do not seem to know from one day to another just what is the law of the land. Nor is it clear any more what laws have to be obeyed. The Methodist Church, for instance, at its General Conference, has just approved a report declaring that Christians, when called upon to obey unjust or immoral laws, should instead follow their consciences and "obey God."

* Editor, *United States News and World Report,* and columnist. The selection is from the New York *Herald-Tribune* (May 6, 1964). Copyright, 1964, New York Herald Tribune Inc., and from *United States News and World Report* (August 5, 1963), p. 104. Copyright, 1963, U.S. News & World Report, Inc. By permission.

Similar sentiments have been voiced by two Negro preachers of prominence, Martin Luther King and Rep. Adam Clayton Powell. But when Govs. Barnett of Mississippi, and Wallace of Alabama decided to ignore a court order and act according to their consciences, they were immediately denounced as "racists" or "extremists" or as "lawless" individuals.

The resolution adopted by the Methodists was offered by the Rev. Harold A. Bosley, of New York, and his committee on Christian social concerns. It reads as follows: "In some instances, where legal recourse is unavailable or inadequate for redress of grievances from laws or their applications that, on their face, are unjust or immoral, the Christian conscience will obey God rather than man."

Resistance to law has been frequent in the racial controversy in recent months. Disobedience has been encouraged in the form of street demonstrations, sit-ins, stall-ins and lie-ins. It has been openly asserted by the leaders of various groups that an individual has a right to decide for himself what is an unjust law. . . . Meanwhile, every individual has the right to test any law as to its constitutionality. If he is wrong, he must be punished, but this doesn't deter even governors of states from taking the risks involved. . . .

We pride ourselves on being a nation governed by law. We boast of a society based on order—preserved by the volition of the citizenry or, if necessary, by force of law.

Yet we see minority groups today pretending that they cannot express their will effectively except through marches in the streets or "lie-down" and "sit-in" demonstrations which interfere forcibly with motor traffic or the carrying on of private business.

What has become of our famed system of communication for the expression of ideas on controversial questions—through the press, through television, through radio, in meeting halls and auditoriums, and even in the pulpits? Have all these facilities been unavailable to minority groups?

Why have so many clergymen, Negro and white, forsaken the pulpit and the spiritual way of inculcating ideas of justice and morality? One minister, a white man of prominence, who was himself arrested as a participant in a "demonstration," told a congressional committee the other day that everything was peaceful until the "counter demonstrators" arrived on the scene. But isn't it natural that "counter demonstrators" should want to express themselves, too? . . .

Do the Negro ministers—those who on Sundays encourage the members of their congregations to participate in the marches—really feel that people of other races cannot be impressed with the merits of their cause except through so-called "non-violent demonstrations" which so often lead to violence?

The dangers of the course which certain Negro leaders have adopted must in due time become apparent. If the only way to get attention for any cause is to organize provocative "demonstrations," what lesson does this teach to a nation which believes in a government of "law and order"? Will not other groups of citizens, intent on attaining their objectives, be encouraged to adopt similar tactics? . . .

We hear the cry: "But we've waited a hundred years, we can't wait any longer!"

Yet what happened in those hundred years? Was there no Congress or Supreme Court in session to proclaim "the law of the land" in the usual manner? Was anyone prevented from challenging the laws or the court decisions in a formal way through the judicial or legislative processes established by our Constitution? Was there in those decades no discussion in the press and no public debate on the principles involved in the racial controversy? Would the ruling in the 1954 desegregation decisions of the Supreme Court have been achieved earlier if Negro "demonstrations" had been organized and many participants had been arrested for disturbing the peace?

Government is, in fact a system developed by evolution. We believe in rule by the majority. The minds and hearts of a majority, however, cannot be won by disregarding the fundamental precepts of government itself—that "law and order" must be preserved while the facilities of debate and lawful communication are made available to all citizens, no matter how unpopular their causes may be.

But constitutional guarantees become worthless if the process of "law and order" is forsaken and we substitute the pressures of the mob in the precincts of government itself.

Letter to Martin Luther King

A GROUP OF CLERGYMEN

Following is the text of the public statement on Negro demonstrations directed to Dr. Martin Luther King Jr. by eight Alabama clergymen.

APRIL 12, 1963

We clergymen are among those who, in January, issued "An Appeal for Law and Order and Common Sense," in dealing with racial problems in Alabama. We expressed understanding that honest convictions in racial matters could properly be pursued in the courts, but urged that decisions of those courts should in the meantime be peacefully obeyed.

Since that time there has been some evidence of increased forbearance and a willingness to face facts. Responsible citizens have undertaken to work on various problems which cause racial friction and unrest. In Birmingham, recent public events have given indication that we all have opportunity for a new constructive and realistic approach to racial problems.

However, we are now confronted by a series of demonstrations by some of our Negro citizens, directed and led in part by outsiders. We recognize the natural impatience of people who feel that their hopes are slow in being realized. But we are convinced that these demonstrations are unwise and untimely.

We agree rather with certain local Negro leadership which has called for honest and open negotiation of racial issues in our area. And we believe this kind of facing of issues can best be accomplished by citizens of our own metropolitan area, white and Negro, meeting with their knowledge and experience of the local situation. All of us need to face that responsibility and find proper channels for its accomplishment.

Just as we formerly pointed out that "hatred and violence have no sanction in our religious and political traditions," we also point out that such actions as incite to hatred and violence, however technically peaceful those actions may be, have not contributed to the resolution of our local problems. We do not believe that these days of new hope are days when extreme measures are justified in Birmingham.

We commend the community as a whole, and the local news media and law enforcement officials in particular, on the calm manner in which these demonstrations have been handled. We urge the public to continue to show restraint should the demonstrations continue, and the law enforcement officials to remain calm and continue to protect our city from violence.

We further strongly urge our own Negro community to withdraw support from these demonstrations, and to unite locally in working peacefully for a better Birmingham. When rights are consistently denied, a cause should be pressed in the courts and in negotiations among local leaders, and not in the streets. We appeal to both our white and Negro citizenry to observe the principles of law and order and common sense.

Signed by:

C. C. J. CARPENTER, D.D., LL.D., *Bishop of Alabama.*

JOSEPH A. DURICK, D.D., *Auxiliary Bishop, Diocese of Mobile-Birmingham*

Rabbi MILTON L. GRAFMAN, *Temple Emanu-El, Birmingham, Alabama*

Bishop PAUL HARDIN, *Bishop of the Alabama-West Florida Conference of the Methodist Church*

Bishop NOLAN B. HARMON, *Bishop of the North Alabama Conference of the Methodist Church*

GEORGE M. MURRAY, D.D., LL.D., *Bishop Coadjutor, Episcopal Diocese of Alabama*

EDWARD V. RAMAGE, *Moderator, Synod of the Alabama Presbyterian Church in the United States*

EARL STALLINGS, *Pastor, First Baptist Church, Birmingham, Alabama*

Letter From Birmingham City Jail

MARTIN LUTHER KING *

April 16, 1963

My Dear Fellow Clergymen,

While confined here in the Birmingham City Jail, I came across your recent statement calling our present activities "unwise and untimely." Seldom, if ever, do I pause to answer criticism of my work and ideas. . . . But since I feel that you are men of genuine good will and your criticisms are sincerely set forth, I would like to answer your statement in what I hope will be patient and reasonable terms. . . .

I am in Birmingham because injustice is here. Just as the 8th century prophets left their little villages and carried their "thus saith the Lord" far beyond the boundaries of their home town, and just as the Apostle Paul left his little village of Tarsus and carried the gospel of Jesus Christ to practically every hamlet and city of the Graeco-Roman world, I too am compelled to carry the gospel of freedom beyond my particular home town. Like Paul, I must constantly respond to the Macedonian call for aid.

Moreover, I am cognizant of the interrelatedness of all communities and states. I cannot sit idly by in Atlanta and not be concerned about what happens in Birmingham. Injustice anywhere is a threat to justice everywhere. We are caught in an inescapable network of mutuality tied in a single garment of destiny. Whatever affects one directly affects all indirectly. Never again can we afford to live with the narrow, provincial "outside agitator" idea. Anyone who lives inside the United States can never be considered an outsider anywhere in this country.

You deplore the demonstrations that are presently taking place in Birmingham. But I am sorry that your statement did not express a similar concern for the conditions that brought the demonstrations into being. I am sure that each of you would want to go far beyond the superficial social analyst who looks merely at effects, and does not grapple with underlying causes. I would not hesitate to say that it is unfortunate that so-called demonstrations are taking place in Birmingham at this time, but I would say in more emphatic terms that it is even more unfortunate that the white power structure of this city left the Negro community with no other alternative.

In any nonviolent campaign there are four basic steps: 1) collection of the facts to determine whether injustices are alive; 2) negotiation; 3) self-purification; and 4) direct action. We have gone through all of these steps

* Distinguished Negro leader. President of the Southern Christian Leadership Conference; winner of the Nobel Peace Prize for 1964.

in Birmingham. There can be no gainsaying of the fact that racial injustice engulfs this community. Birmingham is probably the most thoroughly segregated city in the United States. Its ugly record of police brutality is known in every section of this country. Its unjust treatment of Negroes in the courts is a notorious reality. There have been more unsolved bombings of Negro homes and churches in Birmingham than any city in this nation. These are the hard, brutal, and unbelievable facts. On the basis of these conditions Negro leaders sought to negotiate with the city fathers. But the political leaders consistently refused to engage in good faith negotiation. . . .

As in so many experiences of the past, we were confronted with blasted hopes, and the dark shadow of a deep disappointment settled upon us. So we had no alternative except that of preparing for direct action, whereby we would present our very bodies as a means of laying our case before the conscience of the local and national community. We were not unmindful of the difficulties involved. So we decided to go through a process of self-purification. We started having workshops on nonviolence and repeatedly asked ourselves the questions, "Are you able to accept blows without retaliating?" "Are you able to endure the ordeals of jail?" . . .

You may well ask, "Why direct action? Why sit-ins, marches, etc.? Isn't negotiation a better path?" You are exactly right in your call for negotiation. Indeed, this is the purpose of direct action. Nonviolent direct action seeks to create such a crisis and establish such creative tension that a community that has constantly refused to negotiate is forced to confront the issue. It seeks so to dramatize the issue that it can no longer be ignored.

I just referred to the creation of tension as a part of the work of the nonviolent resister. This may sound rather shocking. But I must confess that I am not afraid of the word tension. I have earnestly worked and preached against violent tension, but there is a type of constructive nonviolent tension that is necessary for growth. Just as Socrates felt that it was necessary to create a tension in the mind so that individuals could rise from the bondage of myths and half-truths to the unfettered realm of creative analysis and objective appraisal, we must see the need of having nonviolent gadflies to create the kind of tension in society that will help men rise from the dark depths of prejudice and racism to the majestic heights of understanding and brotherhood. So the purpose of the direct action is to create a situation so crisis-packed that it will inevitably open the door to negotiation. We, therefore, concur with you in your call for negotiation. Too long has our beloved Southland been bogged down in the tragic attempt to live in monologue rather than dialogue. . . .

My friends, I must say to you that we have not made a single gain in civil rights without determined legal and nonviolent pressure. History is the long and tragic story of the fact that privileged groups seldom give up their privileges voluntarily. Individuals may see the moral light and voluntarily give up their unjust posture; but as Reinhold Niebuhr has reminded us, groups are more immoral than individuals.

We know through painful experience that freedom is never voluntarily given by the oppressor; it must be demanded by the oppressed. Frankly I have never yet engaged in a direct action movement that was "well timed," according to the timetable of those who have not suffered unduly from the disease of segregation. For years now I have heard the word "Wait!" It rings in the ear of every Negro with a piercing familiarity. This "wait" has almost always meant "never." It has been a tranquilizing Thalidomide, relieving the emotional stress for a moment, only to give birth to an ill-formed infant of frustration. We must come to see with the distinguished jurist of yesterday that "justice too long delayed is justice denied." We have waited for more than 340 years for our constitutional and God-given rights. The nations of Asia and Africa are moving with jet-like speed toward the goal of political independence, and we still creep at horse and buggy pace toward the gaining of a cup of coffee at a lunch counter.

I guess it is easy for those who have never felt the stinging darts of segregation to say wait. But when you have seen vicious mobs lynch your mothers and fathers at will and drown your sisters and brothers at whim; when you have seen hate-filled policemen curse, kick, brutalize, and even kill your black brothers and sisters with impunity; when you see the vast majority of your 20 million Negro brothers smothering in an air-tight cage of poverty in the midst of an affluent society; when you suddenly find your tongue twisted and your speech stammering as you seek to explain to your six-year-old daughter why she can't go to the public amusement park that has just been advertised on television, and see tears welling up in her little eyes when she is told that Funtown is closed to colored children, and see the depressing clouds of inferiority begin to form in her little mental sky, and see her begin to distort her little personality by unconsciously developing a bitterness toward white people; when you have to concoct an answer for a five-year-old son asking in agonizing pathos: "Daddy, why do white people treat colored people so mean?"; when you take a cross country drive and find it necessary to sleep night after night in the uncomfortable corners of your automobile because no motel will accept you; when you are humiliated day in and day out by nagging signs reading "white" men and "colored"; when your first name becomes "nigger" and your middle name becomes "boy" (however old you are) and your last name becomes "John," and when your wife and mother are never given the respected title "Mrs."; when you are harried by day and haunted by night by the fact that you are a Negro, living constantly at tip-toe stance never quite knowing what to expect next, and plagued with inner fears and outer resentments; when you are forever fighting a degenerating sense of "nobodiness"—then you will understand why we find it difficult to wait. There comes a time when the cup of endurance runs over, and men are no longer willing to be plunged into an abyss of injustice where they experience the bleakness of corroding despair. I hope, sirs, you can understand our legitimate and unavoidable impatience.

You express a great deal of anxiety over our willingness to break laws. This is certainly a legitimate concern. Since we so diligently urge people to obey the Supreme Court's decision of 1954 outlawing segregation in the public schools, it is rather strange and paradoxical to find us consciously breaking laws. One may well ask, "How can you advocate breaking some laws and obeying others?" The answer is found in the fact that there are two types of laws: There are *just* laws and there are *unjust* laws. I would be the first to advocate obeying just laws. One has not only a legal but a moral responsibility to obey just laws. Conversely, one has a moral responsibility to disobey unjust laws. I would agree with Saint Augustine that "An unjust law is no law at all."

Now what is the difference between the two? How does one determine when a law is just or unjust? A just law is a man-made code that squares with the moral law or the law of God. An unjust law is a mode that is out of harmony with the moral law. To put it in the terms of Saint Thomas Aquinas, an unjust law is a human law that is not rooted in eternal and natural law. Any law that uplifts human personality is just. Any law that degrades human personality is unjust.

All segregation statutes are unjust because segregation distorts the soul and damages the personality. It gives the segregator a false sense of superiority and the segregated a false sense of inferiority. To use the words of Martin Buber, the great Jewish philosopher, segregation substitutes an "I-it" relationship for the "I-thou" relationship, and ends up relegating persons to the status of things. So segregation is not only politically, economically, and sociologically unsound, but it is morally wrong and sinful. Paul Tillich has said that sin is separation. Isn't segregation an existential expression of man's tragic separation, an expression of his awful estrangement, his terrible sinfulness? So I can urge men to obey the 1954 decision of the Supreme Court because it is morally right, and I can urge them to disobey segregation ordinances because they are morally wrong.

Let me give another example of just and unjust laws. An unjust law is a code that a majority inflicts on a minority that is not binding on itself. This is *difference* made legal. On the other hand a just law is a code that a majority compels a minority to follow that it is willing to follow itself. This is *sameness* made legal.

Let me give another explanation. An unjust law is a code inflicted upon a minority which that minority had no part in enacting or creating because they did not have the unhampered right to vote. Who can say the legislature of Alabama which set up the segregation laws was democratically elected? Throughout the state of Alabama all types of conniving methods are used to prevent Negroes from becoming registered voters and there are some counties without a single Negro registered to vote despite the fact that the Negro constitutes a majority of the population. Can any law set up in such a state be considered democratically structured?

These are just a few examples of unjust and just laws. There are some instances when a law is just on its face but unjust in its application. For instance, I was arrested Friday on a charge of parading without a permit. Now there is nothing wrong with an ordinance which requires a permit for a parade, but when the ordinance is used to preserve segregation and to deny citizens the First Amendment privilege of peaceful assembly and peaceful protest, then it becomes unjust.

I hope you can see the distinction I am trying to point out. In no sense do I advocate evading or defying the law as the rabid segregationist would do. This would lead to anarchy. One who breaks an unjust law must do it *openly, lovingly* (not hatefully as the white mothers did in New Orleans when they were seen on television screaming "nigger, nigger, nigger") and with a willingness to accept the penalty. I submit that an individual who breaks a law that conscience tells him is unjust, and willingly accepts the penalty by staying in jail to arouse the conscience of the community over its injustice, is in reality expressing the very highest respect for law.

Of course there is nothing new about this kind of civil disobedience. It was seen sublimely in the refusal of Shadrach, Meshach, and Abednego to obey the laws of Nebuchadnezzar because a higher moral law was involved. It was practiced superbly by the early Christians who were willing to face hungry lions and the excruciating pain of chopping blocks before submitting to certain unjust laws of the Roman Empire. To a degree academic freedom is a reality today because Socrates practiced civil disobedience.

We can never forget that everything Hitler did in Germany was "legal" and everything the Hungarian freedom fighters did in Hungary was "illegal." It was "illegal" to aid and comfort a Jew in Hitler's Germany. But I am sure that, if I had lived in Germany during that time, I would have aided and comforted my Jewish brothers even though it was illegal. If I lived in a Communist country today where certain principles dear to the Christian faith are suppressed, I believe I would openly advocate disobeying these anti-religious laws. . . .

In your statement you asserted that our actions, even though peaceful, must be condemned because they precipitate violence. But can this assertion be logically made? Isn't this like condemning the robbed man because his possession of money precipitated the evil act of robbery? Isn't this like condemning Socrates because his unswerving commitment to truth and his philosophical delvings precipitated the misguided popular mind to make him drink the hemlock? Isn't this like condemning Jesus because His unique God consciousness and never-ceasing devotion to His will precipitated the evil act of crucifixion? We must come to see, as Federal courts have consistently affirmed, that it is immoral to urge an individual to withdraw his efforts to gain his basic constitutional rights because the quest precipitates violence. Society must protect the robbed and punish the robber.

I had also hoped that the white moderate would reject the myth of time. I received a letter this morning from a white brother in Texas which said: "All Christians know that the colored people will receive equal rights eventually, but is it possible that you are in too great of a religious hurry? It has taken Christianity almost 2,000 years to accomplish what it has. The teachings of Christ take time to come to earth." All that is said here grows out of a tragic misconception of time. It is the strangely irrational notion that there is something in the very flow of time that will inevitably cure all ills. Actually time is neutral. It can be used either destructively or constructively. I am coming to feel that the people of ill will have used time much more effectively than the people of good will.

We will have to repent in this generation not merely for the vitriolic words and actions of the bad people, but for the appalling silence of the good people. We must come to see that human progress never rolls in on wheels of inevitability. It comes through the tireless efforts and persistent work of men willing to be co-workers with God, and without this hard work time itself becomes an ally of the forces of social stagnation.

We must use time creatively, and forever realize that the time is always ripe to do right. Now is the time to make real the promise of democracy, and transform our pending national elegy into a creative psalm of brotherhood. Now is the time to lift our national policy from the quicksand of racial injustice to the solid rock of human dignity.

You spoke of our activity in Birmingham as extreme. At first I was rather disappointed that fellow clergymen would see my nonviolent efforts as those of the extremist. I started thinking about the fact that I stand in the middle of two opposing forces in the Negro community. One is a force of complacency made up of Negroes who, as a result of long years of oppression, have been so completely drained of self-respect and a sense of "somebodiness" that they have adjusted to segregation, and of a few Negroes in the middle class who, because of a degree of academic and economic security, and because at points they profit by segregation, have unconsciously become insensitive to the problems of the masses. The other force is one of bitterness and hatred and comes perilously close to advocating violence. It is expressed in the various black nationalist groups that are springing up over the nation, the largest and best known being Elijah Muhammad's Muslim movement. This movement is nourished by the contemporary frustration over the continued existence of racial discrimination. It is made up of people who have lost faith in America, who have absolutely repudiated Christianity, and who have concluded that the white man is an incurable "devil."

I have tried to stand between these two forces saying that we need not follow the "do-nothingism" of the complacent or the hatred and despair of the black nationalist. There is the more excellent way of love and nonviolent protest. I'm grateful to God that, through the Negro church, the dimension of nonviolence entered our struggle. If this philosophy had not emerged I am convinced that by now many streets of the South would be flowing with floods of blood. And I am further convinced that if our white brothers dismiss us as "rabble rousers" and "outside agitators"—those of us who are working through the channels of nonviolent direct action—and refuse to support our nonviolent efforts, millions of Negroes, out of frustration and despair, will seek solace and security in black nationalist ideologies, a development that will lead inevitably to a frightening racial nightmare.

Oppressed people cannot remain oppressed forever. The urge for freedom will eventually come. This is what has happened to the American Negro. Something within has reminded him of his birthright of freedom; something without has reminded him that he can gain it. Consciously and unconsciously, he has been swept in by what the Germans call the *Zeitgeist,* and with his black brothers of Africa, and his brown and yellow brothers of Asia, South America, and the Caribbean, he is moving with a sense of cosmic urgency toward the promised land of racial justice. Recognizing this vital urge that has engulfed the Negro community, one should readily understand public demonstrations.

The Negro has many pent-up resentments and latent frustrations. He has to get them out. So let him march sometime; let him have his prayer pilgrimages to the city hall; understand why he must have sit-ins and freedom rides. If his repressed emotions do not come out in these nonviolent ways, they will come out in ominous expressions of violence. This is not a threat; it is a fact of history. So I have not said to my people, "Get rid of your discontent." But I have tried to say that this normal and healthy discontent can be channeled through the creative outlet of nonviolent direct action. Now this approach is being dismissed as extremist. I must admit that I was initially disappointed in being so categorized.

But as I continued to think about the matter I gradually gained a bit of satisfaction from being considered an extremist. Was not Jesus an extremist in love? "Love your enemies, bless them that curse you, pray for them that despitefully use you." Was not Amos an extremist for justice—"Let justice roll down like waters and righteousness like a mighty stream." Was not Paul an extremist for the gospel of Jesus Christ—"I bear in my body the marks of the Lord Jesus." Was not Martin Luther an extremist—"Here I stand; I can do none other so help me God." Was not John Bunyan an extremist—"I will stay in jail to the end of my days before I make a butchery of my conscience." Was not Abraham Lincoln an extremist—"This nation cannot survive half slave and half free." Was not Thomas Jefferson an extremist—"We hold these truths to be self evident that all men are created equal."

So the question is not whether we will be extremist but what kind of extremist will we be. Will we be extremists for hate or will we be extremists for love? Will we be extremists for the preservation of injustice—or will we be extremists for the cause of justice? In that dramatic scene on Calvary's hill three men were crucified. We must never forget that all three were crucified for the same crime—the crime of extremism. Two were extremists for immorality, and thus fell below their environment. The other, Jesus Christ, was an extremist for love, truth, and goodness, and thereby rose above His environment. So, after all, maybe the South, the nation, and the world are in dire need of creative extremists. . . .

I hope the Church as a whole will meet the challenge of this decisive hour. But even if the Church does not come to the aid of justice, I have no despair about the future. I have no fear about the outcome of our struggle in Birmingham, even if our motives are presently misunderstood. We will reach the goal of freedom in Birmingham and all over the nation, because the goal of America is freedom. Abused and scorned though we may be, our destiny is tied up with the destiny of America.

Before the pilgrims landed at Plymouth, we were here. Before the pen of Jefferson etched across the pages of history the majestic words of the Declaration of Independence, we were here. For more than two centuries our foreparents labored in this country without wages; they made cotton "king"; and they built the homes of their masters in the midst of brutal injustice and shameful humiliation—and yet out of a bottomless vitality they continued to thrive and develop. If the inexpressible cruelties of slavery could not stop us, the opposition we now face will surely fail. We will win our freedom because the sacred heritage of our nation and the eternal will of God are embodied in our echoing demands.

I must close now. But before closing I am impelled to mention one other point in your statement that troubled me profoundly. You warmly commended the Birmingham police force for keeping "order" and "preventing violence." I don't believe you would have so warmly commended the police force if you had seen its angry violent dogs literally biting six unarmed, nonviolent Negroes. I don't believe you would so quickly commend the policemen if you would observe their ugly and inhuman treatment of Negroes here in the city jail; if you would watch them push and curse old Negro women and young Negro girls; if you would see them slap and kick old Negro men and young Negro boys; if you will observe them, as they did on two occasions, refuse to give us food because we wanted to sing our grace together. I'm sorry that I can't join you in your praise for the police department. . . .

It is true that they have been rather disciplined in their public handling of the demonstrators. In this sense they have been rather publicly "nonviolent." But for what purpose? To preserve the evil system of segregation. Over the last few years I have consistently preached that nonviolence demands that the means we use must be as pure as the ends we seek. So I have tried to make it clear that it is wrong to use immoral means to attain moral ends. But now I must affirm that it is just as wrong, or even more so, to use moral means to preserve immoral ends. . . . T. S. Eliot has said that there is no greater treason than to do the right deed for the wrong reason.

I wish you had commended the Negro sit-inners and demonstrators of Birmingham for their sublime courage, their willingness to suffer, and their amazing discipline in the midst of the most inhuman provocation. One day the South will recognize its real heroes. They will be the James Merediths, courageously and with a majestic sense of purpose, facing jeering and hostile mobs and the agonizing loneliness that characterizes the life of the pioneer. They will be old, oppressed, battered Negro women, symbolized in a 72-year-old woman of Montgomery, Alabama, who rose up with a sense of dignity and with her people decided not to ride the segregated buses, and responded to one who inquired about her tiredness with ungrammatical profundity: "My feets is tired, but my soul is rested." They will be young high school and college students, young ministers of the gospel and a host of the elders, courageously and nonviolently sitting in at lunch counters and willingly going to jail for conscience sake. One day the South will know that when these disinherited children of God sat down at lunch counters they were in reality standing up for the best in the American dream and the most sacred values in our Judeo-Christian heritage, and thus carrying our whole nation back to great wells of democracy which were dug deep by the founding fathers in the formulation of the Constitution and the Declaration of Independence.

Yours for the cause of Peace and Brotherhood
M. L. KING JR.

The Limits of Disobedience

JOHN DICKINSON *

The question of the meaning of sovereignty and legal order takes on special importance in periods where an existing sovereignty begins to be threatened on a significant scale with disobedience to its laws and decrees. At such a time we are faced with the possibility, if not as yet with the certainty, of the break-down and disappearance of sovereignty through

* Late professor of law, University of Pennsylvania, formerly U.S. Assistant Attorney General. The selection is from pp. 48–59 of "A Working Theory of Sovereignty II," *Political Science Quarterly*, Vol. 43 (1928), pp. 32–63. By permission.

increasing disobedience; and only a firm grasp of the significance of sovereignty for legal order will enable us intelligently to balance the cost of obedience.

Suppose, for example, that we do not accept the doctrine of sovereignty. We will then insist that laws do not derive their validity from the stamp of the sovereign, but that a rule may be validly a law which is directly contrary to the rule which the sovereign is seeking to enforce. But if this is the case, and if we must look not to the sovereign but to some other source to assure us what is the law, where else are we to look? Mr. Laski has suggested the only possible answer,—we must look within, each man to his own individual conscience.[1] If we use this method of approach we have no choice but to say that the validity of all law is derived from the conscience of the individual. The question of obedience or resistance then becomes a simple one. All that is involved is for each individual to set side by side and compare the law as promulgated by the sovereign with what his own conscience tells him is the law, and if there is a discrepancy between the two precepts, then he is not merely morally justified, he is legally authorized, to disobey.

There are but two factors to be taken in account in solving the problem, —the sovereign's pronouncement on the one hand and the individual's own conception of the law,—i.e., of what is right,—on the other. His career as a member of civil society becomes a continuous process of such comparisons, and he stands at every moment on the brink of disobedience and resistance. "The only ground upon which the individual can give or be asked his support for the state is from the conviction that what it is aiming at is, in each particular action, good. . . . It deserves his allegiance, it should receive it, only where it commands his conscience. . . . Its purpose is at each stage subject to examination." [2] The individual is thus invited to assume habitually what Mr. Laski has elsewhere called the "Athanasius attitude." [3]

[1] "The individual is ultimately the supreme arbiter of his behaviour; and he most fully realizes the purposes of the state when he offers to it the substance, whatever that may be, of his judgment."—*A Grammar of Politics,* p. 63. "The state is for [the individual] sovereign only where his conscience is not stirred against its performance." —*Authority in the Modern State,* p. 43.

[2] *Ibid.,* p. 46. A more extreme statement is that of Thoreau, "Civil Disobedience," *Writings* (Boston, 1906): "Must the citizen, even for a moment or in the least degree, resign his conscience to the legislator? Why has every man a conscience then? I think we should be men first and subjects afterwards." Vol. IV, p. 358. "There will never be a really free and enlightened state until the state comes to recognize the individual as a higher and independent power from which all its own power and authority are derived and treats him accordingly." *Ibid.,* p. 387.

[3] I would urge against this position the criticism that it reverses the proper order of the burden of proof, that it shifts improperly the presumption of validity. The presumption must be in favor of state action; the burden of proof on the refractory individual. The state must not continually be justifying itself to the individual; the individual must justify himself morally in the exceptional cases when he feels morally compelled to resist the state.

The doubt which suggests itself in connection with this attitude is that possibly it may be too naïve,—that possibly it may not be sophisticated enough to comprehend the full challenge of civil society. It is the primitive attitude of Antigone,[4] rather than the mature comprehension of Socrates. Its capital defect is that it leaves fundamentally out of account the chief and most difficult factor in the whole problem—the question, namely, of the advantage, not merely to all individuals but to each individual, of having a legally ordered society to live in, and of the price which he must perforce pay to get it. This factor is the thing which really causes all the difficulty; and it is the major factor. If there were no question but of a conflict between two opposing wills, the will of the citizen as one individual and the will of the sovereign as another, the problem would be quite easy; the individual could not fairly be expected to surrender his will until convinced intellectually and morally that he was wrong. But so to state the problem is to simplify it out of all recognition. It is not a question of a bare conflict between the individual and the sovereign; the conflict must be regarded as rather between the individual and all that the sovereign stands for. The individual may be convinced and reasonably convinced that the sovereign is wrong, unfairly, brutally wrong; but the deeper question must at once arise of what is involved in disobeying the sovereign.

For sovereignty, as we have seen, is a prerequisite of legal order; a prerequisite, that is, of a condition of affairs where the disputes which will honestly and inevitably arise between man and man, and which will as often be due to a real and involuntary difference in intellectual outlook as to a clash between purely selfish purposes, are settled peaceably by a publicly authorized arbiter, and, so far as possible, by impartial rules, rather than by the rough arbitrament of force and chance. The very essence and meaning of civil society is precisely the fact that the former method rather than the latter is the one which habitually prevails; and this essential method of civil society is just the thing which we strike at whenever we disobey or resist the sovereign.

The question of obedience thus raises far more than the mere question of the agreement or disagreement in a particular case between the sovereign's law applying to the case in hand, and what the individual's private conscience tells him the law ought to be; properly approached, it brings

[4] Antigone submits to her punishment, not like Socrates under a sense that it is something owed to civil society, but merely because she must bow to superior force; and she insists on the justice of her position, and protests against the injustice of her punishment, to the bitter end: "What rule of divine justice have I transgressed? . . . It is my piety which wins me the name of impious. But if my death be, as it might seem, the pleasure of the gods, I will suffer death ere I confess that I have sinned; and if, on the other hand, the gods do not approve of my death, and these men are the guilty ones, may they suffer no more woes than they have unjustly done to me."—Sophocles, *Antigone,* lines 921–928.

dominantly into the foreground the large issues of the desirability of preserving public authority and civil society itself. This is the great truth so clearly put by Socrates, when in answer to Crito's plea for disobedience he represents the City as standing before him and saying, "Tell us, Socrates, what is it you mean to do? Nothing more nor less than to overthrow us by this attempt of yours,—to overthrow the laws and the whole commonwealth so far as in you lies. For do you imagine that a city can stand and not be overthrown, when the decisions of the judges have no power, when they are made of no effect and destroyed by private persons?"

In other words, something of vastly superior consequence is involved than the essential rightness or wrongness in the given case of any particular exercise of sovereign power; what is involved, fundamentally, is the value and validity of civil society in contrast with the freedom, the flexibility, the experimentalism, of anarchy, whether the latter take the form of benevolent cooperation or of forceful competition. Civil society cannot stand when the decisions of the judges are made of no effect by private persons; and the Athanasius attitude, to be defensible, must balance not particular differences of opinion between the individual conscience and the sovereign will, but the value of the end which conscience has at stake as against the value of civil society.[5]

For there are of course ends which from time to time do validly outweigh the maintenance for the time being of the orderly processes of civil society. Revolution, like war, is no doubt entitled to a place as one of the indispensable ingredients of progress in the existing, and perhaps in any, state of human nature. The only point I am insisting on is that revolution should always be recognized for what it is,—a lapse into anarchy. Only so, in any specific case, can the wisdom of taking the plunge be fairly assessed; only so can the full meaning of the alternative between obedience and resistance be grasped in all its awful implications.[6] The chief defect in the doctrine of

[5] This point is often made by Mr. Laski himself, e. g.: "A right to disobedience . . . is . . . reasonably to be exercised only at the margins of political conduct. No community could hope to fulfil its purpose if rebellion became a settled habit of the population."—*A Grammar of Politics,* p. 62. "The real obligation of obedience is to the total interest of our fellow-men."—*Ibid.,* p. 64. "The point at which resistance becomes an expedient factor is not a matter for definition or prophecy; it will vary with the circumstances of each age. All we can say is that at times in the history of a state there may well come a point where the maintenance of order seems to some group of men worthless as an end compared to achieving, by other than constitutional means, some good deemed greater than peace."—*Authority in the Modern State,* pp. 53–54.

[6] This was recognized, for example, by Benjamin Constant: "Obedience to law is a duty, but, like all duties, it is not absolute, it is relative; it rests on the supposition that the law emanates from a legitimate source and is confined within just limits. This duty does not cease when the law departs from this rule only in certain respects. We ought to sacrifice a great deal for the sake of the public peace; we should render ourselves guilty in the eyes of morality if, by too inflexible attachment to our rights we should

the denial of sovereignty is that it glosses over with thin sugarcoating this fundamental alternative. The doctrine that there exists somewhere a law above, and independent of, the law of the sovereign, and capable of being discovered for himself by each private individual so as to justify disobedience to the positive law,[7] carries with it the implication that civil society itself exists, and can exist, apart from and independently of obedience to the sovereign; and that therefore resistance by the individual to the sovereign is not necessarily anything like so serious and ultimate a thing as an assault on civil society is readily seen to be. The essential meaning of resistance is obscured, the price which it entails belittled. And at the same time the price that we must pay for civil society itself is belittled. For the demand which civil society makes that private individual will and purpose be always subordinated to the will of the authorized public representative of the society, on no other and no better ground than merely that the one is private and the other public, is by implication denied, if we accept the doctrine that civil society does not depend for its existence and functioning on obedience to its constituted representative. A view of civil society is thus produced which evades the necessity for political organization,—which tolerates the claim of separate and discrete groups within the state to be independent of the jurisdiction of, and immune from interference by, the state, and which in pursuance of the same conviction is capable of seeing in an unorganized "society of nations" a substantial substitute for an organized

---

disturb the peace as soon as it seemed to us that they were being infringed upon in the name of law." If we "say that we obey laws only in so far as they are just, we shall find ourselves authorizing resistance to law in the most senseless and culpable instances, and anarchy will reign." . . . This quotation from his *Cours de Politique Constitutionelle* (additions et notes: "Des Droits Individus") are given in Elizabeth W. Schermerhorn, *Benjamin Constant* (Boston and New York, 1924), p. 381. For an excellent statement of the issues involved in disobedience, see T. H. Green, *Lectures on the Principles of Political Obligation,* §§ 143–147, in *Works,* edited by Nettleship (London, 1906), vol. II, pp. 454–459.

[7] This view possesses a perennial appeal for extreme reformers, e. g., the abolitionists before the American Civil War. Thus one of their platforms declares that since slavery is contrary to the natural rights of man, and since "the moral laws of the Creator are paramount to all human laws . . . therefore, Resolved, that we . . . owe it to the Sovereign Ruler of the Universe, as a proof of our allegiance to him, in all our civil relations and offices, whether as private citizens or as public functionaries sworn to support the Constitution of the United States, to regard and to treat the third clause of the second section of the fourth article of that instrument, whenever applied to the case of a fugitive slave, as utterly null and void, and consequently as forming no part of the Constitution of the United States whenever we are called upon or sworn to support it."—*Emancipator Extra,* Tract No. 1, reprinted in K. H. Porter, *National Party Platforms* (New York, 1924), pp. 13–14. . . . This view has naturally been favored by Roman Catholic writers as in accord with the historic position of that body. Thus Orestes A. Brownson, an American Roman Catholic, denied the right of revolution except when the Church "as the representative of the highest authority on earth, determines when resistance is proper and prescribes its forms and extent." *Works,* ed. by Henry F. Brownson (Detroit, 1884), vol. XV, pp. 397–398.

League. The theory seeks to have its cake of order without having to pay the price or organization.

This was the theory that dominated the thought of the Western world throughout the medieval centuries. It is a theory the defectiveness of which is in large part cured if we are able to accept a presupposition which to the mind of the Middle Ages was a commonplace,—the presupposition, namely, that there not merely exists a body of law above and independent of human choice, but that the precepts of that law are fixed, definite and capable of being as clearly perceived in identical form by every human intelligence as are the elementary truths of mathematics.[8] Men obviously need no sovereign to exercise a prerogative of choice in order to tell them whether twice two is five or four. If the laws which distinguish right from wrong are equally well defined by "nature," we need no sovereign to tell us whether the issue of watered stock by a corporation is illegal, or whether or not relief by injunction is a lawful remedy to apply in a labor dispute. Men thought, not so long ago, that the one right answer to every such question could be reached by mathematical demonstration. If this were so, there would be no need for a sovereign law-declaring agency.

But during the past few centuries there has been growing doubt as to whether it is really so; and the conflict between the faith and the doubt is quaintly reflected in the inconsistency of a central passage of Locke's *Second Treatise of Civil Government:* "In the state of Nature there are many things wanting. Firstly, there wants an established, settled, known law. . . . For though the law of Nature be plain and intelligible to all rational creatures, yet men, being biased by their interest, as well as ignorant for want of study of it, are not apt to allow of it as a law binding to them in the application of it to their particular cases." [9] In other words, the law of nature is there, but we need an authoritative human organ to tell us what it is.[10] "Those who are united into one body and have a common established law and judicature to appeal to . . . are in civil society with one another, but those who have no such common appeal are in the state of nature."

Even, then, if we grant the existence of a "law" that is not of men's making, but recognize that room remains for possible differences of opinion as to its specific precepts, we shall still have to admit the need for political organization, the need for a sovereign to "declare" that law authoritatively;

[8] See my *Administrative Justice and the Supremacy of Law* (Cambridge, 1927), pp. 115 *et seq. Cf.* Bynkershoek, "If men were reasonable, they would know the law accurately without more."—*De Foro Legatorum,* chap. iii. *Opera Minora,* ed. secunda (Leyden, 1744).

[9] *Second Treatise of Civil Government,* chap. ix, § 124.

[10] The same criticism is applicable to the theory of the "sovereignty of reason" put forward by Constant, Cousin, Guizot, and other French liberals of the first half of the nineteenth century. See C. E. Merriam, *History of Sovereignty Since Rousseau* (New York, 1900), chap. v. "Reason" requires an authoritative interpretation, and so an authoritative interpreter, unless anarchy is to result.

and we shall then be driven forward to face the important practical problems incidental to devising a mechanism of organization best adapted to cause the precepts of the sovereign to conform to the precepts of the "higher" law. But this is a task which the doctrine of resistance minimizes and discourages. If each individual is entitled to search in his own conscience for the precept of the higher law applicable to the case in hand, and then to disobey the sovereign should his inquiry lead to a different conclusion from that which that sovereign has reached, the importance of having a sovereign who will reach the right conclusion in the first place is vastly decreased; for if no law made by the sovereign need be obeyed unless it is a good law, the question of whether the sovereign makes bad laws becomes of relatively secondary consequence. From this point of view, therefore, the real guaranty of good government is the "right" of resistance, not the perfecting of the governmental machinery adapted to produce the best results under given circumstances.

In answer to this theory it should be sufficient to point out that the whole history of progress in the art of government has consisted in the gradual substitution of the latter for the former of these guaranties. Revolution was during long ages the only effective way by which the ordinary acts of government could be corrected; the efforts of many centuries have been spent on devising less wasteful and more orderly methods of control. These efforts have proceeded on the assumption that it is not compatible with the existence of civil society to leave to each individual the protection of his own rights; that so long as the normal conditions of civil order prevail, the sovereign, as the organ of the community, must be entitled to the obedience of the individual precisely because, and for no other reason than because, the sovereign *is* the organ of the community; and that therefore the protection of the individual under normal circumstances must be found not in the "right" of resistance, but in the manner and plan whereby sovereign power is organized and constituted.

The fact that in civil society the individual is thus not entitled to set his own idea of the "higher" precepts which the government should follow against the sovereign's version of them, does not mean that there are no such precepts.[11] Whether they constitute a body of "higher law" or not, is of course a wholly different question; but nothing that has been said implies that there are no canons of morality and justice which the sovereign ought to embody in his positive laws. On the contrary, the institution of sovereignty exists primarily because of the need of an organ to focus and formulate these fundamental, but more or less vague and disputed, canons into

[11] This seems to be the heart of Mr. Laski's misunderstanding: "Within the sphere of law, there is therefore . . . no such thing as an unjust command."—*Grammar of Politics,* p. 50. There is no such thing as an illegal law, and "within the sphere of law" no question arises as to whether a law, otherwise proved to be a law, is just; but this emphatically does not mean that there is no such thing as an unjust law.

precise and uniform rules which on the one hand have the fixity and generality necessary for a rule of law, and which on the other hand represent the moral conceptions that command acceptance among the most influential members of the community rather than views which are held merely by isolated private thinkers.

In a realm of ideas where there is so much room for differences of opinion as in connection with the precepts of morality, it is absolutely necessary to have such an authoritative declaration of the rule before there can properly be any thought of enforcing it as a rule of community action. It may, and doubtless often will, result that the rule selected by the sovereign for enforcement, precisely because it will be a rule reflecting the morality of the crowd or the morality of the wealthy or military class, will offend the consciences of the individuals who constitute the most enlightened and morally advanced element of the community. Under such circumstances is not the right of this class to resist essential in order to secure moral progress? As a last resort and in extraordinary situations where the stake is sufficiently high, the answer must certainly be, yes; but always with full recognition of the fact that such resistance constitutes rebellion, and entails for the time being a dissolution of the conditions of civil order.

Under a properly adjusted constitution, the necessity should seldom occur, because such a constitution would, on the one hand, provide adequate channels for the views of this class to exert an influence upon the sovereign as far as is compatible with the obvious fact that laws must be made to fit the average rather than the exceptional man; and because, on the other hand, under such a constitution the sovereign would doubtless be wise enough to limit to the narrowest point his interference with those kinds of individual action from which moral improvement can properly be expected to occur.

Is It Ever Right to Break the Law?

CHARLES FRANKEL *

During recent months, public events have repeatedly dramatized an old and troublesome problem. A group of students defies the State Department's ban on travel to Cuba; a teachers' union threatens a strike even though a state law prohibits strikes by public employes; advocates of civil rights employ mass demonstrations of disobedience to the law to advance their cause;

* Professor of Philosophy at Columbia University. Author of *The Democratic Prospect* and other books and articles. The selection is from the *New York Times,* January 12, 1964, printed by the New York Times Company. Reprinted by permission.

the Governor of a Southern state deliberately obstructs the enforcement of Federal laws, and declares himself thoroughly within his rights in doing so. . . .

When is it justified for the citizen to act as his own legislator, and to decide that he will or will not obey a given law?

An answer that covers all the issues this question raises cannot be given here, nor can a set of principles be proposed that will allow anyone to make automatic and infallible judgments concerning the legitimacy or illegitimacy of specific acts of civil disobedience. Such judgments require detailed knowledge of the facts of specific cases, and such knowledge is often unavailable to the outsider. Nevertheless, it is possible to indicate some of the principal issues that are raised by civil disobedience, some of the more common mistakes that are made in thinking about these issues, and, at least in outline, the approach that one man would take toward such issues.

We can begin, it seems to me, by rejecting one extreme position. This is the view that disobedience to the law can never be justified in any circumstances. To take this position is to say one of two things: either every law that exists is a just law, or a greater wrong is always done by breaking the law. The first statement is plainly false. The second is highly doubtful. If it is true, then the signers of the Declaration of Independence, and those Germans who refused to carry out Hitler's orders, committed acts of injustice.

It is possible, however, to take a much more moderate and plausible version of this position, and many quite reasonable people do. Such people concede that disobedience to the law can sometimes be legitimate and necessary under a despotic regime. They argue, however, that civil disobedience can never be justified in a democratic society, because such a society provides its members with legal instruments for the redress of their grievances.

This is one of the standard arguments that is made, often quite sincerely, against the activities of people like supporters of the Congress of Racial Equality, who set about changing laws they find objectionable by dramatically breaking them. Such groups are often condemned for risking disorder and for spreading disrespect for the law when, so it is maintained, they could accomplish their goals a great deal more fairly and patriotically by staying within the law, and confining themselves to the courts and to methods of peaceful persuasion.

Now it is perfectly true, I believe, that there is a stronger case for obedience to the law, including bad law, in a democracy than in a dictatorship. The people who must abide by the law have presumably been consulted, and they have legal channels through which to express their protests and to work for reform. One way to define democracy is to say that it is a system whose aim is to provide alternatives to civil disobedience. Nevertheless, when applied to the kind of situation faced, say, by CORE, these generalizations, it seems to me, become cruelly abstract.

The basic fallacy in the proposition that, in a democracy, civil disobedience can never be justified, is that it confuses the *ideals* or *aims* of democracy with the inevitably less than perfect accomplishments of democracy at any given moment. In accordance with democratic ideals, the laws of a democracy may give rights and powers to individuals which, in theory, enable them to work legally for the elimination of injustices.

In actual fact, however, these rights and powers may be empty. The police may be hostile, the courts biased, the elections rigged—and the legal remedies available to the individual may be unavailing against these evils.

Worse still, the majority may have demonstrated, in a series of free and honest elections, that it is unwavering in its support of what the minority regards as an unspeakable evil. This is obviously the case today in many parts of the South, where the white majority is either opposed to desegregation or not so impatient to get on with it as is the Negro minority. Are we prepared to say that majorities never err? If not, there is no absolutely conclusive reason why we must invariably give the results of an election greater weight than considerations of elementary justice.

It is true, of course, that one swallow does not make a summer, and that the test of legal democratic processes is not this or that particular success or failure, but rather the general direction in which these processes move over the long run. Still, the position that violation of the law is never justifiable so long as there are legal alternatives overstates this important truth. It fails to face at least three important exceptions to it.

In the first place, dramatic disobedience to the law by a minority may be the only effective way of catching the attention or winning the support of the majority. Most classic cases of civil disobedience, from the early Christians to Gandhi and his supporters, exemplify this truth. Civil disobedience, like almost no other technique, can shame a majority and make it ask itself just how far it is willing to go, just how seriously it really is committed to defending the status quo.

Second, there is the simple but painful factor of time. If a man is holding you down on a bed of nails, it is all very well for a bystander to say that you live in a great country in which there are legal remedies for your condition, and that you ought, therefore, to be patient and wait for these remedies to take effect. But your willingness to listen to this counsel will depend, quite properly, on the nature of the injury you are suffering.

Third, it is baseless prejudice to assume that observance of the law is *always* conducive to strengthening a democratic system while disobedience to the law can never have a salutary effect. A majority's complacent acquiescence in bad laws can undermine the faith of a minority in the power of democratic methods to rectify manifest evils; yet a vigorous democracy depends on the existence of minorities holding just such a faith.

Disobedience to bad laws can sometimes jolt democratic processes into motion. Which strengthens one's hope for democracy more—the behavior of the Negroes in Birmingham who broke municipal ordinances when they staged their protest marches, or the behavior of the police, using dogs and fire hoses to assert their legal authority?

Another factor should also be taken into account. In our Federal system, there are often legitimate doubts concerning the legal validity, under our Constitution, of various state or local ordinances. Disobedience to these laws is in many cases simply a practical, though painful, way of testing their legality. But even where no thought of such a test is involved, there is often present a moral issue which no one can easily dodge—least of all the man whose personal dignity and self-respect are caught up in the issue.

A citizen caught in a conflict between local laws and what he thinks will be upheld as the superior Federal law can sometimes afford to wait until the courts have determined the issue for him. But often he cannot afford to wait, or must take a stand in order to force a decision. This is the situation of many Negro citizens in Southern states as they confront the conflict between local and Federal laws.

Yet there is another side to the story. It would be a mistake to conclude from what has been said that civil disobedience is justified, provided only that it is disobedience in the name of higher principles. Strong moral conviction is not all that is required to turn breaking the law into service to society.

Civil disobedience is not simply like other acts in which men stand up courageously for their principles. It involves violation of the law. And the law can make no provision for its violation except to hold the offender liable to punishment. This is why President Kennedy was in such a delicate position last spring at the time of the Negro demonstrations in Birmingham. He gave many signs that, as an individual, he was in sympathy with the goals of the demonstrators. As a political leader, he probably realized that these goals could not be attained without dramatic actions that crossed the line into illegality. But as Chief Executive he could not give permission or approval to such actions.

We may admire a man like Martin Luther King, who is prepared to defy the authorities in the name of a principle, and we may think that he is entirely in the right; just the same, his right to break the law cannot be officially recognized. No society, whether free or tyrannical, can give its citizens the right to break its laws: To ask it to do so is to ask it to proclaim, as a matter of law, that its laws are not laws.

In short, if anybody ever has a right to break the law, this cannot be a legal right under the law. It has to be a moral right against the law. And this moral right is not an unlimited right to disobey any law which one regards as unjust. It is a right that is hedged about, it seems to me, with important restrictions.

First of all, the exercise of this right is subject to standards of just and fair behavior. I may be correct, for example, in thinking that an ordinance against jaywalking is an unnecessary infringement of my rights. This does not make it reasonable, however, for me to organize a giant sit-down strike in the streets which holds up traffic for a week. Conformity to the concept of justice requires that there be some *proportion* between the importance of the end one desires to attain and the power of the means one employs to attain it.

When applied to civil disobedience, this principle constitutes a very large restriction. Civil disobedience is an effort to change the law by making it impossible to enforce the law, or by making the price of such enforcement extremely high. It is a case, as it were, of holding the legal system to ransom. It can arouse extreme passions on one side or the other, excite and provoke the unbalanced, and make disrespect for the law a commonplace and popular attitude.

Although violence may be no part of the intention of those who practice civil disobedience, the risks of violence are present, and are part of what must be taken into account when a program of civil disobedience is being contemplated.

In short, civil disobedience is a grave enterprise. It may sometimes be justified, but the provocation for it has to be equally grave. Basic principles have to be at issue. The evils being combated have to be serious evils that are likely to endure unless they are fought. There should be reasonable grounds to believe that legal methods of fighting them are likely to be insufficient by themselves.

Nor is this the only limitation on the individual's moral right to disobey the law. The most important limitation is that his cause must be a just one. It was right for General de Gaulle to disobey Marshal Pétain; it was wrong for the commanders of the French Army in Algeria, 20 years later, to disobey General de Gaulle.

Similarly, if it is absolutely necessary, and if the consequences have been properly weighed, then it is right to break the law in order to eliminate inequalities based on race. But it can never be necessary, and no weighing of consequences can ever make it right, to break the law in the name of Nazi principles.

In sum, the goals of those who disobey the law have to lie at the very heart of what we regard as morality before we can say that they have a moral right to do what they are doing.

But who is to make these difficult decisions? Who is to say that one man's moral principles are right and another man's wrong? We come here to the special function that civil disobedience serves in a society. The man who breaks the law on the ground that the law is immoral asks the rest of us, in effect, to trust him, or to trust those he trusts, in preference to the established conventions and authorities of our society.

He has taken a large and visible chance, and implicitly asked us to join him in taking that chance, on the probity of his personal moral judgment. In doing so, he has put it to us whether we are willing to take a similar chance on the probity of our own judgment.

Thomas Hobbes, who knew the trouble that rebels and dissenters convinced of their rectitude can cause, once remarked that a man may be convinced that God has commanded him to act as he has, but that God, after all, does not command other men to believe that this is so. The man who chooses to disobey the law on grounds of principle may be a saint, but he may also be a madman. He may be a courageous and lonely individualist, but he may also merely be taking orders and following his own crowd. Whatever he may be, however, his existence tends to make us painfully aware that we too are implicitly making choices, and must bear responsibility for the ones we make.

This, indeed, may be the most important function of those who practice civil disobedience. They remind us that the man who obeys the law has as much of an obligation to look into the morality of his acts and the rationality of his society as does the man who breaks the law. The occurrence of civil disobedience can never be a happy phenomenon; when it is justified, something is seriously wrong with the society in which it takes place.

But the man who puts his conscience above the law, though he may be right or he may be wrong, does take personal moral responsibility for the social arrangements under which he lives. And so he dramatizes the fascinating and fearful possibility that those who obey the law might do the same. They might obey the law and support what exists, not out of habit or fear, but because they have freely chosen to do so, and are prepared to live with their consciences after having made that choice.

Section VIII

Judicial Review

JUDICAL REVIEW, by which is meant the power of American courts and finally of the Supreme Court to set aside national and state legislation as unconstitutional, has served as, and remains, at least potentially, one of the most important restraints upon majority rule provided by our Constitution. (The power of judicial review with respect to federal legislation, as has been seen, was established in the case of Marbury *v.* Madison.)

The legitimacy of that power itself, although the subject of sharp controversy in the past, is no longer a compelling issue today. Much more vigorously controverted is *how* the Court should exercise its power. Should it act with judicial self-restraint and deference to the legislative judgment? This was the view, for example, of Mr. Justice Felix Frankfurter and is the view of Mr. Justice John Harlan. In support of this position, Professor Wallace Mendelson has queried: "Shall doubts be resolved by a handful of 'independent' judges whose libertarian or proprietarian preferences happen for the moment to dominate the bench? Or, . . . by the people and their elected representatives with a minimum of judicial interference?" On the other hand, supporters of the "activist" position, like Professors Fred Rodell and C. Herman Pritchett, maintain—in the language of Pritchett—that the Court "has a positive obligation not to deny the nation the guidance on basic democratic problems which its unique situation equips it to provide."

Topic 20

WHAT ROLE FOR THE SUPREME COURT?

The Case for Judicial Activism

FRED RODELL *

"Of that freedom [freedom of speech] one may say that it is the matrix, the indispensable condition, of nearly every other form of freedom."—Benjamin Cardozo.

"The history of liberty has largely been the history of the observance of procedural safeguards."—Felix Frankfurter.

"What is freedom of speech and of the press; . . . these fundamental canons . . . turn out to be no more than admonitions of moderation."—Learned Hand.

"The idea that they are no more than that has done more to undermine liberty in this country than any other single force."—William O. Douglas.

In the early evening of March 8, 1948, a college student named Irving Feiner was standing on an actual soap box at a street corner in Syracuse, New York, speaking in occasionally abusive language in behalf of Henry Wallace's absurd bid for the United States presidency. Of a crowd of seventy-five or eighty, one or two men threatened Feiner; a policeman thereupon ordered Feiner to shut up and climb down; Feiner refused; he was arrested and sentenced to thirty days in the penitentiary. His conviction, protested up to the Supreme Court, was there upheld, six to three.[1] Said Justice Frankfurter, characteristically in concurrence: "Where conduct is within the allowable limits of free speech, the police are peace officers for the speaker as well as for his hearers. But . . . ." [2] And again: "Enforcement of these [breach-of-peace] statutes calls for public tolerance and intelligent

* Professor of Law, Yale Law School. Author of *Fifty-Five Men: the Story of the Constitution; Woe Unto You, Lawyers; Democracy and the Third Term; Nine Men: A Political History of the Supreme Court from 1790 to 1955;* and of many articles. The selection is from "Judicial Activists, Judicial Self-Deniers, Judicial Review and the First Amendment—Or, How to Hide the Melody of What You Mean Behind the Words of What You Say," *Georgetown Law Journal,* Vol. 47 (1959), pp. 483–490.

[1] Feiner v. New York, 340 U.S. 315 (1951).

[2] Id. at 289 (concurring opinion).

police administration. These, in the long run, must give substance to whatever the Court may say about free speech. But . . . ." [3] Said Justice Black, in dissent: "I think this conviction makes a mockery of the free speech guarantees of the First and Fourteenth Amendments. . . . I will have no part or parcel in this holding which I view as a long step toward totalitarian authority." [4] There were no But's.

This too-little-noted case—*Feiner v. New York* [5]—along with the head-on-colliding quotes italicized above are here intended to highlight what strikes me as the most meaningful split in constitutional law and theory and practice of the mid-twentieth century. It is a split that stems from the thorny question of *who* is ultimately responsible, under our constitutional system, for the protection of the people's basic liberties, especially those that are guaranteed by the first amendment (and, courtesy of judicial injection, by the fourteenth as well). It is a split that has commonly, if a bit dubiously, been dubbed a conflict between "activists" and "passivists" or "self-deniers," on the bench and in the academic bleachers—and as such, its ramifications reach beyond the first amendment (plus the fourteenth) to the whole of the Bill of Rights and even further still. It is a split whose sources stretch back through at least two thousand years of political theory and whose present manifestations have been known to spawn personal feuds out of ideological differences. In its current intensity, it began to get up steam soon after the clash between the Old Court and the New Deal, or just about twenty years ago.

That, of course, was the approximate point in time when a glorious new epoch in constitutional law seemed to loom immediately and infinitely ahead; an inglorious era of economic overlordship by the Court was at an obvious end; the fat reading of the due process clauses plus the thin reading of the commerce clause, to hobble affirmative government, had been hastily abandoned by the Old Court itself, under the Damoclean sword of the Roosevelt Court plan. Now, new Justices sat in the old seats of power, unanimous in the belief that their predecessors, prior to that quick conversion, had been wrong, wrong, wrong. But how and why had they been wrong? There was the rub whose friction caused the split that has rent the new Court for two decades. And if, in seeking to analyze this split, I should seem too simplistic, too primer-minded for the sophisticated, I offer no apology. The agglutinated gloss of judicial self-justification has grow thicker and stickier with the years; my effort is to cut through those layers of verbal varnish and bare the true grain that lies beneath.

What one group of Old-Court critics said—and are still saying—is that the veto-wielding Nine Old Men of the thirties were wrong to substitute

[3] Ibid.
[4] Id. at 323 (dissenting opinion).
[5] 340 U.S. 315 (1951).

their collective judgment for that of Congress (or, to a lesser extent, for that of state legislatures) on *any* type of issue, under the aegis of *any* constitutional clause. These were and are the passivists, the self-deniers, the apostles of undifferentiated judicial self-restraint. With rare exceptions—usually involving a conflict of sovereignties under our fifty-governmented federal system—they would leave the commands of the Constitution to legislative hands, with the judiciary keeping a strict hands-off. At the federal government level, they come very close to contending that the Court should never overrule Congress on constitutional grounds—that is, to disavowing the right of judicial review Marshall asserted in *Marbury v. Madison.*[6] Their chief spokesman on the Supreme Court, since the death of Justice Jackson, is of course Justice Frankfurter,* who has often bemoaned his inability, self-imposed by self-restraint, to vote to strike down, as unconstitutional, legislation which he finds offensive under the Constitution. Most articulate advocate of this view is the venerable Judge Learned Hand, who has touted the propriety of judicial impotence in the face of legislative arrogance, with special emphasis on the field of civil liberties, in court opinions and in two books—*The Spirit of Liberty*[7] and his recently published Harvard lectures, *The Bill of Rights.*[8] Going further back, the patron saints of the indiscriminate self-deniers include Alexander Hamilton, British jurist John Austin, and Harvard Law Professor Thayer who long preached the doctrine from his lecture platform. Justice Holmes selectively interpreted to fit the faith, is also claimed as a past adherent—although it is highly doubtful that either Justice Frankfurter or Judge Hand would ever judicially subscribe to such a typical Holmesian statement of his own credo as: "If in the long run the beliefs expressed in proletarian dictatorship are destined to be accepted by the dominant forces of the community, the only meaning of free speech is that they should be given their chance and have their way." [9]

Arrayed against the formidable if somewhat Anglophilic forces of these whole-hog self-deniers are the allegedly illogical and inconsistent activists. They agree that the Old Court was wrong to veto pre-New Deal and New Deal legislation—but they see the error in narrower and more specific terms. They see it in the type of laws that were vetoed—and all were economic regulations—and in the fuzzy imprecision of the constitutional excuses used to cut those laws down. Thus, the "substantive due process" suitcase was expandable enough to give the Court, as Holmes once noted, *carte blanche* to veto at its pleasure, just as a subjective reading of the com-

[6] 5 U.S. (1 Cranch) 137 (1803).

* Justice Frankfurter is retired from the Court. The present chief spokesman for this point of view is Justice Harlan.

[7] L. Hand, The Spirit of Liberty (2d ed. 1953).

[8] L. Hand, the Bill of Rights (1958). Judge Hand has since died.

[9] Gitlow v. United States, 268 U.S. 652, 673 (1925) (dissenting opinion).

merce clause was invited by such Court-bred convolutions as *in*-commerce-or-*affecting*-commerce-*directly*-or-*indirectly*. Not so easily elastic is the bulk of the Bill of Rights—especially the first amendment with its flat and absolute commands. Hence the activists believe the Court can and should differentiate—that it can and should overrule Congress in the name of the Constitution where the document itself is more precise and, particularly, where the claimed rights at issue are more precious and more personal than those that deal exclusively with matters of money. Chief spokesmen of this view on the current Court, and for many years back, are Justices Black and Douglas. Among its patron saints are Thomas Jefferson, Justice Holmes—differently interpreted than by the self-deniers, with the emphasis here on his civil-liberty dissents—and Justice Stone who, along with his powerful plea for self-restraint in the *Butler* (AAA) case,[10] a strictly economic hassle, also urged in his famous *Carolene Products*[11] footnote that civil liberties be given preferred judicial treatment.

Accused by the self-deniers of result-minded opportunism, the activists are asked how they can reconcile judicial supremacy where civil liberties are at stake with legislative supremacy in the regulation of business and wealth. Behind this question lurks the inarticulate major premise that a constitutional policy ought to be conceptually consistent, regardless of the stuff of life with which it deals. But the activists do not believe that logic should rule, rather than serve, the ends of government nor that jurisprudence should be dominated by a syllogism. They believe that our nation, our civilization, our culture, put—or should put—a higher premium on individual dignities and freedoms than on such material matters as the getting and keeping of money. They believe that this simple but exalted scale of values was deliberately implanted into the Constitution by the Bill of Rights (plus the fourteenth amendment) and, further, that it is their duty as judges to militantly uphold it rather than meekly deplore its occasional legislative neglect.

Indeed—to go back briefly to historical roots—why have a written Constitution at all in a republic, or a representative democracy, that is dedicated to majority rule? Why, that is, except to set up the sheer mechanics of government (two senators per state, four-year terms for a president, etc.) and to sketch in the structure by which two overlapping sovereigns—the nation and the states—might operate together? Why a written Bill of Rights—without the assurance of which, incidentally, most of the original states would never have ratified the Constitution? The answer must be plain even to the judicial self-deniers. The purpose was to lay down certain basic rules that even a majority was not to be privileged to violate by vote—to guarantee certain fundamental personal rights and liberties *against* majority rule,

[10] United States v. Butler, 297 U.S. 1, 78–79 (1936).
[11] United States v. Carolene Prods. Co., 304 U.S. 144, 152–53 (1938).

because they were deemed so essential to civilized government. These were, and are, the minimum democratic decencies that dictatorships view with scorn, the multifarious protections of individuals and minority groups—especially unpopular individuals and minorities—which range in scope from the first amendment freedoms to the various injunctions of fair treatment and fair trial for every criminal defendant, be he accused of kidnapping or Communism.

And the key question, then—to come back in something of a circle to our starting-point—is *who* is to uphold, under the commands of the Constitution, these uniquely guaranteed liberties of unpopular or even despised people against a lynch-minded, let's-get-them majority. Should it be the legislatures, including Congress, which presumably reflect the current majority will? Or should it perhaps be the courts, especially the Supreme Court, to which the last appeals of those who feel they have been unjustly wronged are regularly taken? It is this old poser in political theory—and in practical day-to-day government as well—that divides, even more than does the logic or illogic of selective self-restraint, the advocates of activism under the Bill of Rights, and most particularly under the first amendment, from the apostles of judicial self-denial. The division has taken on an almost explosive quality during roughly the past dozen years, as "loyalty" and "security" laws and programs have sprouted at every level of government—all of them impinging in some measure on freedom of speech, of press, of association, even of thought in the political realm. Books on the subject have burgeoned, two of the most authoritative, in light of the stature of their authors, being Learned Hand's *The Bill of Rights* and William O. Douglas' *The Right of the People*—both of them published last year.

It is Judge Hand's general thesis, as a lifetime member of the self-denying school, that—with rare and rather fuzzily defined exceptions—the last word should be left by the courts to the legislature, especially to Congress, as much when civil liberties are on the line as when the issue is one of economic regulation. After all, legislators no less than judges take oaths to support the Constitution and should be presumed to consider carefully—though surely this is unrealistic—the constitutionality of whatever laws they pass. Beyond that, though—and this is his basic postulate—Judge Hand sees as inherently undemocratic the whole concept of judicial review (of legislative action) in *any* field; to him, it adds up to rule by judges. "For myself," he says, "it would be most irksome to be ruled by a bevy of Platonic Guardians, even if I knew how to choose them . . . ." [12] Yet Judge Hand must have a twinge of awareness that to equate judicial protection of constitutional liberties, even metaphorically, with rule by a bevy of Platonic Guardians is nonsense. As well call the drafters of the Bill of Rights Platonic Guardians Emeritus. Far more significantly, the judge well knows that the vetoing of laws by courts, on whatever ground, is perforce a negative act,

[12] L. Hand, The Bill of Rights 73 (1958).

whereas to rule is to act affirmatively in a sovereign fashion—scarcely an attribute of a declaration that this statute or that is void because it runs counter, for instance, to the commands of the first amendment. The fact is that Judge Hand is so absorbed with the abstract theory of judicial review—as well as with defense of his own long-tenanted position—that, despite flashes of the old eloquence, he never hits the crucial, living issues head-on.

By contrast, Justice Douglas faces in his book—as he has in his opinions over a score of years—the fact-situations that call for solution, the competing claims that come before the Court, and the frankly functional nature of his own choices and decisions. Indeed, this approach is the essence of judicial activism. Conceptual consistency about the right of judicial review takes second place to an honest weighing of the ends to be achieved on the scale of democratic values. On this scale, the civil liberties of the Bill of Rights and the fourteenth amendment weigh heaviest, with the freedoms guaranteed by the first amendment—"in terms absolute," as Douglas puts it—outweighing all the rest. Justice Douglas has no doubt that it is the duty of the courts to defend these freedoms militantly against legislative encroachment or disregard, no matter what the calamity-howlers may holler about the evils of judicial supremacy. To him, it is rather a matter of *constitutional* supremacy. Thus, he does not consider the judiciary the only *who* charged with protection of the people's liberties. It is—or should be—equally the job of legislators, executives and administrators as well. But when lawmakers or law-enforcers fall short of their obligation, that does not entitle the judges to bow deferentially out of the picture. It is then their special duty to restore, by vigilant use of the judicial veto, those constitutional rights of which the people have been improperly deprived. On a realistic note—contrasting starkly with Judge Hand's Philosophic cerebrations—Justice Douglas recognizes that the two elected, and so majority-minded, branches of government are, by their very nature, less apt to obey those mandates of the Constitution which guarantee minority rights against majority rule. Hence, too often it falls finally to the courts to uphold freedom of speech or press or assembly or religion and all the rest. Tough and unpopular as such decisions frequently are, Justice Douglas sees them as the judiciary's most challenging and finest achievements.

Such achievements on the part of the Supreme Court were lamentably rare during the decade after World War II, as the Smith Act and the McCarran Acts and the whole congeries of abominations against the Bill of Rights in the name of national security withstood judicial inspection. They were rare because the self-deniers prevailed, because a Court majority meekly manacled itself against overruling Congress—or, in most instances, the legislatures of the states—even in defense of the first amendment. Despite their numerical superiority, there was an air of peevish futility about the self-deniers' explanations. Said Justice Frankfurter, concurring in the *Dennis* decision: "Civic liberties draw at best only limited strength from legal guaranties. . . . The ultimate reliance for the deepest needs of civilization must be found outside their vindication in courts of law . . . ."[13] Of course, the decision itself made these statements temporarily true; but might not the identical words and reasoning be used to uphold lynch law? And Justice Jackson, expatiating on his self-denying philosophy in a posthumously published book, remarked that "any court which undertakes by its legal processes to enforce civil liberties needs the support of an enlightened and vigorous public opinion . . . . I do not think the American public is enlightened on this subject."[14] Which would make an easy out for any government servant seeking to excuse himself from enforcing an unpopular law. These are not vicious men, these self-deniers; they are timid and bothered and bookish men, under whose passive aegis the vicious men —freedom-flouting and conformity-minded—have had their way to the nation's detriment.

Yet even at the lowest ebb in the Court's defense of personal liberties, there were other and braver voices to be heard, albeit in dissent. Thus, John Lord O'Brian, respected and Republican elder statesman of the bar, concluded his book on *National Security and Individual Freedom:* "If and when our leaders in the Executive, Congressional, *and Judicial* departments awaken to their obligation to protect the freedom of the human spirit, they will, like their great predecessors, respond to that obligation. The public, with the issues clarified will *then* also respond . . . ."[15] Thus, Justice Douglas, protesting the Court's approval of New York's Feinberg Law, under which schoolteachers were fired because of their past associations, reminded: "The Framers knew . . . the strength that comes when the mind is free, when ideas may be pursued wherever they lead. *We* forget these teachings of the First Amendment when *we* sustain this law."[16] Thus, Justice Black magnificently ended his *Dennis* dissent: "There is hope, however, that in calmer times, when present pressures, passions and fears subside, this or some later *Court* will restore the First Amendment liberties to the high preferred place where they belong in a free society."[17] In trying to counter these clear calls for active judicial responsibility, the self-deniers might, and some did, go back for support to the Founding Fathers—for instance, to Alexander Hamilton who opposed a Bill of Rights and who opined, in Federalist Paper No. 84, that liberty of the press "must depend on legislative discretion, regulated by public opinion . . . ."[18] But the activists could readily quote in reply James Madison's statement: "If they [civil

[13] Dennis v. United States, 341 U.S. 494, 555–56 (1951).

[14] Jackson, The Supreme Court in the American System of Government 82 (1955).

[15] O'Brian, National Security and Individual Freedom 83–84 (1955). (Emphasis added.)

[16] Adler v. Board of Educ., 342 U.S. 485, 511 (1952) (dissenting opinion). (Emphasis added.)

[17] 341 U.S. at 581. (Emphasis added.)

[18] The Federalist No. 84, at 538 (Lodge ed. 1888) (Hamilton).

liberties] are incorporated into the Constitution, independent tribunals of justice will consider themselves in a peculiar manner the guardians of those rights; they will be an impenetrable bulwark against every assumption of power in the legislative or executive; they will be naturally led to resist every encroachment upon rights expressly stipulated for in the Constitution by the declaration of rights." [19] Significantly, Madison gave this strong exposition of judicial activism in the very speech in which he proposed a Bill of Rights to the first Congress.

My less than impartial primer draws to a close. The plain and simple fact is that it is not the dictate of history, long-past or recent, which mainly motivates the self-deniers to decline active judicial defense of the first amendment freedoms. Nor is it a repugnance toward illogic or inconsistency in the exercise of the power of judicial review. Nor is it a faith that if the courts take care of the forms, of the procedure, then the substance of liberty will somehow take care of itself. Nor is it even a decent respect for the prerogatives of the other two branches of government, especially the legislative. All these are factors but they are abstract factors; they are word reasons; they are the gloss upon the underlying grain. The crux of judicial self-denial in the civil liberties field is, in a sense, just as negative as the philosophy it espouses—and it is implicit in the But's that so often follow protestations of devotion to civil liberties. These men, these self-deniers, all believe in the first amendment freedoms; the point is that they do not believe in them enough. They do not believe in them enough to fight officially or effectively for their protection and preservation. Indeed—and here is the essence of it —not one of the self-deniers can say, as can the activists, with Thomas Jefferson: "I have sworn upon the altar of God eternal hostility against every form of tyranny over the mind of man." [20]

The Case for Judicial Restraint

WALLACE MENDELSON *

INTRODUCTION

> . . . law is always a general statement, yet there are cases which it is not possible to cover in general terms. In matters therefore where, while it is necessary to speak in general terms, it is not possible to do so correctly, the law takes into consideration the majority of cases, although it is not unaware of the error this involves. And this does not make it a wrong law; for the

[19] 5 The Writings of James Madison 385 (Hunt ed. 1900).

[20] 10 The Writings of Thomas Jefferson 175 (Library ed. 1903).

* Professor of Government, University of Texas. Author of *The Constitution and the Supreme Court* and of *Capitalism, Democracy, and the Supreme Court*. The selection is from his *Justices Black and Frankfurter: Conflict in the Court* (Chicago, University of Chicago Press, 1961), pp. VII–IX, 114–131. By permission.

error is not in the law nor in the lawgiver, but in the nature of the case: the material of conduct is essentially irregular.

ARISTOTLE

The main trouble with the Supreme Court is a general misunderstanding of its role in American government. Without thinking much about such matters, the man in the street assumes that "the law" is crystal clear. He is mistaken. The Constitution comes to us from the eighteenth century. Along with a few later amendments it was written by men wise enough to know they could not prescribe the details of government for an unknowable future. Nor were they in complete accord among themselves on vital issues—just as we are not. And so they often wrote with calculated generality. That is why the Constitution survives while other works of its age—in medicine, engineering, and every other field—have long since passed away. The Founding Fathers, like the amenders, avoided strait-jacketing precision. Their forte was the suggestive, open-ended hint. Not unlike the Delphic oracle, their "meaning" usually depends upon the wisdom of those who contemplate their words.

Even modern legislation is full of ambiguity. Congress dealing merely with present problems on a year-to-year basis cannot anticipate all the eventualities of life. Nor are congressmen, more than the rest of us, known for unanimity on even those issues which they can foresee.

Of course in many contexts the law is clear. To the extent that this is true there is little litigation. What controversy there is will seldom reach the Supreme Court. Cases which go that far generally do so precisely because the law with respect to them is cloudy—and precisely because they involve not a clash of right and wrong, but of competing rights.

That each state shall have two senators is too plain to require judicial interpretation. But what is the meaning of such constitutional terms as "due process of law," "commerce among the several states," or "equal protection of the laws"? These and other basic constitutional phrases have, and doubtless were designed to have, the chameleon's capacity to change their color with changing moods and circumstances. This is why they survive in a world their authors never knew. Short of constitutional amendment, we leave the final burden of "interpreting" such elastic terms to the Supreme Court. This means we expect the judges to solve for us many of the great dilemmas of life. For surely it is plain by now that the old eighteenth-century document does not automatically provide solutions for Atomic Age problems. And so the crucial question is: Where shall the Court find guidance when the light of the law fails? Shall it be past decisions—however out of date? Shall it be the good sense, or moral aspirations of the community, or perhaps natural law? And how may these be ascertained? If none of them, alone or in combination, what then?

We assume, or perhaps we are taught, that somehow the ancient parchment contains within its four corners the answers to all problems. *We* of course cannot read them there, but judges are supposed to have some special vision. Yet, each of us seems convinced that, if a decision does not coincide with his own emotional preference, then the judges must be biased, or worse. The Constitution is infallible, but judges are not—unless they happen to agree with us.

Sooner or later, if our system is to thrive, Americans must recognize that neither the Constitution nor any other legal code provides plain answers to most of the great issues that divide us. Soon or late we must acknowledge that cases which go as far as the Supreme Court usually represent conflicts between highly commendable principles none of which can fully prevail in life on earth. Each is apt to have impressive legal backing. In such conflicts "the law" is far from clear. Yet judges must somehow decide cases. They must solve enigmas that no other agencies of government, nor we ourselves, have been able to solve. This is a fearful responsibility. What Samuel Butler called "the art of life" is also the jurist's art: "to derive sufficient conclusions from insufficient premises."

Until we have a better understanding of the Supreme Court's real function, that institution will be in trouble. For just so long an important element of free government will be in danger. . . .

JUSTICE AND DEMOCRACY

A little learning is dangerous. Many discovered in the Court crisis of the 1930's that judges do not merely find, but sometimes make, the law. We came to see, as Max Lerner said, that judicial babies are not brought by constitutional storks. This secularization of the Court might have been all to the good, if we had also understood that lawmaking is an inherent and inevitable part of the judicial process. Judges, after all, must be more than mimics. Greatness on the bench, as elsewhere, is creativity. "We shall know," Cardozo said, "that the process of judging is a phase of a never ending movement, and that something more is expected of those who play their part in it than imitative reproduction, the lifeless repetition of a mechanical routine." Or, in the words of Curtis Bok, judging is "the play of an enlightened personality within the boundaries of a system." Of course judges sometimes make law. The great problem is how shall they contribute their bit to the law's growth without overstepping the boundaries of the system. Lord Bryce spoke of the need to reconcile tradition and convenience. Dean Pound referred to the competing claims of stability and change. . . .

"That the courts," Frankfurter once bitterly observed, "are especially fitted to be the ultimate arbiters of policy is an intelligent and tenable doctrine. But let them and us face the fact that five Justices of the Supreme Court *are* conscious molders of policy instead of impersonal vehicles of revealed truth."[1] The English apparently learned the lesson ages ago. They have long since reduced the judge's role to a minimum by rejecting judicial, in favor of parliamentary, supremacy. Either way, some human agency will have the "final" word. We give it to a Supreme Court, they give it to a supreme legislature. Assuming that we are to retain our system, the question is: how far and with what materials shall judges build the law? For build it they must.

Two great traditions provide two quite different approaches to these problems. One finds expression in Taney, Waite, Holmes, Brandeis, Learned Hand, Stone, Cardozo, and Frankfurter. These are the humilitarians, the pragmatists. Recognizing that judicial legislation is inevitable, they would hold it to a minimum. . . .

The other tradition finds expression in Marshall, Field, Peckham, Fuller, Sutherland, and Black. These are the activists. For them judicial legislation is not incidental, it is the heart of the judicial process. They see great visions and feel compelled to embed them in the law. Or, more mildly, their creative impulses are guided by their ideals. One of Mr. Justice Black's ardent supporters put it this way: "As procedure is the instrument, not the master of law; so law is the instrument, not the master of justice." Law, then, is simply a tool to be manipulated in accordance with the judge's vision of right and wrong.

An old story has it that when Holmes departed to assume his duties on the Supreme Court he was admonished to do Justice. He responded thoughtfully that his job was merely to enforce the law. At best this little tale is incomplete, but it is significant. In an opinion that seems destined to live as long as the ideals of democracy survive, Justice Holmes and Brandeis rejected their colleagues' narrow conception of free speech, yet concurred in the judgment affirming conviction.[2] Though the accused had claimed protection under the appropriate constitutional provision, she had failed at the trial level to raise the "clear and present danger" issue. Raising it in the Supreme Court was futile, thought Holmes and Brandeis, because "Our power of review in this case is limited not only to the question whether a right guaranteed by the Federal Constitution was denied [in the state court] . . . but to the particular claims duly made below and denied." It may be said, of course, that Holmes and Brandeis had "no feel for the dominant issues"; that, preoccupied with "crochet patches of legalism on the fingers of the case," they let a technicality prevail over Justice. Others may suppose the two great judges, well aware of what was at stake, deemed themselves not free to do Justice, but bound to do justice under law, i.e., in accordance with that very special allocation of function and authority which is the es-

[1] Frankfurter, "Judge Henry W. Edgerton," 43 Cornell Law Quarterly 161 (1957).
[2] *Whitney* v. *California,* 274 U.S. 357, 372 (1927).

sence of Federalism and the Separation of Powers. The point is, one's estimate of a judge hangs on one's conception—articulate or otherwise—of the judicial function.

To those for whom the Supreme Court's first concern is Justice, a great judge on that bench is an activist, one who does not readily permit "technicalities" to frustrate the ultimate. It follows, of course, that in so far as activism prevails the Court is the final governing authority. For, to that extent, its basic job is to impose Justice upon all other agencies of government, indeed upon the community itself. But what is Justice? Not so long ago, activists among the "nine old men" found it in a modified (read perverted) "laissez faire" called rugged individualism. Modern activists see it as a humane and virile libertarianism. Holmes facetiously suggested that its roots are in one's "can't helps." [3]

All this is unacceptable to those who take the more modest view that the Court's chief concern is *justice under law*. For them, the great judge is the humilitarian, the respecter of those "technicalities" which allocate among many agencies different responsibilities in the pursuit of Justice. In this view, the Court's special function is to preserve a constitutional balance between the several elements in a common enterprise. It maintains the ship, others set the course.

While these two views are distinct at their cores, they fuse into one another at their peripheries. Both are deep in American culture. Neither prevails to the complete exclusion of the other even in the work of a single judge. Eventually, the ardent activist gives way to a rule, just as his counterpart on occasion ignores rules for something deemed transcendental. What is important is the judge's inclination, his view of the nature of his role and the depth of his convictions.

Of the "great dissenters" in the days of "laissez-faire" activism only Harlan Stone remained on the bench to see the new libertarian activism after 1938. He was as unpersuaded by the one as by the other. In his view both entailed abuse of the judicial function. At the close of a long career spanning the two quite different eras of judicial Justice, he wrote a trusted friend,

> My more conservative brethren in the old days [read their preferences into legislation and] into the Constitution as well. What they did placed in jeopardy a great and useful institution of government. The pendulum has now swung to the other extreme, and history is repeating itself. The Court is now in as much danger of becoming a legislative and Constitution-making body, enacting into law its own predilections, as it was then.[4]

As Thomas Reed Powell put it, "Four of the Roosevelt appointees were as determined in *their* direction, as four of their predecessors were determined by attraction to the opposite pole." [5]

[3] That is, the things which because of their familiarity one can't help believing.

[4] Quoted in Alpheus T. Mason, *Security through Freedom* (Ithaca, N.Y., Cornell University Press, 1955), pp. 145–46.

[5] Powell, *Vagaries and Varieties in Constitutional Law,* p. 82.

MR. JUSTICE BLACK'S ACTIVISM

Where Mr. Justice Sutherland gave a preferred place to dominant economic interests, Mr. Justice Black gives preference to the "underdog." Both positions spring from the same activist premise. Each finds in the law a special tenderness for a chosen (though different) set of values. Judicial idealism of this sort prospers if there is harmony between the judge's Justice and the prevailing ideals of the community. Disharmony brings disaster. The old Court rode high while "laissez faire" was in the air. It destroyed itself by clinging too long to moribund views. But anachronism may not be the most serious risk. Perhaps, in some eras—possibly today—there are no plainly dominant ideals. Maybe society is too perplexed, too pluralistic, too ridden with conflicting values to be captured meaningfully in any ideological common denominator. Moreover, there is always some discrepancy between thought and action. Sometimes the only function of an ideal is to appease the conscience, while institutions take more convenient forms.

Plainly, Mr. Justice Black leans one way when "liberal" values are at stake and another way in the face of "conservative" claims—be the issue one of constitutional law, statutory interpretation, or evaluation of evidence. This tendency no doubt is what critics have in mind when they charge the Court with judicial legislation. For, if at most one colleague goes the whole way with him, Mr. Justice Black is obviously a leader—perhaps the backbone—of the new Court's powerful, "liberal" wing. His humane sympathy for the common man, his courage, creative vigor, and perseverance mark him as a dedicated being in pursuit of utopian ends. But is the bench a proper vehicle to use in pursuing them?

Surely it is an idealized view of the American legislative and constitution-making process that finds the product inevitably favoring New Deal values. It was no less a fantasy, of course, for some of the "nine old men" to find the law so often favoring quite different interests. Activism, whether of the old or new variety, may be consistent with the legislator's function, but is it compatible with the basic judicial job of settling "cases" and "controversies" impartially?

Apologists for the modern version of activist Justice seem to concentrate upon its First Amendment aspects and ignore its economic implications as in the FELA, FLSA, ICC, NLRB, and Sherman Act cases. This permits them to rest upon—or hide behind—the hallowed generalities of democratic dogma. Even so, they do not argue that the Constitution guarantees absolute freedom of expression, or that any explicit limitation can be found in the written document. *Choice then is inevitable.* Yet we are not told why a legislative choice between competing interests here is, *a priori,* less worthy of respect than elsewhere. To put it differently, the activist position assumes that courts are somehow inherently more competent to achieve a sound balance of interests in First Amendment cases than in others.

Perhaps freedom of expression and religion are so overwhelmingly important that we must weight the scales of justice in their favor. But what of a judge who is also an activist in economic matters? Is there any point in free discussion if its legislative fruits—the accommodations of the democratic way of life—are to be undone by judicial fiat? Surely the free speech that produced the FLSA compromise, for example, was a waste of time, if all judges—like some—were to reject it for one of its extreme components. Ironically, those who are least respectful of a legislative balance of interests in speech cases are the very ones who show least respect for legislative compromise in the economic domain. A burning faith in democracy and impatience with its results is not a new quality among idealists.

Democracy does not contemplate vast governmental authority in hands that are free both of the legislator's political responsibility and the judge's checkrein of precedent. For a healthy society both stability and change are indispensable. Our separation of governmental functions imposes major responsibility for the one upon courts; for the other upon legislatures. If the judiciary is to be a free-wheeling, legislative body, it will inevitably forfeit "some of the credit needed to fulfill a role much more unique." For as Professor Jaffe suggests: [6]

> Our society *is* a class society, at the least a society of vigorously competing interests. It is also an exceedingly mobile society, richly creating new opportunities, malignantly generating insecurities. It is a society which, in making unprecedented demands on government for change, places a heavy strain on the agencies of stability. To compose the constantly clashing demands for new opportunity our society sets up a representative legislature. To compose the day-to-day differences between man and man, and between man and organized society, it relies upon a nonrepresentative body of professionals. The warrant for their great power is the universal conviction that there is a knowable law which they can and will apply by the exercise of reason. The faith in judicial objectivity is an ultimate source of personal security and social cohesion. But once it comes to be believed by one or another of the great social classes that the Court is an organ of another class, its function is impaired. This is peculiarly the case when the Court is a constitutional one and participates in the very creation of major social premises. To secure wholehearted and widespread acceptance of its pronouncements it has need of all the credit it can amass; to squander it on schemes for social betterment is foolhardy.

In short there are special American reasons for the rejection of Plato's "philosopher-king" in favor of Aristotle's Rule of Law. If the latter is never fully attainable, if "reason" above "personal preference" is an illusion, "to dispel it would cause men to lose themselves in an even greater illusion: the illusion that personal power can be benevolently exercised." [7]

[6] L. L. Jaffe, "Mr. Justice Jackson," 68 Harvard Law Review 940, 994–95 (1955).
[7] T. Arnold, "Professor Hart's Theology," 73 Harvard Law Review 1298, 1311 (1960).

Such creativity destroyed the old Court—and brought the associated state chief justices, among others, to condemn the new one for judicial legislation. But Chief Justice Marshall, too, was condemned for "serving what in his conception [was] the largest good" in his day. To his admirers Hugo Black is another John Marshall: one who—before most of his contemporaries—saw and accommodated the needs of his age. Others see in him the shadow of Sutherland: a wilful judge who with honorable intent abused his power in pursuit of a mirage. Only time can render a true verdict. . . .

MR. JUSTICE FRANKFURTER'S RESTRAINT

Mr. Justice Frankfurter is deeply humilitarian. Plainly this is an acquired characteristic, a judicial mold superimposed upon a powerfully active and thoroughly libertarian personality. If to some his modesty seems exaggerated—breast-beating it has been called—that may be the measure of the struggle within him or within the Court. Just as Holmes was more skeptical, so he was less vocal in his humility. In any case, there can be no doubt of the deep Holmesian mark upon Mr. Justice Frankfurter. Before he took his seat upon the bench he was the intimate personal and professional confidant of Holmes, as well as Brandeis, during the whole, long course of their struggle against the activism of Sutherland and company. The shared ardors of that contest must have reinforced what Professor Frankfurter was learning as teacher of federal jurisdiction at Harvard; namely, that since the Supreme Court cannot review more than a drop in the flood of American litigation, by long established principle that drop must be selected, not on the basis of Justice to any litigant, but in the interest of balance among the various elements in the governmental structure. Moreover, if the Court takes jurisdiction on the one ground and decides on the other, balance is jeopardized and though Justice (in its then current version) be done for a few, the result is hardly fair to the many whose cases, however worthy, cannot for physical limitations hope to reach the judicial summit. What Paul Freund has said of Mr. Justice Brandeis is relevant here.

> [H]e would not be seduced by the quixotic temptation to right every fancied wrong which was paraded before him. The time was always out of joint but he was not [commissioned] to set it right. . . . Husbanding his time and energies as if the next day were to be his last, he steeled himself, like a scientist in the service of man, against the enervating distraction of countless tragedies he was not meant to relieve. His concern for jurisdictional and procedural limits reflected, on the technical level, an essentially Stoic philosophy. For like Epictetus, he recognized "the impropriety of being emotionally affected by what is not under one's control." [8]

The basic articulate premise of government in the United States is the diffusion of power. Ultimate political control is spread broadly among the

[8] *On Understanding the Supreme Court,* p. 65.

people. This is the foundation of democracy. Governmental power is divided between nation and states. This is Federalism. What is given to each is parceled out among three branches to accomplish the Separation of Powers. The purpose is not merely (as schoolboys emphasize) to avoid a tyrannical concentration of power. We seek, as well, the alignment of form to special function and, above all, that unique democratic efficiency, the promise that, if decisions be slow, they will be acceptable to those who must live with them.

For Mr. Justice Frankfurter, dispersion of the power to govern is not just a sophomoric slogan. It is the essence of our system. That is why he is so mindful of the political processes, state responsibility and the division of labor between legislative, executive, administrative, and judicial agencies. In Professor Jaffe's thoughtful account, the Justice is "forever disposing of issues by assigning their disposition to some other sphere of competence."

But this is only half the problem. Familiarity obscures for us what to outsiders is a marked characteristic of American government: our habit of dressing up the most intricate social, economic, and political problems in legal jargon and presenting them to the courts for "adjudication." In view of this, a foreign observer long ago concluded that, if asked where he found the American aristocracy, i.e., the governing class, he would reply "without hesitation . . . that it occupies the judicial bench and bar." Perhaps the short of it is that behind and overshadowing our open commitment to the fragmentation of power lies a brooding, inarticulate distrust of popular government. This finds expression in judicial review, or judicial supremacy. Whatever the name, the essence is clear: *concentration in a single agency*—significantly, that farthest removed from the people—of power to override all other elements of government, whether at the national, state, or local level. Neither Congress nor the President, no administrative agency, no governor, no state court or legislature, not a single city or county functionary is immune from the centralized power of judicial review. Indeed, in some eras the Court has been so domineering—in the name of Justice—that from time to time dissenters have felt compelled to remind it that the judiciary is "not the only agency of government that must be assumed to have capacity to govern." Equally pointed reminders have come from the outside. Most of the great leaders of American democracy, Jefferson, Jackson, Lincoln, Bryan, and the two Roosevelts, among others, have challenged the practice of judicial review. But, except perhaps in some academic circles, the principle has withstood abuse and criticism. It stands only a shade less firmly grounded in our polity than its counterpart, the dispersion of power.

The Supreme Court, then, is caught between basic principles that look in different directions. Mr. Justice Frankfurter seems more sensitive to the pinch than most, though doubtless no one in his position is immune. What is the judge's role in such an impasse? A common "compromise" has been to emphasize diffusion of power or judicial supremacy according to the nature of the interest before the Court. At least since the Civil War some judges have demonstrated a marked propensity to assert their supremacy for the benefit of "private property," while others have shown a tendency to distrust the principle of diffusion only when "personal liberty" is at issue. For Mr. Justice Frankfurter such compromises only underscore the lawless quality of the Court's power. Deeply libertarian in private thought and action, he sees what partisans do not see: that if effective transcendental arguments may be made for the social priority of personal liberty, no less powerful considerations in the abstract would sustain the primacy of economic interests. What Wilmon Sheldon said of philosophers seems relevant to those who hold to either extreme. They are generally right in what they affirm of their own vision and generally wrong in what they deny in the vision of others. There is more subtlety, more depth, and more complexity in our culture than such one-sided polemics dream of. We may be proud of the golden thread of liberalism that runs through American thought, but it is futile to pretend that the "acquisitive instinct" and the old Whiggish concern for property are not as deep in our culture. As Daniel Webster put it long ago, "Life and personal liberty are, no doubt, to be protected by law; but property is also to be protected by law, and is the fund out of which the means for protecting life and liberty are usually furnished." President Hadley of Yale spoke for many when he explained the Constitution as a "set of limitations on the political power of the majority in favor of the political power of the property owner." Such suggestions of the primacy of economic interests are wormwood to libertarians, but the disease is deep. Man must eat and, not less important, he must "know where his next meal is coming from." Our cold war experience in the "backward" areas of the world suggests that those who must choose are far more interested in economic security than in civil liberty.

In any event it is important that neither is fungible and neither in the abstract is ever at stake in litigation. Typically, some finite facet of one or both is imperiled, and certainly in the kind of cases that now reach the Supreme Court the context is often such that intelligent men may differ as to whether a legitimate interest or its abuse is involved. This is what Holmes meant when he said that "general propositions do not decide concrete cases." Or, in Mr. Justice Cardozo's words, "Many an appeal to freedom is the masquerade of privilege or inequality seeking to entrench itself behind the catchword of a principle." For the purpose of settling specific litigation abstract arguments as to the relative importance of personal as against proprietary interests are as futile as medieval arguments about realism and nominalism. They cut no wood. Morris Cohen has called "attention to the fact that the traditional dilemmas, on which people have for a long time taken opposite stands, generally rest on difficulties rather than real contradictions, and that positive gains . . . can be made not by simply trying to prove that one side or the other is the truth, but by trying to get at the difficulty and determining in what respect and to what extent each side is justified." [9] This principle of polarity is the foundation of Mr. Justice Frankfurter's jurisprudence. He cannot be true to the American tradition and ignore the diffusion of power or judicial supremacy. Least of all can he accept reconciliation which raises now one and then another cluster of interests to a "preferred position" and correspondingly defers others.

Despite unqualified language in some parts of the Bill of Rights, no past or present member of the Court has even suggested that its liberties are unlimited. As with the "rights of property," the basic question always has been how and where to locate boundaries. Brandeis taught us anew, when we were in danger of forgetting it, that law is born of fact. *"Ex facto jus oritur*. That ancient rule must prevail in order that we may have a system of living law." The facts, after all, make up the issue. The precise problem of a minimum wage case,[10] for example, is evaded, not solved, by invoking the abstraction "liberty of contract," just as the *Terminiello* case is not solved by "reiterating generalized approbations of freedom of speech." A Brandeis concern for facts is as relevant in the one situation as in the other, if the Court is to decide real, not hypothetical, cases. It follows for Mr. Justice Frankfurter that judicial intrusion upon governmental policy is permissible only when the special facts of a concrete case leave no room for doubt. Since uncertainty entails choice, constitutional doubt must be resolved in favor of the views of those to whom primary governing authority has been given—and the people to whom they must answer.

This maxim of judicial self-restraint is not limited to constitutional law. It finds expression also in Mr. Justice Frankfurter's doctrine of "expertise" in the administrative law cases; in his willingness to accept legislative compromise—however uninspired—in the statutory interpretation cases; in his constant efforts to prevent federal, judge-made law from intruding upon local management of local affairs; and in his insistence in the *certiorari* cases that the Supreme Court stick to its limited and very special business. In the eyes of one critic, this demonstrates that "Mr. Justice Frankfurter has no feel for the dominant issues; he operates best when weaving crochet patches of legalism on the fingers of the case . . . it is a calamity that his skills happen to be petty skills." [11] Another has written that "the ex-professor . . . remained a rather narrow academician, engrossed in the trivia of formal legal propriety . . . to the disregard of the tough stuff of judicial statesmanship." [12] Obviously these critics are ardent supporters of Mr. Jus-

[9] Morris Cohen, *Reason and Nature,* 2d ed. (New York, Harcourt, Brace & Co., 1953), p. 11.

[10] See, for example, *Adkins* v. *Children's Hospital,* 261 U.S. 525 (1923).

[11] Walton Hamilton, quoted in Fred Rodell, *Nine Men* (New York, Random House, 1955), p. 271.

[12] *Ibid.*

tice Black. It is ironical that the very characteristic which won for Felix Frankfurter an appointment to the bench—his insistence that the "dominant issues," i.e., policy-making, should be left to the democratic process—is now considered a vice by his critics. Obviously they like extensive judicial legislation, provided it is of the "new" libertarian, rather than the old, proprietarian, variety. To put it crudely, much depends upon whose ox is being gored or whose ideals are at stake.

If, as tradition holds, the law is a jealous mistress, it also has the feminine capacity to tempt each devotee to find his own image in her bosom. No one escapes entirely. Some yield blindly, some with sophistication. A few more or less effectively resist—Cardozo, because he could not quite forget that ethic of self-denial which man has never mastered; Holmes, from the hopeful scepticism of an inquiring mind; Frankfurter, largely, perhaps, from remembrance of things past. Surely wilfulness on the bench prior to 1937 was a catalyst in the making of all the "Roosevelt judges." Some of them with appropriate apologetics seemed to fly to an opposite wilfulness. Mr. Justice Frankfurter has tried to subsume will to law and, where the law is vague, judicial will to the will, or conscience, of the community. If he falters, is it that his grasp is short, or that his reach is long? The discrepancy, a poet tells us, is "what a heaven's for." Meanwhile, such a judge must carry a heavier burden than does he whose commitment to proprietarian or libertarian abstractions—whose sense of Justice—is automatically decisive. "Believing it still important to do so," Mr. Justice Frankfurter has

> tried to dispel the age-old illusion that the conflicts to which the energy and ambition and imagination of the restless human spirit give rise can be subdued . . . by giving the endeavors of reason we call law a mechanical or automatic or enduring configuration. Law cannot be confined within any such mold because life cannot be so confined.[13]

The Justice has lived too long with legal problems to be fooled by the simple antinomy. Abraham Lincoln made the point when he cut short the ranting of a northern extremist, "Mr. ———, haven't you lived long enough to know that two men may honestly differ about a question and both be right?" In this paradox lies the genius of our system.

> Often "the American Way of Life" is pictured in terms of rigid adherence to some ideology, ignoring that our search for "a more perfect union" has been directed less to seeking final solutions than at establishing a tolerable balance of conflict among ourselves.[14]

Tolstoi saw that a great leader never leads. Does a great judge? At least for cases that reach the Supreme Court the law is seldom clear. The typical controversy entails a clash of interests, each of which has some, but no

[13] Frankfurter, *Of Law and Men*, p. 28.

[14] Samuel Lubell, *Revolt of the Moderates* (New York, Harper & Bros., 1956), p. 239.

plainly proponderant, legal foundation. Yet the Court is expected to give a decision. And so perhaps in the end the intrinsic problem is this: for whom or in what direction shall doubt be resolved? Some have made uncertainty the servant of selected business interests. Others have been guided by more generous considerations. In Mr. Justice Frankfurter's view this "sovereign prerogative of choice" is not for judges. He would resolve all reasonable doubt in favor of the integrity of sister organs of government and the people to whom they must answer. He would adhere, that is, to the deepest of all our constitutional traditions, the dispersion of power—though, as in the "flag salute" cases, the immediate result offend his own generous heart's desire. He is wary of judicial attempts to impose Justice on the community; to deprive it of the wisdom that comes from self-inflicted wounds and the strength that grows with the burden of responsibility. It is his deepest conviction that no five men, or nine, are wise enough or good enough to wield such power over the lives of millions. In his view, humanitarian ends are served best in that allocation of function through which the people by a balance of power seek their own destiny. True to the faith upon which democracy ultimately rests, the Justice would leave to the political processes the onus of building legal standards in the vacuum of doubt. For in his view only that people is free who chooses for itself when choice must be made.

Section IX

Politics in a Democracy

THE CONSTITUTION which established the basic framework of our government did not mention political parties. The Framers, to be sure, took cognizance of the potential power of organized public opinion and political parties and attempted to curb their influence through the electoral college, the indirect election of senators, checks and balances and other devices. Yet, today, the force of both public opinion and political parties is recognized as a vital concomitant of our democratic and constitutional system. Some writers, in fact, consider the condition of political parties to be the best index of the vitality of the democracy within any society.

A question of major importance, regarding the organization and functioning of our political parties, was dealt with some years ago by the Committee on Political Parties of the American Political Science Association. In 1950, it submitted a Report titled "Toward a More Responsible Two-Party System." (It was published as a Supplement in the *American Political Science Review,* Vol. XLIV, No. 3, Part 2, September, 1950.) The "thesis" of the Committee was stated as follows:

"Historical and other factors have caused the American two-party system to operate as two loose associations of state and local organizations, with very little national machinery and very little national cohesion. As a result, either major party, when in power, is ill-equipped to organize its members in the legislative and the executive branches into a government held together and guided by the party program. Party responsibility at the polls thus tends to vanish. This is a very serious matter, for it affects the very heartbeat of American democracy. It also poses grave problems of domestic and foreign policy in an era when it is no longer safe for the nation to deal piecemeal with issues that can be disposed of only on the basis of coherent programs."

The Committee categorically insisted that "an effective party system requires, first, that the parties are able to bring forth programs to which they commit themselves and, second, that the parties possess sufficient internal cohesion to carry out these programs." It made a number of specific recommendations designed to realize this objective.

James M. Burns' argument is in essential agreement with the philosophy of The Committee on Political Parties. On the other hand, the J. Roland Pennock and Stedman-Sonthoff articles raise some serious doubts about that philosophy and its proposed implementation.

Topic 21

"RESPONSIBLE" PARTIES

The Need for Disciplined Parties

JAMES MACGREGOR BURNS *

OUR MULTI-PARTY SYSTEM

In any democracy a major party seeks control of the government. To achieve that goal it bids for support throughout the community. To gain that support the party must broaden its platform through a series of compromises with organized groups and with unorganized voters. No narrow program will do the job. Constantly searching for the beliefs that bind diverse groups, the party's policy-makers define the issues that transcend the claims of special interests and find response among great masses of the people. Since the politicians attempt to attract as many "customers" as possible, the party system becomes, in the words of Lord Bryce, "the best instrument for the suppression of dissident minorities democracy has yet devised." For in a democracy the parties can hold a minority in check without stifling its creative function in the polity.

In the United States especially, a major party must find the common denominator among a large and varied group of voters, for it hopes to pluck the biggest plum of all at the next election—the Presidency. To elect a Chief Executive it must produce an electoral majority, and in doing so it forces adjustments among minority groups. As Carl Becker has said, "the fundamental compromises are, in the first instance, made not between the major parties but within them." Once having gone through this process of compromise in each of their camps, the two parties can offer the voters a relatively simple "either-or" choice rather than a confused array of alternatives. The two parties take up new ideas and attract new voters in order to survive in rigorous competition, and in doing so they display the inclusiveness that is central to democracy.

* Professor of Political Science at Williams College. Formerly Legislative Assistant, United States Congress. Author of *Roosevelt: The Lion and the Fox, John Kennedy: A Political Profile,* and co-author of *Government by the People.* The selection is from James M. Burns, *Congress on Trial* (New York, Harper & Brothers, 1949), pp. 33–44. Copyright, 1949, by Harper & Brothers. By permission.

Such, ideally, are the benefits of a two-party system. But in the United States we do not enjoy these benefits because our two-party system breaks down in the legislative branch. What we have in Congress might better be called a multi-party system. Instead of a grand encounter between the rallied forces of the two great parties in House and Senate, the legislative battle often degenerates into scuffles and skirmishes among minority groups. On matters of vital public policy the major parties fail to hold their lines. They leave the field in possession of the pressure politicians and other members of Congress who are faithful to a locality or to a special interest but not to the national platform of their party.

A glance at virtually any House or Senate roll call will demonstrate the inability of the party to enforce discipline even if it should try. In recent years the Democratic party has been especially vulnerable to the disruptive effects of bloc voting, but the Republicans too are rarely able to prevent at least a few of their adherents from crossing party lines. Party irresponsibility also affects the shaping of bills in committee and on the floor before the final roll call is reached. Indeed, it is hardly proper even to use the term "party responsibility" in discussing Congress, for the most rudimentary underpinnings of such responsibility do not exist. The party members in Congress have no common political program; as Pendleton Herring has said, "On the majority of issues the party takes no stand." And if there were such a program, little machinery exists in House or Senate to enforce it.

As a result of this situation we have in Congress, as far as public policy is concerned, a group of splinter parties. They are the Southern Democratic party, the Farmers' party, the Labor party, the New Deal party, the Liberal Republican party, the Veterans' party, the Silver party, and many others, along with the faithful adherents of the Republican and Democratic parties. A President of the United States is a Democrat or Republican, but key Senators and Representatives are more than likely to vote as members of a multi-party system.

This congressional patchwork is neither new nor accidental. It is rooted in American political organization. As national institutions, our parties are decrepit. They are coalitions of state and local party organizations, pulling together in awkward harmony every four years in an attempt to elect a President, going their own way the rest of the time.

The bosses who run the party machines are concerned more with private spoils than with public policy. The pressure groups that work through and around the parties are interested in their own designs, which may or may not coincide with the general welfare.

Lacking central control and discipline, the major party cannot hold its congressmen responsible to the broad majority of the voters in the nation who put the party into power. The national committee and chairman of the party have little control over national policy. They can do nothing for the congressman—he feels no responsibility to them.

Senators and Representatives can blithely disregard the national political platform; if they bother to pay it lip service, they usually do so because the program is so broad as to permit the widest leeway. In their states and districts the congressmen are responsible to fragments of the party—fragments that assume a variety of shapes under the impact of economic, sectional, ideological, and other forces.

BRITAIN: PARTY GOVERNMENT IN ACTION

We have much to learn from the English on this matter of political organization in a democracy. For over the course of many years they have forged a system of party government in the full sense of the term. That system serves three cardinal purposes. It unites the various branches of the government in order to carry out the will of a popular majority. It staves off the thrusts for power of minority groups. And as recent events have made clear, it offers the voters a genuine choice between two fairly distinct programs, rather than the Tweedledum-Tweedledee alternatives that often characterize political encounters in the United States. . . .

The difference between the British system and ours is not, of course, one of personality, but one of basic political organization. There the party is supreme. Its role in national life is so meaningful and decisive that most Englishmen vote in terms of the party program and record, rather than on the basis of the personality, salesmanship, and promises of the individual candidate.

On first look such a scheme might seem to bear an authoritarian stamp. But in fact the British party system is an almost ideal form of representative government. By forcing candidates for Parliament to run on the national platforms, it gives the voter a real choice between two opposing programs. And the voter expects the successful candidate to support that program once he takes his seat in the Commons, for faithfulness to that cause is part of the bargain between voter, candidate, and party. The parties make no pretense of responding to every ripple of public opinion, or to every pressure of some organized minority. They have the more vital function of expressing the broad political aspirations of a majority of the people. While in this country Congress often seems to represent every group except the majority, in Britain the major parties, operating at the highest level of political organization, give the national welfare right of way over minority interests.

Despite the omnipotence of party in Britain, the legislature is not a dead letter. On the contrary, Parliament enjoys enormous prestige in that country and throughout much of the world. "It has occupied the centre of the political stage for centuries," Jennings has written. "So much of the history of freedom is part of the history of Parliament that freedom and parliamentary government are often considered to be the same thing." . . .

How to explain the contrast between party domination of the legislative in Britain and the constant disruption of party lines in Congress? The answer, in part, lies in the greater homogeneity of the British people that permits a more cohesive political structure. But that is not the whole answer, for Britain too has her sectional rivalries that cut across parties, her special interests that would use either party in their quest for influence. The main reason for that contrast is the organization of political power in Britain as compared with America.

The Conservative Party, and to an even greater extent the Labour Party, are centralized agencies. Ample control over funds, program, and the choice of candidates is lodged in the national office of each party. Because each is responsible for judgment and action on a national scale it requires its parliamentary members to vote in national terms. In contrast to the loose decentralized party structure of the United States, continually disintegrating in Congress under the impact of organized minorities, the British parties have the means of holding their M.P.'s in line.

It is not a matter simply of enforcement machinery. Discipline in the British party rests also on the fact that, except perhaps in times of fast-moving political developments, its program is a genuine compromise among the various groups making up the party. That program is carefully devised not only to consolidate the support of the rank and file but to attract independent voters as well. On the theory that an M.P. is more easily led than driven, it may even make concessions to local and sectional interests. But those concessions are never so fundamental as to endanger seriously the party's loyalty to its national program. It is precisely in this respect—at least as far as discipline in the legislative body is concerned—that the American parties differ so drastically from their British counterparts.

MAKE-BELIEVE MAJORITIES

Lacking the party rule that invigorates the British parliamentary system, Congress is often unable to furnish majorities for even the most urgent measures. While Parliament automatically musters enough votes to enact the program of the party in power, or else must face dissolution, the majority party in Congress cannot control its own rank and file. Hence bills in Congress get stymied in committee; they survive in one chamber only to stall in the other; a few fail in conference between Senate and House. When measures become marooned somewhere in the winding legislative channels, the villain of the piece may well be a minority group holding a strong position in committee or chamber, and the majority may be powerless to come to the rescue.

How, then, do bills get passed? Partly as a result of the appeals and threats of a President acting as chief legislator as well as chief executive. The President's control of patronage, his means of mobilizing public opinion, the authority of his office often enable him to drive measures through the legislature. In many cases, too, legislation is enacted largely as a result of bi-party coalitions responding to group pressures of some sort. Such important measures as the McNary-Haugen proposals for farm surplus control in the 1920's, the Smoot-Hawley tariff of 1930, the Economy Act of 1933, the National Industrial Recovery Act of the same year, the Employment Act of 1946, the Greek-Turkish aid bill of 1947, to name only a few, were passed by Congress as a result of bi-party support.

Least significant of all in the enactment of legislation seems to be the party as such. Half a century ago A. Lawrence Lowell set out to discover how often more than nine-tenths of the party members in Congress voted on the same side of a question. He found such party cohesion in less than eight per cent of the important bills considered by the Thirty-Eighth Congress, elected in 1862; and party influence on legislation was even less in other samples he studied.

Party cohesion is still slight today. And as for straight party voting—where every Republican lines up on one side of an issue and every Democrat on the opposite side—it would be difficult indeed to find an example of such voting on an important issue (aside from "organizing" the House or Senate) in the last quarter century.

In the absence of party voting Congress at times falls back on curious methods of producing majorities. One of these might be termed the "majority by threat." It is the most primitive of all means of securing a working combination. Rather than agreeing on a common program, blocs threaten to withhold their votes from bills backed by other blocs unless support is forthcoming for their own.

It is a sort of log-rolling in reverse, with the advocates of a measure saying in effect: "If you dare to vote against our bill, we will vote against yours." Thus in 1937 the labor bloc in Congress threatened to oppose agricultural legislation unless farm representatives supported a wages and hours bill. In considering the price control bill of 1942 the majority leader issued a similar warning to the farm group. There is a vast difference between such attempts to win votes through fugitive alliances in reverse, and the effecting of agreement by intra-party action based on awareness of a broad but genuine identity of interest.

Another crude method of achieving joint action on bills is "evasion by delegation"—the consignment of broad powers of decision to the President when congressional blocs cannot agree on a closely defined policy. Not because of the need for administrative discretion but because of its own failure to find a basis for agreement, Congress passes important policy-making powers on to the Chief Executive.

An example of such delegation is found in the consideration of the National Industrial Recovery Act in 1933; protectionist and anti-protectionist Senators were at odds over an embargo provision, and as a "compromise" they left the matter to the discretion of Mr. Roosevelt. This type of delegation is a form of legislative abdication.

Such behavior by congressional majorities should not be confused with genuine majority rule. It is one thing for a party to present its platform and candidates to the voters and, when vested with power, to make specific policies in terms of the approved program. It is quite another matter when bi-party majorities, operating without the endorsement of a majority of the voters, capture the machinery of law-making. Such majorities in Congress raise hob with the representative process. They have little responsibility to the people. They may gain their ends and disappear overnight. Their actions may be good or bad, but in either case the bi-party coalitions can ignore with impunity the national party platforms which, however vague and irresolute, at least must pass some kind of public inspection. Bi-party blocs cannot long provide real majority rule. The fleeting majorities that they muster are often not truly representative of the majority of the voters.

If these coalitions do not provide real majority rule, what does? In a democracy majority rule is assumed to be the best means of discovering and satisfying the "public interest." But what kind of majority? There are many types—the majority required to pass an amendment to the Constitution, that needed to push a bill through Congress, that involved in electing a President, and others.

VIRTUES OF A POPULAR MAJORITY

The most democratic, stable, and effective type of majority, however, is a popular majority—namely, one half of all the pooled votes throughout the nation, plus one (or more). This is a different sort of majority than that represented by a coalition in Congress responding to minorities organized in the various states and districts. "No public policy could ever be the mere sum of the demands of the organized special interests," says Schattschneider; ". . . the sum of the special interests, especially the organized special interests, is not equal to the total of all interests of the community, for there are vital common interests that cannot be organized by pressure groups."

Not only do pressure groups often fail to represent fairly the interests of many of their own members. Also in the interstices of the pressure groups one finds voting fragments that see their main stake in the well-being of the community at large. The marginal members of pressure groups, those who are not members of pressure groups, and the voters who are torn between allegiance to competing pressure groups—all these have significant weight in a nation-wide popular election, but far less weight in the sum total of local elections. In short, they are far more influential in choosing Presidents (even with the electoral college) than in choosing members of Congress.

Consequently, a popular majority tends to be more representative and democratic than a "segmented" majority. It is more stable too, because it cannot be manipulated by a few pressure politicians who are able to mobilize organized interests in various states and districts. A simple, mass, nation-wide, popular majority is often feared as leading to the "tyranny of the majority." Actually it is the safest kind of majority. Building a nation-wide coalition of twenty or more millions of voters is no mean feat. It requires the presidential candidate to find a basis of harmony among diverse groups and to widen his platform to attract those groups and the millions of independent voters. A popular majority, like democratic politics in general, furnishes its own checks and balances.

The nation-wide political party is the natural vehicle for a popular majority. But it is also a rickety one. "Coalition fever" in Congress reflects the weakness of the American parties—their inertia, their slackness, their fear of assuming leadership. Organized interest groups display precisely the traits that the parties should display but do not—discipline over their representatives in office, alertness, the capacity to submerge internal differences in a united drive toward the more decisive group objectives. The special interests operate through either or both major parties with a cynical disregard for the party platform. "In a Republican district I was Republican; in a Democratic district I was a Democrat; and in a doubtful district I was doubtful," said Jay Gould, "but I was always Erie."

Similarly with the organized interests of today. It would be inconceivable for a dairy Senator from Wisconsin, a silver Congressman from Colorado, a cotton Senator from Alabama to desert their respective groups to uphold the party platform or the general welfare. In a Congress lacking sturdy party organization, many of the nation's pressure groups seem to enjoy greater representation than the majority of the voters.

Responsibility and Majority Rule

J. ROLAND PENNOCK *

Although, as Lippmann recognized, parties in fact must be judged on the basis of very general and vague standards, it has been widely felt to be the ideal that they should take clear stands on specific issues. Then, of course, party members in the executive and legislative branches would have to adhere to these positions; that is to say, they would have to accept party "discipline," for otherwise the whole system would be ineffectual.[1] In other words, those who would stress the role of political parties as instrumentalities of government, as opposed to mere nominating devices, must emphasize the elements of program and discipline.

Now it is clear that party government, in this sense seldom very effective in this country, is today at a low ebb.[2] There are also evidences that voters are both less inclined to vote a straight party ticket and readier to shift their support from one major party to the other than once was the case. The 1950 election in New York City, in which a plurality of the voters supported a Republican candidate for Governor, a Democrat for Senator, and an Independent for Mayor, was a spectacular instance of what appears to be a growing tendency.[3]† It may also be noted that, even apart from the controversial literature that the American Political Science Association's committee re-

* Professor and Chairman, Department of Political Science, Swarthmore College. Author of *Administration and the Rule of Law* and of *Liberal Democracy: Its Merits and Prospects.* The selection is from "Responsiveness, Responsibility, and Majority Rule," *The American Political Science Review,* Vol. XLVI (Sept. 1952), pp. 790–807. By permission.

[1] There is a very extensive literature setting forth and defending this position. It has, of course, been given its most authoritative recent expression by the Committee on Political Parties of the American Political Science Association in "Toward a More Responsible Two-Party System," Supplement to *The American Political Science Review,* cited above.

[2] See Julius Turner, *Party and Constituency: Pressures on Congress,* The Johns Hopkins University Studies in Historical and Political Science, Series 69, No. 1 (Baltimore, 1951), pp. 28–34, and especially Table 3, p. 28.

[3] It is true that this phenomenon may itself be a consequence of the indeterminate nature of the parties; but it pretty effectively disposes of the argument that strong parties are needed because of the voters' inability to distinguish between individual candidates.

† The 1964 election produced ticket splitting on an unprecedented scale. Republican candidates for governor ran ahead of their party's Presidential candidate by 42% of the vote in Rhode Island, 27% in Massachusetts, 24% in Michigan and behind by 12% in Iowa. In the contest for the U.S. Senate, Republican candidates led their ticket by 32% in Hawaii, 20% in Vermont, 16% in Pennsylvania, 14% in Nebraska, and fell behind by 24% in Virginia and 13% in Florida. The greatest disparity was in the vote for Senator and Governor in Rhode Island and Washington. In order to elect Democratic Senators and Republican Governors at least one third of the voters split their ticket in Washington and over 44% did so in Rhode Island. See *Congressional Quarterly,* Vol. XXII, No. 45 (November 6, 1964).

port, "Toward a More Responsible Two-Party System," has elicited, numerous students of politics have come to question the workability of the party responsibility theory as applied to this country. Witness, for example, Professor Lasswell's statement that "America is far too diversified, articulate, and swift to abide the elephantine routines of party obligation." [4]

These facts pose a real problem. If the theory is sound, the situation must be bad. . . . In the first place, the system of government through the agency of disciplined political parties may run counter to the principle of majority rule, at least in the sense of responsiveness to the majority of the electorate. If the party that controls the legislature and executive submits to group discipline and supports whatever is agreed upon by a majority of its own membership, it is clear that this majority of a majority may itself represent only a minority of the electorate. (This problem can be ameliorated, of course, if the party caucus refuses to bind itself by a bare majority vote.) Nor is such a hypothetical case at all improbable. There can be little doubt that it has recently been exemplified in Great Britain. The nationalization of steel is quite clearly an instance, for in 1950 a majority of the voters cast their ballots for candidates who were opposed to this program. It may even be questioned whether most of the nationalization program carried out between 1945 and 1950 had the support of the majority of the voters, in view of the fact that the popular majority for Socialism in 1945 was, at most, a matter of some 65,000 votes, from nearly 25 million.[5] Since the nationalization program was clearly the least popular plank in Labour's platform, their majority, if it is to be counted at all, must be attributed to other factors.*

It may be replied that the British voters cast their ballots with their eyes open and must be presumed to have preferred other parts of the Labour program *with* nationalization to opposition programs *without* it. This is perfectly true. It is also true, however, that to force such a harsh alternative upon the voters might not be necessary under a looser party system. And, furthermore, even with disciplined parties, clear programs, and sharp issues, one must be chary indeed about interpreting the results of national elections in terms of particular issues. Did the British electorate express itself in favor of Labour's nationalization program? In view of the fact that anyone who approved of the rest of Labour's program more than he disapproved of nationalization had no alternative but to vote for the latter along with the former, such a conclusion would clearly be unjustified; yet it is the conclusion called for by the orthodox theory.

[4] Harold D. Lasswell, *National Security and Individual Freedom* (New York, 1950), p. 120.

[5] See the excellent analysis by R. B. McCallum and Alison Readman, *The British General Election of 1945* (London, 1947), pp. 250–253.

* In the election of 1964 the Labor Party, with 44.1% of the popular vote, won a majority of 4 in the House of Commons. The Conservatives polled 43.4% and the Liberal Party 11.2% of the vote. With disciplined parties the nationalization of steel may prevail in the House of Commons although the two parties opposing this measure received 54.5% of the vote in the election.

As a footnote, we may observe that the system of direct primaries not only makes it more difficult to enforce party regularity in the legislature, but also makes the result of such enforcement more unrepresentative, more contrary to rule by the majority of the voters. And yet—and this, for present purposes, is the significant point—the institution of the direct primary is aimed directly at the objective of securing responsiveness to the majority will. The potential conflict between party government and majority rule, in other words, is once more indicated.

A second consequence of the party government system may be briefly noted: it encourages sharp reversals of policy. Again the case of British nationalization of the steel industry is in point. Clearly, in this instance, a decision of basic importance was taken, and acted upon, before it had a sufficiently strong basis in public opinion to be stable. While the example of steel is by no means unique,[6] it is exceptional. The reason it is exceptional, however, is that even in Britain parties, although disciplined, are not highly programmatic. More often than not a decision between them does not contribute greatly to the clarification of the majority opinion about issues, because the parties hedge, or agree, on the issues. In other words, party responsibility does not necessarily mean greater clarity as to issues, as is frequently assumed to be the case. Under such circumstances accountability is not furthered.

An oft-remarked effect of disciplined parties is to diminish the power and importance of the individual legislator. Insofar as a collective judgment is substituted for individual judgment, the sense of responsibility of the individual legislator tends to be weakened. Furthermore, and this would be particularly true in the United States where legislative membership is not the sole avenue to top executive positions in the government, a system that weakens the position of the individual legislator would make it more difficult to interest able and responsible men in running for legislative office.

It is time we looked at the other side of the picture. If the system of strong, programmatic parties tends to conflict with the objective of responsiveness to the will of the majority, encourages instability of policy or avoids this evil only on pain of losing its claimed advantage of greater accountability, and if it diminishes the number of responsible individuals in the legislature, what of the situation with weak parties? Is it unresponsive or irresponsible? Although these questions are too large to be given anything like a complete answer in this article, it is hoped that examination from the point of view of the preceding analysis can suggest partial answers.

The American system of loose and undisciplined parties which vie, on scarcely even terms, with pressure groups and other associations for giving expression to public opinion, is frequently referred to as government by

[6] Cf. the account of the effects of changes of governments on housing programs in Britain during the twenties, in Barbara Wootton, *Freedom Under Planning* (Chapel Hill, 1945), pp. 131–133.

consensus, or by "concurrent majorities." By permitting representatives to regroup themselves from issue to issue, with relatively little regard for party affiliation, the very looseness of the American system fosters the maximum response to majority will. (It may be observed in passing that the total product of the legislative process under this system is likely to bear more resemblance to a patchwork quilt than to a woven blanket. The significance of this fact will be discussed at a later stage in the argument.) At the same time, the system of checks and balances tends to make it difficult to secure the enactment of legislation unless it is very strongly supported by public opinion generally or, in the absence of such support, at least is not vigorously opposed by any of the great pressure groups. It will be apparent that this second feature of American government considerably modifies the first (the party system itself). The two must be considered together.

What can be said of the legislative process under the system of government prevailing in this country? As Professor Bailey has said, "one generalization is that the process is almost unbelievably complex." [7] A bill is drafted, perhaps by a legislator, more likely by the staff of an administrative agency, a pressure group, or a policy-leading group such as the National Planning Association or the Committee for Economic Development, or by some combination of two or more such agencies. If it is an important bill with substantial backing, it will be the subject of extensive hearings and subsequent executive deliberations by committees in both houses of Congress. The testimony of experts from within and without the government, arguments and persuasive efforts of all kinds, the views of concerned administrative agencies and of the President, will all be presented. The staff experts of the congressional committees themselves are likely to play an influential role. There will be abundant opportunities for amendment at various stages along the legislative path in an effort to adjust conflicting interests; and especially if the measure is highly controversial, it is unlikely to emerge from the legislative mill in its original form. The result is typically the product of many minds and many interests, acting with the aid of extensive research facilities to bring to bear the relevant facts and to point out distortions or omissions in each other's arguments and factual presentations. The process is designed to maximize the opportunities for criticism, for fresh ideas and insights, and for achieving a result that will receive the widest possible acceptance. By this same token, however, the product is likely to be quite different from what would have been desired by any of the interested groups in the first instance—perhaps quite different from what any of them would still consider ideal. Final votes in all probability may not divide sharply along party lines. Such a situation, it is sometimes held, is bad because no "recognizable group, interest, or individual" can be held responsible.[8]

[7] Stephen Kemp Bailey, *Congress Makes a Law* (New York, 1950), p. 236.
[8] Bailey, p. 237.

Now it seems clear that the legislative process we have just described involves considerable pains to achieve action that is responsible in the sense of being explicable, rationally supportable. Decision follows only after there has been ample opportunity for investigation and deliberation. The issue before us, then, is whether it is to be condemned because of a failure to meet the test of responsibility in the first sense—answerability. With respect to this question, several observations suggest themselves. In the first place, it would appear that the lack of an identifiable group, interest, or individual as responsible for a given act is certainly not *ipso facto* bad, because such a lack may indicate virtually unanimous support. Surely all unanimous-consent legislation is not to be condemned because of the absence of opposition! In other words, the kind of lack of responsibility that can be attributed to the legislative process as described above, as it operated in the enactment of the Employment Act of 1946, for example, is a function of facts that add to the generality of its acceptability. Responsibility for steel nationalization in England was clear; but it was purchased at the price of such low acceptability that the decision did not stick. Nationalization of the mines, not to mention "cradle-to-the-grave" security, on the other hand, had bipartisan support from the outset. It is hard to view with dissatisfaction the consequent diffusion of responsibility.

If we look again at the example of the Employment Act of 1946, it appears that the only way in which responsibility could have been made clearer would have been either to have had a different final Act—for instance, something more like the original bill—or to have had the whole idea defeated. That is to say, if the result had been more pleasing to one or the other of the (relatively) extreme groups, responsibility would have been clearer. Yet such an achievement would have been more displeasing to the defeated groups, less close to modal opinion, and therefore more likely to prove unstable. Certainly it would have been less representative of public opinion.

We must look further, however, at this matter of answerability. Its purpose, of course, is to enable the electorate to control policy. If something is done which the electorate disapproves, there should be a workable way for the voters to express that disapproval and bring about a change. Legislation which has received very general approval, which represents a substantial consensus, is much less likely than bare majority legislation to become the subject of popular disapproval. The very process that beclouds accountability makes it less essential. Nevertheless, the proof of the pudding is in the eating; that which was approved as a bill may be condemned in operation. Suppose, for example, that we are again beset by severe unemployment and that the President and Congress, lacking the spur of the strong words of the original Full Employment Bill, take inadequate steps to meet the crisis. How can those who are concerned about the situation produce a change? Are they any worse-situated in this respect than they would be if the backers of the law that was enacted had all been members of the same political party, or were otherwise easily identifiable? It would not seem so. In any case, through pressure groups, letters to their representatives, and other avenues of opinion expression, the voters will express their demand for action. If satisfaction is not forthcoming before election time, they will demand that candidates at the primaries (and later at the general election) express themselves on the issue. Incumbents who are up for reëlection and have failed to press for action of the kind demanded will have to account for their failure. In all probability, they will have to campaign against candidates who promise to take a different line. It is unusual, in this country, for important legislation to be repealed, for the reason that transient majorities are seldom able to secure enactment of their projects; but the history of any major field of legislation is a history of major enactments followed, from time to time, by modifications in the form of amendatory legislation, frequently produced by just such a process as has been described.[9]

Indeed, the whole theory that the political party is the primary agency for the enforcement of responsibility with respect to particular issues appears to be somewhat outmoded in contemporary America.[10] When issues were relatively few and simple, it made a great deal of sense. Half a century ago, a few great but relatively simple questions, such as those involving tariffs and trusts, were predominant. It calls for no listing of the issues that face Congress today to prove that the present situation is very different. When each of the major parties must give some indication of its position on such issues as the Point Four program, military aid, the Brannan Plan, price and wage control, aid to education, and how to balance the values of security and liberty, it is unlikely that an election can give a clear indication of what a majority of the public wants.[11] Opinions cluster sufficiently to admit of considerable polar differentiation (but not polar opposites) in any given region, and a slight degree of such differentiation clearly exists nationally; but this is all that can be said. Southern Democrats will vote for a pro-labor presidential candidate only because they can elect Congressmen who will join with Republicans to defeat his policies. Nor is this situation confined to the Democratic Party. The basic condition it reflects has nothing to do with

[9] See Fred W. Riggs, *Pressures on Congress; A Study of the Repeal of Chinese Exclusion* (New York, 1950), for an excellent study of a successful repeal movement.

[10] We may also hazard the guess that even in Great Britain its vitality is on the decline. However, the sharp class-consciousness of British politics contributes greatly to the solidarity of parties and to the difficulty of achieving government by consensus.

[11] It is true, of course, that attitudes on many of these subjects tend to cluster, so that a person's views on health insurance, for instance, may give a very good indication of what his position will be with regard to tax policy. Unless this situation existed, our party system would be completely unworkable. Even after making due allowance for this fact, however, the situation is incompatible with the existence and survival of programmatic major parties.

party organization or the form of government; it lies in the number and complexity of issues facing the country and the almost equal number and variety of group interests comprising the electorate. Such a plurality of views cannot be forced into the confines of dichotomous statement.

Moreover, today's public is far more articulate than were the enfranchised masses of half a century ago. Mr. Lippmann's choice between tweedledum and tweedledee is indeed about all that can be expressed in a general election, but this is only the beginning of popular expression in a modern democracy. Or, often enough, it is the last stage, giving formal sanction to policy determinations that represent responses to popular demands more discriminating and more varied than can be expressed at the polls. These determinations are often made in the selection of candidates. Once more, the device of the primary election is only the crude club that, in accordance with Friedrich's "law of anticipated reactions," leads party managers to find candidates who will achieve maximal voter response. Frequently, to be sure, a change in public opinion does not call for a change in the party candidates, much less a change in the party in power; all that is required is a shift in the position of the incumbents. Thus Senator Taft, not generally thought of as one of the most flexible members of Congress, has made numerous changes of tack; [12] one would have to be exceedingly naïve not to see a connection between these changes and Taft's appraisal of popular sentiment in Ohio and in the nation. Certainly readers of this article will need no reminders of the manifold avenues by which public opinions are brought to bear upon policy determinations in this country.[13] They operate at all levels, from the precinct to the administrator; they use all kinds of techniques and all manner of organization. And the difficulties of achieving democratic and responsible policy-making at the legislative level through the sole agency—or even the dominant agency—of the political party are greatly magnified when it comes to the administrative level, where so much of the policy-determining process today takes place.

Before concluding this discussion, we must deal with an objection that is commonly raised against weak political parties. It is said that they facilitate log-rolling in the legislature, since individuals and groups in the legislature are relatively free to shift alignments from issue to issue, and that they encourage competitive bidding for popular support by being free with promises of *largesse*. Since both of these practices might properly be designated as

[12] See his volume, *A Foreign Policy for Americans* (New York, 1951).

[13] For an excellent account of them, see David B. Truman, *The Governmental Process; Political Interests and Public Opinion* (New York, 1951). See also Riggs, *Pressures on Congress,* for a valuable case study. His discussion of the "catalytic group" is especially interesting (pp. 43–46). Riggs also gives concrete evidence in support of what was said (above, pp. 795–796) about the effect given to intensity of demand by the American system (*Pressures on Congress,* pp. 197–199).

irresponsible, it is pertinent to consider them in the present context; and the two points are closely enough related to be treated together. That both conditions are far too characteristic of the American scene is painfully evident. The question of whether the existence of disciplined political parties, even if it were attainable, would improve the situation, calls for consideration. A glance at the record is enough to raise serious doubts about the proposed remedy. We may look at what happened in the United States during the early period of the New Deal, when President Roosevelt was in an exceedingly strong position with his party. The inconsistencies and contradictions that were involved in the New Deal program are an old story. Combinations in restraint of trade were at once attacked (strengthened anti-trust enforcement) and fostered (N.R.A.); credit was relaxed (Federal Reserve Board policy) and tightened (pressure from Treasury and F.D.I.C. inspectors); efforts were made to stimulate international economic cooperation (trade agreements program) while we wrecked the International Monetary Conference.[14] A relatively strong party leadership did nothing to prevent such mutually contradictory policies then; and there is nothing to indicate that today such leadership would prevent one arm of the government from spending public money to support the prices of agricultural commodities in a time of great farm prosperity, while other arms struggle to keep down wages and prices.

The situation in England is not radically different. The existence of strong parties there did not prevent the Conservatives in the 1951 campaign from promising to cut expenditures, but to maintain the social services and build more houses. Nor did strong parties hinder the Labour Government from pursuing inconsistent objectives, such as seeking to replenish capital goods while greatly expanding consumption, trying to stimulate private investment while threatening nationalization, and opposing nationalization of British interests abroad while pursuing a nationalization policy at home. Surely the vices of bidding for votes by pursuing opposing objectives at the same time are by no means confined to governments lacking disciplined parties.

As long as political parties can hope to defeat their opponents by winning the votes of groups from within the other party, or from independents, they will be tempted to try to do so by promising good things to the groups they are courting. In fact, the stronger is the discipline of a given party, the better it can afford to make such promises even when they run counter to the interests of some of its constituent elements. We are confronted here with a problem of democracy, not a problem of a particular party system.[15]

[14] In some of these cases the mutually opposing policies were in effect at the same time, while in others they came in fairly rapid succession.

[15] It is not within the province of this article to offer solutions to this problem. It may be pointed out, however, that government by consensus places power in the hands

Moreover, a strongly disciplined, two-party system can be obtained only by creating a sharp division of the population along class-conscious lines.[16] If the parties are evenly balanced, both competitive bidding for votes and frequent reversals of policy (assuming programmatic parties) are the natural results. If one party or the other gains marked ascendancy, the logical outcome is class rule and exploitation, rather than responsible search for the means of achieving the greatest possible general acceptability.

All of this does not mean that political parties are not important. They are one of the kinds of organization essential to the political process. They are indispensable; but without supplementation they would be woefully inadequate. Moreover, I am not concerned to argue whether or not some strengthening might be both possible and desirable. Some of the recommendations of the Committee on Political Parties are undoubtedly advisable. Possibly most of them are. But, and this *is* part of what I am concerned to argue, they would not accomplish as much as the Committee appears to believe; and it would not be desirable that they should. Tightly disciplined and programmatic political parties would be as inadequate for the task of political brokerage in America as the belief that we could create them would be unrealistic.

Party Responsibility—A Critical Inquiry

MURRAY S. STEDMAN, JR., AND HERBERT SONTHOFF *

MAJORITY RULE OR CONSENSUS?

There may be wide agreement with the assumption in the Report of the Committee on Political Parties of the American Political Science Asso-

---

of any major group to secure the modification of policies opposed to its interests. Where inconsistent programs merely defeat each other, no great harm is done to the general public. Where they do have a harmful general effect, other powerful groups are likely to be aroused and to take effective action. Moreover, the process of political education proceeds by experience. It is often discouragingly slow, but it is sometimes surprisingly effective. It is notable that, following the war, we did attain a balanced budget, and even a budget surplus. That the return of a semi-war economy has reversed the situation is hardly a matter for surprise. Whether any government can avoid some form of inflation under such conditions is doubtful. It is not irrelevant to remark, however, that it can come nearer to accomplishing this result if it is able to borrow from abroad.

[16] Conceivably the same result could be obtained by a regional division, with the threat of civil war or national disintegration.

* Dr. Stedman now teaches at Trinity College. He formerly taught at Brown and Columbia Universities and Swarthmore College. He is the author of *Religion and*

ciation[1] that *the present two party system is irresponsible,* although the precise meaning of "irresponsible" may vary greatly. Yet the essence of the assumption is that the American party system is an inadequate mechanism for translating popular wishes into action or specific policy. This charge rests on several beliefs which are open to considerable doubt. It assumes that the problem of popular responsibility is largely the mechanical one of organization, i.e., that responsibility is "effective" only when there exist clear lines of responsibility.[2] If, as the allegation presupposes, responsibility is a matter of discipline, it becomes a fairly narrow and rigid premise. . . .

CENTRALIZED PARTIES

Another assumption is that *more responsible parties would require a very high degree of centralization of the internal party structure.* It has long been noted by students of Congress that party discipline on important issues is either weak or nonexistent. . . . The advocates of party government desire not only to facilitate executive-legislative co-ordination, but also to guarantee such co-ordination through highly centralized national parties.

Such a degree of centralization would be unprecedented in American history. However, only a centralized organization could possibly commit itself to and subsequently execute a specific program. To be successful, the national party would have to control rigidly such matters as patronage, finances, the nominating processes, and local party subsidiary organizations. The locus of power would be at the national rather than at the state or local level, as is the case today.

To make this change in power relationships, the national parties would have to possess sanctions to penalize recalcitrant state and local party leaders whose faith in the national "line" might otherwise waver. Such control would go far beyond the kind envisaged, for example, by the unsuccessful "purges" of 1938, since it would not be limited merely

Politics in America and co-author of *Discontent at the Polls* and *The Dynamics of Democratic Government.* Herbert Sonthoff formerly taught at Swarthmore College. The selection is from their article "Party Responsibility—A Critical Inquiry," *Western Political Quarterly,* Vol. IV (September, 1951), pp. 454–468, *passim.* By permission.

[1] "Toward A More Responsible Two-Party System." Supplement to *The American Political Science Review,* Vol. XLIV, No. 3 (September, 1950), hereafter referred to as *Report.*

[2] "Party responsibility is the responsibility of both parties to the general public, as enforced in elections. Party responsibility to the public, enforced in elections, implies that there be more than one party, for the public can hold a party responsible only if it has a choice. . . . Party responsibility also includes the responsibility of party leaders to the party membership, as enforced in primaries, caucuses and conventions." *Report,* p. 2.

to congressional candidates. It would affect the nominating process generally. Quite logically, therefore, the advocates of party government stress the need for great control over local party organizations, including the power to refuse to seat "disloyal" elements at national conventions, and to exclude such elements from the national committees. Furthermore, as the *Report* states, ". . . consideration should be given to the development of additional means of dealing with rebellious and disloyal state organizations."

From this line of reasoning it follows that only the closed primary could be endorsed, for only if the national party could control the local nominating process could it choose candidates loyal to itself. It is clear that such a change would require tremendous revision of existing primary statutes. For example, the four states of Pennsylvania, New York, California, and Washington all use different procedures to nominate to statewide offices. It is hardly possible to determine objectively which of the four systems produces the best qualified candidates. Yet, most proposals for party centralization imply a drastic change of the primary, perhaps in the face of hostile public opinion.

The logic of the argument carries much further, however, than merely urging the closed primary or some particular form of it. It also implies a threat to the direct primary as an institution. If nominations are to be determined in accordance with criteria established by the national party, it is difficult to see what, if any, purpose is served by retaining the direct primary. But the abolition of the primary would have particularly serious effects in those states, counties, and cities which are essentially one-party areas. In those localities, the only meaningful choice for the voter is between candidates of the same party. This may be true not only of the choice between candidates, but also of the choice between programs. The net effect of the disappearance of primaries in such a situation would be to take from the voter his only effective weapon for registering protest. In two-party areas the ending of the direct primary would presumably have less serious results, but such an action might create more problems than it would solve.

Proponents of stronger national parties usually contend that such parties would weaken the hold of local bosses and pressure groups, thus achieving a separation of national from local issues. To be sure, if local organizations lost control of the nominating process, their power would be drastically reduced. It does not follow, however, that a greater separation of national from state and local politics would be achieved. Neither as a matter of principle nor as a matter of applied psychology is there any great support for the contention that the national parties would lose interest in local patronage. It is probable that the first of the existing national parties to reorganize itself would be able to extend its patronage power into hitherto sacrosanct areas. In passing, the question may be raised whether the whole idea of party government is compatible with any kind of nonpartisan approach to local government. If the answer is negative, one can visualize a vast new area of spoils opening up for the benefit of national organizations.

The danger of the idea of party government is not that stronger national parties per se would be created. The danger is that the national leaders, in order to build an ever more extensive base for their own operations, might take over, so far as possible, all existing state and local organizations. Such a development would clearly imply more than the death of the direct primary. To propose it raises very serious challenges to the federal pattern itself and to many real advances made in state and local governments during the past half century. Quite possibly, because of its widespread character the centralized type of bossism, even under the name of "party government," might be even more objectionable than the existing local bossism.

In view of the almost proverbial contempt in which many professional students of politics hold party machines, a word in their defense may appear unusual. Still, we need to reflect on the positive services they perform in terms of the organization of local voter interest; and we should also consider the extent to which the usual connotation of the term "politician," which has become almost an expletive, impedes a realistic understanding of the functional role the politician plays in the crystallization of political opinion and in the political process on the grass roots level generally. It is an open question whether greater responsibility of the political party to the voter is obtained by strengthening the internal chains of party command through closer adherence to an obligatory party platform. The role of the local leader also requires examination; for another belief seemingly held by the proponents of stronger parties is that the public will abandon the idea of the politician as a broker. It is urged that the public will prefer an automaton committed beyond all else to the party program, and thus will cast aside the traditional politician's role of middleman. The implications of this line of thought are far-reaching. What is being urged is nothing less than a revolutionary transformation in the role and function of the party, of the candidates, and of the electorate. . . .

DISCIPLINED PARTIES AND BIPARTISAN POLICY

Let us hypothesize a very strong, disciplined party system in this country. Furthermore, let us imagine that for one reason or another the President and one or both houses represent different parties. What might be expected to occur in the highly important area of foreign affairs? Bipartisanship on foreign policy is often criticized on three principal grounds: First, that it is undemocratic in that the minority party by its acquiescence may contribute to its own demise; second, that it is immoral in that a totally false and misleading impression of national unity may be created; third, that it is incompatible with party government.

It is the last charge which concerns us here and needs examination. Under our present party arrangement, with one or two exceptions the major parties have always co-operated in periods of external crisis. Cooperation was never a hundred per cent complete; but a working majority of each major party usually agreed with its counterpart as to the basic policies to be followed. Whatever opposition existed was likewise usually bipartisan; that is, it was not confined to a single party. A most significant demonstration of approval of bipartisan foreign policy, so obvious as often to be overlooked, occurred in the 1948 elections. Whatever else the presidential election of that year showed, it conclusively demonstrated support for Truman's "bipartisan" foreign policy by repudiating the proposals of Henry A. Wallace.

In principle, the proponents of party government are driven to the position that bipartisanship is per se an evil. They condemn the present practice where, instead of aligning themselves solidly on different sides of great policy issues, Senators and Representatives split into pro and con bipartisan blocs. Party allegiance becomes subordinate to sectional and regional interests.

Few would argue that such an arrangement is an unmixed blessing. On the credit side, however, it offers the tremendous advantage of very great flexibility. It does not suffer from the rigidity which the existence of a really strong, well-organized opposition party would entail. The basis of consensus is broad enough to allow for compromise and thus, among other things, plays down any process of aggrandizement by the President at the expense of Congress. Some critics of the existing system express the fear that our traditional form of government may break down as the result of a series of crises in which congressional inability to co-operate with the executive is followed by presidential dictatorship. These fears appear grossly exaggerated. Nevertheless, in the absence of cabinet responsibility under a parliamentary type of government, the prospect of a breakdown in democratic procedures would surely be aggravated rather than lessened by the existence of strongly disciplined and highly dedicated parties. If such a doctrinaire congressional-presidential impasse would be unfortunate in domestic affairs, it could conceivably be disastrous in the area of foreign policy.

Section X

President and Congress

THE OFFICE of the president is now the most powerful, responsible, and difficult in the democratic world. Yet, the author of a classic study of the American party system, after observing our convention method of nominating candidates for the presidency and the considerations which controlled its action, characterized the process as "a colossal travesty of popular institutions." The correctness of M. Ostrogorski's appraisal is clearly a matter of importance. The issue is discussed by James Bryce, Harold Laski, and Pendleton Herring. Theodore C. Sorensen, on the other hand, reflects upon the problems, process, pressures, and "politics" of decision-making in the White House.

The gap between the Congress and the President has to some extent been bridged by political parties intent upon controlling all the branches of government. Nevertheless, as recent experience has shown, our system makes possible stalemate on important issues with responsibility difficult to establish. Furthermore, the role of the president in the legislative process, even when Congress is composed predominantly of members of his own party, is uncertain and varying. Under these circumstances, various measures to improve, or even drastically alter, legislative-executive organization and relations, to make government more responsive to the wishes of a "majority" as expressed in elections, have been advocated.

Among these measures have been the suggestions for congressional reform urged by Senator Joseph S. Clark. On the other hand, John Fischer has emphasized "the unwritten rules of American politics" involving an "informal, highly elastic, and generally accepted understanding" by the terms of which "all of the contending interest groups recognize and abide by certain rules of the game." This, he calls, the "Doctrine of the Concurrent Majority."

Two additional issues which have commanded considerable attention in recent years are discussed: the uses and abuses of (1) the filibuster, and (2) congressional investigations (particularly in regard to alleged subversive activities).

Topic 22

CHOOSING A PRESIDENT

Why Great Men Are Not Chosen President

JAMES BRYCE *

Europeans often ask, and Americans do not always explain, how it happens that this great office, the greatest in the world, unless we except the Papacy, to which any one can rise by his own merits, is not more frequently filled by great and striking men. In America, which is beyond all other countries the country of a "career open to talents," a country, moreover, in which political life is unusually keen and political ambition widely diffused, it might be expected that the highest place would always be won by a man of brilliant gifts. But from the time when the heroes of the Revolution died out with Jefferson and Adams and Madison, no person except General Grant, had, down till the end of last century, reached the chair whose name would have been remembered had he not been President, and no President except Abraham Lincoln had displayed rare or striking qualities in the chair. Who now knows or cares to know anything about the personality of James K. Polk or Franklin Pierce? The only thing remarkable about them is that being so commonplace they should have climbed so high.

Several reasons may be suggested for the fact, which Americans are themselves the first to admit. One is that the proportion of first-rate ability drawn into politics is smaller in America than in most European countries. This is a phenomenon whose causes must be elucidated later: in the meantime it is enough to say that in France, where the half-revolutionary conditions that lasted for some time after 1870 made public life exciting and accessible; in Germany, where an admirably-organized civil service cultivates and develops statecraft with unusual success; in England, where many persons of wealth and leisure seek to enter the political arena, while burning questions touch the interests of all classes and make men eager observers of the combatants, the total quantity of talent devoted to parliamentary or administrative work has been larger, relatively to the population, than in

* British Ambassador to the United States, 1907–1913. Formerly President of the American Political Science Association. Author of *The Holy Roman Empire, Modern Democracies, The American Commonwealth,* etc. The selection is from James Bryce, "Why Great Men Are Not Chosen President," *The American Commonwealth* (New York, The Macmillan Co., 1922–23), Vol. 1, Ch. 8. By permission.

America, where much of the best ability, both for thought and for action, for planning and for executing, rushes into a field which is comparatively narrow in Europe, the business of developing the material resources of the country.

Another is that the methods and habits of Congress, and indeed of political life generally, give fewer opportunities for personal distinction, fewer modes in which a man may commend himself to his countrymen by eminent capacity in thought, in speech, or in administration, than is the case in the free countries of Europe. . . .

A third reason is that eminent men make more enemies, and give those enemies more assailable points, than obscure men do. They are therefore in so far less desirable candidates. It is true that the eminent man has also made more friends, that his name is more widely known, and may be greeted with louder cheers. Other things being equal, the famous man is preferable. But other things never are equal. The famous man has probably attacked some leaders in his own party, has supplanted others, has expressed his dislike to the crochet of some active section, has perhaps committed errors which are capable of being magnified into offences. No man stands long before the public and bears a part in great affairs without giving openings to censorious criticism. Fiercer far than the light which beats upon a throne is the light which beats upon a presidential candidate, searching out all the recesses of his past life. Hence, when the choice lies between a brilliant man and a safe man, the safe man is preferred. Party feeling, strong enough to carry in on its back a man without conspicuous positive merits, is not always strong enough to procure forgiveness for a man with positive faults.

A European finds that this phenomenon needs in its turn to be explained, for in the free countries of Europe brilliancy, be it eloquence in speech, or some striking achievement in war or administration, or the power through whatever means of somehow impressing the popular imagination, is what makes a leader triumphant. Why should it be otherwise in America? Because in America party loyalty and party organization have been hitherto so perfect that any one put forward by the party will get the full party vote if his character is good and his "record," as they call it, unstained. The safe candidate may not draw in quite so many votes from the moderate men of the other side as the brilliant one would, but he will not lose nearly so many from his own ranks. Even those who admit his mediocrity will vote straight when the moment for voting comes. Besides, the ordinary American voter does not object to mediocrity. He has a lower conception of the qualities requisite to make a statesman than those who direct public opinion in Europe have. He likes his candidate to be sensible, vigorous, and, above all, what he calls "magnetic," and does not value, because he sees no need for, originality or profundity, a fine culture or a wide knowledge. Candidates are selected to be run for nomination by knots of persons who, however expert as party tacticians, are usually commonplace men; and the choice between those selected for nomination is made by a very large body, an assembly of nearly a thousand delegates from the local party organizations over the country, who are certainly no better than ordinary citizens. . . .

It must also be remembered that the merits of a President are one thing and those of a candidate another thing. An eminent American is reported to have said to friends who wished to put him forward, "Gentlemen, let there be no mistake. I should make a good President, but a very bad candidate." Now to a party it is more important that its nominee should be a good candidate than that he should turn out a good President. A nearer danger is a greater danger. As Saladin says in *The Talisman,* "A wild cat in a chamber is more dangerous than a lion in a distant desert." It will be a misfortune to the party, as well as to the country, if the candidate elected should prove a bad President. But it is a greater misfortune to the party that it should be beaten in the impending election, for the evil of losing national patronage will have come four years sooner. "B" (so reason the leaders), "who is one of our possible candidates, may be an abler man than A, who is the other. But we have a better chance of winning with A than with B, while X, the candidate of our opponents, is anyhow no better than A. We must therefore run A." This reasoning is all the more forcible because the previous career of the possible candidates has generally made it easier to say who will succeed as a candidate than who will succeed as a President; and because the wirepullers with whom the choice rests are better judges of the former question than of the latter.

After all, too, a President need not be a man of brilliant intellectual gifts. His main duties are to be prompt and firm in securing the due execution of the laws and maintaining the public peace, careful and upright in the choice of the executive officials of the country. Eloquence, whose value is apt to be overrated in all free countries, imagination, profundity of thought or extent of knowledge, are all in so far a gain to him that they make him "a bigger man," and help him to gain over the nation an influence which, if he be a true patriot, he may use for its good. But they are not necessary for the due discharge in ordinary times of the duties of his post. Four-fifths of his work is the same in kind as that which devolves on the chairman of a commercial company or the manager of a railway, the work of choosing good subordinates, seeing that they attend to their business, and taking a sound practical view of such administrative questions as require his decision. Firmness, common sense, and most of all, honesty, an honesty above all suspicion of personal interest, are the qualities which the country chiefly needs in its first magistrate.

So far we have been considering personal merits. But in the selection of a candidate many considerations have to be regarded besides the personal merits, whether of a candidate, or of a possible President. The chief of these considerations is the amount of support which can be secured from different States or from different "sections" of the Union, a term by which the Americans denote groups of States with a broad community of interest. State feeling and sectional feeling are powerful factors in a presidential election. The Middle West and Northwest, including the States from Ohio to Montana, is now the most populous section of the Union, and therefore counts for most in an election. It naturally conceives that its interests will be best protected by one who knows them from birth and residence. Hence *prima facie* a man from that section makes the best candidate. A large State casts a heavier vote in the election; and every State is of course more likely to be carried by one of its own children than by a stranger, because his fellow-citizens, while they feel honoured by the choice, gain also a substantial advantage, having a better prospect of such favours as the administration can bestow. Hence, *cæteris paribus,* a man from a large State is preferable as a candidate. The problem is further complicated by the fact that some States are already safe for one or other party, while others are doubtful. The Northwestern and New England States have usually tended to go Republican; while nearly all of the Southern States have, since 1877, been pretty certain to go Democratic. *Cæteris paribus,* a candidate from a doubtful State, such as New York and Indiana have usually been, is to be preferred.

Other minor disqualifying circumstances require less explanation. A Roman Catholic, or an avowed disbeliever in Christianity, would be an undesirable candidate. For many years after the Civil War, any one who had fought, especially if he fought with distinction, in the Northern army, enjoyed great advantages, for the soldiers of that army rallied to his name. The two elections of General Grant, who knew nothing of politics, and the fact that his influence survived the faults of his administration, are evidence of the weight of this consideration. . . .

These secondary considerations do not always prevail. Intellectual ability and strength of character must influence the choice of a candidate. When a man has once impressed himself on the nation by force, courage, and rectitude, the influence of these qualities may be decisive. They naturally count for most when times are critical. Reformers declare that their weight will go on increasing as the disgust of good citizens with the methods of professional politicians increases. . . .

We may now answer the question from which we started. Great men have not often been chosen Presidents, first because great men are rare in politics; secondly, because the method of choice may not bring them to the top; thirdly, because they are not, in quiet times, absolutely needed. Let us close by observing that the Presidents, regarded historically, fall into three periods, the second inferior to the first, the third rather better than the second.

Down till the election of Andrew Jackson in 1828, all the Presidents had been statesmen in the European sense of the word, men of education, of administrative experience, of a certain largeness of view and dignity of character. All except the first two had served in the great office of secretary of state; all were known to the nation from the part they had played. In the second period, from Jackson till the outbreak of the Civil War in 1861, the Presidents were either mere politicians, such as Van Buren, Polk, or Buchanan, or else successful soldiers, such as Harrison or Taylor, whom their party found useful as figureheads. They were intellectual pigmies beside the real leaders of that generation—Clay, Calhoun, and Webster. A new series begins with Lincoln in 1861. He and General Grant, his successor, who cover sixteen years between them, belong to the history of the world. Even the less distinguished Presidents of this period contrast favourably with the Polks and Pierces of the days before the war, if they are not, like the early Presidents, the first men of the country. If we compare the twenty Presidents who were elected to office between 1789 and 1900 with the twenty English prime ministers of the same period, there are but six of the latter, and at least eight of the former whom history calls personally insignificant, while only Washington, Jefferson, Lincoln, and Grant can claim to belong to a front rank represented in the English list by seven or possibly eight names. It would seem that the natural selection of the English parliamentary system, even as modified by the aristocratic habits of that country, had more tendency to bring the highest gifts to the highest place than the more artificial selection of America.

Crises Produce Great Presidents

HAROLD J. LASKI *

The big problem that is raised by the American method of nominating presidential candidates is whether it puts a premium, as Lord Bryce argued, against the opportunity of first-rate men to receive consideration. I do not think his case is proved by making a list of first-rate men, Clay and Calhoun and Webster, for example, who missed nomination. The answer to that

* Late Professor of Political Science at The London School of Economics. Formerly Chairman of the British Labor Party Executive Committee. Author of numerous books on politics including *Grammar of Politics, Democracy in Crisis, State in Theory and Practice,* and *The American Democracy*. This selection is from Harold J. Laski, *The American Presidency* (New York, Harper & Bros., 1940), pp. 49–53. Copyright, 1940, by Harper & Bros.

argument is, first, that many first-rate men have become president by reason of the system; and second, that the reasons which stopped others would have been powerful reasons against their elevation in any representative democracy. . . .

Granted, this is to say, the greatness of the prize, and the necessity of popular election, it is difficult to see what other method than the nominating convention is available; more, it is true to say that, on balance, it has worked well rather than badly. The criticisms that are brought against it are rather, in their real substance, criticisms of the place of the presidency in the American constitutional scheme than of the method whereby the president is chosen. It is regrettable that an inexperienced man may come to reside in the White House; the answer is that few of those who have reached it have been inexperienced men. If it be said that men like Harding and Coolidge were unfit for the great post they secured, the answer is that the first had considerable experience both in the Ohio legislature and in the Senate, while the second had been a successful Massachusetts politician, twice occupying the governorship, for twenty years. If we take the presidents of the twentieth century, there is not one who had not been prepared for presidential office by a long experience of politics. . . .

It must be remembered that, in making the choice, there are two fundamental considerations in the background of which the meaning of "availability" must be set. The first is that the party choosing a candidate wants, if it can, to win; and second, it knows that if it does win, and its nominee becomes president, there is great likelihood of its having to adopt him a second time, since not to do so is to condemn an Administration for which it has to bear responsibility. While, therefore, it is quite true that a party convention provides an opportunity for the art of such a dubious wire-puller as Mr. Daugherty, it is also true that the managers of a great party are anxious to avoid, if they can, the consequences of success in that type of manipulation. . . .

All in all, I doubt whether the methods of the system are very different from those of other countries. They are, perhaps, more open and crude than in Great Britain. There is no generosity in the fight for power. There is a passionate determination on the part of organized interests to get the "safe" man who can be relied upon to live up to the commitments exacted from him. There is the fierce conflict of rival ambitions. There is the organization of every sort of cabal to win a victory for its man. Press and radio and platform are vigorously manipulated to this end. Immense promises are made, pretty ugly deals are effected. Yet I suggest that anyone who knows the life of a political party from within Great Britain will not feel inclined to cast a stone at the American system. It fits, well enough, the medium in which it has to work. It achieves the results that the needs of the people require.

For there is at least one test of the system that is, I think, decisive. There have been five considerable crises in American history. There was the need to start the new republic adequately in 1789; it gave the American people its natural leader in George Washington. The crisis of 1800 brought Jefferson to the presidency; that of 1861 brought Abraham Lincoln. The War of 1914 found Woodrow Wilson in office; the great depression resulted in the election of Franklin Roosevelt. So far, it is clear, the hour has brought forth the man. It is of course true, as Bagehot said, that "success in a lottery is no argument for lotteries." I agree that no nation can afford a succession of what Theodore Roosevelt termed "Buchanan Presidents"—men whose handling of the issues is uncertain and feeble. But the answer is that the nation has never had that succession; an epoch of Hardings and Coolidges produces, by the scale of the problems to which it gives rise, its own regeneration. The weak president, as I have argued, comes from the fact that a strong predecessor has set the feet of the nation on level ground. He is chosen because, after a diet of strong occasions, a nation, like an individual, turns naturally to the chance of a quiet time. "Normalcy" is always certain to be popular after crises. The issue is whether, when crisis comes, the system can discover the man to handle it. On the evidence, this has so far been very remarkably the case. To urge that it is chance is, I think, a superficial view. It is the outcome of the national recognition that energy and direction are required, and the man chosen is the party response to that recognition. . . . The more deeply we penetrate the working of the system the more clearly does it emerge that the result is inherent in its nature.

The Uses for National Conventions

PENDLETON HERRING *

The usefulness of our national nominating conventions has at times seemed obscure. Most of the criticism of party conventions grows out of the belief that they are held to discuss policy as well as to nominate candidates. Such a belief misinterprets the structure of our party system. . . . The behavior of any organization must be interpreted in the light of the elements that compose it if any understanding is to be achieved. To expect bands of local chieftains and their henchmen to come together and act as

* Director Social Science Research Council. Formerly Professor of Government, Harvard University, and Professor, Harvard Graduate School of Public Administration. Author of *Group Representation Before Congress, Public Administration and the Public Interest, Presidential Leadership,* and other works. The selection is from Pendleton Herring, *The Politics of Democracy: American Parties in Action* (New York, Rinehart & Co., Inc., 1940), Ch. 16. By permission of the publisher.

a deliberative national unit once every four years is to expect the impossible.

Our conventions could be orderly if they were the apex of a well-organized hierarchy. The most dignified, orderly, and impressive assembly for selecting an individual for a high office is the College of Cardinals. Even this august assembly is not without its political undercurrents, but it can function with its unexampled success because it is the final expression of a remarkably well-disciplined body. . . .

Our political parties are built not on the rock of faith but rather on the broad mud flats of popular desires and individual ambitions. The party convention is no better than the loose and undisciplined local and state organizations that send their delegates to bargain. If we cannot do much to change these underlying factors the question then is to consider anew what can be done with the materials at hand.

Judged as strictly rational and intellectual performances, these huge assemblies are flat failures; but are they to be measured by such standards?

Let us first hear some of the critics. No recent writer is more outspoken than Herbert Agar. He states that "the position of the average delegate at a national convention has neither dignity nor sense." "Never a wholly adequate device, the nomination convention," he says, "is now an anachronism." He deplores the absence of serious discussion of public problems and the "atmosphere of lightminded carousal." This comes in for heartiest condemnation. "The delegates even showed signs of being ashamed of their own immoderate antics. They wondered whether the way to run a great political party is to get drunk and ride donkeys into hotel lobbies. . . . They knew they ought to be doing serious work. Yet there was no serious work to do, so they took refuge in idiocy." The author quotes Milton on the noises of Hell and concludes that conventions are worse. Agar's reaction is that of a cultured and sensitive man who evidently does not enjoy rough-housing. He would feel equally ill at ease at an American Legion convention or a conclave of the Elks.

Many of us would certainly prefer to see conventions less noisy, more thoughtful and "full of argument and heart-searching and high seriousness." My purpose here, however, is not to exhort delegates to be sober and meditative, but rather to raise the question as to whether a convention is primarily an intellectual activity. . . .

The attention of commentators has been focused most eloquently on sins of omission. The following views of Lord Bryce serve as a classic critique upon the shortcomings of the party convention:

> It goes without saying that such a meeting is capable neither of discussing political questions and settling a political programme, nor of deliberately weighing the merits of rival aspirants for the nomination. Its programme must be presented to it cut and dry, and this is the work of a small committee. In

> choosing a candidate, it must follow a few leaders. And what sort of leaders do conventions tend to produce? Two sorts—the intriguer and the declaimer. . . . For men of wisdom and knowledge, not seconded by a commanding voice and presence, there is no demand, and little chance of usefulness, in these tempestuous halls. . . . Large popular gatherings . . . are excitable in virtue of their size. . . . A national convention . . . is the hugest mass meeting the world knows of. . . . The struggle in a convention is over men, not over principles.

Such a sweeping denunciation hardly stands close scrutiny. The men influential in "these tempestuous halls" are the same men who serve as political leaders in Congress and the state governments. A huge mass meeting cannot be judged by its incapacity to perform tasks appropriate to a small committee. Unless we are to substitute for the convention a small executive council, we must accept the characteristics resulting from size. Moreover, its positive qualities are worthy of our respect. It is an indigenous institution and can be best evaluated with respect to our own peculiar needs.

What has our experience with national party conventions demonstrated their basic purpose to be? It is to find a man whom a majority of the voters will agree to support.

Farley has given us a perfect picture of the professional politician's attitude toward the selection of a candidate. On his way to the Elks' convention Farley called upon the national Committeeman of South Dakota, Bill Howe. Farley relates:

> . . . We sat in a lunchroom at Aberdeen on a roasting-hot day. Bill was a canny politician who had been in the game for years; he knew it backward and forward. We sat there for some time, exchanging generalities, without disclosing what either of us really had in mind. Just before it was time to go, Bill plumped his fat fist on the table and growled in a deep voice, "Farley, I'm damn' tired of backing losers. In my opinion, Roosevelt can sweep the country, and I'm going to support him."

The desire to find a winner and thereby help the ticket back home is a force of no small importance. The primary task of the delegates is to find a winning candidate. The convention is designed to unite diverse sections and rival leaders behind a man, and to whip up the enthusiasm of party workers to fight for his election. This involves not questions of public policy but problems of party strategy. In view of the rivalries, the frank self-seeking, and the bitter jealousies arising in our party conventions, the ultimate adjustment almost invariably reached is a triumph of popular government.

The value of the convention lies in its permitting the rank and file of the party to participate physically and emotionally in a common enterprise. Here are the men who must carry the brunt of the campaign. Here they have their chance to meet, to shout together, to act together, to feel together. The excitement and the turmoil of the convention fulfill a useful purpose. The relationship of follower and leader is seldom an intellectual bond. A common bond of sympathy, a common symbol, is easily grasped and equally binding.

The party convention places a premium on party harmony. It reveals in a beating glare of publicity any thin spots and holes in the party fabric. Hence the impetus of the whole procedure is toward agreement. Prolonged dispute is greatly feared. As William G. McAdoo explained to the 1932 convention, when shifting the California delegation to Roosevelt: "Sometimes in major operations where skillful surgery is required, the life of the patient may be destroyed if there is unnecessary delay. We believe, therefore, that California should take a stand here tonight that will bring this contest to a swift and, we hope, satisfactory conclusion—a stand, we hope, which will be promotive of party harmony." A convention must try to unify a party not inherently unified. Its purpose is not to examine intellectual differences but to seek terms of agreement. When differences cannot be reconciled, the politicians seek unity in the face of disagreement. A party convention offers them the opportunity to negotiate and human materials with which to work.

As just noted, the basic function of the convention is to focus national attention upon the task of selection that is going forward, and then to align the regular party politicians behind a man who will lead them to victory. To do this the methods must be such as to attract and hold the attention of the great mass of citizens. Experience indicates that prizefights, football games, and similar sporting spectacles have characteristics that please the populace. Debating societies have a more limited following. The intellectually inclined may view this as an unfortunate situation. If a political spectacle is the way to arouse public attention, that is reason enough for the average politician.

The party convention may likewise be viewed as an excellent implement for compromise. Compromise in politics is not achieved simply through argumentation. The process entails bargaining and manipulation as well. There are various levels and types of compromise. To reach such peaceful adjustments of interest requires an area for movement and something with which to trade and barter. The party convention creates a human situation and provides scope under general rules of the game for elaborate interrelationships. Here concessions of many types can be made and victories in various terms are possible. The range of satisfactions is great, and disappointment on one count may be compensated for on another. There must be something wherewith to compromise. . . .

No one would think of planning an industrial development, an army campaign, or an educational program by devices similar to a party convention. No one can accurately regard our conventions as deliberative or planning agencies. Our conventions are a romantic and flamboyant attempt to get a high degree of popular participation in the high drama of democracy. It is not an institution to be dismissed contemptuously because of its noise and apparent confusion. It is characteristic of our free political system; the Nazis had pageantry of a different sort. Those who prefer order found it at Nuremberg.

There is much that is not heroic in our system. The heroic mold has seemed ill suited to the peaceful routine of minding one's own business and working for a living. If we are approaching more dangerous times we will have less use for negative candidates selected because they came from the tactically important states with large electoral votes. Our easygoing, rough-and-tumble politics of compromise and barter may give way to a more efficient and effective control from the top. The demands made upon government may force our political parties to attempt a more authoritarian line. There would be no point in carefully devising a program unless the party leaders were determined to carry it through. This would entail sanctions to make such power effective. Our party conventions have sought not the strongest or wisest candidate but rather the man who would best serve to unite the party and attract the voters. This is one consequence of treating the presidency as a symbol as well as a job.

A party convention is a parley of state bosses accompanied by their henchmen carrying with them local jealousies and favoritisms. A convention might possibly become a meeting dominated by a clique of politicians in command of a national machine. Instead of selecting a compromise candidate, they might decide to put before the country their strong man who would—through all the arts of persuasion—be sold to the public as the leader.

The party convention is not an inappropriate device for serving our present purposes. In fact, it is admirably suited to testing the talents of our politicians. It demands organizational skill and manipulative genius—both of which qualities are exceedingly useful in democratic government. . . .

Much more can and should be done to give men of reason and knowledge a more strategic position within the party structure. Parties can aid in the political education of their own membership. Questions of public policy must now be thought of in national and even international terms. This means that the inadequacies of the local politician become more evident. Social and economic necessities push us forward in demanding more intelligence in the conduct of political affairs. Yet we would be shortsighted indeed if we placed our faith in the expert as the only man with the answer. The party convention is one institutional expression of human beings competing by their wits and emotions for some of the prizes available under popular government.

Demands of the Presidential Office

THEODORE C. SORENSEN *

THE UNIQUENESS OF WHITE HOUSE DECISIONS

To begin with, White House decision-making is not a science but an art. It requires, not calculation, but judgment. There is no unit of measure which can weigh the substantive consequences of a decision against the political consequences, or judge the precise portions of public opinion and congressional pressure, or balance domestic against foreign, short-range against long-range, or private against public considerations.

Every decision a President makes involves uncertainty. Every decision involves risk. Almost every decision involves an element of prediction and at least latent disagreement with others. Bismarck believed that it was these "doubts and anxieties," not the burdens of the daily schedule, which were so wearing on a political official.

Elaborate guides to decision-making in private business or even in public administration are of little help in the White House. For the breadth and scope of presidential decisions cannot be matched in any large corporation or Cabinet department, or even in the halls of Congress. For the President alone is ultimately accountable for the lives of more than 2.5 million American servicemen, for the deeds of 2.5 million federal employees, and he alone is ultimately held accountable to 190 million citizens, to more than 40 foreign allies and, in a very real sense—as custodian of the nuclear trigger—to all men and to all mankind.

His decisions do not merely differ in degree from the decisions of others. No one else faces so many complex issues where the solutions are so remote, so dependent on the undependable, and so tinged with potential disaster. No one else, as Woodrow Wilson said, bears such multiple responsibilities in so many different and conflicting areas. No one else knows in advance that his decisions will be subject to such scrutiny, to such calumny, or to what Professor Neustadt calls such irreversibility.

In an age when not only this nation but also its chief adversary possess the capacity to inflict unacceptable disaster on another power in a matter of minutes, it is foolish to compare the role of the current President with that of any other man, including even his thirty-three predecessors. When President Kennedy, for example, reviewed with the nation his decision to resume

* Former Special Counsel to President John F. Kennedy. The selection is from *Decision-Making in the White House* (New York, Columbia University Press, 1963), *passim*. By permission.

nuclear testing in the atmosphere, every citizen could understand his stated desire to examine every alternative, to demand a thorough justification, and to consider all the consequences. But no one, not even those who served with him in high position, could truly know the weight of his responsibility or all the forces that induced his conclusion.

For every course he examines, there will always be some opposition in the country, in the Congress, and even among his advisers. There will always be one adviser to say, after the fashion of certain columnists and commentators, that "on the one hand" consider this but "on the other hand" think of that. Idealists on his staff will rule out expediency. Realists will disregard morality. Some will counsel speed; others will counsel delay—yet even delay will constitute a decision.

As each President nears a final answer, he realizes that this choice is only the beginning. For each new decision sets a precedent, begetting new decisions, foreclosing others, and causing reactions which require counteraction. Roosevelt, according to Madam Perkins, "rarely got himself sewed tight to a program from which there was no turning back." And President Kennedy, aware of the enormous hazards in the confrontation with the Soviets over Cuba in October, 1962, made certain that his first move did not close out either all his options or all of theirs.

But too often a President finds that events or the decisions of others have limited his freedom of maneuver—that, as he makes a choice, that door closes behind him. And he knows that, once that door is closed, it may never open again—and he may then find himself in a one-way tunnel, or in a baffling maze, or descending a slippery slope. He cannot count on turning back—yet he cannot see his way ahead. He knows that if he is to act, some eggs must be broken to make the omelet, as the old saying goes. But he also knows that an omelet cannot lay any more eggs.

PRESIDENTIAL POLITICS

We can turn now to the major forces or sources of influence which shape the presidential decision itself, grouped under three frames of reference: presidential politics, presidential advisers,* and the presidential perspective.

Some purists—if not realists—may blush at the fact that politics heads the list. But we are discussing our prime political office and the nation's prime politician, a man who has been chosen by his party as well as the people. Some Presidents may assert that they are "above politics," yet politics, in its truest and broadest sense, still colors their every decision (including the decision to appear nonpolitical). Some issues have been traditionally deemed to be outside of politics, but considerations of public and congressional support still affect their disposition.

* This excerpt omits the discussion of "presidential advisers."

There is nothing dishonorable about the influence of politics on White House decisions. In a nation governed by the consent of the governed, it is both honorable and indispensable. While limitations of responsibility and accuracy should always be present, to say that we should remove such issues as Berlin or Red China from politics is to say they should be removed from public accountability and scrutiny. To charge that a President is politically motivated when he advocates a tax cut or a strong civil rights measure is simply to charge that he is doing what every elected official is elected to do.

Politics pervades the White House without seeming to prevail. It is not a role for which the President sets apart certain hours. It is rarely the sole subject of a formal presidential meeting. It is instead an ever-present influence—counterbalancing the unrealistic, checking the unreasonable, sometimes preventing the desirable, but always testing what is acceptable.

PUBLIC OPINION

But democratic government is not a popularity contest; and no President is obliged to abide by the dictates of public opinion. Our political idealism may be filled with assumptions of human virtue and wisdom, but our political history is filled with examples of human weakness and error.

Public opinion is often erratic, inconsistent, arbitrary, and unreasonable—with a "compulsion to make mistakes," as Walter Lippmann put it. It rarely considers the needs of the next generation or the history of the last. It is frequently hampered by myths and misinformation, by stereotypes and shibboleths, and by an innate resistance to innovation. It is usually slow to form, promiscuous and pervidious in its affection, and always difficult to distinguish. For it rarely speaks in one loud, clear, united voice.

A President, therefore, must remember that public opinion and the public interest do not always agree. The value to this nation of a foreign aid program, for example, is not determined by its popularity. Last year's trade expansion bill could not have awaited a spontaneous public demand. Voter enthusiasm for our space effort is high after each flight of a Soviet or American astronaut, but in between flights new doubts and complaints will emerge. And almost any pollster in any state will find that most voters want higher federal expenditures in their areas of interest, lower expenditures elsewhere, and a balanced budget always.

No President could simply respond to these pressures. He has a responsibility to lead public opinion as well as respect it—to shape it, to inform it, to woo it, and win it. It can be his sword as well as his compass. An aroused public opinion was more effective in 1962, for example, in helping create a climate favorable to the rescission of steel prices, than any statutory tool. President Kennedy's televised explanations of his decisions on Berlin, nuclear testing, and the Cuban quarantine achieved on each occasion a new national consensus that discouraged any adversary's hopes for disunity. . . .

In 1961 he resisted the recommendation that he declare a full-scale national emergency over the threat to Berlin, recognizing that this resort to ultimate powers and public response had to be selectively used. For similar reasons, he has generally resisted urgings of disappointed partisans who would have him stir up the public against a Congress which is controlled (at least nominally) by his own party and which has consistently enacted four-fifths of his program.

In short, presidential appeals for public support must be at the right time and with the right frequency, if they are to be effective. On other occasions he may need to alienate a portion of his public support, for serving as President of all the people does not mean offending none of them. But this also cannot be done too often if he is to maintain his position, and it should not be done for meaningless or hopeless causes. . . .

One important distinction should be kept in mind. In domestic affairs, a presidential decision is usually the beginning of public debate. In foreign affairs, the issues are frequently so complex, the facts so obscure, and the period for decision so short, that the American people have from the beginning—and even more so in this century—delegated to the President more discretion in this vital area; and they are usually willing to support any reasonable decision he makes.

But public opinion cannot be taken for granted. Some Presidents have tried to change it, others have rushed to catch up with it, but none has repeatedly defied it. "With public sentiment on its side," Lincoln said with some exaggeration, "everything succeeds; with public sentiment against it, nothing succeeds." Franklin D. Roosevelt wrote: "I cannot go any faster than the people will let me." And President Kennedy is acutely aware of Jefferson's dictum: "Great innovations should not be forced on slender majorities." . . .

No President respects public opinion simply out of fear of impeachment or even solely out of a desire for reelection—for the same principle is followed in both his terms. Instead both his conscience and his common sense, both his principles and his political judgment, compel him to seek, to the extent possible, the approval of the voters who elected him and who can defeat his party, the consent of the governed who are affected by his decision and on whose consent its success may depend.

Every President must, therefore, be a keen judge of public opinion. He must be able to distinguish its petty whims, to estimate its endurance, to respond to its impatience, and to respect its potential power. He must know how best and how often he can appeal to the public—and when it is better left undisturbed.

No President reaches that summit of public favor without believing he possesses (and he usually does) an extraordinary instinct for public opinion.

He does not rely on the views expressed in his mail, or in public petitions, or by pickets in front of the White House, for they all too often reflect only a tiny organized group. He does not rely on opinion polls, which, outside of testing comparative candidate strengths, are still an inexact measure of the voters' views. He does not rely on the crowds that greet him on his travels, knowing they are usually a disproportionately partisan sample. Nor does he generalize from conversations with visitors, reports from his advisers, or his reading and viewing of mass media. His political intuition is in part an amalgamation of all of these—but he is likely to regard his own invisible antennae as somehow more sensitive than any. (President McKinley, according to Speaker Cannon, retained his popularity by "keeping his ear so close to the ground he got it full of grasshoppers.")

I no longer believe those who say that a poor politician could be a good President, "if he could only be appointed to the job." Without the qualities required of a successful candidate—without the ability to rally support, to understand the public, to express its aspirations—without the organizational talent, the personal charm, and the physical stamina required to survive the primaries, the convention, and the election—no man would make a great President, however wise in other ways he might be.

PRESSURE GROUPS, CONGRESS, AND THE PRESS

Each President must also judge when to oppose or accommodate a single segment of public opinion—a region or state, an occupation or age group, an industry or profession, a pressure group or lobby. Some will have views the President respects, such as nuclear scientists on nuclear tests. Some will have influence he seeks to enlist, such as the organization of older citizens on behalf of his health bill. Some will have sufficient power to cause him concern, at least in their own sphere of influence. (The least respected and least effective lobbies in Washington, I might add, are those which rush forward to testify on every measure of every kind, whether directly related or not to the interests of their members. It is doubtful, for example, that President Roosevelt was either heartened or dismayed by the 1934 resolution of a bankers' organization stating that its members would stand solidly behind the President on all emergency measures that did not infringe on their interests.)

There will always be a small but noisy group of critics intolerant of the gap between hope and possibility, complaining of a lack of leadership when long-awaited measures are not immediately enacted, while an equally small and vocal group will wail that each step forward the President takes is a gross usurpation of power.

The amount of pressure generated by those concerned over import competition must be balanced against the less active but larger number of persons benefiting from both exports and imports. The political or congressional attacks induced by a contractor whose weapons system has been discontinued must be weighed against the long-range costs of continuing an outmoded system.

The task is not always one of choosing between two interests. No President, even if he so wished, could suspend the laws in response to complaints —with respect to desegregation or anti-trust, for example. But he may find it desirable to accept amendments to a tax measure, or to reach informal understandings on concessions regarding a trade bill, in order to secure the passage of those bills with the support of a diverse coalition; or he may warn his appointees against exhibiting an attitude toward business or labor that is so hostile it might dampen the economic climate.

A President's own ties with some economic or other interest group may give him additional bargaining power with that group or reduced influence with another. A President with close ties to business, for example, will meet less resistance to his anti-inflation or anti-trust efforts. On the other hand, while it should not be impossible to find an equitable constitutional formula to settle the church-school aid problem, it is difficult for that formula to be suggested by the nation's first Catholic President.

Pressure groups usually have less direct effect on the President than on his relations with the Congress—a large and separate topic but a major arena of presidential politics. While this discussion is concerned primarily with White House decisions, members of the Congress will inevitably attempt to affect those decisions in much the same way as the White House attempts to affect the decisions of the Congress: i.e., legislators will privately or publicly lobby, pressure, encourage, or discourage the President and his advisers, with respect to his legislative program or budget, both before and after their passage through the Congress.

As is true of public opinion and segments thereof, the views of one or more members of Congress must sometimes be resisted, sometimes reshaped, sometimes ignored, and sometimes accepted, depending not only on the validity of those views but on the power of those who express them and on the extent to which they are shared throughout the Congress. Presidents have differed in the degree of their deference to (or domination of) congressional opinion, according to their own legislative experience, their control of their party, and their party's control of the Congress, but all Presidents since Washington have noted the change in climate that occurs when Congress adjourns.

Finally, presidential politics includes attention to the American press and other media. Their selection and description of particular events—far more than their editorials—help to create or promote national issues, to shape the minds of the Congress and public, and to influence the President's agenda and timing. Ever since George Washington expressed the wish in 1777 "that our Printers were more discreet in many of their publications," our Presidents and the press have engaged in what the jargon of the Cold War would call a "contest for men's minds."

The winning side of this contest is debatable. The advent of television has given the President great resources for directly reaching the public, but even presidential corrections rarely catch up with those misstatements which now and then appear in the press. For example, the great newspaper chain which headlined a totally false scare story about Soviet planes overflying the southeastern United States has never acknowledged its error.

I have often been asked why President Kennedy, unlike his predecessor, should bother to read so many newspapers when so much of their important information and arguments—excluding overseas statements and events that occurred during the night—is at least twenty-four hours old to him. Obviously this would be even more true of weekly and monthly magazines. He reads them, I believe, partly to gain new insights for himself but primarily to know what the public and the Congress are reading, to see how his actions or choices appear to others without his access to the facts. For any President, any politician dependent on public opinion, is concerned with how that opinion is shaped, with how, to use a current phrase, the news is being "managed" in the only place it can be managed, the media editorial offices.

A President cannot afford to be modest. No one else sits where he sits or knows all that he knows. No one else has his power to lead, to inspire, or to restrain the Congress and country. If he fails to lead, no one leads. "The buck," in Truman's words, "stops here."

A President knows that his name will be the label for a whole era. Textbooks yet unwritten and school-children yet unborn will hold him responsible for all that happens. His program, his power, his prestige, his place in history, perhaps his reelection, will all be affected by key decisions. His appointees, however distinguished they may be in their own right, will rise or fall as he rises or falls. Even his White House aides, who see him constantly, cannot fully perceive his personal stakes and isolation. And no amount of tinkering with the presidential machinery, or establishment of new executive offices, can give anyone else *his* perspective.

Consequently, self-confidence and self-assertion are more important than modesty. The nation selects its President, at least in part, for his philosophy and his judgment and his conscientious conviction of what is right—and he need not hesitate to apply them. He must believe in his own objectives. He must assert his own priorities. And he must strive always to preserve the power and prestige of his office, the availability of his options, and the long-range interests of the nation. . . .

BY WAY OF SUMMARY

Unlike the leaders of autocracy, the President of our democracy must contend with powerful pressures of public opinion, with co-equal branches of the government, and with a free and critical press. He cannot allocate resources, or ignore traditions, or override departments in whatever manner he wishes. His allies cannot be treated as satellites, his mistakes cannot be concealed, his critics cannot be silenced.

But over the long haul, democratic decision-making, for all its faults and failures, will, I believe, produce superior decisions. True, a totalitarian leader can exercise absolute command over his advisers and absolute compulsion over ideology. But he cannot command good advice and he cannot compel new ideas. Suppression and terror may suffice for the efficient control of machinery, but they cannot improve the decisions of men.

For great and lasting decisions in human affairs can only be made by those exposed to human value judgments. Consistently wise decisions can only be made by those whose wisdom is constantly challenged. The voluntary unity of free men and nations is ultimately more solid than the forced uniformity of repression. In the long run, there can be no wisdom without dissent, no progress without diversity, no greatness without responsibility.

Topic 23

CONGRESSIONAL REFORM?

"Tyranny of the Minorities"

JOSEPH S. CLARK *

PROLOGUE TO REFORM

The customs, manners, rules and procedures of the Congress owe much to the American tradition of thinking in sectional and local social, economic and political terms. Americans, like most human beings, share a conviction that "The Lord helps those who help themselves." Until recently we were content to protect ourselves from alleged governmental restraint on our personal activities by Congressional devices designed to give minority interests (other than the Negro) a veto on the legislative process. The durability of these devices is also a tribute to the curious notion that to do nothing does not constitute a decision. The fear that the creation of a national legislature with the capacity to act might produce wrong decisions overlooks the fact that to do nothing in the modern world may itself represent a decision as disastrous as any affirmative action.

This strain of negativism runs deep. One may recall the interminable delays in enacting the constitutional amendments providing for the income tax, the direct election of Senators and women suffrage; and how long we waited for child labor legislation, unemployment compensation and a host of economic and social welfare measures passed a generation earlier in most other Western democracies.

While Congressional political lag has always existed—indeed, through failure to solve the slavery question it played its part in bringing on the Civil War—it did not become glaringly apparent until the Great Depression of the 1930s. Prior to that time the system worked tolerably well. Each section got its interests taken care of by logrolling. Our wealth made the price supportable. World affairs did not require decisive action by the Congress. The really vital interests of the nation were not adversely affected. The system operated through a national legislature so organized that sectional and eco-

* United States Senator from Pennsylvania. The selection is from *Congress: The Sapless Branch* by Senator Joseph S. Clark.

nomic interests were able to protect themselves from objectionable government policy during a period in which no vigorous government policy of any kind was required in the national interest.

A governmental system that is not capable of producing a coherent legislative program is not likely to appear deficient to a people imbued with a firm distaste for strong government and not confronted with crisis. It produced a government that did not interfere with the expanding economy, which was then the main interest of most influential Americans. Understandably, it was not then perceived that an arrangement which gave minority interests a stranglehold on national policy through control over Congressional procedures might, when crisis arrived, prove to be inoperable.

It is in the nature of minorities, as Joseph Chamberlain once said, "to devise some ingenious machinery by which [they] may be saved from the natural consequences of being outnumbered." Such ingenious machinery is the very nerve center of the present control of the Congress. It will not do to defend this machinery as a protection against "the tyranny of the majority," for it is nothing of the sort. It is a built-in defense for maintaining a status quo no longer tenable in the face of present conditions at home and abroad. And it violates every principle of popular rule on which free governments are based. It is the "tyranny of the minorities" we suffer from.

The central defect of the modern Congress is that it permits a minority determined on inaction to frustrate the will of the majority which desires to act. All the majority wants to do is to work the will of the people it represents. Minority obstructionism has merely reinforced that Congressional lag which gets us into trouble. We can reflect soberly today on the results of the bitterest Senate filibuster of the nineteenth century, which in 1890–91 defeated a bill, already passed by the House, to give the federal government supervision over Congressional elections. How much rancor and discord in our century would have been avoided had the majority in the Senate been able to pass this bill, aimed at eliminating Negro disqualification and intimidation in the South.

Those who delight in the fear of "majority tyranny" should seek election to a major governmental post under conditions of genuine political competition. They would soon learn how varied are the interests that must be conciliated if success is to be achieved at the polls. There is nothing monolithic and therefore no basis for "tyranny" in the majorities put together by Congressmen from two-party states and districts today. Potential tyranny is a characteristic of minorities like the John Birch Society or the Communists, not the mark of the representatives of a major party seeking the support of a national electorate.

It is the dynamics of democratic politics, not the erection of legal barriers to action, that make for moderation in our public life and provide the real protection from majority tyranny. In fact, while both major parties have extremists in their ranks, those extremists have never represented orthodoxy in the parties to which they belonged. Their very power emerged from their exploitation of devices aimed at protecting the minority. Huey Long and his one-man filibusters, or Joe McCarthy arrogating to himself the investigatory power of the Senate and temporarily usurping executive prerogatives, never seriously threatened to assume leadership of either party. There is an old saying in England that the House of Commons has more sense than anyone in it. The same thing can be said of any legislative body where a consensus is permitted to develop and take action. It is, therefore, a grave error not to establish procedures which permit the good sense of a majority to prevail.

Congressional preoccupation with legal checks on the majority is superimposed on functional checks implicit in the separation of powers, including the Presidential veto. Moreover, our strongly held respect for minorities gives them additional protection. It is the strength of that tradition which provides the moral support for the effort to integrate the Negro into American life. It is indeed ironic that this effort on behalf of our most disadvantaged minority is frustrated by devices ostensibly aimed at preventing "majority tyranny."

The obstructionist policies encouraged by those same devices are in the long run self-defeating. In 1925 Vice President Dawes advised the Senate that "under the inexorable laws of human nature and human reaction, the Senate rules, unless changed, could only lessen the effectiveness, prestige, and dignity of that body." There can be no doubt that the Dawes warning was prophetic, if unheeded. A legislature which denies itself the power to act, particularly when the obstacles to action are so obvious and so publicly demeaning as the filibuster, merits only disrespect and the loss of popular esteem it has achieved.

Max Lerner's harsh description is a typical reaction:

> Congress has become a problem child of the American governmental family. It is noisy, volatile, vulnerable to pressure groups and lobbies, often parochial in its outlook, jealous of its prerogatives, insecure about its position, implacable in its vendettas, bewildered by its mounting tasks. It has lost its reputation for great debate, has become intractable to party leadership and discipline and incapable of disciplining itself, and in recent generations it has developed fewer examples of the great leadership it once possessed.

Vesting the veto power in a minority goes far to destroy that spirit of desirable compromise which is one of the hallmarks of a democratic legislative assembly. A minority bent on inaction finds it unnecessary to compromise with a majority which is powerless to act. The Congress of the United States is, within very broad limits, favorably disposed to accommodate a wide spectrum of opinion. There is no compulsion to agree on moderate and reasonable action, however, when the rules offer hope that nothing at all need be agreed to. Defiance by the minority breeds in the end vindictiveness in the majority. Neither sentiment is congenial to useful action.

The risk of tyranny by the majority over the minority is today small indeed. Tocqueville's fears of democracy have proved groundless. It is a minority, not a majority, which imposes sterile uniformity. Today the Negro minority is tyrannized by a white minority. National democracy has had no fair chance to do justice. . . .

As Henry Steele Commager has noted,

> For well over a century now, this pernicious doctrine [states' rights] has been invoked for two major purposes . . . to weaken government and to endanger freedom. A states' rights philosophy which is never inspired by generosity, never excited by a passion for freedom or for justice, never exalted by magnanimity but takes refuge in narrowness, selfishness and vindictiveness, exhausts its claim to tolerance.

There is no greater nonsense circulated today than the theory that the states are the defenders of freedom and the national government its enemy. The fact is just the opposite. The growth of the power of the national government has secured an increase in individual freedom, social, economic and political. The effect of national power has been benign, not malign. It is a shame that the Congress has not sensed this basic political truth until long after it occurred to both the Supreme Court and the President. The use of states' rights as a rallying cry for those who desire to perpetuate an inept Congress unable to deal with pressing national problems is a cry to perpetuate plutocracy and greed and to protect those who are today violating civil rights and civil liberties with impunity. To rely upon the states for a solution of problems essentially national in their scope, such as education, unemployment, and social security is to insure that these problems will not be solved. Those who advocate states' rights are, therefore, in the vanguard of the opponents of Congressional reform. As long as they can keep the Congress negative their status quo philosophy is safe. It is state debt and state government employment which have risen almost astronomically in the postwar years, not the federal government's. Yet this enormous increase has not been sufficient to make appreciable inroads toward solution of the domestic problems which beset us. Letting the states do it is tantamount to letting the problems remain unsolved.

Closely related to the states' rights argument is the nightmare of "federal control" over individual liberties which haunts the dreams of our conservative friends. This is a sheer hallucination. I cannot think of one current program in which the "heavy hand of the federal government reaching out into our private lives" has actually been restrictive of our personal freedoms or detrimental to our economy—if, that is, one accepts the need for a justly organized society in a civilized world. The problem of protecting liberty against the demands of society is difficult and delicate, as John Stuart Mill made clear long ago. "Government, like dress," said Tom Paine, "is the badge of lost innocence." Sometimes the choice between liberty and order is difficult. In the great struggle for civil rights for all Americans, for example, it has been argued that equal access to public accommodations is an infringement on the liberty of the individual who owns or manages the facility. I would argue that the individual right of every American to the use of that facility is an *expansion* of basic liberty, not a *denial* of liberties. But the question is not easy.

The concern over minority rights and regional interests is understandable enough in view of our history. For the descendants of Southern planters, steerage immigrants, British convicts, African slaves and New England Puritans to live and work in peace and harmony, and pursue happiness together, is no easy thing. No other nation has had to attempt it. On the whole we have been successful, but we still have some miles to go on the road to the good society.

The motto carved on the New Senate Office Building is "The Senate is the Living Symbol of the Union of the States." That pretty well sums up the Congressional attitude. But time and history and world responsibility have made us a nation, and it is time that in our thinking and in our behavior we recognized contemporary fact. We must move toward national federalism, accepting the federal structure, but emphasizing the national.

There are many who persist in the mistaken view that the problems of Congress, like the poor, will always be with us. But the Congress has not always been as incapable of action as it is now, and majority rule has not always been so successfully thwarted. Like the tradition of Jim Crow in the South, which is not nearly so old as it is iniquitous, there is a tendency to accept as age-old and hallowed traditions the habits of a few decades. Most of the unfortunate traditions of Congress are not very old and not very hallowed. In a culture confronted with constant change it is surprising that so many still believe change in Congress is not possible.

Procedural reform in the Congress has a history at least as old as the practices which led to it. In the past hundred years, important procedural reforms have often been successfully accomplished as the need became clear. . . .

[Senator Clark then points out, with respect to the House of Representatives, that in 1860 "a largely technical revision of the rules in the interest of clarity was adopted" and that, in 1880, the 167 rules were consolidated into 44 "thus securing 'accuracy in business, economy of time, order, uniformity and impartiality.' " In 1890, the Reed Rules were adopted which "placed the speaker in control of the House with almost dictatorial powers." In 1910, however, drastic reform destroyed "a large part of the system of strong party government, party discipline and majority rule."

With respect to the Senate, in 1913, new rules "gave a majority of a committee authority to call meetings and dispose of pending business, a power hitherto vested in the chairman. They placed in the majority power to name subcommittees, to elect conferees to meet with Representatives of the House and generally democratized Senate procedures."

Under the Legislative Reorganization Act of 1946, the committee structure of both Houses was simplified but "some of the most important recommendations" for reform were defeated. Senator Clark quotes the language of this Legislative Committee Report as "prophetic":

"Devised to handle the simpler task of an earlier day, our legislative machinery and procedures are by common consent no longer competent to cope satisfactorily with the grave and complex problems of the post-war world. They must be modernized if we are to avoid an imminent breakdown of the legislative branch of the national government. . . . Democracy itself is in grave danger of disintegrating from internal dissentions under the terrific pressures of the post-war world."

Senator Clark concludes: "So it is again today."]

INTERNAL REFORMS FOR CONGRESS

The main objectives of internal Congressional reform are, specifically, four:

1. To change the party leadership structure so that within both parties and in both houses a majority will decide party policy and enforce party discipline against recalcitrant members.

2. To change the rules and procedures of both houses so that a majority *can* act when it is ready to act.

3. To substitute cooperation for competition in the relations between the two houses, and between the whole Congress and the President.

4. To establish and enforce high ethical standards for members of Congress.

Nothing less than such drastic treatment will restore the Congress to vigorous, working, democratic health. But I am neither so naïve nor so egotistical as to expect my colleagues to agree with me in the absence of a strong popular demand for Congressional reform. I do not think that the Congressional Establishment will respond to the arguments in this book, cast off lethargy and obstructionism and reform itself. A great deal of public prodding is needed. . . .

The question of discipline is necessarily involved and the conference is the place to settle it. Hardly a Senator today would support the old practice of the binding caucus. "King Caucus" is dead in the Congress for the foreseeable future. Moreover, both parties are divided into liberal and conservative blocks so that substantial agreement would be impossible and revolt certain on all controversial measures if an attempt to bind were made.[1] Finally, the Establishment, even with its wings clipped, as I hope in due course they will

[1] This situation should not, however, prevent votes being taken by the conference from time to time to enable the leadership to determine the strength which could be summoned for the passage of particular measures.

be, will probably always be strong enough within the legislative committees to prevent dictation of policy by the conference.

Nevertheless, there is a practical area where the conference should exercise discipline. No institution should countenance members who are consistently out of sympathy with its objectives and the Congressional Democratic Conference should be no exception. Senators and Representatives who are unwilling to support the Presidential candidate of their party in the campaign simply have no place in the Congressional Conferences of their party after the election. Congressmen who are unwilling to support the platform planks of their party in the area of jurisdiction of a particular committee have no business serving as members of that party on that committee; and far less should they have the right through seniority to become or remain chairmen of such committees.

There is plenty of precedent for the exercise of such discipline. . . . After the election of 1924, the Republicans in the Senate, in the second session of the Sixty-eighth Congress, passed a resolution that Senators who had campaigned against President Calvin Coolidge that year "be not invited to future Republican conferences and be not named to fill any Republican vacancies on Senate Committees."

Senator La Follette, who had run for the Presidency against Coolidge, and Senators Ladd, Brookhart and Frazier were expelled from the Republican conference. They were permitted to retain the committee assignments they had theretofore held, but placed at the bottom of the committee seniority list. Senator Ladd was demoted as chairman of the then important Committee on Public Lands and Surveys.

There are other precedents. In 1859 Stephen A. Douglas of Illinois, then the only Democratic Senator from a non-slaveholding state holding the chairmanship of an important committee touching the public business of the government, was dropped from the chairmanship of the Committee on Territories, a position he had held ever since he entered the Senate. At the beginning of the opening session in 1866, the Republicans demoted Senators Cowan of Pennsylvania, Dixon of Connecticut and Doolittle of Wisconsin as chairmen of their respective committees, because they had failed to support Republican party policy in voting to override President Andrew Johnson's veto of the Civil Rights Bill. In 1871 Charles Sumner of Massachusetts, at the instance of President Grant, was not only deposed as chairman of the Foreign Relations Committee, but left off the committee entirely. . . .

In our own day Senator Wayne Morse of Oregon was disciplined by the Republicans for political independence in 1953 by removal from membership on the Armed Services and Labor Committees. When he later joined the Democratic party, he was restored to the Labor Committee, but at the bottom of the list. Later he was placed on the Foreign Relations Committee. In the House the Democratic party conference seems to be even less effective than in the Senate. . . .

There are fewer examples in House history than in the Senate of demotion of committee chairmen and discipline of committee members. The most famous one resulted from the revolt of the Progressives of Wisconsin against the regular conservative Republican leadership in the early 1920's. It came to a head after the Presidential election of 1924 in which Senator Robert La Follette, a Bull Moose Republican, ran for the Presidency on a third ticket.

In the "lame duck" session of Congress held in December, 1924, after the election of President Calvin Coolidge that November, ten Representatives from Wisconsin who had supported Senator La Follette for the Presidency were deprived of committee posts to which they had previously been chosen as Republicans. One of them, John M. Nelson, was removed as chairman of the Committee on Elections and dropped from the committee. Another, Florian Lampert, was removed as chairman of the Committee on Patents, but allowed to remain on the committee on the bottom of the seniority list. In 1949 Speaker Sam Rayburn caused John Rankin of Mississippi and Edward Hébert of Louisiana to be removed from the House Un-American Activities Committee for "antics" which displeased him and, it might be added, most of the country as well.

In each case in both houses these demotions caused enormous controversy. In many cases they have not received the praise of historians. Vengeance was perhaps a motive in some of them. But for an institution, like the Congress, which exalts precedent, the precedents are there. And in each instance the party leadership recommended the action taken by the caucus. . . .

[Senator Clark then recommends a whole series of particular intra-party organizational reforms basically designed to establish the primacy of majority views in each party in the selection of committee members. He adds:]

A major requirement of Congressional reform is a change in the rules, customs, procedures and floor action of the two houses with the end in view of making it easier for both bodies to act effectively when a majority is ready for action. The ultimate purpose of rules reform is to remove as many of these obstacles as is feasible while retaining adequate opportunity for careful consideration in committee and full debate on the floor of all bills under serious consideration.

In the House the problem seems simple. Floor action is expeditious and needs no significant change. "Reed's Rules" plus the reforms connected with the overthrow of Speaker Joseph Cannon in 1910 took care of that many years ago.

The problem in the House is to pry loose from the legislative committees and the Rules Committee bills which are part of the program of the President or whose passage is desired by a clear majority of the House. The presently available techniques to solve this problem have proved inadequate in practice.

Three methods of achieving the desired result which worked well in the past but were abandoned might be restored by changes in the House rules. The first would be to reinstate the twenty-one-day rule which resulted in the passage of much important legislation during its short lifetime in the Truman administration.* The second would be to decrease the number of names on a discharge petition required to bring a bill from committee to the calendar from 218, or a majority of the whole House, to 150, which was the requirement from 1924 to 1935. The third would be to remove from the Rules Committee the power to determine whether a bill shall go to conference if one member of the House objects on the floor to a motion to appoint conferees, thus leaving the decision to the whole House.

Of course, even with restricted powers, it is essential to have the Rules Committee an ally and not an enemy of the leadership. The best way to do this would seem to be to demote its chairman and any other members who are unwilling to commit themselves to the winning party's platform and candidate in 1964, as well as members of the minority party who are disloyal to their own national leader and platform. While demotion in the case of other committees should be confined to those who are unwilling to support the platform in the area of the committee's jurisdiction, the Rules Committee covers the waterfront, having authority to send to the floor or pickle *any* proposed legislation on *any* subject. This vast power should never be permitted to be exercised by a committee containing members disloyal to the platform of the party to which they ostensibly belong.

The result of these suggested changes would be to democratize committee action in the House and make the committees subject to the will of a majority of that body. Whether the majority of the House would be prepared to follow the platform of the majority party or of the President is quite a different story. The composition of the House might well be such that no such result would follow. But at least so far as internal operations are concerned the President and his party would fight under ground rules which are in the tradition of our American democracy rather than the outmoded result of control of the House by an ancient oligarchical and plutocratic minority unresponsive to the popular will.

Before discussing needed changes in Senate rules and methods of operation something should be said about the custom of seniority, a controversial subject in both houses and in the country at large.

There is an unwritten custom, sometimes violated in practice, that length

* Under this rule, the chairman of a legislative committee could call up for action a bill his committee had reported favorably at any time after the lapse of 21 calendar days—if the Rules Committee in the meantime, had failed to grant a rule.

of service in the House and Senate determines eligibility for appointment to committees, and that the majority senior member of a committee succeeds automatically to a vacancy in the chairmanship. The latter half of the custom is more scrupulously observed than the former. . . .

In the House the Speaker, the Democratic members of the Ways and Means Committees and the Republican Committee on Committees give some weight to factors other than seniority in making initial assignments. This is because there are, with each new Congress, so many new Representatives with equal seniority to be fitted into committee vacancies. Former members returning to the House after an earlier defeat or resignation are usually given priority in the choice of committee posts, but lose for all time their seniority on defeat or resignation.

The seniority rule has come in for much adverse public comment largely because it tends to give power to elderly conservative members of both houses, mostly from the South when the Democrats control the Congress, who are apt to use their power to defeat or delay the enactment of the program of their party and of the President. . . .

When one considers how much the luck of the draw contributes to achieving a committee chairmanship, the geographical distribution in the House is not subject to serious criticism. While there is some overweighting from the South, it must be remembered that the next time the Republicans carry the House these Southern chairmen will be replaced by Northerners and Westerners. On grounds of ideology the story is different. In the area of their committees' jurisdiction four chairmen hold views not in accord with the platform of their party. In terms of age one notes three chairmen over eighty and five more who have seen three score years and ten go by.

The difficulty is not so much in the seniority system itself as in the failure to exercise party discipline in a manner which would require chairmen to conform to the platform of their party in the area of the committee's jurisdiction or resign and seek service on another committee.

Nor is there any apparent correlation between age and ideology. Representatives Cellar and Patman, among the older chairmen, are as liberal as Representatives Smith and Cannon are conservative. And Chairman Cannon, while he delights in cutting the heart out of appropriations recommended by any administration, voted for both the civil rights and tax bills in 1963.

Nevertheless, a rule that would require chairmen to relinquish their positions as such on reaching age seventy or seventy-five while still remaining as members of the committee, as Senator Theodore Francis Green did voluntarily on the Senate Foreign Relations Committee a few years ago, would avoid the embarrassment of the public display of a slowing down of mental agility and energy which are recognized by all save the elderly chairman himself—and which slow down and sometimes prevent the effective conduct of committee business. There would be a few cases where such a rule would deprive the committee of a useful chairman, but there would be many more where the result would be wholly salutary. Such a rule should apply both to the House and to the Senate. . . .

Seniority is a convenient method of eliminating internal politics in both Houses. It is, in a sense, a lazy man's way of avoiding a struggle and a decision. It makes it possible for the most senior Congressman around to get what he wants without a struggle. But it also gives other Congressmen an excuse not to start a fight. The constituents pleading for action to get a committee off dead center can always be told, "What can I do?"

That invariable following of the seniority rule can do great damage to the legislative process is clear beyond doubt. History is full of instances where incompetent or senile men have obstructed the national interest through their positions as committee chairmen attained through seniority. Even worse are the instances, several of which presently exist, where extremely capable men have used their power as committee chairmen, acquired through seniority, to obstruct and often to defeat the programs of their own party and the President that party sent to the White House.

The remedy is not to eliminate seniority, but rather to curb and regulate it. Primarily this could be done by the exercise of party discipline as recommended earlier in this chapter. Another effective step would be always to fill committee vacancies, regardless of seniority, with men known to be in sympathy with party policy in the area of the committee's jurisdiction. This, of course, requires a Steering Committee or Committee on Committees responsive to a party conference prepared to support party programs.

A third reform to curb the evil effects of seniority would be to provide by rule that the chairmen of all standing committees should be chosen at the beginning of each Congress by secret ballot of the committee members of the majority party. Nine times out of ten the choice would be the senior Senator or Representative. But in the tenth case a recalcitrant chairman would be deposed or a prospective recalcitrant candidate for the chairmanship relying on seniority defeated. And in the other nine cases the chairman chosen because of seniority would bend over backward to be fair, to assure his continued tenure against the threat of demotion by his colleagues.

Finally, the evil effects of seniority or indeed of arbitrary action by chairmen could be curbed by enacting by rule a "Committee Bill of Rights." Some committees presently have rules of procedure which are in accord with normal parliamentary practice. Others do not. It would help very much in the latter cases to provide by rule that a majority of the members of a committee could convene meetings, fix the agenda, call up bills for consideration, regulate the conduct of hearings and terminate debate within the committee after a reasonable time. Ordinarily these matters are left to the chairman, and properly so. But the power of the majority to act if the chairman fails to do so should be clearly established.

Because these procedures were followed in the Senate Committee on Interstate and Foreign Commerce, the Public Accommodations title of President Kennedy's Civil Rights Bill was promptly considered and favorably reported in the fall of 1963. Because they were not, much of the rest of the bill was never reported by the Senate Judiciary Committee.

In the House the absence of effective committee procedures enables the chairman of the Interior Committee to pickle indefinitely the Senate-passed Wilderness Bill, and the chairman of the Rules Committee to delay for months major legislation already approved by the appropriate standing committee.

The seniority system, then, is a serious obstacle to effective Congressional performance of duty. But the remedies for the evil are close at hand. All that is needed is to put them into effect and thus bring the system under control. There is no need to throw the baby out with the bath water. Properly regulated, the seniority system has its uses, principally in minimizing internal conflict between members of Congress. . . .

A useful reform would be to prohibit any Senator from holding the floor for more than two hours, except when floor managing a bill or by unanimous consent. We have no time or need in the modern world for marathon speeches. . . . A motion to take up a bill on the calendar made by the Majority Leaders should be determined by vote without debate. At present such a motion is subject to unlimited debate, thus giving the opponents of the bill two chances to filibuster instead of only one, i.e., (1) when the motion to take up is made the pending business and (2) after the motion is finally approved and unlimited debate begins on the bill and amendments.

The Senate should adopt a rule requiring debate to be germane when legislation which the leadership wishes to expedite has been made the pending business. No other legislative body in the world, so far as I have been able to discover, operates without a rule of germaneness. The principle is well laid down in Jefferson's Manual and was originally followed in the Senate: "No one is to speak impertinently or *beside the question,* superfluously or tediously." Some years ago the Parliamentarian ruled Jefferson need no longer be followed. No one can prevent a Senator from being tedious, but it should be possible to require him to stick to the subject. . . .

Rule XXIV of the Senate should be amended by adding a new paragraph reading: "A majority of the Senate members of a committee or conference shall have indicated by their votes their sympathy with the bill as passed and their concurrence in the prevailing opinion of the Senate on matters of disagreement with the House of Representatives which occasion the appointment of the committee."

This sound, democratic principle, which is recognized in Jefferson's Manual, Cleaves' Manual, and the Watkins and Riddick book on Senate procedure, has been violated on a number of important occasions in recent years. Thus the Senate has been represented on particular bills, as it was in 1959 on the question of extending the temporary unemployment compensation law, by Senators who voted against the Senate position and in favor of the House position on the bill as a whole or particular provisions of it.

Under the existing situation, if a Senator wishes to protest that the practices as stated in the manuals are not being adhered to, he must publicly challenge one or more of the conferees. This has been done successfully on several occasions, but for obvious reasons it has usually created personal ill will, which might be avoided if a Senate rule incorporated the principle and it could be invoked by a point of order.

The need for the change at present is largely, but not entirely, confined to instances where the Senate overrules its Finance Committee on a tax bill. In these instances the senior members of the Committee, who would normally be the conferees, would in all likelihood have voted with the minority on the floor.

Perhaps the most important needed change in Senate rules is the liberalization of Rule XXII, which presently provides for terminating debate, only on the affirmative vote of two-thirds of the Senators present. The latest effort to decrease the number of Senators required to bring debate to an end from two-thirds to three-fifths, advocated by Senator Anderson, or to a simple majority, urged by Senator Humphrey, failed in February, 1963, although fifty-six Senators were on record in support of the Anderson resolution. . . .

The single most desirable change in the present attitude of both houses, a change which would do more than any other to bring the President and the Congress together on a program for the country, would be passage of a concurrent resolution committing both houses to bring to a vote on its merits any legislative proposal on which the President requests prompt action within six months of the date his proposed legislation is sent down to Capitol Hill. In this way the original intention of the framers of the Constitution could be resuscitated. The Executive would report annually on the State of the Union and how he had performed his duty to see that the laws should be faithfully executed as provided in Article II of the Constitution. He would make his recommendations for needed legislation to the Congress; send down his budget; and the legislative arm would promptly act on those recommendations—accepting some, modifying others, rejecting still others. It would then pass and send to the President for veto or approval such other laws as in its wisdom, exercising its extensive powers under Article I of the Constitution, it thought should be enacted. . . . So might the public business be expeditiously dispatched.

Until the Congress accepts this obligation there is little hope that our tripartite system of checks and balances with all its frustrations, with all its roadblocks to needed action, with all its futilities and with all its callous disregard of the public interest can measure up to the responsibilities placed on it in the modern world.

The mechanics could be simple enough. Any committee member, citing the concurrent resolution, would be authorized to move within the committee to report out favorably the bill submitted by the President. When the bill reached the floor, the Majority Leader would promptly motion it up. If a committee failed to act, a discharge motion or petition could be filed to bring the bill to the floor. The resolution would provide that these motions to report and take up would by-pass any reference to the House Rules Committee and would not be subject to Senate filibuster. The motion for the previous question would terminate debate in both houses.

Walter Lippmann has made a similar suggestion. "To make our system work, it is essential that the initiative of the President be respected by Congress, and when he says a measure is of great national importance, his proposals should be accorded enough priority to bring them to a vote and a decision within a reasonable time—say three months."

Such are my personal recommendations for turning the Congress into an effective working partner with the executive and judicial branches of our federal government. But to convert such a program into reality a very large part of Congress will have to take a serious interest in reform. To rally support and achieve solid results, Senate Concurrent Resolution 1 was introduced early in January, 1963, by thirty Senators. Senator Clifford Case and I were the principal sponsors. Modeled on the LaFollette-Monroney resolution of 1945, it called for the creation of a joint Congressional committee of seven members from each House to make an over-all study of needed Congressional reorganization and to report back its recommendations to the Congress within a year of its passage. . . .

The need for such a study is obvious, and I have no doubt some sort of study will be authorized, if not immediately, then in the foreseeable future. . . . One way or another the massive job of Congressional reorganization and reform must get under way before it is too late and Congressional government breaks down under the strain of modern pressures for action.

Government by Concurrent Majority

JOHN FISCHER *

Every now and then somebody comes up with the idea that the party system in American politics is absurd because our two great parties don't stand for clearly contrasting principles, and that we would be better off if we had a conservative party and a radical or liberal party. It is a persuasive argument, especially for well-meaning people who have not had much first-hand experience in politics. You have probably heard it; it runs something like this:

"Both of the traditional American parties are outrageous frauds. Neither the Republicans nor the Democrats have any fundamental principles or ideology. They do not even have a program. In every campaign the platforms of both parties are simply collections of noble generalities, muffled in the vaguest possible language; and in each case the two platforms are very nearly identical.

"Obviously, then, both parties are merely machines for grabbing power and distributing favors. In their lust for office they are quite willing to make a deal with anybody who can deliver a sizable block of votes. As a result, each party has become an outlandish cluster of local machines and special interest groups which have nothing in common except a craving for the public trough.

"This kind of political system"—so the argument runs—"is clearly meaningless. A man of high principles can never hope to accomplish anything through the old parties, because they are not interested in principle. Moreover, the whole arrangement is so illogical that it affronts every intelligent citizen.

"We ought to separate the sheep from the goats—to herd all the progressives on one side of the fence and all the conservatives on the other. Then politics really will have some meaning; every campaign can be fought over clearly defined issues. The Europeans, who are more sophisticated politically than we simple Americans, discovered this long ago, and in each of their countries they have arranged a neat political spectrum running from Left to Right."

This argument pops up with special urgency whenever a third party

* Editor of *Harper's Magazine*. Author of *Why They Behave Like Russians,* and many articles on politics. The selection is from John Fischer, "Unwritten Rules of American Politics," *Harper's Magazine Reader* (Chicago, Bantam Books, 1953).

appears—Theodore Roosevelt's in 1912, Robert LaFollette's in 1924, or Henry Wallace's in 1948. And it sounds so plausible—at least on the surface—that many people have wondered why these splinter parties have always dwindled away after the election was over. Indeed, many veteran third-party enthusiasts have been able to account for their failure only by assuming a perverse and rock-headed stupidity among the American electorate.

There is, however, another possible explanation for the stubborn durability of our seemingly illogical two-party system; that it is more vigorous, more deeply rooted, and far better suited to our own peculiar needs than any European system would be; that it involves a more complex and subtle conception than the crude blacks and whites of the European ideological parties. There is considerable evidence, it seems to me, that our system—in spite of certain dangerous weaknesses—has on the whole worked out more successfully than the European.

Perhaps it is the very subtlety of the American political tradition which is responsible for the almost universal misunderstanding of it abroad. Every practicing American politician grasps its principles by instinct; if he does not, he soon retires into some less demanding profession. Moreover, the overwhelming majority of citizens have a sound working knowledge of the system, which they apply every day of their lives—though many of them might have a hard time putting that knowledge into words. There are almost no foreigners, however (except perhaps D. W. Brogan), who really understand the underlying theory. Even the editors of the London *Economist*—probably the most brilliant and well-informed group of journalists practicing anywhere today—display their bewilderment week after week. To them, and to virtually all other European observers, our whole political scene looks arbitrary, irrational, and dangerous.

Another reason for this misunderstanding lies in the fact that surprisingly little has been written about the rules of American politics during our generation. The newspapers, textbooks, and learned journals are running over with discussions of tactics and mechanics—but no one, so far as I know, has bothered to trace out the basic tradition for a good many years.

THE DOCTRINE OF THE CONCURRENT MAJORITY

In fact, the most useful discussion of this tradition which I have come across is the work of John C. Calhoun, published nearly a century ago. Today of course he is an almost forgotten figure, and many people take it for granted that his views were discredited for good by the Civil War. I know of only one writer—Peter F. Drucker—who has paid much attention to him in recent years. It was he who described Calhoun's ideas as "a major if not the only key to the understanding of what is specifically and uniquely American in our political system"; and I am indebted to Mr. Drucker for much of the case set forth here.

Calhoun summed up his political thought in what he called the Doctrine of the Concurrent Majority. He saw the United States as a nation of tremendous and frightening diversity—a collection of many different climates, races, cultures, religions, and economic patterns. He saw the constant tension among all these special interests, and he realized that the central problem of American politics was to find some way of holding these conflicting groups together.

It could not be done by force; no one group was strong enough to impose its will on all the others. The goal could be achieved only by compromise—and no real compromise could be possible if any threat of coercion lurked behind the door. Therefore, Calhoun reasoned, every vital decision in American life would have to be adopted by a "concurrent majority"—by which he meant, in effect, a unanimous agreement of all interested parties. No decision which affected the interests of the slaveholders, he argued, should be taken without their consent; and by implication he would have given a similar veto to every other special interest, whether it be labor, management, the Catholic church, old-age pensioners, the silver miners, or the corngrowers of the Middle West.

Under the goad of the slavery issue, Calhoun was driven to state his doctrine in an extreme and unworkable form. If every sectional interest had been given the explicit, legal veto power which he called for, the government obviously would have been paralyzed. (That, in fact, is precisely what seems to be happening today in the United Nations.) It is the very essence of the idea of "concurrent majority" that it cannot be made legal and official. It can operate effectively only as an informal, highly elastic, and generally accepted understanding.

Moreover, government by concurrent majority can exist only when no one power is strong enough to dominate completely, *and then only when all of the contending interest groups recognize and abide by certain rules of the game.*

UNWRITTEN RULES OF AMERICAN POLITICS

These rules are the fundamental bond of unity in American political life. They can be summed up as a habit of extraordinary toleration, plus "equality" in the peculiar American meaning of that term which cannot be translated into any other language, even into the English of Great Britain. Under these rules every group tacitly binds itself to tolerate the interests and opinions of every other group. It must not try to impose its views on others, nor can it press its own special interests to the point where they seriously endanger the interests of other groups or of the nation as a whole.

Furthermore, each group must exercise its implied veto with responsibility and discretion; and in times of great emergency it must forsake its veto right altogether. It dare not be intransigent or doctrinaire. It must make every conceivable effort to compromise, relying on its veto only as a last resort. For if any player wields this weapon recklessly, the game will break up—or all the other players will turn on him in anger, suspend the rules for the time being, and maul those very interests he is trying so desperately to protect. That was what happened in 1860, when the followers of Calhoun carried his doctrine to an unbearable extreme. Much the same thing, on a less violent scale, happened to American business interests in 1933 and to the labor unions in 1947.

This is the somewhat elusive sense, it seems to me, in which Calhoun's theory has been adopted by the American people. But elusive and subtle as it may be, it remains the basic rule of the game of politics in this country—and in this country alone. Nothing comparable exists in any other nation, although the British, in a different way, have applied their own rules of responsibility and self-restraint.

It is a rule which operates unofficially and entirely outside the Constitution—but it has given us a method by which all the official and Constitutional organs of government can be made to work. It also provides a means of selecting leaders on all levels of our political life, for hammering out policies, and for organizing and managing the conquest of political power.

The way in which this tradition works in practice can be observed most easily in Congress. Anyone who has ever tried to push through a piece of legislation quickly discovers that the basic units of organization on Capitol Hill are not the parties, but the so-called blocs, which are familiar to everyone who reads a newspaper. There are dozens of them —the farm bloc, the silver bloc, the friends of labor, the business group, the isolationists, the public power bloc—and they all cut across party lines.

They are loosely organized and pretty blurred at the edges, so that every Congressman belongs at different times to several different blocs. Each of them represents a special interest group. Each of them ordinarily works hand-in-hand with that group's Washington lobby. In passing, it might be noted that these lobbies are by no means the cancerous growth which is sometimes pictured in civics textbooks. They have become an indispensable part of the political machine—the accepted channel through which American citizens make their wishes known and play their day-to-day role in the process of government. Nor is their influence measured solely by the size of the bankrolls and propaganda apparatus which they have at their disposal. Some of the smallest and poorest lobbies often are more effective than their well-heeled rivals. For example, Russell Smith, the one-man lobby of the Farmers Union, was largely responsible for conceiving and nursing through Congress the Employment Act of 1946, one of the most far-reaching measures adopted since the war.

Now it is an unwritten but firm rule of Congress that no important bloc shall ever be voted down—under normal circumstances—on any matter which touches its own vital interests. Each of them, in other words, has a tacit right of veto on legislation in which it is primarily concerned. The ultimate expression of this right is the institution—uniquely American—of the filibuster in the Senate. Recently it has acquired a bad name among liberals because the Southern conservatives have used it ruthlessly to fight off civil rights legislation and protect white supremacy. Not so long ago, however, the filibuster was the stoutest weapon of such men as Norris and the LaFollettes in defending many a progressive cause.

Naturally no bloc wants to exercise its veto power except when it is absolutely forced to—for this is a negative power, and one which is always subject to retaliation. Positive power to influence legislation, on the other hand, can be gained only by conciliation, compromise, and endless horse-trading.

The farm bloc, for instance, normally needs no outside aid to halt the passage of a hostile bill. As a last resort, three or four strong-lunged statesmen from the corn belt can always filibuster it to death in the Senate. If the bloc wants to put through a measure to support agricultural prices, however, it can succeed only by enlisting the help of other powerful special interest groups. Consequently, it must always be careful not to antagonize any potential ally by a reckless use of the veto; and it must be willing to pay for such help by throwing its support from time to time behind legislation sought by the labor bloc, the National Association of Manufacturers, or the school-teachers' lobby.

The classic alliance of this sort was formed in the early days of the New Deal, when most of the Roosevelt legislation was shoved onto the statute books by a temporary coalition of the farm bloc and urban labor, occasionally reinforced by such minor allies as the public power group and spokesmen for the northern Negroes. Mr. Roosevelt's political genius rested largely on his ability to put together a program which would offer something to each of these groups without fatally antagonizing any of them, and then to time the presentation of each bill so that he would always retain enough bargaining power to line up a Congressional majority. It also was necessary for him to avoid the veto of the business group, which viewed much of this legislation as a barbarous assault upon its privileges; and for this purpose he employed another traditional technique, which we shall examine a little later.

This process of trading blocs of votes is generally known as log-rolling, and frequently it is deplored by the more innocent type of reformer. Such pious disapproval has no effect whatever on any practicing politician. He knows that log-rolling is a sensible and reasonably fair device, and that without it Congress could scarcely operate at all.

In fact, Congress gradually has developed a formal apparatus—the committee system—which is designed to make the log-rolling process as smooth and efficient as possible. There is no parallel system anywhere; the committees of Parliament and of the Continental legislative bodies work in an entirely different way.

Obviously the main business of Congress—the hammering out of a series of compromises between many special interest groups—cannot be conducted satisfactorily on the floor of the House or Senate. The meetings there are too large and far too public for such delicate negotiations. Moreover, every speech delivered on the floor must be aimed primarily at the voters back home, and not at the other members of the chamber. Therefore, Congress—especially the House—does nearly all its work in the closed sessions of its various committees, simply because the committee room is the only place where it is possible to arrange a compromise acceptable to all major interests affected.

For this reason, it is a matter of considerable importance to get a bill before the proper committee. Each committee serves as a forum for a particular cluster of special interests, and the assignment of a bill to a specific committee often decides which interest groups shall be recognized officially as affected by the measure and therefore entitled to a hand in its drafting. "Who is to have standing before the committee" is the technical term, and it is this decision that frequently decides the fate of the legislation.

Calhoun's principles of the concurrent majority and of sectional compromise operate just as powerfully, though sometimes less obviously, in every other American political institution. Our cabinet, for example, is the only one in the world where the members are charged by law with the representation of special interests—labor, agriculture, commerce, and so on. In other countries, each agency of government is at least presumed to act for the nation as a whole; here most agencies are expected to behave as servants for one interest or another. The Veterans' Administration, to cite the most familiar case, is frankly intended to look out for Our Boys; the Maritime Board is to look out for the shipping industry; the National Labor Relations Board, as originally established under the Wagner Act, was explicitly intended to build up the bargaining power of the unions.

Even within a single department, separate agencies are sometimes set up to represent conflicting interests. Thus in the Department of Agriculture under the New Deal the old Triple-A became primarily an instrument of the large-scale commercial farmers, as represented by their lobby, the Farm Bureau Federation; while the Farm Security Administration went to bat for the tenants, the farm laborers, and the little subsistence farmers, as represented by the Farmers Union.

This is one reason why federal agencies often struggle so bitterly against each other, and why the position of the administration as a whole on any question can be determined only after a long period of interbureau squabbling and compromise. Anyone who was in Washington during the war will remember how these goings-on always confused and alarmed our British allies.

Calhoun's laws also govern the selection of virtually every candidate for public office. The mystery of "eligibility" which has eluded most foreign observers simply means that a candidate must not be unacceptable to any important special interest group—a negative rather than a positive qualification. A notorious case of this process at work was the selection of Mr. Truman as the Democrats' Vice Presidential candidate in 1944. As Edward J. Flynn, the Boss of the Bronx, has pointed out in his memoirs, Truman was the one man "who would hurt . . . least" as Roosevelt's running mate. Many stronger men were disqualified, Flynn explained, by the tacit veto of one sectional interest or another. Wallace was unacceptable to the businessmen and to the many local party machines. Byrnes was distasteful to the Catholics, the Negroes, and organized labor. Rayburn came from the wrong part of the country. Truman, however, came from a border state, his labor record was good, he had not antagonized the conservatives, and—as Flynn put it—"he had never made any 'racial' remarks. He just dropped into the slot."

The same kind of considerations govern the selection of candidates right down to the county, city, and precinct levels. Flynn, one of the most successful political operators of our time, explained in some detail the complicated job of making up a ticket in his own domain. Each of the main population groups in the Bronx—Italians, Jews, and Irish Catholics—must be properly represented on the list of nominees, and so must each of the main geographical divisions. The result was a ticket which sounded like the roster of the Brooklyn Dodgers: Loreto, Delagi, Lyman, Joseph, Lyons, and Foley.

Comparable traditions govern the internal political life of the American Legion, the Federation of Women's Clubs, university student bodies, labor unions, Rotary Clubs, and the thousands of other quasi-political institutions which are so characteristic of our society and which give us such a rich fabric of spontaneous local government.

The stronghold of Calhoun's doctrine, however, is the American party—the wonder and despair of foreigners who cannot fit it into any of their concepts of political life.

"NOT TO DIVIDE BUT TO UNITE"

The purpose of European parties is, of course, to divide men of different ideologies into coherent and disciplined organizations. The historic role of the American party, on the other hand, is not to divide but to unite. That task was imposed by simple necessity. If a division into ideological parties had been attempted, in addition to all the other centrifugal forces in this country, it very probably would have proved impossible to hold the nation together. The Founding Fathers understood this thoroughly; hence Washington's warning against "factions."

Indeed, on the one occasion when we did develop two ideological parties, squarely opposing each other on an issue of principle, the result was civil war. Fortunately, that was our last large-scale experiment with a third party formed on an ideological basis—for in its early days that is just what the Republican party was.

Its radical wing, led by such men as Thaddeus Stevens, Seward, and Chase, made a determined and skillful effort to substitute principles for interests as the foundations of American political life. Even within their own party, however, they were opposed by such practical politicians as Lincoln and Johnson—men who distrusted fanaticism in any form—and by the end of the Reconstruction period the experiment had been abandoned. American politics then swung back into its normal path and has never veered far away from it since. Although Calhoun's cause was defeated, his political theory came through the Civil War stronger than ever.

The result is that the American party has no permanent program and no fixed aim, except to win elections. Its one purpose is to unite the largest possible number of divergent interest groups in the pursuit of power. Its unity is one of compromise, not of dogma. It must—if it hopes to succeed—appeal to considerable numbers on both the left and the right, to rich and poor, Protestant and Catholic, farmer and industrial worker, native and foreign born.

It must be ready to bid for the support of any group that can deliver a sizable chunk of votes, accepting that group's program with whatever modifications may be necessary to reconcile the other members of the party. If sun worship, or Existentialism, or the nationalization of industry should ever attract any significant following in this country, you can be sure that both parties would soon whip up a plank designed to win it over.

This ability to absorb new ideas (along with the enthusiasts behind them) and to mold them into a shape acceptable to the party's standpatters is, perhaps, the chief measure of vitality in the party's leadership. Such ideas almost never germinate within the party itself. They are stolen —very often from third parties.

Indeed, the historic function of third parties has been to sprout new issues, nurse them along until they have gathered a body of supporters worth stealing, and then to turn them over (often reluctantly) to the major parties. A glance at the old platforms of the Populists, the Bull Moosers, and the Socialists will show what an astonishingly high percentage of their once-radical notions have been purloined by both Republicans and Democrats—and enacted into law. Thus the income tax, child-labor laws, minimum wages, regulation of railroads and utilities, and old-age pensions have all become part of the American Way of Life.

While each major party must always stand alert to grab a promising new issue, it also must be careful never to scare off any of the big, established interest groups. For as soon as it alienates any one of them, it finds itself in a state of crisis.

During the nineteen-thirties and -forties the Republicans lost much of their standing as a truly national party because they had made themselves unacceptable to labor. Similarly, the Democrats, during the middle stage of the New Deal, incurred the wrath of the business interests. Ever since Mr. Truman was plumped into the White House, the Democratic leadership has struggled desperately—though rather ineptly—to regain the confidence of businessmen without at the same time driving organized labor out of the ranks. It probably would be safe to predict that if the Republican party is to regain a long period of health, it must make an equally vigorous effort to win back the confidence of labor. For the permanent veto of any major element in American society means political death—as the ghosts of the Federalists and Whigs can testify.

WEAKNESSES OF THE AMERICAN POLITICAL SYSTEM

The weaknesses of the American political system are obvious—much more obvious, in fact, than its virtues. These weaknesses have been so sharply criticized for the past hundred years, by a procession of able analysts ranging from Walter Bagehot to Thomas K. Finletter, that it is hardly necessary to mention them here. It is enough to note that most of the criticism has been aimed at two major flaws.

First, it is apparent that the doctrine of the concurrent majority is a negative one—a principle of inaction. A strong government, capable of rapid and decisive action, is difficult to achieve under a system which forbids it to do anything until virtually everybody acquiesces. In times of crisis, a dangerously long period of debate and compromise usually is necessary before any administration can carry out the drastic measures needed. The depression of the early thirties, the crisis in foreign policy which ended only with Pearl Harbor, the crisis of the Marshall program all illustrate this recurring problem.

This same characteristic of our system gives undue weight to the small but well-organized pressure group—especially when it is fighting *against* something. Hence a few power companies were able to block for twenty years the sensible use of the Muscle Shoals dam which eventually became the nucleus of TVA, and—in alliance with the railroads, rail unions, and Eastern port interests—they [held] up development of the St. Lawrence Waterway. An even more flagrant example is the silver bloc, representing only a tiny fraction of the American people. It has been looting the Treasury for a generation by a series of outrageous silver subsidy and purchase laws.

The negative character of our political rules also makes it uncommonly difficult for us to choose a President. Many of our outstanding political operatives—notably those who serve in the Senate—are virtually barred from a Presidential nomination because they are forced to get on record on too many issues. Inevitably they offend some important interest group, and therefore become "unavailable." Governors, who can keep their mouths shut on most national issues, have a much better chance to reach the White House. Moveover, the very qualities of caution and inoffensiveness which make a good candidate—Harding and Coolidge come most readily to mind—are likely to make a bad President.

An even more serious flaw in our scheme of politics is the difficulty in finding anybody to speak for the country as a whole. Calhoun would have argued that the national interest is merely the sum of all the various special interests, and therefore needs no spokesmen of its own—but in this case he clearly was wrong.

In practice, we tend to settle sectional and class conflicts at the expense of the nation as a whole—with results painful to all of us. The labor troubles in the spring of 1946, for instance, could be settled only on a basis acceptable to *both* labor and management: that is, on the basis of higher wages *plus* higher prices. The upshot was an inflationary spiral which damaged everybody. Countless other instances, from soil erosion to the rash of billboards along our highways, bear witness to the

American tendency to neglect matters which are "only" of national interest, and therefore are left without a recognized sponsor.

Over the generations we have developed a series of practices and institutions which partly remedy these weaknesses, although we are still far from a complete cure. One such development has been the gradual strengthening of the Presidency as against Congress. As the only man elected by all the people, the President inevitably has had to take over many of the policy-making and leadership functions which the Founding Fathers originally assigned to the legislators. This meant, of course, that he could no longer behave merely as an obedient executor of the will of Congress, but was forced into increasingly frequent conflicts with Capitol Hill.

Today we have come to recognize that this conflict is one of the most important obligations of the Presidency. No really strong executive tries to avoid it—he accepts it as an essential part of his job. If he simply tries to placate the pressure groups which speak through Congress, history writes him down as a failure. For it is his duty to enlist the support of many minorities for measures rooted in the national interest, reaching beyond their own immediate concern—and, if necessary, to stand up against the ravening minorities for the interest of the whole.

In recent times this particular part of the President's job has been made easier by the growth of the Theory of Temporary Emergencies. All of us—or nearly all—have come around to admitting that in time of emergency special interest groups must forego their right of veto. As a result, the President often is tempted to scare up an emergency to secure legislation which could not be passed under any other pretext. Thus, most of the New Deal bills were introduced as "temporary emergency measures," although they were clearly intended to be permanent from the very first; for in no other way could Mr. Roosevelt avoid the veto of the business interests.

Again, in 1939 the threat of war enabled the President to push through much legislation which would have been impossible under normal circumstances.

ELEMENTS OF STRENGTH

Because we have been so preoccupied with trying to patch up the flaws in our system, we have often overlooked its unique elements of strength. The chief of these is its ability to minimize conflict—not by suppressing the conflicting forces, but by absorbing and utilizing them. The result is a society which is both free and reasonably stable—a government which is as strong and effective as most dictatorships, but which can still adapt itself to social change.

The way in which the American political organism tames down the extremists of both the left and right is always fascinating to watch. Either party normally is willing to embrace any group or movement which can deliver votes—but in return it requires these groups to adjust their programs to fit the traditions, beliefs, and prejudices of the majority of the people. The fanatics, the implacable radicals cannot hope to get to first base in American politics until they abandon their fanaticism and learn the habits of conciliation. As a consequence, it is almost impossible for political movements here to become entirely irresponsible and to draw strength from the kind of demagogic obstruction which has nurtured both Communist and Fascist movements abroad.

The same process which gentles down the extremists also prods along the political laggards. As long as it is in a state of health, each American party has a conservative and a liberal wing. Sometimes one is dominant, sometimes the other—but even when the conservative element is most powerful, it must reckon with the left-wingers in its own family. At the moment the Republican party certainly is in one of its more conservative phases; yet it contains such men as Senators Morse, Aiken, Flanders, and Tobey, who are at least as progressive as most of the old New Dealers.* They, and their counterparts in the Democratic party, exert a steady tug to the left which prevents either party from lapsing into complete reaction.

The strength of this tug is indicated by the fact that the major New Deal reforms have now been almost universally accepted. In the mid-thirties, many leading Republicans, plus many conservative Democrats, were hell-bent on wiping out social security, TVA, SEC, minimum-wage laws, rural electrification, and all the other dread innovations of the New Deal. Today no Presidential aspirant would dare suggest the repeal of a single one of them. In this country there simply is no place for a hard core of irreconcilable reactionaries, comparable to those political groups in France which have never yet accepted the reforms of the French Revolution.

This American tendency to push extremists of both the left and right toward a middle position has enabled us, so far, to escape class warfare. This is no small achievement for any political system; for class warfare cannot be tolerated by a modern industrial society. If it seriously threatens, it is bound to be suppressed by some form of totalitarianism, as it has been in Germany, Spain, Italy, Russia, and most of Eastern Europe.

* [This was written in 1948.]

In fact, suppression might be termed the normal method of settling conflicts in continental Europe, where parties traditionally have been drawn up along ideological battle lines. Every political campaign becomes a religious crusade; each party is fanatically convinced that it and it alone has truth by the tail; each party is certain that its opponents not only are wrong, but wicked. If the sacred ideology is to be established beyond challenge, no heresy can be tolerated. Therefore it becomes a duty not only to defeat the enemy at the polls, but to wipe him out. Any suggestion of compromise must be rejected as treason and betrayal of the true faith. The party must be disciplined like an army, and if it cannot win by other means it must be ready to take up arms in deadly fact.

Under this kind of political system the best that can be hoped for is a prolonged deadlock between parties which are too numerous and weak to exterminate one another. The classic example is prewar France, where six revolutions or near-revolutions broke out within a century, where cabinets fell every weekend, and no government could ever become strong enough to govern effectively. The more usual outcome is a complete victory for one ideology or another, after a brief period of electioneering, turmoil, and fighting in the streets; then comes the liquidation of the defeated.

Because this sort of ideological politics is so foreign to our native tradition, neither Socialists, Communists, nor Fascists have ever been accepted as normal parties. So long as that tradition retains its very considerable vitality, it seems to me unlikely that any third party founded on an ideological basis can take root. The notion of a ruthless and unlimited class struggle, the concept of a master race, a fascist élite, or a proletariat which is entitled to impose its will on all others—these are ideas which are incompatible with the main current of American political life. The uncompromising ideologist, of whatever faith, appears in our eyes peculiarly "un-American," simply because he cannot recognize the rule of the concurrent majority, nor can he accept the rules of mutual toleration which are necessary to make it work. Unless he forsakes his ideology, he cannot even understand that basic principle of American politics which was perhaps best expressed by Judge Learned Hand: "The spirit of liberty is the spirit which is not too sure that it is right."

Topic 24

THE FILIBUSTER

The Public Business Must Go Forward

JACOB K. JAVITS *

[At the opening of the 1959 session of Congress, some Democratic and Republican Senators, including Senator Javits, proposed a substantial change in Senate Rule XXII so that debate could be shut off by a simple majority of the whole Senate membership. The Senate rejected this proposal and adopted a plan by which cloture could be made operative by vote of two-thirds of the senators on the floor. While Javits' argument and that of Lindsay Rogers were addressed to the old Rule, they have retained their essential force insofar as the prevailing Rule still requires an extraordinary majority to impose an end to debate, and remains a source of continuing controversy. One such controversy, in fact, arose in the Senate in 1964 over the civil rights bill. In this instance, after a 75-day filibuster, cloture was achieved by a vote of 71 to 29, the necessary two-thirds margin (with four votes to spare).]

After careful study of the hearing testimony and of the historic conceptions of the function of the Senate, I am convinced that rule XXII needs amendment to end its veto power on behalf of a small minority; while at the same time assuring the opportunity for full debate and discussion of any subject in the Senate, which has been called the greatest deliberative body on earth.

I do not believe that the present rule XXII serves the purpose of deliberation within the Senate or of education of the public generally. No one questions those two objectives. What I do question is a delegation of the power and responsibility of the majority to a determined minority, which has been and can be again and again an arbitrary block to action, contrary to the will of the majority of this body and of the people to whom they are responsible. Indeed, it seems to me prophetic that this report is filed at an hour of basic crisis in the defense of our country when the weapons which challenge us are precisely so mortally dangerous because of the speed with which they may be effectively used to destroy us. In such a time—and there is nothing temporary about this new frame of reference—there is a justifiable demand for making our organs of decision conform to the challenge. How appropriate, then, to consider

* United States Senator from New York. The selection is from *Proposed Amendments to Rule XXII of the Standing Rules of the Senate* (Senate Report No. 1509, 85th Congress, 2d Session), pp. 9–19. By permission.

now a rule of debate which can and has paralyzed decision in the Senate and which can be used by a determined minority to paralyze it on any subject—not alone civil rights. Rule XXII as now written was archaic long before the first Russian earth satellite was launched and is even more so now.

Careful research on the development of the United States Government from its initial period under the Articles of Confederation, through the Constitutional Convention of 1787, when studied in the light of the contemporaneous writings of the Founding Fathers, convinces me that the power which now stems from rule XXII was not even contemplated at the time. On the contrary, from the expressed views of Madison, Hamilton, and others, a method of parliamentary procedure premised on rule XXII would have been violently opposed had it been suggested.

For the premise of rule XXII violates fundamental parliamentary law. It is at odds with early Senate procedures, British Parliamentary practice, and, almost without exception, is contrary to all our State legislative rules of procedure.

In the early Senate, simple majority cloture was used and the "previous question" as a parliamentary device was available under Senate rules and in Jefferson's Senate Manual to close debates. Even after reference to the "previous question" was dropped from the standing rules (in 1806), the presiding officer's power to rule on questions of relevancy and order could have prevented abuse through unrestrained irrelevancies. The conjunction of the lack of cloture and the lack of enforcement of a rule of relevancy (after 1872) made possible the modern veto-type filibuster.

Its fullest development and its most flagrant abuses have occurred following the Civil War in opposition to civil rights legislation—mostly in the last 35 years. While rule XXII did not prevent enactment of the Civil Rights Act of the last session, I believe it did profoundly affect its final formulation. . . .

The realistic effect of [both the old and new rule XXII] is that a small minority of Senators, if sufficiently determined, can by use of a filibuster absolutely prevent the Senate from taking action (in the only way it can—by voting) even though a great majority of Senators desires to come to a vote. Voting is the final method of resolution of national issues contemplated in the Constitution. Protracted speaking which is not intended to illuminate that decision, but to prevent its occurrence, makes a mockery of freedom of speech by confusing it with freedom to obstruct. It does not require great imagination to grasp the significance of this potential power in the hands of Members bent on influencing enactment or the course of particular proposals, without the necessity for persuasion.

The basic issue underlying the problem of cloture is whether we shall permit the Senate, resting as it does on the premise of majority rule, to function at all; to fulfill its legislative purpose; or whether we shall permit the Congress to be stultified by the undemocratic and, in essence, unparliamentary device of filibuster in the Senate—even though cloaked in the senatorial toga of rule XXII. . . .

THE POWER OF THE FILIBUSTER AS A VETO, WITH A CASE HISTORY OF THE CIVIL RIGHTS BILL OF 1957

The *ability* to carry on a filibuster can affect the kind of legislation passed by the Senate even though no actual filibuster is undertaken. The incidence of a filibuster or the certain knowledge that a filibuster would be organized has made the majority come to terms before. The mere threat that a filibuster of great length would be undertaken against some proposal or unless amendment to a bill was accepted has in effect resulted in the majority of the Senate acquiescing in changes in legislation which otherwise they would probably not have considered wise or desirable.

Careful study of the legislative background and history of the civil rights bill of 1957 and the changes that occurred during the long Senate debate bears out this conclusion and illustrates the pervasive and subtle effect of rule XXII. . . . It became apparent that a bloc of Senators had selected part III as the most objectionable feature of the bill from their viewpoint; and that they were prepared to use every parliamentary device to prevent the enactment of a law which would contain the authorization for the Attorney General on his own motion to enforce through civil action (as an alternative to criminal prosecutions in existing law) the provisions of the 14th amendment to the Constitution. I believe that a number of Senators, among whom were some who favored the retention of part III, felt that insistence on part III would inevitably force the Senators from the South into a filibuster, with the ensuing possibility that no bill at all might be passed. . . .

I have no doubt that if part III had been retained in the bill the Senate would have faced the necessity of a long filibuster which could be blocked only if a large majority were sufficiently determined to sit out the long dreary months that would have been involved. In that interim, no other business could have been transacted and Congress would have been at a standstill. In these times, with important pending legislation, this was a risk to which, naturally, Members of the Senate should give thoughtful consideration. The determined proponents of part III were fully aware of the consequences of insisting upon it. Schedules were worked out for around-the-clock coverage of the Senate floor, Members had beds installed in their offices, the staff details were worked out for a 24-hour operation. Senator Russell of Georgia, the leader of the southern bloc of Senators, was interviewed on a nationwide television program, Face the Nation, on July 21, 1957. Pertinent excerpts of the interview transcript inserted in the Congressional Record of July 22, 1957, indicate clearly the position of the minority:

> Mr. SHADEL. But, Senator, is there any feeling in the Senate that this bill is going to go through, as is, without modifications?
>
> Senator RUSSELL. Not on my part because I will certainly die fighting it in my tracks before this vicious bill could go through, and I would feel the same way if it were aimed at any section of the country. . . .
>
> Mr. LAWRENCE. Well, would it be the intention of the South, under the circumstances that I can foresee and that you can foresee at the moment, to talk this bill to death?
>
> Senator RUSSELL. I can't say that, Mr. Lawrence, without seeing the bill and if it has these very vicious provisions in it, well, you may be sure that we will use every means at our command to fight it to the very death because it is a very vicious piece of legislation in its present form.

Decision by ordeal was imminent.

No one who participated in the Senate's deliberations could escape the sense of drama, or the mounting tension and concern over the threat inherent in a filibuster. It was in this atmosphere that crucial decisions were made resulting in a number of changes in the legislation, including the elimination of part III. In closing on this point, I should like to add that Little Rock has demonstrated that the decision taken by the Senate to eliminate part III was unwise and that the risk of a stubborn filibuster should have been faced. . . .

Close observers of the legislative process in Congress are aware of this force—of the filibuster—in other legislative compromises which have been adopted, and could cite other examples of the effect of the filibuster on legislation. Vice President Charles G. Dawes, a keen student of Senate proceedings, described the effect of the filibuster in the following words:

> The right of filibuster does not affect simply legislation defeated but, in much greater degree, legislation passed, continually weaving into our laws, which should be framed in the public interest alone, modifications dictated by personal and sectional interest as distinguished from the public interest.

It is no answer to say, as some do say, that such power prevents or softens bad legislation. Of course, it may do that; because legislative proposals subject to a successful filibuster do not get enacted. If any specific action is bad, inaction may be preferred. If all change were bad, then whatever inhibited it would be wise. But the millennium is not here and events do not wait, even if governments do. This built-in stalemate as a permanent method of procedure is opposed to our American spirit and genius.

If the men who conceived our Constitution had thought we needed the concurrence of the majority of two Houses, the assent of the President, and in addition the forbearance of 33 Senators to make law, I assume they would have said so. If this additional check on governmental action is necessary, let us amend the Constitution. The standing rules of the Senate were not drafted in Philadelphia in 1787. The American people neither concurred in them nor agreed to be bound by them—nor did the States. In each Congress, as adopted or acquiesed in, and, to the extent they are constitutional, they bind our Senate procedure so long as they remain unchanged, but they are not the supreme law. They are not the bulwark of free speech and States rights; nor are they immutable. . . .

One may, of course, argue that the existence of rule XXII by which any substantial group of Senators can conduct a filibuster so as to act as a veto, constitutes a "power" which may be exercised on behalf of the States represented by the filibustering Senators; but it is the power neither of persuasion nor of public education. It is an arbitrary power unsanctioned by the Constitution and indeed in direct conflict with its spirit.

Far from securing any constitutional balance, rule XXII seriously disturbs it. The Constitution, in article I, section 5, clause 1, states that—

> A majority of each [House] shall constitute a quorum to do business.

That is, 49 Senators are sufficient for the transaction of legislative business. A majority of this quorum is required to assent to the passage of a normal bill. Yet cloture may not be invoked unless at least 64 Members are present and vote for cloture. Legislation of the most profound national effect requires the assent of fewer than half of those required to bring a filibuster to a reasonable close so that that very legislation may be acted upon. I fail to see what balance is here maintained by continuance of the present rule. Alexander Hamilton in arguing, in the Federalist Papers, for the adoption of the Constitution he had helped frame, set forth the need for a totally different balance (Federalist Papers No. 22):

> To give a minority a negative upon the majority (which is always the case where more than a majority is requisite to a decision), is, in its tendency, to subject the sense of the greater number to that of the lesser. . . . This is one of those refinements which, in practice, has an effect the reverse of what is expected from it in theory. The necessity of unanimity in public bodies, or of something approaching toward it, has been founded upon a supposition that it would contribute to security. But its real operation is to embarrass the administration, to destroy the energy of the Gov-

ernment, and to substitute the pleasure, caprice, or arifices of an insignificant, turbulent, or corrupt junto, to the regular deliberations and decisions of a respectable majority. . . . The public business must, in some way or other, go forward. If a pertinacious minority can control the opinion of a majority respecting the best mode of conducting it, the majority, in order that something may be done, must conform to the views of the minority; and thus the sense of the smaller number will overrule that of the greater, and give a tone to the national proceedings. Hence, tedious delays; continual negotiation and intrigue; contemptible compromises of the public good, and yet, in such a system, it is even happy when such compromises can take place: for upon some occasions things will not admit of accommodation: and then the measures of government must be injuriously suspended, or fatally defeated. It is often, by the impracticability of obtaining the concurrence of the necessary number of votes, kept in a state of inaction. Its situation must always savor of weakness, sometimes border upon anarchy. . . .

When the concurrence of a large number is required by the Constitution to the doing of any national act, we are apt to rest satisfied that all is safe, because nothing improper will be likely to be done; but we forget how much good may be prevented, and how much ill may be produced, by the power of hindering the doing what may be necessary; and of keeping affairs in the same unfavorable posture in which they may happen to stand at particular periods.

. . . There was a great question of the proper balance of State representation in the Congress in 1787. A study of the debates of the Constitutional Convention shows very clearly that the decision to establish 2 Houses, one to be based on a reference to population, and the other to have 2 Senators from each State regardless of size or population, was the compromise between the delegates from big States and the delegates from the small States. This was the only basis on which the small States would agree to join the Federal Union. This was the great compromise that gave the small States an equal measure of legislative power with the more populous States in this body.

As far as the big States are concerned, according to Madison and others devoted to the principle of proportional representation, they had given enough and more than enough when they finally agreed that each State should have two votes in the Senate. No one then dreamed that in the future Senators would want to upset this balance and add an additional check by a small minority of one-third upon the power of a majority of the Senate as so constituted. This, of course, was long prior to the time when John C. Calhoun developed his theory of concurrent majorities under which legislation favored by a majority in the country as a whole or in the Congress would be subject to the veto of a majority of each and every sectional interest in the country.

This kind of balance, which the opponents of civil-rights legislation wish to retain in the Senate, is a modern version of Calhoun's "concurrent majorities." It was such a sectional right of veto and interposition that Calhoun and other States-rights advocates urged during the debates, in and out of Congress, that led up to the Civil War. This type of imbalance, however, finds no support in the Constitution nor in current practice outside of rule XXII.[1]

Senator Underwood of Alabama said, with respect to the filibuster against the Dyer anti-lynching bill, as follows:

> We are not disguising what is being done on this side of the Chamber. It must be apparent, not only to the Senate but to the country, that an effort is being made to prevent the consideration of a certain bill, and I want to be perfectly candid about it. It is known throughout the country generally as a "force" bill. . . .
>
> *I do not say that captiously. I think all men here know that under the rules of the Senate when 15 or 20 or 25 men say that you cannot pass a certain bill, it cannot be passed. . . .*
>
> I want to say right now to the Senate that if the majority party insists on this procedure they are not going to pass the bill, and they are not going to do any other business. . . .
>
> You know you cannot pass it. Then let us go along and attend to the business of the country. [Emphasis supplied.]

Shortly thereafter he posed the dilemma which the Senate faced even more concisely:

> There is but one way for the Senate now to get down to work and transact the business of the Government before the 4th of March, and that is to get a final disposition of this force bill before anything else is done. Pass it if you can; abandon it if we force you to do so. . . .
>
> So long as the Senate has the rules that it has now, you know just as well as I know that I am standing here that you cannot pass it; and, more than that, the country does not want you to pass it.

The reality of the use of the filibuster as a veto has been borne out by the experience of the intervening years. As my colleague, Senator Kuchel, of California, put it last summer in the hearings before this subcommittee:

> How can any reasonable person uphold such tactics as those which occurred some years ago when the Senate ludicrously debated for 2 weeks a motion to amend the Chaplain's prayer?

Permitting a Senator or a group of Senators to talk for hours and days on any conceivable subject or on no subject in order to consume time and prevent the Senate from voting, affords no dignity to the Senate and

[1] The paralyzing effect of the minority veto is clearly evident in the deliberations of the United Nations Security Council.

adds nothing to its deliberative function. Reading recipes for "pot licker," "fried oysters," quoting from Aesops Fables,[2] and otherwise talking in utter irrelevancies does nothing to enhance the Senate's standing as a great deliberative body.

Senators have a right—and freely exercise it—to express their views on any question before the Senate or before the country. Without doubt it would be a violation of the letter and the spirit of the Constitution to deny or even seriously abridge the right of debate. But, it is also a most flagrant violation of the spirit of the Constitution to clothe this body with forms of procedure by which it may be blocked in the exercise of the legislative powers, and thereby suspended of every other function except that of speaking. The Senate has a duty to debate, but it is likewise a constitutional duty of a majority of this body to act, and with some reasonable expedition. We are obligated not only to pass laws, but also to pass them in time to meet the public need and the general welfare of the country.

Some observers have declared that, far from enhancing the Senate's deliberative function, the right to filibuster has all but destroyed it. Vice President Dawes, for example, said of the veto power of the filibuster:

> The Senate is not and cannot be a properly deliberative body, giving due consideration to the passage of all laws, unless it allots its time for work according to the relative importance of its duties, as do all other great parliamentary bodies. It has, however, through the right of unlimited debate surrendered to the whim and personal purposes of individuals and minorities its right to allot its own time. Only the establishment of majority cloture will enable the Senate to make itself a properly deliberative body. This is impossible when it must sit idly by and see time needed for deliberation frittered away in frivolous and irrelevant talk, indulged in by individuals and minorities for ulterior purposes.

Yet, the Senators who argue that rule XXII should be retained in its present form support this retention as necessary to its deliberative character. I certainly agree that the Senate is a forum of great debate, deliberation, and revision; but I submit that it owes nothing to rule XXII for achieving this distinction. It has achieved that eminence despite the rule.

[2] During the filibuster against the extension of a skeletonized NRA, Senator Long discussed various recipes at great length. This talk continued for 15½ hours and included the reading of long passages from works of Victor Hugo and a reading and discussion of the United States Constitution, article by article, without any necessary reference to the pending business. (See *Congressional Record,* vol. 79, pt. 8, pp. 9122 et seq.)

On June 20, 1936, Senator Rush D. Holt of West Virginia successfully filibustered against passage of a coal conservation bill by reading Aesops Fables to the Senate. The Senate finally adjourned, sine die, without ever voting on the bill.

Barrier Against Steamrollers

LINDSAY ROGERS *

"The Senate of the United States is the only legislative body in the world which cannot act when its majority is ready for action." Thus Woodrow Wilson early in 1917 when a Senate filibuster killed his proposal to arm American merchant ships. The "little group of willful men" were successful only because we then had "short sessions" of Congress that had to come to an end on March 4. The check was not a catastrophe. The ships were armed under authority conferred by an old statute that had been forgotten.

In 1917 the Senate was powerless to end a debate so long as any senator insisted on holding the floor, but debate can now be ended by a vote of two-thirds of the "Senators duly chosen and sworn." It is this much-debated Rule XXII that the Northern liberals hope to change in order to prevent Southern senators from using a filibuster to prevent the passage of drastic civil-rights legislation.

The Northern liberals propose two amendments. The first of these is that two days after a petition has been filed to end debate, two-thirds of the Senate present and voting may so decree. This is not very important; if such a cloture resolution were up, practically all of the "Senators duly chosen and sworn" would be present and vote. But the Northern liberals have a further proposal: that fifteen days after the filing of a petition to end debate, a majority of the entire Senate may so decree. Garrulity would still be permitted; each senator could speak for an hour, but under such circumstances only the filibusterers would do so. Then a vote. No longer could a filibuster interpose a veto as it has sometimes done in the past.

Such a change in the rule would, I think, be a mistake. Not so, says [former] Senator Irving M. Ives (R., New York), who maintains that "the principle of majority rule is at stake." It is only in the Senate of the United States, exclaims Senator Clifford P. Case (R., New Jersey), that an opposition must be beaten down by "physical exhaustion" and where "the medieval practice of trial by ordeal still survives."

With great respect to Senator Ives, the term "majority rule" is meaningless as he uses it. Does he want to amend the Constitution so that the Senate would advise and consent to the ratification of a treaty by a

* Consultant to the Senate Committee on Foreign Relations and former Professor of Public Law at Columbia University. Author of *The American Senate, Crisis Government, The Pollsters,* and other works. The selection is from "Barrier Against Steamrollers," *The Reporter,* Vol. 20 (January 8, 1959), pp. 21–23. By permission.

majority instead of a two-thirds vote? Is he uneasy because of the theoretical possibility that the minority which defeats a treaty (or a proposed Constitutional amendment) might come from the seventeen smallest states with a total population less than that of New York? Or that a Senate majority might be drawn from twenty-five states with a population of less than twenty-nine millions? We elect Presidents not by a national popular majority or even plurality, but by counting the ballots federally; each state's Presidential electors do the choosing. Fifty-one per cent may be a numerical majority, but in many cases it is not the majority that our Constitutional practices contemplate. Our Federal arrangements take account of what has been called "the gravity and the impact of the decision." Thus, when one great section of our country opposes a proposed decision, attention may well be paid to "gravity" and "impact."

And when Senator Case brands the Senate as the only legislative assembly in which verbal avoirdupois plays a role along with numbers, so what? The Northern liberals have sometimes insisted on "trial by ordeal." Senator Paul H. Douglas (D., Illinois) boasts that in 1954 he "spoke for three days against the offshore oil bill and in 1956 for four days against the natural gas bill. In each case, with my colleagues of the so-called liberal group, we kept the discussion going for approximately a month." Mr. Douglas applauds "stunts such as Senator Morse's record-breaking, 22½-hour speech delivered without sitting down or leaving the Chamber." The stunters were not attempting "to prevent a vote from being taken." They simply "believed that in these cases many of our colleagues were not fully acquainted with the real issues which were at stake." This is not a veto, Mr. Douglas insists, but only an endeavor to educate senators who were poorly informed. I would allow a substantial group of senators who are well informed, who come from a great section of the country, and who are united in purpose, to impose a veto unless two-thirds of their colleagues are prepared to overrule them.

BLOCKING THE STEAMROLLER

Gladstone called the Senate "the most remarkable of all the inventions of modern politics," and it has remained remarkable in that, contrary to the fate of practically every other upper chamber, it has not become secondary and suffered a loss of authority either by Constitutional amendment or by custom. It is the only legislative body in the world made up of representatives from commonwealths no one of which without its consent can be deprived of its equal representation and whose rights, even though steadily dwindling, still remain substantial. Where in other assemblies is there anything resembling our Senate's rule that its members must not "refer offensively to any State of the Union"?

The filibuster is a weapon that the Constitutional framers who constructed the Senate failed to anticipate but one that they would view with favor. "A dependence on the people is, no doubt, the primary control on the government," Number 51 of *The Federalist* tells us; "but experience has taught mankind the necessity of auxiliary precautions." The framers sought to have "in the society so many separate descriptions of citizens as will render an unjust combination of the majority of the whole very improbable, if not impracticable." The filibuster is no more than a modern "auxiliary precaution" against what one more than one-third of the senators may consider an "unjust combination" of the majority; and I am not impressed when I am told that no other legislative body in the world allows a minority to have such a formidable weapon of defense.

With us the Executive holds office for a fixed term and never appears before the legislature to account for his actions. Hence, it is "an auxiliary precaution" that there be some place in the congressional system at which a party steamroller will meet an effective barrier. The House of Representatives cannot serve this purpose. There, debate is often more severely limited and freedom of decision is more restricted than in any other legislative chamber in the world. A two-thirds majority can suspend the rules, and after forty minutes of discussion, it can pass a measure with no opportunity to offer amendments. A special order from the Rules Committee can allocate time for debate between the majority and minority and require that the House can say only "Yes" or "No." Since the senators number only ninety-eight and show more qualities of prima donnas than do representatives, they would refuse to shackle themselves as do members of the House when they approve a special order from the Committee on Rules; senators would insist that they be permitted to vote on amendments. But without the possibility of parliamentary obstruction—that is, filibustering—a party steamroller, driven by a President and party leaders, could on occasion move almost as ruthlessly on the Senate side as it does on the House side of the Capitol.

Thirty-odd years ago in a book called *The American Senate,* which now occasionally enjoys what William James called the immortality of a footnote, I argued the case for the filibuster. I began the book during the Harding administration and finished when Coolidge was in the White House—the era of the Teapot Dome scandals. The Republican Party machine was then powerful enough to prevent any investigation by a House committee, and Republicans in the Senate were not anxious to uncover wrongdoing. The Republican leaders knew that Senator Thomas J. Walsh of Montana and other Democrats could hold up important business; hence they had to consent to the thoroughgoing inquiry that was demanded. As to whether the threatened filibuster that brought about this result was in the public interest, it is sufficient to remark that three out of ten cabinet members were permitted or pressed to resign, and that there were several indictments and two suicides.

Those desiring Federal civil-rights legislation talk a great deal about the high-handed behavior of a minority. The Southern senators, it is charged, are able to defy "not only a majority in the Senate, but a majority in the country at large." Probably a majority in the country at large is willing for more civil-rights legislation to be passed, but we must not forget that one of the main reasons the framers of the Constitution provided two senators for each state, large or small, was precisely in order to protect the rights of sections against a majority in the country at large.

December 5, 1958, marked the twenty-fifth anniversary of an event on which the Northern liberals might pause to reflect: the end of national prohibition, which was, perhaps, in President Herbert Hoover's phrase, an experiment "noble in motive" but which was certainly a spectacular and disastrous failure. In 1918, when the state legislatures began to vote on the proposed prohibition amendment, saloons were illegal in approximately ninety per cent of the area of the nation, which contained nearly two-thirds of the population of the country. Temperance societies and the Anti-Saloon League (the most powerful pressure group that ever worked on Congress and state legislatures) insisted that aridity be complete. The "drys" marched to a battle that they won. Then they lost the war.

One concluding observation. Ours is the only major country with a two-party system where the laws that get on the Federal statute books, or that fail to get there, usually have bipartisan support and bipartisan opposition. In academic quarters one sometimes hears laments that American political parties are not "disciplined"; that their leadership is sometimes shadowy or undiscoverable, and that they do not present to the electorate clashing bodies of doctrine. But in a country as vast as the United States, with different sectional interests, a political providence has been good in seeing to it that a party majority does not pass party legislation which is opposed by a powerful and determined party minority; that on policies our parties prefer concessions to Pyrrhic victories. The filibuster is undemocratic if "democracy" means that anywhere, and particularly in a federal system, any majority should be able to do what it wishes on any issue at any time. Do the Northern liberals thus define "democracy"? Federalism was the means of forming the nation and it remains the means of preserving it. Congress, as well as the Supreme Court, is the Federal system's manager, and a Senate filibuster is well worth while if, on occasion, it prevents the Congressional manager from being tyrannical.

Minorities Should Not Be Coerced

WALTER LIPPMANN*

Although the question before the Senate is whether to amend the rules, the issue is not one of parliamentary procedure. It is whether there shall be a profound and far-reaching constitutional change in the character of the American government. The proposed amendment to Rule XXII would enable two-thirds of the Senate to close the debate and force any measure, motion, or other matter to a vote.† If the amendment is carried, the existing power of a minority of the states to stop legislation will have been abolished.

"Stripped of all mumbo-jumbo and flag waving," says "The New York Times," the issue "is whether the country's highest legislative body will permit important measures to be kept from a vote through the activities of a few leather-throated, iron-legged members who don't want democratic decision." This is an unduly scornful and superficial way to dispose of a great constitutional problem. For the real issue is whether any majority, even a two-thirds majority, shall now assume the power to override the opposition of a large minority of the states.

In the American system of government, the right of "democratic decision" has never been identified with majority rule as such. The genius of the American system, unique I believe among the democracies of the world, is that it limits all power—including the power of the majority. Absolute power, whether in a king, a president, a legislative majority, a popular majority, is alien to the American idea of "democratic decision."

The American idea of a democratic decision has always been that important minorities must not be coerced. When there is strong opposition, it is neither wise nor practical to force a decision. It is necessary and it is better to postpone the decision—to respect the opposition and then to accept the burden of trying to persuade it.

For a decision which has to be enforced against the determined opposition of large communities and regions of the country will, as Americans

* Newspaper columnist. Formerly newspaper editor. Author of *Public Opinion, A Preface to Politics, A Preface to Morals, The Good Society, Public Philosophy,* and numerous other books. The selection is from a column by Walter Lippmann in the *New York Herald Tribune,* March 3, 1949. Copyright, 1949, New York Herald Tribune, Inc. By permission.

† This has reference to a proposal before the Senate in 1949 to enable two-thirds of *all* Senate members to close debate which was, in fact, adopted. In 1959, the rule was liberalized to permit cloture by two-thirds of those present and voting. The proposal presently being urged would enable a simple majority of the Senate membership to terminate debate.

have long realized, almost never produce the results it is supposed to produce. The opposition and the resistance, having been overridden, will not disappear. They will merely find some other way of avoiding, evading, obstructing or nullifying the decision.

For that reason it is a cardinal principle of the American democracy that great decisions on issues that men regard as vital shall not be taken by the vote of the majority until the consent of the minority has been obtained. Where the consent of the minority has been lacking, as for example in the case of the prohibition amendment, the "democratic decision" has produced hypocrisy and lawlessness.

This is the issue in the Senate. It is not whether there shall be unlimited debates. The right of unlimited debates is merely a device, rather an awkward and tiresome device, to prevent large and determined communities from being coerced.

The issue is whether the fundamental principle of American democratic decision—that strong minorities must be persuaded and not coerced—shall be altered radically, not by constitutional amendment but by a subtle change in the rules of the Senate.

The issue has been raised in connection with the civil rights legislation. The question is whether the vindication of these civil rights requires the sacrifice of the American limitation on majority rule. The question is a painful one. But I believe the answer has to be that the rights of Negroes will in the end be made more secure, even if they are vindicated more slowly, if the cardinal principle—that minorities shall not be coerced by majorities—is conserved.

For if that principle is abandoned, then the great limitations on the absolutism and tyranny of transient majorities will be gone, and the path will be much more open than it now is to the demagogic dictator who, having aroused a mob, destroys the liberties of the people.

Topic 25

CONGRESSIONAL INVESTIGATIONS

A Defense of Investigations

JAMES BURNHAM *

In the past, congressional investigations have been intermittently and sometimes sharply attacked. The 1923–24 investigations into the oil industry and the Departments of the Navy and Justice were condemned by Owen J. Roberts, speaking before the American Bankers Association, as mere "propaganda for nationalization." The *Wall Street Journal* dismissed them as a "political smokescreen." The *New York Times* declared that Congress was "investigation-mad," and was trying to introduce "government by clamor [and] hole in corner gossip." The *Times* (in February, 1924) upheld Attorney General Daugherty as a sturdy patriot who was defending "decency [and] honor . . . , the honor which ought to prevail among gentlemen, if not among politicians."[1] In the same month the Communist *Daily Worker* created the label, "smelling committees."

A few years earlier Walter Lippmann, in his book, *Public Opinion,*[2] had described investigations as "that legalized atrocity . . . where Congressmen starved of their legitimate food for thought, go on a wild and feverish man-hunt, and do not stop at cannibalism." In 1925 the influential legal authority, J. H. Wigmore, characterized the investigators as "on the level of professional searchers of the municipal dunghills." The investigators to whom Wigmore was thus referring (Senators Walsh, Wheeler, Borah and LaFollette) were also termed, in the contemporary press, "scandal-mongers," "mud-gunners," "assassins of character." Their inquiries were described as "lynching bees," "poisoned-tongued partisanship, pure malice, and twittering hysteria," and "in plain words, contemptible and disgusting."

A decade later the New Deal inquiries into investment, banking, utilities,

* Editor of the *National Review.* Author of *The Managerial Revolution, The Machiavellians,* and *Web of Subversion.* The selection is from *Congress and the American Tradition* (Chicago, Henry Regnery Company, 1959), pp. 236–252. By permission.

[1] Within six months Daugherty had resigned in disgrace, after the investigators had shown that during his two and a half years in Washington on a $15,000 salary, his personal holdings had shifted from a $19,000 debt to a $100,000 fortune.

[2] Published in 1922.

and munitions were the targets for denunciations comparable in content though less colorful in rhetoric. Long before, congressional investigating methods had been eloquently criticized even from the floor of Congress itself. In 1860, during the course of the Senate inquiry into John Brown's raid on Harper's Ferry, Senator Charles Sumner defended a contumacious witness, Thaddeus Hyatt, who had been "incarcerated in the filthy jail" for having refused to answer the committee's questions: [3] "To aid a committee of this body merely in a legislative purpose, a citizen, guilty of no crime, charged with no offense, presumed to be innocent, honored and beloved in his neighborhood, may be seized, handcuffed, kidnapped, and dragged away from his home, hurried across State lines, brought here as a criminal, and then thrust into jail." . . .

Generally speaking, as these prominent instances suggest, it has been the gored ox that has bellowed. Whether well-grounded or not, vigorous congressional inquiries usually threaten institutionalized as well as individual interests. The spokesmen and friends of these interests, along with the individuals directly involved, fight back as best they are able. Usually the best defense, in a public polemic, is to drop the question of one's own private concern out of sight, and to counterattack either with *ad hominem* grapeshot or with seemingly general considerations of propriety, morals and political philosophy.

It was natural enough that the *Wall Street Journal,* the American Bankers Association, the *New York Times* (as edited in the 1920's) and the Hearst press (with large Hearst mining interests in the background) should look with initial disfavor on a probing of oil leases by a partisan and already suspect Public Lands Committee. The established banking and investment interests, the utility holding companies, and the great industrial corporations that had armed the nation for the first world war could not, even though cowed by the long depression, welcome the inquiries of the 1930's into their carefully unpublic ways. John Brown was a martyred hero of the abolitionists, who had provoked and financed his raid on Harper's Ferry. The abolitionist Senators from New England could hardly have been expected to further an investigation, headed by a Senator from Virginia, which was likely to confirm the formal case against Brown and to uncover the links in the conspiracy. . . .

Hugo L. Black, writing in 1936 when he was an investigator and not a Supreme Court Justice, summed up the natural response: "The instant that a resolution [authorizing an investigation] is offered, or even rumored, the call to arms is sounded by the interest to be investigated." [4]

[3] Here and below, the quotations of the Harper's Ferry debate are taken from *Congressional Globe,* 36th Congress, 1st session, March 12, 1860, pp. 1100–09; and Part 4, June 15, 1860, pp. 3006–7.

[4] Hugo L. Black, "Inside a Senate Investigation" (*Harper's,* February, 1936).

II

I do not mean to suggest that all of these past criticisms of inquiries have been subjectively biased or hypocritical. It may be presumed that Dean Wigmore was concerned primarily with the investigative procedures that are too coarse and unrestrained for so judicially oriented a mind as his was. Mr. Lippmann has been long and persistently critical of investigations differing widely in subject-matter and political direction. For that matter, most of the critics have doubtless been sincere enough when they voiced their criticisms.

At the same time we may note that until recent years, most of the attacks on the investigations, like the defending replies, seem to be part of the general political struggle in the nation over issues and problems that have successively arisen. The impetus of the attacks has been specific: against this particular inquiry or related set of inquiries. The legislative inquiry as an accredited institution of the American political system has not been in dispute. The critics did not question Congress' autonomous right to investigate, with adequate compulsory sanctions, in its own way and on its own sovereign authority. . . .

During the past decade the attack on the investigations has assumed a very different character. Although it has arisen primarily out of inquiries dealing with Communism and other forms of subversion, it is no longer specific or limited. In fact, it is no longer an attack on investigations, but on the investigatory power, and it has come in waves from all directions: from journalists, cartoonists, publicists and academicians; from the courts; from the executive; and even from within Congress itself.

As pictured by the most influential liberal cartoonists, led by Herblock and Fitzgerald, the typical congressional investigator is either a gangster, a Star Chamber hanging-judge, or a rubber-truncheoned fascist. Thousands of editorials, articles, monographs, lectures and sermons have condemned the investigating committees, their methods, their results and their most prominent members. In 1955 two general books—Alan Barth's *Government by Investigation* and Telford Taylor's *Grand Inquest*—broadened the adverse critique that had been undertaken by such preliminary studies as Robert K. Carr's *The House Committee on Un-American Activities.* A number of organizations—among them Americans for Democratic Action, the American Civil Liberties Union and the Committee for an Effective Congress—have in these recent years made the defects of investigations and investigators a principal element of their public agitation. For several years prior to his death in 1957, the figure of Senator Joseph R. McCarthy of Wisconsin became the symbolic target for this massive campaign against the investigatory power—a campaign which began, however, before McCarthy's entry on the national stage, as it continues after his exit.

III

The opponents and critics of congressional investigations do not explicitly call for the abolition of the investigatory power; that is, they do not state that Congress should be altogether deprived of the right and power to make investigations. They argue, rather, that the investigations should be curbed, limited and controlled in such ways as to prevent violations of rights, demagogic exploitation, encroachments on the executive or judiciary, and other excesses. The restrictive proposals go along such lines as the following:

(A.) *Some topics should be outside the purview of investigations.* These prohibited subjects would include all private affairs, rather broadly defined.[5] It has also been urged that all the varied matters included under "espionage" and "subversion" should be put under the exclusive jurisdiction of the Federal Bureau of Investigation and other security agencies: that is, should be shifted wholly out of the legislative into the executive branch.

(B.) *Investigating committee proceedings should be governed by detailed rules for the protection of the rights and privileges of witnesses, similar to the rules governing judicial actions.* Witnesses should have right to counsel, to confront accusers, to cross-examine, to call rebuttal witnesses and submit rebuttal evidence, to obtain full transcripts, and so on.[6]

It should perhaps be added that many of the rules proposed by the critics—such as the requirement of a committee quorum for all hearings and for all decisions in preparation of hearings—are virtually impossible under the real conditions of congressional activity. Others, drawn from courtroom practice, are inappropriate to an investigation, which by the nature of the case, is partly a "fishing expedition" in which the issues are not known fully in advance—unlike a court action, where the issue is defined in the indictment. And it is seldom remarked that the loose investigatory procedures, though they undoubtedly sometimes violate what would generally be regarded as individual rights and are often

[5] Thus extending a principle recognized by the Supreme Court in Kilbourn v. Thompson (1881).

[6] Actually, many such procedural rules have in fact been adopted by the committees, either through customary practice or on formal action. The House Committee on Un-American Activities—to cite one of the most controversial instances—operates in accordance with a printed list of fourteen rules in addition to the governing rules of the House itself.

disturbing to individual pleasure and convenience, at the same time frequently offer witnesses unusual liberties that they do not possess in the courtroom: to make long statements; to argue with interlocutors; to bring in hearsay, subjective motivation, mitigating circumstances; to delay and repeat; to become the accuser and to counterattack.

(C.) *The self-incrimination clause of the Fifth Amendment should have total application to inquiry proceedings.* That is, a witness, without any motivating explanation on his part or any objective indication that the refusal is well-grounded, should have the right to refuse to answer any question whatever on the ground that by answering it he risks possible incrimination. This blanket restraint on the investigatory function seems to be accepted at present by the courts and by Congress. It is further and persistently being proposed that the grounds for a refusal to testify should also include the First Amendment guarantees of freedom of belief and speech. Historically there is no foundation for applying these amendments to congressional inquiries. "These guarantees," observe Messrs. Kelly and Harbison, "were historically associated almost entirely with the business of the courts. And the substantive guarantees of the Bill of Rights—freedom of speech, press, and the like—appeared to apply to the content of congressional legislation, not to the mode of enacting it." [7]

(D.) *All phases of congressional investigations should be subject to review and adjudication by the courts.* For a hundred and fifty years the Supreme Court shied as far away as it could from intervention in the legislature's investigatory power, finally summing up its traditional recognition of legislative autonomy therein by its sweeping decision in McGrain *v.* Daugherty (1927). In the late 1940's, by refusing to review three lower court decisions that reasserted congressional autonomy in investigations,[8] the Court held fast to McGrain *v.* Daugherty against the rising liberal clamor. Then, in a series of decisions that began with Christoffel *v.* United States (1950) and reached a high point in Watkins *v.* United States (1957), the Supreme Court asserted what would be by implication its general right to define the rules, limits, methods, scope and sanctions of the investigatory power. On the meaning of the Watkins case, which reversed the decision of both the District Court and the Court of Appeals, dissenting Justice Tom C. Clark wrote that the Supreme Court was appointing itself "Grand Inquisitor and supervisor of congressional investigations."

[7] Alfred H. Harbison and Winfred A. Kelly, *The American Constitution* (New York, Norton & Co., 1955), p. 908.

[8] United States *v.* Bryan (1947), United States *v.* Josephson (1948), Barsky *v.* United States (1948). In the latter two decisions there had been a sharp division in the Court of Appeals.

(E.) *Congressional investigators who get out of bounds should be disciplined.* This proposal, a frequent exhortation of the critics of Congress, is difficult to apply, because of the explicit words of Article I, Section 6 of the Constitution: "[Senators and Representatives] shall in all Cases, except Treason, Felony and Breach of the Peace, be privileged from Arrest during their Attendance at the Session of their respective Houses, and in going to and returning from the same; and for any Speech or Debate in either House, they shall not be questioned in any other Place." Since these words seem to put members of Congress, so far as their official acts go, out of reach of the courts, traditional doctrine has left their due punishment to the ballot. As a disciplinary supplement, the new critics urge—though so far unsuccessfully—that too savage investigators might be tamed by being deprived of committee chairmanships, or even of membership on committees that conduct investigations.

The temporary focusing of the problem in Senator Joseph McCarthy provoked a novel, and momentous sanction. In 1954, through combined pressure from a liberal-led public opinion and the executive branch, Congress was induced to turn its investigatory power against itself; and then, by the Senate vote of an unprecedented censure against one of its own members, to make common cause with its critics.

[The fact is] that a true investigatory power cannot exist unless the investigator (individual or institution) is equipped with immunity, autonomy, and the power of compulsion. The public critique and the Supreme Court decisions since 1950, though not openly directed against the investigatory power itself, have attacked and much weakened these three conditions of its effective operation.

The power of compulsion is meaningless unless there is assured, speedy punishment for contumacious witnesses. Such punishment, under the now prevailing court rulings and congressional practice, is neither sure nor speedy. It can be postponed indefinitely when it is not avoided altogether, by legal technicalities, the plea of civil rights, or Congress' own unwillingness to pursue the matter vigorously. Thus, with very little personal hazard, witnesses may defeat the ends of a current inquiry: there will be a new Congress with new interests, before the question of punishment is decided one way or the other.

The investigator's immunity and autonomy do not mean that he can properly do anything that he wishes, but that the major decisions about what he can properly do will be his. More specifically applied to congressional investigation: that Congress shall itself decide when an investigation has a legislative purpose, what sort of evidence is relevant to that purpose and from whom, how evidence and information may be most fruitfully gathered. Quite possibly this is too great a license to be granted without restriction to any single institution. That is not here at issue, but merely the historical observation that in recent years the investigatory power of Congress, at the same time that it has emerged as the first among the remaining congressional powers, has been shorn and blunted by a many-sided and continuing attack. The public controversy over the investigatory power has often failed to distinguish between two types of inquiry that are profoundly different in their political meaning: investigations into the activities of private citizens, associations and institutions, on the one hand; and on the other, investigations of the administration of the government—that is, of the executive branch and the bureaucracy. A particular inquiry may bridge the two types (as in a study of the relation between a government regulatory agency and the industry it is supposed to regulate), but the functional distinction remains clear.

Most of the formal arguments that are advanced against investigations concern, primarily or exclusively, the first type. It is alleged that the civil rights or personal life of private citizens who appear as witnesses are violated, and that the protection of these private rights is a duty that takes precedence over the possible public gains from investigating this or that subject-matter. That is to say, the argument is cast in the form of: individual liberty *vs.* despotism.

For Americans, an argument in this form has roots in both tradition and rhetoric. It is persuasive to many citizens even apart from their opinion on the particular content of the investigations which provoke the controversy. And it is a fact that an unchecked investigatory power always threatens and sometimes subverts what Americans wish to regard as inviolable individual rights.

But inquiries into the doings of the executive and the bureaucracy are of a different order, in which private and individual rights are only coincidentally at stake. By making an artificial amalgam between the two types of investigation, we smear the second with the doubtful or negative feelings attached to the first. Objectively, the principal similarity between the two is the mere fact that both express the investigatory power of the legislature.

Traditionally it has never been questioned, either in doctrine or practice, that the legislature possesses the power, as it was put in early years, "to inquire into the honesty and efficiency of the executive branch." Under the American system it is this that is the heart of the investigatory power. It is conceivable that, without a major constitutional transformation, Congress could cede all investigations of the affairs of private citizens to the executive and judiciary. But if it lost the power to investigate the executive, Congress would retain only the name of legislature.

The late Senator George Norris, once the dean of liberals, accurately remarked during the controversies of 1924: "Whenever you take away from the legislative body of any country in the world the power of investigation, the power to look into the executive department of the government, you have taken a full step that will eventually lead into absolute monarchy [9] and destroy any government such as ours."

Woodrow Wilson's distaste for the practices of Congress did not lead him to obscure the basic relations:

> Quite as important as legislation is vigilant oversight of administration. . . . An effective representative body [ought] to serve as [the nation's] eyes in superintending all matters of government. . . . There is some scandal and discomfort, but infinite advantage, in having every affair of administration subjected to the test of constant examination on the part of the assembly which represents the nation. . . . Congress is the only body which has the proper motive for inquiry. . . . It is the proper duty of a representative body to look diligently into every affair of government and to talk much about what it sees. It is meant to be the eyes and the voice and to embody the wisdom and will of its constituents. Unless Congress have and use every means of acquainting itself with the acts and the dispositions of the administrative agents of the government, the country must be helpless to learn how it is being served. . . . The only really self-governing people is that people which discusses and interrogates its administration.[10]

Professor McGeary has put the situation still more bluntly: "An administrator's knowledge that at some future time he and his activities might be subjects of congressional investigation has probably been the principal external deterrent to wrong-doing in the executive branch." [11]

Scholars who have taken refuge in the United States from totalitarian regimes have been still more deeply impressed with the crucial role of legislative investigations into the operations of the executive. Dr. Henry W. Ehrmann, a refugee from Nazism, concludes that a lack of this power was a prime factor both in the failure of German pre-Nazi parliamentarism and in the bureaucratic sclerosis of the French political system.[12] He recalls the judgment of Germany's great sociologist, Max Weber: "In his criticism of the political situation in Imperial Germany, [Weber] attributed greater responsibility for the unsatisfactory results of constitutional life to the lack of parliamentary investigation than to any

[9] In the traditional American vocabulary, "absolute monarchy" was the term often used to refer to "despotism."

[10] Woodrow Wilson, *Congressional Government,* pp. 277–303 *passim.*

[11] N. Nelson McGeary, "Historical Development," a contribution to the symposium on congressional investigations in *University of Chicago Law Review,* Vol. 18, No. 3, Spring 1951; p. 430.

[12] Henry W. Ehrmann, "The Duty of Disclosure in Parliamentary Investigation: A Comparative Study" (*Univ. of Chicago Law Review,* Vol. 2, No. 2, Feb. 1944), pp. 117–53.

other single factor. The German parliament was condemned to dilettantism as well as ignorance."

Under Weber's influence, a right of parliamentary inquiry was introduced into the Weimar Constitution, but, as in the case of the inquiry function in France, there was no real power of compulsion to back it up. In both countries it could therefore have only minor political significance. "The unsatisfactory results in both France and Germany can easily be explained by the insufficient powers obtained by the parliamentary committees."

It is against this background that we may evaluate the progressive undermining of the investigatory power during the past decade by the executive as well as by liberal publicists and the courts. The executive under Presidents Franklin Roosevelt, Truman and Eisenhower has challenged the investigatory power in the most direct of ways: with respect to an ever expanding mass of data, it has simply refused to supply information to the investigating committees.

These refusals have been formally motivated by: the doctrine of "the separation of powers"; the need for secrecy; various laws, and in particular a "housekeeping act" of 1789 originally passed to authorize executive departments to set up files and records; an alleged traditional practice within the American system. These considerations were systematically stated in a memorandum submitted in May, 1954 by Attorney General Herbert Brownell to President Eisenhower, and countered by a Staff Study of the House Committee on Government Operations, dated May 3, 1956.

The executive's argument from tradition is undoubtedly specious. It is true that a number of Presidents, beginning with the first, have denied the universal right of Congress to call for testimony and documents from the executive branch. Among them have been Presidents otherwise so various as Andrew Jackson, John Tyler, Abraham Lincoln, Grover Cleveland and Calvin Coolidge. Washington would seem to have declared—in theory—a complete executive immunity to the investigatory power: "The executive ought to communicate such papers as the public good would permit and ought to refuse those, the disclosure of which would injure the public." Jackson, when Congress wished to look more closely into the working of his Spoils System, replied indignantly: "For myself, I shall repel all such attempts as an invasion of the principles of justice, as well as of the Constitution; and I shall esteem it my sacred duty to the people of the United States to resist them as I would the establishment of a Spanish inquisition." Even Calvin Coolidge denounced with unwonted sharpness the investigatory feelers directed by the Couzens committee at Secretary Andrew Mellon's administration of the Treasury Department. . . .

This earlier occasional practice—which like so much in the older American tradition commends itself to ordinary common sense—has now been blown up into a polished routine. By an administrative fiction, the "confidential" relation between President and subordinates—which in the past meant a literal personal relation between man and man—has been extended to the entire bureaucracy, so that the executive now claims a right to order any official or employee of the bureaucracy to refuse to testify to an investigating committee, or to withhold almost any sort of document or record pertaining to any department or agency.

In explaining Congress' 1958 attempt to restore the traditional interpretation of the 1789 housekeeping act as a mere authorization to preserve public records, Representative John E. Moss of California commented:

> The "housekeeping act" has been twisted and tortured by federal officials seeking to withhold information from the public and from the Congress. . . .
>
> A few of the recent examples of misuse of the act include the withholding by the Treasury Department of information about imports and exports; the attempt by the Agriculture Department to impose censorship as the price for cooperation in the making of newsreel and television films about agricultural subjects; the withholding of information by the Farmers' Home Administration and the Rural Electrification Administration on loans of public money.

Mr. Moss added a revealing datum: "Each of the ten Cabinet departments opposed this amendment to restore the traditional interpretation." [13]

With the shibboleths of secrecy, security and "classification," the executive has still further darkened the screen constructed out of the claims of constitutional privilege and separation of powers. Whenever the executive (or the bureaucracy) wishes to hide information from congressional scrutiny, it is only necessary to declare it "classified." Sometimes, granted the conditions of our age, this procedure is justified—as, for example, in the case of advanced military experiments, or the Federal Bureau of Investigation's "raw" (*i.e.*, unevaluated) security files on individuals [14]—but the secrecy labels have been extended over a considerable portion of the nation's ordinary business, which thus becomes removed from congressional (and thereby also from public) scrutiny.

The results are sometimes curious, from a traditional point of view.

[13] *New York Times*, Aug. 17, 1958.

[14] Common sense would agree that it would be improper to turn over such files to a large and factionally minded congressional committee. But even in this case there are solutions other than total executive immunity: *e.g.*, the British practice of showing the confidential material to a small parliamentary committee of authoritative and trusted members. Something of this sort was done in Washington during the 1953 conflict over the appointment of Charles Bohlen as Ambassador to Moscow.

The executive, for example, will call on Congress to vote appropriations for foreign aid, but will decline to furnish the information about what has been, is being and is intended to be done with the forign aid. On the basis of a special commission study, like the 1957 "Gaither report," the executive will demand certain armament funds; but will not show Congress the report which supplies the motivation. The executive will insist on Senate confirmation of a military treaty, like those establishing the North Atlantic or the Southeast Asia treaty organizations, without disclosing the commitments that the treaty entails. Thus, inevitably, the weakening of the congressional investigatory power leads to a correlated further weakening of the congressional share in the power of the purse, the war power and the treaty power.

It would be wrong to exaggerate the stage that the contest has reached. The investigatory power is bruised and shaken, but it is still vigorous. In fact, it is just because the investigatory power is so vigorous, because it retains more vitality than any other of the congressional powers, that it is so sharply under attack. It becomes easier to see why Dr. Ehrmann, reflecting on the experiences of many nations, concluded the study to which we have made reference with the summary judgment: "Certainly 'government by investigation is not government,' but government without investigation might easily turn out to be democratic government no longer."

A Threat to Civil Liberties?

LLOYD K. GARRISON *

Congressional investigations are a peculiarly American invention, born of the separation of the executive and legislative branches. They have served the country well and we could not do without them; but in recent years some of them have developed excesses which have caused their friends both in and out of Congress much concern.

In the way they treat witnesses and persons accused by witnesses, the committees may be likened to a poker, cool at one end and hot at the other. At the cool end, we see them performing their earliest historical function of checking up on the executive branch, seeking information and scrutinizing this or that activity. Congress has been at this salutary

* Noted New York lawyer and part-time Professor of Law at New York University. Former dean of the University of Wisconsin School of Law. The selection is from "Congressional Investigations: Are They a Threat to Civil Liberties?" *American Bar Association Journal,* Vol. 40 (February, 1954), pp. 125–128. By permission.

task since 1792, and in the course of it questions of civil liberties have seldom been presented.

At the cool end also are those investigations where the object is to get facts needed for the shaping of legislation. It was not till 1827 in the House and 1859 in the Senate that investigations of this sort, backed by the subpoena power, were instituted, but they have grown apace with the increasing complexity of legislative problems. In these inquiries, private citizens have been witnesses more often than government employees, and private rather than official acts more often the subject of examination; but where Congress has had a clear legislative end in view and the committees have sincerely sought light on defined and specific problems, questions of civil liberties have rarely arisen.

In both the executive and the legislative fields the process of investigation may shift toward the warmer end of the poker where the committees' motives are less simple and direct than those which have just been described. The bias against particular agencies or private groups has at times been so strong that their representatives or members have been treated less than fairly. Liberals and conservatives alike have complained of this sort of treatment.

The hot end of the poker begins to burn when the committee's target is no longer an agency or group but a single individual. There the individual, on trial for his actions, associations or beliefs, stands isolated and virtually defenseless. He may contend that no legislative purpose can be served by the investigation, or that given questions are not relevant to the subject matter of the inquiry, or that a subpoena of his private records is too broad; but these defenses are for practical purposes worthless (see the illuminating analysis by Judge Wyzanski in the March, 1948, issue of the *Record of The Association of the Bar of the City of New York*).

The witness may of course claim his privilege against self-incrimination and suffer the inferences which the public generally, and it may be justifiably, draws from such a plea. Apart from this he is substantially at the mercy of the committee. In extreme cases, where the investigation may destroy his livelihood, regardless of the truth of the charges, and the committee knows this or even encourages such a result, the committee's action may come close to being a bill of attainder. "A bill of attainder" said the Supreme Court in the post-Civil War case of Cummings *v.* Missouri, 4 Wall. (U.S.) 277, 323, "is a legislative Act which inflicts punishment without a judicial trial"; and a similar pronouncement was made in the companion case of *Ex parte* Garland, 4 Wall. (U.S.) 333. In those cases the Court reversed the convictions of Cummings, a Roman Catholic priest, and of Garland, a lawyer, for practicing their callings without swearing that they had never taken arms against the United States or abetted its enemies.

These cases were reaffirmed in 1945 in United States *v.* Lovett, 328 U.S. 303, where the Court said at page 318 that "When our Constitution and Bill of Rights were written, our ancestors had ample reason to know that legislative trials and punishments were too dangerous to liberty to exist in the nation of free men they envisaged. And so they proscribed bills of attainder." The Court accordingly held unconstitutional an act of Congress prohibiting salary payments to three named employees charged by a Committee with disloyalty. The Court said that: "What is involved here is a Congressional proscription of Lovett, Watson and Dodd, prohibiting their ever holding a government job. Were this case to be not justiciable, Congressional action, aimed at three named individuals, which stigmatized their reputation and seriously impaired their chance to earn a living, could never be challenged in any court. Our Constitution did not contemplate such a result" (page 314).

PERSONS UNDER INVESTIGATION SHOULD NOT BE DENIED RIGHTS

When a congressional committee in an investigation aimed at particular individuals "stigmatizes their reputation" and "seriously impairs their chance to earn a living," to use the language of the Court, the action is not far in effect as well as in spirit from the action condemned by the Constitution, even though the committee does not directly inflict the punishment but leaves that task to others, having reason to expect its due performance. The very fact that the committee's action, though close to a bill of attainder, is not literally one, emphasizes the need of affording defendants in these "legislative trials," to the fullest possible extent, the basic protections extended to accused criminals by the Bill of Rights.

And not to defendants only. Innocent outsiders may be, and in late years frequently have been, accused by witnesses in the course of particular investigations without an opportunity to appear and be heard in their own defense; and even where that opportunity has been given the defense has never yet caught up with the accusation.

In the light of these abuses numerous reforms have been proposed in recent years by leaders of the Bar, law teachers, The Association of the Bar of the City of New York, students of government, and members of Congress from both sides of the aisle. The proposals are of three sorts.

The first would bring the executive and legislative branches closer together in knowledge and understanding, so as to lessen the number of investigations and to improve their temper and narrow their scope. Outstanding is Senator Kefauver's bill for a question period in Congress comparable to that in the House of Commons, but adapted to the American scene. It seems to me wholly admirable in concept and in detail. It would not, however, affect investigations of individuals unconnected with the government, where the most severe abuses have occurred.

The second type of proposal relates to the all-important question of personnel. One measure, for example, would concentrate investigations in the hands of the standing committees and their subcommittees. This was intended by the Legislative Reorganization Act of 1946, but has not been fully accomplished. The great objection to special committees is that the person who proposes the resolution invariably is appointed chairman and then runs the show, whatever his qualifications.

Another set of proposals relating to personnel would sharply (and I think rightly) curtail the power of the chairman. Thus it is suggested that a majority of the committee should be required to authorize certain important steps, such as initiating an investigation, defining its scope, issuing subpoenas, finding a witness in contempt, deciding whether a given hearing should be public or in executive session, releasing or making use of testimony given in executive session, and approving the text of interim and final reports. Plainly there is need of a greater assumption of responsibility by committee members in spite of the heavy pressure for time under which all members labor. There is general agreement that all investigating committees should be provided with expert staff and counsel. It has also been proposed, with obvious justification, that committeemen and staff members should be precluded from speaking or writing about the committee's work for compensation, and that predictions and conclusions, which have so frequently prejudiced individuals, ought not to be publicly aired in advance of the report.

The third type of proposal has to do with procedural rules, of whose importance we as lawyers are particularly aware. The rules most frequently advocated are that a person who believes he has been injured by the testimony of another should have the right to appear and be heard, to call witnesses on his own behalf and to cross-examine his accusers, with the aid of counsel and of committee subpoenas if need be. These elementary rights, the core of our Anglo-Saxon system of discovering the truth, are long overdue in congressional investigations. They are needed not merely to protect the individual but even more importantly to bring out the truth in the public interest. They must obviously be subject to limitations and controls, lest the time of committees be unduly wasted and the proceedings get out of hand. These limitations and controls will not be easy to work out, and some degree of flexibility and room for experimentation seems desirable, But the practical problems, such as they may be, ought not to be allowed to delay action where the principle at stake is so clear.

At least one committee has successfully conducted an investigation in which all parties were given the right to examine and cross-examine witnesses and to rebut adverse testimony. This was the House Judiciary Committee's subcommittee on the study of monopoly power, under the chairmanship of Representative Celler. Concededly it operated in the cooler zone of seeking light on specific legislative problems and did not have to cope with the emotions and tensions that are aroused where a committee's object is to expose the activities, associations or beliefs of a particular individual. But even in investigations of the latter sort, where the rights in question are so essential to the ascertainment of the truth, there is no reason to suppose that the successful experience of the Celler committee could not be duplicated, given a competent chairman and rules of reasonable limitation.

WHAT SHOULD BE THE SCOPE OF INVESTIGATIONS

Now I turn to the question of the scope and reach of congressional investigations. This is of basic importance because even if rights of the sort just discussed are granted, they will necessarily fall short of those prevailing in courts of law, given the practical requirements of committee operation. Moreover the existence of these rights will not prevent the mere making of an accusation from irretrievably injuring the reputation of the person accused, however innocent he may later prove himself to be. This difficulty might be cured if it were possible to establish some closely safeguarded procedure, comparable to that of a grand jury, where charges could be sifted in private before any person was subjected to the humiliation of being publicly interrogated or denounced. But it is doubtful whether such a procedure could be worked out. Probably the nearest thing to it is the frequent practice of examining witnesses in executive session before a decision is reached as to whether to call them publicly; but this procedure in turn is unsatisfactory: because of time pressure, the attendance at executive sessions is generally meager and but little attention can be given to weighing the evidence after it is in; leaks to the watchful and sometimes prying press may occur, to the prejudice of the witness; and, particularly if the witness is a well-known person, the fact that he has been called is almost sure to become public knowledge and in and of itself is harmful to him. Finally—and this applies of course to public as well as executive sessions—the triers of the facts are politicians, of whom it can be said with certainty that they are neither juries nor judges.

These difficulties are inherent in trying to convert legislative investigations of individuals into the semblance of judicial trials. The judicial safeguards against falsehood and harassment which we so rightfully revere simply cannot, in full measure, be adapted to investigating committees. It follows from this that Congress should exercise the utmost restraint in launching investigations of individuals where by the very nature of the process, even after all practical procedural reforms have been made, full justice cannot be done and truthful conclusions cannot be assured. It does not follow, however, that there are any areas of American life which should permanently and under all circumstances be blocked off from the scrutiny of committees. Congress would not stand for such a limitation and the public interest would not be served by it. We need only recall a few of those investigations in which the careers of individuals were shattered but the country was the gainer: Teapot Dome, for example, and the King Committee's recent investigation of the Bureau of Internal Revenue, and other inquiries into alleged frauds upon the government. Similarly, some of the exposures of Communist infiltration into government, illustrated by examples of particular individuals, helped to illuminate the nature and objectives of the Communist Party and the steps that the government must take in self-defense.

What is needed is not a fixed limitation upon the scope of congressional investigations, but the assumption of a greater degree of responsibility by Congress as a whole for what is done in its name. Even the Supreme Court upon occasion has had to be admonished to exercise self-restraint within its sphere of power. The time is surely ripe for a congressional stock-taking of that which it is permitting its committees to do, particularly in the field of alleged subversion, where because of the natural anxieties of our citizens and the dazzling glare of publicity committee activities are heavily concentrated.

In this most sensitive field of inquiry, the investigations have proliferated out into the community in an ever-widening circle, embracing all manner of people unconnected with the government or with the defense effort, in walks of life far removed from any possibility of sabotage, espionage or interference with the economy, and far removed also from any serious likelihood of federal regulation. It is in these investigations that the maximum harm can be done to innocent individuals with the least gain to the country. I suppose that wherever in private life a Communist member is made to suffer from public exposure some damage, potential or actual, is done to the Party, and this may be chalked up as a gain; but we must measure the cost on the other side of the ledger. There is, to begin with, the injury to those who, having been called to testify, are not shown to have had any connection with the Party, or whose connection with it was at some time in the past. More seriously, the spreading ambit of these inquiries into men's beliefs and associations, past and present, contributes to the general state of timidity and conformity that is creeping over the land and sapping our vitality as a nation. Nothing is more un-American than timidity and conformity. And nothing is more risky in the age in which we live.

We are living as Toynbee puts it, in a "time of troubles." In such a time it is above all things important that we, the people of the United States, should remain clear-headed, unafraid, resourceful in our thinking as in our actions, and ready to change old policies, and, if need be, invent new ones, as circumstances may require. The censorship of books, attacks upon schools, colleges, newspaper editors and clergymen, the browbeating of those both in and out of government who dare to criticize the conduct of investigations, the multiplication of loyalty oaths and tests for various kinds of private employment, the building up of multitudinous dossiers on the private lives of citizens, the use against individuals of the undisclosed contents of reports prepared by secret agents, the increasingly intolerant treatment of immigrants and aliens, the excessive encroachments upon executive functions, and the spreading abroad of fear, suspicion and confusion—in these developments lie serious risks to our national sanity and our capacity to deal boldly and creatively with a world in ferment.

It would be unfair to ascribe to congressional investigations all of these threats to our true security. Many of them stem from state and municipal actions, and many are initiated or furthered by private groups. But what Congress does affects the whole body politic more powerfully than any other influence; the dramas of the committee rooms radiate outward to a watching and listening public and profoundly affect for good or evil the patterns of thought and emotion which in the end will shape our destinies.

So I say that there is no more urgent need than for Congress to assume responsibility not merely for improving the procedures of its committees but for passing upon the scope and reach and aims of their investigations.

What, then, specifically should be done? Two possible courses, among many which have been proposed, suggest themselves. The first would be for Congress to establish a joint standing Committee on Investigations, composed of leading members of both houses, to which all requests for investigations would be referred for study and recommendation. The joint Committee would first consider whether or not there was need of the investigation, balancing gains and risks from an over-all national standpoint. The joint committee would also consider how the investigation could best be conducted, whether by a standing committee or a special committee, or (as has often been suggested) by outside experts or officials together with Senators and Representatives, or by officials or outside experts alone, with or without the grant of particular powers. The joint committee would also consider whether any special procedures or safeguards should be adopted, consistent with the practical requirements of the task to be done, and having in mind the extent to which the rights of individuals might be adversely affected. The joint Committee would be required to report within a stated time, and its report would be recommendatory only, final responsibility being borne by the particular house involved.

A second step forward could be taken by Congress's adoption of minimum standards for the conduct of all investigating committees, defining the functions of chairmen and the duties of members, and the rights of witnesses and persons accused by witnesses. The makings of these minimum standards already exist in various pending bills introduced by Senators and Congressmen who have given long and patient study to the matter. Several committees have, in addition, adopted rules of procedure of their own which mark a real step forward. Common agreement should be possible, and the standards when adopted could from time to time be improved by particular committees and by Congress itself after adequate experimentation.

There will of course be many difficulties in the way of any reform: the vested interests of particular committees, the ambitions of individual Senators and Congressmen. But Congress is responsive to the will of an informed people.

Section XI

The Welfare State

IN AN AGE of vast and proliferating government regulation and enterprise, an issue of persistent and increasing importance is: What are the economically efficient and politically democratic limits of what has come to be known as the welfare state? This issue receives the attention of three scholars in the pages that follow.

Topic 26

THE DEMOCRATIC LIMITS OF THE WELFARE STATE

The Limits of Intervention

LOUIS M. HACKER *

The current debate on the limits of intervention (Is the welfare state inevitable? Can we stop short of socialism?) is taking place in a fog through which light shines only occasionally. In consequence, voices seem disembodied and values unreal as historical experience and political and economic truths are sacrificed to the demands of urgency. It has been said, for example, by a recent writer, that our modern world is unique because of "the decline of competition, the recurrence of periods of depression and the persistence of demands for basic economic reforms," [1] and that first call upon economic and political statesmanship is the resolution of our "pressing immediacies"

* Professor of Economics and former Dean of the School of General Studies at Columbia University. Author of *The Shaping of the American Tradition* and *The Triumph of American Capitalism*. The selection is from Louis M. Hacker, "The Limits of Intervention," *The American Scholar,* Vol. 19 (Autumn,, 1950), pp. 481–486. By permission.

[1] K. William Kapp, "Economic Planning and Freedom" in *Weltwirtschaftliches Archiv,* Band 64, Heft 1 (Hamburg, 1950).

—to wit, stability, security and full employment. National planning stands high on any agenda.[2]

Why urgency? These analyses, or reproaches, are almost as old as historical man himself. The Gracchi talked in the same vein; so did the rebels and popular leaders of the early fourteenth and sixteenth centuries. The complaints against monopoly and depression fill the pages of our first economic literature; the demands for "basic economic reform"—to mention only the best known of the viewers-with-alarm—go back as far as Harrington in the seventeenth century, and their number is legion in the nineteenth (Saint-Simon, Owen, Fourier, Proudhon, Cabet, Marx, Morris, Bellamy).

Another question: Dare a democracy ever yield to a sense of urgency? If we believe in unlimited debate, the examination of choices, and the peaceful persuasion and full support of a majority of the electorate—as well as the conversion of the majority by a minority—can we at any time say that emergency measures are in order? A fair charge against Lincoln was that he suspended habeas corpus and imposed martial law in Northern districts that were not even threatened by invasion. Even when Britain was so threatened, after the fall of France, its government never abridged the constitutional guarantees of the British people.

These questions, however, are not my immediate interest here. I am addressing myself to that of intervention: Are there limits to it? In fact, how far can public authority legitimately go before it changes our world entirely from the one we have to another with completely different codes of behavior, morality and welfare? . . .

The middle-of-the-roaders, the faint of heart, Mr. Arthur M. Schlesinger, Jr.'s "vital centrists," hope we can stop in midcareer and that "the welfare state" will be a working compromise between no-intervention and full-intervention. But the fox has been flushed, the hounds are in full cry, and away we go over hill and dale, not meaning to pull up until we are in at the kill. "Kill" is the wrong word, of course, except to the cynical. The happy huntsmen are convinced we can plan for stability and security, and at the same time maintain full consumer choices, a free market, and the right to invest—which means to take risks. *Our* welfare state will not be dominated by the police.

The British Labor government has formally declared that its grand plan encompasses only these three ideas: direction over investment, location of industry, and foreign exchange. It does not mean to nationalize entirely, and never without compensation. No policeman here—certainly as far as the Englishman's fundamental rights are concerned. But let us see.[3]

[2] J. B Condliffe, *The Commerce of Nations* (New York, 1950).

[3] Mr. Harold Wilson, President of the British Board of Trade, reported in The London *Times,* Jan. 20, 1950: "Basic controls, such as those of the location of industry, foreign exchange and the volume of investment, will be maintained as permanent in-

You want to start a newspaper and you begin making your rounds of the very many public offices involved. You learn, in time, that your investment plans, for share capital to erect buildings and furnish equipment, cannot have top priority ("More important to build houses for workers"); that paper shortages forbid the launching of new publishing ventures ("Purchases from the dollar area must be rigorously controlled by import licenses"); that all trained workers already have jobs and trade-union contracts ("A planned economy is based on high employment"). Socialism has a job to be done; first things come first, and dissent—which has always been a luxury—must wait its turn. There is no open attack on liberty. It is only that the sustenance it requires for survival simply becomes more difficult, if not impossible, to obtain. . . .

And as regards the brave challenge: "The art of political economy . . . must take account of criteria other than wealth"—this has been the stand of every Utopian from Plato up to and beyond William Morris. Without wealth—achieved not through privilege but by starting risky ventures—how can men launch new and cheaper ways of making goods and creating services? And unless we do so, will the cruel poverty which plagues so large a part of the population of the earth's surface, causing disease, starvation and early death, ever be abolished? Only a fool will deny that great deficits everywhere exist in the areas of health, education, child care—all the social services. The point is a simple one: Unless we continue to expand and create new engines of production—tearing down obsolescent plants, erecting more efficient factories and mills, building hydroelectric irrigation and flood-control projects, laying out more systems of communication—and make it possible, in consequence, to turn out more and cheaper hard and soft goods, we cannot pay for social security. The fascinating and frightening lesson of Britain's National Health Act is that its people need health services, but that the British economy will go bankrupt if its socialist leaders continue trying to pay for the health program at the expense of plant modernization. At this point in our development we simply cannot afford socialism—at any rate, Christian socialism, which is a morality and not a method for organizing production.

All this being so, how far may we expect the state to go? It has traditional roles which all of us in a democratic society are accustomed to see performed. It provides for the national defense; it maintains and upholds an incorruptible judiciary guided by the Rule of Law; it encourages and safeguards freedom of religion, communication and association; it gives minority groups protection and permits them to be heard; it employs the police power to defend and improve the life, health and morals of its people. The state can and should

struments to ensure the maintenance of our economic position and the fulfillment of our full employment programme."

go further; and, having said this, one should also be prepared to say: There are other functions which are the proper concerns, but also the limits, of state intervention. I record them here, not necessarily in the order of their importance.

1. The protection of private property is an important function of the state. If we are committed to the encouragement of innovation in order to increase production; if we are ready to agree that capital formation in a poor world is still a crying need; if we concede that the maintenance of unequal wage and salary scales is one of the ways through which savings can occur; if, from historical experience, we are prepared to recognize that unless risks can be taken—and fortunes made by the successful—the idea of economic progress must be abandoned, then private property and private business decision must be assured. In a free society, the existence of free consumer choices always will keep resources scarce. Unless we build our foundations on the vision of an ideal Spartan world—Plato's and More's and Marx's Utopias—there will always continue to be a relative dearth of goods. It is idle to talk of the abolition of wages as an ultimate goal, for the surfeit of plenty of which all well-intentioned romanticists have dreamed (Marx was the worst of the lot!) can never be realized.

The existence of unequal wages is one of the great social incentives: in fact, unequal wage scales are further developed in the Soviet Union than in most capitalist countries. Unequal wage and salary scales—leading to private fortunes—are a great spur to innovation. Short of a war period (the caterpillar tractor, the jet plane, atomic energy), it still is to be demonstrated that a planned and regulated economy is a more favorable climate for innovation than capitalism. The very nature of socialism—the timidity of functionaries, the vested interests of labor unions and cooperatives, the curious cost-accounting procedures—stifles innovation. Capitalism is not on trial here; its achievements, as far as production is concerned, have been magnificent. If the state means to concern itself with social welfare, it must permit adventurers to invest, take risks, and save for further investments from their successful ventures.

2. All this does not mean that privilege is to be tolerated. Tariffs that have outlived their usefulness (encouraging infant industries) must be abolished; monopolies and unfair trade practices are to be fought; patents are proper, but they should not be privately suppressed; excessive fortunes and idle funds should be regarded with suspicion. Every political thinker worthy of the name, from Aristotle to John Stuart Mill, was aware of the fact that no society could endure for long, or ward off social discontent, unless it constantly preoccupied itself with the question of the redistribution of wealth and income. There was always a wealthy group in the top layer and a poor one in the bottom. In between was to remain that broad sector of the middle class

which had the fluidity and opportunity to reach above or—if unsuccessful—to fall below.

Redistribution, through taxation, keeps opportunity alive and makes possible the regular emergence of new adventurers or innovators. So does the maintenance of the luxury industries, although in a minor way. Mandeville, in part, was right: the luxury industries are useful—not, of course, because they give employment, but because they help the profligate and stupid to speed the processes of redistribution. (J. M. Keynes was either cynical or entirely despairing when he applauded Mandeville.) Taxation, of course, is a two-edged sword: it always threatens the life of incentive.

3. Given the possession of that awful weapon, fiscal power, the state has a great responsibility: the protection of society's credit structure is in its hands. The state cannot be heedless in the management of its own finances. So completely—for good or ill—does it dominate central banking today that any recklessness on its part must have a blighting effect on enterprise at once. A sound monetary and credit system and a manageable public debt are the first concerns of virtuous lawmakers; otherwise, economic chaos inevitably follows. The history books are filled with too many familiar examples to require their recital here.

This warning, particularly, must be taken to heart by new or underdeveloped nations. The formula of inflation (or repudiation) and price and exchange controls seems such a simple and magical one; but only one's own people—and not for long—can be bemused by it. Certainly the stranger—the foreign investor and trader—will smell danger at once. That great and wise young man, Alexander Hamilton, America's first secretary of the Treasury, knew how vital it was that the young republic's public and private credit be built on an indestructible foundation. He paid off the revolutionary foreign and domestic debts; the prewar commercial claims of English merchants were to be honored; the new public debt was to be secured by a sinking fund; a central bank was established to regulate the currency; and long-term foreign funds and short-term financing flowed into the United States, to make its formative years secure.[4]

It would be idle to maintain that lawmakers must ever close their minds to the occasional necessity for unbalanced budgets. The experiences of the 1930's and the teachings of Keynes and his disciples are valuable here: deficit financing in bad years, surpluses in good ones. But what shall we say of a government which, during the greatest peacetime period of prosperity in its history, complacently draws up a budget calling for a deficit of five billions of dollars?

I am arguing for fiscal integrity; but I am not saying that state fiscal intervention should never take place. In a young or growing economy, there are

[4] See my own *England & America: The Ties that Bind. An Inaugural Lecture* (Oxford, 1948) for a fuller exposition of this point.

many areas where private capital cannot enter because it is not powerful enough. Indeed, in the underdeveloped countries—in the new nations of India and Israel, for example, and in Latin America—public investment will undoubtedly occur. Private investment, with foreign funds, however, is more efficient, and because it is willing to take risks is less likely to be badgered by the cautious or the foolish. An illuminating contrast is that between the building of the railroads by foreign private capital in the United States after the Civil War, on the one hand, and, on the other, the current efforts of the British Labor government to push its great groundnuts project in Africa. In both cases, financial failure initially took place. In the United States, the railroads were built despite the losses suffered by British, German and Swiss investors; in Britain, the plans for the development of Africa have come under such sharp criticism that the government has been forced to narrow and limit its outlays.[5]

4. Up to this point, I have mentioned the economic responsibilities of the state; there remains to be discussed an important social one. All cultures have had dependent or unemployable persons. Their care becomes a public duty in a world such as ours which advances in medical knowledge and develops a more refined social conscience, prolongs the age of child dependency, increases life expectation and therefore the numbers of the old, and has large numbers of the chronically and permanently ill. A distinction should be drawn between the sick and those chronically and permanently ill; between the unemployed and the unemployables. Invalidity, dependent mothers and children, and the aged (where there do not exist adequate pension programs) are a public concern and should be budgeted for.

On the other hand, the sick can be taken care of more efficiently and at less cost by private-insurance and group-medicine devices. And the unemployed can be protected by pension funds and schemes. There is a large area of joint enterprise, participated in by industry and labor, which we are beginning to explore in the United States. This, it seems to me, is a more fruitful experimentation than state programs. The welfare funds currently being set up in many of our industries place administration and responsibility where they belong; and they have the great virtue of preserving the independence of the unions.

If we mean what we say about our liberties, then pluralistic loyalties need encouraging: devolution of power, and not its concentration, is the key to proper political thinking. The welfare state (or socialism) produces the reverse, and sooner or later because it has fiscal authority over all the social services, as well as over credit, production and exchange, it must

[5] Because I favor foreign investments, I know I will be charged with "imperialism." Two of the greatest troublemakers of modern times have been Hobson and Lenin, who popularized, and cast obloquy on, this concept. See my *England & America,* heretofore referred to.

weaken the independence of associations (trade unions, trade associations) and convert them into pale satellites without lives of their own.

5. Finally, I wish to mention what may be called the psychological duty of the state: the preservation of opportunity. There will not be an active and contented citizenry unless opportunity flourishes, unless people can climb up and down the ladder of economic success and social recognition. The founder of the Medicis began as a wool comber; the first Astor was a butcher boy; the first Vanderbilt, a ferryman. Innovators must have the chance to start, and their talents demand social acceptance. In our world of great institutional organization—the guidance of public offices, corporations, trade unions—the surest way to maintain opportunity is through the creation and defense of full educational facilities.

The state must educate, therefore, because education is expensive and should be universal. Plato's Academy, the Stoics, Peter Abelard, could meet their pupils over a covered walk or in a room; the gathering together of teachers and scholars for discourse constituted early education. But when education requires libraries, laboratories and elaborate equipment; when education begins with infancy and does not end until death; when it tries to reach whole populations to train for the effective citizenship of all rather than the leadership of the few—then we cannot escape public outlays.

Outlays are one thing; supervision is another. This is not the place to examine closely the complicated question of educational policy. The elimination of privately-administered educational institutions would be a tragedy, if we really mean what we say about wanting to uphold a democratic society and to produce free men. Authority does not start in the schools; it begins in the family, probably. But certainly the perversion of young minds can be effectively completed, and their thought forever controlled, by those who dominate education.

The state undoubtedly will have to subsidize higher education (scholarships would be the best way), but educational administration should be in the hands of local agencies (where the schools are public) and in the hands of faculties (where the schools are private). If the schools can be kept independent, the Big Policeman will be kept cut down to size.

The preservation of liberty is no longer an abstract question. Political theorists, up to now, have always assumed that threats to it came from irresponsible authority. But liberty can be put in jeopardy equally by a state which starts out with benevolent intentions. Socialism's aim is not power but welfare; yet in striving to achieve welfare it threatens innovation, sacrifices fiscal integrity, and dries up opportunity. The state has positive functions; but, if we are interested in economic progress and the maintenance of liberty, there should be specific limits on intervention. To define functions is also to limit them.

Empirical Problems and Particular Goals

CHARLES E. LINDBLOM *

Mr. Hacker asks: "Is the welfare state inevitable? Can we stop short of socialism?" But these factual questions he chooses not to answer. Instead he defines the *proper* limits of government intervention, and we can only guess whether the inevitable is improper.

For present purposes, I am inclined to believe that he has asked the wrong questions, but answered the right ones (though wrongly). Leaving prediction aside, I shall comment on his proposals for proper policy.

To ask how far government should go is something like asking how fast an automobile should be driven. I think Mr. Hacker is, in effect, saying that he cannot agree that fifty miles per hour is a proper maximum, even if it was once so considered. But he cannot, on the other hand, approve speeds of much over seventy miles per hour because he knows the hazards of high velocity.

As ordinarily asked and answered, such questions come close to being nonsense. Ninety miles per hour is no further from an optimum than forty or sixty. It all depends on traffic, weather, the effectiveness of brakes, the vision and reaction time of the driver, the technical characteristics of the automobile, and a number of other variables which not only can be changed, but are, in fact, always changing.

Similarly, the proper limits on government in economic life depend on a number of changeable and ever-changing conditions about which Mr. Hacker says almost nothing. Limits on intervention should depend on at least the following variables:

1. *The community's objectives or values.* These objectives change frequently, and the functions of government ought to change with them.
2. *The specific kinds of problems with which the community must deal.* It is incredible that the common prescriptions for the limits of government intervention have not been rewritten since Hiroshima. While national security has dictated a government monopoly of a potential major source of industrial energy, we idiotically turn out the same old slogans.
3. *The degree to which power in government can be held responsible.* This, in turn, depends upon such factors as the degree of consensus in the com-

* Professor of Economics, Yale University. Author of *Unions and Capitalism* and other books and articles. The selection is from Charles E. Lindblom, "Empirical Problems and Particular Goals," *The American Scholar,* Vol. 19 (Autumn, 1950), pp. 486–488. By permission.

munity, the level of party responsibility, and the extent of citizen participation in politics. Again, these are not only varying but variable.

4. *The effectiveness of alternative nongovernmental techniques for reaching individual and community objectives.* Would it have been sensible, for example, to debate the ambitious extension of government power involved in the establishment of the Federal Reserve System without first diagnosing the performance of private banking as of 1913?

If we first become reasonably clear about our values and objectives, the determination of the proper limits on government power then becomes a technical problem, largely empirical rather than moral—approached in the same way that we determine optimum driving speeds by examining, among other things, night blindness among drivers.

The converse of this proposition is that the limits of intervention cannot successfully be discussed with terms which reduce complicated empirical questions to relatively simple problems of morality. . . .

It is high time we stopped talking about socialism. Mr. Hacker is against socialism, but this assurance gives me very little idea of what he is actually against. If socialism means increased government intervention in economic life, he is not opposed. If it means more equality—social and economic—he is not opposed. If it means democratization of industrial life, I infer that he is not opposed to that either. If his objection to socialism simply reflects his belief that too much is too much, we can dispense with the term and get down to the job of defining "too much."

On the other hand, if Mr. Hacker's repeated objections to socialism record his opposition to nationalization of industry, I suggest that he is beating a dead horse. We in the United States have long ago agreed that nationalization was a suitable specific organizational technique in certain limited circumstances. Among democratic socialists here and abroad, this is about all that is today being claimed for nationalization. What specific industries are well suited to nationalization is a technical question on which sweeping generalizations are worthless.

I would therefore conclude that social policies should be designed neither to "save" capitalism from socialism, nor to substitute socialism for capitalism. We live in an economy as much socialist as capitalist—and I can say this easily because neither of the terms means anything in particular. Policy should now be directed to choosing and developing the best of specific alternative social techniques, public and private, to achieve particular social goals. My guess is that policy so designed would be less timid than Mr. Hacker's.

Defense of the Welfare State

MAX LERNER *

I find Professor Hacker less persuasive in his introductory remarks than he is when he tackles the main matter at hand. He asks, to start with, "why the urgency" about economic reform, and points out that the reformist analyses and reproaches "are almost as old as historical man himself." It is a little as if a writer on medicine were to ask "why the urgency" in the efforts to improve medical science, and were to point out that the diagnoses of disease and the calls for cure "are almost as old as historical man himself."

More than a decade ago I wrote a book called *It Is Later Than You Think.* I would not in today's crisis diminish in the slightest degree the sense of urgency implied in that title. I am certain that Professor Hacker will not deny the reality of the contemporary struggle between an all-out totalitarianism, which aims to put the whole economy, and with it the whole human mind and personality, under rigid public direction, and, on the other hand, the effort to find a way of organizing the economy effectively without destroying freedom. The problem is at once economic, political and moral. When Professor Hacker says with disdain that "socialism—at any rate, Christian socialism . . . is a morality and not a method for organizing production," he does it less than justice by denying its economic and political aspect; yet its moral emphasis—the effort at a greater economic security and stability, the effort to meet the threat of corporate power-aggregates, the effort to create access to opportunity for all—is not in our day a negligible emphasis. In most areas of the world the problem that Professor Hacker is inclined to dismiss with an air of tiredness as old stuff of the utopian brand is a problem as real as livelihood and freedom. If we ignore it or abdicate it, we may find soon that we have lost the battle for the allegiance of men, and with it the chance to explore further the best ways of organizing an economy for common ends through democratic means.

Professor Hacker gets some telling effects from the English dilemma by pointing out that if your choice is between paying for social security or using the same limited funds to renovate obsolescent machinery, it is no solution to let the machinery go on obsolescing. What he does not add is that America, with a national income approaching three hundred billion dollars a year, is not faced by anything like so cruel a choice. I have noted a tendency

* Professor of American Civilization at Brandeis University. Author of *It Is Later Than You Think, American Civilization,* and other books; newspaper columnist. The selection is from Max Lerner, "State Capitalism and Business Capitalism," *The American Scholar,* Vol. 19 (Autumn, 1950), pp. 488–491. By permission.

on the part of many of the critics of the New Deal and Fair Deal to use the case of England as a whipping boy. They attribute to socialism all the present ills of England, and by a transposition they imply that Americans, too, will have to live under austerity, and ration orange juice and gasoline, if they move further toward socialism. On the other hand, they attribute to pure capitalism all the productive achievements and material prosperity of America today, and by a transposition they imply that if contemporary Britain had not followed after the strange gods of socialism, the British, too, would have today a bull market, roads crowded with burnished autos, shop windows crammed full of luxuries, the highest living standards in history, a Byzantine lushness of life, and money to burn.

It should be pointed out for the historical record that there is a difference in the resources of the two countries, both natural and human. It should also be pointed out that the obsolescence of British machinery, British railway equipment, British coal mining equipment, was notorious long before the labor governments were even heard of. Writing in 1915, Thorstein Veblen, in his *Imperial Germany and the Industrial Revolution,* gave a classic analysis of Britain's lag in terms of "the penalty for taking the lead." Whether he was right or wrong in his analysis, the fact of the British lag was recognized thirty-five years ago. Professor Hacker, who has had a first hand acquaintance with Britain as exchange professor at Oxford, should know that the bankruptcy of Britain is not the consequence of the labor government, but that the labor government is the consequence of the bankruptcy of Britain. That bankruptcy came under capitalist auspices, and was nourished by the fearful material and human expenditures of two world wars. British socialism, to the extent that it exists, is a particular kind of socialism that comes in the wake of a deficit economy. That is why Aneuran Bevan was so roundly cheered at a British Labor party conference when he said that "the language of priorities is the religion of socialism." Because the British problem was one of priorities, it does not follow that it is—or would be—the American problem as well.

The case of America presents, not the problem of deficits, but the problems of distribution, stability, security. What Professor Hacker calls deficits in the areas of health, education, child care, and the social services are (for the case of America) deficits not for all the people but only for some of the people. The New Deal and Fair Deal have already gone a considerable distance toward wiping them out, and the Cassandra-like prophecies which have dogged us since 1934—that we could do so only by eating into risk capital and investment capital—have proved utterly empty. Always we were asked the question: "Where will the money come from?"—the question that Professor Hacker is still asking. Would it be acrimonious to suggest that not only has the community found the money to establish these services, but that in the process both the volume of capital and the profits of private enterprise have been increased? And I would suggest also that to go farther along the same road, and wipe out wholly the deficits in the areas of health, education, child care and all the social services would, far from destroying the private sectors of the economy, build an even stronger base under their prosperity.

I hope I am not unfair to Professor Hacker when I say that he seems to miss the dynamic elements in the American economy. Like other critics of the Welfare State, his thinking seems to go back to the presuppositions of the wage-fund economic theorists—that there is a static fund of income upon which the society can draw as upon a bank account, and that if you withdraw it for social security, for public medical services, for farm subsidies, for public-housing construction, for hydroelectric dams, you may overdraw your account. What we have found in the case of America since the beginning of the New Deal is that the psychological factors are the crucial ones in an economy, as in all human living. John Maynard Keynes understood this, and that is why he evolved a new—if still crude—psychological language of the "propensities" to save and spend and consume. Given a strong base of resources, managerial ability, technology and labor power, as we have in America, the extent of potential national product and national income in the calculable future is such as to stagger the imagination. In that sense, the most recent report of the Committee of Economic Advisers to the President was not a utopian or a whimsical report, but a realistic assessment of what can be accomplished in the next fifty years, based upon what we have accomplished in the past twenty years. The psychological atmosphere of confidence, employment and social construction achieved by the New Deal gave a fillip to the managerial group, as well as to the workers and the consumers. That is why America has managed at once to move toward a Welfare State and to increase its national income.

But the psychological factor is only one of a complex of factors that made this possible. It would be as foolish to attribute the results to government intervention as it would be to insist that America's current prosperity is due to the boldness and imaginativeness of "risk taking capital." The wealth of a nation lies in the state of its industrial arts, its technological advance, its managerial skills, its labor force. All of these may be called "socialist" in the sense that they are all community possessions. They come from social sources and they should pay a social dividend. To an extent they are doing so in America. Wages and living standards are high, profits are unexampled, new industries and new millionaires are being created. And all of this is being done within what has been called the "strait jacket" of the New Deal and the Fair Deal.

But there are lumps in the porridge. Professor Hacker, I am sure, will agree with me when I enumerate them. The biggest lump is the fact that much of our present prosperity is the result of armament economics.

Second, there is the glaring fact of corporate monopoly. Since the 1880's the free American economy has been growing less free. The path of monopoly is strewn with the graves of small enterprises. Every year the area of concentrated corporate power gets greater; the area of small business enterprise shrinks. The monopolies are governments in themselves and bureaucracies in themselves. They levy their toll, as Thurman Arnold has pointed out, not only on their rivals, but also on the consumer. They are the American form of feudalism.

The third lump is boom-and-bust. The American economy has gone periodically through fevers and chills. To the extent that we carry over the planlessness of the past, to that extent we shall continue the alternation of boom-and-bust.

The fourth lump is that so-called "risk taking capital" has tended to stay out of the areas of risk, and to play it safe. It has not pushed with boldness into the possibilities of large scale investment with low profit margins. Some of the critics of American capitalism from inside have pointed out that it has not taken advantage of doing a larger volume of business on a lower margin of profit. It has tended to charge what the traffic will bear. The replacement of Commonwealth and Southern by the TVA has shown that the government is sometimes in a better position to take risks than private capital is. In the entire field of housing today there is very little risk left. The risks are all guaranteed by public funds, and the profits are the reward, not of risk, but of capital.

It is to correct these still crucial defects of our economy that we must continue along the path of economic reform.

This means exploring further what John Stuart Mill called the "limits of the province of government." Professor Hacker has mapped out with considerable cogency the five major duties of the state, and then he has drawn a line as with a flaming sword, with the injunction: "thus far and no farther at your mortal peril."

I cannot have his certitude about how definite these limits are. I think it is a matter for many decades of further experience and further experiment and the further use of the inquiring mind.

Western Europe, especially Britain, has been experimenting with the socialism of the deficit economy. America alone, as I have said, has the resources for experimenting with a better organization of a surplus economy.

It will not do to debate the issue as if it were a clear one between "capitalism" and "socialism." The fact is that in the modern Western State, whether in Britain or America, whether in Israel or India (both of which have become Western states), there are elements both of capitalism and of socialism. Perhaps it would be better to say that there are elements of business capitalism and of state capitalism. The problem is how to form an amalgam of them which will achieve the best form of welfare economy.

Britain has moved reluctantly toward a larger public sector—that is, a sector of state capitalism. It has done so from necessity in the interest of sheer survival, although the Marxist tradition of the Labor party has given the new developments a dogmatic welcome. America has moved, also under the spur of necessity, toward enlarged sectors of public action in the economy. Dogmatically we abhor every such step. We call it "socialism" and many worse names as well. But under the spur of the great depression, and the thrust of the democratic welfare impulse, which is very strong in the American tradition, we have nevertheless kept moving. Our problem has been, not sheer survival, as in the case of Britain, but stability and security.

I don't think that Professor Hacker is justified in ridiculing the concept of a mixed economy, such as will be found in Professor Schlesinger's *Vital Center* and in Irwin Ross's book on the mixed economy, *Strategy for Liberals.* Our whole historic instinct has been to cling to the private sector wherever we can, to move toward the public sector only when we must. There is no danger within the American tradition and the American psychology that we will embrace socialism either out of dogmatic enthusiasm or subservience to the state. The greater danger lies in the fact that the great power structures in America are the aggregates of corporate power; that they function very much as governments function; that, more than ever, they control the agencies of public opinion and influence the direction of education and belief; that the business system in America is invested with power, and that property is invested with sanctity and with grace. My own anxiety is not that we will slip unaware into socialism, but that we will not have the courage to challenge those who fear the valid extensions of the public sector.

Section XII

Democracy Evaluated

THAT GOVERNMENTS derive "their just powers from the consent of the governed" appears to many Americans so self-evident as to require no demonstration. But in a world in which democracy as understood and valued in the West is under challenge, it is essential to subject this premise to continuing examination.

The section begins with a thought-provoking selection from Norman L. Stamps' book, *Why Democracies Fail,* in which he presents and analyzes what he considers to be serious and disturbing weaknesses in traditional democratic assumptions and practices.

It follows with Lenin's critique of "capitalist" democracy, reflecting a point of view which, it must be recognized, commands acceptance in a vast area of the world. Lenin also provides a description of a socialist and communist society as envisaged *before* the Bolshevik revolution. What happened in practice under Stalin, with respect to Lenin's image of proletarian democracy, is examined by Khrushchev in his 1956 speech (denouncing Stalin). The more general statement, that follows, presents an *official* Soviet interpretation of the meaning and content of so-called proletarian democracy today.

A thoroughgoing analysis of, and penetrating reply to, the Communist case are presented from the writings of Reinhold Niebuhr, H. B. Mayo, and Morris R. Cohen. Finally, H. B. Mayo emphasizes the positive and fundamental values that are inherent in, and promoted by, democracy. [In earlier topics consideration was given to the value and limits of free expression. The case for free speech is obviously an integral part of the case for democracy and arguments which support one will ordinarily support the other.]

It may be asked why a book called *Basic Issues of American Democracy* should include excerpts from official Soviet sources. An answer, it is suggested, may be found in John Stuart Mill's famous essay *On Liberty:* "They [who] have never thrown themselves into the mental position of those who think differently from them and considered what such persons may have to say . . . do not, in any proper sense of the word, know the doctrine which they themselves profess," or, at best their conclusion is held "in a manner of a prejudice, with little comprehension or feeling of its rational grounds." It must be borne in mind, too, that the most serious challenge to American democracy today is being made in the name and under claim of a superior form of Soviet "democracy"—a claim that demands critical evaluation.

Topic 27

THE DECLINE OF DEMOCRACY

Why Democracies Fail

NORMAN L. STAMPS *

At the end of World War I it appeared as though democracy had reached its greatest triumph. Lord Bryce in his *Modern Democracies,* first published in 1921, pointed out that "A century ago there was in the Old World only one tiny spot in which the working of democracy could be studied." [1] This was in "a few of the ancient rural cantons of Switzerland" but "nowhere else in Europe did the people rule." However, within a hundred years "nearly all the monarchies of the Old World have been turned into democracies," twenty new republics have sprung up in the Western hemisphere, and five new democracies developed out of colonies within the British dominions. Lord Bryce added that more than a hundred representative assemblies were at work legislating for self-governing communities but that the most significant change in the last hundred years was "the universal acceptance of democracy as the normal and natural form of government." The word, democracy, which had formerly awakened dislike or fear, was now a word of praise; and the old question as to what is the best form of government had become almost obsolete.[2]

THE CLIMAX OF "CLASSIC CONSTITUTIONALISM"

This almost universal confidence in the ultimate triumph of popular government was not merely the mood of this generation but was instead the climax of an ever-widening and deepening conviction that democracy was the predestined form of government for all civilized nations. Jeremy Bentham, James and John Stuart Mill, Thomas Paine, and Thomas Jefferson believed that, given widespread educational opportunities, the whole world would eventually become democratic. . . .

* Late Professor of Government at Rutgers University. The selection is from *Why Democracies Fail* (Notre Dame, Indiana, University of Notre Dame Press, 1957), *passim.* By permission.

[1] James Bryce, *Modern Democracies* (New York, 1924), I, 3.

[2] *Ibid.,* pp. 3–4.

Even W. E. H. Lecky, whose own misgivings concerning democracy effectively protected him against any suspicion of wishful thinking, wrote in 1896:

> I do not think that anyone who seriously considers the force and universality of the movement of our generation in the direction of democracy can doubt that this conception of government will necessarily, at least for a considerable time, dominate in all civilized countries, and the real question for politicians is the form it is likely to take, and the means by which its characteristic evils can be best mitigated.[3]

The World War increased, rather than diminished, belief in the irresistible triumph of popular government. Woodrow Wilson gradually became convinced that the selfish ambition of irresponsible kings and military rulers was a major cause of the conflict. When America entered the war the absolute Tsarist regime in Russia had been replaced by a provisional government committed to the selection of a constituent assembly, and Wilson announced in his message to Congress that a major aim of the allied cause was to "make the world safe for democracy." At the end of the war military defeat had brought an end to the reign, not only of the Romanov, but also to the Hapsburg and Hohenzollern dynasties; and the victory of the Entente powers was attributed partially to the democratic spirit of their peoples. Thus the return of peace coincided with the establishment of democratic constitutions all over Europe.

THE RUDE AWAKENING

It was hardly expected that a rapid spread of dictatorship should begin at this time; yet there were signs of approaching danger. . . . A few close students of government noted that the universal acceptance of democracy was not a tribute to the smoothness of its working and that discontent was everywhere rife. For example, Lord Bryce, writing in 1921, concluded that there were few countries "in which freedom seems safe for a century or two ahead";[4] but such statements were exceptional at this time. Although a provisional government committed to the election of a constituent assembly had triumphed over Russian Tsarism in March, 1917, a Communist dictatorship

[3] William Edward Hartpole Lecky, *Democracy and Liberty* (New York, 1913), I, 256.

[4] *Modern Democracies* (1921), II, 603. *The New Democratic Constitutions of Europe* (London, 1929). In 1913 A. Lawrence Lowell had written: "Many people feel that because popular government is new it must be lasting. They know it is a vital part of the spirit of the age, which they assume to be permanent. But that is the one thing the spirit of the age never is. It would not deserve its name if it were; and when any spirit of the age has become universally recognized, it is time to scan the horizon for signs of a new era." *Public Opinion and Popular Government* (New York, 1913), p. 303.

of the proletariat under Lenin soon took its place. In 1922 Mussolini made his famous "march on Rome" and began the gradual consolidation of power which was eventually to turn Italy into a totalitarian state. However, defenders of democracy, for the most part, were undisturbed by these developments. It was explained that party government had never taken root in Italy or Russia and that these countries had merely turned from one form of dictatorship to another. . . . By 1938 all of central and eastern Europe and all Mediterranean countries were under dictatorial rule. . . .

EMPIRICAL CAUSES OF DICTATORSHIP

There is perhaps no single set of causes for dictatorship. In modern Europe absolutism has appeared in very different countries, under different circumstances, and for very different reasons. Although in each country it was imposed to deal with a crisis of some kind, there was no similarity in social structure, economic organization, national tradition, or race. . . .

EXECUTIVE IMPOTENCE

Perhaps the greatest operational weakness of popular government has been its inability to provide effective political leadership within the traditional institutional framework. In the eighteenth and nineteenth centuries there was a reaction against executives, and during this period legislatures everywhere gained in power. The struggle was first an attempt to establish parliaments as a counterpoise to the Crown and then, as election came to be looked upon as the primary basis of authority, to dominate the executive and bring the specialized bureaucracy under parliamentary control. Thus the memory of an old regime of executive absolutism caused the assembly to be jealous of its power and to be constantly on the alert against the new executive in order to prevent its reversion to the old type.

Today there is a reaction against weak executive power because social and economic conditions are of such a nature as to demand swift and drastic executive action. Perhaps one of the most dramatic cleavages between constitutional intent and political reality has been that legislative supremacy has so frequently led to the establishment of dictatorship. This is because government requires the concentration of political power in a small compact group. A multi-membered assembly, torn by party dissensions and subject to the fluctuating moods of public opinion, is incapable of governing. The most such an assembly can do is control the government it places in the chair of authority. It is an interesting fact that in no European country has the aggrandizement of a strong constitutional executive led towards authoritarian rule. It is instead a weak executive, incapable of providing effective government, that has been replaced by a strong executive free from legislative control.

In Italy the country was faced with serious economic difficulties. There was mounting unemployment, economic dislocation brought about by the war, a seething discontent not only on the part of workers but also of veterans who returned home to find that they had no jobs and that the sacrifices they had made benefited the profiteers. The socialists, who had opposed the war, benefited from the general disappointment felt in the peace treaties and Italy's failure to secure the colonial territories she had expected. Although the cost of living was still rising, employers sought to reduce wages on the theory that labor costs had increased during the war far beyond their real value. The government apparently, because of successive splits in the party system, was unable to agree upon a consistent policy of any kind. . . . Although there was chaos and an obvious need for drastic action, the government did nothing. Although Mussolini had only thirty-five deputies in the Chamber, he finally challenged the government itself. It was only then that the cabinet decided to take action, but it was too late. The king, upon being advised that the Fascists had infiltrated the army and the police, refused to permit the government to declare martial law, accepted the cabinet's resignation, and asked Mussolini to become premier.

PARTY STALEMATE

The major cause of executive impotence has been party deadlock in the legislature. Since parliamentary government makes the executive dependent upon and responsible to a majority in the representative assembly, all governmental activity becomes paralyzed if the assembly becomes divided into so many factions that there cannot be found a stable majority for the executive's support. For example, there were twelve parties in the Italian Parliament before the Fascist revolution and fifteen in the German Reichstag in 1928. As this paralysis crept in, the people in country after country lost hope that effective action ever would be produced and "parliamentarism" became a by-word for inefficiency and inaction.

This fact raises a number of fundamental issues concerning the party system and its functions in the governmental system. In the first place, what is the purpose of parties and what should be the subject of party controversy? Acting alone the individual citizen can do nothing, and it appears obvious that a principal aim of political parties is to organize the chaotic public will and educate the private citizen to political responsibility. However, not everything can be the subject of party controversy. By following obstructionist tactics a party can paralyze the work of an assembly and sabotage parliamentary institutions. Even though a minority and regularly defeated when votes are taken, such a party can delay debates and prevent the majority from bringing them to a conclusion, hurl insults, resort to disorderly conduct and a program of violence, and employ other techniques designed to prevent the normal operation of democratic institutions. Obviously a government must remove such obstacles; for it will otherwise be unable to act decisively and its opponents may profit from the chaos and confusion which they have caused; yet if the government goes too far in cutting off the fringes of dissent, it will have thereby destroyed the very principles upon which democracy is based. Democracy assumes that the minority will accept the rule of the majority and that the majority, in turn, will not rule too oppressively. In other words, both the majority and minority have rights but they also have obligations. It is the duty of the majority as represented in the government to govern and of the minority to confine its opposition to appeals to public opinion. Although the *raison d'être* of the opposition is to discuss and criticize and thereby educate public opinion, it does not have the right to follow obstructionist tactics.

There is also the question concerning how to correlate party responsibility with executive action. For example, the multiple party system in Germany was furthered by proportional representation so that there were regularly between ten and fifteen parties in the Reichstag. The result was that no government could command a majority in the legislature and that any combination of parties for the assumption of responsibility could always be defeated by a combination of those in opposition. Moreover, the electoral system discouraged a spirit of moderation and cooperation among the parties, not only because it gave representation to extremist groups, but also because each party was able to win seats on its own program without compromising its position and without taking into consideration the marginal voter. . . .

Party stalemate also raises a question concerning the proper function of the legislature. A parliament is an admirable instrument for the expression of grievances and for the discussion of large principles. Its purpose is to discuss and guide the general conduct of the government, but it does not exist in order to govern. As a matter of fact, it may be argued that a legislative assembly is too numerous and too incoherent even to legislate directly and that it is bound by its nature to accept or reject proposals offered to it by the executive power. This is the view set forth by John Stuart Mill in a famous passage of *Representative Government:*

> Instead of the function of governing, for which it is radically unfit, the proper office of a representative assembly is to watch and control the government: . . . to be at once the nation's Committee of Grievances and its Congress of Opinions. . . . Nothing but the restriction of the function of representative bodies within these rational limits, will enable the benefits of popular control to be enjoyed in conjunction with the no less important requisites (growing ever more important as human affairs increase in scale and complexity) of skilled legislation and administration.[5]

[5] *Representative Government* (Everyman's Library; New York, 1936) pp. 239–241.

In any case, a legislative chamber composed of five or six hundred people of divergent political outlook cannot really govern; but it can prevent the government from doing so. . . .

LACK OF AGREEMENT ON FUNDAMENTAL MATTERS

Democracy is a delicate form of government which rests upon conditions which are rather precarious. For representative institutions to function successfully there must be a wide area of agreement on fundamental matters and a willingness to compromise on others. The great advantage which the British government had during the nineteenth century was that the differences which divided the two parties were on methods of action rather than on deep-seated principles. The Whigs and Tories, Liberals and Conservatives were united in their desire to preserve the monarchy, the established Church, and the main tenets of the economic system. . . . In other words, the two parties were in agreement as to the kind of state they wanted, and there was little difference in their social composition. Being in agreement on the broad and general principles which ought to guide the policies of government, they could proceed to disagree on the best means of achieving the aims or goals they both had in common. There were, of course, differences of opinion, but they were concerned primarily with matters of degree and emphasis rather than with the fundamental structure of society or the form of government. Under such circumstances government by discussion and majority vote works best because compromise is possible at all pivotal points and because the minority can meet defeat at the polls in good temper since it need not regard the decision as either a fatal or a permanent surrender of its vital interests.

It is impossible to overestimate the extent to which the success of parliamentary government is dependent upon a considerable measure of agreement on fundamentals. The device of alternating government and opposition is possible only because the minority consents to lose and is willing to accept the rule of the majority. The opposition party is willing to do this because it can, when it comes to office again, take up the threads of its activity more or less where it left them. It is prepared to accept the risks of the next election because it knows that in the meantime the fundamental contours of the state will remain unchanged and that eventually it is certain of office again.

When differences of opinion within a state become irreconcilable and passionate and when individuals or groups refuse peaceably to lose, constitutional government breaks down. For example, in Portugal a substantial portion of the people refused to accept the republic and wanted a monarchy. Under such circumstances it was impossible for the republican system to operate because the government was compelled, in order to maintain the regime, to cut off the fringes of dissent and thus itself became authoritarian.

Under such circumstances the dominant interest in the state establishes control by force and governs by coercion rather than by consent.[6] Only a firmly established government is capable of being constitutionalized. . . .

Constitutionalism imposes limitations on the organs of government and diffuses powers in order to prevent a dangerous concentration at the top. This limitation may be enforced in a number of ways. For example, in some countries it is partially enforced by a supreme court which acts as the guardian of the constitution and repels encroachments by other agencies of the government. In other countries there are special administrative courts which prevent the executive from exceeding and abusing such powers as he has. Sometimes the existence of a federal system helps curtail and balance the powers of the central government, and sometimes this limitation is enforced by the different political groups which together exercise supreme guardianship in the legislature. However, in all countries reliance must ultimately be based upon a nation's sense of its heritage, upon a common understanding that certain things are not done, and upon an insistence that the time-honored procedure must be followed. In other words, all legal and theoretical rules rest on the expectation that every major group in the country will agree to be bound by the constitution and will not attempt to force its will beyond these limits. In the last analysis this agreement must be voluntary; for a state either collapses or becomes a dictatorship when a considerable number of people refuse to accept the constitution.

A voluntary agreement of this kind is possible only when the contending political forces within a country are not too far apart on fundamental principles. This does not mean that there cannot be spirited debates over important issues for the electorate to decide; but when mutual animosity and differences of opinion reach the point "where one political party feels that its very life is threatened by the possible victory of another important party, then constitutional barriers are easily brushed aside and the grim struggle for political, and sometimes physical, survival begins." [7]

POLITICAL INEXPERIENCE AND EXPLOITATION

It is impossible to operate a democratic government when the people are not interested in public affairs and when people have not had experience in self-government. There must be not only a passion for liberty but also a

[6] One of the techniques used by most dictators is to distinguish between the "real" and the empiric. There is an underlying something which is the real country and which the party will bring forth. Thus the "real" Portugal is altogether different from the existing Portugal. Both the Russian and the German, as well as most other, dictatorships have used this device. For example, Lenin said that the peasants are ignorant and probably would rush back into private property, but the "real" Russia is crying to be communized.

[7] Neumann, *European and Comparative Government,* p. 593.

desire to preserve the conditions of liberty. This means that the people must possess enough of the common to sustain the common weal against the fierce conflicts of interests and factions. When class lines are strongly held and when a sense of class exploitation reaches deep into the masses of the population, democratic institutions are hard to establish and maintain. In Italy and Germany proportional representation made it possible for political parties representing narrow class interests to secure a larger representation in the legislature; and although political parties even in Germany did not have a strict class basis in the Marxian sense, they did tend to reflect narrow group interests and to develop platforms appealing to specific local, economic, or occupational interests to a much greater extent than in hardly any other country.[8] . . .

Marxist parties, unlike the Labor party in England, are not inclined to advocate a gradual approach to socialism.

> They oppose "reform" and believe in revolution. When they become powerful they regard the political conflict as a sheer struggle between themselves and the reactionary right, in which latter category they tend to include all who do not share their own allegiance. Marxism and fascism breed one another and in the clash, whichever wins, democracy loses.[9]

The situation that developed in Spain prior to the civil war is only one of many illustrations that could be given. Democracy puts the common interest, and not merely some majority interest, above the divisive interests of all groups.

Democracy requires a process of maturation. Where its spirit has long been awake, as in Switzerland, Scandinavia, England, and the United States, the movement towards dictatorship has never succeeded. It may be that these countries were not so profoundly shaken by the universal crisis and that, if pressure had been further intensified, they too would have followed the same road. There are catastrophic conditions under which democracy cannot flourish or even endure. On the other hand, in immature republics, such as Weimar Germany, where there was no established democratic tradition, there was a greater willingness to follow the leader and to submit to authority. In these countries the people, faced with an economic and spiritual crisis, were more inclined to vote for political parties pledged to change not merely the government but the whole system of government.

NATURE OF CONSTITUTIONAL DEVELOPMENT

There can be little doubt that conditions prevailing in the nineteenth century presented a more favorable environment for the operation of parliamentary institutions. The problems of government were simpler than they

[8] Hermens, *Democracy or Anarchy?*, pp. 35–43, 241–244, 290–292.
[9] MacIver, *The Web of Government*, p. 191.

are today; public opinion was more homogeneous; agriculture was still the predominant occupation of men; and the representation of geographical areas had a meaning it has since lost. The electorate was then smaller, and an elaborate party organization was not needed. The issues discussed in the nineteenth century were of a character which the average man found interesting and intelligible without the possession of special knowledge, and lent themselves to eloquent debate in the legislature.[10]

Today the character of discussion has changed. It is indeed difficult to dramatize or to interest public opinion in matters such as the details of industrial reorganization, currency reform, grants-in-aid for housing, and other matters of this kind which require a special knowledge not available to the ordinary man. Moreover, as life becomes more technical and complicated it becomes increasingly difficult for legislators to understand thoroughly the details of the legislation concerning which they are called upon to pass; yet the amount of legislation passed each year has increased to such an extent that representatives are overwhelmed with work and find it increasingly difficult to find the time for adequate discussion of legislative projects. The broad outlines of legislative procedure were laid down at a time when the main tasks of the state were few in number and negative in character. There was a suspicion of too much government, and legislative procedure developed forms which were designed to prevent a majority from riding roughshod over its opponents. Hence the amplitude of debate, the resentment of an assembly against steps designed to limit its initiative or freedom of discussion, and the power of a minister to make any question, no matter how insignificant, a question of confidence. Moreover, the very nature of political democracy precludes the possibility of swift and comprehensive action. Based as it is on a process of discussion, new measures cannot be undertaken until they have received the support of public opinion; a political party is naturally hesitant to promote novel ideas because of the possibility of defeat; and the number of interests to be consulted and the time required to do so is always great. . . .

NATURE OF THE PARTY SYSTEM

A democratic party system is based upon the idea that man is a rational animal capable of intelligent choice and that, having heard the arguments, he will make a wise decision; but when emotion takes the place of reason, when party organization reaches the point where party spirit completely

[10] Professor Harold J. Laski, *Democracy in Crisis* (Chapel Hill, 1933), p. 70, says: "The debates of the nineteenth century did not, I think, arouse greater interest or secure wider publicity because their level was higher; it was rather because their subject matter was, in itself, calculated to arrest the attention of a non-technical audience."

dominates his mind, or when there is no longer the possibility that he will exercise a choice, then the democratic process tends to break down. It is undoubtedly true that the number of independent voters who record the general movements of opinion by changing their votes from time to time is always small; but party organization can become so intensive that it precludes a reasonable opportunity for all groups to appeal to the electorate and to influence its judgment by intellectual argument. Under such circumstances the electorate tends to become fixed in its allegiances and inflexible in its attitudes. There can be no swing of the pendulum but a constant stalemate with the added threat of civil war. The cry is then heard for a party above parties, for a "movement" which will encompass all others and bring about a "new unity."

Democracy is based upon the assumption that the party can penetrate the associations to which an individual belongs, that it can teach its programmes, and that the individual will consider the alternatives with an open mind; but the total party attempts to indoctrinate its members thoroughly, to cover the whole of men's minds, and to mold their minds so as to leave them in no position to exercise a free choice. When parties become emotional absolutes, they cease to be a part of the system of rational discussion. . . .

MATERIAL CONDITIONS FOR DEMOCRACY

Democracy is a delicate form of government which rests upon conditions that are rather precarious. It makes certain assumptions about the capacities and virtues of men, and it presumes the presence of certain material and intellectual conditions favorable to the exercise of these capacities and virtues. John Stuart Mill, whose devotion to liberty cannot be doubted, pointed out that a people might desire liberty and yet be unable or unwilling to fulfill its conditions.[11] There must be a wide range of interest and a capacity to relate one's own immediate interest to a more general pattern. The only possible government is some kind of oligarchy when people are deeply divided by racial, religious, or other differences. . . .

ECONOMIC THEORIES OF DICTATORSHIP

1. The Marxian explanation. Perhaps the most popular explanation for the rise of dictatorship has been derived from Marxian philosophy. According to this view, every state has a class basis. Political democracy, therefore, is nothing more than a concealed dictatorship which permits the capitalists to delude the workers; and so long as it can be carried on it is, from the

[11] See his *Representative Government* (Everyman's Library, New York, 1936), esp. pp. 175–184, 218–227.

capitalist point of view, the most efficient and acceptable form of government. However, the growth of working-class organizations and universal suffrage have produced a clash between the working-class and the owners of property, and the capitalist is compelled to resort to open force to maintain his position. Thus fascism is an effort to save capitalism and give it a longer life by preventing the establishment of socialism. "The creation of a fascist party is, then, a desperate expedient only resorted to by a capitalist class in the face of the most urgent danger from the workers." [12] . . .

2. *Polarization of an authoritarian left and right.* It has also been contended that certain conditions inherent in democracy itself create an antidemocratic spirit and that as time goes on there is a tendency for the adherents of democracy to decrease and for the supporters of dictatorship to increase. This is because the left develops a fear of majority rule believing that if the decision were left to the ballot box that they would lose. There is no government more conservative than a democratic regime because the people are by nature suspicious of change and because drastic reforms cannot be undertaken until the great body of the people has become convinced of the need for change. The result is that the left begins to despair of winning a majority at the polls and the demand for and a readiness to accept a dictatorship on the Russian pattern are greatly enhanced. On the other hand, the middle classes also fear majority rule because it means the enthronement of the "have-nots." With the development of communication and education, there is a constant increase in the number of people whose ideas are antidemocratic. Out of this situation will come an authoritarian movement, either from the left or from the right and probably from both, which will sap the democratic structure [13]. . . .

THE PROPAGANDA THEORY

To prove their assertion that fascism was a gigantic capitalist plot, Marxian writers are compelled to fall back upon the propaganda theory which asserts that the masses were manipulated by the clever use of propaganda. They are encouraged in this view by many statements made by leading Fascists and Nazis themselves. As is well known, Hitler was particularly interested in propaganda techniques. *Mein Kampf* is largely a treatise on the art of political propaganda; and, along with Dr. Joseph Goebbels, Hitler became the world's foremost exponent of propaganda as a method of controlling opinion. The Nazis carefully employed most of the devices dis-

[12] John Strachey, *The Coming Struggle for Power* (New York, 1933), p. 262; see also by the same author, *The Menace of Fascism* (New York, 1933).

[13] See Hans Kelsen, "The Party Dictatorship," *Politica,* II (March, 1936), 19–32; Charles E. Merriam, *The New Democracy and the New Despotism* (New York, 1939), p. 197.

covered by modern psychology and drew upon the experience made available by modern advertising. Nazi theory proceeded upon the assumption that man is not a rational animal, that he is subject to emotion rather than to reason, that political pronouncements should not be deliberative but present exclusively the idea or view which they are designed to advance, and that propaganda was useful mainly to manipulate opinion and as a weapon in the struggle for power. . . .

THE NATURE OF MODERN SOCIETY

Although it has been fashionable in recent years to speak of dictatorship as an incomprehensible freak and as a reaction against the whole trend of western civilization, conditions inherent in the very nature of modern industrial society pose new problems and help explain the contemporary crisis of democracy. In many countries dictatorship has emerged after the breakdown of established institutions. In other countries it represents a protest against what has become a questionable economic system, a shattered social order, or the injustice of the preceding system. Thus dictatorship has grown out of democracy, is not completely divorced from the past, and is a reaction to modern conditions. The question arises as to what factors inherent in the nature of modern society have contributed to the decline of democracy and the establishment of dictatorship.

ISOLATION OF THE INDIVIDUAL

The rise of capitalism destroyed the old medieval social system together with the stability and relative security it offered. Although the individual was freed from the authority of the medieval church and the absolutist state, he was also uprooted with a consequent feeling of insecurity and reduced to becoming a mere cog in a vast machine. Modern man is unable to make decisions affecting the most important aspects of his life, and his feeling of isolation and powerlessness are enhanced by the fear of mass unemployment and the threat of war.

Everywhere he goes and in everything he does he comes into contact with vast impersonal forces. Although he lives in a large city together with thousands of others, he is not integrated into the community and has a terrible feeling of frustration and isolation. At his job he is merely a small part of a vast operation. When he goes to the department store, no one is particularly happy because he came. The clerks who wait on him are employees of a large concern; and, unlike the proprietor of a small store, they do not care whether he buys anything or not. If he joins a trade union to further his economic interests, the union is also likely to be a huge organization in which he cannot play an important role. The individual, therefore, stands alone, confused, frustrated, and overawed by a consciousness of his lack of importance and powerlessness.

Erich Fromm has shown how every aspect of modern life is calculated to produce a sense of insecurity, doubt, aloneness, and anxiety and that such feelings exist among all classes. The paradox of contemporary society is that "as man becomes more independent, self-reliant and critical he becomes more isolated, alone and afraid" and hence more susceptible to "any custom and any belief, however absurd and degrading, if it only connects the individual with others." Dr. Fromm says that the appeal of fascism can be partially explained by the desire to "escape into submission" from the heavy burden and strain of freedom; for "if we do not see the unconscious suffering of the average atomized person, then we fail to see the danger that threatens our culture from its human basis: the readiness to accept any ideology and any leader, if only he promises excitement and offers a political structure and symbols which allegedly give meaning and order to an individual's life. The despair of the human automaton is fertile soil for the political purposes of Fascism." [14]

It has sometimes been said that men everywhere are desirous of freedom, but an unemotional investigation would subject this statement to considerable doubt. There is, to be sure, the desire for a negative freedom: to be rid of certain oppressions, such as colonial administrators or domestic secret-police forces; but the positive desire to govern oneself and to make constant decisions on matters of public concern is not too widespread in the world. As soon as certain grievances have been eliminated, many people are content to leave the government in the hands of "those who know best."

INCREASED BURDEN ON THE ELECTORATE

Democratic theory assumes that the intellectual qualities of the people are such that they can judge effectively the general quality of the men who seek their votes. Historical experience seems to confirm that the electorate can give a great and simple answer to a great and simple question; but in modern society the number of policies requiring electoral decision have been vastly increased and their nature has become progressively complicated. Hence it has become increasingly difficult to interpret the meaning of election results. One has only to sample the literature on [British and American elections] to see how many factors play a role and how difficult it is to say precisely what it was that "the people" thought about the matters discussed in the campaign. In a sense this has always been true. Opinions seldom carry weight in pure proportion to their intrinsic merit. The average man has always made his decision on the basis of a general impression; and trivial matters, rather than important questions of principle, have always influenced

[14] *Escape from Freedom* (New York, 1941), p. 256.

his vote. Nevertheless it is far more difficult today to say definitely that an election decides anything other than the personnel of key office holders; and in a multi-party country, such as France, it cannot be said that even this issue is decided by an election. The average man is likely to think that parties exist not because there are two sides to every question but because there are two sides to a political office—an inside and an outside; and he is also likely to feel that it is impossible for him to exert an effective influence on the policies of the government.

GROWTH OF BUREAUCRACY

The assumption of new functions by the state has resulted in the growth of a vast and complicated administrative machine. To deplore and denounce this development is futile; for the economic functions of the modern state cannot be abandoned, have been dictated by public opinion, and have come into being in all modern states as a response to real problems. On the other hand, it is equally ridiculous to ignore this new expansion of administration and argue, as many people do, that because it is necessary, no problem exists.

The increasing complexity of the economic system, the growth of public regulation, the nationalization of industry, and an increasing demand for all kinds of social services have produced a mighty bureaucracy which is highly specialized and which has had professional training in administration. Gone are the days when, as President Jackson said, a government job was either so simple or could be made so simple that the average man could perform it satisfactorily. As administration becomes more and more a closed profession and as the power of this group increases, the ordinary voter is less likely to feel that he lives under a system which makes him one of the governors as well as one of the governed. . . .

Red tape and bureaucratic inefficiency are problems facing all modern governments—democratic and dictatorial as well. A study of the speeches and of the changes made in party rules at the Nineteenth Communist Party Congress held shortly before Premier Stalin's death confirms that most of the evils ordinarily associated with bureaucracy were a matter of chief concern.[15] However, in a democracy there is the added problem of how to keep this huge administration responsible and sensitive to public opinion. Even in Britain this is today a matter of chief concern. It is generally admitted that ministers are more dependent on their permanent civil servants than at any previous time, that ministers probably have little knowledge of what is done

[15] Harry Schwartz, "Anatomy of the Russian Communist Party," *New York Times Magazine* (March 22, 1953), p. 12; Merle Fainsod, *How Russia Is Ruled* (Cambridge, Mass., 1953), pp. 327–353; Victor Kravchenko, *I Chose Freedom* (New York, 1946), esp. pp. 316–331.

in their names or under their nominal responsibility, and that the traditional methods for controlling the administration are far from satisfactory. Members of the House of Commons are finding it increasingly difficult to discuss intelligently much of the highly technical legislation which they are called upon to pass, and they are finding the traditional methods of control over the processes of administration increasingly unsatisfactory. . . .

When one contemplates the size and complexity of the governmental machine in any modern state, it is indeed a tribute to the political capacity of the people if the government can be operated at all within a democratic framework. It is impossible to go on forever piling bureau upon bureau and constantly increasing the number of boards. The individual citizen will become lost in a maze! Yet a way must be found to restore the idea that he is one of the governors as well as one of the governed. It has been suggested that this can perhaps best be done by creating an opportunity for him to participate, at least to some extent, in the decisions of bodies which most intimately affect his daily life. It is no longer a question as to whether "big government" is a good thing; for the welfare state and its bureaucratic machine are already here. It is instead a question as to whether new administrative techniques can be developed rapidly enough to meet the challenge of the social service state.

GROWTH OF ORGANIZED ECONOMIC POWER

Since the individual standing alone can accomplish nothing, he joins an association to further his interests. Today there are trade unions, employers' organizations, professional societies, agricultural associations, and many other special interest groups. "If we wish to get a correct picture of the social and economic structure of the modern world," Professor E. H. Carr tells us,

> We must think not of a number of individuals cooperating and competing within the framework of a state, but a number of large and powerful groups, sometimes competing, sometimes cooperating, in the pursuit of their group interests, and of a state constantly impelled to increase the strength and scope of its authority in order to maintain the necessary minimum of cohesion in the social fabric. We can no longer base our thinking, like the classical economists, on the isolated independent individual. The subject of modern economics is a man in society, man as a member of a number of collective groups struggling for power, of which the most powerful, the most highly organised and the most broadly based is the state.[16]

The existence of these many groups increases the opportunity for participation by the citizen, but it also raises the question as to what their relationships should be to society as a whole and how these various organizations are to be integrated into community life.

[16] *Conditions of Peace* (New York, 1943), pp. 74–75.

To vast numbers of people political rights have lost their former importance because of the feeling that the unorganized majority of the electorate can accomplish nothing against the overriding force of organized economic power. Even in Great Britain the opinion is growing that politics consist of a bargaining process between the forces representing organized capital and organized labor. It would be an exaggeration to say that the Conservative and Labor parties are nothing more than two machines representing respectively the combined forces of organized capital and organized labor, for electoral considerations compel both major parties to broaden their appeal to include a great deal more than a narrow special group interest. Yet there is considerable evidence to substantiate the charge that political policies are influenced in a major degree by the vested interests who supply the bulk of party funds and only to a minor degree by the opinions of the electorate whom they claim to represent. . . .

Under modern conditions it is more difficult to preserve a sense of community because the individual instead of becoming a civic-minded person is likely to be the supporter of a special interest group. Thus what was formerly a uniform and homogeneous opinion under simpler conditions may become broken up into a number of highly specialized functional organizations. . . .

EXERCISE OF DICTATORIAL POWER EASIER

If the nature of modern society has made the emergence of dictatorship psychologically possible, it has also made the exercise of autocratic power easier than in any preceding period. The telephone, telegraph, railways, motor cars, aeroplanes, and other means of transportation and communication make it possible for governments to regulate and control vast areas and huge populations. The military weapons used by a modern army, such as tanks and machine guns, make it possible for a small number of men to dominate a huge population. Gone are the days when an aroused citizenry can take to the streets and overthrow a government which still has the support of the army. The growth of large-scale business organizations has also facilitated centralized governmental control, for it is easier for the state to regulate a small number of huge corporations than to check on a large number of small business men. The emphasis placed upon "scientific management" in modern industry and the development of a huge business bureaucracy have meant that the responsibility for making key decisions has become progressively centered in fewer and fewer hands and that the average person becomes increasingly accustomed to being led by others and gives up his own interpretation of events for those which others give him. The nationalization of industry offers no solution to this problem because in any highly industrial society men are bound to be part of a highly disciplined and authoritative organization. Thus "a modern industrial democratic state has been a house divided against itself, an autocratically governed industry over against a political democracy." [17]

It is impossible to discuss here all the changes brought about by the Industrial Revolution and their psychological effects, but it is easy to see that the cumulative result may be inimical to democracy. Having witnessed how science has conquered terrible diseases, how transportation advances and construction marvels have overcome the former impediments of both distance and space, and how government itself has performed functions previously considered impossible, people no longer feel that the insecurity they experience or the disasters they fear are due to the uncontrollable forces of nature. They are instead inclined to believe that the government can do anything. Such an attitude is fertile ground for the demagogue because the people are credulous and are not likely to detect that he promises more than he can deliver. Moreover, the electorate is likely to be too impatient because it believes all problems are capable of solution and because it is likely to feel that hardships and inconveniences are due to the greed, selfishness, or incompetence of other men or else to the inadequacies of the economic and political system. Thus the emotionally charged propaganda of the demagogue claiming that a particular group is selfishly causing the trouble and ought to be brought under control has a powerful effect.[18] The spread of industry has brought a higher standard of living together with the increase and diffusion of knowledge, but it may in the long run have the effect of discouraging democratic institutions. As a matter of fact, both fascism and communism are so closely connected with contemporary sociological and psychological conditions that they could hardly have come at any other time.

THE PSYCHOLOGY OF DICTATORSHIP

A complete analysis of political forces must include not only sociological facts but their relationship to opinion. Although there is always an economic and social aspect to political activity, politics has its roots in psychology. A study of symbols and myths may contribute as much to our knowledge of political institutions as a study of the historical background, economic institutions, and the environmental setting. In any case, there is always the human element which must be understood in assessing political movements. In recent years a number of observers, employing a socio-psychological ap-

[17] A. D. Lindsay, *The Modern Democratic State* (New York, 1943), pp. 186–187. See also Karl Mannheim, *Man and Society in an Age of Reconstruction* (New York, 1941).

[18] For example, the Nazis focused their attention on the Jews, the Communists on the capitalists.

proach, have deduced interpretations of the nature of man and his reactions to contemporary conditions which help explain the popularity of dictatorships. . . .

CHARISMATIC LEADERSHIP

Leadership has always been a great factor in the history of human communities. Carlyle, Maurras, Nietzsche, and Leopold von Ranke saw history as largely the work of great state builders. Charisma is an irrational belief which arises in situations which the average man cannot grasp and understand rationally. In periods of civil strife, religious turmoil, and profound social and economic upheavals, men are often unable to perceive the factors which have caused their misery and distress. Under such circumstances they are likely to look for a leader who will fend off misery and deliver them from destitution. An examination of the idolatrous utterances made by party members, university professors, army officers, business men, and ordinary workers indicates quite clearly that contemporary leaders are revered and that they are thought of as possessing qualities lacking in ordinary mortals. In Nazi Germany hero-worship was formulated into a definite theory, for there were "Führers" for every branch of activity. However, Hermann Goering's description in *Germany Reborn* is similar to the adoration of the person of the dictator in other countries:

> Just as the Roman Catholic considers the Pope infallible in all matters concerning religion and morals, so do we National Socialists believe, with the same inner conviction, that for us the Leader is, in all political and other matters concerning the national and social interests of the people, simply infallible. Wherein lies the secret of this enormous influence which he has on his followers? . . . It is something mystical, inexpressible, almost incomprehensible, which this unique man possesses, and he who cannot feel it instinctively will not be able to grasp it at all. For we love Adolf Hitler, because we believe deeply and unswervingly that God has sent him to us to save Germany.[19]

A similar attitude also existed in Italy where Mussolini was proclaimed as a genius, a creative force who united in his person the irrational elements of the will of history, a man in the Messianic sense who was also the exemplary Italian in whom the people found its representative. . . .

Although the theory of historic materialism denies that an individual can have any influence on the progress of events, the same phenomenon has occurred in the Soviet Union. Although Beatrice and Sidney Webb did not consider Stalin a dictator, they found "the deliberate exploitation by the governing junta of the emotion of hero-worship, of the traditional reverence of the Russian people for a personal autocrat. . . . Scarcely a speech is

[19] Hermann Goering, *Germany Reborn* (London, 1934), pp. 79–80.

made or a conference held, without a naïve—some would say a fulsome—reference to 'Comrade Stalin' as the great leader of the people."[20] At the time when the Webbs wrote, the deification of Lenin, which began soon after his death, had become a fixed feature of Soviet national life; . . .

However, extravagant statements of adoration are not confined to rulers in dictatorial countries. One is reminded of the American business man who said that President Franklin D. Roosevelt was "the greatest leader since Jesus Christ."[21] When one reads how thousands wept as they walked in the streets upon the death of Kemal Ataturk, how many of the common people were struck with a sincere grief by the passing of Stalin, or about the emotional feeling of many, if not most, Americans upon the death of President Franklin D. Roosevelt,[22] there can be no doubt about the existence of charisma. Power has a peculiar fascination to the human mind. The masses apparently dote on a leader who by the mystery of magnetism inspires respect, who makes himself into their national symbol, and who makes them feel great through their kinship with him. The belief in one man's power to perform miracles is undoubtedly promoted and encouraged by both the leader and his followers, but there is no question that millions do sincerely believe in it. The fact that the worship of the ruler is a recurring idea in history would also seem to indicate that the masses derive an emotional satisfaction in the experience of hero-worship. The question arises, therefore, as to what are the exigencies in contemporary life responsible for the return of personal leadership and the psychological conditions which have created it. . . .

Even in democratic countries the masses have found it easier to fix their allegiance to a single personality than to a group of legislators whom it is hard to make responsible. Almost everywhere the executive has increased in power and prestige as compared with the legislature; and although this development is to some extent the inevitable result of social and economic changes which have produced a tremendous growth in the functions and activities of government, it has also been furthered by an extension of the suffrage. In both Britain and the United States the exploitation of personality has gone on increasingly as the franchise was widened to include a larger number of citizens. Ever since the days of Gladstone and Disraeli British electors have tended to vote for individual candidates, not on their merits, but in terms of whom they will support to be the prime minister. This de-

[20] *Soviet Communism: A New Civilisation?* (New York, Charles Scribner's Sons, 1936), p. 438. For a profound criticism of the Webbs on the ground that their ideas are anti-democratic, see Shirley R. Letwin, "Representation Without Democracy: The Webbs' Constitution," *The Review of Politics,* XVI (July, 1954), 352–375.

[21] John T. Flynn, "Other People's Money," *New Republic,* LXXXV (December 11, 1935), 129.

[22] For a discussion, see Harold Orlansky, "Reactions to the Death of President Roosevelt," *The Journal of Social Psychology,* XXVI (1947), 235–266.

velopment has also been furthered by the increased use of the press and radio. Today everything that a British prime minister or an American president says or does is news. Every party must have a great leader, and in the hands of the publicity experts he becomes almost divinely inspired. . . . In the same manner the eyes of the entire nation are fixed upon the President of the United States. The masses expect him to manage Congress and to secure favorable action on a well-rounded legislative program. Rightly or wrongly they tend to give him all the credit for successes but they also blame him for all the failures or shortcomings during his administration whether they can be attributed to his own personal actions or not. . . .

In so far as the growth of large cities has reduced the opportunity for personal participation by the citizen in local self-government, an important training ground of democracy has been lost; and in so far as modern education has failed to produce a well-rounded individual capable of critically analyzing political issues and devoted to participating in community life and taking an active interest in civic affairs, it has failed to produce the type of man upon which democracy depends.

FREUDIAN CONCEPTIONS

Sigmund Freud, the founder of psychoanalysis, developed a theory of human nature and behavior which, when given an application to social problems, has challenged the older forms of social psychology and produced new insights for explaining the emergence of dictatorship.[23] Space does not permit an extensive discussion of Freud's ideas and the social and political implications involved. However, his most important contribution lies in the emphasis he placed upon unconscious motivation and the role of irrational factors in human conduct. His discoveries have caused us to revise our conception of human nature and to see more clearly wherein the democratic theorists of the eighteenth and nineteenth centuries held a much too simple and optimistic view of man and placed too great an emphasis upon his rational nature.

Freud's psychology of society starts from the experience of the individual. There is developed inside the human psyche a father-hatred because it is the father who intervenes and prevents the child from possessing mother completely. In some respects the father is a terrible figure because it is he who brings the element of fear into a child's life through punishment and who teaches him a consciousness of guilt. At the same time, the child has a feeling of respect and admiration for the father, and this hate-love attitude

[23] Freud's most important books which make direct contributions to the social sciences are: *Group Psychology and the Analysis of the Ego* (London, 1922); *The Future of an Illusion* (London, 1928); *Civilization and Its Discontents* (London, 1930); and *The Problem of Anxiety* (New York, 1936).

is called ambivalence. The father is the most powerful member of the family; he is generally a kindly and benevolent person; the child is dependent on the father for the necessities of life and indeed thinks of him at first as an all-powerful person.

In the normal family an equilibrium is reached, but in every individual the experience of his early years is entangled with his whole personality. After he becomes an adult, he often wishes that he could return to his childhood when all of his wants were satisfied without effort on his part. After leaving the all-embracing comforts of the home, he is constantly seeking the loving mother and the father whom he respects and admires. Thus the king is an unconscious symbol of the father and the queen of the mother. A successful statesman has frequently been called "the father of his country." It is possible to substitute a symbol or an idea for an individual, but in times of stress and strain a people may not remain content with a "symbolic" leader and demand the destruction of the institutions standing between them and emotional reality. It may be that they will demand a "savior" or a "leader" who will stand in the same emotional relationship to them as that in which a father used to stand. Thus freedom is not really what people want, and dictatorship is merely the effort of a strained people to bring about order. It is the result of an emotional need which people feel, especially at a time when political conditions appear to be outside of human control, for a dominating personality. . . .

If men are cold, hungry, and impoverished and if there is also a vast incomprehensible menace, such as an economic crisis or war, they are seized by a paralyzing fear because the situation seems to leave no room for action. The very nature of the crisis makes an individual feel helpless and like a little child. He is inhibited from taking any action on his own because he does not know what is happening; and even if sources of information are available to the ordinary person, he is incapable of understanding.

> How could the Turkish peasant understand the complications of the world situation in 1922, the Italian the economic crisis, the Russian the famine and civil war which swept over him, the German worker the complex results of war and economic crisis? He is reduced to the position of a child in an incomprehensible world; his reaction resembles that of the ordinary adult in the face of illness.[24]

EVALUATION OF PRESENT KNOWLEDGE

If the conclusions reached in the preceding discussion are sound, dictatorship is the result of an intrinsic weakness of contemporary democracy which is partly institutional but which is mainly psychological and moral. The failure of democratic leadership to muster necessary electoral and legislative

[24] Spearman, *Modern Dictatorship,* p. 104.

support made it impossible for the executive to mobilize the power of the state or to develop and fulfill any broad public policy; and this crisis in authority in turn brought democratic government into contempt even among its supporters and had the effect of strengthening the antidemocratic elements in society. The contemporary crisis of democracy, therefore, is mainly spiritual and psychological. Its roots must be found in the loss of a common unity, in the inability of parties and interest groups to achieve agreement on fundamental common aims, and in their failure to find and accept a common moral purpose. . . .

The truth is that democracy has failed where it did not produce satisfactory results. Of all forms of government democracy is the most delicate requiring a long period for maturation and growth and presupposing the inculcation of an appropriate philosophy without which it cannot withstand the forces of disruption. When the pressures impinging on the government's stability are moderate, it can adjust to them and undergo gradual reformation or evolution; but when they are extreme, the desperate civil conflict generally culminates in the elevation of a tyrant.

The "best form of government," as Aristotle said, is relative to circumstances. Under right conditions and favorable circumstances democracy undoubtedly is the best form of government and secures the most satisfactory results. However, when these conditions are not present, democracy may at the same time be one of the worst kinds of government. It is sometimes forgotten that the judgment of both Plato and Aristotle was against democracy; and although they were unfamiliar with modern "representative democracy," the reasons for their adverse judgment and the circumstances out of which it arose may be instructive to us at the present time.

At no time has democracy been widely adopted in practice nor is it likely to be in the future. History does not teach us that men really wish to govern themselves but that they want to be well governed and expect results from the government in power. . . .

CONCLUSION

It is impossible to state with certainty the future of democracy in the modern world. Man as a free agent has the capacity to choose and the ability to influence his destiny. However, the social sciences lack certainty, and the present state of our knowledge can take us only a small way in determining the outcome.

Emphasis has been placed upon our lack of knowledge and the need for more study because existing theories do not seem to explain adequately political events and because profound changes taking place at the present time are little understood and their significance often ignored. However, there is a sense in which a solution to the crisis does not depend upon more knowledge. As Professor Hans J. Morgenthau has pointed out, "Politics is an art and not a science, and what is required for its mastery is not the rationality of the engineer but the wisdom and moral strength of the statesman." [25] The political conflicts in the modern world are only partially economic; they are not technical problems to be resolved through a blueprint; and they are similar to irrational forces that have previously dominated the aspirations of man. Man is a rational creature, but he is also influenced by prejudice and emotion; and it is impossible to predict with certainty whether the immediate future lies with the democratic leader or the tyrannical demagogue. The question confronting the modern world is whether it has the capacity to produce the statesmen who have the political wisdom to act successfully, who have the moral judgment to choose among expedient actions the least evil ones, and who have the imagination to build a new society which will reconcile man's political nature with his moral aspirations and his weakness with his strength.

[25] *Scientific Man vs. Power Politics* (Chicago, 1946), p. 10.

Topic 28

COMMUNISM AND DEMOCRACY

State and Revolution

V. I. LENIN *

Marx's doctrines are now undergoing the same fate, which, more than once in the course of history, has befallen the doctrines of other revolutionary thinkers and leaders of oppressed classes struggling for emancipation. During the lifetime of great revolutionaries, the oppressing classes have invariably meted out to them relentless persecution, and received their teaching with the most savage hostility, most furious hatred, and a ruthless campaign of lies and slanders. After their death, however, attempts are usually made to turn them into harmless saints, canonizing them, as it were, and investing their name with a certain halo by way of "consolation" to the oppressed classes, and with the object of duping them; while at the same time emasculating and vulgarizing the real essence of their revolutionary theories and blunting their revolutionary edge. At the present time the bourgeoisie and the opportunists within the Labor Movement are co-operating in this work of adulterating Marxism. They omit, obliterate, and distort the revolutionary side of its teaching, its revolutionary soul, and push to the foreground and extol what is, or seems, acceptable to the bourgeoisie. . . .

THE STATE AS THE PRODUCT OF THE IRRECONCILABILITY OF CLASS ANTAGONISMS

Let us begin with the most popular of Engels' works, *The Origin of the Family, Private Property, and the State*. Summarizing his historical analysis Engels says:

The State in no way constitutes a force imposed on Society from outside. Nor is the State "the reality of the Moral Idea," "the image and reality of Reason" as Hegel asserted. The State is the product of Society at a certain stage of its development. The State is tantamount to an acknowledgment that the given society has become entangled in an insoluble contradiction with

* Outstanding leader of the Russian Bolshevik Revolution. First Chairman of the Council of People's Commissars, U.S.S.R. Author of *Imperialism: The Highest Stage of Capitalism* and numerous other books and articles. *State and Revolution*, written in 1917, is presented here in abridged and rearranged form.

itself, that it has broken up into irreconcilable antagonisms, of which it is powerless to rid itself. And in order that these antagonisms, these classes with their opposing economic interests, may not devour one another and Society itself in their sterile struggle, some force standing, seemingly, above Society, becomes necessary so as to moderate the force of their collisions and to keep them within the bounds of "order." And this force arising from Society, but placing itself above it, which gradually separates itself from it—this force is the State.

Here, we have, expressed in all its clearness, the basic idea of Marxism on the question of the historical role and meaning of the State. The State is the product and the manifestation of the irreconcilability of class antagonisms. When, where and to what extent the State arises, depends directly on when, where and to what extent the class antagonisms of a given society cannot be objectively reconciled. And, conversely, the existence of the State proves that the class antagonisms *are* irreconcilable. . . .

According to Marx, the State is the organ of class *domination,* the organ of oppression of one class by another. Its aim is the creation of order which legalizes and perpetuates this oppression by moderating the collisions between the classes. But in the opinion of the petty-bourgeois politicians, the establishment of order is equivalent to the reconciliation of classes, and not to the oppression of one class by another. To moderate their collisions does not mean, according to them, to deprive the oppressed class of certain definite means and methods in its struggle for throwing off the yoke of the oppressors, but to conciliate it. . . .

But what is forgotten or overlooked is this:—If the State is the product of the irreconcilable character of class antagonisms, if it is a force standing above society and "separating itself gradually from it," then it is clear that the liberation of the oppressed class is impossible without a violent revolution, and without the destruction of the machinery of State power, which has been created by the governing class and in which this "separation" is embodied. . . .

What does this force consist of, in the main? It consists of special bodies of armed men who have at their command prisons, etc. We are justified in speaking of special bodies of armed men, because the public power peculiar to every State "is not identical" with the armed population, with its "self-acting armed organization." . . .

BOURGEOIS DEMOCRACY

In capitalist society, under the conditions most favorable to its development, we have a more or less complete democracy in the form of a democratic republic. But this democracy is always bound by the narrow framework of capitalist exploitation, and consequently always remains, in reality, a democracy only for the minority, only for the possessing classes, only for the rich. Freedom in capitalist society always remains more or less the same as it was in the ancient Greek republics, that is, freedom for the slave owners. The modern wage-slaves, in virtue of the conditions of capitalist exploitation, remain to such an extent crushed by want and poverty that they "cannot be bothered with democracy," have "no time for politics"; that, in the ordinary peaceful course of events, the majority of the population is debarred from participating in public political life. . . .

Democracy for an insignificant minority, democracy for the rich—that is the democracy of capitalist society. If we look more closely into the mechanism of capitalist democracy, everywhere—in the so-called "petty" details of the suffrage (the residential qualification, the exclusion of women, etc.), in the technique of the representative institutions, in the actual obstacles to the right of meeting (public buildings are not for the "poor"), in the purely capitalist organization of the daily press, etc., etc.—on all sides we shall see restrictions upon restrictions of democracy. These restrictions, exceptions, exclusions, obstacles for the poor, seem slight—especially in the eyes of one who has himself never known want, and has never lived in close contact with the oppressed classes in their hard life, and nine-tenths, if not ninety-nine hundredths, of the bourgeois publicists and politicians are of this class! But in their sum these restrictions exclude and thrust out the poor from politics and from an active share in democracy. Marx splendidly grasped the *essence* of capitalist democracy, when, in his analysis of the experience of the Commune, he said that the oppressed are allowed, once every few years to decide which particular representatives of the oppressing class are to represent and repress them in Parliament! . . .

In a democratic Republic, Engels continues "wealth wields its power indirectly, but all the more effectively," first, by means of "direct corruption of the officials" (America); second, by means of "the alliance of the government with the stock exchange" (France and America). At the present time, imperialism and the domination of the banks have reduced to a fine art both these methods of defending and practically asserting the omnipotence of wealth in democratic Republics of all descriptions. . .

We must also note that Engels quite definitely regards universal suffrage as a means of capitalist domination. Universal suffrage, he says (summing up obviously the long experience of German Social-Democracy), is "an index of the maturity of the working class; it cannot and never will, give anything more in the present state." The petty-bourgeois democrats such as our Socialist-Revolutionaries and Mensheviks and also their twin brothers, the Social-Chauvinists and opportunists of Western Europe, all expect a "great deal" from this universal suffrage. They themselves think and instil into the minds of the people the wrong idea that universal suffrage in the "present state" is really capable of expressing the will of the majority of the laboring masses and of securing its realization. . . .

Take any parliamentary country, from America to Switzerland, from France to England, Norway and so forth; the actual work of the State is done behind the scenes and is carried out by the departments, the chancelleries and the staffs. Parliament itself is given up to talk for the special purpose of fooling the "common people." . . .

Two more points. First: when Engels says that in a democratic republic, "not a whit less" than in a monarchy, the State remains an "apparatus for the oppression of one class by another," this by no means signifies that the *form* of oppression is a matter of indifference to the proletariat, as some anarchists "teach." A wider, more free and open form of the class struggle and class oppression enormously assists the proletariat in its struggle for the annihilation of all classes.

Second: only a new generation will be able completely to scrap the ancient lumber of the State—this question is bound up with the question of overcoming democracy, to which we now turn.

DICTATORSHIP OF THE PROLETARIAT

The forms of bourgeois States are exceedingly various, but their substance is the same and in the last analysis inevitably the *Dictatorship of the Bourgeoisie*. The transition from capitalism to Communism will certainly bring a great variety and abundance of political forms, but the substance will inevitably be: the *Dictatorship of the Proletariat*. . . .

The State is a particular form of organization of force; it is the organization of violence for the purpose of holding down some class. What is the class which the proletariat must hold down? It can only be, naturally, the exploiting class, i.e., the bourgeoisie. The toilers need the State only to overcome the resistance of the exploiters, and only the proletariat can guide this suppression and bring it to fulfillment, for the proletariat is the only class that is thoroughly revolutionary, the only class that can unite all the toilers and the exploited in the struggle against the bourgeoisie, for its complete displacement from power. . . .

But the dictatorship of the proletariat—that is, the organization of the advance-guard of the oppressed as the ruling class, for the purpose of crushing the oppressors—cannot produce merely an expansion of democracy. *Together* with an immense expansion of democracy—for the first time becoming democracy for the poor, democracy for the people, and not democracy for the rich—the dictatorship of the proletariat will produce a series of restrictions of liberty in the case of the oppressors, exploiters and capitalists. We must crush them in order to free humanity from wage-slavery; their resistance must be broken by force. It is clear that where there is suppression there must also be violence, and there cannot be liberty or democracy. . . .

The replacement of the bourgeois by the proletarian State is impossible without a violent revolution. . . . There is [in *Anti-Dühring*] a disquisition on the nature of a violent revolution; and the historical appreciation of its role becomes, with Engels, a veritable panegyric on violent revolution. . . . Here is Engels' argument:

> That force also plays another part in history (other than that of a perpetuation of evil), namely a *revolutionary* part; that, as Marx says, it is the midwife of every old society when it is pregnant with a new one; that force is the instrument and the means by which social movements hack their way through and break up the dead and fossilized political forms—of all this not a word by Herr Dühring. Duly, with sighs and groans, does he admit the possibility that for the overthrow of the system of exploitation force may, perhaps, be necessary, but most unfortunate if you please, because all use of force, forsooth, demoralizes its user! And this is said in face of the great moral and intellectual advance which has been the result of every victorious revolution! And this is said in Germany where a violent collision—which might perhaps be forced on the people—should have, at the very least, this advantage that it would destroy the spirit of subservience which has been permeating the national mind ever since the degradation and humiliation of the Thirty Years' War. And this turbid, flabby, impotent, parson's mode of thinking dares offer itself for acceptance to the most revolutionary party which history has known!

In the *Communist Manifesto* are summed up the general lessons of history, which force us to see in the State the organ of class domination, and lead us to the inevitable conclusion that the proletariat cannot overthrow the bourgeoisie without first conquering political power, without obtaining political rule, without transforming the State into the "proletariat organized as the ruling class"; and that this proletarian State must begin to wither away immediately after its victory, because in a community without class antagonisms, the State is unnecessary and impossible.

WHAT IS TO REPLACE THE SHATTERED STATE MACHINERY?

In 1847, in the *Communist Manifesto,* Marx was as yet only able to answer this question entirely in an abstract manner, stating the problem rather than its solution. To replace this machinery by "the proletariat organized as the ruling class," "by the conquest of democracy"—such was the answer of the *Communist Manifesto*. . . .

Refusing to plunge into Utopia, Marx waited for the experience of a mass movement to produce the answer to the problem as to the exact forms which this organization of the proletariat as the dominant class will assume and exactly in what manner this organization will embody the most complete, most consistent "conquest of democracy." Marx subjected the experiment of the [Paris] Commune, although it was so meagre, to a most minute analysis in his *Civil War in France*. Let us bring before the reader the most important passages of this work. . . .

> The Commune was the direct antithesis of the Empire. It was a definite form . . . of a Republic which was to abolish, not only the monarchical form of class rule, but also class rule itself.

What was this "definite" form of the proletarian Socialist Republic? What was the State it was beginning to create? "The first decree of the [Paris] Commune was the suppression of the standing army, and the substitution for it of the armed people," says Marx. . . . But let us see how, twenty years after the Commune, Engels summed up its lessons for the fighting proletariat. . . .

> Against this inevitable feature of all systems of government that have existed hitherto, viz., the transformation of the State and its organs from servants into the lords of society, the Commune used two unfailing remedies. First, it appointed to all posts, administrative, legal, educational, persons elected by universal suffrage; introducing at the same time the right of recalling those elected at any time by the decision of their electors. Secondly, it paid all officials, both high and low, only such pay as was received by any other worker. The highest salary paid by the Commune was 6,000 francs (about £240).
>
> Thus was created an effective barrier to place-hunting and career-making, even apart from the imperative mandates of the deputies in representative institutions introduced by the Commune over and above this. . . .

The lowering of the pay of the highest State officials seems simply a naive, primitive demand of democracy. One of the "founders" of the newest opportunism, the former Social-Democrat, E. Bernstein, has more than once exercised his talents in the repetition of the vulgar capitalist jeers at "primitive" democracy. Like all opportunists, like the present followers of Kautsky, he quite failed to understand that, first of all, the transition from capitalism to Socialism is impossible without "return," in a measure, to "primitive" democracy. How can we otherwise pass on to the discharge of all the functions of government by the majority of the population and by every individual of the population. And, secondly, he forgot that "primitive democracy" on the basis of capitalism and capitalist culture is not the same primitive democracy as in pre-historic or pre-capitalist times. Capitalist culture has created industry on a large scale in the shape of factories, railways, posts, telephones, and so forth: and *on this basis* the great majority of functions of "the old State" have become enormously simplified and reduced, in practice, to very simple operations such as registration, filing and checking. Hence they will be quite within the reach of every literate person, and it will be possible to perform them for the usual "working man's wage." This circumstance ought to and will strip them of all their former glamour as "government," and, therefore, privileged service.

The control of all officials, without exception, by the unreserved application of the principle of election and, *at any time,* re-call; and the approximation of their salaries to the "ordinary pay of the workers"—these are simple and "self-evident" democratic measures, which harmonize completely the interests of the workers and the majority of peasants; and, at the same time, serve as a bridge leading from capitalism to Socialism. . . .

The dictatorship of the proletariat, the period of transition to Communism, will, for the first time, produce a democracy for the people, for the majority, side by side with the necessary suppression of the minority constituted by the exploiters. Communism alone is capable of giving a really complete democracy, and the fuller it is the more quickly will it become unnecessary and wither away of itself. In other words, under capitalism we have a State in the proper sense of the word: that is, a special instrument for the suppression of one class by another, and of the majority by the minority at that. Naturally, for the successful discharge of such a task as the systematic suppression by the minority of exploiters of the majority of exploited, the greatest ferocity and savagery of suppression is required, and seas of blood are needed, through which humanity has to direct its path, in a condition of slavery, serfdom and wage labor.

Again, during the *transition* from capitalism to Communism, suppression is *still* necessary; but in this case it is suppression of the minority of exploiters by the majority of exploited. A special instrument, a special machine for suppression—that is, the "State"—is necessary, but this is now a transitional State, no longer a State in the ordinary sense of the term. For the suppression of the minority of exploiters, by the majority of those who were *but yesterday* wage slaves, is a matter comparatively so easy, simple and natural that it will cost far less bloodshed than the suppression of the risings of the slaves, serfs or wage laborers, and will cost the human race far less. And it is compatible with the diffusion of democracy over such an overwhelming majority of the nation that the need for any *special machinery* for *suppression* will gradually cease to exist. The exploiters are unable, of course, to suppress the people without a most complex machine for performing this duty; but *the people* can suppress the exploiters even with a very simple "machine"—almost without any "machine" at all, without any special apparatus—by the simple *organization of the armed masses* (such as the Councils of Workers' and Soldiers' Deputies, we may remark, anticipating a little).

Finally, only under Communism will the State become quite unnecessary, for there will be *no one* to suppress—"no one" in the sense of a *class,* in the sense of a systematic struggle with a definite section of the population. We are not utopians, and we do not in the least deny the possibility and inevitability of excesses by *individual persons,* and equally the need to suppress such excesses. But, in the first place, for this no special machine, no special instrument of repression is needed. This will be done by the armed nation itself, as simply and as readily as any crowd of civilized people, even in modern society, parts a pair of combatants or does not allow a woman to be outraged. And, secondly, we know that the fundamental social cause of excesses which violate the rules of social life is the exploitation of the masses, their want and their poverty. With the removal of this chief cause, excesses will inevitably begin to "wither away." We do not know how quickly and in what stages, but we know that they will be withering away. With their withering away, the State will also wither away.

THE "WITHERING AWAY" OF THE STATE

Engels' words regarding the "withering away" of the State enjoy such a popularity, are so often quoted, and reveal so clearly the essence of the common adulteration of Marxism in an opportunist sense that we must examine them in detail. Let us give the passage from which they are taken.

> The proletariat takes control of the State authority and, first of all, converts the means of production into State property. But by this very act it destroys itself, as a proletariat, destroying at the same time all class differences and class antagonisms, and with this, also, the State.

Engels speaks here of the *destruction* of the capitalist State by the proletarian revolution, while the words about its withering away refer to the remains of a *proletarian* State *after* the Socialist revolution. The capitalist State does not wither away, according to Engels, but is *destroyed* by the proletariat in the course of the revolution. Only the proletarian State or semi-State withers away after the revolution. . . .

A general summary of his views is given by Engels in the following words:—

> Thus, the State has not always existed. There were societies which did without it, which had no idea of the State or of State power. At a given stage of economic development which was necessarily bound up with the break up of society into classes, the State became a necessity, as a result of this division. We are now rapidly approaching a stage in the development of production, in which the existence of these classes is not only no longer necessary, but is becoming a direct impediment to production. Classes will vanish as inevitably as they inevitably arose in the past. With the disappearance of classes the State, too, will inevitably disappear. When organizing production anew on the basis of a free and equal association of the producers, Society will banish the whole State machine to a place which will then be the most proper one for it—to the museum of antiquities side by side with the spinning-wheel and the bronze axe.

FIRST PHASE OF COMMUNIST SOCIETY: SOCIALISM

It is this Communist society—a society which has just come into the world out of the womb of capitalism, and which, in all respects, bears the stamp of the old society—that Marx terms the first, or lower, phase of Communist society.

The means of production are now no longer the private property of individuals. The means of production belong to the whole of society. Every member of society, performing a certain part of socially-necessary labor, receives a certificate from society that he has done such and such a quantity of work. According to this certificate, he receives from the public stores of articles of consumption, a corresponding quantity of products. After the deduction of that proportion of labor which goes to the public fund, every worker, therefore, receives from society as much as he has given it.

"Equality" seems to reign supreme. . . . But different people are not equal to one another. One is strong, another is weak; one is married, the other is not. One has more children, another has less, and so on.

> With equal labor [Marx concludes] and, therefore, with an equal share in the public stock of articles of consumption, one will, in reality, receive more than another, will find himself richer, and so on. To avoid all this, "rights," instead of being equal, should be unequal.

The first phase of Communism, therefore, still cannot produce justice and equality; differences and unjust differences in wealth will still exist, but the *exploitation* of man by man will have become impossible, because it will be impossible to seize as private property the *means of production,* the factories, machines, land, and so on. . . .

"He who does not work neither shall he eat"—this Socialist principle is *already* realized. "For an equal quantity of labor an equal quantity of products"—this Socialist principle is also already realized. Nevertheless, this is not yet Communism, and this does not abolish "bourgeois law," [for Communism] gives to unequal individuals, in return for an unequal (in reality) amount of work, an equal quantity of products.

This is a "defect," says Marx, but it is unavoidable during the first phase of Communism; for, if we are not to land in Utopia, we cannot imagine that, having overthrown capitalism, people will at once learn to work for society *without any regulations by law;* indeed, the abolition of capitalism does not *immediately* lay the economic foundations for such a change. . . .

The State is withering away in so far as there are no longer any capitalists, any classes, and, consequently, any *class* whatever to suppress. But the State is not yet dead altogether, since there still remains the protection of "bourgeois law," which sanctifies actual inequality. For the complete extinction of the State complete Communism is necessary.

THE HIGHER PHASE OF COMMUNIST SOCIETY: COMMUNISM

Marx continues:

> In the higher phase of Communist society, after the disappearance of the enslavement of man caused by his subjection to the principle of division of labor; when, together with this, the opposition between brain and manual work will have disappeared; when labor will have ceased to be a mere means of supporting life and will itself have become one of the first necessities of life when with the all-round development of the individual, the productive forces, too, will have grown to maturity, and all the forces of social wealth will be pouring an uninterrupted torrent—only then will it be possible wholly to pass beyond the narrow horizon of bourgeois laws, and only then will society be able to inscribe on its banner: "From each according to his ability; to each according to his needs."

Only now can we appreciate the full justice of Engels' observations when he mercilessly ridiculed all the absurdity of combining the words "freedom" and "State." While the State exists there can be no freedom. When there is freedom there will be no State.

The economic basis for the complete withering away of the State is that high stage of development of Communism when the distinction between brain and manual work disappears; consequently, when one of the principal sources of modern *social* inequalities will have vanished—a source, moreover, which it is impossible to remove immediately by the mere conversion of the means of production into public property, by the mere expropriation of the capitalists.

This expropriation will make it possible gigantically to develop the forces of production. And seeing how incredibly, even now, capitalism *retards* this development, how much progress could be made even on the basis of modern technique at the level it has reached, we have a right to say, with the fullest confidence, that the expropriation of the capitalists will result inevitably in a gigantic development of the productive forces of human society. But how rapidly this development will go forward, how soon it will reach the point of breaking away from the division of labor, of the destruction of the antagonism between brain and manual work, of the transformation of work into a "first necessity of life"—this we do not and *cannot* know.

Consequently, we are right in speaking solely of the inevitable withering away of the State, emphasizing the protracted nature of this process, and its dependence upon the rapidity of development of the *higher phase* of Communism; leaving quite open the question of lengths of time, or the concrete forms of this withering away, since material for the solution of such questions is not available.

The State will be able to wither away completely when society has realized the formula: "From each according to his ability; to each according to his needs"; that is when people have become accustomed to observe the fundamental principles of social life, and their labor is so productive, that they will voluntarily work *according to their abilities.* "The narrow horizon of bourgeois law," which compels one to calculate, with the pitilessness of a Shylock, whether one has not worked half-an-hour more than another, whether one is not getting less pay than another—this narrow horizon will then be left behind. There will then be no need for any exact calculation by society of the quantity of products to be distributed to each of its members; each will take freely "according to his needs." . . .

The scientific difference between Socialism and Communism is clear. That which is generally called Socialism is termed by Marx the first or lower phase of Communist society. In so far as the means of production become public property, the word Communism is also applicable here, providing that we do not forget that it is not full Communism. . . .

Democracy implies equality. The immense significance of the struggle of the proletariat for equality and the power of attraction of such a battlecry are obvious, if we but rightly interpret it as meaning the *annihilation of classes.* But the equality of democracy is *formal* equality—no more; and immediately after the attainment of the equality of all members of society in respect of the ownership of the means of production, that is, of equality of labor and equality of wages, there will inevitably arise before humanity the question of going further from equality which is formal to equality which is real, and of realizing in life the formula, "From each according to his ability; to each according to his needs." By what stages, by means of what practical measures humanity will proceed to this higher aim—this we do not and cannot know. But it is important that one should realize how infinitely mendacious is the usual capitalist representation of Socialism as something lifeless, petrified, fixed once for all. In reality, it is only with Socialism that there will commence a rapid, genuine, real mass advance, in which first the majority and then the *whole* of the population will take part—an advance in all domains of social and individual life.

Analysis of the Communist Critique

H. B. MAYO *

Marxism may be studied today for at least two good reasons. In the first place, Marx was one of those pioneers, like Darwin or Freud, who

* Professor of Political Science, University of Western Ontario. The selection is from H. B. Mayo, *Democracy and Marxism* (New York: Oxford University Press, 1955), from the Preface and Chs. III and IX with some rearrangement. By permission.

changed the tenor of man's thought; and every student of history and society must sooner or later come to terms with him. His work may be riddled with ambiguities and inconsistencies, but it remains one of the landmarks of human thought, and the critical appraisal of any great system is one way of extending our knowledge. Marx's insight was never so constructive as it was analytic and critical; and certainly his influence has not been wholly beneficial. Yet much the same could be said of the founders of many other systems.

There is a second, but no less important, reason for studying Marxism. Marx's theories have often been refuted, but they are now the official beliefs of a third of the world's population. Hence to discuss them systematically is no mere academic diversion: urgent questions of domestic and international policy compel us to inquire into what the communist part of the world believes, or professes to believe. The democrat ought to know the case of his chief opponent, its strength and its weakness. To reject communism is not enough; it must be rejected soberly, and on the right grounds, with knowledge of what it does and does not contain.

To explain Marxism has naturally involved an examination of the writings of both Marx and Engels, since it is from these two men, joint authors of the *Communist Manifesto* in 1848, that the ideas of modern communism are largely derived. If our study stopped with Marx, however, we could hardly understand modern communism, which differs in many important respects from what Marx taught. Communism today is firmly cast in the Russian mold, and it has thus been necessary to examine also the additions and alterations to Marx's thought made by Lenin and Stalin. Marx once wrote that Russia always runs after the most extreme ideas the West has to offer. In some particulars, indeed, Russian communism, although paying tribute to Marx, flatly contradicts some of his theories.

Marxism as a grand-scale philosophy of history has obvious antidemocratic implications. The theory of an inevitable law of history, a dialectical economic process to which mankind can only conform, is stultifying to a free society. Democracy involves a faith in a future which is open and which can be, in time, what man chooses to make it, whereas Marxism casts the immediate future in an iron mold. So far as the Marxist philosophy of history is believed, even though it is false, to that extent it tends to weaken the will to democracy, encourages a fatalistic submission to communist movements, and postpones freedom of choice for mankind until the far future and the arrival of the classless society. Anyone who really believes in the inevitable victory of communism is lost as a democrat.

But the big guns of the Marxist attack are aimed more directly against democracy. . . . Marxist political theory describes the state as a class state, a mere instrument of exploitation in the hands of the bourgeoisie.

Legal and political systems are called forceful instruments of class rule, with the moral code cunningly devised to operate by persuasion to serve the same class interests. . . .

There is no possible way of operating a constitutional democracy smoothly if this kind of theory is widely believed by the citizens, and Lenin's advice to communists to get into a parliament in order to disrupt it is a natural deduction for anyone who regards bourgeois democracy as a sham. . . .

Nevertheless the Marxist critique may usefully be examined. Marxists can of course find real instances in all democracies of class pressures upon government, and the farther back one goes into history the more numerous the instances become; naturally so, since democracy did not spring full-fledged into being, but has been steadily developing through the years. For that reason, too, Marxists are fonder of citing the past, as revealed in the works of Marx and Engels, than of making fresh analyses of contemporary society.

A plausible case for the Marxist critique can very easily be made. Who can deny on the one hand the tender solicitude of government for business, and on the other, the shorter shrift which labor has so often got as its portion? Who can deny the enormous influence of money and a monied press in molding public opinion and influencing elections and legislatures? Who would feel so confident of receiving justice under the law even today if he were destitute?

Yet even when one has selected all the class elements within the democracies—conditions so much better documented by others than by Marxists—such a case is slowly but surely becoming obsolete. The redeeming feature of the democracies is that they are aware of the existing anomalies and are steadily reducing them; so that to say with the Marxist that the liberal democratic state of today is only a class dictatorship, or that "formal" freedom exhausts the content of democracy for the mass of the population, is a farcical exaggeration which scarcely calls for refutation. One comment suffices. Civil servants are not lackeys of the capitalists, as Lenin thought; their increasing number shows how the welfare state is growing, not how the bourgeoisie is grinding the faces of the poor.

One may go deeper with the inquiry. If Marx's general theory is right, and the economic foundation is all-important, can politics matter at all? Two conclusions are possible. One is that drawn by non-revolutionary socialists such as the Fabians: the political system can be consciously and flexibly adapted to changing economic conditions, and as long as that is done there need never be a violent break with the past. But such a conclusion is distasteful to Marxists and instead their conclusion is that under capitalism the chief purpose of the struggle for political power is to strengthen the class consciousness of the proletariat. Democratic politics has merely an instrumental and temporary function, to enable the proletariat to capture the state machinery in order to "smash" it. The Marxist theory thus reduces democracy to a mere stage before the inevitable dictatorship.

It was of course only too easy in early nineteenth-century England to believe in the ineffectual state and the harsh realities and power of economic life. The state that Marx analyzed was, in truth, grossly class-biased, as was the Russian state against which Lenin inveighed. But historically it is political action that has come in to redress the balance and to make wealth and economic power more and more responsible for public welfare. And every partial political control has also enlarged the area of man's freedom by lessening dependence on purely unplanned and unregulated economic forces. It is, among other reasons, just because the conscious social controls have increased steadily in number and scope since Marx's day that his predictions have proved to be so wide of the mark. . . .

What makes dogmatic Marxism an enemy of *contemporary* democracy is the denial of the autonomy and efficacy of politics *here and now* in any of the liberal democracies. Democracy can be stretched to mean many things, but when it ceases to mean that through political action a free people can shape the policies they desire, including the economic policies, then with Marx we must lapse into sheer economic determinism. This is only another way of saying that the difference between Marxist and democrat is that the latter believes it is possible to achieve economic change by peaceful political means, but that nothing short of revolution will satisfy the Marxist.

The "revisionists" had a keener understanding here than Marx and Lenin. Lenin had written that "the toiling masses are *barred* from participation in bourgeois parliaments . . . ." The statement was nonsense, based upon the working example of no capitalist democracy, and in convenient forgetfulness of Engels' observation that communists thrived on legal methods. Marx was indignant at the Gotha Program, since, although not saying so in as many words, it amounted to a rejection of his theory of the class state, and an affirmation that the state could be used for the benefit of all classes including the workers. The leaders of the Social Democratic party in Germany were aware that they could reasonably expect substantial reforms once the workers were enfranchised. The Social Democratic party, it is true, continued to suffer from a split personality: in practice its program was one of reform, but a section of its membership continued to profess adherence to Marxist theory. Nevertheless the party remained firmly gradualist and democratic in its conduct until the Russian revolution. In the end doctrinaire Leninism drove a section of the proletariat (the communist party) into open hostility toward democracy, while under the influence of revisionist leaders the rest of the workers rallied to the support of constitutional government.

The idea that government is conducted by a ruling class, whose interests are always identified with the national interest, was not invented by Marx but had been an accepted commonplace long before the nineteenth century. Sir Thomas More had defined government as "nothing more than a certain conspiracy of rich men procuring their own commodities under the name and title of a Commonwealth." James Harrington had taken it for granted (in 1656) that "power follows property." Even with the rise of modern democracies, the idea that political power *should* follow property took a long time a-dying, and for that matter still lingers on at the municipal level of government, in the remnants of property qualifications sometimes attached to the vote. But the Marxist accusation that government is merely another arm of the bourgeoisie or, in Lenin's words, "the millionaires" national committees called governments, has become a less and less adequate description of democratic government.

The one thing which Marxism cannot explain in modern democracies is the hostility of business toward its alleged puppet, the state. On ordinary empirical grounds, however, the explanation is easy: the enmity arises because the democratic state is used to benefit all classes, to weight the scales in favor of the weak, and to subject the economy to political direction. . . .

To Marx, the economic forces worked themselves out through the class struggle. Now, the sharpening of the class struggle and the increasing impoverishment which Marx expected have not in fact come about, and there is consequently no sign that the capitalist democracies will ever pass through the period of revolution predicted by Marx. . . .

Perhaps the great depression during the 1930's was the period when, if ever, the danger of proletarian revolution was most to be apprehended, yet nowhere did the revolution occur. In Britain the number of votes cast for the communist party remained negligible, while in the United States the communist vote actually declined. If there is such a thing as a consensus, it is that never again will depressions be allowed to become really severe. The United States and Canada have both officially adopted the Keynesian principles, the former in the Employment Act of 1946, and the latter in the 1945 White Paper on Employment and Income. The specific measures so far proposed are not likely, in themselves, to avert another slump, yet nevertheless once the state has assumed responsibility for a high level of employment, income, and prosperity, more than half the battle has been won. Citizens will rightly expect their government to take adequate remedial measures, and no democratic government will be able to refuse, especially now that the economists are widely publicizing the view (perhaps a little too confidently) that they know how to avert a serious slump, and how to keep on increasing the real income per capita.[1] Should the economic situation require drastic measures, as it may well do, these could lead very far

[1] E.g. Benjamin Higgins, *What Do Economists Know?*, Melbourne, 1951.

indeed away from the kind of capitalist society we have had in the past. Lord Keynes himself foresaw that prospect and did not dodge it.[2]

Marxism is here, again, at sharp odds with democracy, since it teaches that the democracies cannot prevent the crises of boom and slump. Engels was eloquent on the subject:

> Bourgeois economics can neither prevent crises in general, nor protect the individual capitalists from losses, bad debts and bankruptcy, nor secure the individual workers against unemployment and destitution. It is still true that man proposes and God (that is, the extraneous force of the capitalist mode of production) disposes.

All later Marxists have constantly chanted the same refrain: ". . . capitalist society is always an endless horror."[3] Within the framework of capitalism, crises can never be abolished, but will continue to get worse and worse, until the final catastrophic collapse.

As capitalist society changes its character, however—and it is changing all the time—many of the worst objections to it tend to disappear, in particular those stemming from unemployment and gross inequality. "Prosperity demoralizes the workers," as Marx noted, and since increasing impoverishment and the "industrial reserve army" are nowhere in evidence, Marxism loses its trump card. Political action then becomes a matter of degree, a little more or less of public ownership, social security, or piecemeal planning, in the interest of equality and the general welfare. Revolutions are not made by this pragmatic approach to the problems of society.

Since industrial society is nothing if not dynamic and experimental it would be more than remarkable, it would be miraculous, if subsequent development had fitted into the iron prognosis drawn up by Marx a century ago. (The society which Marx studied was moreover largely that of the *early* nineteenth century; that is, many of the Reports and Blue Books which he used referred to the past, and not to the second half of the century, when he studied and wrote.) The increasing economic influence and the growing political influence of the "working class," and of the organized farmers, are two of the outstanding features of the modern world, especially in the more industrialized countries. And these are not revolutionary groups. As we know well, one of the best innoculations against revolution is a flourishing trade-union movement which can see that it is making substantial gains. Marx would no doubt take the stand that all these things do not really lead to a change of system per se, but that is only a matter of definition. What matters is that the going economic and social system under which we now live, whatever it may be called, is quite unlike the society analyzed by Marx and even more unlike the future which he anticipated. . . .

[2] *General Theory of Employment, Interest and Money,* Ch. 24.

[3] Engels, *Anti-Duhring, Handbook,* p. 301; *Lenin, Selected Works,* 1951, I, Part 2, p. 574.

Marx turned to the study of economic history to find the proof for his class-struggle theory. The social scientist of today, however, turns to society not with a thesis to prove but with a question: are the rigidities arising from property relations so serious that industrial society cannot adapt its institutions and ideas to the changing modes of production quickly enough to make a peaceful transition to the future? In less Marxist language: is the social lag between technology on the one hand, and institutions and beliefs on the other, capable of being reduced peacefully? . . .

The functions of the state have always been to provide internal order and protection from external enemies. But they have never been confined to these, and there is no mystery about the process by which the democratic state has gone beyond them to concern itself deeply with the economy. . . . No sharp line can in fact be drawn between politics and the economy. As Adam Smith astutely noted, property and wealth depend upon society and law as well as upon individual effort; and this is especially true in the present highly interdependent society. Business itself has set the example for state intervention by its readiness to seek government protection whenever the chill winds of competition have become too biting. The United States, like all democracies, has always had an empirically collectivist tradition.[4] Modern advertising, too, by its emphasis on "service to the community"—which makes so many advertisements read as though put out by philanthropists—encourages the citizen to judge the performance of business by the test of public welfare. The relief of depressions and the planning of a wartime economy have accustomed the public to state action for the achievement of specific objectives. The logic of democracy and the spread of humanitarianism have generated new demands and, contrary to the Marxist assumption, it has been possible to appeal successfully to reason and conscience in all democratic states, and (equally important) the increasing productivity has assured that the demands could be met.

The ghost of the Great Depression haunts every democracy, and although there may be no great confidence in the ability of private enterprise alone to maintain economic stability and rising living standards, there is every confidence in a partnership of government and business that offers a middle way between rugged competition and total collectivism. One of the reasons why this "middle way" is not better understood is that it changes so fast that theory cannot keep up with it. Nor have we yet discovered a satisfactory word to describe it. (The term "neo-mercantilism" has been suggested, but has some drawbacks.)

As the public interest instead of private profit becomes more and more the criterion of economic action, as taxation regulates income in order to influence demand and promote equity, and as regulation of many kinds

[4] George H. Sabine, "Two Democratic Traditions," *Philosophical Review*, October 1952, pp. 451ff.

becomes a normal concomitant of business, the essentially private nature of the economy is slowly but steadily altered, and the social character of freedom and property is increasingly recognized. What is remarkable about this historic development is not the amount of opposition to trade unions, state regulation, government enterprise, progressive and rising taxation, and the welfare state; what is much more surprising is that private enterprise should put up such a comparatively weak fight as it finds itself taxed, controlled, hampered, and sometimes eliminated by the responsible public authorities. So far has the process gone that it becomes ever more difficult to see any point at which a stand in defense of the past could be made.

The mixed economy we have at present is partly "socialized" and partly in private hands, partly free and partly controlled. Anyone who fails to recognize this, and to make it the very basis of his analysis, is looking at the world through glasses as opaque as those worn by the Marxist. A system and an age are passing away and the resulting conflicts in society are being resolved in other ways than by means of a sharpening class struggle. Nor is it accurate to describe present society as socialist, for the kind of society that is coming about in the Western democracies is a long way removed from socialism as it has traditionally been understood. In Britain many an old-time socialist has been disillusioned by the course of events, while many a younger conservative finds the changed social climate quite congenial. The same process goes on in nearly every country regardless of the political party in power, and serves to show how free societies can adapt themselves peacefully to meet changing conditions. Democracy today is not merely liberalism but liberalism with something added, which may be described as social welfare and the public interest.

Why I Am Not a Communist

MORRIS RAPHAEL COHEN *

What distinguishes present-day Communists is not . . . their professed ultimate goal or their analysis of our economic ills, but their political remedy or program—to wit, the seizure of power by armed rebellion [1] and the

* Late Professor of Philosophy, The City College of New York. President of the American Philosophical Association, 1929. Author of *Reason and Nature, Law and the Social Order, Faith of a Liberal,* and other works. The selection is from Morris Raphael Cohen, "Why I Am Not a Communist," *Modern Monthly* (April, 1934), Vol. 8, No. 3; reprinted in *The Meaning of Marx. A Symposium,* by Bertrand Russell, John Dewey, Morris Cohen, Sidney Hook, and Sherwood Eddy (New York, Rinehart & Co., Inc., 1934). Reprinted with permission of the administrators of the estate of Morris Raphael Cohen.

[1] Since this article was written armed intervention seems to have largely replaced armed rebellion as a technique for the seizure of power.

setting up of a dictatorship by the leaders of the Communist Party. To be sure, this dictatorship is to be in the name of the *proletariat,* just as the fascist dictatorship is in the name of *the whole nation.* But such verbal tricks cannot hide the brute facts of tyrannical suppression necessarily involved in all dictatorship. For the wielders of dictatorial power are few, they are seldom if ever themselves toilers, and they can maintain their power only by ruthlessly suppressing all expression of popular dissatisfaction with their rule. And where there is no freedom of discussion, there is no freedom of thought.

This program of civil war, dictatorship, and the illiberal or fanatically intolerant spirit which war psychology always engenders may bring more miseries than those that the Communists seek to remove; and the arguments to prove that such war is desirable or inevitable seem to me patently inadequate.

Communists ignore the historic truth that civil wars are much more destructive of all that men hold dearest than are wars between nations; and all the arguments that they use against the latter, including the late "war to end war," are much more cogent against civil wars. Wars between nations are necessarily restricted in scope and do not prevent—to a limited extent they even stimulate—co-operation within a community. But civil wars necessarily dislocate all existing social organs and leave us with little social capital or machinery to rebuild a better society. The hatreds which fratricidal wars develop are more persistent and destructive than those developed by wars that terminate in treaties or agreements.

Having lived under the tyranny of the Czar, I cannot and do not condemn all revolutions. But the success and benefits of any revolution depend on the extent to which—like the American Revolution of 1776, the French Revolution of 1789, and the anti-Czarist Revolution of March 1917—it approximates national unanimity in the co-operation of diverse classes. When armed uprisings have been undertaken by single oppressed classes, as in the revolt of the gladiators in Rome, the various peasant revolts in England, Germany, and Russia, the French Commune of 1871, or the Moscow uprising of 1905, they have left a deplorably monotonous record of bloody massacres and oppressive reaction. The idea that armed rebellion is the only or the always effective cure for social ills seems to me no better than the old superstition of medieval medicine that blood-letting is the only and the sovereign remedy for all bodily ills.

Communists may feel that the benefits of their Revolution of 1917 outweigh all the terrific hardships which the Russian people have suffered since then. But reasonable people in America will do well to demand better evidence than has yet been offered that they can improve their lot by blindly imitating Russia. Russian breadlines, and famine without breadlines, are certainly not *prima facie* improvements over American conditions.

At best a revolution is a regrettable means to bring about greater human welfare. It always unleashes the forces that thrive in disorder, the brutal executions, imprisonments, and, what is even worse, the sordid spying that undermines all feeling of personal security. These forces, once let loose, are difficult to control and they tend to perpetuate themselves. If, therefore, human well-being, rather than mere destruction, is our aim, we must be as critically-minded in considering the consequences of armed revolution as in considering the evils of the existing regime.

One of the reasons that lead Communists to ignore the terrific destruction which armed rebellion must bring about is the conviction that "the revolution" is inevitable. In this they follow Marx, who, dominated by the Hegelian dialectic, regarded the victory of the proletariat over the bourgeoisie as inevitable, so that all that human effort can hope to achieve is "to shorten and lessen the birth pangs" of the new order. There is, however, very little scientific value in this dialectic argument, and many Communists are quite ready to soft-pedal it and admit that some human mistake or misstep might lead to the triumph of fascism. The truth is that the dialectic method which Marx inherited from Hegel and Schelling is an outgrowth of speculations carried on in theologic seminaries. The "system" of production takes the place of the councils or the mills of the gods. Such Oriental fatalism has little support in the spirit and method of modern science. Let us therefore leave the pretended dialectic proof and examine the contention on an historical basis.

Historically, the argument is put thus: When did any class give up its power without a bloody struggle? As in most rhetorical questions, the questioner does not stop for an answer, assuming that his ignorance is conclusive as to the facts. Now, it is not difficult to give instances of ruling classes giving up their sovereignty without armed resistance. The English landed aristocracy did it in the Reform Bill of 1832; and the Russian nobility did it in 1863 when they freed their serfs, though history showed clearly that in this way not only their political power but their very existence was doomed (for money income has never been so secure as direct revenue from the land, and life in cities reduced the absolute number of noble families). In our own country, the old seaboard aristocracy, which put over the United States Constitution and controlled the government up to the Jacksonian era, offered no armed resistance when the backwoods farmers outvoted them and removed church and property qualifications for office and for the franchise.

But it is not necessary to multiply such instances. It is more important to observe that history does not show that any *class* ever gained its enfranchisement through a bloody rebellion carried out by its own unaided efforts. When ruling classes are overthrown it is generally by a combination of groups that have risen to power only after a long process. For the parties to a rebellion cannot succeed unless they have more resources than the established regime. Thus the ascendancy of the French bourgeoisie was aided by the royal power which Richelieu and Colbert used in the seventeenth century to transform the landed barons into dependent courtiers. Even so, the French Revolution of 1789 would have been impossible without the co-operation of the peasantry, whose opposition to their ancient seigneurs was strengthened as the latter ceased to be independent rulers of the land. This is in a measure also true of the supposedly purely Communist Revolution in Russia. For in that revolution, too, the peasantry had a much greater share than is ordinarily assumed. After all, the amount of landed communal property (that of the crown, the church, etc.) which was changed by the peasants into individual ownership may have been greater than the amount of private property made communal by the Soviet regime. Even the system of collective farms is, after all, a return to the old *mir* system, using modern machinery. The success of the Russian Revolution was largely due to the landlords' agents who, in their endeavor to restore the rule of the landlords, threw the peasantry into the arms of the Bolshevists. Indeed, the strictly Marxian economics, with its ideology of surplus-value due to the ownership of the means of production, is inherently inapplicable to the case of the peasant who cultivates his own piece of ground.

Even more important, however, is it to note that no amount of repetition can make a truth of the dogma that the capitalist class alone rules this country and like the Almighty can do what it pleases. It would be folly to deny that, as individuals or as a class, capitalists have more than their proportionate share of influence in the government, and that they have exercised it unintelligently and with dire results. But it is equally absurd to maintain that they have governed or can govern without the co-operation of the farmers and the influential middle classes. None of our recent constitutional amendments—not the income-tax amendment, not the popular election of the United States Senators, not woman suffrage, neither prohibition nor its repeal—nor any other major bit of legislation can be said to have been imposed on our country in the interests of the capitalist class. The farmers, who despite mortgages still cling to the private ownership of their land, are actually the dominant political group even in industrial states like New York, Pennsylvania, and Illinois.

The Communist division of mankind into workingmen and capitalists suffers from the fallacy of simplism. Our social structure and effective class divisions are much more complicated. As the productivity of machinery increases, the middle classes increase rather than decrease. Hence a program based entirely on the supposed exclusive interests of the proletariat has no reasonable prospect. Any real threat of an armed uprising will only strengthen the reactionaries, who are not less intelligent than the Communist leaders, understand just as well how to reach and influence our people, and have more ample means for organization. If our working classes find it difficult to learn what their true interests are and do not know how to control their representatives in the government and in the trade unions, there is little prospect that they will be able to control things better during a rebellion or during the ensuing dictatorship.

If the history of the past is any guide at all, it indicates that real improvements in the future will come like the improvements of the past—namely, through co-operation among different groups, each of which is wise enough to see the necessity of compromising with those with whom we have to live together and whom we cannot or do not wish to exterminate.

I know that this notion of compromise or of taking counsel as the least wasteful way of adjusting differences is regarded as hopelessly antiquated and bourgeois, but I do not believe that the ideas of so-called Utopian socialists have really been refuted by those who arrogate the epithet "scientific" to themselves. The Communists seem to me to be much more Utopian and quite unscientific in their claims that the working class alone can by its own efforts completely transform our social order.

I do not have very high expectations from the efforts of sentimental benevolence. Yet I cannot help noticing that the leaders of the Communists and of other revolutionary labor movements—Engels, Marx, Lassalle, Luxemburg, Liebknecht, Lenin, and Trotsky—have not been drawn to it by economic solidarity. They were not workingmen nor even all of workingmen's families. They were driven to their role by human sympathy. Sympathy with the sufferings of our fellow men is a human motive that cannot be read out of history. It has exerted tremendous social pressure. Without it you cannot explain the course of nineteenth-century factory legislation, the freeing of serfs and slaves, or the elimination of the grosser forms of human exploitation. Though some who regard themselves as followers of Karl Marx are constantly denouncing reformers who believe in piecemeal improvement and hope rather that things will get worse so as to drive people into a revolution, Marx himself did not always take that view. Very wisely he attached great importance to English factory legislation which restricted the number of hours per working day, for he realized that every little bit that strengthens the workers strengthens their resistance to exploitation. Those who are most oppressed and depressed, the inhabitants of the slums, do not revolt—they have not energy enough to think of it. When, therefore, Mr. Strachey and others criticize the socialists for not bringing about the millennium when they get into power, I am not at all impressed. I do not believe that the socialists or the Labor Party in England have been free from shameful error. But neither have the Communists, nor any other human group, been free from it. Trite though it sounds, it is nevertheless true that no human arrangement can bring about perfection on earth. And while the illusion of omniscience may offer great consolation, it brings endless inhumanity when it leads us to shut the gates of mercy. Real as are our human conflicts, our fundamental identity of interest in the face of hostile nature seems to me worthy of more serious attention than the Communists have been willing to accord it.

If liberalism were dead, I should still maintain that it deserved to live, that it had not been condemned in the court of human reason, but lynched outside of it by the passionate and uncompromisingly ruthless war spirit, common to Communists and Fascists. But I do not believe that liberalism is dead, even though it is under eclipse. There still seems to me enough reason left to which to appeal against reckless fanaticism.

It is pure fanaticism to belittle the gains that have come to mankind from the spirit of free inquiry, free discussion, and accommodation. No human individual or group of individuals can claim omniscience. Hence society can only suffer serious loss when one group suppresses the opinions and criticisms of all others. In purely abstract questions compromise may often be a sign of confusion. One cannot really believe inconsistent principles at the same time. But in the absence of perfect or even adequate knowledge in regard to human affairs and their future, we must adopt an experimental attitude and treat principles not as eternal dogmas, but as hypotheses, to be tried to the extent that they indicate the general direction of solution to specific issues. But as the scientist must be ever ready to modify his own hypothesis or to recognize wherein a contrary hypothesis has merits or deserves preference, so in practical affairs we must be prepared to learn from those who differ with us, and to recognize that however contradictory diverse views may appear in discourse they may not be so in their practical applications. . . .

The ruthless suppression of dissent within the Communist Party in Russia and the systematic glorification of the national heroes and military objectives of Czarist days suggest that the Bolshevik Revolution was not so complete a break with the Russian past as most of its friends and enemies assumed in earlier days. In any event we have witnessed in the history of the Communist movement since 1917 a dramatic demonstration of the way in which the glorification of power—first as a means of destroying a ruling class, then as a means of defending a beleaguered state from surrounding enemies, and finally as a means of extending Communism to neighboring lands—comes imperceptibly to displace the ends or objectives which once formed the core of Communist thought. Thus, one by one, the worst features of capitalist society and imperialism, against which Communism cut its eye teeth in protest—extreme inequality in wages, speed-up of workers, secret diplomacy, and armed intervention as a technique of international intercourse—have been taken over by the Soviet Union, with only a set of thin verbal distinctions to distinguish the "good" techniques of Communism from the corresponding "bad" techniques used by capitalism. As is always the case, the glorification of power dulls the sense of righteousness to which any movement for bettering the basic conditions of human living must appeal.

The Communist criticism of liberalism seems to me altogether baseless and worthless. One would suppose from it that liberalism is a peculiar excrescence of capitalism. This is, however, not true. The essence of liberalism—freedom of thought and inquiry, freedom of discussion and criticism—is not the invention of the capitalist system. It is rather the mother of Greek and modern science, without which our present industrial order and the labor movement would be impossible. The plea that the denial of freedom is a temporary necessity is advanced by all militarists. It ignores the fact that, when suppression becomes a habit, it is not readily abandoned. Thus, when the Christian Church after its alliance with the Roman Empire began the policy of "compelling them to enter," it kept up the habit of intolerant persecution for many centuries. Those who believe that many of the finer fruits of civilization were thereby choked should be careful about strengthening the forces of intolerance.

When the Communists tell me that I must choose between their dictatorship and Fascism, I feel that I am offered the choice between being shot and being hanged. It would be suicide for liberal civilization to accept this as exhausting the field of human possibility. I prefer to hope that the present wave of irrationalism and of fanatical intolerance will recede and that the great human energy which manifests itself in free thought will not perish.

Topic 29

THE COMMUNIST ALTERNATIVE

"The Cult Of The Individual"

NIKITA S. KHRUSHCHEV *

Comrades! In the report of the Central Committee of the party at the 20th Congress, in a number of speeches by delegates to the Congress, as also formerly during the plenary CC/CPSU [Central Committee of the Communist Party of the Soviet Union] sessions, quite a lot has been said about the cult of the individual and about its harmful consequences.

After Stalin's death the Central Committee of the party began to implement a policy of explaining concisely and consistently that it is impermissible and foreign to the spirit of Marxism-Leninism to elevate one person, to transform him into a superman possessing supernatural characteristics, akin to those of a god. Such a man supposedly knows everything, sees everything, thinks for everyone, can do anything, is infallible in his behavior. Such a belief about a man, and specifically about Stalin, was cultivated among us for many years. . . .

During Lenin's life the Central Committee of the party was a real expression of collective leadership of the party and of the nation. Being a militant Marxist-revolutionist, always unyielding in matters of principle, Lenin never imposed by force his views upon his co-workers. He tried to convince; he patiently explained his opinions to others. Lenin always diligently observed that the norms of party life were realized, that the party statute was enforced, that the party congresses and the plenary sessions of the Central Committee took place at the proper intervals.

In addition to the great accomplishments of V. I. Lenin for the victory of the working class and of the working peasants, for the victory of our party and for the application of the ideas of scientific Communism to life, his acute mind expressed itself also in this—that he detected in Stalin in

* Formerly Chairman of the Council of Ministers of the Union of Soviet Socialist Republics and First Secretary of the Central Committee of the Communist Party of the Soviet Union. This denunciation of Stalin was delivered on February 24–25, 1956 before the 20th Congress of the Communist Party of the Soviet Union, and first published in the United States on June 4, 1956. Although its authenticity has never been officially acknowledged, it has been widely credited in the Communist press throughout the world, and was implicitly admitted by Anastas I. Mikoyan, a leading Soviet official.

time those negative characteristics which resulted later in grave consequences. Fearing the future fate of the party and of the Soviet nation, V. I. Lenin made a completely correct characterization of Stalin, pointing out that it was necessary to consider the question of transferring Stalin from the position of the Secretary General because of the fact that Stalin is excessively rude, that he does not have a proper attitude toward his comrades, that he is capricious and abuses his power. . . .

When we analyze the practice of Stalin in regard to the direction of the party and of the country, when we pause to consider everything which Stalin perpetrated, we must be convinced that Lenin's fears were justified. The negative characteristics of Stalin, which, in Lenin's time, were only incipient, transformed themselves during the last years into a grave abuse of power by Stalin, which caused untold harm to our party.

We have to consider seriously and analyze correctly this matter in order that we may preclude any possibility of a repetition in any form whatever of what took place during the life of Stalin, who absolutely did not tolerate collegiality in leadership and in work, and who practiced brutal violence, not only toward everything which opposed him, but also toward that which seemed, to his capricious and despotic character, contrary to his concepts.

Stalin acted not through persuasion, explanation and patient cooperation with people, but by imposing his concepts and demanding absolute submission to his opinion. Whoever opposed this concept or tried to prove his viewpoint and the correctness of his position was doomed to removal from the leading collective and to subsequent moral and physical annihilation. This was especially true during the period following the 17th Party Congress, when many prominent party leaders and rank-and-file party workers, honest and dedicated to the cause of Communism, fell victim to Stalin's despotism.

We must affirm that the party had fought a serious fight against the Trotskyites, rightists and bourgeois nationalists, and that it disarmed ideologically all the enemies of Leninism. This ideological fight was carried on successfully, as a result of which the party became strengthened and tempered. Here Stalin played a positive role. . . .

Worth noting is the fact that, even during the progress of the furious ideological fight against the Trotskyites, the Zinovievites, the Bukharinites and others, extreme repressive measures were not used against them. The fight was on ideological grounds. But some years later, when socialism in our country was fundamentally constructed, when the exploiting classes were generally liquidated, when the Soviet social structure had radically changed, when the social basis for political movements and groups hostile to the party had violently contracted, when the ideological opponents of the party were long since defeated politically—then the repression directed against them began.

It was precisely during this period (1935–1937–1938) that the practice of mass repression through the Government apparatus was born, first against the enemies of Leninism—Trotskyites, Zinovievites, Bukharinites, long since politically defeated by the party—and subsequently also against many honest Communists, against those party cadres who had borne the heavy load of the Civil War and the first and most difficult years of industrialization and collectivization, who actively fought against the Trotskyites and the rightists for the Leninist party line.

Stalin originated the concept "enemy of the people." This term automatically rendered it unnecessary that the ideological errors of a man or men engaged in a controversy be proven; this term made possible the usage of the most cruel repression, violating all norms of revolutionary legality, against anyone who in any way disagreed with Stalin, against those who were only suspected of hostile intent, against those who had bad reputations. This concept "enemy of the people" actually eliminated the possibility of any kind of ideological fight or the making of one's views known on this or that issue, even those of a practical character. In the main, and in actuality, the only proof of guilt used, against all norms of current legal science, was the "confession" of the accused himself; and, as subsequent probing proved, "confessions" were acquired through physical pressures against the accused. This led to glaring violations of revolutionary legality and to the fact that many entirely innocent persons, who in the past had defended the party line, became victims.

We must assert that, in regard to those persons who in their time had opposed the party line, there were often no sufficiently serious reasons for their physical annihilation. The formula "enemy of the people" was specifically introduced for the purpose of physically annihilating such individuals. . . .

Arbitrary behavior by one person encouraged and permitted arbitrariness in others. Mass arrests and deportations of many thousands of people, execution without trial and without normal investigation created conditions of insecurity, fear and even desperation. This, of course, did not contribute toward unity of the party ranks and of all strata of working people, but, on the contrary, brought about annihilation and the expulsion from the party of workers who were loyal but inconvenient to Stalin. . . .

But can it be said that Lenin did not decide to use even the most severe means against enemies of the Revolution when this was actually necessary? No; no one can say this. Vladimir Ilyich demanded uncompromising dealings with the enemies of the Revolution and of the working class and when necessary resorted ruthlessly to such methods. You will recall only V. I. Lenin's fight with the Socialist Revolutionary organizers of the anti-Soviet uprising, with the counterrevolutionary kulaks in 1918 and with others, when Lenin without hesitation used the most extreme methods against the enemies. Lenin used such methods, however, only against actual class enemies and not against those who blunder, who err, and whom it was possible to lead through ideological influence and even retain in the leadership. Lenin used severe methods only in the most necessary cases, when the exploiting classes were still in existence and were vigorously opposing the Revolution, when the struggle for survival was decidedly assuming the sharpest forms, even including a civil war.

Stalin, on the other hand, used extreme methods and mass repressions at a time when the Revolution was already victorious, when the Soviet state was strengthened, when the exploiting classes were already liquidated and socialist relations were rooted solidly in all phases of national economy, when our party was politically consolidated and had strengthened itself both numerically and ideologically. . . .

Whereas, during the first few years after Lenin's death, party congresses and Central Committee plenums took place more or less regularly, later, when Stalin began increasingly to abuse his power, these principles were brutally violated. This was especially evident during the last 15 years of his life. Was it a normal situation when over 13 years elapsed between the 18th and 19th Party Congresses, years during which our party and our country had experienced so many important events? These events demanded categorically that the party should have passed resolutions pertaining to the country's defense during the Patriotic War [World War II] and to peacetime construction after the war. Even after the end of the war a Congress was not convened for over seven years. Central Committee plenums were hardly ever called. It should be sufficient to mention that during all the years of the Patriotic War not a single Central Committee plenum took place. It is true that there was an attempt to call a Central Commitee plenum in October 1941, when Central Committee members from the whole country were called to Moscow. They waited two days for the opening of the plenum, but in vain. Stalin did not even want to meet and talk to the Central Committee members. This fact shows how demoralized Stalin was in the first months of the war and how haughtily and disdainfully he treated the Central Committee members.

In practice, Stalin ignored the norms of party life and trampled on the Leninist principle of collective party leadership. Stalin's willfulness *vis-à-vis* the party and its Central Committee became fully evident after the 17th Party Congress which took place in 1934. Having at its disposal numerous data showing brutal willfulness toward party cadres, the Central Committee has created a party commission under the control of the Central Committee Presidium; it was charged with investigating what made possible the mass repressions against the majority of the Central Committee members and candidates elected at the 17th Congress of the All-Union Communist Party (Bolsheviks).

The commission has become acquainted with a large quantity of materials in the NKVD archives and with other documents and has established many facts pertaining to the fabrication of cases against Communists, to false accusations, to glaring abuses of socialist legality, which resulted in the death of innocent people. It became apparent that many party, Soviet and economic activists, who were branded in 1937–1938 as "enemies," were actually never enemies, spies, wreckers, etc., but were always honest Communists; they were only so stigmatized and, often, no longer able to bear barbaric tortures, they charged themselves (at the order of the investigative judges—falsifiers) with all kinds of grave and unlikely crimes.

The commission has presented to the Central Committee Presidium lengthy and documented materials pertaining to mass repressions against the delegates to the 17th Party Congress and against members of the Central Committee elected at that Congress. These materials have been studied by the Presidium of the Central Committee.

It was determined that of the 139 members and candidates of the party's Central Committee who were elected at the 17th Congress, 98 persons, *i.e.,* 70 per cent, were arrested and shot (mostly in 1937–1938). (Indignation in the hall.) What was the composition of the delegates to the 17th Congress? It is known that 80 per cent of the voting participants of the 17th Congress joined the party during the years of conspiracy before the Revolution and during the civil war; this means before 1921. By social origin the basic mass of the delegates to the Congress were workers (60 per cent of the voting members).

For this reason, it was inconceivable that a congress so composed would have elected a Central Committee a majority of whom would prove to be enemies of the party. The only reason why 70 per cent of Central Committee members and candidates elected at the 17th Congress were branded as enemies of the party and of the people was because honest Communists were slandered, accusations against them were fabricated, and revolutionary legality was gravely undermined.

The same fate met not only the Central Committee members but also the majority of the delegates to the 17th Party Congress. Of 1,966 delegates with either voting or advisory rights, 1,108 persons were arrested on charges of anti-revolutionary crimes, *i.e.,* decidedly more than a majority. This very fact shows how absurd, wild and contrary to common sense were the charges of counterrevolutionary crimes made out, as we now see, against a majority of participants at the 17th Party Congress. (Indignation in the hall.)

We should recall that the 17th Party Congress is historically known as the Congress of Victors. Delegates to the Congress were active participants in the building of our socialist state; many of them suffered and fought for party interests during the pre-Revolutionary years in the conspiracy and at the civil-war fronts; they fought their enemies valiantly and often nervelessly looked into the face of death. . . .

Mass repressions grew tremendously from the end of 1936 after a telegram from Stalin and [Andrei] Zhdanov, dated from Sochi on September 25, 1936, was addressed to Kaganovich, Molotov and other members of the Political Bureau. The content of the telegram was as follows:

> We deem it absolutely necessary and urgent that Comrade Yezhov be nominated to the post of People's Commissar for Internal Affairs. Yagoda has definitely proved himself to be incapable of unmasking the Trotskyite-Zinovievite bloc. The OGPU is four years behind in this matter. This is noted by all party workers and by the majority of the representatives of the NKVD.

Strictly speaking, we should stress that Stalin did not meet with and, therefore, could not know the opinion of party workers. This Stalinist formulation that the "NKVD is four years behind" in applying mass repression and that there is a necessity for "catching up" with the neglected work directly pushed the NKVD workers on the path of mass arrests and executions. . . .

The mass repressions at this time were made under the slogan of a fight against the Trotskyites. Did the Trotskyites at this time actually constitute such a danger to our party and to the Soviet state? We should recall that in 1927, on the eve of the 15th Party Congress, only some 4,000 votes were cast for the Trotskyite-Zinovievite opposition while there were 724,000 for the party line. During the 10 years which passed between the 15th Party Congress and the February-March Central Committee plenum, Trotskyism was completely disarmed; many former Trotskyites had changed their former views and worked in the various sectors building socialism. It is clear that in the situation of socialist victory there was no basis for mass terror in the country.

This terror was actually directed not at the remnants of the defeated exploiting classes but against the honest workers of the party and of the Soviet state; against them were made lying, slanderous and absurd accusations concerning "two-facedness," "espionage," "sabotage," preparation of fictitious "plots," etc.

At the February–March Central Committee plenum in 1937 many members actually questioned the rightness of the established course regarding mass repression under the pretext of combating "two-facedness." . . .

Using Stalin's formulation, namely, that the closer we are to socialism the more enemies we will have, and using the resolution of the February–March Central Committee plenum passed on the basis of Yezhov's report, the *provocateurs* who had infiltrated the state-security organs together with conscienceless careerists began to protect with the party name the mass terror against party cadres, cadres of the Soviet state and the ordinary Soviet citizens. It should suffice to say that the number of arrests based on charges of counterrevolutionary crimes had grown ten times between 1936 and 1937. . . .

Now, when the cases of some of these so-called "spies" and "saboteurs" were examined, it was found that all their cases were fabricated. Confessions of guilt of many arrested and charged with enemy activity were gained with the help of cruel and inhuman tortures. . . .

An example of vile provocation, of odious falsification and of criminal violation of revolutionary legality is the case of the former candidate for the Central Committee Political Bureau, one of the most eminent workers of the party and of the Soviet Government, Comrade Eikhe who was a party member since 1905. (Commotion in the hall.)

Comrade Eikhe was arrested on April 29, 1938 on the basis of slanderous materials, without the sanction of the Prosecutor of the U.S.S.R., which was finally received 15 months after the arrest. Investigation of Eikhe's case was made in a manner which most brutally violated Soviet legality and was accompanied by willfulness and falsification. Eikhe was forced under torture to sign ahead of time a protocol of his confession prepared by the investigative judges, in which he and several other eminent party workers were accused of anti-Soviet activity. . . . This is the kind of vile things which were then practiced. (Movement in the hall.) . . . Many thousands of honest and innocent Communists have died as a result of this monstrous falsification of such "cases," as a result of the fact that all kinds of slanderous "confessions" were accepted, and as a result of the practice of forcing accusations against oneself and others. . . . In those years repressions on a mass scale were applied which were based on nothing tangible and which resulted in heavy cadre losses to the party. . . .

Mass arrests of party, Soviet, economic and military workers caused tremendous harm to our country and to the cause of socialist advancement. Mass repressions had a negative influence on the moral-political condition of the party, created a situation of uncertainty, contributed to the spreading of unhealthy suspicion, and sowed distrust among Communists. All sorts of slanderers and careerists were active. . . .

Facts prove that many abuses were made on Stalin's orders without reckoning with any norms of party and Soviet legality. Stalin was a very distrustful man, sickly suspicious; we know this from our work with him. He could look at a man and say: "Why are your eyes so shifty today?" or "Why are you turning so much today and avoiding to look me directly in the eyes?" The sickly suspicion created in him a general distrust even toward eminent party workers whom he had known for years. Everywhere and in everything he saw "enemies," "two-facers" and "spies." Possessing unlimited power, he indulged in great willfulness and choked a person morally and physically. A situation was created where one could not express one's own will.

When Stalin said that one or another should be arrested, it was necessary to accept on faith that he was an "enemy of the people." Meanwhile, Beria's gang, which ran the organs of state security, outdid itself in proving the guilt of the arrested and the truth of materials which it falsified. And what proofs were offered? The confessions of the arrested, and the investigative judges accepted these "confessions." And how is it possible that a person confesses to crimes which he has not committed? Only in one way—because of application of physical methods of pressuring him, tortures, bringing him to a state of unconsciousness, deprivation of his judgment, taking away of his human dignity. In this manner were "confessions" acquired. . . .

Comrades, let us reach for some other facts. The Soviet Union is justly considered as a model of a multinational state because we have in practice assured the equality and friendship of all nations which live in our great Fatherland.

All the more monstrous are the acts whose initiator was Stalin and which are rude violations of the basic Leninist principles of the nationality policy of the Soviet state. We refer to the mass deportations from their native places of whole nations, together with all Communists and Komsomols without any exception; this deportation action was not dictated by any military considerations.

Thus, already at the end of 1943, when there occurred a permanent break-through at the fronts of the Great Patriotic War benefiting the Soviet Union, a decision was taken and executed concerning the deportation of all the Karachai from the lands on which they lived.

In the same period, at the end of December 1943, the same lot befell the whole population of the Autonomous Kalmyk Republic. In March 1944, all the Chechen and Ingush peoples were deported and the Chechen-Ingush Autonomous Republic was liquidated. In April 1944, all Balkars were deported to faraway places from the territory of the Kabardino-Balkar Autonomous Republic and the Republic itself was renamed the Autonomous Kabardian Republic.

The Ukrainians avoided meeting this fate only because there were too many of them and there was no place to which to deport them. Otherwise, he would have deported them also. (Laughter and animation in the hall.)

Not only a Marxist-Leninist but also no man of common sense can grasp how it is possible to make whole nations responsible for inimical activity, including women, children, old people, Communists and Komsomols, to use mass repression against them, and to expose them to misery and suffering for the hostile acts of individual persons or groups of persons. . . .

He [Stalin] issued orders to arrest a group of eminent Soviet medical specialists. He personally issued advice on the conduct of the investigation and the method of interrogation of the arrested persons. He said that the academician Vinogradov should be put in chains, another one should be beaten. Present at this Congress as a delegate is the former Minister of State Security, Comrade Ignatiev. Stalin told him curtly, "If you do not obtain confessions from the doctors we will shorten you by a head." (Tumult in the hall.) Stalin personally called the investigative judge, gave him instructions, advised him on which investigative methods should be used; these methods were simple—beat, beat and, once again, beat.

Shortly after the doctors were arrested, we members of the Political Bureau received protocols with the doctors' confessions of guilt. After distributing these protocols, Stalin told us, "You are blind like young kittens; what will happen without me? The country will perish because you do not know how to recognize enemies."

The case was so presented that no one could verify the facts on which the investigation was based. There was no possibility of trying to verify facts by contacting those who had made the confessions of guilt. We felt, however, that the case of the arrested doctors was questionable. We knew some of these people personally because they had once treated us. When we examined this "case" after Stalin's death, we found it to be fabricated from beginning to end. . . .

Comrades: The cult of the individual acquired such monstrous size chiefly because Stalin himself, using all conceivable methods, supported the glorification of his own person. This is supported by numerous facts. One of the most characteristic examples of Stalin's self-glorification and of his lack of even elementary modesty is the edition of his *Short Biography,* which was published in 1948. This book is an expression of the most dissolute flattery, an example of making a man into a godhead, of transforming him into an infallible sage, "the greatest leader, sublime strategist of all times and nations." Finally, no other words could be found with which to lift Stalin up to the heavens. We need not give here examples of the loathesome adulation filling this book. All we need to add is that they all were approved and edited by Stalin personally and some of them were added in his own handwriting to the draft text of the book.

What did Stalin consider essential to write into this book? Did he want to cool the ardor of his flatterers who were composing his *Short Biography?* No! He marked the very places where he thought that the praise of his services was insufficient. . . . Thus writes Stalin himself:

> Although he performed his task as leader of the party and the people with consummate skill and enjoyed the unreserved support of the entire Soviet people, Stalin never allowed his work to be marred by the slightest hint of vanity, conceit or self-adulation. . . .
>
> Stalin's military mastership was displayed both in defense and offense. Comrade Stalin's genius enabled him to divine the enemy's plans and defeat them. The battles in which Comrade Stalin directed the Soviet armies are brilliant examples of operational military skill. . . .

We should also not forget that, due to the numerous arrests of party, Soviet and economic leaders, many workers began to work uncertainly, showed over-cautiousness, feared all which was new, feared their own shadows and began to show less initiative in their work. . . .

Stalin's reluctance to consider life's realities and the fact that he was not aware of the real state of affairs in the provinces can be illustrated by his direction of agriculture. All those who interested themselves even a little in the national situation saw the difficult situation in agriculture, but Stalin never even noted it. Did we tell Stalin about this? Yes, we told him, but he did not support us. Why? Because Stalin never traveled anywhere, did not meet city *kolkhoz* workers; he did not know the actual situation in the provinces. . . .

Some comrades may ask us: Where were the members of the Political Bureau of the Central Committee? Why did they not assert themselves against the cult of the individual in time? And why is this being done only now?

First of all, we have to consider the fact that the members of the Political Bureau viewed these matters in a different way at different times. Initially, many of them backed Stalin actively because Stalin was one of the strongest Marxists and his logic, his strength and his will greatly influenced the cadres and party work.

It is known that Stalin, after Lenin's death, especially during the first years, actively fought for Leninism against the enemies of Leninist theory and against those who deviated. Beginning with Leninist theory, the party, with its Central Committee at the head, started on a great scale the work of socialist industrialization of the country, agricultural collectivization and the cultural revolution.

At that time Stalin gained great popularity, sympathy and support. The party had to fight those who attempted to lead the country away from the correct Leninist path; it had to fight Trotskyites, Zinovievites and rightists, and the bourgeois nationalists. This fight was indispensable. Later, however, Stalin, abusing his power more and more, began to fight eminent party and Government leaders and to use terroristic methods against honest Soviet people. . . .

In the situation which then prevailed I have talked often with Nikolai Alexandrovich Bulganin; once when we two were traveling in a car, he said, "It has happened sometimes that a man goes to Stalin on his invitation as a friend. And, when he sits with Stalin, he does not know where he will be sent next—home or to jail."

It is clear that such conditions put every member of the Political Bureau in a very difficult situation. And, when we also consider the fact that in the last years the Central Committee plenary sessions were not convened and that the sessions of the Political Bureau occurred only occasionally, from time to time, then we will understand how difficult it was for any member of the Political Bureau to take a stand against one or another unjust or improper procedure, against serious errors and shortcomings in the practices of leadership. As we have already shown, many decisions were taken either by one person or in a roundabout way, without collective discussion. . . .

We should, in all seriousness, consider the question of the cult of the individual. We cannot let this matter get out of the party, especially not to the press. It is for this reason that we are considering it here at a closed Congress session. We should know the limits; we should not give ammunition to the enemy; we should not wash our dirty linen before their eyes. I think that the delegates to the Congress will understand and assess properly all these proposals. (Tumultuous applause.)

Comrades! We must abolish the cult of the individual decisively, once and for all; we must draw the proper conclusions concerning both ideological-theoretical and practical work. It is necessary for this purpose, in a Bolshevik manner, to condemn and to eradicate the cult of the individual as alien to Marxism-Leninism and not consonant with the principles of party leadership and the norms of party life, and to fight inexorably all attempts at bringing back this practice in one form or another.

Dictatorship or Democracy?

AN OFFICIAL SOVIET VIEW *

The question of dictatorship or democracy cannot be answered in the abstract as the enemies of socialism do. The most common error in discussions of democracy and dictatorship consists in that the question is put in the abstract. Many are accustomed to think that these concepts are mutually exclusive.

Let us, however, ask the question: *for whom* does democracy exist in a given state and *against whom* or *over whom* is the dictatorship exercised, and we shall see that these concepts, notwithstanding their opposite nature, are compatible. Ancient Athens was a democratic republic in its heyday. It was a democracy for the free men, or the slave-owners, but it was at the same time a dictatorship against the slaves, whom the Athenian state ruthlessly oppressed. In a society divided into hostile classes, the propertied and the propertyless, the haves and have-nots, there never has been "pure" democracy, nor can there ever be. In such a society, democracy, although this cannot be discerned at once, always bears a class nature. It is democracy for a particular class, for particular sections of society, which by no means precludes dictatorship over other classes and strata of society.

All former regimes which called themselves democracies, from the Athens democracy to present day bourgeois democracy, represented a democracy for the small, exploiting minority. This assertion might seem too categorical to those who are accustomed to see in contemporary Western democracy

* From *The U.S.S.R., A Socialist State of Workers and Peasants,* 1958, *passim.*

the only model of democracy "for all." But we have in view actual democracy and not formal. Even in capitalist countries where formally all citizens enjoy equal political rights actually the possibilities of exercising them differ substantially for the propertied and the propertyless. Democracy cannot be judged apart from economics: how the means of production and all wealth of society are distributed among its members, what part they play in production. And if there is great economic inequality between members of society, it will necessarily be reflected in their participation in political life.

And so, we consider it necessary to judge democracy not formally, but by the actual rights enjoyed by members of society, by their real participation in the political life of their country.

With the establishment of Soviet power, all Russia's working people gained political rights. The working people and their organizations received at their disposal public buildings, printeries and stocks of paper, which gave them real freedom of speech, of assembly and of the press. The Soviet state, as no other in the world, has really drawn the broad masses into political activity to help decide state and other public affairs. Besides giving the working people political rights, it also began to demolish all barriers preventing them from exercising the rights. Special mention should be made in this connection of the great efforts exerted by the Soviet state to advance the culture of the masses, abolish illiteracy and extend the network of schools, courses and other educational establishments. While this is usually not considered in examining the question of democracy, is it not clear that the exercise by a people of their political rights largely depends on the degree of their cultural development?

This depends to a still greater degree on the changes in the economic system of society, the abolition of class inequality and of exploitation of man by man. By making the mills and factories, railways and banks the property of the people and by abolishing private ownership in land in the very first months of its existence, the Soviet state created the conditions for ensuring genuine democracy. You may speak all you want about the democratic rights of the people, freedom and equality for all citizens, but if alongside these rights you place the right of private ownership of the means of production and defend its inviolability, then democracy will inevitably remain merely a paper democracy. By gradually turning the means of production into the property of the people, the Soviet state has created the economic basis of genuine democracy. It is on this basis that the people have gained freedom from exploitation, from economic crises and unemployment, freedom from poverty and other freedoms which are of incomparably greater importance to people than legal rights. It is these freedoms that give the people a real possibility of showing what they can do, of developing their abilities and becoming active participants in political life, which is the most important feature of true democracy.

Is the dictatorship of the proletariat compatible with such democracy? It is not only compatible with it; it is also necessary for it. Socialism is not brought into being through a voluntary agreement of all people, including the capitalists, as the old, Utopian Socialists imagined. It is the result of the class struggle of the proletariat against the obsolete capitalist system and its defenders. It is vitally necessary that the proletariat shall win political power in this struggle, and as a consequence, political guidance of society passes into the hands of the proletariat. This is what is called the dictatorship of the proletariat. Such a dictatorship can by no means be identified with one-man rule, or the rule of a few individuals, as the enemies of socialism falsely claim at times. This is dictatorship by a class which in the advanced industrial countries comprises the majority of the population, a class which is supported by the working peasantry and the other sections of the working people, together with whom it makes up the bulk of the people.

The dictatorship of the proletariat has its coercive aspect, which is unavoidable so long as forces of the old order exist and resist socialism. But it represents not merely and not chiefly, coercion. During the Civil War in the Soviet Republic, when the coercive aspect of the dictatorship of the proletariat was most pronounced and it seemed to overshadow all its other aspects, Lenin repeatedly pointed out that the dictatorship meant not only coercion against the exploiting minority of society; it also meant a higher organization of labour than had existed before. Its essence is the organization and discipline of the advanced detachment of the working people, their vanguard, their only leader—the proletariat. Its aim is to build socialism, abolish the division of society into classes, make all members of society working people, make the soil unfavourable for exploitation of man by man. To this end it is necessary to organize and rally the broadest masses round the proletariat, to develop tremendous economic-organizational and cultural-educational work. These functions of the dictatorship of the proletariat constitute its most important aspects.

Some men are prone to regard dictatorship as a negation of law; they assert that any dictatorship, and consequently the dictatorship of the proletariat too, inevitably leads to violation of law, to arbitrary rule and lawlessness. But let us ask them: what law is in question? If they have in mind the law of the old society which has been replaced by socialism then it is indisputable that the Socialist Revolution has broken it, has infringed its very foundations. No revolution can act otherwise, for it does not fit in the framework of the old law. When Cromwell and his supporters sent Charles I to the scaffold did they act on the basis of royal edicts? No. Despite the respect for law, which is a tradition in British history, they were forced to transgress the bounds of the old law.

Breaking with the law of the old order, the Socialist Revolution creates its own, new law. Only people blinded by hatred for socialism will identify the dictatorship of the proletariat with a lawless regime. In reality, the new, socialist state makes its own laws which are in accord with the interests of the people; the laws are enacted by their representatives in conformity with the established procedure. It demands of all organs of government, officials and citizens the strict observance of the laws. The Soviet state has from its inception devoted much effort to developing in all citizens respect for Soviet law. Today, too, visitors to the Kremlin who go into Lenin's study, where everything has been preserved just as it was when the father of the socialist state lived here, can see on his desk, next to the programme of the Communist Party, a pamphlet entitled *Respect the Laws of the Soviet Republic,* published on Lenin's recommendation. In the history of the Soviet state there have been, unfortunately, instances of violation of socialist law, unjustified repressions connected with the cult of personality of J. V. Stalin in the latter period of his activities. But these violations by no means stemmed from the character of the socialist state; they are alien to the nature of the dictatorship of the proletariat. This is strikingly attested to by the fact that the violations were brought to light on the initiative of the leading organs of the Communist Party and the Soviet state themselves, which have taken all measures to rectify them and eliminate their consequences.

And so, the dictatorship of the proletariat by no means denies all law and all democracy. The new, socialist state is a state which is dictatorial and democratic in a new way. It exercises dictatorship over the reactionary forces of the old order and gives democracy to the people, to the working folk. These two functions of the dictatorship of the proletariat are indivisible in their essence.

We might be told that by repressing a part of the population we are violating democracy, departing from its principles. To this we can reply: No, gentlemen, we would be violating democracy for the working people, i.e., for the majority of the population, if we did not curb the exploiting minority. Thus, if in the first years of the revolution the Soviet state, because of falsely understood, abstract democracy, had given freedom of action to the reactionaries, had allowed the bourgeois parties to carry on their activity, their propaganda hostile to socialism, it would have failed in its duty to the working people.

The exceptions, limitations of democracy with regard to the exploiting classes, limitations which are necessary so long as a bitter class struggle goes on, are, however, of a temporary nature. Even during the first years of the revolution Lenin explained that the disfranchisement of the exploiters was not an indispensable feature of the dictatorship of the proletariat, that it had been dictated by the concrete historical conditions in which the Soviet Republic was born in Russia and would be abolished in the future when the conditions had changed. The successes of socialist construction in the USSR, indeed, made it possible to abolish all suffrage restrictions. The present Constitution of the USSR, adopted in 1936, introduced universal suffrage without any restrictions. Thus, democracy for the majority of the population (i.e., for the working people) has become democracy for *all.*

This became possible as a result of the deep-going social and economic changes which brought about the abolition of the exploiting classes in the USSR. The main distinguishing feature of Soviet socialist society is that it is not divided into antagonistic, hostile classes, for it no longer has any exploiting classes. A person travelling across the country from end to end will nowhere find any landed estates, factories or mills belonging to capitalists, and will encounter no peasants working on fields belonging to landlords or kulaks, or workers toiling for a boss.

Statistical tables showing the composition of the population no longer have social categories such as landlords, capitalists, merchants or kulaks. In 1956, 59.5 per cent of the population consisted of factory or office workers, 40.0 per cent were collective farmers or members of producers' co-operatives, and 0.5 per cent were individual peasants or artisans not united in co-operatives. These figures show that in the USSR there are no longer any social groups who live by exploiting the labour of others, that the population is made up of working people. In view of this, the bounds of democracy have been extended and it now embraces the entire population.

The history of the Soviet Union shows that its development proceeds along the line of steadily broadening democracy. In this it differs in principle from the development of many other, non-socialist, states, which follow the path of the gradual contraction, curtailment and limitation of democracy for the broad masses, the common people.

Constant broadening and deepening of democracy is a law governing the development of the socialist state. It stems from its very nature, from the tasks the workers' and peasants' state is called upon to accomplish. This state is an instrument for building communist society. Communism can be built only if the broad masses are very active politically and are highly conscious of the meaning of this cause. The development of socialist democracy is a means for raising the political activity and consciousness of the masses. The more conscious are the masses of the tasks confronting the country and the more actively they take part in accomplishing them, the stronger is the socialist state.

How the Soviet State Is Organized and How It Functions

Now let us see Soviet democracy in action. For this we first have to get an idea of how the Soviet state is organized and how it functions.

State power in the USSR belongs to the Soviets of Working People's Deputies. Article 2 of the Constitution of the USSR reads: "The political foundation of the USSR is the Soviets of Working People's Deputies, which grew and became strong as a result of the overthrow of the power of the landlords and capitalists and the conquest of the dictatorship of the proletariat." The Soviets form a well-knit system of organs of state power. The highest level of this system is the USSR Supreme Soviet, which is the highest organ of state power in the Soviet Union. Next come the Supreme Soviets of the Union Republics, the constituent members of the Union of Soviet Socialist Republics and the Supreme Soviets of the Autonomous Republics. Local organs of state power are the territorial, regional, district, city, rural and other Soviets of Working People's Deputies, of which there are close to 60,000 in the country.

All these organs of state power are elected by the people directly for a term of from 2 to 4 years, in accordance with the fixed basis of representation. Elections in the USSR are universal, direct and equal by secret ballot. All citizens who have reached the age of 18 have the right to vote, except insane persons and persons convicted by a court of law, whose sentence includes deprivation of electoral rights. Every citizen who has reached the age of 23 is eligible for election to the Supreme Soviet of the USSR; the minimum age for election to the Supreme Soviets of the Union and Autonomous Republics is 21 and to local Soviets 18.

The USSR has no restrictions of electoral rights of citizens on account of their race or nationality and women enjoy the same electoral rights as men. There are no domicile, property, educational or other voting qualifications. Neither national origin, nor religious convictions, property status, nor social origin can bar anyone from political activity. All citizens take part in the elections on an equal footing, each elector having one vote. The territory of the USSR and of each republic, region, district, etc., is divided into election districts, the number depending on the size of the population. Each district elects one deputy by direct vote. The election procedure ensures the complete secrecy of voting: the ballots are not numbered and are filled in by the voters in special booths, to which no one is admitted except the voter. This precludes any pressure on the electorate.

Candidates are nominated by public meeting of factory and office workers, by general membership meetings of collective farmers, etc. The right to nominate candidates is secured to public organizations and societies of the working people: Communist Party organizations, trade unions, co-operatives, youth organizations and cultural societies. All who wish can take part in discussing the merits or demerits of the nominees.

The turnout at the polls in the USSR is much higher than in any non-socialist country. For example, in the elections to local Soviets in 1957, 99.9 per cent of the electors went to polls in a number of republics. The proportion of ballots cast for the candidates is also very high. This is explained by the fact that candidates are nominated jointly by Party and non-Party organizations which enjoy great prestige among the people.

The relations between deputies and electors rest on a different basis than in most non-socialist countries. The deputy's ties with his voters do not end after the election. A deputy is a servant of the people who carries out their will. He is frequently given a mandate by his constituents. It is the duty of the deputy to render an account to the voters of the work done by himself and the Soviet of which he is a member as a whole. He can be criticized by the electors and be recalled if he ignores the will of the electors. . . .

The principal and most precious gain of Soviet power is that the masses have become aware that they are the masters of their country. This is the source of the great interest the working masses take in all questions of the country's life. It also means that they feel really free.

D. Zavarkin, wire drawer, A. Subbotin, steel melter, and I. Turtanov, senior rolling mill foreman, of the Sickle and Hammer Steel Mill, have published in the press a reply to George Meany, American trade-union leader, who crudely attacked socialist democracy. This is what the Soviet workers wrote of their understanding of freedom: "For us it is above all freedom from exploitation, it is political and national equality, it is the right to work, the right to take part in administering the state. . . .

We want to draw attention to the fact that the authors of this letter regard the mill director as a representative of their own class. In the Soviet Union there is no class enmity between the director of an establishment and the workers. Although a factory director is appointed by the state, he does not consider himself unaccountable to the people. The plant community controls the work of the management in various ways. Such right is possessed in the first place by the plant's Party organization, which consists of the most active and politically conscious part of the personnel. The trade-union organization, which usually embraces all workers and other employees, also has considerable rights. The relations between the management and the workers are governed by a collective agreement concluded annually by the trade-union committee and the management. The agreement stipulates the mutual obligations of the sides for carrying out the production plan, improvement in the organization of work and safety measures, wages and work quotas, satisfaction of the material and cultural needs of the workers, etc. Trade unions exercise regular control over the fulfilment of the collective agreement. If the management systematically violates the agreement, the trade union can take it to task by turning to a higher economic organization or take the matter to court. . . .

Since the workers regard their plant as their own, a people's enterprise, they are much concerned with improving its work: they take an active part in discussing and drawing up production plans and see to their fulfilment. Suffice it to say that the workers of over 9,000 enterprises energetically participated in drawing up the Sixth Five-Year Plan.

Production conferences and workers' meetings are an important form of participation by workers and other employees in the management of production. At production conferences, which are called jointly by the plant's trade-union committee and management major problems of the operation of the plant or shop are discussed. The scope of these conferences can be judged from the fact that in the first six months of 1956 over five million proposals for improvements in production were adopted by their participants, with nearly four-fifths of them introduced at once.

In the USSR trade unions are an important element of socialist democracy; they serve for the millions of factory and office workers as a school of management, a school of communism. Trade-union activists (functionaries serving without pay) elected at meetings and conferences, from group organizers to members of regional committees, number over 16 million. . . .

Slightly less than half of the entire population of the Soviet Union consists of peasants united in collective farms. A collective farm is not only an economic enterprise but also a social community. Unlike state enterprises, which are owned by the whole people, collective farms are owned by their members in common. The members themselves elect the board and the chairman, and they themselves settle all of the farm's important questions. General meetings of the collective farm's members are usually held two or three times a year, and the meetings elect delegates to check on the work of the board and decide some important problems in the interval between meetings. This, as it were, is a collective-farm *parliament.*

And so, real democracy, which actually obtains, is expressed not alone in democratic forms of state organization. It is also expressed in that the working people manage production both through their representatives and directly, by taking part in production conferences, meetings of workers and collective farmers. Business-like criticism of shortcomings at all levels, from the USSR Supreme Soviet to a workers' or collective farmers' meeting, is a real embodiment of socialist democracy.

Some people are accustomed to seeing democracy only in countries where there is an organized opposition to the government. Their idea of a model democracy is a system under which anyone can make a speech at a square or in a park, whether he preaches religious dogmas or criticizes the government. But do supporters of such a view ever think how effective such a form of democracy is and what influence it has on life? It is by no means our intention to deny traditional forms of democracy existing in other countries, but we categorically reject them as the sole criterion of democracy.

It is understandable, for example, that organized opposition to the government is of great importance in countries where there are antagonistic classes, where the government does not express the interests and aspirations of a considerable part or the majority of the population. This compels these sections to defend their interests through opposition to the government's policy. But what significance can such a criterion have for a socialist country, where there are no antagonistic classes, where the government considers itself and actually is the servant of the people? Obviously, under these conditions the dissatisfaction of one part of the population or another with shortcomings in the work of state organs is expressed in a different form, in the form of criticism and self-criticism.

The view that democracy implies the existence of many parties is a rather widespread delusion abroad. "If you have only one party, the Communist Party," we are told, "you can have no genuine democracy! In what way is the will of the people expressed if they are deprived of the possibility of setting up other parties?"

Our answer to this line of reasoning is first that it is wrong to think that the degree of democracy is determined everywhere and at all times by the existence of several parties. It is quite natural that in countries where a struggle is going on between antagonistic classes many political parties arise, expressing and defending the interests of different classes. But this is no real guarantee of democracy. The degree of democracy is determined not by the number of parties in a country but by what class is actually in power, by the *policy* pursued by the government. Only a state in which the ruling party follows a policy that accords with the interests of the people may be called a truly democratic state.

Socialist democracy does not reject in principle the possibility of the existence of several parties. Alongside the Communist Party, which plays the leading role, there are other parties in China, Rumania, Bulgaria and the German Democratic Republic. . . . Obviously, what is meant are genuinely democratic parties, expressing the interests of the working people, because the Communists in no way consider themselves bound to give freedom of action to enemies of the working people merely to comply with the demands of formal democracy.

As to the Soviet Union, here the whole course of historical development has resulted in the Communist Party remaining the only party in the country. All the other parties which claimed to lead the masses proved bankrupt, while the Communist Party won the undivided trust of the people as the only one expressing their aspirations and hopes. The victory of Socialism in the USSR has brought about the moral and political unity of the people; the exploiting classes vanished from the face of the Soviet land and together with them, vanished the soil favourable for the existence of parties other than the Communist Party.

The Communist Party of the Soviet Union unites now in its ranks close to eight million men and women. These are not a kind of privileged stratum of Soviet society, but the finest representatives of all strata who consider their membership in the Party as a duty to be in the front ranks everywhere, on the most difficult tasks. As the ruling party, the Communist Party gives guidance to state organs, including the USSR Government. But this guidance is not in the nature of some back-stage dictation. It is done through Communists who are members of state bodies and who decide questions with full observance of the standards set by the USSR Constitution. If we are to speak not of the formal aspects but the essence of the matter, we must stress that the Communist Party's guidance makes it possible to reflect and bring out the will of the people most fully in the activity of state organs. The Communist Party, which is a public organization, the advanced detachment of the working people, listens very attentively to the voice of the masses, expresses their aspirations and embodies in its decisions solutions to urgent problems of social development. Indicative, for example, is the fact that it was on the initiative of the Central Committee of the CPSU that the question of reorganizing industrial management, a question that had fully matured for Soviet society, was submitted for discussion to the whole people.

Around the Communist Party are numerous public organizations among which a particularly important part is played by the trade unions, the YCL, co-operatives and various cultural societies. Thanks to the activities of these organizations and to the leadership of the Communist Party the political activity and organization of the people in the Soviet Union is at a higher level than in any other country. . . .

CO-OPERATION OF NATIONS

. . . Tsarism and capitalism left a terrible legacy to the young Soviet Republic: not only colonial backwardness of the borderlands in which non-Russian peoples lived, but also bitter strife between the peoples, discord between the nations. Long years of national oppression engendered among many peoples mistrust of everything Russian; on top of this came strife between the oppressed peoples themselves: between Georgians and Armenians and Azerbaijans, and so on. Matters reached such lengths that in 1919–1920, when the Mensheviks, Mussavatists and Dashnaks [1] dominated in Transcaucasia, wars were fought between Georgia and Armenia and between Azerbaijan and Armenia; there were even wars within the republics as, for example, the defeat and sacking of South Ossetia by the Georgian Mensheviks, etc.

How did the Soviet state succeed in cutting this Gordian Knot, in solving the problem of relations between nationalities, which according to the French writer Henri Barbusse was a "sanguinary vicious circle in all modern history?" . . . This is a new multi-national state without precedent in history. Its salient feature is first that it is founded on the *voluntary* unity of the

[1] Mussavatists were members of a bourgeois-landlord nationalist party in Azerbaijan, Dashnaks were members of an Armenian bourgeois-nationalist party.

peoples. The voluntary nature of the union is underscored by the fact that under the Constitution of the USSR each Union Republic retains the right of secession from the USSR. The equality of all peoples is another cornerstone of the multi-national Socialist state. All Soviet Socialist Republics making up the USSR enjoy equal rights. The Constitution of the USSR precludes national inequality. It proclaims the equality of citizens of the USSR, irrespective of nationality or race, in all spheres of economic, government, cultural, political and other public activities. Any direct or indirect restriction of the right of, or conversely, the establishment of any direct or indirect privileges for citizens on account of their race or nationality, as well as any advocacy of racial or national exclusiveness or hatred are declared a crime punishable by law.

But the concept of equality, which seems so simple, has two aspects. One is equality under the law, proclaimed in the USSR at the very inception of Soviet power, and the other is actual equality, which depends on the degree of economic, political and cultural development of a people. If Soviet power had limited itself to the proclamation of legal equality, the equality would have remained only formal since many peoples and tribes, owing to their backwardness, would have been unable to exercise the rights granted them by law. But in this, as in other spheres, Soviet power provided the peoples the material conditions to enable them to exercise the democratic rights proclaimed in the Constitution. It has accomplished a truly titanic task in eliminating the economic, political and cultural backwardness inherited by many peoples from the old system. This required great effort and even sacrifices on the part of the Russian people, as the most developed people in Russia. Thanks to its fraternal, unselfish assistance the peoples in the borderlands were able swiftly to develop their industry and agriculture and to create their own culture, national in form and Socialist in content. . . .

Some of our enemies urge that we hurry and take measures for the withering away of the state, which follows from the teaching of Marx and Engels. We can tell these uninvited zealots of Marxism that they needn't hope that like little Red Riding Hood we shall not notice the sharp fangs of the big bad wolf! Marxists-Leninists are by no means proponents of preserving the state for the state's sake, they know that in time the state will wither away. But imperialist states still exist and they continue to entertain hopes of smashing the Socialist world by force of arms. Under these conditions the Soviet people will continue to strengthen the economic and defensive power of their state in every way. . . .

THE STATE AND FREEDOM OF THE INDIVIDUAL

Today there are few people who deny the greatness of the social and economic changes effected by the USSR. But not rare by far is the view that these changes have been brought about at the cost "of destroying personal freedom," "suppression of the individual," etc.

Socialism and the individual—there are few questions that arouse so much misgiving among people who live outside the Soviet Union and the People's Democracies. Not infrequently even progressive-minded people ask whether the establishment of Socialism does not signify the suppression of personal interests and desires of people, restriction of their personality, etc.

We do not conceal the fact that we had to make no little sacrifices and suffer privation in the struggle for the victory of Socialism, a struggle which was resisted in every way by the defenders of the obsolete system. But no one can refute the historical fact that it is the great social revolution which smashed the chains fettering man and opened the way for the economic and cultural advancement of the USSR peoples. The new social system set up in the USSR has given real scope for the display of personal initiative, freedom for development of the creative forces of the millions. And we can proudly say that no preceding era, even the eras of the greatest revolutions and national-liberation movements of the past, can be compared with our era for the degree of understanding by the people of the tasks confronting them, for the host and power of the masses who have stirred and have risen to make history.

Having liberated the working people from exploitation and having ensured the satisfaction of their rising material and cultural requirements, Socialism created the most favourable conditions for the development of the personal abilities and talents of millions of people. In Socialist society the purpose of expansion of production is to serve man and his requirements.

The economic foundation of the Socialist system is public ownership of the means of production, which far from disuniting, unites people, helps to bring them closer together. Relations of comradely co-operation and Socialist mutual assistance of people free from exploitation are created in the process of collective labour. This eliminates the "war of all against all" and ends the operation of the jungle law of capitalist competition. . . .

The rights of the individual are secured in a special chapter, (Chapter X), of the USSR Constitution. Here we find the rights and freedoms which are usually recorded in constitutions of democratic states, for example, freedom of speech, of the press and of assembly, inviolability of the person, inviolability of the home, etc., but in addition there are also rights which are usually not found in constitutions of non-Socialist states. These are the rights of USSR citizens to work, i.e., the right to guaranteed employment and payment for their work in accordance with its quantity and quality; the right to rest and leisure; the right to maintenance in old age and also in case of sickness or disability; the right to education.

The right of citizens to work, to rest and leisure, education and material maintenance, secured to them by the USSR Constitution, reflect the great gains of Socialism. But these rights are important not only by themselves. Still more important is the confidence of Soviet citizens in the feasibility of these rights, in that the steady development of the Socialist economic system will ensure them in the future, as today, the possibility of working fruitfully and improving their living standards. The Soviet citizen knows that he is threatened neither by economic crisis, nor unemployment, nor the danger of being evicted from his home because of inability to pay rent. He knows that in case of sickness the state will provide him free medical aid and state social insurance agencies will pay him sick benefits. He knows that his children will be able to receive an education.

All this gives the Soviet citizen firm confidence in the morrow and creates favourable conditions for the development of his personal abilities and talents. . . . Only in Socialist society where there is no private ownership of the means of production, no exploitation of man by man, no crises and unemployment, are the common people able to develop their talents, to find application for them, to display their initiative.

Socialist democracy raises high the dignity of the working man and woman and this shows its genuinely popular character. In our country work has acquired social significance; the man of labour feels he is a public figure. The initiative of front-rankers in production is supported by the Socialist state, which raises high the dignity of men of labour. Millions of people have been decorated with government orders and medals for their valorous labour. Thousands of working folk in town and country wear the Gold Star of the Hero of Socialist Labour. The names of workers and peasants who gained glory by their labour are recorded in the annals of our country alongside the names of famous scientists, artists and thinkers of whom we are proud.

Socialist democracy opens boundless scope for the application of the creative forces of the people not only in the sphere of material production, but also in all social, political and cultural spheres.

What Is Evil in Communism

REINHOLD NIEBUHR *

The real tragedy of our age lies in the fact that the Marxist alternative to the injustices of our society should have generated cruelties and injustices so much worse than those which Marxism challenged, and should neverthe-

* Professor Emeritus, Union Theological Seminary. Author of *The Children of Light and The Children of Darkness, Moral Man and Immoral Society,* fifteen other books, and numerous articles. This compilation is taken from the writings of Reinhold Niebuhr cited at the end of each selection below. A substantial portion of this article is also reprinted in *Reinhold Niebuhr on Politics* edited by Harry R. Davis and Robert C. Good (New York, Charles Scribner's Sons, 1960).

less be able to gain the devotion of millions of desperate people in Europe and particularly in Asia upon the basis of the original dream, as if the dream had not turned into a nightmare.[1]

What makes communism so evil and what are the sources of its malignancy? We are bound to ask the question because we are fated as a generation to live in the insecurity which this universal evil of communism creates for our world. The timid spirits ask another question: is communism really as evil as we now think; or are we tempted by the tensions of our conflict with it to exaggerate our negative judgments about it, somewhat as we did in judging the Kaiser's Germany, which we erroneously regarded as evil as Hitler's Germany subsequently proved to be.

It is important to analyze the nature of the communist evil both for the sake of those who take its evil for granted but do not bother to diagnose its nature or trace its sources; and for the sake of those deluded spirits who imagine that communism is but a different version of a common democratic creed, a difference which might be resolved if a dissipation of the war psychosis would permit us to engage in the enterprise. We must analyze it too for the sake of those who assess the degree of evil in communism correctly but prove their confusion in regard to its nature by comparing it with something much less evil than itself, as for instance the former State Department official who asserted that communism was "nothing but" the old Russian imperialism in a new form. This judgment obscured the difference between the comparative ordinate and normal lust for power of a great traditional nation and the noxious demonry of this worldwide secular religion.

MONOPOLY OF POWER

If we seek to isolate more specifically the various causes of an organized evil which spreads terror and cruelty throughout the world and confronts us everywhere with faceless men who are immune to every term of moral and political persuasion we must inevitably begin with the monopoly of power which communism established. Disproportions of power everywhere in the human community are fruitful of injustice, but a system which gives some men absolute power over other men results in evils which are worse than injustice. Marxism did not indeed plan the highly centralized power structure of communism, but Marx did plan for a "dictatorship of the proletariat"; and the progressive moral deterioration of such a dictatorship was inevitable rather than fortuitous for two reasons.

The *first* is that when society is divided into the powerful and the powerless there is no way of preventing the gradual concentration of the monopoly of power. The monopoly of a class becomes the monopoly of the party which claims to be the vanguard of the whole class; the monopoly of the party

[1] "The Soviet Reality," *Nation,* Vol. CLXXI (September 23, 1950) p. 270. By permission.

becomes the monopoly of a small oligarchy who speaks at first for the class to other classes who have been robbed of power. But their authority inevitably degenerates into a monopoly of power exercised over their party and class because no one in the whole community has the constitutional means to challenge and check the inevitable extension of power after which the most powerful grasp. The dictatorship of the oligarchy further degenerates into the dictatorship of a single tyrant.[2]

Let us recall how this tyranny developed. The Marxist dogma provided for a "dictatorship of the proletariat." According to the dogma, this dictatorship was necessary because the messianic class, the workers, was bound to be insecure until its class enemies were "liquidated." . . . The theory was that the workers would exercise a dictatorship to eliminate their class enemies, but they would enjoy a perfect brotherhood among themselves. They would not need courts and policemen because they would put down any anti-social behavior by spontaneous action.

It is well to note the utopian touch in the vision of a democracy within a dictatorship, because it is the first clue to the question why the Marxist utopia turned into a hell. The visionaries did not consider the ordinary problems of a community, the competition of interests, the arbitration of rights, the adjudication of conflict. The only cause for conflict, namely property, was abolished. But meanwhile, the community on the other side of the revolution needed to be organized. It could not rely on spontaneous action. The embryo of the dictatorship lay in the party. The dogma assumed that, while the workers were the messianic class, they needed the party to inform them of the logic of history and what good things it intended for them. The workers had an essential righteousness, but evidently no wisdom. Lenin declared that they, left to themselves, could not rise above a "trade union psychology." How right he was. The Marxist dogma would always outrage the common sense of common men. It could be believed only by the ideologists. These were the secular prophets who became the priest-kings of the utopian state.

So we proceed from the dictatorship of the workers to the dictatorship of the party. But the party must also be organized. Everywhere the need for government which the dogma had defined as merely an instrument of oppression, makes itself felt. Without integration, the masses are merely a mob. The party must have a "central committee." The committee is even now the governing group in theory. But the committee was too large for executive action. The ruling group within the committee was first a mere class war improvisation. But naturally, its powers grew rather than diminished. The real oligarchs emerged. They had the power. It is this "democratic centralism" of Lenin to which the present oligarchs would fain return, after ex-

[2] *Christian Realism and Political Problems* (New York, Charles Scribner's Sons, 1953), pp. 34, 35. By permission.

periencing the baneful effects of absolute tyranny. It must be observed, however, that Lenin, while more subtle than Stalin, was potentially a dictator. He did not allow real discussion even within the ruling group. Above all, he did not allow "factions." He was the charismatic leader who knew the logic of history better than his colleagues. Had he not prophesied correctly?

But without real freedom, either within the party or in the community, there was nothing to prevent a shrewd manipulator, Stalin, from bringing all the organs of power into his single hands, from liquidating even the oldest prophets who did not agree with him, and from terrorizing a whole generation of newer oligarchs—many of whom owed their positions to his favor and had helped to eliminate his foes. It is this absolute monopoly of power which proved to be so vicious and which is now defined by the euphemism, "the cult of personality." The present oligarchs would like to eliminate the possibility of a return to such a tyranny, yet meanwhile they try to maintain their own power and preserve the dogma which sanctifies it.[3]

Togliatti, the Italian Communist leader, the French Communists, and even the lowly American Communist Party dare to criticize the present leadership and ask the embarrassing question: "What were the present leaders doing when all these atrocities of Stalin were perpetrated?" Khruschev has asserted that no one could protest, for fear of his life. Nothing can change the impact of this confession.[4]

One must confess, incidentally, an ironic satisfaction in observing orthodox Marxists, who believe that history moves only in terms of "objective conditions," placing all the blame for a horrible tyranny upon the failure of a single individual. They have practiced "the cult of the individual" in reverse. Meanwhile the "objective conditions" which generated the evil are still with them. It is the monopoly of power which proved even more grievous in a revolutionary movement than all history proved it to be when it was used to defend the status quo.[5]

THE MARXIST THEORY OF THE STATE

A *second* reason for the excessive concentration of power is that the Marxist theory wrongly assumes that economic power inheres solely in the ownership of property and obscures the power of the manager of property. It therefore wrongly concludes that the socialization of property causes economic power to evaporate when in fact it merely gives *a single oligarchy a monopoly of both economic and political power.*[6]

[3] "Is This the Collapse of a Tyranny?" *Christianity and Society,* Vol. XVI (July 9, 1956), p. 5. By permission.

[4] *Ibid,* p. 4.

[5] "Nikita Khrushchev's Meditation on Josef Stalin," *Christianity and Crisis,* Vol. XVI (July 9, 1956), p. 90. By permission.

[6] *Christian Realism and Political Problems,* p. 36.

The Marxian theory of the state is very simple. The state is the instrument of class oppression. It will therefore disappear with the disappearance of classes. "In the course of its development," declared Marx, "the working class will replace the old bourgeois society . . . and there will no longer be any real political power, for political power is precisely the official expression of class antagonisms in bourgeois society." Lenin, proclaiming the same faith, says, "We do not expect the advent of an order of society in which the principle of the subordination of the minority to the majority will not be observed. But striving for socialism, we are convinced that it will develop into communism, . . . all need for force will vanish, and for the subjection of one man to another, and one part of the population to another, since people will grow accustomed to observing the elementary conditions of social existence without force and without subjection." One might multiply such citations indefinitely. They all look forward to a kind of anarchistic Utopia despite the explicit disavowals of utopianism that are found in Marxism.

Obviously the crucial point in this interpretation of the function of force in society is that it is regarded not as a necessity of social cohesion but simply as an instrument of class oppression. This implies that human egoism is not congenital but merely the product of a particular class organization of society. Nothing is more paradoxical in Marxian theory than that it prompts its adherents to a cynically realistic analysis of human motives in the present instance and yet persuades them to look forward to a paradise of brotherhood after the revolution. For the period after the revolution every orthodox Marxian is a liberal. The eighteenth-century faith in the perfectibility of man is expressed with the greater abandon for having been tentatively veiled and qualified. . . .

Stalin's power is a double refutation of the Marxian theory of the state. The fact that the power is necessary refutes the Communists, who regard the growth of an oligarchy as merely the fruit of Stalin's perfidy. Every society must finally define its course and assert its will not only against foreign foes but against dissenters within its own household. In a socialist society, such dissent is derived not merely from remnants of capitalist ideology but from varying interpretations of the purpose and program of socialism made by different schools of Marxist thoughts. The instincts of self-preservation within a great community will generate an irrefutable logic of their own against which doctrinaire creeds are powerless. In exactly the same way, French ideals of a bourgeois world revolution were compounded with patriotism in the period after the French Revolution.

But the degree of Stalin's power, its irresponsible and autocratic character, refutes the Marxian theory of the state in another sense. The Marxian thesis that the state will wither away after the capitalist enemies of socialism are destroyed prompts Marxists to maximize the power of the state and to relax ordinary human precautions against the exercise of irresponsible power. Since the state is involved in a process of self-destruction, it is believed that its power can safely be increased. This power will supposedly enhance the efficiency of the Communist community in defeating its internal and external foes; and when this has been done, the state will wither away.

Every government is tempted to confuse its own prejudices with the general welfare and to corrupt its rule by the lust for power. "Power tends to corrupt," declared Lord Acton quite truly, "and absolute power corrupts absolutely." The validity of this observation escapes utopians, who imagine that they have found a way to eliminate power and coercion from society. Hence they allow the power of their state to grow unduly, vainly imagining that the heart which beats under the tunic of a commissar is of different stuff from the hearts of ancient kings.[7]

IMPERIALISM

Around a central dogma which ascribes all historic evil to the institutions of property and promises redemption from every ill through the socialization of property are clustered a whole series of ancillary and derivative dogmas.[8]

Marxism projects an ideal community in which the rivalry between nations will be abolished because that rivalry is ascribed purely to economic causes. Therefore, the socialization of property is expected to guarantee not only a classless national community but also a harmonious international community.[9]

The vexations and tyrannical rule of Russia over the smaller communist states is completely obscured and denied by the official theory. Hamilton Fish Armstrong reports Bukharin's interpretation of the relation of communist states to each other as follows: "Bukharin explained at length that national rivalry between Communist states was 'an impossibility by definition.' 'What creates wars,' he said, 'is the competition of monopoly capitalism for raw materials and markets. Capitalist society is made up of selfish and competing national units and therefore is by definition a world at war. Communist society will be made up of unselfish and harmonious units and therefore will be by definition a world at peace. Just as capitalism cannot live without war, so war cannot live with Communism.' " It is difficult to conceive of a more implausible theory of human nature and conduct.[10]

Nations, as individuals who are completely innocent in their own esteem, are insufferable in their human contacts. The whole world suffers from the pretensions of the communist oligarchs.[11] The result of such a delusion is a

[7] "Russia and Karl Marx," *Nation,* Vol. CXLVI (May 7, 1938), pp. 530, 531. By permission.

[8] *Christian Realism and Political Problems,* p. 46.

[9] *The Structure of Nations and Empires* (New York, Charles Scribner's Sons, 1959), p. 240. By permission.

[10] *The Irony of American History* (New York, Charles Scribner's Sons, 1952), p. 20. By permission.

[11] *Ibid,* p. 42.

meretricious compound of Russian nationalism with Communist dreams of world dominion; and the creation of a tyrannical oligarchy devoid of either internal or external checks upon its power.[12] The illusions enable communists to pose as liberators of every class or nation which they intend to enslave; and to exploit every moral and political weakness of the civilized world as if they had the conscience of civilization in their keeping.[13] The thesis that imperialism is purely the fruit of "capitalism" and therefore non-capitalist nations are non-imperialistic and internationalist "by definition" has been refuted through the flagrant imperialism of Russia.[14]

THE MANIPULATION OF DESTINY

Another pretension of communism is usually obscured by the stock criticism against Marxism. It is rightly accused of being deterministic, that is, of underestimating the freedom of man and of emphasizing the determined character of his culture and of his convictions, which are said to be rooted in his economic interest. This determinism is at least half true and not nearly as dangerous as a supplementary and contradictory dogma according to which history works toward a climax in which the proletarian class must by a "revolutionary act" intervene in the course of history and thereby change not only history but the whole human situation. For after this act man is no longer both creature and creator of history but purely the creator who "not only proposes but also disposes." This idea involves monstrous claims of both omnipotence and omniscience which support the actual monopoly of power and aggravate its evil. Molotov illustrated the pretensions of omniscience when he declared that the communists, guided by "Marxist-Leninist science," know not only the inner meaning of current events but are able to penetrate the curtain of the future and anticipate its events. This tendency of playing God to human history is the cause for a great deal of communist malignancy.

The seemingly opposite tendency to regard men as the product of economic circumstance supports the pretension; for it makes it possible for an elite to pretend to be the manipulators of the destiny of their fellow men. The pretension reveals the similarity between the Nazi evil, based upon the pretension of Nietzsche's "superman," who makes his power self-justifying, and this kind of superman whose power is ostensibly justified by the fate which appoints him as the creator of historical destiny. Some of the communist fury is the consequence of the frustration of the communist oligarchs, when they discover history to be more complex than anticipated in their logic and find that opposing forces, which are marked for defeat in their

[12] "Hazards and Resources," *Virginia Quarterly Review,* Vol. XXV (Spring 1949), p. 204. By permission.
[13] *Christian Realism and Political Problems,* p. 37. [14] *Ibid,* p. 46.

apocalypse, show a more stubborn strength and resistance than they anticipated.

THE DOMINION OF DOGMA OVER FACTS

The Marxist dogmatism, coupled with its pretensions of scientific rationality, is an additional source of evil. The dogmas are the more questionable because the tyrannical organization prevents a re-examination of the dogmas when the facts refute them. Thus communist irrationality and dogmatism consist of a rigorous adhesion to dogma in defiance of the fact. The communists test every historical fact with ostensible precision and coolness, but their so-called science looks at the world through the spectacles of inflexible dogma which alters all the facts and creates a confused world picture. The greatest danger of communist policy comes from the fact that the communists do not know what kind of a world they live in, and what their foes are like. Their own rigorous dogma obscures the facts and their tyrannical system prevents, for motives of fear, the various proconsuls of their imperium from apprising the men in the Kremlin of the truth.

The rigor of the communist dogmatism creates an ideological inflexibility, consonant with the monolithic political structure. The combination of dogmatism and tyranny lead to shocking irrationalities in communist trials, where the victims were made to confess to the most implausible charges. Since the communist dogma allows for no differences of opinion among the elect, every deviation from orthodoxy is not only branded as treason but is attributed to some original sinful social taint.

It is instructive that the actual monopoly of power accentuates the evil in the ideological pretensions of communism while these pretensions give a spiritual dimension to the evils which flow from a monopoly of power. Thus the evil of communism flows from a combination of political and "spiritual" factors, which prove that the combination of power and pride is responsible for turning the illusory dreams of yesterday into the present nightmare, which disturbs the ease of millions of men in our generation.[15]

COMMUNISM AND NAZISM

It is deeply ironic that our modern culture, which dreams of the gradual elimination of "methods of force" in favor of "methods of mind" and of the progressive triumph of democratic government over all forms of tyranny, should encounter two forms of tyranny in one generation. It is baffling, as well as ironic, that the two forms of tyranny, Nazism and communism, should be so similar in practice and yet so dissimilar in theory. Unless we

[15] *Christian Realism and Political Problems,* pp. 39–42, as rewritten in *Reinhold Niebuhr on Politics,* edited by Harry R. Davis and Robert C. Good. By permission.

are perfectly clear how such contradictory theories of man's moral and political problem can issue in practically identical political institutions and moral behavior, we will not fully comprehend the breadth and depth of our contemporary crisis.

Nazism was the fruit of moral cynicism. Communism is the product of moral and political utopianism. Nazism believed (or believes) that a nation has the right to declare that there are no standards of justice beyond its own interest. Communism dreams of a universal society in which all nations will be related to each other in a frictionless harmony, if indeed nations will not disappear entirely in a universal brotherhood. Nazism raises the self-worship, to which all ethnic groups are prone, to explicit proportions in its theory of a "master race." Communism believes that ethnic distinctions are irrelevant in an ideal society.

Nazism regards power as the final justification of any action. According to its theory a nation which has the power to organize an imperial society beyond its own borders, proves its right to do so by its success. Communism dreams of an ideal society in which the state "will wither away" and in which every form of coercion, force and power will gradually become irrelevant. Nazism believes in an elite class which manages the affairs of the mass of men. Communism is fiercely equalitarian in theory and hopes for the abolition of all class distinctions. The "dictatorship of the proletariat" is, in theory, provisional. For the dictatorship of a small oligarchy, which has in fact established itself in the communist state, there is no place at all in communist theory.

The contrast in theory between the two systems is practically complete. The question is how almost identical political institutions can develop from these contradictory theories. Nazi theory and practice are consistent. The practice follows by logical necessity from the theory. Communism boasts that it has created a new unity of theory and practice. Yet it presents the modern world with the most shocking disparity between the two.

We have seen that the root of communist utopianism lies in the Marxist analysis of the cause of human egoism. If it should be true that a particular economic institution (private property) is the cause of all human egoism, it would follow of course that the elimination of that institution would make men completely social and would abolish all frictions and competitions in human society. A propertyless society would have no use for the coercive functions of the state. It would wither away. If it should be true that this desirable end cannot be achieved without a world-wide revolution of the propertyless classes against the property owners, the idyllic paradise to be attained would seem to justify the ruthless policies pursued in the conflict. It would seem also to justify a provisional dictatorship, which will give cohesion and striking power to the cohorts of redemption. If this provisional dictatorship seems to have inordinate power, the utopian need not worry over-much about the perils of such power, because, according to his theory, all political power will atrophy in the day when a complete victory has been won.

Thus, communism, as we know it, is a political system in which a provisional moral cynicism, which countenances the defiance of the moral experience of the human race, is justified by a moral utopianism which dreams of the achievement of an ideal world in which property, government, nationality and ethnic distinctions will all disappear. Since the communist hope is an illusion, the objective observer must recognize the provisional cynicism as no different than the basic cynicism of the Nazis even as he knows that a supposedly provisional dictatorship follows the same practices as one which claimed permanent tenure.

While it is important to recognize that diametrically opposite conceptions of human nature may thus produce common unscrupulous and ruthless political practices and despotic political institutions, it is nevertheless important to bear the differences in basic theory in mind. One reason for doing this is that the corruption of an ideal may be politically more dangerous than a frankly cynical political program.[16] Most of our polemic against communism sounds like something left over from the propaganda warfare against Nazism. We think we are making the ultimate condemnation of communism if we insist that its totalitarianism is identical with that of Nazism. Thereby we obscure its greater danger, which is derived from the fact that it is a corruption of a utopian dream and does not stem from the pure moral cynicism which the Nazis avowed.[17]

The Nazis were, for instance, frustrated in their senseless self-worship. It is ridiculous to ask a subject people to violate their sense of self-respect by holding the conqueror in religious veneration. The Russian will-to-power is more subtly related to the communist cause. Russia comes to every nation, which it intends to subjugate, as a "liberator" from "fascist" and "imperialist" oppression. Russian nationalism was related to the liberal dream of the eighteenth century. The difference between the nationalism of the Nazis and the nationalism of the Russian communists is the difference between the "honest" moral cynic and the misguided or self-deceived idealist, who fails to recognize to what degree self-interest corrupts even the most ideal motives. A corrupted ideal may be more potent than a frank defiance of all ideal values. The proof of that higher potency is given by the fact that Russia's so-called "fifth columns" in the Western world are composed not of the miserable traitors who constituted the Nazi dominated "Bund," nor yet of mere Communist Party hacks. They contain thousands of misguided idealists, who still think that Russia is the midwife of an ideal society, about to be born.

[16] "Two Forms of Tyranny," *Christianity and Crisis,* Vol. VIII (February 2, 1948), pp. 3, 4. By permission.

[17] "The Soviet Reality," *op. cit.,* p. 270.

But there is an even more important reason for noting the difference between the utopian and the cynical bases of these two forms of tyranny. It will not do to fight a despotism, which had its inspiration in utopianism, merely by calling attention to the crass corruption of the original ideal. It is necessary for a democratic civilization to recognize the weakness in its own life which gave power and plausibility to this dream.[18]

COMMUNISM AND LIBERALISM

The fact is that Marxism, in its pure form, has been the most potent critic of liberal illusions. Who understands the pretensions of "rational objectivity" in social conflict better than a real Marxist? Or for that matter the invalidity of an absolute distinction between the covert and the overt use of force? Yet the provisional realism of the Marxists quickly results in new illusions and confusions.[19] Those of us who once used Marxist collectivism to counter the error of liberal individualism, Marxist catastrophism to counter false liberal optimism, and Marxist determinism to challenge the sentimentality of liberal moralism and idealism, must now admit that the "truths" which we used to challenge "error" turned out to be no more true (though also no less true) than the liberal ones. But they were more dangerous.[20]

For example, our liberal or democratic culture, which maintained a critical attitude toward political power, became increasingly uncritical toward economic power, assuming it to be the source of justice. Thus property rights were made more absolute in an industrial and commercial society than they were in the older agrarian society despite the fact that a technical civilization created new perils of economic power which did not exist in an agrarian civilization. It was this error which invited, in a sense, first the legitimate criticism, but then the counter-error, of Marxism. For a religious veneration of the institution of property led to a new religion which sought the redemption of mankind through the abolition of property. Since Marxism erroneously assumed that economic power inhered altogether in the ownership of property, failing to recognize that the power of the manager of economic process would persist even in a society devoid of private property, its policy of socialization merely resulted in turning both economic and political power over to a single oligarchy, thus increasing the danger of tyranny. This error, added to all of its other miscalculations of human nature and history, accentuated its drift toward despotism.[21]

[18] "Two Forms of Tyranny," *op. cit.*, pp. 4, 5.
[19] *Christianity and Power Politics* (New York, Charles Scribner's Sons, 1940), p. 91. By permission.
[20] "Communism and the Clergy," *Christian Century*, Vol. LXX (August 19, 1953), p. 937. Copyright 1953 Christian Century Foundation. Reprinted by permission.
[21] "Two Forms of Tyranny," *op. cit.*, p. 5.

THE OPEN SOCIETY

A democratic or open society is not a perfect society; on the contrary it allows its imperfections to be published abroad. It is a society which permits and even encourages criticism of itself in the light of universal standards. Such a society has at hand the means of peaceful self-correction. Such a society keeps alive the concern for objective truth and it can never be deceived into substituting the fiat of the state for objective truth. Such a society enables persons to keep their integrity as persons without constant fear of the secret police. Such a society permits minorities to organize for the purpose of changing its policies and even its structure. Such a society is uncorrupted by officially planned terror against its most independent minds and its bravest spirits.[22] Yet we are committed even to the proposition that there are no human institutions, including religious ones, which can safely be made immune to democratic criticism and which can be allowed to dictate the terms and the limits of the unity of the culture. We are committed to democracy as a method of holding all sources of power under restraint and all sources of authority under criticism.[23] The reason this final democratic freedom is right is that there is no historical reality, whether it be church or government, whether it be the reason of wise men or specialists, which is not involved in the flux and relativity of human existence; which is not subject to error and sin, and which is not tempted to exaggerate its errors and sins when they are made immune to criticism.[24]

[22] "What Is at Stake?" *Christianity and Crisis,* Vol. I (May 19, 1941), p. 1. By permission.

[23] "The Contribution of Religion to Cultural Unity," Hazen Pamphlet No. 13 (1945), p. 4. By permission.

[24] *The Children of Light and the Children of Darkness* (New York, Charles Scribner's Sons, 1944), p. 70, 71. By permission.

Topic 30

DEFENSE OF DEMOCRACY

Justification of Democracy

H. B. MAYO *

In this discussion, I propose to examine the values which are inherent in or implied by *any* democracy; those values which follow logically or emerge from the actual working of a democratic system. Those values will then constitute a large part of the justification for democracy. . . .

DEMOCRACY IS "FOR" THE PEOPLE

One broad implication of democracy almost inevitably follows from the system: government by the people is likely to aim also at government *for* the people, and not only because democracy is partly so defined, as in Lincoln's well-known phrase. . . .

Of itself, this does not take us very far—it merely puts the emphasis on the *people*. In some way, what is done to and for them is most important of all; the sights are trained on them, and not upon a collectivity, an organic state, a divine monarch, a particular class, or the like. The utilitarians in their emphasis on the happiness of the greatest number, and all democratic politicians in stressing the welfare or service of the people, belong in some sense to the same tradition of government for the people. Some of the support for democracy, and the opposition too, has come from those who hoped or feared, as the case might be, that it would turn out to be *for* the people.

So much has the idea of government *for* the people sunk into the modern mind that dictators nowadays profess to rule for the benefit of their people, a method of justification for despotism used far less often in earlier days. The definition of democracy given by Soviet spokesmen usually follows this line: if the policies of a government are for the benefit of the people, instead of for "their most bitter enemies," then the

* Professor of Political Science, University of Western Ontario. Author of *An Introduction to Marxist Theory*. The selection is from *An Introduction to Democratic Theory* by Henry B. Mayo.

government is a democracy. But this definition will not do. It abolishes the distinction entirely between benevolent despotism and democracy, while in the absence of the political freedoms and effective choice—which are distingushing features of democracy—we have only the dictator's word for it that his policies are in fact for the people.

The Soviet definition leads into two ancient errors: one is that the wishes of the people can be ascertained more accurately by some mysterious methods of intuition open to an elite rather than by allowing people to discuss and vote and decide freely. The other error goes deeper: that in some way the rulers know the "real" interest of the people better than the people and their freely chosen leaders would know it themselves. All fanatics believe the same.

When Aristotle spoke of the state continuing that men might live well and said that the purpose of the *polis* was to promote the "good" life, he too laid the democrat's emphasis on "*for* the people" (though in this case on a concept of their virtue). Historical experience shows, I think, a rather high positive correlation between rule *by* and *for* as representative democracy has broadened. After votes for women were secured, more women's-rights legislation of all kinds followed; with every widening of the franchise, more legislation followed to benefit the enfranchised voters. Common sense and a knowledge of political methods would confirm this: after all, a politician comes to office by bidding for votes, by offering something he believes the voters want. He has room for "statesmanship" in the debate and competition, which give him the chance to persuade them to want what he thinks they need. The cynic might call this mass bribery, but it scarcely rivals the class bribery of the earlier limited franchise. There is too much evidence that special-interest legislation was a corrupt and delicate art, brought to a much finer flower of perfection in the days before universal suffrage.

Yet this first implication—that democracy works out for (or is designed for) the people—is undeniably vague. What sectional interest or policy, after all, is not defended on the ground that it is *for* the people? Yet vague as it is, it is not useless, and may be said to constitute one of the values of democracies, a value which many people rate highly. In this context, however, I shall treat it as a highly general, preliminary value, and proceed to identify more specific values of democracy.

THE SPECIFIC VALUES OF A DEMOCRATIC SYSTEM

The values of democracy are two-fold: (a) those underlying the principles considered separately; and (b) the values of the system as a whole. The task is to identify the values in both cases, so that, these being isolated, we may see what values we are committed to when we embrace democracy. In isolating these values we are not, of course, committing ourselves to every institution in every democracy, since obviously any actual democracy contains much that is unique and adventitious derived from its particular history. . . .

(1) *The first value is the peaceful voluntary adjustment of disputes.* Life in any human society contains a perpetual conflict of interests and opinions, whether the conflict is suppressed or conducted openly. If anyone doubts this, let him look around him or read history. A democracy is unique in recognizing the political expression of such conflicts as legitimate, and in providing for their peaceful adjustment through the negotiations of politics, as an alternative to their settlement by force or fiat. Every political theory either provides means for this peaceful settlement within a political system, or else it must call upon a *deus ex machina* to impose order, an authority from outside the system of conflict, as Hobbes expected the monarch of the Leviathan to rule, as Bolingbroke looked to his Patriot King, as Plato looked to his Guardians, as the Germans looked to the Führer and as Marx once or twice spoke of the state as standing "above society."

Democracy makes unique provision for the peaceful adjustment of disputes, the maintenance of order, and the working out of public policies, by means of its "honest broker" or compromise function. The policy compromises are worked out as the representatives bid for electoral support, amid the constant public debate, agitation, and politicking that go on in the context of political liberties, until in time many policies pass from dispute to virtual unanimity in settled law; . . .

Democracy is thus institutionalized peaceful settlement of conflict (ballots for bullets, a counting instead of a cracking of heads), a settlement arrived at *pro tem* with the widest possible participation because of the adult suffrage and the political freedoms. It is distinguished from elite systems or borderline cases (with *some* freedoms, *some* choice, etc.) by the difference in degree, by the recognition of the legitimacy of many diverse political interests and the extent of public participation in the settlement of disputes.

Here, then, is a value, characteristic of democracy, which will be prized by all who prefer voluntary to imposed adjustment and agreement. It is not a value, however, to those (if there are any such) who believe that force is preferable; nor would democracy be valued by those who believe that the ideally best policies are always preferable even if they have to be imposed from above.

(2) *The second value is that of ensuring peaceful change in a changing society.* This is so closely related that it may be regarded as an application of the first to the special circumstances of the modern world.

The value makes a stronger appeal today than in earlier, more static, periods, that is, it has a greater element of plausibility now, because we accept the normality, even inevitability, of rapid technological change. Tomorrow the stars. (In suggesting that technology is an independent variable, initiating social and political changes though not fully determining their extent or direction, we need not ignore other determinants such as population changes or such mechanisms as the entrepreneurial function.)

We know from experience that social changes of many kinds inevitably follow the technological. The democratic political method—flexible, responsive to public opinion and to the influence of leadership, open to controversy—ensures political adaptation to this determinant of change. Almost by definition, because of the electoral changes of policy-makers, there is less "political lag" in the many adjustments which are required in law and policy to meet rapidly changing circumstances. . . .

(3) *The third value is the orderly succession of rulers.* Democracy not only presides over social conflict and change, but at the same time solves an even older political problem: that of finding, peacefully, legitimate successors to the present rulers. Hobbes, for instance, thought that the problem of succession was the chief difficulty with a monarchical system. Democracy is pre-eminently an answer to the question which no alternative system can answer convincingly in the modern climate of opinion: how to find and change the rulers peaceably and legitimately. The methods of self-appointment, of hereditary succession, of co-option by an elite, and of the *coup d'état* are not contemporaneously plausible in their philosophic justifications, apart altogether from the practical difficulties inherent in them, to which abundant historical experience testifies.

It was with these three social values in mind—peaceful adjustment, change, succession—that Judge Learned Hand could write of democracy and free elections:

> It seems to me, with all its defects our system does just that. For, abuse it as you will, it gives a bloodless measure of social forces—bloodless, have you thought of that?—a means of continuity, a principle of stability, a relief from the paralyzing terror of revolution.[1]

(4) *The fourth value is that of the minimum of coercion.* A fourth value may be constructed by reference to the extent and quality of coercion involved in a democracy. . . . It is not only that almost by definition the greater number approves of the policy decisions, so that always the smaller number is coerced. This is the least of the argument, which depends much more on the existence of political freedoms and the way in which policies are made. For one thing there is great value

[1] Learned Hand, *The Spirit of Liberty,* ed. Irving Dillard, New York, 1952 and 1959, p. 76.

in a safety valve, in being able to let off steam and to contribute to the debate and the politicking even though one is finally outvoted. We may follow the fashion and call it a catharsis, a working-off harmlessly of buried feelings of aggression, guilt, or the like. An ill-treated minority does normally feel differently—less coerced—if political equality is recognized and if it has to give only conditional obedience to policies which it may criticize and which it can entertain a reasonable hope of altering either by persuasion or by political influence. (This does not, however, always satisfy "permanent" minorities. . . .)

We may go further. The normal democratic policy is in a sense a decision which gives no claimant everything he asks for; is not a mere mechanical compromise but a new policy, shaped from the continuing dialogue and struggle of the political process. Some go so far as to call the method "creative discussion." From this it is only a short step to saying that there is more value in decisions which we make, or help to make, than in having "wiser" decisions made *for* us, and which we must be compelled to obey.

> To try to force people to embrace something that is believed to be good and glorious but which they do not actually want, even though they may be expected to like it when they experience its results—is the very hall mark of anti-democratic belief.[2]

One might plausibly assume then that nearly everybody would accept this value—that *ceteris paribus,** it is better to coerce fewer people than more, to get voluntary observance rather than coerced obedience, to substitute what Wordsworth called the "discipline of virtue" for the "discipline of slavery": "order else cannot subsist, nor confidence nor peace." The notion of willing obedience reasonably, freely, and conditionally given would also agree with ideas of self-discipline, responsibility, and the like, of which we hear so much.

(5) *The fifth value is that of diversity.* The argument here depends initially on whether diversity of beliefs and action, and a wider area of choice, are of themselves good. Many will dispute their value, since diversity and variety can result in more of both the good and the bad, and free choice implies the freedom to choose badly. Ruskin thought that liberty of choice destroyed life and strength, and hence democracy was destructive. Human freedom has destructive as well as creative possibilities. But is there not at least some prima facie case for diversity and variety per se, as there is for freedom?

In the first place there is always diversity in any society, even if not to the extent of as many opinions as there are men. Democracy merely

[2] Cf. A. D. Lindsay, *The Modern Democratic State,* Oxford, 1943, pp. 45, 241, 275. Schumpeter, *Capitalism, Socialism and Democracy* (New York, 1950), p. 237.

* Other things being equal.

recognizes its existence, and legitimatizes the different opinions and interests. . . .

In the second place, the value of open channels and political liberties is that by implication an inevitable variety will result. Here, too, as far as ideas are concerned, we may fall back upon the arguments used by Mill in his defense of liberty of opinion. We do rightly, on grounds of experience, to be suspicious of man's ability to know beforehand what new idea or proposal or way of behaving should be strangled at birth by the authorities and what allowed to live. The true and the good often repel in their very novelty.

In the third place, however, we can only say that "other things being equal," a wider choice is *ipso facto* good; it is a necessary condition for moral improvement, for reaching closer to the truth (so long as we assume we have not already reached perfection or the *summum bonum*). . . .[3]

By maintaining an open society, democracy may then be called good because its freedoms give flexibility and a wide variety of choice. The argument may rest not only on the formal principles of democracy, but also on the empirical tendency for the political freedoms to extend beyond the purely political. The tendency is strong and ever present since political discussion includes the very topic of what is political, and because in their bidding for votes, parties and candidates tend to compete in granting substantive favors, including repeal of restrictive laws in some fields, and promotion of positive policies in others, e.g., on behalf of education, the arts and sciences. It is partly because of this tendency that democracy is sometimes called a "way of life." . . .

(6) *The sixth value is the attainment of justice.* Justice has been rated highly by political philosophers as a value to be attained in many societies. Its achievement is often regarded as the central core of political morality, and the defense of democracy on this ground must be that it is the system best able to produce justice. There are several relevant points in the case.

First, let us grant that the best we can hope for in any practicable political system is not that injustice will never be committed (a perfectionist ideal) but that it can be seen, corrected if possible, and avoided the next time beforehand. (The dilemma could perhaps be avoided if democracy were by definition, or could be in practice, unanimous rule.

[3] A subsidiary value from diversity may be formulated: a wider range of temptations gives more opportunities of strengthening the character. For this reason Morris Cohen could write: "the very essence of civilization [is] that we should increase the temptation and with it the power of self-control." *Reason and Law,* Glencoe, Ill., 1950, p. 52. Rousseau started from the same point: morality for the individual implies liberty of choice. Unfortunately, he tended to merge individual liberty in the community, though in this he was not far from one of the ideals of the Greek city-state.

There would then be no others within the system to judge the decisions to be unwise or unjust. But even then, a later generation could pass such judgment, as could persons in other states. Unanimity or universality is no guarantee of rightness or justice.) The link with democracy lies in the political liberties—the procedures, the publicity, and possibilities of redress. What the U.S. Supreme Court once said of liberty may be true of justice too: "the history of liberty has largely been the history of the observance of procedural safeguards."

No political system, lacking perfection, can be entitled to unconditional allegiance. There may come a time when any individual may feel bound in conscience to withhold his obedience; and it comes to much the same thing to say that no political system can lay down, beforehand, the institutional rules for justified disobedience or rebellion. In this respect, democracy again makes perhaps the best claim for obedience to an unjust law because of the political freedoms, provisional obedience, and chances of redress. It is certainly not illogical to obey a particular bad law if it is part of a general system of which we approve, and where we have the liberty of protest and persuasion, and the reasonable hope for redress. We must beware of posing the problem of obeying bad laws too sharply, and on this we may look to Locke for some sensible observations. Allegiance and obedience are never explainable on the ground that the political system gives us, as individuals, everything that we want.

Second, the likelihood of injustice under democracy is much less than where the political freedoms are suppressed, and where none of the usual political safeguards exist. Democracy provides some representation of all substantial groups and interests (though not always strictly in proportion to their numbers, and still less to their "importance"); injured interests, being vocal and able to muster power through influencing votes and through many other recognized and legitimate ways, are seldom likely to be ignored when policy decisions are being made. . . .

Third, democracy involves political compromise or harmony by the adjustment of conflicting claims. This may fairly enough be called "relative" justice, even though it does not approach the kind of harmony or "right relationship" of classes which constituted so much of Plato's idea of justice. In any case "absolute" justice is an ideal beyond the reach of democratic politics, partly because it involves less than full satisfaction of some claims (or "rights") but also partly because absolute justice in any other sense is beyond any system of government. Only relative justice, the relative attainment of any of our highest ideals, is feasible in any political system. The best word to use perhaps is equity, with its connotation of both justice and flexibility. . . .

(7) [*Another*] *value consists of the freedoms found in a democracy. . . .*

The case for democracy, on the ground that it promotes freedoms, is chiefly in terms of the political freedoms. Whether freedoms will be extended to other spheres is not guaranteed by the logic of the democratic system, but is merely a likelihood or probability, a tendency for the political freedoms to carry over into other spheres. The presumption is extremely strong that they will do so, as they did in Athens if we may take the word of Pericles on the social freedom which the citizens enjoyed. It is the same sort of (weaker) tendency by which equality tends to be carried over from the political to other spheres. As Duverger puts it:

> The history of the development of civil rights in France shows a link between the existence of a liberal regime and that of a democratic regime with free elections. This same link is to be found in most of the countries in the world, so that the following general statement may be formulated: civil rights in a country exist in direct proportion to the degree of democracy to be found there. This is not a logical connection but one based on actual fact.[4]

The case can go somewhat deeper. The inescapable conditions of social life impose restrictions on one's freedom of action: freedoms conflict with other goods which we value highly, and sometimes with one another. The essential function of co-ordinating freedoms with one another and with other goods is performed by all governments, but the claim on behalf of democracy is that democratic co-ordination maximizes freedoms. And—paradoxical though it may sound—the maximizing of freedoms does not necessarily mean that the laws are few. To protect and even extend freedoms may demand an elaborate network of laws. We may start with Hobbes's dictum about the silence of the law, but a political theory cannot end there.

It is perhaps worth mentioning again that the political freedoms of a democracy may be valued highly in their own right, and not only for the instrumental reason that they give citizens a share in political power, or are necessary to promote social welfare. There is eloquent testimony that such freedoms may be valued intrinsically, given by many refugees from Nazi Germany and from the Soviet Union and its satellites. Those of us living in democracies, having been born free, and never having been deprived, must often make a greater effort in order to appreciate our birthright. To those who value political freedoms, for whatever reason, the justification for democracy is strong; to those who place a higher intrinsic value upon *other* freedoms, it can at least be said that democracy has a marked tendency to extend the freedoms from the political to other spheres if only because there are channels for the political extension of freedoms.

(8) *Finally, a value may be constructed for democracy from the de-*

[4] Maurice Duverger, *The French Political System* (Chicago, 1958), p. 161.

ficiencies of alternative systems. Any alternative is inevitably a system in which some kind of minority makes the policy decisions—always of course a properly qualified minority, since no one advocates that the numerical minority should rule merely *because* they are a minority.

In the contemporary world there is a strong, almost universal aversion to the idea that any kind of minority has any right or title to rule. Not only are the almost unrecognized postulates of our political thinking against it, but also the rational objections: What minority? What credentials? Who will judge the credentials? Nor must we make the mistake of merely assuming that because democracy is imperfect, any minority alternative is better because it is made so by definition. We cannot get from a definition to a feasible and perfect political system.

COMMENTS ON THE JUSTIFICATION

Obviously, only those who prize those values listed above, and who believe they are inseparable from or most likely to be promoted by a democracy, will find the values cogent arguments for a democratic system. Thus, apart altogether from considerations of the social and other empirical conditions necessary for democracy, we have not proved that democracy is logically always and everywhere the best political system. I do not think it can be proved, in any logical sense of proof, and that is why I have not attempted it. Instead we may agree with Aristotle that the best form of government is relative to circumstances. The case for democracy is a case, not a demonstration like a Euclidean theorem. By taking this attitude we avoid making a political system itself into an absolute value, as well as the mistake of completely identifying any existing democracy with the theoretical model.

Again, all the values noted are not always and only found in actual democratic systems. Political systems do not always work as their distinguishing principles might lead us to think. Absolute monarchies, for instance, may occasionally be noted for the freedoms and diversity which they permit, as in the rich literary, artistic, and scientific life of eighteenth-century France. But those values noted above follow from the logic of a democratic system, whereas they do not follow from the logic of other systems. . . .

SOME CRITICISMS OF DEMOCRACY

A common opinion has it that democracy has lost much of its appeal in the modern world because its attitudes or character are thought not to agree with the findings of psychology. At any rate, there is a substantial corpus of pessimistic writing to that effect.

For one thing, it is alleged that a whole body of psychological doctrine, starting with Freud, has undermined belief in the rationality of man by showing that much of our behavior is determined at the unconscious mental level. If political decisions cannot be partly rational—in both the economic sense of means to ends and the sense of choosing ends—it is hard to see how we can justify democracy. Another fashionable school of thought purports to show that people are "naturally" and not "culturally" afraid of what Gide called the "anguish of freedom"—of choice, self-discipline, and the responsibility that the democratic method presupposes.

Then, again, so it is said, sociology and the discovery of "iron laws of oligarchy" in virtually every type of large-scale social organization including political parties tend to the same pessimistic conclusion of the inherent unsuitability of democratic principles and attitudes for any large-scale organization, and *a fortiori* for one as large as a political system. This kind of social determinism is seen at its most determinist and pessimistic in the classic by Michels on *Political Parties:* the iron law of oligarchy is "the fundamental sociological law of political parties." No remedy can be found: all organizations in time will become oligarchic. The charge of inevitable oligarchy, or something very similar, is brought not only by Michels but also by writers such as Pareto, Mosca, and Burnham, and is supported by much empirical evidence drawn from the study of political parties, trade unions, and business organizations. The charge is based on different concepts such as that of the "managerial elite," the inevitable trends to bureaucracy, the "organization man," the nature of large-scale technology, and so forth. The concept of the "sociology of knowledge" has contributed also to the same end—e.g., here and there in the works of Karl Mannheim—by suggesting that social factors determine man's beliefs and actions.

What are we to say to these impressive arguments? For myself, I do not find that they support the anti-democratic conclusions so often drawn. Take the "iron law of oligarchy." There is nothing in democratic theory which cannot come to terms with leadership in organizations, political or any other kind. It is no great news that large-scale organizations are led by the leaders. This sociological finding, for which so many—sometimes conflicting—causes are given and from which different conclusions are drawn, is only devastating to a primitive or direct type of democratic system, and scarcely affects a representative system. A democracy does not require everyone to be politically active, or show all the democratic attitudes, and can make full allowance for the realities of leadership and parties. (A democracy does, however, presuppose that political action is not determinist, but that human choice and attitudes do count, causally; that human choice can control and mold the impersonal forces at work in society, and within limits shape them to human ends.)

A fuller answer may be attempted to the charge based upon psychology. We can, in the first place, readily admit that any democracy may contain a proportion of undemocratic personalities, judged by the standards set forth above or by other standards. How high the proportion can get before a democracy becomes unworkable, we simply do not know. Doubtless the proportion will vary with the kind of political circumstances at different times, including the urgency and magnitude of the policies to be made, the quality of political leadership, and so forth. We do know, however, that democracy need not presuppose any large proportion of the politically active, or even a high proportion of voters. Despite Aristotle, not every man is (or need be) a political animal.

Then, too, we can point to the going democracies, some of which have been successful for a considerable time; and to the many attempts at self-government—even those that have failed—all of which must be explained away by the psychological pessimists. Those who assert that man is not psychologically able to work democracy often forget that full representative democracy is, for all practical purposes, a comparatively new political system. It takes time for the masses of men to adjust to new political forms, and to adapt to the ideas and the moral climate which accompanies democracy—the autonomy, the discussion, the political equality and freedoms, and the majority principle—until they become "second nature." Life in the past seems to have been lived more by "instinct" (or custom) and government has been more readily accepted with resignation, instead of approached with the idea that it can be popularly created and controlled. Every democracy trails clouds of these older traditions into the present. Democracy, as Morley said, "stands for a remarkable revolution in human affairs." Then, too, there is still the cogent point that so much of man's "unfitness" for democracy may be simply his "unfitness" for, or painful adjustment to, a scientific and industrial urban way of living.

In pointing thus to experience with democracy and self-government, we do not need to posit any primitive "instinct to freedom," nor yet to assume any universal psychological or other needs which only democracy can satisfy. There is a set of psychological *wants* that are democratic, but they are a function of the values of democracy, i.e., they are culturally learned and (as yet) certainly not universal. Men may come to democracy to fulfill different needs—as they go to religion for different reasons. It is enough if the needs thus fulfilled, in their overt expression as wants, are compatible with democracy. (Those who have been led to take a pessimistic view of man's capacity for democracy have, I think, been led astray by making two additional mistakes: first, by founding their psychological theory upon clinical experience with the unfit; and second, by assuming that democracy presupposes that all, or even a large proportion of, citizens need be politically active. They have been better at their psychology, their technical expertise, than in their understanding of politics.)

We can also point to the psychological evidence in *favor* of man's capacity for democracy—including those persons who value the procedures of democracy more highly than any of its substantive objectives. While it may be true that "every man bears within himself a dormant fascist," it is equally true that we are all animals in our unconscious. It is what is in our consciousness that counts, and the business of any society is to make a civilized consciousness.

Our conclusions can be modest. We need conclude only that there is nothing in the demands which democracy makes upon men, or in the kind of personality which it requires and promotes, that is at variance with what we know with a fair degree of reliability of psychology. This may not be saying much, because we may not know much for certain; most psychology is local and western and not universal. On the other hand, if we do not know much, it is hard to feel that arguments drawn from psychological theories are very damaging to democracy. We must assume, however, that the democratic character "does not form against the grain" in enough people [to make it impossible] to work the system successfully. Compatibility, then, is a justifiable assumption, and a quite sufficient one. "Man has no nature: what he has is . . . history." (And it may help to recall that anthropology finds something very like democracy in some early primitive societies, whence some assert that democracy is the oldest form of government, while some make the cheerful assumption that democracy is the norm at which the political animal most naturally will arrive.) . . .

THE CHARGE OF INCOMPETENCE

The second class of contemporary criticism, commanding a wide following, may for convenience be grouped under the head of "incompetence." A host of such specific charges used to be directed at the existing democracies before World War II, most of them being associated with Fascism and Nazism, both of which despised democracy but avoided the Marxist diagnosis of putting the blame on the capitalists and the economic system. The charges were focused instead around the allegation that democracy is incompetent and inefficient—in dealing with serious economic problems, in its unstable domestic and foreign policies, and in its inability to prepare for war. The breakdown of democracy in Germany and Italy, and its relative economic failure everywhere in the depression of the 1930's, was usually adduced as supporting evidence of incompetence. (The Marxist criticism is almost the opposite, that democracy *is* efficient in terms of its own "real" underlying principles—giving the *bourgeoisie* their way, and maintaining class rule for the time being.)

The alleged incompetence of democracy is accounted for in several ways. For one thing, the democratic system is inevitably slow—taking too long to act, to hammer out a policy in the endless debates, electioneering, and politicking. This slow method is quite unsuited for dealing with emergencies requiring quick decision. Nothing gets done, except during a war, and then only at the cost of suspending democracy.

For another, the political system of democracy is said to be inherently unsuited to the complexities and large scale of the modern world, whatever may perhaps have been its usefulness in a simpler age, when political units were small or when *laissez faire* prevailed and the services provided by government were few. When a government does a few things, mistakes hardly matter; but when many things, failures are always serious and may be calamitous. This particular criticism is indeed made the basis of pessimistic predictions of the prospects of democracy by both its friends and its enemies: by its friends who fear that "increasing" government may destroy democracy, and by its enemies who hope that it will do so.

Then again, democracy is said to fail on the score of leadership. The talents for vote-getting are not those of ruling—of making "wise" decisions. Democracy emphasizes and rewards the former, and bonuses opportunism of parties and politicians as they have the money or cunning to influence the votes. But good government, wise policies, are needed to ensure the success of any system, and only good leaders can provide these desiderata.

Moreover, even if competent leaders should occasionally find themselves in office—combining the roles of politicians and statesmen—they are hopelessly handicapped by the methods of democratic politics. Democracy diffuses responsibility for policies, whereas responsibility must be concentrated in order to "get things done," i.e., to decide policies, to make them into a consistent pattern, and to see they are carried out efficiently. A casual reference to the near-chaos or deadlock in some multi-party systems—usually that of France—is taken to be enough to document the case against democratic leadership.

The very principle of compromise which is, so to speak, built into the democratic system further militates against efficiency, consistency, and "good" government. Compromise is also made the basis of the charge that democracy lacks "principle" (compromise is said to be the exaltation of "no principle"), while in addition it stands for and invites unlimited sectionalism, pressures, and group selfishness. Alternatively, democracy is sometimes accused of being organized deceit and hypocrisy

—professing high principles and the public interest but always deviating from them in the compromises of politics—an inevitable tendency (so it is said), since, not being able to accomplish anything important, politicians must pretend that the trivial things they actually do are important.

Democracy is also confusing to the citizens, who cannot understand the complexities and subtleties of its policy-making or methods of operation. It has, moreover, no ideology, no body of agreed and simple doctrine, no great aims or purposes, by which to inspire devotion and sacrifice and to command the enthusiastic loyalty, if not the understanding, of the masses. The result is bound to be disillusion and apathy among the public, and in the end a collapse of the system from its own defects —to give way to more militant, inspiring, and demanding faiths, supporting other newer systems which are the "wave of the future." Where the democratic system has worked, after a fashion, its success is accounted for by extraneous or fortuitous factors which have, as it were, managed to keep a bumbling and incompetent system afloat in spite of its defects.

The case is familiar and at first sight formidable. (I pass over the virtues sometimes grudgingly granted to democracy, e.g., that it solves the problem of peaceful succession of rulers.) And it would obviously be foolish to deny an element of truth here and there in these criticisms. Before coming to grips with the main charge of incompetence, two oft-forgotten points of considerable importance should be recalled.

(a) Much of democratic government—though by no means all—is conducted in the white glare of publicity, and faults are exaggerated. The very function of an opposition is to oppose, and to do so as noisily and as effectively as possible. Because of the political liberties allowed, every democracy produces critics of the system and of its most fundamental principles. Mistakes of policy and abuses of the system, both real and imaginary, are freely ventilated—often to loud and profitable applause. By contrast, only praise and flattery are allowed in a dictatorship, and since the mistakes and evils go uncriticized, one tends to assume they are nonexistent. The old observation is still true that under a popular government everyone speaks ill of the people with freedom and without fear; whereas no one speaks of an absolute prince without a thousand fears and precautions.

(b) The critics of democracy all too often fail to apply the same standards to democracy as to its rivals. The very highest, often perfectionist, standards are used to judge democracy—as when moral purists attack the United States for the mote and make generous excuses for the Soviet beam, or denounce the scandals of democratic politics, forgetting the institutionalized corruption of other political systems. (This kind of criticism also subtly shifts the ground of attack from incompetence to moral turpitude.)

Nevertheless, even when due allowance has been made for the exaggeration of faults and the use of the double standard, the charge of incompetence raises a question which goes to the very root of the theory of democratic politics. Incompetence, or the lack of political wisdom, constitutes in fact the gravamen of the most serious charge (other than the Marxist) and is also the oldest of the criticisms against democracy —modern versions being seldom more than glosses on Plato, with a few topical illustrations added. In the end, the quasi-Platonic criticism is directed against the principle of political equality, and rests upon a particular view of the nature of politics. This principle of political equality, so it is said, is based on the assumption of equality of political wisdom among the citizens—which is absurd. Political wisdom is distributed unequally, and some obviously know more than others. The masses of the citizens are ignorant, and even if most of them can be made technically literate, their judgment on public policy (if it can be called judgment) is necessarily incomplete and faulty.

Whatever validity Plato's critique of the assumption of equal political wisdom had against Athenian democracy, the modern version has far less force against the indirect, representative democracy with which we are familiar. Political wisdom of a high order on every complex issue is not required of all citizens in a system where the people do not make the policy decisions, but instead elect and authorize representatives to do this for them. The wisdom is needed by the leaders (though there is admittedly the problem of how the leaders may persuade the citizens to follow them). The modern criticism ought, then, to be directed against the democratic method of choosing its leaders (politicians). And often it is in fact so directed—as when it becomes an attack upon the universal suffrage, which is alleged to have been responsible for the rise of Hitler, to make the conduct of enlightened foreign policy impossible, to lower and destroy moral and cultural values alike.[5]

Democracy, like any other political system, must produce "adequate" leaders, adequate to ensure the continuance of the system, and thus to realize its values; adequate to meet the short- and long-term problems, whether economic or international or whatever they may be. Democracy obviously stands or falls by its method of selecting its leaders, and rests on the explicit assumption that elections are the best, or least bad, method of choosing the wisest and best. Behind the elections there is, of course, the pre-selection of candidates by parties—using all the polit-

[5] For a survey of the criticisms of democracy on cultural grounds by Carlyle, Ruskin, Arnold, Stephen, Maine, and Lecky see Benjamin E. Lippincott, *Victorian Critics of Democracy*, Minneapolis, 1938. Tocqueville and Henry Adams should also be consulted.

ical criteria of "availability," electoral appeal, and so forth; an elaborate and severely competitive pre-selection process that is usually ignored by the critics.

Let us grant that we need more investigations into democratic leadership: how it is in fact found and brought forward; in what political "talent" consists; whether there is a large stock of "talent"; whether the system does in fact make good use of its "talent"; whether a traditional ruling class is necessary (as Schumpeter argued); whether businessmen as a class are inherently poor political leaders (as Adam Smith believed); whether democratic leadership tends to compare unfavorably with leadership in other systems, and many similar questions. H. L. Mencken was much more severe than Adam Smith on what he called the plutocracy. Bryce too, a friendly critic, thought that the chief fault of democracy was "The power of money to pervert administration or legislation."

The theoretical argument against democratic wisdom is not, however, to be turned aside by empirical studies of leadership, even if their results should happen to be favorable to democracy. Questions of philosophy and principle are also at stake. Plato, it will be recalled, supported his critique by extended argument on the kind of knowledge required, and hence on the difficulty of acquiring wisdom, and on the training and qualifications of the guardians. The philosopher-rulers were to be an aristocracy in the better sense of the word, who by a combination of experience and knowledge received their title to rule just because they *were* qualified.

Fundamentally, two quite different views of the nature of politics and government—the question of what politics and political leadership are *about*—are involved. In the one case, the "proper end" and the implementing policies can only be known with difficulty, by the philosophers; in the democratic view the ends and policies are many and conflicting, the task of ruling is not conceived as holding society, willy-nilly, to the highest ideals, but of achieving the tolerable and the acceptable for the time being, of permitting progress to whatever ideals may be cherished and which the public may be persuaded to accept. Knowledge of the *summum bonum* is not excluded from a democracy, but it must be married to political persuasion in the politician or pressure group.

It is, however, when we come to consider practical minority-rule alternatives to democracy that the nature of the elite critique is more clearly revealed. Not only do all such critiques start by assuming differences in political capacity and wisdom—so much is admitted to exist—but they go on to assert that the "wise elite" can be identified and their rule validated. This is precisely the insuperable difficulty, since there are no accepted credentials for such wisdom.

> Nor will I forsake the faith of our fathers in democracy, however I must transmute it, and make it unlovely to their eyes, were they here to see their strangely perverse disciple. If you will give me scales by which to weigh Tom and Dick and Harry as to their fitness to rule, and tell me how much each shall count, I will talk with you about some other kind of organization. Plato jumped hurdles that are too high for my legs. . . .[6]

Even if an elite is once selected, methods of continuing its recruitment and training must be invented. (The nearest approach to a dominant elite today is the self-selected communist party in some countries.) The selection of an elite cannot be done by mass voting, or else we should be back again at democracy, yet somehow the whole of the citizens must be able to recognize the presence of such wisdom and the rulers who have it; and must accept and continue to accept the validity of their rule, i.e., its legitimacy. It is no wonder that even Plato flinched at this task, and resorted to his "myths" and "conditioning" once the initial philosopher-kings were installed. Nor can it be seriously maintained today that we can accept the rule of some kind of aristocracy based on and validated by wealth, blood, intellect, military prowess, or priestly power. (Think of the difficulty of getting an I.Q. rating accepted as conferring a right to rule.) We know that none of these is necessarily accompanied by political wisdom.

Further, the elite alternative assumes that the wisest and best, once found, will accept rule and responsibility, and will continue to exercise it wisely, their virtue and judgment alike remaining incorruptible by power. These are large assumptions, for which we are not in the market. Architects of Utopia may ignore the peril, but we know too much today about the corrupting influence of power upon those aloof from and out of touch with the governed, exacting obedience, yet unaccountable to anyone except their consciences or their God. It is for this reason that it seems so true that "Great men are nearly always bad men." In the end such rulers can only reduce the stature of their subjects, and they are left trying vainly—as Mill put it—to "do great things with little people." Only a democracy provides institutional safeguards against the corruption of power in an elite, by its freedoms and elections answering the old question *quis custodiet ipsos custodes?* * Elites and dictators both good and bad, are shrewd enough not to take chances by asking for a free renewal of their mandate. They fall a prey to all the evils of the "cult of the individual," having "no remedy for the personality defects which they may bring into their exalted station." [7]

[6] Learned Hand, *op. cit.* p. 77. See also Charles E. Merriam, *Systematic Politics,* Chicago, 1945, pp. 187ff.

* Who will watch over the rulers?

[7] F. Hermens, *The Representative Republic,* Notre Dame, 1958, p. 83.

Section XIII

The Bases of American Foreign Policy

Participation in two world wars in one generation suggests that the survival of America as an independent and democratic nation is inextricably linked with developments abroad.

On what premises and assumptions should American foreign policy be based? Should we agree with Wilson that "we dare not turn from the principle that morality and not expediency is the thing that must guide us, and that we will never condone iniquity because it is most convenient to do so."? Or, must we distinguish between "moral sympathies and the political interests which [we] must defend"? Or, should we seek a "coincidence between national self-interest and supranational ideals."? The issue is discussed by Professors Hans J. Morgenthau, Robert E. Osgood, and H. B. Mayo.

Topic 31

IDEALS AND NATIONAL INTEREST

The Primacy of the National Interest

HANS J. MORGENTHAU *

Moral principles and the national interest have contended for dominance over the minds and actions of men throughout the history of the modern state system. The conduct of American foreign affairs in particular has from

* Professor of Political Science, University of Chicago. Author of *Scientific Man vs. Power Politics, Politics Among Nations, In Defense of the National Interest,* and of

its very beginning been deeply affected by the contest between these two principles of political action. Perhaps never before or after have the practical alternatives which flow from these two principles been stated with greater acumen and persuasiveness than in the Pacificus articles of Alexander Hamilton, and it is for the light which Hamilton's arguments shed upon our problem—as well as for the analogy between the situation to which they apply and some of the situations with which American foreign policy must deal in our time—that we might dwell at some length upon the situation which gave rise to the Pacificus articles, and upon the philosophy which they express.

In 1792 the War of the First Coalition had ranged Austria, Prussia, Sardinia, Great Britain and the United Netherlands against revolutionary France, which was tied to the United States by a treaty of alliance. On April 22, 1793, Washington issued a Proclamation of Neutrality, and it was in defense of that proclamation that Hamilton wrote the Pacificus articles. Among the arguments directed against the Proclamation were three derived from moral principles. Faithfulness to treaty obligations, gratitude toward a country which had lent its assistance to the colonies in their struggle for independence, and the affinity of republican institutions, were cited to prove that the United States must side with France. Against these moral principles, Hamilton invoked the national interest of the United States:

> There would be no proportion between the mischiefs and perils to which the United States would expose themselves, by embarking in the war, and the benefit which the nature of their stipulation aims at securing to France, or that which it would be in their power actually to render her by becoming a party.
>
> This disproportion would be a valid reason for not executing the guaranty. All contracts are to receive a reasonable construction. Self-preservation is the first duty of a nation; and though in the performance of stipulations relating to war, good faith requires that its ordinary hazards should be fairly met, because they are directly contemplated by such stipulations, yet it does not require that extraordinary and extreme hazards should be run. . . .
>
> The basis of gratitude is a benefit received or intended which there was no right to claim, originating in a regard to the interest or advantage of the party on whom the benefit is, or is meant to be, conferred. If a service is rendered from views relative to the immediate interest of the party who performs it, and is productive of reciprocal advantages, there seems scarcely, in such a case, to be an adequate basis for a sentiment like that of gratitude. . . . It may be affirmed as a general principle, that the predominant motive of good offices from one nation to another, is the interest or advantage of the nation which performs them.

---

many articles in the field of international relations. The selection is from Hans J. Morgenthau, "The Primacy of the National Interest," *The American Scholar,* Vol. 18 (Spring, 1949), pp. 207–210 and from "Another 'Great Debate': The National Interest of the United States," *The American Political Science Review,* Vol. XLVI (December, 1952), pp. 961–988. Reprinted by permission of *The American Scholar* and of *The American Political Science Review.*

> Indeed, the rule of morality in this respect is not precisely the same between nations as between individuals. The duty of making its own welfare the guide of its actions, is much stronger upon the former than upon the latter; in proportion to the greater magnitude and importance of national compared with individual happiness, and to the greater permanency of the effects of national than of individual conduct. Existing millions, and for the most part future generations, are concerned in the present measures of a government; while the consequences of the private actions of an individual ordinarily terminate with himself, or are circumscribed within a narrow compass. . . .

The philosophy of this discussion provided the guiding principles of American foreign policy for more than a century. That philosophy has found expression in the *Federalist* and Washington's Farewell Address, no less than in many diplomatic documents. It was eclipsed by a conception of foreign policy whose main representatives were McKinley, Theodore Roosevelt and Admiral Mahan. In that second period, moral principles were invoked side by side with the national interest to justify American expansion within and outside the Western hemisphere. Yet, as before with Gladstone's similar emphasis upon the moral obligations of British foreign policy, it so happened that by a felicitous coincidence what the moral law demanded of the United States was always identical with what its national interest seemed to require.

It is a distinctive characteristic of the third conception of American foreign policy, propounded by Woodrow Wilson, that this identity between the national interest and moral principles is consciously abandoned, and that the sacrifice of the national interest for compliance with moral principles is made the earmark of a worthy foreign policy. In his address at Mobile on October 27, 1913, Wilson declared: "It is a very perilous thing to determine the foreign policy of a nation in the terms of material interest. It not only is unfair to those with whom you are dealing, but it is degrading as regards your own actions. . . . We dare not turn from the principle that morality and not expediency is the thing that must guide us, and that we will never condone iniquity because it is most convenient to do so."

"Only a free people . . ." he said in his message of April 2, 1917, "prefer the interest of mankind to any interest of their own. . . . We have no selfish ends to serve. . . . We are but one of the champions of the rights of mankind." And in his message of January 22, 1917, he had opposed "a peace that will serve the several interests and immediate aims of the nations engaged."

It stands to reason that no statesman in actual performance could have lived up to such principles without ruining his country. Whenever, therefore, Wilson had to apply these moral principles to situations, especially in the Western hemisphere, where the national interest was of long standing and well-defined, he applied them in actions which might as well have been justified in terms of the national interest. Where, however, the national interest was new and not yet clearly defined—as with regard to Europe at the end of the First World War—Wilson started with the assumption, which was a subtly isolationist one, that no specific national interest of the United States was affected by any particular settlement of European issues, and ended up with half-hearted, uneasy compromises between moral principles and the national interests of the more influential European states. Such compromises could not fail to shock the adherents of the Wilsonian principles, to disappoint the nations whose interests had not been fully satisfied, and to remain unintelligible to those sectors of the American public which, following the Federalist tradition of the national interest, had not been affected by the idealism of Wilson's "new diplomacy."

Thus the twenties witnessed a revival of the conception of the national interest, however erroneously defined. Under Franklin D. Roosevelt, Wilsonianism was revived in the foreign policy of Cordell Hull, while the President came closest to identifying the national interest with moral principles, the characteristic of the second period of American foreign policy. It is with the Truman Doctrine that a fourth conception of foreign policy has come to dominate the conduct of American foreign affairs. The Truman Doctrine is Wilsonian in that it proclaims universal moral principles—such as promotion of free and democratic governments everywhere in the world—as standards of American foreign policy. It is within the Federalist tradition in that it finds the containment of Russian power at some point required by the national interest. Yet, by defining that point in terms of its moral principles and not in those political and military terms which the national interest would demand, it vitiates its consideration of the national interest and cannot help being eclectic and immature as a philosophy, and half-hearted, contradictory and threatened with failure in actual operation. . . .

The man in the street, unsophisticated as he is and uninformed as he may be, has a surer grasp of the essentials of foreign policy and a more mature judgment of its basic issues than many of the intellectuals and politicians who pretend to speak for him and cater to what they imagine his prejudices to be. During the recent war the ideologues of the Atlantic Charter, the Four Freedoms, and the United Nations were constantly complaining that the American soldier did not know what he was fighting for. Indeed, if he was fighting for some utopian ideal, divorced from the concrete experiences and interests of the country, then the complaint was well grounded. However, if he was fighting for the territorial integrity of the nation and for its survival as a free country where he could live, think, and act as he pleased, then he had never any doubt about what he was fighting for. Ideological rationalizations and justifications are indeed the indispensable concomitants of all political action. Yet there is something unhealthy in a craving for ideological intoxication and in the inability to act and to see merit in action except under the stimulant of grandiose ideas and far-fetched schemes. Have our intellectuals become, like Hamlet, too much beset by doubt to act and, unlike Hamlet, compelled to still their doubts by renouncing their sense of what is real? The man in the street has no such doubts. It is true that ideologues and demagogues can sway him by appealing to his emotions. But it is also true, as American history shows in abundance and as the popular success of Ambassador Kennan's book demonstrates, that responsible statesmen can guide him by awakening his latent understanding of the national interest.

Yet what is the national interest? How can we define it and give it the content which will make it a guide for action? This is one of the relevant questions to which the current debate has given rise.

It has been frequently argued against the realist conception of foreign policy that its key concept, the national interest, does not provide an acceptable standard for political action. This argument is in the main based upon two grounds: the elusiveness of the concept and its susceptibility to interpretations, such as limitless imperialism and narrow nationalism, which are not in keeping with the American tradition in foreign policy. The argument has substance as far as it goes, but it does not invalidate the usefulness of the concept.

The concept of the national interest is similar in two respects to the "great generalities" of the Constitution, such as the general welfare and due process. It contains a residual meaning which is inherent in the concept itself, but beyond these minimum requirements its content can run the whole gamut of meanings which are logically compatible with it. That content is determined by the political traditions and the total cultural context within which a nation formulates its foreign policy. The concept of the national interest, then, contains two elements, one that is logically required and in that sense necessary, and one that is variable and determined by circumstances.

Any foreign policy which operates under the standard of the national interest must obviously have some reference to the physical, political and cultural entity which we call a nation. In a world where a number of sovereign nations compete with and oppose each other for power, the foreign policies of all nations must necessarily refer to their survival as their minimum requirements. Thus all nations do what they cannot help but do: protect their physical, political, and cultural identity against encroachments by other nations.

It has been suggested that this reasoning erects the national state into the last word in politics and the national interest into an absolute standard for political action. This, however, is not quite the case. The idea of interest is indeed of the essence of politics and, as such, unaffected by the circumstances of time and place. Thucydides' statement, born of the experiences of ancient Greece, that "identity of interest is the surest of bonds whether between states or individuals" was taken up in the nineteenth century by Lord Salisbury's remark that "the only bond of union that endures" among nations is "the absence of all clashing interests." The perennial issue between the realist and utopian schools of thought over the nature of politics, to which we have referred before, might well be formulated in terms of concrete interest *vs.* abstract principles. Yet while the concern of politics with interest is perennial, the connection between interest and the national state is a product of history.

The national state itself is obviously a product of history and as such destined to yield in time to different modes of political organization. As long as the world is politically organized into nations, the national interest is indeed the last word in world politics. When the national state will have been replaced by another mode of organization, foreign policy must then protect the interest in survival of that new organization. For the benefit of those who insist upon discarding the national state and constructing supranational organizations by constitutional fiat, it must be pointed out that these new organizational forms will either come into being through conquest or else through consent based upon the mutual recognition of the national interests of the nations concerned; for no nation will forego its freedom of action if it has no reason to expect proportionate benefits in compensation for that loss. This is true of treaties concerning commerce or fisheries as it is true of the great compacts, such as the European Coal and Steel Community, through which nations try to create supranational forms of organization. Thus, by an apparent paradox, what is historically relative in the idea of the national interest can be overcome only through the promotion in concert of the national interest of a number of nations.

The survival of a political unit, such as a nation, in its identity is the irreducible minimum, the necessary element of its interests vis-à-vis other units. Taken in isolation, the determination of its content in a concrete situation is relatively simple; for it encompasses the integrity of the nation's territory, of its political institutions, and of its culture. Thus bipartisanship in foreign policy, especially in times of war, has been most easily achieved in the promotion of these minimum requirements of the national interest. The situation is different with respect to the variable elements of the national interest. All the cross currents of personalities, public opinion, sectional interests, partisan politics, and political and moral folkways are brought to bear upon their determination. In consequence, the contribution which science can make to this field, as to all fields of policy formation, is limited. It can identify the different agencies of the government which contribute to the determination of the variable elements of the national interest and assess their relative weight. It can separate the long-range objectives of foreign policy from the short-term ones which are the means for the achievement of the former and can tentatively establish their rational relations. Finally, it can analyze the variable elements of the national interest in terms of their legitimacy and their compatibility with other national values and with the national interest of other nations. . . .

We have said before that the utopian and realist positions in international affairs do not necessarily differ in the policies they advocate, but that they part company over their general philosophies of politics and their way of thinking about matters political. It does not follow that the present debate is only of academic interest and without practical significance. Both camps, it is true, may support this same policy for different reasons. Yet if the reasons are unsound, the soundness of the policies supported by them is a mere coincidence, and these very same reasons may be, and inevitably are, invoked on other occasions in support of unsound policies. The nefarious consequences of false philosophies and wrong ways of thinking may for the time being be concealed by the apparent success of policies derived from them. You may go to war, justified by your nation's interests, for a moral purpose and in disregard of considerations of power; and military victory seems to satisfy both your moral aspirations and your nation's interests. Yet the manner in which you waged the war, achieved victory, and settled the peace cannot help reflecting your philosophy of politics and your way of thinking about political problems. If these are in error, you may win victory on the field of battle and still assist in the defeat of both your moral principles and the national interest of your country.

Any number of examples could illustrate the real yet subtle practical consequences which follow from the different positions taken. We have chosen two: collective security in Korea and the liberation of the nations that are captives of Communism. A case for both policies can be made from both the utopian and realist positions, but with significant differences in the emphasis and substance of the policies pursued.

Collective security as an abstract principle of utopian politics requires that all nations come to the aid of a victim of aggression by resisting the aggressor with all means necessary to frustrate his aims. Once the case of aggression is established, the duty to act is unequivocal. Its extent may be affected by concern for the nation's survival; obviously no nation will commit outright suicide in the service of collective security. But beyond that elemental limitation no consideration of interest or power, either with regard to the aggressor or his victim or the nation acting in the latter's defense, can qualify the obligation to act under the principle of collective security. Thus high officials of our government have declared that we intervened in Korea not for any narrow interest of ours but in support of the moral principle of collective security.

Collective security as a concrete principle of realist policy is the age-old maxim, "Hang together or hang separately," in modern dress. It recognizes the need for nation A under certain circumstances to defend nation B against attack by nation C. That need is determined, first, by the interest which A has in the territorial integrity of B and by the relation of that interest to all the other interests of A as well as to the resources available for the support of all those interests. Furthermore, A must take into account the power which is at the disposal of aggressor C for fighting A and B as over against the power available to A and B for fighting C. The same calculation must be carried on concerning the power of the likely allies of C as over against those of A and B. Before going to war for the defense of South Korea in the name of collective security, an American adherent of political realism would have demanded an answer to the following four questions: First, what is our interest in the preservation of the independence of South Korea; second, what is our power to defend that independence against North Korea; third, what is our power to defend that independence against China and the Soviet Union; and fourth, what are the chances for preventing China and the Soviet Union from entering the Korean War?

In view of the principle of collective security, interpreted in utopian terms, our intervention in Korea was a foregone conclusion. The interpretation of this principle in realist terms might or might not, depending upon the concrete circumstances of interest and power, have led us to the same conclusion. In the execution of the policy of collective security the utopian had to be indifferent to the possibility of Chinese and Russian intervention, except for his resolution to apply the principle of collective security to anybody who would intervene on the side of the aggressor. The realist could not help weighing the possibility of the intervention of a great power on the side of the aggressor in terms of the interests engaged and the power available on the other side.

The Truman administration could not bring itself to taking resolutely the utopian or the realist position. It resolved to intervene in good measure on utopian grounds and in spite of military advice to the contrary; it allowed the military commander to advance to the Yalu River in disregard of the risk of the intervention of a great power against which collective security could be carried out only by means of a general war, and then refused to pursue the war with full effectiveness on the realist grounds of the risk of a third world war. Thus Mr. Truman in 1952 was caught in the same dilemma from which Mr. Baldwin could extricate himself in 1936 on the occasion of the League of Nations sanctions against Italy's attack upon Ethiopia only at an enormous loss to British prestige. Collective security as a defense of the *status quo* short of a general war can be effective only against second-rate powers. Applied against a major power, it is a contradiction in terms, for it means necessarily a major war. Of this self-defeating contradiction Mr. Baldwin was as unaware in the 'thirties as Mr. Truman seemed to be in 1952. Mr. Churchill put Mr. Baldwin's dilemma in these cogent terms: "First, the Prime Minister had declared that sanctions meant war; secondly, he was resolved that there must be no war; and thirdly, he decided upon sanctions. It was evidently impossible to comply with these three conditions." Similarly Mr. Truman had declared that the effective prosecution of the Korean War meant the possibility of a third world war; he resolved that there must be no third world war; and he decided upon intervention in the Korean War. Here, too, it is impossible to comply with these three conditions.

Similar contradictions are inherent in the proposals which would substitute for the current policy of containment one of the liberation of the nations presently the captives of Russian Communism. This objective can be compatible with the utopian or realist position, but the policies designed to secure it will be fundamentally different according to whether they are based upon one or the other position. The clearest case to date for the utopian justification of such policies has been made by Representative Charles J. Kersten of Wisconsin who pointed to these four "basic defects" of the "negative policy of containment and negotiated coexistence":

> It would be immoral and unchristian to negotiate a permanent agreement with forces which by every religious creed and moral precept are evil. It abandons nearly one-half of humanity and the once free nations of Poland, Czechoslovakia, Hungary, Rumania, Bulgaria, Albania, Lithuania, Latvia, Estonia and China to enslavement of the Communist police state.
>
> It is un-American because it violates the principle of the American Declaration of Independence, which proclaims the rights of all people to freedom and their right and duty to throw off tyranny.
>
> It will lead to all-out World War III because it aligns all the forces of the non-Communist world in military opposition to and against all the forces of the Communist world, including the 800,000,000 peoples behind the Iron Curtain.
>
> The policy of mere containment is uneconomic and will lead to national bankruptcy.

This statement is interesting for its straightforwardness and because it combines in a rather typical fashion considerations of abstract morality and of expediency. The captive nations must be liberated not only because their captivity is immoral, unchristian, and un-American, but also because its continuation will lead to a third world war and to national bankruptcy. To what extent, however, these considerations of expediency are invalidated by their utopian setting will become obvious from a comparison between the utopian and the realist positions.

From the utopian point of view there can be no difference between the liberation of Estonia or Czechoslovakia, of Poland or China; the captivity of any nation, large or small, close or far away, is a moral outrage which cannot be tolerated. The realist, too, seeks the liberation of all captive nations because he realizes that the presence of the Russian armies in the heart of Europe and their cooperation with the Chinese armies constitute the two main sources of the imbalance of power which threatens our security. Yet before he formulates a program of liberation, he will seek answers to a number of questions such as these: While the United States has a general interest in the liberation of all captive nations, what is the hierarchy of interests it has in the liberation, say, of China, Estonia, and Hungary? And while the Soviet Union has a general interest in keeping all captive nations in that state, what is the hierarchy of its interests in keeping, say, Poland, Eastern Germany, and Bulgaria captive? If we assume, as we must on the historic evidence of two centuries, that Russia would never give up control over Poland without being compelled by force of arms, would the objective of the liberation of Poland justify the ruin of western civilization, that of Poland included, which would be the certain result of a third world war? What resources does the United States have at its disposal for the liberation of all captive nations or some of them? What resources does the Soviet Union have at its disposal to keep in captivity all captive nations or some of them? Are we more likely to avoid national bankruptcy by embarking upon a policy of indiscriminate liberation with the concomitant certainty of war or by continuing the present policy of containment?

It might be that in a particular instance the policies suggested by the answers to these questions will coincide with Representative Kersten's proposals, but there can be no doubt that in its overall character, substance, emphasis, and likely consequences a utopian policy of liberation differs fundamentally from a realist one.

The issue between liberation as a utopian principle of abstract morality *vs.* the realist evaluation of the consequences which a policy of liberation would have for the survival of the nation has arisen before in American history. Abraham Lincoln was faced with a dilemma similar to that which confronts us today. Should he make the liberation of the slaves the ultimate standard of his policy even at the risk of destroying the Union, as many urged him to do, or should he subordinate the moral principle of universal freedom to considerations of the national interest? The answer Lincoln gave to Horace Greeley, a spokesman for the utopian moralists, is timeless in its eloquent wisdom. "If there be those," he wrote on August 22, 1862,

> who would not save the Union unless they could at the same time save slavery, I do not agree with them. If there be those who would not save the Union unless they could at the same time destroy slavery, I do not agree with them. My paramount object in this struggle *is* to save the Union, and is *not* either to save or to destroy slavery. If I could save the Union without freeing *any* slave I would do it, and if I could save it by freeing *all* the slaves, I would do it; and if I could save it by freeing some and leaving others alone I would also do that. What I do about slavery, and the colored race, I do because I believe it helps to save the Union; and what I forbear, I forbear because I do *not* believe it would help to save the Union. I shall do *less* whenever I shall believe what I am doing hurts the cause, and I shall do *more* whenever I shall believe doing more will help the cause. I shall try to correct errors when shown to be errors; and I shall adopt new views so fast as they appear to be true views.

> I have here stated my purpose according to my view of *official* duty; and I intend no modification of my oft-expressed *personal* wish that all men everywhere could be free.

The foregoing discussion ought to shed additional light, if this is still needed, upon the moral merits of the utopian and realist positions. . . .

The realist recognizes that a moral decision, especially in the political sphere, does not imply a simple choice between a moral principle and a standard of action which is morally irrelevant or even outright immoral. A moral decision implies always a choice among different moral principles, one of which is given precedence over others. To say that a political action has no moral purpose is absurd; for political action can be defined as an attempt to realize moral values through the medium of politics, that is, power. The relevant moral question concerns the choice among different moral values, and it is at this point that the realist and the utopian part company again. If an American statesman must choose between the promotion of universal liberty, which is a moral good, at the risk of American security and, hence, of liberty in the United States, and the promotion of American security and of liberty in the United States, which is another moral good, to the detriment of the promotion of universal liberty, which choice ought he to make? The utopian will not face the issue squarely and will deceive himself into believing that he can achieve both goods at the same time. The realist will choose the national interest on both moral and pragmatic grounds; for if he does not take care of the national interest nobody else will, and if he puts American security and liberty in jeopardy the cause of liberty everywhere will be impaired.

Finally, the political realist distinguishes between his moral sympathies and the political interests which he must defend. He will distinguish with Lincoln between his "*official* duty" which is to protect the national interest and his "*personal* wish" which is to see universal moral values realized throughout the world. . . .

The contest between utopianism and realism is not tantamount to a contest between principle and expediency, morality and immorality, although some spokesmen for the former would like to have it that way. The contest is rather between one type of political morality and another type of political morality, one taking as its standard universal moral principles abstractly formulated, the other weighing these principles against the moral requirements of concrete political action, their relative merits to be decided by a prudent evaluation of the political consequences to which they are likely to lead.

These points are re-emphasized by the foregoing discussion. Which attitude with regard to collective security and to the liberation of the captive nations, the utopian or the realist, is more likely to safeguard the survival of the United States in its territorial, political, and cultural identity and at the same time to contribute the most to the security and liberty of other nations? This is the ultimate test—political and moral—by which utopianism and realism must be judged.

Ideals and Self-Interest

ROBERT ENDICOTT OSGOOD *

There is no virtue in a nation's being able to achieve its ends if those ends are not worth achieving. Obviously, I am not just interested in the stability and effectiveness of America's foreign relations as one might be interested in the adjustment of the Hopi Indians to their social and physical environment, without passing any judgment on the moral purpose and consequence of such an adjustment. . . .

SELF-INTEREST WITHOUT IDEALS IS SELF-DEFEATING

Fundamentally, there is no justification for ideals beyond the ideals themselves. They are matters of faith, not empirical propositions. But, if one assumes the worth of the Christian-liberal-humanitarian ideals, as this essay does, then it is relevant to understand that the calculation and pursuit of national self-interest without regard for universal ideals is not only immoral but self-defeating. Any assessment of the conditions for achieving a nation's international ends which ignores this fact is unrealistic.

If one believes that the enrichment of the individual's life, and not the aggrandizement of the state, is the ultimate goal of politics, if one believes that the object of survival is not mere breathing but the fulfilment of the liberal and humane values of Western civilization, then the preservation and the promotion of American power and interests cannot be an end in itself; it is but a means to an end. This is not just a theoretical consideration. It has practical implications for the conduct of America's foreign relations, and for her domestic affairs too, in the present time of troubles.

National security, like danger, is an uncertain quality; it is relative, not absolute; it is largely subjective and takes countless forms according to a variety of international circumstances. Under the complex circumstances of a world-wide power conflict the bounds of self-preservation are vastly extended, until there is scarcely any aspect of foreign policy that does not involve the nation's safety. Under the impact of persistent fear and tension

* Associate Professor of Political Science, University of Chicago. This selection is from Robert Endicott Osgood, *Ideals and Self Interest in America's Foreign Relations* (Chicago, University of Chicago Press, 1953), pp. 20, 442–444, 446–451, & 23.

national security becomes even more protean and nebulous, so that the notion of self-defense tends to become absorbed in the notion of self-assertion, and the assertion of national pride, honor, prestige, and power tends to become an end in itself. But when the preservation or aggrandizement of national power becomes an end in itself, the search for security will have defeated its very purpose; for according to the values which America professes to exemplify, power is meaningless unless it is a means to some ultimate goal.

If American power becomes an end in itself, American society, no less than international society, will suffer; for unless American security is measured by ideal standards transcending the national interest, it may take forms that undermine the moral basis of all social relations. If the Christian, humanitarian, and democratic values, which are the basis of America's social and political institutions, are valid at all, they are as valid outside American borders as within. Consequently, if they cease to compel respect in America's foreign relations, they will, ultimately, become ineffective in her domestic affairs. The resulting destruction of America's moral fiber through the loss of national integrity and the disintegration of ethical standards would be as great a blow to the nation as an armed attack upon her territory.

I do not mean that the standard of conduct in America's internal affairs varies in direct proportion with her standard in foreign relations. Clearly, this is not the case, for the relative anarchy of international society imposes severe limitations upon human morality, which, fortunately, do not apply to relations among groups and individuals within the structure of American society. Nevertheless, since the validity of the moral and ethical principles which form the bonds of American society is derived from their universal applicability, it would be unrealistic to suppose that the American people can maintain the vitality of these principles within their national borders while they are allowed to languish outside. If national self-interest becomes an all-consuming end in America's outlook upon international relations, it will necessarily jeopardize the strength and stability of liberal and humane values within the United States.

Woodrow Wilson and other American idealists understood the profound moral and psychological bond between America's international and her national behavior. Their mistake was in confusing what was ideally desirable with what was practically attainable. To expect nations to conform to the moral standards obeyed by groups and individuals within nations is not only utopian but, as Theodore Roosevelt asserted, ultimately destructive of both universal principles and the national advantage. But it is equally true that to reduce what is ideally desirable to what is practically attainable is to deprive the popular conscience of a standard of moral judgment which is indispensable to the progress and stability of all social relations, whether within or among nations. This is the moral dilemma posed by the impact of man's egoism upon his desire for perfection. In the past, American Realists have been too prone to ignore this dilemma by investing the unpleasant realities of national egoism with the character of normative principles. . . .

HUMAN NATURE DEMANDS THAT IDEALS SUPPLEMENT REASON

A view of international relations which imagines that nations can in the long run achieve a stable and effective foreign policy solely by a rational calculation of the demands of national self-interest is based upon an unrealistic conception of human nature, for it is certainly utopian to expect any great number of people to have the wit to perceive or the will to follow the dictates of enlightened self-interest on the basis of sheer reason alone. Rational self-interest divorced from ideal principles is as weak and erratic a guide for foreign policy as idealism undisciplined by reason. No great mass of people is Machiavellian, least of all the American people. Americans in particular have displayed a strong aversion to the pursuit of self-interest, unless self-interest has been leavened with moral sentiment.

A genuine realist should recognize that the transcendent ideals expressed in the traditional American mission, no less than America's fundamental strategic interests, are an indispensable source of stability in America's foreign relations. The vitality and the persistence of the liberal strain of American idealism—whether manifested in anti-imperialism, the peace movement, internationalism, the search for disarmament, or anti-fascism—is evidence of this fact. However naive or misguided the proponents of this central strain of American idealism may have been during the last half-century, they have, nevertheless, tenaciously preserved its vital core, which constitutes its universal validity; and their continual reassertion of that vital core of moral purpose—a reassertion kindled by a lively conscience and a profound faculty for self-criticism—has been one of the strongest, most consistent, and most influential aspects of America's international conduct. If American idealism has, at times, been an unsettling influence upon foreign policy, it is because it has lacked the discipline of political realism; but this is largely due to America's relative isolation and security in the past, not to any fatal antithesis between realism and idealism. One can well imagine American idealism being moderated by a less utopian view of international politics—indeed signs of this development are already apparent—but a steady and effective foreign policy devoid of moral appeal is scarcely conceivable.

If the present international tension puts a premium upon a rational comprehension of the thrust of national power and self-interest in world politics, it equally demands an unwavering devotion to ideal ends transcending the national interest in order that reason be given direction and purpose. For example, we have observed that, according to a realistic view of international relations, the American people must be prepared to compromise their ideals in the short run in order to preserve and promote them in the long run. We have stated that compromise will become increasingly necessary, the longer the polarized power struggle persists; and that, therefore, the need for clear, calm reason will become correspondingly great. However, unless the people realize that reason is only the instrument for effecting compromises and not the standard for judging their effectiveness, some anxious citizens, in their growing concern for the national security, may become so habituated to compromise that they will lose sight of the ideal criteria of judgment which determine whether a compromise achieves its purpose. They may blindly settle upon the half-loaf or reject the loaf altogether, when three-quarters of the loaf is available. As fear may constrict ideals to an inflexible pattern, reason may so continually stretch ideals to suit expediency that they will lose all shape and elasticity. The end result will be the same: the undermining of that idealistic element of stability in foreign relations, which reason alone cannot supply. . . .

A preoccupation with expediency leads men to seek the minimum risk and effort in the expectation of a limited return; it dulls imagination and saps initiative. A purely selfish attitude tends to confine attention to those manifestations of power which bear directly and immediately upon the national interest; it tends to obscure those positive, constructive measures which cope with the basic social and psychological conditions behind such manifestations. Rational self-interest, by itself, fails to inspire boldness or breadth of vision. It may even corrode the national faith and paralyze the will to resist. In a sense, the collapse of France was the collapse of pure rational expediency, as expressed in the popular slogan "Why die for Danzig?" It is no accident that those American isolationists in the period preceding Pearl Harbor who were most insistent that the United States shape its foreign relations strictly according to its selfish interests were also the ones who were most blind to the real requirements of American self-interest, and the least willing to take measures that recognized the dependence of American security upon the survival of Great Britain and France; whereas those idealists who were most sensitive to the Fascist menace to Western culture and civilization were among the first to understand the necessity of undertaking revolutionary measures to sustain America's first line of defense in Europe.

In other words, a realistic conception of human nature must recognize that national egoism unenlightened by idealism may lead men to view America's self-interest too narrowly to achieve or preserve security itself, for idealism is an indispensable spur to reason in leading men to perceive and act upon the real imperatives of power politics. It limbers the imagination and impels men to look beyond the immediate circumstances of the power struggle. It places the status quo in the perspective of ultimate goals. It frees the reason to examine broadly and perceptively the variety of means for adjusting the instruments of national purpose to the ever-changing international environment. Idealism illuminates the basic human aspirations common to all people and thus sharpens men's insight into the psychological sources of national power. It excites the human sympathies which inspire men to enlarge the area of mutual national interest among peoples sharing common values. Idealism is the driving force, the dynamic element, which can dispel the inertia of habit and move men to adopt the bold, constructive measures necessary for surmounting the present crisis and the crises beyond. In the long run, it is the only impulse that can sustain the people's willingness to make the personal and national sacrifices that are indispensable for sheer survival.

THE EXPEDIENCY OF IDEALISM

A true realist must recognize that ideals and self-interest are so closely interdependent that, even on grounds of national expediency, there are cogent arguments for maintaining the vitality of American idealism.

Ideals are as much an instrument of national power as the weapons of war. All manifestations of national power, including the threat of coercion, operate by influencing the thoughts and actions of human beings, whether by frightening them or by converting them. Since men are motivated by faith and moral sentiment as well as by fear and the instinct of self-preservation, the strength of America's moral reputation and the persuasiveness of the American mission are as vital a factor in the power equation as planes, ships, and tanks. One has only to recall the consequences of the rise and fall of America's moral reputation during and after World War I to understand the force of American idealism among foreign peoples.

The persuasiveness of the American mission is especially significant under the present circumstances, when the competition of ideologies is such a conspicuous feature of the power struggle between the Russian and the American orbits and when the effectiveness of American policy depends so heavily upon winning the moral and intellectual allegiance of vast numbers of people in the throes of social and nationalistic revolution. If in the eyes of millions of people living in underdeveloped areas of the world the United States ceases to stand for a positive and constructive program of social and material progress, if American ideals no longer mean anything beyond smug generalities and hypocritical rationalizations of selfish national advantage, then all the wealth and military power the United States can muster will not render these people an asset to the free world. If the nations within the Western Coalition conclude that America has lost all passion for improving the lot of common people for the sake of the people themselves, if they believe that Americans have lost interest in the vision of world peace in their overriding concern for their national self-interest, then no display of shrewd power politics will win for the United States the popular trust and admiration which American leadership requires.

Moreover, no coalition can survive through a common fear of tyranny without a common faith in liberty. If the leader of the Western Coalition ceases to sustain that faith, then who will sustain it? Because the United States is unavoidably thrust into a position of global leadership, her standards of conduct must, inevitably, have a great influence in setting the moral tone of international relations in general. Consequently, it behooves America to conduct its foreign relations in a way that will encourage the kind of international environment compatible with its ideals and interests.

That kind of environment cannot exist apart from a widespread respect for the universal ideals of peace, brotherhood, and the essential dignity of the individual. To perceive this one has but to imagine the unmitigated anarchy that would ensue if every nation identified the interests of all nations with its own interests and pursued its own independent security as a self-sufficient end without relation to universal goals; for if every nation made expediency its sole guide in foreign relations, and if every nation anticipated that every other nation was motivated solely by the improvement of its own welfare, the only bond among nations would be the concurrence of their interests. But there is no automatic harmony of interests among nations, and unadorned reason is a weak instrument for achieving the tolerance and fair play indispensable to a contrived harmony. If national self-interest were the sole standard of conduct common to nations, an improvement in the power position of one nation would set off a wave of distrust among the rest; and, eventually, the pressure of international conflict would loosen what moral and ethical restraints man has succeeded in placing on his collective behavior; international society would disintegrate into a Hobbesian state of anarchy. In the light of this prospect, it is apparent that America's moral leadership is an indispensable instrument of her survival.

We may admit the expediency of America's reputation for idealism, but we should not imagine that America's ability to gain the moral and intellectual allegiance of foreign peoples is merely a problem in the technique of propaganda. To be sure, skilful propaganda can make a vast difference in the effectiveness of America's leadership. American ideals must be interpreted with resourcefulness and imagination, according to the particular needs and aspirations of different peoples. But, no matter how clever American propaganda may be, if it is not consistent with American actions, it will be of little value as an instrument of policy and may well alienate its intended converts. At the same time, the actions of the United States must, in the long run, reflect the actual state of American opinion; for no foreign program, least of all one of international benevolence, will survive long in a democracy if it is contrary to public opinion, and it would be extremely unrealistic to expect Americans to support such a program for its propagandistic worth if they did not also believe in its moral worth. It follows that a sincere and widespread devotion to positive ideals of human betterment is a prerequisite for effective propaganda, for Americans cannot pretend to be idealists without being truly idealistic. American idealism cannot be exported like American machinery and weapons. The United States is a democracy, and, therefore, official propaganda, in its broad outlines, must be believed to be effective. Otherwise, it will be undermined at home, foreign peoples will see that it is undermined, and American idealism will be marked down as deception and hypocrisy. Therefore, genuine conviction becomes necessary in order to sustain the appearance of idealism demanded by sheer national expediency. It is fortunate for the survival of democratic government that this paradox exists. . . .

To recognize the points of coincidence between national self-interest and supranational ideals is one of the highest tasks of statesmanship. The last half-century of Anglo-American relations demonstrates that men can recognize and even multiply the points of coincidence by patiently building upon a foundation of mutual self-interest to enlarge the area of international confidence and respect. It seems likely that the greatest advances in international morality in the foreseeable future will be brought about by men with enough vision and good will to temper the more immediate or extreme demands of national self-interest with the superior demands of a long-run interest in international compromise and the rational, peaceful settlement of differences. In this imperfect world it is neither too much nor too little to expect that man's recognition of the coincidence of ideals with national self-interest may mitigate and enlighten the thrust of national egoism. . . .

What Unites the West?

H. B. MAYO *

We are often told that behind the conflict of power between Russia and the West there is an irreconcilable ideological conflict; that two fundamentally different philosophies and ways of life are at stake; and that the tension can be resolved only when one or the other ideology is stamped out by war. On the one side, obvious to all, is the philosophy of communism,

* Professor of Political Science, University of Western Ontario. The selection is from H. B. Mayo, *Democracy and Marxism* (New York: Oxford University Press, 1955), from Ch. IX. By permission.

the confused and odious ideology upon which the U.S.S.R. and its satellites are, or profess to be, united. On the other there is something called "Western civilization." Exactly what kind of *Weltanschauung* the West stands for is not easy to say; and no wonder, since within it there is something to everyone's taste. It is a rich *smorgasbord* of philosophies, religions, political, economic, and social systems. Is there, behind this surface diversity, agreement among the Western allies upon any kind of fundamental principles?

Private enterprise or free competition is often said to be the basic principle that unites the West. Yet Yugoslavia and Norway are dissenters, and several other countries in the Western camp have had socialist governments at one time or another, and may have them again at the next election; while almost everywhere the capitalist countries have diluted the pure milk of private enterprise and competition. Western Europeans, for the most part, have no intention of fighting an atomic war in defense of private enterprise; and still less is this slogan (or principle) likely to attract support from the masses in the uncommitted countries of the Far East.

Is the West united on the principle of national sovereignty? Curiously enough it is the communist countries which have become notorious for their beating of the nationalist drums, whether in Russia, Yugoslavia, or China. But even more important is the fact that the really strong popular support for a merging of national sovereignties, for schemes of federalism, and for eventual world government comes from within the Western countries themselves. To say that the West stands for complete national sovereignty and the Soviet Union for internationalism is not only to distort the truth but also to invite Western democrats to desert their own side *en masse*.

Is religion something that unites the Western allies? Hardly any part of the globe is more secular in outlook than the Western world. Secularism is often associated with the enjoyment of creature comforts, the good things of this world. In our day the emphasis is on a constantly rising standard of living, measured in such terms as more leisure and a larger output of goods and services. If judged by their actions (and their advertising) the Western peoples seem to attach paramount importance to these material standards. But on this very point the West and the Soviet Union are, for once, in agreement, since both make a fetish of higher productivity and standards of living.

An even more difficult question arises. On which religion are we united —the Jewish, the Moslem, or the Christian? Is Turkey not in the alliance? Is Israel not a friendly neighbor? And if the Christian, which of the innumerable bodies into which Christendom is divided? No doubt if we all belonged to the same church it would unite us; but we do not.

There has been a strong move afoot to put up a fourth uniting principle called "Western values." But as one philosopher has said:

> These western values are supposed to consist of toleration, respect for individual liberty, and brotherly love. I am afraid this view is grossly unhistorical. If we compare Europe with other continents, it is marked out as the persecuting continent.[1]

Western history has often shown us the opposite qualities: intolerance, blind obedience to authority, and ruthless self-interest. Values of all kinds can be found in our blood-stained past, but which ones we select depends entirely on our *present* beliefs, and it is precisely the unity of these present beliefs which may be questioned.

Are we bound together by a belief in peaceful change as opposed to violence and revolution? Peaceful political change is a principle adhered to only in the democracies—how does one get a change of government or policy in Spain or the Argentine?—and so is included within the wider principle of democracy. The claim that democracy is the unifying principle of the West, although stronger than the others, is not without weaknesses. A number of democracies stand aloof from the Western alliance, while one of the allies (Yugoslavia) adheres to an ideology similar to that of the Soviet Union; one is authoritarian in a clerico-Fascist way (Spain); and South Africa—which must also be counted in the Western camp—introduces an embarrassing racial complication. Clearly we cannot, without qualification, equate the West with democracy.

Nevertheless, the more powerful of the Western nations *are* democracies. The United States, Britain, Canada, for example, do substantially believe in and practice the democratic principles of constitutionalism, political freedom, toleration, and maintain the traditional cultural and civil liberties. Enough other countries are with them on these matters to justify the claim that in a broad general sense the Western cause is the cause of democracy. If the Western allies should triumph, democracy would gain enormously in prestige and influence, and communism in turn would suffer the ignominious fate of Nazism and Fascism.

The agreement is not unanimous, however, by all the nations in the alliance, but is only a kind of majority-nation opinion; and even that does not extend beyond political democracy. One should not, like the Marxists, decry political democracy merely because one believes it is not enough, but it is as well to realize that the Western world differs widely on how far democracy should be extended into the economic and social sphere. Any one interpretation, if pushed too far, may endanger the solidarity of the alliance.

What, then, does unite the West? The answer is simple. It is fear of a possible enemy, the threat of possible aggression, and so the Western nations have allied and armed for self-protection. This may seem a negative sort of union, and of course it is negative to those who favor liberating crusades on behalf of great principles, and the enthusiasm which belief in cosmic ulti-

[1] B. Russell, *New Hopes for a Changing World,* London, 1951, p. 118.

mates can give. What is often forgotten, however, is that resistance to a common enemy has usually been the chief bond between allies, a classic example having occurred in the Second World War, when the democracies and the Soviet Union fought together against the Nazis.

Such an alliance also has its positive side, since when all the exceptions are allowed for, the Western cause remains, broadly speaking, the cause of democracy. Moreover, each nation within the alliance is also protecting its independence, its way of life, its own ideals, however these may be defined. And while defending what is our own we defend also the essential principle of diversity.

A great deal of nonsense is talked about the need for a faith to unite the West against communism. Many people are frantically looking around for a faith or an idea that can command general assent and inspire the West to the fervor of enthusiasm formerly displayed by the Nazis, and now by communists. But it is more than doubtful whether such an ideal set of values or ultimate principles can be found to command general agreement. Nor is it possible to adopt beliefs merely because they would be useful in the cold war: beliefs on such a scale can be manufactured to order only in the totalitarian states. The very search for a Western faith is a tacit admission that we are not already agreed upon our ideology. The common impression that an ideological conflict has lead to international friction is probably mistaken. It seems nearer the truth that the friction and fears came first and the clash of ideologies has been called upon in order to bolster morale.

If the preceding argument is sound, then it is misleading and self-deceptive to speak of ideological Western unity where none exists, because such talk tends to gloss over the differences within the Western alliance, and to assume that all are democratic, or share some other common philosophy, solely because they are anti-Soviet and reject communism. It is also dangerous, because it leads to a fanaticism and a warlike spirit which can make war more likely. Inflammatory crusading talk may not easily be deflected from the rash aim of liberation to the proper but humdrum job of defense. And if an ideological war should come it will be a war of extermination, not of mere defeat, since the only thorough way to extinguish a heresy (for the time being) is to kill off the heretics. Christian Europe tried this barbarous method long ago, and there are more heretics today than ever. Heresies rarely stay dead. Moreover, an uncompromising ideological attitude will keep us fighting forever all over the globe, since as soon as one "bad" principle or philosophy is destroyed another is bound to spring up and offend us. Already there has been friction among the allies, caused by this talk of "our" ideology. Even the total preparation for an ideological war, and the atmosphere of conformity created, are giving rise to a tendency which, if carried far enough, could convert the West into military states indistinguishable from military tyrannies.

But the most serious immediate danger is this: for the West to adopt the language and attitude of Russia, with constant emphasis on a messianic message, is to make it almost impossible to come to any sort of peaceable *modus vivendi*. Questions of moral principle should not be ignored in international relations; but if it is a mistake to ignore them, it is an even worse mistake to elevate every clash of interest into a conflict of sacred principles. In that way we become intransigent, publicly committed beforehand on every issue, until every compromise, every trivial concession, every negotiation is interpreted as surrender, betrayal, or appeasement.

What we tend to forget is that it is not necessary to agree on our metaphysics first in order to live together without fighting. Differences on ultimates divide Jew from Gentile, Catholic from Protestant, Moslem from Hindu, atheist from believer. And none of these differences is likely to be settled in any foreseeable future. But the slumbering volcanoes need not erupt. We have learned to live together within the democracies, despite the gulfs that divide us, united in our common humanity, in the desire for law and order, and in the procedural agreement to differ.

So in the international sphere. An international community does not necessarily presuppose that we all think alike on fundamentals. We are all united in our will to survive, and it is (or ought to be) perfectly possible to live in a world at peace without deciding whose ultimates are right. War will settle not which side is right but merely which is the more powerful; although victory will no doubt lend prestige to the ideas of the winner. . . .

Section XIV

What Policy for America?

HAVING GIVEN consideration to the appropriate roles of "national interest" and of moral or ideological principles in the formulation of American foreign policy, our inquiry turns, more specifically, to certain contemporary issues, namely: What are the meaning, implications, advantages, and risks of "coexistence" between the U.S. and the U.S.S.R.; and what basic directions should our foreign policies take to preserve our security and freedom, and maintain and extend them so far as possible throughout the world, while preserving peace, in an age of incredibly destructive military power?

Topic 32

FREEDOM AND SURVIVAL IN THE ATOMIC AGE

Peaceful Coexistence in the Nuclear Age

NIKITA S. KHRUSHCHEV *

To perceive today's world accurately, one must see the dividing line following a political, economic and social principle. On the one hand are the capitalist, the imperialist, countries, which have preserved and still preserve the old social system of exploitation and oppression. At the head of these countries stand monopolists who want to save the exploiter system from ruin and want to perpetuate it. On the other hand, countries are gaining strength and

* Extracts from the speech delivered by the former Soviet Premier at the Sixth Congress of the Socialist Unity Party of East Germany, Berlin, January 16, 1963, *The Current Digest of the Soviet Press,* Vol. XV, No. 4 (Feb. 20, 1963), pp. 15–18. Translated by *The Current Digest of the Soviet Press,* published weekly at Columbia University by the Joint Committee on Slavic Studies, appointed by the American Council on Learned Societies and the Social Research Council. Copyright 1963. By permission.

developing where the working people have overthrown capitalism, have wiped out its oppression and exploitation, have established the rule of the people and are following the path of building socialism and communism. The number of these countries will grow, while the capitalist world will shrink. . . .

It is not only we who say that the balance of forces in the world has changed in favor of socialism. In effect, our enemies also admit this when they speak of the "balance of fear." We do not adhere to the doctrine of "balance of fear," but one cannot help but note such conclusions by enemies. These conclusions are nothing but an admission by the ruling circles of the imperialist powers that the might of the world system of socialism has grown. Their talk of "balance" is no longer the thesis of "rolling back communism" and so on. We not only declare but know well that the forces of socialism and peace are mightier than the forces of imperialism. (*Applause.*)

Comrades! Permit me to dwell on some important and pressing questions of the world Communist movement. First of all, I wish to speak about the interrelationship of the struggle for peace, for peaceful coexistence, and the revolutionary struggle of the working class, of all the working people, for the victory of socialism on earth.

As matters stand in our times, the struggle for peace has become a most important condition of the struggle for socialism. Not one problem of the revolutionary movement of the working class, of the national-liberation movement, can now be considered in isolation from the struggle for peace, for preventing world thermonuclear war. This is precisely the important lesson for the tactics of the world Communist movement that stems from the recent events in the Caribbean. . . .

A feature of our era is the fact that the struggle for peace has become more than ever a major historical task not only of the working class but also of all other strata of the population. This is the knot in which the interests of all mankind intertwine. In the face of the menace of thermonuclear war, the most diverse mass movements form a single torrent—movements that can unite in the common striving to deliver mankind from the catastrophe of war. The international working class and the socialist countries are the leading and organizing force of this torrent. This is not because the countries of socialism have simply seized upon the popular slogan of struggle for peace. No, the fact is that the objective interests of the socialist countries, the interests of the world movement of the working class, of the national-liberation movement, are indivisible from the struggle to prevent thermonuclear war. . . .

The concentration and centralization of capital lead to monopolies and to the greater and greater decay of capitalism, and this prepares the conditions for a transition to a higher social system—socialism. In the course of its development capitalism, as Marx said, creates its own gravedigger in the person of the working class.

Life has fully confirmed the correctness of Marxist-Leninist teaching. According to this teaching, the working class gains victory over capitalism not by unleashing wars between states but in class struggle against the exploiters. . . .

This is not at all what is wanted by those fledgling theoreticians who are attempting to form a "theory" to the effect that the path to the victory of socialism lies through war between states, through destruction, bloodshed and the deaths of millions of people. If the Communists had been guided by such a "theory," they would not have attracted the popular masses but repelled them. Such a "theory" is particularly repellent in our age of missiles and nuclear weapons. Marxist-Leninists have always paid a great deal of attention to questions of war and peace and have always considered these questions from a specifically historical point of view. One must not solve questions of war and peace without taking account of the actual situation. One must have the courage to look the real facts in the face and to weigh with scientific precision what modern war would do if it were not averted. According to calculations by foreign economists and military specialists, the U.S.A. has about 40,000 nuclear bombs and warheads. As is known, the Soviet Union has more than enough of these goods. What would happen if all these nuclear weapons burst over people's heads? According to calculations by scientists, 700,000,000 to 800,000,000 people would die in the first strike alone. Not only the large cities of the two leading nuclear powers—the U.S.A. and the U.S.S.R.—but also the cities of France, Britain, Germany, Italy, China, Japan and many other countries would be wiped from the face of the earth and destroyed. The consequences of a nuclear war would have their effect on the life expectancy of many generations of people, would produce disease and death and lead to the most monstrous development of mankind. I am not saying all this to frighten anyone, I am simply citing scientific data. And these data must be reckoned with.

There is no doubt that if a thermonuclear war were unleased by the imperialist maniacs, the capitalist system that gave rise to the war would perish in it. But would the socialist countries and the cause of the struggle for socialism throughout the world gain from a world thermonuclear catastrophe? Only people who deliberately close their eyes to the facts can think this. As far as the Marxist-Leninists are concerned, they cannot think in terms of a communist civilization built upon the ruins of the world's cultural centers, on ravaged earth contaminated by thermonuclear fallout. This is not to mention the fact that for many people there would be no question of socialism at all, since they would have been removed from the face of our planet.

I will tell you a secret: Our scientists have developed a 100-megaton bomb. But according to the calculations of our military people, a 100-

megaton bomb cannot be dropped on Europe. If our probable opponent unleashes a war, where is it to be dropped? On West Germany or France? The explosion of such a bomb on this territory would destroy you and several other countries as well. Therefore it would seem that such a weapon could be used by us only outside Western Europe. I am saying this in order to provide a more realistic idea of what terrible means of destruction are now in existence.

Nor is the 100-megaton bomb the limit. If I may express myself thus, it is the limit from the point of view of probable military usefulness. This is because still more powerful means of destruction might also present a great danger to those who decide to use them.

In brief, comrades, as I said in the report to the session of the U.S.S.R. Supreme Soviet, to hurry into the next world is not recommended, since no one has ever come back to tell us that life is better there than it is here. (*Amused stir. Prolonged applause.*) We do not want a heavenly kingdom but an earthly one, the kingdom of labor. It is for this kingdom that we are fighting, and we will spare no effort in this; we will fight and we will win. (*Stormy, prolonged applause.*) . . . .

The principle of peaceful coexistence between states with different social systems, as proclaimed by Lenin, we have considered and now consider to be the only correct one. Its importance has been confirmed and is still being confirmed by the whole practice of international relations.

The policy of peaceful coexistence has acquired particularly great importance in contemporary conditions. When there was only one socialist state in the world, surrounded on all sides by imperialist states, the policy of peaceful coexistence was used to gain time, to obtain a breathing space in which to strengthen proletarian rule and build socialism in our country. Now that the nature of war has changed, and now that there is a new alignment of forces in the world arena in favor of the forces of peace and socialism, the policy of peaceful coexistence has much more important goals and tasks and has an essentially new content. Its final goal is the attainment of the most favorable conditions for the victory of socialism over capitalism in peaceful economic competition.

Some people distort our Marxist-Leninist stand, trying to make it seem that by proclaiming a policy of peaceful coexistence we are thus appealing to revolutionary forces, to the Communist Parties in capitalist countries, that they abandon the class struggle, the struggle for the establishment of the rule of the working class and the working people and the national-liberation struggle of the peoples. This is a stupid invention and a slander.

The Soviet Union supports the just wars of peoples not only in its declarations and statements. This support has been expressed more than once in material terms. Many peoples have used our weapons in their liberation struggle and have achieved victory, have freed themselves from the colonial yoke. The colonial peoples' wars for their liberation are holy wars, and therefore we have been, are now and always will be, on the side of the peoples who are fighting for their independence. (*Prolonged applause.*)

The advocates of the so-called theory of the victory of socialism through war also deny the possibility of taking the peaceful path toward the victory of socialism, claiming that this is a retreat from Marxism. For the information of these devotees of the Stalin cult, it should be said that Stalin himself, in a conversation with British Communists after World War II, spoke of a peaceful, parliamentarian path to the victory of socialism. This was written into the Program of the Communist Party of Great Britain. The leaders of the British Communist Party know that this formulation was proposed by Stalin.

The Albanian leaders * allege that the C.P.S.U. is in favor only of the peaceful path and rejects the path of armed struggle. One might ask the Albanian leaders this: Can they name an instance when a Communist Party in any country believed there was a revolutionary situation in the country and when the Communists of that country decided to undertake an uprising, but the C.P.S.U. came out against the method of armed struggle? Do the Albanians have such an example? No, they cannot give an example of this, for none exists.

The Albanian leaders think it is possible to stir up a revolution artificially, when it suits them, and that a revolution does not require the necessary objective and subjective conditions. According to their theory, everything is managed very simply: Heroes emerge, and they come along and start the uprising. But such things have not happened in history, nor will they happen in the future. This "theory," if you will pardon the expression, has nothing in common with Marxism.

As far as the C.P.S.U. is concerned, we stand on Marxist-Leninist positions. Certain preconditions are needed for a victorious revolution. If a revolutionary situation should arise, the working class, headed by its vanguard, must make use of it to gain power. If the exploiting classes have recourse to violence against the people, the people have the right to use the most decisive measures, including armed struggle, in the interests of the victory of socialism.

The struggle in capitalist countries is an internal matter for the workers' movement in each country. Only the party of the proletariat in the individual capitalist country, and not other states and parties, has the right and is in a position to determine revolutionary tactics and the forms and methods of struggle.

A precise analysis of the concrete situation and a correct appraisal of the alignment of class forces are necessary for the revolutionary tactics of

* This is a covert way of referring to the differences between the Soviet Communist Party and the Chinese Party.

the working class. Everyone knows what flexible tactics the Bolsheviks used under Lenin's leadership in preparing for the October Revolution in Russia. . . .

[Khrushchev traces Lenin's policies from that of "peaceful development of the revolution" to a "demand for an immediate armed uprising (on October 25, 1917) to replace the slogan of peaceful development of the revolution."]

Who could fix the date of the uprising so precisely and thereby ensure its success? This could be done only by the Party of Bolsheviks armed with Marxism-Leninism, and by no one else. It was done by the leader of the working class, the leader of the Communist Party—the great Lenin. (*Stormy applause.*) . . .

In order to specify the exact time for the beginning of an uprising, it is necessary to have all the data: One must have an exact picture of the alignment and interaction of the class forces in the country. For this one needs first of all close ties with the masses, needs a good barometer that shows the revolutionary mood of the masses in the country in the given period of time. . . .

This is a clear example of the flexible tactics used by the vanguard of the working class, an example of mastery of all forms of struggle, both peaceful and nonpeaceful, an example of the ability to change one form for another rapidly and without warning. . . .

In order that the revolution truly gain victory, the revolutionary situation must ripen and there must be among the people, and particularly among the vanguard—the working class, which is the best-organized force in the capitalist world—a mature understanding of the need for revolution. It would be frivolous to think that one or two bold, intelligent and dedicated revolutionaries suffice to bring about the success of a revolution. The overthrow of the rule of the exploiting classes requires not individual heroes but the action of the broad masses of the people headed by a revolutionary party; it requires the specific conditions for the maturation of the revolution, the attack on capitalism and the victory of the working class, for the transfer of power to the working people, to the people as a whole. . . .

ABOLITION OF COLONIALISM AND PERSPECTIVES OF THE FURTHER DEVELOPMENT OF THE NEWLY-INDEPENDENT COUNTRIES *

Comrades! The peoples that have won national independence have become a mighty new force in the struggle for peace and social progress.

The national-liberation movement is striking more and more telling blows at imperialism and helping to strengthen peace and to speed mankind's de-

* The following material is from a speech delivered at a meeting of the Party organizations in the Higher Party School, the Academy of Social Sciences and the

velopment along the path of social progress. At present Asia, Africa and Latin America are the major focal centers of revolutionary struggle against imperialism. In the postwar period some 40 countries have won national independence. Almost 1,500,000,000 people have cast off colonial slavery. . . .

Take Asia, for example, that ancient cradle of human civilization. What inexhaustible forces are latent in the peoples of that continent! And can the Arab peoples, with their heroic traditions, and all the peoples of the Near and Middle East that have liberated themselves or are liberating themselves from political and economic dependence on imperialism, play any lesser role in the accomplishment of the tasks now confronting mankind?

One of the remarkable phenomena of our time is the awakening of the peoples of Africa. Dozens of states of North and Central Africa have already achieved independence, the south of Africa is beginning to seethe, and there is no doubt that the fascist dungeons in the Union of South Africa will crumble and that Rhodesia, Uganda and other parts of Africa will become free.

The forces of the national-liberation movement are multiplying enormously in connection with the fact that still another active front of active struggle against American imperialism has formed in recent years. This front is Latin America. Only recently this enormous continent was identified by a single concept—America. This concept to a large extent accorded with the fact: Latin America was bound hand and foot by Yankee imperialism. Today the Latin American people are showing by their struggle that the American continent is not the manorial domain of the U.S.A. Latin America is reminiscent of an active volcano. The lava of the liberation struggle has swept away dictatorships in a number of countries of Latin America. The thunder of the heroic Cuban revolution has reverberated throughout the world. The Cuban revolution is not only repelling the onslaught of the imperialists; it is deepening and broadening and marks a new and higher stage of the national-liberation struggle, in which the people take power and become the masters of their wealth. Solidarity with revolutionary Cuba is a duty not only of the peoples of Latin America but also of the socialist countries, of the entire international Communist movement and of the proletariat of all parts of the world.

The national-liberation movement is an anti-imperialist movement. With the collapse of the colonial system, imperialism has become considerably weaker. Vast territories and enormous masses of people have ceased or are

---

Institute of Marxism-Leninism, C. C., CPSU, on January 6, 1961, *The Current Digest of the Soviet Press,* Vol. XIII, No. 4 (February 22, 1961), pp. 11–13. Translation from *The Current Digest of the Soviet Press,* published weekly at Columbia University by the Joint Committee on Slavic Studies, appointed by the American Council on Learned Societies and the Social Science Research Council.

ceasing to serve as a reserve for it, as a source of cheap raw materials and cannon fodder. With the support of the socialist states and all international progressive forces, the Asian, African and Latin American countries are more and more frequently inflicting defeats on the imperialist powers and coalitions. . . .

Speaking at the Second All-Russian Congress of Communist Organizations of Peoples of the East in 1919, V. I. Lenin stated: "Whereas the Russian Bolsheviks managed to make a breach in old imperialism, to take on the uncommonly difficult but uncommonly noble task of blazing new paths of revolution, you representatives of the working masses of the East will be faced with an even greater and even newer task" ("Works" [in Russian], Vol. XXX, pp. 137–138). Lenin saw this task as one of arousing revolutionary energy for the independent activity and organization of the working masses regardless of the stage they had attained, of using the Communist teaching in the specific conditions of their countries and of merging with the proletarians of other countries in common struggle ("Works" [in Russian], Vol. XXX, p. 141).

When Lenin advanced this task, it had not yet been carried out anywhere in practice and it was impossible to learn from any book how specifically it should be carried out. Today the Communist Parties of the countries which are fighting for national independence, or which have already won it, have incomparably more favorable conditions, since there is already vast experience in the application of the theory of Marxism-Leninism in the conditions of countries and regions that capitalism had doomed to prolonged backwardness. . . .

The renovation of the world on the principles of freedom, democracy and socialism, in which we are participants, is a great historical process in which various revolutionary democratic movements unite and cooperate, with the socialist revolutions exerting the determining influence. The successes of the national-liberation movement are due in great measure to the victories of socialism in the struggle against imperialism and, in turn, strengthen the international positions of socialism in the struggle against imperialism. It is this truly Leninist conception of these historical processes that forms the basis of the policy of the Communist Parties and socialist states, a policy aimed at strengthening the close alliance with the peoples who are fighting for independence or have already won it.

Bourgeois and revisionist politicians claim that the national-liberation movement is developing independently of the struggle of the working class for socialism, and of the support of the socialist states, and that the colonialists themselves are bestowing freedom on the peoples of the former colonial countries. These fabrications are employed to isolate the young independent states from the countries of the socialist camp, to prove that they should, supposedly, play the role of a kind of "third force" in the international arena and not oppose imperialism. Needless to say, such claims are utter chicanery. . . .

Communists are revolutionaries, and it would be bad if they failed to see the new opportunities that are arising and did not find new methods and forms that lead most surely to achievement of the established goal. Special note should be taken of the idea of the formation of national democratic states. . . . It is important to stress that in view of the enormous variety of specific conditions in the countries whose peoples have risen to independent historical development, varied forms of meeting the tasks of social progress cannot fail to arise.

The correct application of Marxist-Leninist theory in the liberated countries lies precisely in taking into account the specific features of the economic, political and cultural life of the peoples and finding forms for uniting all the healthy forces of a nation and ensuring the guiding role of the working class in the national front, in the struggle for decisively uprooting imperialism and the vestiges of feudalism, and clearing the way for the ultimate movement toward socialism.

At present, when imperialist reaction is trying to foist a policy of anticommunism on the young independent states, special importance attaches to truthful elucidation of Communist views and aspirations. Communists support the general democratic measures of the national governments. At the same time Communists explain to the masses that these measures are not at all socialist ones.

No one is closer to or understands better the aspirations of the peoples who are breaking the fetters of colonialism than the working people of the socialist countries and the Communists of the whole world. Our very outlook, and the interests of toiling mankind for which we are fighting, impel us to do everything we can in order that the peoples may take the correct path to progress and the flowering of their material and spiritual forces. By our policy we must strengthen the confidence of the peoples in the socialist countries.

The aid of the U.S.S.R. and the other socialist countries that have won independence pursues but one aim—to help strengthen the positions of these countries in the struggle against imperialism, develop the national economy and improve the life of the peoples. Pointing out the enormous interest of the working class of the advanced countries in "bringing independence as quickly as possible" to the colonial countries, F. Engels wrote: "One thing is beyond doubt: The victorious proletariat cannot impose any benefaction on any other people without thereby undermining its own victory" (K. Marx and F. Engels, "Works" [Russian ed.] Vol. XXVII, pp. 238 and 239).

The internationalist duty of the victorious working class is to help the peoples of the economically underdeveloped countries to smash the chains of colonial slavery binding them and to give all-round support in their struggle against imperialism and for the right to self-determination and independent development. But it by no means follows that socialist aid exerts no influence on the prospect of further development of the countries that have won freedom.

The Soviet Union has been and remains the sincere friend of the colonial peoples and has always championed their rights, interests and aspirations to independence. We will continue to strengthen and develop economic and cultural cooperation with the countries that have taken the path of independent existence. . . .

The peoples of the socialist countries, Communists and progressives the world over, see it as their duty to destroy the last vestiges of the colonial system of imperialism, to protect from encroachments of the colonial powers the peoples who are winning freedom and to help these peoples realize their ideals of liberation. . . .

Forty-one years ago the First Congress of the Comintern was held here in Moscow. Communist Parties and left-wing socialist organizations from 30 countries were represented at it. Not counting the Communist Parties of the Republics that today form the U.S.S.R., there were only five Communist Parties in all of Europe then. There were no Communist Parties in Asia, Africa, Australia and Oceania. On the American continent there was only the Communist Party of Argentina. Today there are Communist or Workers' Parties in 87 countries. They unite more than 36,000,000 persons. The ideas of communism have captured the minds of millions of people in all corners of the globe. This is fine, very fine, comrades!

The Meaning of Coexistence

SIR WILLIAM HAYTER *

Hatred of class enemies is necessary, because it is not possible to become a good fighter for your people or for communism if one does not know how to hate enemies. . . . Yes, comrades, a harsh class struggle is now in progress throughout the world.

N. S. Khrushchev, speaking to the Central Committee of the Communist Party of the Soviet Union, 21 June 1963.

It is a great mistake to deceive ourselves about the realities of East-West relations. In the euphoria induced by the signature of the Test-Ban Agreement many optimists in the West persuaded themselves that the Cold War

* British Ambassador to Moscow from 1953 to 1957. At present Warden of New College, Oxford. The selection is from *Survey* (January, 1964), pp. 23–29. By permission.

between the Soviet Union and ourselves had ended, or at least was ending. The Soviet leaders, it was thought, had finally realised that their interests and ours, on most major points, coincided; war must be avoided; China was a common enemy; Russia was joining the Western world.

There are certain obvious arguments in favour of this view. The row with China is genuine and deep-seated. It is now seen to have hinged largely on the Soviet desire to avoid the spread of nuclear weapons, a desire shared by the West. This desire in turn is inspired by a common realisation, common that is to Russia and the West but not to China, that nuclear war must be avoided at almost any price. Russia and the West proclaim the peaceful co-existence of states with differing social systems, a concept to which China pays only rather tight-lipped lip service.

All this is true. But it is not the whole truth, and even on this partial truth misleading conclusions and misleading interpretations are often based. The Russians, more informed than the Chinese, less ruthless, more sated, with more to lose, have reached, rather belatedly and less demonstratively, the view long held in the West that nothing can be gained by nuclear warfare and that its outbreak would imperil not only the existing world order, to which they are not particularly attached, but the whole fabric of their own society, about which they mind very much. They are therefore ready to go to great lengths to prevent the outbreak of nuclear war. They are firm believers in the deterrent, their own of course principally, as a means of preventing a deliberate attack. But they also believe that it is possible to make suitable arrangements with the West, of a technical kind, to prevent a chain of accidents leading to a nuclear war. These arrangements should include measures against all wars between the opposing blocs; they do not believe, it seems, in the possibility of limited or conventional wars involving themselves and the Western Alliance, though minor wars not involving the Great Powers are seen as possible and in certain cases, e.g. 'just' anti-colonial wars, desirable.

Further than that the Soviet leaders do not go. Much misunderstanding has been created by the words 'peaceful co-existence'. Sir Winston Churchill was once heard to say 'I thought Anthony had invented peaceful co-existence, but it seems Lenin thought of it first.' He did indeed, and he meant by it something quite different from anything that the Earl of Avon would have had in mind. Lenin believed it was a temporary phase, affecting only inter-State relations, through which States with differing social systems would have to pass as part of the dialectical process, to be resolved by frightful clashes in which one system (communism of course) would conquer the other. The only modification which Khrushchev has imported into this doctrine is that these frightful clashes need not necessarily involve international war. There will be no hot war, but the Cold War will go on. There can be no reconciliation. The texts are quite explicit on this point. The Moscow

Declaration of December 1960, still the most authoritative of all recent communist doctrinal pronouncements, lays down that 'peaceful co-existence of countries with differing social systems does not mean conciliation of socialist and bourgeois ideologies. On the contrary, it implies intensification of the struggle of the working class, of all the Communist Parties, for the triumph of socialist ideas.' Mr. Khrushchev himself has recently reaffirmed this in blunter terms, in the speech from which the quotation at the head of this article is taken, and again at the Kremlin reception celebrating the signature of the Test-Ban Treaty.

All right, you may say, but why worry? The Russians are not going to make war on us, and if they dislike our ideas and are going to make propaganda against us, need this rob us of our sleep? We can cope with it; as long as there is not going to be a war, the rest is manageable. Hard words break no bones.

Roughly speaking, I myself believe this to be true. But it is important to realise the conditions under which it is, or remains, true. The first is the condition of deterrence. The Russians say that the reason why war is not now inevitable, as Lenin used to think it was, is that the communist bloc is too strong to attack. This is the deterrent doctrine in its simplest form, and it is really very difficult to controvert, especially if you put it the other way round (that the capitalist bloc is too strong to attack) and add the two together. But of course for it to continue to work both blocs must in fact remain too strong to attack.

This is the first condition. What others are needed to make peaceful coexistence tolerable? Provided there is no war, does it really not matter that we can never reach a real position of conciliation, of friendship with the Soviet Government? Does the class war, the 'intensified struggle for the triumph of socialist [sic. communist] ideas,' really not threaten us with mortal danger? I do not believe ultimately that it does, but we ought to consider what is involved here, both in the intentions of the Soviet leaders and in the realities which actually confront us.

The general Soviet view of the world is, I think, clear enough. Put crudely, it can be summarised in three propositions. The world is divided into two eternally antagonistic systems which are bound to try to destroy each other. Communism will win in the end, but only at the price of tremendous efforts in which all communists everywhere must participate. In this deathly struggle all methods are permissible except those which involve a risk of nuclear war.

Having renounced war, what weapons do the Soviet leaders think they possess and how effective are they likely to be? They must, at times, regret having given up the military arm; it will be recalled that Stalin explained to the Yugoslav leaders, in the middle forties, how impossible it had been to establish communism in France and Italy, despite the massive Communist Parties in those two countries, because the Red Army had not been able to extend so far the good work it had been doing in Eastern Europe. But those good old days are past. What can be done now?

Mr. Khrushchev has perhaps been less frank about this to the world at large than Stalin was to his Yugoslav friends. Publicly, the only admitted weapon is economic competition. The Soviet economy is going to 'overtake and surpass' capitalism in this, that, and the other sphere by this, that, and the other date. This will demonstrate the superiority of communism over capitalism for all to see, the light will dawn, capitalism will collapse, presumably out of sheer shame at being beaten at its own game, and communism will be established automatically everywhere (Mr. Khrushchev's second doctrinal innovation at the twentieth CPSU congress was to establish that communism could in fact come to power by peaceful or parliamentary means and not necessarily by violent revolution).

If this were all there would indeed be no cause for worry, and this for three reasons. First, the 'overtaking and surpassing' is still a long way off. Statistics, particularly when projected into the future, can prove anything, but no one who has had any experience of living recently in Russia and in America, or even Western Europe, can feel that the time when the standard of living in the former will cause shame and envy in the latter is at all imminent. Secondly, if Russia did ever catch up it is very unlikely that this fact alone would cause Western countries to change their present political and economic systems, with which, by and large, they are not dissatisfied, and which are in any case evolving rapidly. There is no reason why even material superiority in the Soviet Union should persuade the populations of the Western countries that their way of life, their political systems, their legal, cultural, personal, and political freedoms must be sacrificed. Finally, increased Russian prosperity in itself should be encouraging, not alarming, to the West. Russia, on the basis of her natural resources and population, ought always to have been one of the prosperous countries of the world. Hitherto she has been held back from this position by incompetence of one kind or another. If this incompetence is now overcome and she assumes her normal place among the 'have' nations of the world, her behaviour may well become less alarming to her neighbours and she may even have more to spare for the 'have-nots'. Indeed, China is already accusing her, prematurely perhaps, of lining up with the 'haves' (the Western Alliance) against the 'have-nots' whom China herself aspires to lead.

So if economic competition were Russia's only weapon we should not have much to fear. What else is there? The present phase of decolonisation plainly gives Russia certain advantages. The Soviet leaders' proclaimed hatred of colonialism is quite uninhibited by the fact that Moscow now controls the largest remaining colonial empire in the world; in Soviet eyes, the Soviet colonies in Asia are not colonies but rather backward countries which are being 'led forward to socialism'. So their conscience is untroubled and they can indulge their hatred of other imperialisms in all-out support for the most extreme demands of the emerging countries. This support wins them some popularity there, and it is undoubtedly the case that as decolonisation proceeds Moscow is able to exercise influence in areas which it could not previously penetrate. Decolonisation, however, has not been brought about by Moscow; it is a product of other causes, not to be analysed here, and the end of the process is in sight, though there are still difficult passages ahead. The gap left by the withdrawal of Western control from Asia and Africa had to be filled by someone; the really significant fact is that, so far at least, it has been filled not by Soviet or Chinese control but by local control. The Western Empires have not been succeeded by Communist Empires, and the question whether the newly emergent countries will or will not succumb eventually to communism thus takes its place within the larger question of communist prospects of success in the world as a whole.

Here we come back to the quotation from Mr. Khrushchev at the head of this article, the 'harsh class struggle' which, he thinks, is now in progress throughout the world. What are the chances of communist victory in this struggle, and what can Russia do, what is she doing, to help? What would be the effect of communist victories in one country or another? These questions are mostly unanswerable, but one or two points can be made. As already mentioned, the twentieth CPSU congress did adopt the novel view that communism could in certain circumstances achieve power by non-violent, non-revolutionary means. This was no doubt tactically wise. Communists, by continuing to insist on violence as an essential element in their policy, were almost inviting the use of violence against themselves. Furthermore, a legitimate non-communist government overthrown by violence would be in a strong moral position to invoke outside support, which would be more difficult to justify in the case of the arrival in power of communism by due constitutional process. Nevertheless this new doctrine was officially approved at a time when its practical application was becoming increasingly unlikely. In the confused period after the end of the Second World War communism made immense popular gains, and was able for the first time to achieve the support of mass parties in a number of important countries. These gains were facilitated by the prestige which the Soviet Union had won during the war and by the discredit into which the pre-war regimes had in many places fallen. But by the early fifties this tide had reached its highest point. Stalin's post-war policies had begun to alienate all but the faithful, the world's economies began to recover from the dislocations of the war, and political and economic regimes in the West were restabilising. Communist Parties in Western countries now seem stagnant, defensive, sometimes divided, sometimes losing rather than gaining members. They remain useful allies for Soviet foreign policy. They continue to be valuable organisations for Soviet espionage and even for sabotage, perhaps in peace-time and certainly in the event of war with the USSR. But their chances of obtaining power by constitutional means in any Western country have virtually disappeared. Even in the new countries they seem to have made no significant headway against the much stronger forces of what the communists angrily call 'bourgeois nationalism'.

This is of course not to say that communism can never again come to power in a country outside the bloc. It can, and Cuba is a recent example. There may be others, and perhaps Latin America is one of the few areas where communism could even now come to power with mass popular support. Moreover there are other methods than the ballot box, not all of them involving violence or even illegality, by which communist power could be established in a State; by infiltration of other parties, for instance, by gradual penetration of key organs of government, by capturing the leadership of popular movements whose original or ostensible ends had nothing to do with communism, or eventually by the support of guerrilla forces. These are all, primarily, internal movements requiring certain internal conditions for their success. But there is no doubt that Moscow, so far as it can, will help to create these conditions and will support these movements with funds, advice, personnel, arms where necessary, the creation of suitable front organisations and, in the event of success as in Cuba, with open political and military backing.

Let us admit, therefore, that although popular support for communism in the world at large is probably now stagnant or even declining, there is always the possibility that new communist regimes may come into being in one part or another of the world. What would be the likely effect of that? This question is certainly unanswerable, but there are two points, rather contradictory in their effect, that are worth considering. First, communist regimes, once established, are very difficult to overthrow from within. There is only one case in history of a communist regime being overthrown by internal forces alone, without outside intervention, and that is Hungary in 1956, a very special case with very special circumstances not likely to be repeated. A good example to the contrary is Cuba, where a newly-established communist regime survived unshaken not only rather half-hearted onslaughts from without but the public humiliation of its Soviet champion. This irremovability of communist governments is a permanent disadvantage from which the West must suffer and continue to suffer in the Cold War. Its own system necessarily and inherently provides for the possibility of alternative parties coming to power; if one of these parties happens to be the Communist Party it is likely to stay in power, however much popular support it subsequently alienates. One cannot see communists happily playing the game of the Ins and Outs, and it is perhaps their refusal to abide by the rules of this game which on occasion justifies sending them off the field.

What would be the effect on the world situation of communist regimes winning control of a number of countries now governed by other regimes? There is no doubt that a series of Cubas in, say, Latin America or South-East Asia would seem to involve, and perhaps really would involve, a considerable change in the world balance of power. The slight doubt about the reality of the change arises of course from the new relationship between the different governments of the communist world. In Stalin's day it was safe to assume that all communist regimes, all Communist Parties, owed fealty and obedience to Moscow unless, like Tito, they were in open schism. This assumption is obviously no longer valid, and it cannot now be taken absolutely for granted that all new communist regimes everywhere would put the interests of the Soviet Union, or even of the world communist movement, ahead of their own national, local, or personal advantage.

Still, it is probably wiser to assume that communist regimes, if established with or without Soviet support in countries previously part of the non-communist world, would find themselves in some kind of mutual interdependence with the Soviet Union. Since this is so, the question which will sooner or later pose itself is whether, and if so in what circumstances, the West could or should intervene to prevent the establishment, or the consolidation, of such regimes. The answer will no doubt depend on the circumstances in which the question arises, and the precedents are confusing. In Cuba, American intervention was confined to ineffective support of an ineffective indigenous counter-revolution and to the prevention of the installation of Soviet nuclear weapons. In Guatemala it went rather further. Again in Jordan and the Lebanon, in the summer of 1958, British and American armed forces were sent in at the request of the local Governments to provide support against threats that were partly internal, partly external. The threats in this case were not communist, but the action taken provides perhaps a useful guide to the limits of probable Western reactions in comparable cases of threatened communist takeover. These limits no doubt would fall short of the Soviet action in Hungary in 1956, where Soviet forces were openly sent in to overthrow a Government that was legitimate and still communist, but slipping, and to replace it by a more subservient communist regime. Similar action was threatened but not actually taken in Poland at about the same time. Here again the communist system encourages a form of ruthless determination denied to the West. Probably the furthest the latter would go would be to support with armed forces a legal Government still in power which asked for such support. The Governments of South Vietnam and South Korea provide not very happy precedents for this, and so, less unhappily, do British and, later, American support for Greek Governments faced with communist attack. In Cuba the difficulty was that there was no indigenous regime that the United States could bring themselves to support; the position might well be different in, say, Venezuela.

So, in general, the position seems to be this. The international conflict will continue, indefinitely so far as can be foreseen. But it will not be prosecuted by open war, since Russia has recognised this as too dangerous and China is too weak to wage it without Russian help. All other methods will be used, but they are less likely to be effective in winning friends and influencing people than the Red Army was in Europe in 1944 and 1945. Communism on the whole is on the decline, but of its very nature retains certain advantages over those who believe in more liberal systems of government, and these advantages may bring it occasional, perhaps isolated, victories which if they are too numerous could, but will not necessarily, change the balance of power in the world. The Western Powers, in deciding their reactions to such victories, are likely to be influenced not only by consideration of their own interests but in part also by their restraining inhibitions. Nevertheless there is no reason to despond. The strength of Western institutions has proved itself and has increased in the last decade; the new countries are evolving their own institutions, which are not those of Marxism-Leninism, and are remaining independent of Moscow; and on the whole Mr. Khrushchev's prophecy that our grand-children will all be communists seems unlikely to be fulfilled.

Topic 33

NEW DIRECTIONS IN FOREIGN POLICY

Inaugural Address

JOHN F. KENNEDY *

MY FELLOW CITIZENS:

We observe today not a victory of party but a celebration of freedom—symbolizing an end as well as a beginning—signifying renewal as well as change. For I have sworn before you and Almighty God the same solemn oath our forebears prescribed nearly a century and three quarters ago.

The world is very different now. For man holds in his mortal hands the power to abolish all forms of human poverty and to abolish all form of human life. And, yet, the same revolutionary beliefs for which our forebears fought are still at issue around the globe—the belief that the rights of man come not from the generosity of the state but from the hand of God.

We dare not forget today that we are the heirs of that first revolution. Let the word go forth from this time and place, to friend and foe alike, that the torch has been passed to a new generation of Americans—born in this century, tempered by war, disciplined by a cold and bitter peace, proud of our ancient heritage—and unwilling to witness or permit the slow undoing of those human rights to which this nation has always been committed, and to which we are committed today.

Let every nation know, whether it wish us well or ill, that we shall pay any price, bear any burden, meet any hardship, support any friend or oppose any foe in order to assure the survival and success of liberty.

This much we pledge—and more.

To those old Allies whose cultural and spiritual origins we share, we pledge the loyalty of faithful friends. United, there is little we cannot do in a host of new co-operative ventures. Divided, there is little we can do—for we dare not meet a powerful challenge at odds and split asunder.

To those new states whom we now welcome to the ranks of the free, we pledge our word that one form of colonial control shall not have passed

* Delivered at the United States Capitol, January 20, 1961.

merely to be replaced by a far more iron tyranny. We shall not always expect to find them supporting our every view. But we shall always hope to find them strongly supporting their own freedom—and to remember that, in the past, those who foolishly sought to find power by riding on the tiger's back inevitably ended up inside.

To those peoples in the huts and villages of half the globe struggling to break the bonds of mass misery, we pledge our best efforts to help them help themselves, for whatever period is required—not because the Communists are doing it, not because we seek their votes, but because it is right. If the free society cannot help the many who are poor, it can never save the few who are rich.

To our sister republics south of our border, we offer a special pledge—to convert our good words into good deeds—in a new alliance for progress—to assist free men and free Governments in casting off the chains of poverty. But this peaceful revolution of hope cannot become the prey of hostile powers. Let all our neighbors know that we shall join with them to oppose aggression or subversion anywhere in the Americas. And let every other power know that this Hemisphere intends to remain the master of its own house.

To that world assembly of sovereign states, the United Nations, our last best hope in an age where the instruments of war have far outpaced the instruments of peace, we renew our pledge of support—to prevent its becoming merely a forum for invective—to strengthen its shield of the new and the weak—and to enlarge the area to which its writ may run.

Finally, to those nations who would make themselves our adversary, we offer not a pledge but a request: that both sides begin anew the quest for peace, before the dark powers of destruction unleashed by science engulf all humanity in planned or accidental self-destruction.

We dare not tempt them with weakness. For only when our arms are sufficient beyond doubt can we be certain beyond doubt that they will never be employed.

But neither can two great and powerful groups of nations take comfort from their present course—both sides overburdened by the cost of modern weapons, both rightly alarmed by the steady spread of the deadly atom, yet both racing to alter that uncertain balance of terror that stays the hand of mankind's final war.

So let us begin anew—remembering on both sides that civility is not a sign of weakness and sincerity is always subject to proof. Let us never negotiate out of fear. But let us never fear to negotiate.

Let both sides explore what problems unite us instead of belaboring the problems that divide us.

Let both sides, for the first time, formulate serious and precise proposals for the inspection and control of arms—and bring the absolute power to destroy other nations under the absolute control of all nations.

Let both sides join to invoke the wonders of science instead of its terrors. Together let us explore the stars, conquer the deserts, eradicate disease, tap the ocean depths and encourage the arts and commerce.

Let both sides unite to heed in all corners of the earth the command of Isaiah—to "undo the heavy burdens . . . (and) let the oppressed go free."

And if a beachhead of co-operation can be made in the jungles of suspicion, let both sides join in the next task: creating, not a new balance of power, but a new world of law, where the strong are just and the weak secure and the peace preserved forever.

All this will not be finished in the first 100 days. Nor will it be finished in the first 1,000 days, nor in the life of this Administration, nor even perhaps in our lifetime on this planet. But let us begin.

In your hands, my fellow citizens, more than in mine, will rest the final success or failure of our course. Since this country was founded, each generation has been summoned to give testimony to its national loyalty. The graves of young Americans who answered that call encircle the globe.

Now the trumpet summons us again—not as a call to bear arms, though arms we need—not as a call to battle, though embattled we are—but a call to bear the burden of a long twilight struggle, year in and year out, "rejoicing in hope, patient in tribulation"—a struggle against the common enemies of man: tyranny, poverty, disease and war itself.

Can we forge against these enemies a grand and global alliance, north and south, east and west, that can assure a more fruitful life for all mankind? Will you join in that historic effort?

In the long history of the world, only a few generations have been granted the role of defending freedom in its hour of maximum danger. I do not shrink from this responsibility—I welcome it. I do not believe that any of us would exchange places with any other people or any other generation. The energy, the faith and the devotion which we bring to this endeavor will light our country and all who serve it—and the glow from that fire can truly light the world.

And so, my fellow Americans: Ask not what your country will do for you—ask what you can do for your country.

My fellow citizens of the world: Ask not what America will do for you, but what together we can do for the freedom of man.

Finally, whether you are citizens of America or of the world, ask of us the same high standards of strength and sacrifice that we shall ask of you. With a good conscience our only sure reward, with history the final judge of our deeds, let us go forth to lead the land we love, asking His blessing and His help, but knowing that here on earth God's work must truly be our own.

What Kind of Peace?

JOHN F. KENNEDY *

"There are few earthly things more beautiful than a University," wrote John Masefield, in his tribute to the English Universities—and his words are equally true here. He did not refer to spires and towers, to campus greens and ivied walls. He admired the splendid beauty of the University, he said, because it was "a place where those who hate ignorance may strive to know, where those who perceive truth may strive to make others see."

I have, therefore, chosen this time and this place to discuss a topic on which ignorance too often abounds and the truth is too rarely perceived—yet it is the most important topic on earth: world peace.

What kind of peace do I mean? What kind of peace do we seek? Not a Pax Americana enforced on the world by American weapons of war. Not the peace of the grave or the security of the slave. I am talking about genuine peace—the kind of peace that makes life on earth worth living—the kind that enables men and nations to grow and to hope and to build a better life for their children—not merely peace for Americans but peace for all men and women—not merely peace in our time but peace for all time.

I speak of peace because of the new face of war. Total war makes no sense in an age when great powers can maintain large and relatively invulnerable nuclear forces and refuse to surrender without resort to those forces. It makes no sense in an age when a single nuclear weapon contains almost ten times the explosive force delivered by all of the allied air forces in the Second World War. It makes no sense in an age when the deadly poisons produced by a nuclear exchange would be carried by the wind and water and soil and seed to the far corners of the globe and to generations yet unborn.

Today the expenditure of billions of dollars every year on weapons acquired for the purpose of making sure we never need to use them is essential to keeping the peace. But surely the acquisition of such idle stockpiles—which can only destroy and never create—is not the only, much less the most efficient, means of assuring peace.

I speak of peace, therefore, as the necessary rational end of rational men. I realize that the pursuit of peace is not as dramatic as the pursuit of war—and frequently the words of the pursuer fall on deaf ears. But we have no more urgent task.

* Remarks of the President at American University, Washington, D.C., June 10, 1963.

Some say that it is useless to speak of world peace or world law or world disarmament—and that it will be useless until the leaders of the Soviet Union adopt a more enlightened attitude. I hope they do. I believe we can help them do it. But I also believe that we must re-examine our own attitude—as individuals and as a Nation—for our attitude is as essential as theirs. And every graduate of this school, every thoughtful citizen who despairs of war and wishes to bring peace, should begin by looking inward—by examining his own attitude toward the possibilities of peace, toward the Soviet Union, toward the course of the Cold War and toward freedom and peace here at home.

First: Let us examine our attitude toward peace itself. Too many of us think it is impossible. Too many think it unreal. But that is a dangerous, defeatist belief. It leads to the conclusion that war is inevitable—that mankind is doomed—that we are gripped by forces we cannot control.

We need not accept that view. Our problems are manmade—therefore, they can be solved by man. And man can be as big as he wants. No problem of human destiny is beyond human beings. Man's reason and spirit have often solved the seemingly unsolvable—and we believe they can do it again.

I am not referring to the absolute, infinite concept of universal peace and good will of which some fantasies and fanatics dream. I do not deny the values of hopes and dreams but we merely invite discouragement and incredulity by making that our only and immediate goal.

Let us focus instead on a more practical, more attainable peace—based not on a sudden revolution in human nature but on a gradual evolution in human institutions—on a series of concrete actions and effective agreements which are in the interest of all concerned. There is no single, simple key to this peace—no grand or magic formula to be adopted by one or two powers. Genuine peace must be the product of many nations, the sum of many acts. It must be dynamic, not static, changing to meet the challenge of each new generation. For peace is a process—a way of solving problems.

With such a peace, there will still be quarrels and conflicting interests, as there are within families and nations. World peace, like community peace, does not require that each man love his neighbor—it requires only that they live together in mutual tolerance, submitting their disputes to a just and peaceful settlement. And history teaches us that enmities between nations, as between individuals, do not last forever. However fixed our likes and dislikes may seem, the tide of time and events will often bring surprising changes in the relations between nations and neighbors.

So let us persevere. Peace need not be impracticable—and war need not be inevitable. By defining our goal more clearly—by making it seem more manageable and less remote—we can help all peoples to see it, to draw hope from it, and to move irresistibly toward it.

Second: Let us re-examine our attitude toward the Soviet Union. It is discouraging to think that their leaders may actually believe what their propagandists write. It is discouraging to read a recent authoritative Soviet text on *Military Strategy* and find, on page after page, wholly baseless and incredible claims—such as the allegation that "American imperialist circles are preparing to unleash different types of wars . . . that there is a very real threat of a preventive war being unleashed by American imperialists against the Soviet Union . . . (and that) the political aims of the American imperialists are to enslave economically and politically the European and other capitalist countries . . . (and) to achieve world domination . . . by means of aggressive wars."

Truly, as it was written long ago: "The wicked flee when no man pursueth." Yet it is sad to read these Soviet statements—to realize the extent of the gulf between us. But it is also a warning—a warning to the American people not to fall into the same trap as the Soviets, not to see only a distorted and desperate view of the other side, not to see conflict as inevitable, accommodation as impossible and communication as nothing more than an exchange of threats.

No government or social system is so evil that its people must be considered as lacking in virtue. As Americans, we find communism profoundly repugnant as a negation of personal freedom and dignity. But we can still hail the Russian people for their many achievements—in science and space, in economic and industrial growth, in culture and in acts of courage.

Among the many traits the peoples of our two countries have in common, none is stronger than our mutual abhorrence of war. Almost unique, among the major world powers, we have never been at war with each other. And no nation in the history of battle ever suffered more than the Soviet Union suffered in the course of the Second World War. At least 20 million lost their lives. Countless millions of homes and farms were burned or sacked. A third of the nation's territory, including nearly two-thirds of its industrial base, was turned into wasteland—a loss equivalent to the devastation of this country east of Chicago.

Today, should total war ever break out again—no matter how—our two countries would become the primary targets. It is an ironical but accurate fact that the two strongest powers are the two in the most danger of devastation. All we have built, all we have worked for, would be destroyed in the first 24 hours. And even in the Cold War, which brings burdens and dangers to so many countries, including this Nation's closest allies—our two countries bear the heaviest burdens. For we are both devoting massive sums of money to weapons that could be better devoted to combating ignorance, poverty and disease. We are both caught up in a vicious and dangerous cycle in which suspicion on one side breeds suspicion on the other, and new weapons beget counter-weapons.

In short, both the United States and its allies, and the Soviet Union and its allies, have a mutually deep interest in a just and genuine peace and in halting the arms race. Agreements to this end are in the interests of the Soviet Union as well as ours—and even the most hostile nations can be relied upon to accept and keep those treaty obligations, and only those treaty obligations, which are in their own interest.

So, let us not be blind to our differences—but let us also direct attention to our common interests and to the means by which those differences can be resolved. And if we cannot end now our differences, at least we can help make the world safe for diversity. For, in the final analysis, our most basic common link is that we all inhabit this planet. We all breathe the same air. We all cherish our children's future. And we are all mortal.

Third: Let us re-examine our attitude toward the Cold War, remembering that we are not engaged in a debate, seeking to pile up debating points. We are not here distributing blame or pointing the finger of judgment. We must deal with the world as it is, and not as it might have been had the history of the last eighteen years been different.

We must, therefore, persevere in the search for peace in the hope that constructive changes within the Communist bloc might bring within reach solutions which now seem beyond us. We must conduct our affairs in such a way that it becomes in the Communists' interest to agree on a genuine peace. Above all, while defending our own vital interests, nuclear powers must avert those confrontations which bring an adversary to a choice of either a humiliating retreat or a nuclear war. To adopt that kind of course in the nuclear age would be evidence only of the bankruptcy of our policy—or of a collective death-wish for the world.

To secure these ends, America's weapons are non-provocative, carefully controlled, designed to deter and capable of selective use. Our military forces are committed to peace and disciplined in self-restraint. Our diplomats are instructed to avoid unnecessary irritants and purely rhetorical hostility.

For we can seek a relaxation of tensions without relaxing our guard. And, for our part, we do not need to use threats to prove that we are resolute. We do not need to jam foreign broadcasts out of fear our faith will be eroded. We are unwilling to impose our system on any unwilling people—but we are willing and able to engage in peaceful competition with any people on earth.

Meanwhile, we seek to strengthen the United Nations, to help solve its financial problems, to make it a more effective instrument of peace, to develop it into a genuine world security system—a system capable of resolving disputes on the basis of law, of insuring the security of the large and the small, and of creating conditions under which arms can finally be abolished.

At the same time we seek to keep peace inside the non-communist world, where many nations, all of them our friends, are divided over issues which weaken western unity, which invite communist intervention or which threaten to erupt into war. Our efforts in West New Guinea, in the Congo, in the

Middle East and in the Indian subcontinent, have been persistent and patient despite criticism from both sides. We have also tried to set an example for others—by seeking to adjust small but significant differences with our own closest neighbors in Mexico and in Canada.

Speaking of other nations, I wish to make one point clear. We are bound to many nations by alliances. Those alliances exist because our concern and theirs substantially overlap. Our commitment to defend Western Europe and West Berlin, for example, stands undiminished because of the identity of our vital interests. The United States will make no deal with the Soviet Union at the expense of other nations and other peoples, not merely because they are our partners, but also because their interests and ours converge.

Our interests converge, however, not only in defending the frontiers of freedom, but in pursuing the paths of peace. It is our hope—and the purpose of Allied policies—to convince the Soviet Union that she, too, should let each nation choose its own future, so long as that choice does not interfere with the choices of others. The communist drive to impose their political and economic system on others is the primary cause of world tension today. For there can be no doubt that, if all nations could refrain from interfering in the self-determination of others, the peace would be much more assured.

This will require a new effort to achieve world law—a new context for world discussions. It will require increased understanding between the Soviets and ourselves. And increased understanding will require increased contact and communication. One step in this direction is the proposed arrangement for a direct line between Moscow and Washington, to avoid on each side the dangerous delays, misunderstandings, and misreadings of the other's actions which might occur at a time of crisis.*

We have also been talking in Geneva about other first-step measures of arms control, designed to limit the intensity of the arms race and to reduce the risks of accidental war. Our primary long-range interest in Geneva, however, is general and complete disarmament—designed to take place by stages, permitting parallel political developments to build the new institutions of peace which would take the place of arms. The pursuit of disarmament has been an effort of this Government since the 1920's. It has been urgently sought by the past three Administrations. And however dim the prospects may be today, we intend to continue this effort—to continue it in order that all countries, including our own, can better grasp what the problems and possibilities of disarmament are.

The one major area of these negotiations where the end is in sight—yet where a fresh start is badly needed—is in a treaty to outlaw nuclear tests. The conclusion of such a treaty—so near and yet so far—would check the spiraling arms race in one of its most dangerous areas. It would place the

* Such arrangement was, in fact, concluded.

nuclear powers in a position to deal more effectively with one of the greatest hazards which man faces in 1963, the further spread of nuclear arms. It would increase our security—it would decrease the prospects of war. Surely this goal is sufficiently important to require our steady pursuit, yielding neither to the temptation to give up the whole effort nor the temptation to give up our insistence on vital and responsible safeguards.

I am taking this opportunity, therefore, to announce two important decisions in this regard.

First: Chairman Khrushchev, Prime Minister Macmillan and I have agreed that high-level discussions will shortly begin in Moscow looking toward early agreement on a comprehensive test ban treaty.* Our hopes must be tempered with the caution of history—but with our hopes go the hopes of all mankind.

Second: To make clear our good faith and solemn convictions on the matter, I now declare that the United States does not propose to conduct nuclear tests in the atmosphere so long as other states do not do so. We will not be the first to resume. Such a declaration is no substitute for a formal binding treaty—but I hope it will help us achieve one. Nor would such a treaty be a substitute for disarmament—but I hope it will help us achieve it.

Finally, my fellow Americans, let us examine our attitude toward peace and freedom here at home. The quality and spirit of our own society must justify and support our efforts abroad. We must show it in the dedication of our own lives—as many of you who are graduating today will have a unique opportunity to do, by serving without pay in the Peace Corps abroad or in the proposed National Service Corps here at home.

But whatever we are, we must all, in our daily lives, live up to the age-old faith that peace and freedom walk together. In too many of our cities today, the peace is not secure because freedom is incomplete.

It is the responsibility of the Executive Branch at all levels of government —local, state and national—to provide and protect that freedom for all of our citizens by all means within their authority. It is the responsibility of the Legislative Branch at all levels, wherever that authority is not now adequate, to make it adequate. And it is the responsibility of all citizens in all sections of this country to respect the rights of all others and to respect the law of the land.

All this is not unrelated to world peace. "When a man's ways please the Lord," the Scriptures tell us, "he maketh even his enemies to be at peace with him." And is not peace, in the last analysis, basically a matter of human rights—the right to live out our lives without fear of devastation—the right to breathe air as nature provided it—the right of future generations to a healthy existence?

While we proceed to safeguard our national interests, let us also safeguard human interests. And the elimination of war and arms is clearly in the inter-

* The nuclear test ban treaty was agreed to, signed in Moscow on August 5, and ratified by the United States Senate on September 24, 1963.

est of both. No treaty, however much it may be to the advantage of all, however tightly it may be worded, can provide absolute security against the risks of deception and evasion. But it can—if it is sufficiently effective in its enforcement and if it is sufficiently in the interests of its signers—offer far more security and far fewer risks than an unabated, uncontrolled, unpredictable arms race.

The United States, as the world knows, will never start a war. We do not want a war. We do not now expect war. This generation of Americans has already had enough—more than enough—of war and hate and oppression. We shall be prepared if others wish it. We shall be alert to try to stop it. But we shall also do our part to build a world of peace where the weak are safe and the strong are just. We are not helpless before that task or hopeless of its success. Confident and unafraid, we labor on—not toward a strategy of annihilation but toward a strategy of peace.

Old Myths and New Realities

JAMES WILLIAM FULBRIGHT *

Mr. President, there is an inevitable divergence, attributable to the imperfections of the human mind, between the world as it is and the world as men perceive it. As long as our perceptions are reasonably close to objective reality, it is possible for us to act upon our problems in a rational and appropriate manner. But when our perceptions fail to keep pace with events, when we refuse to believe something because it displeases or frightens us, or because it is simply startlingly unfamiliar, then the gap between fact and perception becomes a chasm, and action becomes irrelevant and irrational.

There has always—and inevitably—been some divergence between the realities of foreign policy and our ideas about it. This divergence has in certain respects been growing, rather than narrowing; and we are handicapped, accordingly, by policies based on old myths, rather than current realities. This divergence is, in my opinion, dangerous and unnecessary—dangerous, because it can reduce foreign policy to a fraudulent game of imagery and appearances; unnecessary, because it can be overcome by the determination of men in high office to dispel prevailing misconceptions by the candid dissemination of unpleasant, but inescapable, facts.

Before commenting on some of the specific areas where I believe our policies are at least partially based on cherished myths, rather than objective facts, I should like to suggest two possible reasons for the growing diver-

*Senator from Arkansas. Chairman of the Foreign Relations Committee of the United States Senate, in which this address was delivered on March 25, 1964.

gence between the realities and our perceptions of current world politics. The first is the radical change in relations between and within the Communist and the free world; and the second is the tendency of too many of us to confuse means with ends and, accordingly, to adhere to prevailing practices with a fervor befitting immutable principles.

Although it is too soon to render a definitive judgment, there is mounting evidence that events of recent years have wrought profound changes in the character of East-West relations. In the Cuban missile crisis of October 1962, the United States proved to the Soviet Union that a policy of aggression and adventure involved unacceptable risks. In the signing of the test ban treaty, each side in effect assured the other that it was prepared to forego, at least for the present, any bid for a decisive military or political breakthrough. These occurrences, it should be added, took place against the background of the clearly understood strategic superiority—but not supremacy—of the United States.

It seems reasonable, therefore, to suggest that the character of the cold war has, for the present, at least, been profoundly altered: by the drawing back of the Soviet Union from extremely aggressive policies; by the implicit repudiation by both sides of a policy of "total victory"; and by the establishment of an American strategic superiority which the Soviet Union appears to have tacitly accepted because it has been accompanied by assurances that it will be exercised by the United States with responsibility and restraint. These enormously important changes may come to be regarded by historians as the foremost achievements of the Kennedy administration in the field of foreign policy. Their effect has been to commit us to a foreign policy which can accurately—though perhaps not prudently—be defined as one of "peaceful coexistence."

Another of the results of the lowering of tensions between East and West is that each is now free to enjoy the luxury of accelerated strife and squabbling within its own domain. The ideological thunderbolts between Washington and Moscow which until a few years ago seemed a permanent part of our daily lives have become a pale shadow of their former selves. Now instead the United States waits in fascinated apprehension for the Olympian pronouncements that issue from Paris at 6-month intervals while the Russians respond to the crude epithets of Peiping with almost plaintive rejoinders about "those who want to start a war against everybody." These astonishing changes in the configuration of the postwar world have had an unsettling effect on both public and official opinion in the United States. One reason for this, I believe, lies in the fact that we are a people used to looking at the world, and indeed at ourselves, in moralistic rather than empirical terms. We are predisposed to regard any conflict as a clash between good and evil rather than as simply a clash between conflicting interests. We are inclined to confuse freedom and democracy, which we regard as moral principles, with the way in which they are practiced in America—with capitalism, federalism, and the two-party system, which are not moral principles but simply the preferred and accepted practices of the American people. There is much cant in American moralism and not a little inconsistency. It resembles in some ways the religious faith of the many respectable people who, in Samuel Butler's words, "would be equally horrified to hear the Christian religion doubted or to see it practiced."

Our national vocabulary is full of "self-evident truths" not only about "life, liberty, and happiness," but about a vast number of personal and public issues, including the cold war. It has become one of the "self-evident truths" of the postwar era that just as the President resides in Washington and the Pope in Rome, the Devil resides immutably in Moscow. We have come to regard the Kremlin as the permanent seat of his power and we have grown almost comfortable with a menace which, though unspeakably evil, has had the redeeming virtues of constancy, predictability, and familiarity. Now the Devil has betrayed us by traveling abroad and, worse still, by dispersing himself, turning up now here, now there, and in many places at once, with a devilish disregard for the laboriously constructed frontiers of ideology.

We are confronted with a complex and fluid world situation and we are not adapting ourselves to it. We are clinging to old myths in the face of new realities and we are seeking to escape the contradictions by narrowing the permissible bounds of public discussion, by relegating an increasing number of ideas and viewpoints to a growing category of "unthinkable thoughts." I believe that this tendency can and should be reversed, that it is within our ability, and unquestionably in our interests, to cut loose from established myths and to start thinking some "unthinkable thoughts"—about the cold war and East-West relations, about the underdeveloped countries and particularly those in Latin America, about the changing nature of the Chinese Communist threat in Asia and about the festering war in Vietnam.

The master myth of the cold war is that the Communist bloc is a monolith composed of governments which are not really governments at all but organized conspiracies, divided among themselves perhaps in certain matters of tactics, but all equally resolute and implacable in their determination to destroy the free world.

I believe that the Communist world is indeed hostile to the free world in its general and long-term intentions but that the existence of this animosity in principle is far less important for our foreign policy than the great variations in its intensity and character both in time and among the individual members of the Communist bloc. Only if we recognize these variations, ranging from China, which poses immediate threats to the free world, to Poland and Yugoslavia, which pose none, can we hope to act effectively upon the bloc and to turn its internal differences to our own advantage and to the advantage of those bloc countries which wish to maximize their independence. It is the responsibility of our national leaders both in the executive branch and in Congress, to acknowledge and act upon these realities, even at the cost of saying things which will not win immediate widespread enthusiasm.

For a start, we can acknowledge the fact that the Soviet Union, though still a most formidable adversary, has ceased to be totally and implacably hostile to the West. It has shown a new willingness to enter mutually advantageous arrangements with the West and, thus far at least, to honor them. It has therefore become possible to divert some of our energies from the prosecution of the cold war to the relaxation of the cold war and to deal with the Soviet Union, for certain purposes, as a normal state with normal and traditional interests.

If we are to do these things effectively, we must distinguish between communism as an ideology and the power and policy of the Soviet state. It is not communism as a doctrine, or communism as it is practiced within the Soviet Union or within any other country, that threatens us. How the Soviet Union organizes its internal life, the gods and doctrines that it worships, are matters for the Soviet Union to determine. It is not Communist dogma as espoused within Russia but Communist imperialism that threatens us and other peoples of the non-Communist world. Insofar as a great nation mobilizes its power and resources for aggressive purposes, that nation, regardless of ideology, makes itself our enemy. Insofar as a nation is content to practice its doctrines within its own frontiers, that nation, however repugnant its ideology, is one with which we have no proper quarrel. We must deal with the Soviet Union as a great power, quite apart from differences of ideology. To the extent that the Soviet leaders abandon the global ambitions of Marxist ideology, in fact if not in words, it becomes possible for us to engage in normal relations with them, relations which probably cannot be close or trusting for many years to come but which can be gradually freed of the terror and the tensions of the cold war.

In our relations with the Russians, and indeed in our relations with all nations, we would do well to remember, and to act upon, the words of Pope John in the great Encyclical, Pacem in Terris:

"It must be borne in mind," said Pope John, "that to proceed gradually is the law of life in all its expressions, therefore, in human institutions, too, it is not possible to renovate for the better except by working from within them, gradually. Violence has always achieved only destruction, not construction, the kindling of passions, not their pacification, the accumulation of hate and ruin, not the reconciliation of the contending parties. And it has reduced men and parties to the difficult task of rebuilding, after sad experience, on the ruins of discord."

Important opportunities have been created for Western policy by the development of "polycentrism" in the Communist bloc. The Communist nations, as George Kennan has pointed out, are, like the Western nations, currently caught up in a crisis of indecision about their relations with countries outside their own ideological bloc. The choices open to the satellite states are limited but by no means insignificant. They can adhere slavishly to Soviet preferences or they can strike out on their own, within limits, to enter into mutually advantageous relations with the West.

Whether they do so, and to what extent, is to some extent at least within the power of the West to determine. If we persist in the view that all Communist regimes are equally hostile and equally threatening to the West, and that we can have no policy toward the captive nations except the eventual overthrow of their Communist regimes, then the West may enforce upon the Communist bloc a degree of unity which the Soviet Union has shown itself to be quite incapable of imposing—just as Stalin in the early postwar years frightened the West into a degree of unity that it almost certainly could not have attained by his own unaided efforts. If, on the other hand, we are willing to reexamine the view that all Communist regimes are alike in the threat which they pose for the West—a view which had a certain validity in Stalin's time—then we may be able to exert an important influence on the course of events within a divided Communist world.

We are to a great extent the victims, and the Soviets the beneficiaries, of our own ideological convictions, and of the curious contradictions which they involve. We consider it a form of subversion of the free world, for example, when the Russians enter trade relations or conclude a consular convention or establish airline connections with a free country in Asia, Africa, or Latin America—and to a certain extent we are right. On the other hand, when it is proposed that we adopt the same strategy in reverse—by extending commercial credits to Poland or Yugoslavia, or by exchanging Ambassadors with a Hungarian regime which has changed considerably in character since the revolution of 1956—then the same patriots who are so alarmed by Soviet activities in the free world charge our policymakers with "giving aid and comfort to the enemy" and with innumerable other categories of idiocy and immorality.

It is time that we resolved this contradiction and separated myth from reality. The myth is that every Communist state is an unmitigated evil and a relentless enemy of the free world; the reality is that some Communist regimes pose a threat to the free world while others pose little or none, and that if we will recognize these distinctions, we ourselves will be able to influence events in the Communist bloc in a way favorable to the security of the free world.

There are numerous areas in which we can seek to reduce the tensions of the cold war and to bring a degree of normalcy into our relations with the Soviet Union and other Communist countries—once we have resolved that it is safe and wise to do so. We have already taken important steps in this direction: the Antarctic and Austrian treaties and the nuclear test ban treaty, the broadening of East-West cultural and educational relations, and the expansion of trade. . . .

A modest increase in East-West trade may serve as a modest instrument of East-West detente—provided that we are able to overcome the myth that trade with Communist countries is a compact with the Devil and to recognize that, on the contrary, trade can serve as an effective and honorable means of advancing both peace and human welfare.

Whether we are able to make these philosophic adjustments or not, we cannot escape the fact that our efforts to devise a common Western trade policy are a palpable failure and that our allies are going to trade with the Communist bloc whether we like it or not. The world's major exporting nations are slowly but steadily increasing their trade with the Communist bloc and the bloc countries are showing themselves to be reliable customers. Since 1958 Western Europe has been increasing its exports to the East at the rate of about 7 percent a year, which is nearly the same rate at which its overall world sales have been increasing. . . .

The inability of the United States to prevent its partners from trading extensively with the Communist bloc is one good reason for relaxing our own restrictions, but there is a better reason: the potential value of trade —a moderate volume of trade in nonstrategic items—as an instrument for reducing world tensions and strengthening the foundations of peace. I do not think that trade or the nuclear test ban, or any other prospective East-West accommodation, will lead to a grand reconciliation that will end the cold war and usher in the brotherhood of man. At the most, the cumulative effect of all the agreements that are likely to be attainable in the forseeable future will be the alleviation of the extreme tensions and animosities that threaten the world with nuclear devastation and the gradual conversion of the struggle between communism and the free world into a safer and more tolerable international rivalry, one which may be with us for years and decades to come but which need not be so terrifying and so costly as to distract the nations of the world from the creative pursuits of civilized societies.

There is little in history to justify the expectation that we can either win the cold war or end it immediately and completely. These are favored myths, respectively, of the American right and of the American left. They are, I believe, equal in their unreality and in their disregard for the feasibilities of history. We must disabuse ourselves of them and come to terms, at last, with the realities of a world in which neither good nor evil is absolute and in which those who move events and make history are those who have understood not how much but how little it is within our power to change. . . .

I believe that the Cuban missile crisis of 1962, involving a confrontation with nuclear weapons and intercontinental missiles, was a test of our courage, and we acquitted ourselves extremely well in that instance. . . . [But] the problem of Cuba is difficult . . . and heavily burdened with the deadweight of old myths and prohibitions against "unthinkable thoughts." I think the time is overdue for a candid reevaluation of our Cuban policy even though it may also lead to distasteful conclusions.

There are and have been three options open to the United States with respect to Cuba: first, the removal of the Castro regime by invading and occupying the island; second, an effort to weaken and ultimately bring down the regime by a policy of political and economic boycott; and finally, acceptance of the Communist regime as a disagreeable reality and annoyance but one which is not likely to be removed in the near future because of the unavailability of acceptable means of removing it.

The first option, invasion, has been tried in a halfhearted way and found wanting. It is generally acknowledged that the invasion and occupation of Cuba, besides violating our obligations as a member of the United Nations and of the Organization of American States, would have explosive consequences in Latin America and elsewhere and might precipitate a global nuclear war. I know of no responsible statesman who advocates this approach. It has been rejected by our Government and by public opinion and I think that, barring some grave provocation, it can be ruled out as a feasible policy for the United States.

The approach which we have adopted has been the second of those mentioned, an effort to weaken and eventually bring down the Castro regime by a policy of political and economic boycott. This policy has taken the form of extensive restrictions, against trade with Cuba by United States citizens, of the exclusion of Cuba from the inter-American system and efforts to secure Latin American support in isolating Cuba politically and economically, and of diplomatic efforts, backed by certain trade and aid sanctions, to persuade other free world countries to maintain economic boycotts against Cuba.

This policy, it now seems clear, has been a failure, and there is no reason to believe that it will succeed in the future. Our efforts to persuade our allies to terminate their trade with Cuba have been generally rebuffed. The prevailing attitude was perhaps best expressed by a British manufacturer who, in response to American criticisms of the sale of British buses to Cuba, said: "If America has a surplus of wheat, we have a surplus of buses."

In cutting off military assistance to Great Britain, France, and Yugoslavia under the provisions of Section 620 of the Foreign Assistance Act of 1963, the United States has wielded a stuffed club. The amounts of aid involved are infinitesimal; the chances of gaining compliance with our boycott policy are nil; and the annoyance of the countries concerned may be considerable. What we terminated with respect to Britain and France, in fact, can hardly be called aid; it was more of a sales promotion program under which British and French military leaders were brought to the United States to see—and to buy—advanced American weapons. Terminating this program was in itself of little importance; Britain and France do not need our assistance. But terminating the program as a sanction against their trade with Cuba can have no real effect other than to create an illusory image of "toughness" for the benefit of our own people.

Free world exports to Cuba have, on the whole, been declining over recent years, but overall imports have been rising since 1961. . . .

I should like to make it very clear that I am not arguing against the desirability of an economic boycott against the Castro regime but against its feasibility. The effort has been made and all the fulminations we can utter about sanctions and retaliation against free world countries that trade with Cuba cannot long conceal the fact that the boycott policy is a failure.

The boycott policy has not failed because of any "weakness" or "timidity" on the part of our Government. This charge, so frequently heard, is one of the most pernicious myths to have been inflicted on the American people. The boycott policy has failed because the United States is not omnipotent and cannot be. The basic reality to be faced is that it is simply not within our power to compel our allies to cut off their trade with Cuba, unless we are prepared to take drastic sanctions against them, such as closing our own markets to any foreign company that does business in Cuba, as proposed by Mr. Nixon. We can do this, of course, but if we do, we ought first to be very sure as apparently Mr. Nixon is, that the Cuban boycott is more important than good relations with our closest allies. . . .

The prospects of bringing down the Castro regime by political and economic boycott have never been very good. Even if a general free world boycott were successfully applied against Cuba, it is unlikely that the Russians would refuse to carry the extra financial burden and thereby permit the only Communist regime in the Western Hemisphere to collapse. We are thus compelled to recognize that there is probably no way of bringing down the Castro regime by means of economic pressures unless we are prepared to impose a blockade against nonmilitary shipments from the Soviet Union. Exactly such a policy has been recommended by some of our more reckless politicians, but the preponderance of informed opinion is that a blockade against Soviet shipments of nonmilitary supplies to Cuba would be extravagantly dangerous, carrying the strong possibility of a confrontation that could explode into nuclear war.

Having ruled out military invasion and blockade, and recognizing the failure of the boycott policy, we are compelled to consider the third of the three options open to us with respect to Cuba: the acceptance of the continued existence of the Castro regime as a distasteful nuisance but not an intolerable danger so long as the nations of the hemisphere are prepared to meet their obligations of collective defense under the Rio Treaty.

In recent years we have become transfixed with Cuba, making it far more important in both our foreign relations and in our domestic life than its size and influence warrant. We have flattered a noisy but minor demagogue by treating him as if he were a Napoleonic menace. Communist Cuba has been a disruptive and subversive influence in Venezuela and other countries of the hemisphere, and there is no doubt that both we and our Latin American partners would be better off if the Castro regime did not exist. But it is important to bear in mind that, despite their best efforts, the Cuban Communists have not succeeded in subverting the hemisphere and that in Venezuela, for example, where communism has made a major effort to gain power through terrorism, it has been repudiated by a people who in a free election have committed themselves to the course of liberal democracy. It is necessary to weigh the desirability of an objective against the feasibility of its attainment, and when we do this with respect to Cuba, I think we are bound to conclude that Castro is a nuisance but not a grave threat to the United States and that he cannot be gotten rid of except by means that are wholly disproportionate to the objective. Cuban communism does pose a grave threat to other Latin American countries, but this threat can be dealt with by prompt and vigorous use of the established procedures of the inter-American system against any act of aggression.

I think that we must abandon the myth that Cuban communism is a transitory menace that is going to collapse or disappear in the immediate future and face up to two basic realities about Cuba: first, that the Castro regime is not on the verge of collapse and is not likely to be overthrown by any policies which we are now pursuing or can reasonably undertake; and second, that the continued existence of the Castro regime, though inimical to our interests and policies, is not an insuperable obstacle to the attainment of our objectives, unless we make it so by permitting it to poison our politics at home and to divert us from more important tasks in the hemisphere.

The policy of the United States with respect to Latin America as a whole is predicated on the assumption that social revolution can be accomplished without violent upheaval. This is the guiding principle of the Alliance for Progress and it may in time be vindicated. We are entitled to hope so and it is wise and necessary for us to do all that we can to advance the prospects of peaceful and orderly reform.

At the same time, we must be under no illusions as to the extreme difficulty of uprooting long-established ruling oligarchies without disruptions involving lesser or greater degrees of violence. The historical odds are probably against the prospects of peaceful social revolution. There are places, of course, where it has occurred and others where it seems likely to occur. In Latin America, the chances for such basic change by peaceful means seem bright in Colombia and Venezuela and certain other countries; in Mexico, many basic changes have been made by peaceful means, but these came in the wake of a violent revolution. In other Latin American countries, the power of ruling oligarchies is so solidly established and their ignorance so great that there seems little prospect of accomplishing economic growth or social reform by means short of the forcible overthrow of established authorities.

I am not predicting violent revolutions in Latin America or elsewhere. Still less am I advocating them. I wish only to suggest that violent social revolutions are a possibility in countries where feudal oligarchies resist all meaningful change by peaceful means. We must not, in our preference for the democratic procedures envisioned by the Charter of Punta del Este, close our minds to the possibility that democratic procedures may fail in certain countries and that where democracy does fail violent social convulsions may occur.

We would do well, while continuing our efforts to promote peaceful change through the Alliance for Progress, to consider what our reactions might be in the event of the outbreak of genuine social revolution in one or more Latin American countries. Such a revolution did occur in Bolivia, and we accepted it calmly and sensibly. But what if a violent social revolution were to break out in one of the larger Latin American countries? Would we feel certain that it was Cuban or Soviet inspired? Would we wish to intervene on the side of established authority? Or would we be willing to tolerate or even support a revolution if it was seen to be not Communist but similar in nature to the Mexican revolution or the Nasser revolution in Egypt?

These are hypothetical questions and there is no readily available set of answers to them. But they are questions which we should be thinking about because they have to do with problems that could become real and urgent with great suddenness. We should be considering, for example, what groups in particular countries might conceivably lead revolutionary movements, and if we can identify them, we should be considering how we might communicate with them and influence them in such a way that their movements, if successful, will not pursue courses detrimental to our security and our interests.

The Far East is another area of the world in which American policy is handicapped by the divergence of old myths and new realities. Particularly with respect to China, an elaborate vocabulary of make believe has become compulsory in both official and public discussion. . . . The point is that, whatever the outcome of a rethinking of policy might be, we have been unwilling to undertake it because of the fear of many Government officials, undoubtedly well founded, that even the suggestion of new policies toward China or Vietnam would provoke a vehement public outcry.

I do not think the United States can, or should, recognize Communist China, or acquiesce in its admission to the United Nations under present circumstances. It would be unwise to do so, because there is nothing to be gained by it so long as the Peiping regime maintains its attitude of implacable hostility toward the United States. I do not believe, however, that this state of affairs is necessarily permanent. As we have seen in our relations with Germany and Japan, hostility can give way in an astonishingly short time to close friendship; and, as we have seen in our relations with China, the reverse can occur with equal speed. It is not impossible that in time our relations with China will change again—if not to friendship, then perhaps to "competitive coexistence." It would therefore be extremely useful if we could introduce an element of flexibility, or, more precisely, of the capacity to be flexible, into our relations with Communist China.

We would do well, as former Assistant Secretary Hilsman has recommended, to maintain an "open door" to the possibility of improved relations with Communist China in the future. For a start, we must jar open our minds to certain realities about China, of which the foremost is that there really are not "two Chinas," but only one—mainland China; and that it is ruled by Communists, and is likely to remain so for the indefinite future. Once we accept this fact, it becomes possible to reflect on the conditions under which it might be possible for us to enter into relatively normal relations with mainland China. One condition, of course, must be the abandonment by the Chinese Communists, tacitly, if not explicitly, of their intention to conquer and incorporate Taiwan. This seems unlikely now; but far more surprising changes have occurred in politics, and it is quite possible that a new generation of leaders in Peiping and Taipei may put a quiet end to the Chinese civil war, thus opening the possibility of entirely new patterns of international relations in the Far East.

Should such changes occur, they will open important opportunities for American policy; and it is to be hoped that we shall be able and willing to take advantage of them. It seems possible, for instance, that an atmosphere of reduced tensions in the Far East might make it possible to strengthen world peace by drawing mainland China into existing East-West agreements in such fields as disarmament, trade, and educational exchange. . . .

The situation in Vietnam poses a far more pressing need for a reevaluation of American policy. Other than withdrawal, which I do not think can be realistically considered under present circumstances, three options are open to us in Vietnam: First, continuation of the antiguerrilla war within South Vietnam, along with renewed American efforts to increase the military effectiveness of the South Vietnamese Army and the political effectiveness of the South Vietnamese Government; second, an attempt to end the war, through negotiations for the neutralization of South Vietnam, or of both North and South Vietnam; and, finally, the expansion of the scale of the war, either by the direct commitment of large numbers of American troops or by equipping the South Vietnamese Army to attack North Vietnamese territory, possibly by means of commando-type operations from the sea or the air.

It is difficult to see how a negotiation, under present military circumstances, could lead to termination of the war under conditions that would preserve the freedom of South Vietnam. It is extremely difficult for a party to a negotiation to achieve by diplomacy objectives which it has conspicuously failed to win by warfare. The hard fact of the matter is that our bargaining position is at present a weak one; and until the equation of advantages between the two sides has been substantially altered in our favor, there can be little prospect of a negotiated settlement which would secure the independence of a non-Communist South Vietnam. . . .

It seems clear that only two realistic options are open to us in Vietnam in the immediate future: the expansion of the conflict in one way or another, or a renewed effort to bolster the capacity of the South Vietnamese to prosecute the war successfully on its present scale. The matter calls for thorough examination by responsible officials in the executive branch; and until they have had an opportunity to evaluate the contingencies and feasibilities of the options open to us, it seems to me that we have no choice but to support the South Vietnamese Government and Army by the most effective means available. Whatever specific policy decisions are made, it should be clear to all concerned that the United States will continue to meet its obligations and fulfill its commitments with respect to Vietnam.

These, I believe, are some, although by no means all, of the issues of foreign policy in which it is essential to reevaluate longstanding ideas and commitments in the light of new and changing realities. In all the issues which I have discussed, American policy has to one degree or another been less effective than it might have been because of our national tendency to equate means with ends and therefore to attach a mythological sanctity to policies and practices which in themselves have no moral content or value except insofar as they contribute to the achievement of some valid national objective. I believe that we must try to overcome this excessive moralism, which binds us to old myths and blinds us to new realities and, worse still, leads us to regard new and unfamiliar ideas with fear and mistrust.

We must dare to think about "unthinkable" things. We must learn to explore all of the options and possibilities that confront us in a complex and rapidly changing world. We must learn to welcome rather than fear the voices of dissent and not to recoil in horror whenever some heretic suggests that Castro may survive or that Khrushchev is not as bad a fellow as Stalin was. We must overcome our susceptibility to "shock"—a word which I wish could be banned from our newspapers and magazines and especially from the *Congressional Record.*

If Congress and public opinion are unduly susceptible to "shock," the executive branch, and particularly the Department of State, is subject to the malady of chronic and excessive caution. An effective foreign policy is one which concerns itself more with innovation abroad than with conciliation at home. A creative foreign policy—as President Truman, for one, knew—is not necessarily one which wins immediate general approval. It is sometimes necessary for leaders to do unpleasant and unpopular things, because, as Burke pointed out, the duty of the democratic politician to his constituents is not to comply with their every wish and preference but to give them the benefit of, and to be held responsible for, the exercise of his own best judgment.

We must dare to think about "unthinkable things," because when things become "unthinkable," thinking stops and action becomes mindless. If we are to disabuse ourselves of old myths and to act wisely and creatively upon the new realities of our time, we must think and talk about our problems with perfect freedom, remembering, as Woodrow Wilson said, that "The greatest freedom of speech is the greatest safety because, if a man is a fool, the best thing to do is to encourage him to advertise the fact by speaking."